A Companion to the Worlds of the Renaissance

BLACKWELL COMPANIONS TO EUROPEAN HISTORY

This series provides sophisticated and authoritative overviews of the scholarship that has shaped our current understanding of Europe's past. Each volume comprises between twenty-five and forty concise essays written by individual scholars within their area of specialization. The aim of each contribution is to synthesize the current state of scholarship from a variety of historical perspectives and to provide a statement on where the field is heading. The essays are written in a clear, provocative, and lively manner, designed for an international audience of scholars, students, and general readers.

The *Blackwell Companions to European History* is a cornerstone of Blackwell's overarching *Companions to History* series, covering British, American, and World History.

Published
A Companion to the Worlds of the Renaissance
Edited by Guido Ruggiero

In preparation
A Companion to the Reformation World
Edited by R. Po-chia Hsia

BLACKWELL COMPANIONS TO HISTORY

Published
A Companion to Western Historical Thought
Edited by Lloyd Kramer and Sarah Maza

In preparation
A Companion to Gender History
Edited by Teresa Meade and Merry E. Weisner-Hanks

BLACKWELL COMPANIONS TO BRITISH HISTORY

Published
A Companion to Britain in the Later Middle Ages
Edited by S. H. Rigby
A Companion to Eighteenth-Century Britain
Edited by H. T. Dickinson
A Companion to Early Twentieth-Century Britain
Edited by Chris Wrigley

In preparation
A Companion to Roman Britain
Edited by Malcolm Todd
A Companion to Tudor Britain
Edited by Robert Tittler and Norman Jones
A Companion to Stuart Britain
Edited by Barry Coward
A Companion to Nineteenth-Century Britain
Edited by Chris Williams
A Companion to Contemporary Britain
Edited by Paul Addison and Harriet Jones

BLACKWELL COMPANIONS TO AMERICAN HISTORY

Published
A Companion to the American Revolution
Edited by Jack P. Greene and J. R. Pole
A Companion to 19th-Century America
Edited by William L. Barney
A Companion to the American South
Edited by John B. Boles
A Companion to American Indian History
Edited by Philip J. Deloria and Neal Salisbury
A Companion to American Women's History
Edited by Nancy A. Hewitt
A Companion to Post-1945 America
Edited by Jean-Christophe Agnew and Roy Rosenzweig
A Companion to the Vietnam War
Edited by Marilyn Young and Robert Buzzanco

In preparation
A Companion to Colonial America
Edited by Daniel Vickers
A Companion to 20th-Century America
Edited by Stephen J. Whitfield
A Companion to the American West
Edited by William Deverell
A Companion to American Foreign Relations
Edited by Robert Schulzinger

BLACKWELL COMPANIONS TO WORLD HISTORY

In preparation
A Companion to the History of Africa
Edited by Joseph Miller

A COMPANION TO THE WORLDS OF THE RENAISSANCE

Edited by

Guido Ruggiero

Blackwell
Publishing

© 2002 by Blackwell Publishers Ltd
a Blackwell Publishing company

Editorial Offices:
108 Cowley Road, Oxford OX4 1JF, UK
  Tel: +44 (0) 1865 791100
350 Main Street, Malden, MA 02148-5018, USA
  Tel: +1 781 388 8250

First published 2002 by Blackwell Publishers Ltd

Library of Congress Cataloging-in-Publication Data

A companion to the worlds of the Renaissance / edited by Guido
Ruggiero.
    p. cm. – (Blackwell companions to history)
Includes bibliographical references and index.
    ISBN 0–631–21524–7 (alk. paper)
    1. Renaissance. 2. Renaissance–Italy. 3. Power (Social sciences)–Italy. 4. Power (Social sciences)–Europe. 5. Europe–Economic conditions–16th century. 6. Italy–Civilization–1268–1559. 7. Europe–Social conditions–16th century. 8. Italy–Social conditions–1268–1559. 9. Italy–Intellectual life–1268–1559. I. Ruggiero, Guido, 1944– II. Series.
    CB367. C65 2002
    940.2′1–dc21

                                                              2001005176

A catalogue record for this title is available from the British Library.

Typeset in 10/12 pt Galliard
by Kolam Information Services Pvt Ltd, Pondicherry, India
Printed and bound in Great Britain by T. J. International Ltd, Padstow, Cornwall

For further information on
Blackwell Publishers, visit our website:
www.blackwellpublishers.co.uk

Contents

Contributors

James S. Amelang is Professor of Early Modern History at the Universidad Autónoma of Madrid. The author of several works on the social and cultural history of early modern Barcelona, most recently he has published The Flight of Icarus: Artisan Autobiography in Early Modern Europe (1998). He is presently preparing a general history of early modern Spain, and for the more distant future, plans to work on aspects of the history of urban discourse in early modern Europe.

Karl Appuhn is an Assistant Professor in the History Department at the University of Oregon. His research is primarily concerned with the environmental history of the Renaissance, with a particular focus on the political, economic, and intellectual dimensions of human attempts to control nature. He has written articles about forest management and land surveying in Renaissance Venice. He is currently working on a history of flood control in Venice.

Thomas F. Arnold is program manager with the Alliance for Lifelong Learning, a not-for-profit online educational joint project of Oxford, Stanford, and Yale Universities. From 1993 to 2001 he was Assistant Professor of History at Yale, where he taught Renaissance Italy. His specialty is military history, and particularly the possibility that Renaissance Europeans invented a new military culture that continues to shape warfare down to the present.

Gene Brucker was Professor Emeritus of History at the University of California, Berkeley prior to his retirement. Among his many books on medieval history and the Renaissance are *Renaissance Florence* (1969, 1983), and *Giovanni and Lusanna: Love and Marriage in Renaissance Florence* (1986).

Peter Burke is Professor of Cultural History, University of Cambridge, and Fellow of Emmanuel College. He has been publishing studies of the Renaissance for nearly forty years, including *Culture and Society in Renaissance Italy* (1972, fourth edition 2001), *The Renaissance* (1987, second edition 2000) and *The European Renaissance* (1998). His current research interests include the social history of language and he is working on a comparative study, provisionally entitled *Languages and Communities in Early Modern Europe*.

Linda T. Darling is Professor of History at the University of Arizona, where she has taught Middle Eastern history since 1989. Her current research interests include an examination of provincial fiscality in the seventeenth century and its impact on provincial politics, taking Syria-Lebanon as a case study.

William Eamon is Professor of History and director of the University Honors Program at New Mexico State University, where he teaches courses on the history of science and medicine and on early modern history. He is the author of *Science and the Secrets of Nature: Books of Secrets in Medieval and Early Modern Culture* (1994; Italian translation 1999) and about forty articles on various themes relating to the history of science, medicine, and magic. He is currently completing a book titled *The Charlatan's Tale: A Renaissance Surgeon's World*.

James R. Farr is Professor of History at Purdue University. He received his PhD from Northwestern University in 1983, served as Editor of *French Historical Studies* from 1991–2000, and is the author of three books, *Hands of Honor: Artisans and Their World in Dijon, 1550–1650* (1988), *Authority and Sexuality in Early Modern Burgundy, 1550–1730* (1995), and *Artisans in Europe, 1300–1914* (2000).

Joanne M. Ferraro is Professor of History at San Diego State University. A specialist in the history of marriage, family, and gender in early modern Italy, she is the author of *Family and Public Life in Brescia, 1580–1650, The Foundations of Power in the Venetian State* (1993), and *Marriage Wars in Late Renaissance Venice* (2001).

David C. Gentilcore is Reader in History, Department of History, University of Leicester. He is interested in the social and cultural history of early modern Italy, in particular the (often strained) relationship between beliefs and practices at different levels of society. He is the author of *From Bishop to Witch: the System of the Sacred in Early Modern Italy* (1992) and *Healers and Healing in Early Modern Italy* (1998), and is currently preparing a study of medical charlatanism.

Gregory Hanlon is Professor of History at Dalhousie University in Halifax, Canada. He is author of *L'Univers des gens de bien: Culture et comportements des élites urbaines en Agenais-Condomois au XVIIe siècle* (1989), *Confession and Community in Seventeenth-century France: Catholic and Protestant Coexistence in Aquitaine* (1993), *The Twilight of a Military Tradition: Italian Aristocrats and European Conflicts, 1560–1800* (1998), and *Early Modern Italy, 1550–1800: Three seasons in European History* (2000). He is currently researching a book called *Peasant Lives in rural Tuscany: Human nature in historical time, 1610–1670*.

R. Po-chia Hsia is Edwin Earle Sparks Professor of History at Pennsylvania State University. He previously taught at Columbia, Cornell, University of Massachusetts, and New York University. He has received fellowships from the United States and Germany, and has held visiting professorships and research positions in Germany and the Netherlands. Elected in 2000 to the Academia Sinica (Taiwan), he is currently researching the history of Sino-European relations from the 16th to the 18th centuries. His books include *Society and Religion in Munster 1535–1618* (1984), *Social Discipline in the Reformation: Central Europe 1550–1750* (1989), and *The World of Catholic Renewal 1540–1770* (1998).

Mary Lindemann is Professor of History at Carnegie Mellon University in Pittsburgh. She is a specialist in the history of seventeenth- and eighteenth-century Europe, in particular Germany and the Low Countries, and in the history of medicine. Her publications include *Patriots and Paupers: Hamburg, 1712–1830* (1990), *Health and Healing in Eighteenth-Century Germany* (1996), and *Medicine and Society in Early Modern Europe* (1999).

John A. Marino is Associate Professor of History at the University of California, San Diego. He is the author of Pastoral Economics in the Kingdom of Naples (1988). He is the editor of *Early Modern Italy, 1550–1796* (2002), *Early Modern History and the Social Sciences: Testing the Limits of Braudel's Mediterranean* (2002), and has co-edited/co-translated *Good Government in Spanish Naples* (1990). He specializes in the early modern history of Naples, Spanish Italy, and the Mediterranean.

John Jeffries Martin, is Professor of History at Trinity University, where he teaches courses on medieval and early modern Europe. He is the author of *Venice's Hidden Enemies: Italian Heretics in a Renaissance City* (1993) and the editor of *The Renaissance: Italy and Abroad* (2002). He is currently writing a book on the history of sincerity and constructions of the individual in western Europe from the Renaissance to the Enlightenment.

Ian Frederick Moulton is Associate Professor of English at Arizona State University West. He is the author of *Before Pornography: Erotic Writing in Early Modern England* (2000), a study of the representation of sexuality and gender in 16th century England and Italy, as well as a number of articles on early modern literature and culture. He is currently preparing a translation of *La Cazzaria*, an erotic academic dialogue from Renaissance Italy.

Robert Muchembled is Professor of History at the University of Paris North. He is project co-ordinator for the ESF program *Cultural Exchange in Europe 1400–1700*, and author of numerous books and articles. These include *Culture Populaire* (1998) and *History of the Devil* (forthcoming).

Edward Muir is the Clarence L. Ver Steeg Professor in the Arts and Sciences and a member of the History Department at Northwestern University. He is the author of *Civic Ritual in Renaissance Venice*, *Mad Blood Stirring: Vendetta in Renaissance Italy*, and *Ritual in Early Modern Europe*. He co-edited with Guido Ruggiero three volumes of articles translated from the Italian journal, *Quaderni Storici*. He is currently engaged in a study of the forms of neighborly trust in Italian Renaissance communities.

John M. Najemy is Professor of History at Cornell University. His chief research interests have been in the political and intellectual history of Renaissance Florence. He is the author of *Corporatism and Consensus in Florentine Electoral Politics, 1280–1400* (1982), *Between Friends: Discourses of Power and Desire in the Machiavelli-Vettori Letters of 1513–1515* (1993), and essays on Florentine political thought, civic humanism, Machiavelli, and Alberti. He is currently writing a history of Florence from 1250 to 1555 (forthcoming) and editing a volume on the Renaissance.

Loren Partridge is Professor of Art History and Italian Studies at the University of California, Berkeley where he has taught Italian Renaissance art and architecture for over thirty years. Recent books include (with Randolph Starn) *Arts of Power: Three Halls of State in Italy 1300–1600* (1992), *The Renaissance in Rome* (1996), *Michelangelo: The Sistine Chapel Ceiling, Rome* (1996), and *Michelangelo; The Last Judgment: A Glorious Restoration* with contributions by F. Mancinelli and G. Colalucci (1996). He is currently writing a monograph on the Villa Farnese at Caprarola, and a general survey of italian Renaissance art.

Matthew Restall is Associate Professor of Colonial Latin American History and Women's Studies and Director of Latin American Studies at the Pennsylvania State University. His publications, which focus mostly on the history of colonial Yucatán, include *The Maya World: Yucatec Culture and Society, 1550–1850* (1997) and *Maya Conquistador* (1998). His new book, *Seven Myths of the Spanish Conquest*, comes out this year, and he is currently writing a study of Africans in colonial Yucatán.

Ingrid D. Rowland is Andrew W. Mellon Professor in the Humanities at the American Academy in Rome. She is author of *The Culture of the High Renaissance: Ancients and Moderns in Sixteenth-Century Rome* (1998), *The Ecstatic Journey: Athanasius Kircher in Baroque Rome* (2000), *The Correspondence of Agostino Chigi* (2001), and translator of *Vitruvius' Ten Books on Architecture* (1999). She is currently writing a biography of the southern Italian philosopher Giordano Bruno.

Guido Ruggiero is Josephine Berry Weiss Chair in the Humanities and Professor of History and Women's Studies at the Pennsylvania State University. His previous publications include *Binding Passions: Tales of Magic Marriage and Power at the End of the Renaissance* (1993), *The Boundaries of Eros: Sex Crime and Sexuality in Renaissance Venice (1985)* and *Violence in Early Renaissance Venice* (1980). He has also edited two series of books: *Studies in the History of Sexuality* and *Selections from Quaderni Storici.*

Randolf Starn is Professor of History and Italian Studies, currently Director of the Center for Italian Studies, at the University of California, Berkeley. He has taught and written extensively on Renaissance Italy and the history of Renaissance culture. A collection of his essays, *Varieties of Cultural History,* will appear in 2002.

James Grantham Turner is Professor of English at the University of California, Berkeley. He has published numerous articles on literature, art, and culture from the 16th to the 18th centuries, and edited a volume of essays on Renaissance sexuality and gender. His books include *One Flesh: Paradisal Marriage and Sexual Relations in the Age of Milton* (1987, 1993), *Libertines and Radicals in Early Modern London: Sexuality, Politics and Literary Culture, 1630–1685* (2001), and *Schooling Sex: Libertine Literature and Erotic Education in Italy, France, and England, 1534–1685* (forthcoming).

Matthew Vester is Assistant Professor of History at West Virginia University. He received his PhD in 1997 from the University of California, Los Angeles. He has published articles on early modern fiscal politics and is completing a book manuscript on political culture (institutions, informal political networks, representations of power, and local political associations) in the sixteenth-century Savoyard states. A second area of his research examines interactions between villages, state officials, municipalities, and the feudal nobility in the late Renaissance alpine duchy of Aoste/Aosta.

Elissa B. Weaver is Professor of Italian at the University of Chicago. Her research interests include Italian medieval and early modern literature, women's literature, Renaissance theater and epic-chivalric poetry. She is author of *Convent Theatre in Early Modern Italy: Spiritual Fun and Learning for Women* (2002) and editor of *Francesco Buoninsegni and suor Arcangela Tarabotti, Satira Antisatira* (1998), *Beatrice del Sera, Amor di virtú, commedia in cinque atti (1548)* (1990).

Linda Woodbridge, Professor of English at Pennsylvania State University since 1994, she previously taught at the University of Alberta for 24 years, where she chaired the English department. Her books include *Women and the English Renaissance: Literature and the Nature of Womankind, 1540–1620, The Scythe of Saturn: Shakespeare and Magical Thinking*, and *Vagrancy, Homelessness, and English Renaissance Literature*. She has served as president of the Shakespeare Association of America. In 2001–2002 she is a long-term fellow at the Folger Shakespeare Library in Washington, DC.

Introduction
Renaissance Dreaming: In Search of a Paradigm

Guido Ruggiero

In many ways the Renaissance was always a fantasy, a dream. Even before it gained the name "renaissance," intellectuals from the fourteenth century on dreamed that they were giving birth anew to the glories of ancient civilization and rediscovering lost worlds and peoples on the borders of their known world, even if they tended to call the age in which they lived, when they called it anything at all, "modern." In itself their idea that an ancient world could be recreated was little more than a fantasy, a dream that we can smile at from the perspective of our newer and even more hubristic dreams of being at the end of time or being postmodern. But for all the unlikelihood of that dream it struck a deep and resonant chord, which was so powerful that it was replayed with interesting variations in the societies and cultures that followed, gaining ever more power.

The term "renaissance" was used only occasionally at the time; the sixteenth-century artist and famous biographer of artists, Giorgio Vasari, was most notable for using the Italian *rinascita* ("rebirth" or "renaissance") to describe the rebirth of ancient art in Italy in the period. But it was the Enlightenment and the French who popularized the term "renaissance" (*renaître, renaissance*), reflecting the French origin of the word and concept. In that French Enlightenment dreaming, the Renaissance became an Apollonian age of reason and measure when brilliant men broke free from a long dark age of superstition and backwardness (a Germanic Middle Age or Dark Age) to create a brilliant civilization modeled on ancient culture. The Enlightenment's Renaissance still has its appeal today, but, of course, in the cultural world of the Enlightenment the Renaissance became a place where French aristocratic *philosophes* minimally disguised as fifteenth- and sixteenth-century upper-class Italians rationally discussed ancient learning and ways of dealing with life's problems, creating a measured and controlled art, architecture, and civilization that gave rebirth to ancient Rome and Greece and the classic. To put it simply, it was to a great extent the French Enlightenment's dream of itself, dreamt into the past.

But, of course, it was not just a French dream. American thinkers such as Thomas Jefferson were also dreaming of societies, especially republican societies, where good men with a strong civic sense, who were disciplined by civic morality, could build stable and secure states that would endure. For him and many of his peers one of the most important dreams of all was the Enlightenment vision of the Renaissance, a dream that they re-conceived in a revolutionary American context and built into the constitution of the United States and into the ideology that went along with it. Little wonder that the early political world of the United States featured Palladian architecture, governmental forms based on models deemed Renaissance – especially the mixed government made famous by Venice – and an emphasis on the civic virtues that were believed to have typified the upper classes of the most famous and stable Renaissance city-states. Meanwhile, back in the mother country that the American revolutionaries had rejected, the Renaissance was being dreamed as well, but stripped as much as possible of its Frenchness. For the English upper classes the manners and aristocratic style of the Renaissance gained ground on the republican and measured rationalism of the French Enlightenment vision, without entirely displacing them. Benvenuto Cellini and Lorenzo de' Medici became dashing, dramatic heroes of the period, and the English aristocracy could imagine itself in that world as the swashbuckling unbridled Cellini or the bright poet and ruler Lorenzo the Magnificent, even secretly enjoying some of the seamier and darker sides of Renaissance mores and sexual life. The long-established practice of the continental tour for wellborn young Englishmen, which regularly took them to Italy to encounter the surviving glories of Renaissance and ancient civilization, contributed to this Renaissance dreaming, especially as for many it seems to have been a period of exploration and pleasure before they settled down to the strict conventions and responsibilities of life at home as an English aristocrat. In England the Renaissance was perhaps imagined more ambiguously than in France or the new republic of the United States, and for many there it encapsulated the dream of beauty, freedom, and sexual pleasure associated with youth, and a vibrant creativity and aristocratic ease.

Perhaps the most impressive dream of all, however, was that of the Swiss historian Jacob Burckhardt, who in his classic work *The Civilization of the Renaissance in Italy* not only projected his fantasies of an ideal nineteenth-century European civilization on to the Renaissance, but did so with a range and verve that make his vision a powerful and compelling one even today. Times had changed in nineteenth-century Europe, however; virtually perfect Renaissance republics were replaced with city-states under strong-willed tyrants who ruled cleverly, providing order and a certain discipline to society, making the state a work of art – hardly strange in an age that longed for order and strong-willed rulers and where the modern disciplines were being invented. Aristocratic men became more secular in their approach to life and spread their talents widely, seeing themselves as glorious Renaissance amateurs capable of doing everything pretty well, with ease and grace. The most noble (literally) legacy of this attitude was perhaps the revival of the Olympics as a competition for aristocratic amateur athletes who took part as just one more aspect of their brilliant and varied lives of privilege. No matter that across the span of the twentieth century scholars have demolished Burckhardt's dream in nearly every way possible; it still finds its supporters and even the most hard-nosed scholars – myself included – cannot always avoid a wistful acknowledgment of its power or resist slipping momentarily under its spell, for Burckhardt's was quite literally a noble dream, one might almost claim the last noble dream of the European aristocracy.

But so compelling are some visions that they will not fade; like them, the Renaissance dream seems continually to return, adapting itself to changing times. In its various forms in the second half of the twentieth century it has been demolished by archival and social historians (and justly so), attacked by new cultural historians (with equal justice) and reviled by feminists, democrats, and those who seek a less Eurocentric approach to the past (with yet more justice). It has been reincorporated into the Middle Ages, dissolved into the early modern period, obliterated by the premodern, and largely ignored by history done from a local or a world perspective. But tellingly, it is still dreamed.

So what are we to make of this dream? That question is a central theme in this volume. Is there some way to dream the Renaissance today that will do justice to the important understanding of that past already achieved? And at the same time can we do justice to the powerful new ways of thinking about the past in general that have developed over the last century? In sum, can we set an agenda and develop a way of seeing the Renaissance that can be useful for scholars at the turn of the twenty-first century, helpful in understanding a rich complex past, and still worth dreaming in our own times?

One thing is clear: not only has Burckhardt's dream, for all its enduring appeal, been hopelessly shattered, but those who have attempted to reduce it to an inner defensible core have inadvertently limited the concept of the Renaissance to a pale shadow of its former complex brilliance – so much so that the calls for giving up on the Renaissance have actually gained strength in response to that defensive posture. If we reduce the Renaissance to merely a movement led by upper-class intellectuals who styled themselves humanists we may have a defensible periodization of traditional intellectual history (although it might well be argued that even that seriously deforms and underestimates the complexity and richness of high culture in the period), but we have cut away so much of the era that there is little left to characterize it in any significant way, or even dream about it. Moreover, that defensive stance cuts the period off from the newer approaches to history and has a dangerous tendency to leave the Renaissance as a dream to be dreamt only by those who would roll back history and scholarship to the study of great ideas produced by great white European males. Certainly such dreams can, and will, be dreamt, but one hopes that even the most traditional might also be attracted by complex, rich dreams that resonate with contemporary approaches to the past, rather than holding only to older ones that have been shorn of their richness and color in large part because their time is well and truly past.

For this volume I asked several outstanding scholars to dream widely and imaginatively about the Renaissance and they have done so with impressive results. To help them in this project, I made some suggestions for rethinking and redreaming the Renaissance that were designed to introduce and often reintroduce into our view of the period a wide range of issues that are central to it, and that also reflect the methodological developments and intellectual concerns of our own time. Both approaches are necessary, I believe, in order to construct a vision of a period that is useful, meaningful and pleasing – the ultimate goals of this volume – for if we are going to do something as difficult as study the Renaissance we might as well insist on having our cake and eating it too. In fact, if I thought that the Renaissance could not fulfill both requirements, I would join the large group of people clamoring for its demise. But it is precisely because the term still has the potential to blend together modern scholarly concerns, the rich texture of the past, and our deepest dreams, without sacrificing any one for another, that I think it is worth saving, rethinking, and redeploying in our cultures at the beginning of the twenty-first century.

There are three broad themes in this project of rethinking and redeploying the Renaissance as a meaningful periodization of history: first, "Encounters" – the multiple encounters with other worlds both ancient and contemporary that transformed Europe and the world; second, "Imitation" – the widespread fascination with things and ways of doing things Italian, particularly in the areas of culture, economy, and politics (along with the resistance to that fascination), which deeply affected the organization and ways of understanding society; and third, "Reconstruction" – the way society gradually recreated itself in response to rapid urbanization and growth in wealth (punctuated with equally rapid economic crises), demographic disasters, and wars that literally destroyed older social structures and ideologies, ultimately creating the ancient regime in Europe and recreating an aristocratic society based on social hierarchy and family.

Virtually all these changes were viewed at the time in terms of rebirth or reform, at least at first. Even time itself, in going forward in a sense went back, at least as it was reified in the form of the new mechanical clock whose circular movements measured time's movement ahead by continually returning to the beginning. The "new" was a category that aroused deep suspicions at the time. That heartfelt need to look backwards and to go back, shared by elite and popular cultures, makes a strong case for retaining the label "Renaissance" for the period. This is so even if one admits that the period was one where slowly and reluctantly the "new" broke through such resistance in many areas – with new worlds, new diseases, and new sciences to name perhaps only the most obvious. Still, there is no doubt that most people of the period, if they could have chosen, would still have preferred to change by going back. Over and over again they chose re-turn (to the good old ways and customs), re-form (to the proven and correct forms), and if necessary re-volt (the violent re-volution at times necessary to overturn new corruptions and regain a golden past); thus, although the term was rarely used at the time, "renaissance" seems a label that fits their time particularly well.

Of course, labels of historical periods suffer the same limitations as any very broad generalization. The Enlightenment was certainly not all that enlightened; one may legitimately wonder how many people living in the romantic period were romantic or how many people living in the twenties of the twentieth century heard them roar. But an important caveat about periodization is that it is merely a suggestive way of thinking very broadly about, and breaking up, time, whose ceaseless flow and infinite detail in and of itself has no meaning (and periodization may in fact merely be a condition of the way our mind works to understand change), unless there lies behind time itself some cosmic plan or divine vision not available to our secular age. In fact, one might consider throwing out periodization entirely, but broad generalizations – when one keeps in mind what they cannot do and what they are not – certainly can help in grasping large masses of information. And if periods are thoughtfully framed and loaded with subgeneralizations they offer some of the best broad knowledge that we have, and perhaps more interestingly they suggest ways of thinking critically not just about historical periods but our own lives in time.

But rather than claim too much for historical periods, let it suffice to say that this volume attempts to open out and redeploy the concept of Renaissance in order to make it work as a broad frame for a certain period of time – one that, depending upon where one was, stretched from the early fourteenth century to the early seventeenth century and perhaps a bit beyond. The essays here try to take that broad concept and fill it out with generalizations more finely tuned to particularly Renaissance concerns and at the same time suggest agendas for rethinking and research that will not only refine our thinking about the period but also change it. For the best scholarship does not confirm our knowledge, but rather tests it, tries it, wrestles and plays with it, and eventually breaks beyond it, otherwise it would be doomed to become a dull game of dusty certainties and, I fear, of ideas that are well and truly dead.

Let me attempt to anticipate how this volume handles the three broad themes of "Encounters," "Imitation," and "Reconstruction." Centrally, the Renaissance can be seen as a period that opened Europe to contact with other worlds – cultural, social, economic, temporal. It first tried to incorporate and reintegrate those worlds within an inherited common vision (of one unified world revealed by the Bible and ordered by the Christian God), but was slowly forced to deal with a much more pluralistic reality replete with decidedly troubling concepts such as "the new," "the alien," "the other," and "the many." Perhaps the first intellectual contact that helped to define the original paradigm of the Renaissance was the temporal contact with the ancient world, a world that was at once perceived as other, foundational, and recoverable in the present. At this level another world – the past – became a model for the present and its ideologies, culture, and values. In many ways this keen awareness of the past was one of the main motors of Renaissance humanism, reform ideology, and political beliefs, as well as a stimulus to a radical rethinking of the social hierarchy.

Of course this encounter with the past was not new in the Renaissance. All through the Middle Ages and especially from the late eleventh century on, scholars (mainly clerics) were intensely engaged in attempting to recover classical culture and learning. Two things were significant, however, in the ongoing program to recover what was perceived as the superior knowledge of classical times. First, although clerics did not withdraw from this pursuit, upper-class men, and even some of the middling classes, along with a few women as well, eagerly joined the hunt. Second, in the northern Italian homeland of the early Renaissance, these new hunters for ancient treasures lived in flourishing city-states, urban centers that often were consciously legitimating their existence and their governments as the true bearers of ancient traditions originating in classical civilizations. Imagine reading a text by Cicero that argued that the highest morality was to be achieved by serving one's city and living an active life of civic virtue, and imagine the difference between reading this as a monk deep in the countryside in a medieval monastery, or as a member of the ruling class in a vibrant Renaissance city-republic like Florence. Both readers might have the same text and the same ability to read the scholarly Latin, but the text has a radically different meaning in the two settings. Because of the urban and political character of Florence and of many other Renaissance cities, the ancient meaning of many classical texts that had also been written in vibrant city-states could be re-appreciated – very much in the sense of a re-naissance. But that is not the whole story. For despite the dreams that such re-readings might create a true rebirth of classical culture, the urban setting, although in many way closer to the ancient world than was the rural world of the Middle Ages, was still clearly *not* the ancient world. And that meant that the lack of fit between ancient ideas and modern re-creations could prompt creative new ways of thinking about politics, society, and culture in the name of going back to the past. Tellingly, the new slid through these cracks in the fit between ancient texts and modern readings, an unwelcome and often unexpected serpent. And this meant that the Renaissance would never return to the ancient paradise of the classical world, but rather would eventually be thrown unwillingly up against the cold world of the new and the modern.

This encounter with another world was not without its conflicts – the pagan nature of much ancient culture comes immediately to mind. Nevertheless, on the whole, the Renaissance began with a fairly smooth incorporation of this "other" in large part because it was perceived as previous and superior: "other" yet at the same time first and familiar. But a host of more threatening "others" was waiting on Europe's geographical and perceptual borders and much of the Renaissance reformulation of society and culture would be consciously done in the context of contacts and conflicts with those "others." Internally, there were Jews, Moors, "heretics," and marginal people (certain of the poor and the peasants, who were increasingly perceived as threatening). In addition, people suffering from certain kinds of illness (the plague, syphilis, and madness perhaps most significantly), women and their sexuality (also increasingly feared), along with sodomites and others were also perceived as sexually dangerous and "other" in this context. Although not necessarily "others" from a modern perspective, these groups – some of whom had already been marginalized in the Middle Ages – were now more ruthlessly and systematically labeled and treated as "others" who should be either safely isolated, eliminated, or controlled.

More noted in this context were perhaps the encounters with others beyond the borders of Europe: first "Turks" and Africans, then Asians and finally the pseudo-Asians of what would eventually become the "New World" – "Indians." These meetings were often begun on a note of optimism, on the assumption that soon these people would be converted to Christianity (or even that they had once been Christian, converted by Christ's Apostles); others assumed that such encounters were simply part of God's master plan for universal Christian redemption and perhaps a precursor of the much awaited end of time. In a second stage of these interactions Renaissance Europe attempted to impose its dreams of itself on these other worlds, often with devastating and unexpected results, a process that has been strangely re-enacted in diverse ways by later colonial and "modern" western societies and cultures. But with time Europe had reluctantly to face and come to grips with a much more complex world; in the process it crucially also had to rediscover itself in a much deeper and more self-reflective way. And of course, that reluctant acceptance of the alienness of others was reinforced in the heart of Europe itself with the confessional battles that divided the ideological unity of Christendom – a unity that had been largely an ideology itself. Nonetheless, the breaking down of that apparent unity helped to focus concern on the idea of multiple worlds, multiple cultures and, crucially, dangerous "others" that once more had to be isolated, dominated, and even at times eliminated. Thus during the Renaissance the attitude to other worlds moved fitfully but inexorably from confidence and assimilation to conflict and domination. Rather paradoxically the Renaissance might be seen as ending with the formation of European states fully committed and ready to dominate and "civilize" (read "Europeanize") the other worlds they had come into contact with – perhaps the ultimate move of modernity. Here the dream of the Renaissance reveals a potentially darker side, sliding at times all too easily towards nightmare.

A second facet of the Renaissance as a period that has often been noted, but perhaps not given the weight it deserves, is the degree to which Italy was looked to as a leader of this period, much as France was seen as a leader in the Enlightenment or England in the Victorian period – the theme that I have labeled "Imitation." One thing that makes this harder to see is the evident fact that Italy did not exist as a country in the period or even as a geographic entity. We are actually speaking about a group of diverse city-states in the north of Italy (along with the virtually undefinable court/city/religious-center Rome) perceived as leading Europe culturally. This unlikely grouping – a true imagined community, perhaps – set the scene for seeing the Renaissance as a revival of classical culture, one based on humanism and its less noted but perhaps equally important formulation of an urban and civic focus for culture. These closely related cultural developments had a tremendous impact on the high culture of Europe and, through European expansion, on the culture of the world. Less noted, however, has been the way Italy led, and was imitated, in other fields, such as economic techniques and strategies, the articulation of bureaucracies and governmental structures, the development of new ideologies of power and social hierarchy, and even in seemingly more mundane areas like rethinking the illicit and the perverse. Little wonder that at the end of the sixteenth century and during the first years of the seventeenth in England the two pillars of Italy were Machiavelli and Aretino – the one representing the danger of taking the Italian model in politics too far and the other embodying the danger of following the illicit models of that dangerously seductive country. Little wonder too that French cookbooks followed and at the same time attempted to break free from Italian models, and that Italian artists, lawyers, bureaucrats, merchants, and adventurers fanned out across Europe and beyond in the period, finding themselves the much sought after (and occasionally reviled) bearers of what we might still call the civilization of the Renaissance.

But crucially, imitation is never perfect. The slippages and imperfections caused by attempting to translate concepts, forms, and things across cultures and space means that imitation often creates something unexpectedly new, innovative, and at times even threatening. Moreover, as aspects of culture both material and spiritual are imitated or recreated in different cultures and societies they gain other resonances and meanings; I suggest that much that was new and even revolutionary in the Renaissance may be traced back to imperfect imitation. Perhaps the most notable area where this can be seen is in religious thought and enthusiasms, where the ancient texts to which scholars turned in Italy, in other areas and contexts took on unanticipated and ultimately revolutionary dimensions. In many ways, then, the Renaissance may be seen as a period when things Italian gained a cultural and broader preeminence in Europe and beyond, only to slowly lose pride of place to newer chauvinisms, incipient forms of national pride, and local resistance. Thus the Renaissance period might be seen as ending with the successful rejection of what at the time still seemed Italian.

Finally, the Renaissance as a period was deeply marked by social realignments across the board. What disguises the intense social conflict and change is the fact that superficially things look much the same at the end of the period as they looked at the beginning – this "Reconstruction" of an aristocratic and hierarchical society won out in the end; so one could be tempted to say that little or nothing had changed. In fact, the period begins with a conflict in Italy between newer urban merchant-banker elites and older traditional aristocracies, which was soon won by the former. But not content merely to have wrested power and position economically and politically from that traditional aristocracy, these new elites set out to create a social ideology that would confirm them as the true elites of society. A goodly part of the agenda of early humanism and civic culture was concerned with finding in the ancient world an intellectual rationale for the ideological shift that would put these new urban leaders on top of society, not just because they were powerful, but because they deserved in any case to be on top. In turn, it was that ideological component that made humanism and Italian civic culture for all their seductive brilliance so potentially destabilizing for the rest of Europe, at least until local adaptations were able to domesticate them. Still, urban culture in many ways became the culture of the Renaissance throughout Europe and in some telling ways in the rest of the world as well, often with unsettling results.

Meanwhile, back in Italy, as the Renaissance progressed the merchant-banker elites of Italy slowly transformed themselves into a new aristocracy, in the process creating new forms of courtly society, new forms of art and patronage, new forms of cultural display, and new forms of manners and civility for society, virtually all, of course, in the name of returning to the old. Much of this is reflected in the splendor of the courts of Renaissance Italy, a splendor quickly noticed and emulated in the rest of Europe – especially because in much of Europe courts had never really gone out of fashion or lost their vitality. There is a certain irony, however, in the fact that Italian etiquette books and books on courtly manners in the sixteenth century would become the benchmarks for courtly society throughout Europe when one considers that the Italians were relative newcomers to such courtly traditions and, often, to aristocratic ways.

But there was a darker side to this renaissance of aristocratic sensibilities, because in Italy this new aristocracy was concerned to define clearly and effectively the boundaries that separated its members from the rest of society. This is no surprise when one considers that most of them had recently arrived at the top of the social hierarchy and were anxious to defend their newly won status and the power that often went hand and hand with it. And below them at each social level in turn, there was also considerable anxiety to demarcate and confirm social distinctions. This clearly was a much broader phenomenon, tied up as it was with obvious economic, demographic, and social dislocations of the late Renaissance in Europe in general. The general phenomenon of the late Renaissance that we might label as boundary forming – between social groups, between countries and territories, between insiders and outsiders, between the licit and the illicit, between confessional beliefs to name only the most obvious – was probably so overdetermined that historians will be able to debate for much of the twenty-first century about what the primary factors were in this drive to define European society more clearly. Most notably, however, along with a strengthening separation of insiders from outsiders noted above, the divisions of social hierarchy were entrenched more deeply, with harder boundaries being drawn at the upper social levels and the lower levels being virtually defined out of society. In many ways peasants and marginal people (the undeserving poor) were culturally "reconstructed" as dangerous others and as the lowly uncivilized at the margins of European society. One curious example of how far this way of seeing things went was the movement to send internal missions within Europe to certain rural areas to convert the peasants there to Christianity and a Christian way of life – missions consciously modeled on those to the "others" of the New World. Peasants and the now "undeserving" poor had become "others," Europe's own dangerous Indians, as it were. From top to bottom, social redefinitions of society had a profound impact on the Renaissance; by the end of these changes we have a new regime, which from the perspective of the American and French Revolutions a little more than a century and a half later, would become the ancient regime. But from the perspective of the Renaissance that seemingly ancient regime was the culmination of a long, complex, often violent, realignment of European society.

At the level of the family there were also dramatic changes and conflicts, masked by a seeming continuity. Certainly at the end of the Renaissance the family was still the benchmark of social organization and discipline, based upon heterosexual reproduction and intergenerational inheritance strategies to preserve wealth and power through the male line. But that apparent continuity masks great changes and conflicts that are still matters of intense scholarly debate. Still, certain things seem clear. Narrowing gaps in the age difference between marital partners offered a greater possibility for companionate marriages and changed the age dynamic dramatically in upper-class marriages – making marriage a much less alien phenomenon to the modern observer than it was in the early and High Renaissance. Simply put, the earlier Renaissance ideal of marriage between a 30-year-old man and a 14-year-old girl had a dramatically different dynamic from a marriage between a 22-year-old woman and a 25-year-old man, which had become the ideal for the upper classes by the end of the period. Equally significant, at levels below the elite, urbanization and greater mobility for individuals meant that in many larger families supportive structures were severely weakened and had to be replaced by other forms of social support and discipline. Changes in Renaissance guild life and forms of religious community were closely intertwined with these developments, as were forms of male and female sociability in general beyond the family. It may well be that such changes played a crucial and largely unrecognized role in recasting many of the poor as no longer deserving charity (and as increasingly other and dangerous) and in the rapid articulation of disciplining agencies and drives, especially in Renaissance cities. Finally, as the age difference between husband and wife became less and the age at marriage went up, problems such as the number of illegitimate births seemed to increase. It seems also that throughout the Renaissance the strong call to restrict women to the home and place them more securely under the control of males, won out – not as absolutely, however, as was once assumed, but still enough so that at the end of the period in most of Europe, especially among the upper classes, one half of the population was essentially locked away – a form of confinement that would be long in undoing.

Encounter, Imitation, and Reconstruction: these processes, this turmoil, such basic change warrant a period of their own, I would argue. And the dynamic, destructive, regenerative reformulation of Europe and the world that it involved seems, paradoxically, to call for its traditional name: The Renaissance. It was quite simply a period and a movement that sprang from the often violent and conflicted rebirth of worlds cultural, social, and geographical. To make this renaissance a happy dream may be difficult, for like all periods of history it had its nightmarish sides as well. But if we are to come close to the past in any meaningful way we need to face the negative as well as the positive; in fact, some of the most useful critical thinking may grow out of an unflinching look at the darker sides of the Renaissance. And, less practically speaking, it does seem that brooding on the negative aspects of an earlier age resonates well with our skeptical and pessimistic perspective on the world, and may provide an aesthetic dimension to the Renaissance more attuned to our times.

Yet perhaps it would be best to end this rethinking of the Renaissance by returning to its dreaming to suggest some more positive visions of the period. In terms of "Encounters" one might suggest that for all the negative effects of European encounters with other worlds, those encounters reflected an original confidence that meeting and understanding others was ultimately a project that was valuable and doable. Accepting that example in an age where the trend seems to be to fear or destroy others, and to emphasize the unbridgeability of gaps, while thinking critically about the areas where the Renaissance failed in this project, might make redreaming the Renaissance particularly useful. Redreaming Italy and imitating it might seem to have little to offer, even if, curiously, it seems that at the moment that is exactly what is happening in much of the world, with the popularity of things Italian, with Italian style, food, and material culture having a wide following. But behind the Renaissance vision of a superior culture and way of life to be found in the Italian, there lay a deeper faith that social and cultural life could be improved and that that was a worthy and necessary project for civil life in communities. Once again we seem to have lost track of that vision. If market values and consumption add something to our social and cultural lives, we take what pleasure we can in that gift from those driving forces, but perhaps it would be interesting to redream this aspect of the Renaissance and try to modify our more cynical attitude with that kind of optimism about how society and culture might go together to make life in modern society meaningful and rewarding. Finally, in a time where we have great faith in the fact that we have abolished social hierarchy and created individuals capable literally of fashioning themselves, a closer critical look at how social hierarchy worked and individuals interacted with family and society in a very different time may not only expose the flaws in our own dreams, but suggest rather different agendas for change than the ones currently fashionable in what is left of radical circles. Which is all just to suggest that rethinking the Renaissance and redreaming it too is not merely an arcane project for a few university professors, but something useful and potentially enjoyable to consider for a new millennium.

The essays of this volume have not tried to cover every aspect of the Renaissance. Rather, the goal was to rethink the Renaissance along the lines of the broad themes outlined above, combining recent scholarship with the strengths of the more traditional, and offering new agendas for thinking critically about the period. In the first section of the volume the essays focus on the course of events in various parts of the world at the time, with a special attention to how they might fit into a Renaissance paradigm. Readers will quickly see that these essays have not been forced into the vision of the Renaissance outlined above; rather that vision served as merely a point of departure from which each essay develops its own perspective and agenda. The first essay, by Gene Brucker, reflects well the social and cultural vision of the Italian Renaissance that has been one of dominant ways of looking at the period from the 1960s on, and which Brucker himself in many ways pioneered and established as he trained a generation of students at Berkeley. Research in the rich archives of Italy to deepen and enrich the understanding of the political, social, and economic workings of the Italian Renaissance has been the key to his work and to that of a host of other scholars who earned this approach a central position in post-war Renaissance scholarship. In fact, much of this work was so tightly focused on archival data and a close analysis of local events or social conditions that questions of periodization were largely ignored. In this essay, however, Brucker takes a broader look at the way the political and social interacted with, and in many ways structured, the cultural, and advances a powerful overview of how the Renaissance worked as a period in Italy. In the process he also provides some rationale for the often lamented Florentine focus of much of this scholarship.

Randolph Starn's essay on the European Renaissance reflects a newer vision of the period, based on many of the ideas central to the new cultural history. It is not surprising that he does so, since he, as one of the leaders of the group who founded the cutting edge journal *Representations*, has played a significant role in formulating that approach. Significantly, however, in this essay Starn blends traditional scholarship with a deeper rethinking, and places change ahead of structure in his historical analysis; thus genealogies (echoing Foucault) and process are the key to his analysis of the Renaissance. In a way the Renaissance is for Starn a constant process of a society and culture discovering and creating itself in space and time. Thus, tellingly, it was less the "New World" that had to be discovered in Starn's vision – it was already known by its inhabitants – but rather it was Europe that had to be created and the genealogy of this creation traced here was one of the most crucial aspects of the Renaissance forced upon Europe by its encounters with a larger world. Following the pioneering work of Stephen Greenblatt, Starn also treats the genealogy of the individual, nicely problematizing this concept in the process and providing a provocative new twist on the idea of Renaissance self-fashioning. In the end, as one might expect given his emphasis on cultural dynamics over cultural structures, the Renaissance becomes a series of open-ended sets of practices that in many ways set out the main themes of this book.

The next three essays in the volume follow in the footsteps of Starn's interest in how other worlds were constructed and encountered in the Renaissance and, as in his essay, they provide some stimulating ways of reconsidering what was occurring not only in those other places but in Europe as well. Linda Darling, whose work on the Middle East contributed to a renaissance of interest in the area in our period, breaks down the traditional Eurocentrism of the idea of Renaissance. Working mainly from a cultural perspective she argues persuasively that the term can be usefully applied to developments in the Middle East and beyond and to the relationships between the Middle East and Mediterranean and European cultures, societies, and economies. Refreshingly and challengingly she also presents a Renaissance economic world centered in the Middle East with Europe as merely another trading partner and peripheral competitor. Matthew Restall offers an even more forceful essay, which calls into question the Eurocentrism of the traditional visions of the Renaissance. Noted for his path-breaking studies of the languages and documents written in Mesoamerican languages, especially Nahuatl, Restall in this essay looks closely at two areas especially associated with the Renaissance in Europe – urban planning and literacy – and argues that in both areas the New World in many ways led the Old. Perhaps most striking is his claim that the most innovative urban designs in Renaissance Europe were actually modeled on New World urban models. Whether or not one is willing to go all the way with Restall and accept that "it was in Spanish America, therefore, that the 'real' renaissance was created" his essay suggests that the relationship between "other" worlds and Europe needs to be rethought as much more reciprocal and interdependent than has been the case, a theme that runs through all these essays.

Peter Burke's essay nicely weaves these themes into an innovative look at the way geography shaped Renaissance society and culture, without falling into geographical determinism. Noted for his evocative essays on the Renaissance that have repeatedly provoked new ways of thinking about the period and new issues to investigate, Burke looks at how the Renaissance was diffused over space and time. The themes of both encounters and imitation come out strongly here as he examines how culture, people, and things move and are literally translated from place to place in the period. Perhaps influenced by literary theory as well as geography, he argues that when thinking about these movements of the Renaissance we need to shift our focus from diffusion to reception and from adoption to adaptation, much as Starn, Darling, and Restall do in their essays. Tellingly, Burke also suggests, echoing Starn, that rather than looking at humanism, the traditional cultural centerpiece of Renaissance scholarship, as a system of ideas about philology, the dignity of man, and ancient learning, we should look at it as a set of cultural practices more concerned with the collecting of coins, writing letters in classical Latin, and teaching Latin grammar – an interpretation that will return later in the essay of Ingrid Rowland.

The second part of the volume examines some of the more significant worlds and ways of power in the Renaissance. Looking quickly at the list of topics covered it should be clear that this section follows the lead of contemporary scholars who are breaking new ground by suggesting that significant technologies and strategies of power can be found throughout society and culture. And that is particularly true in the Renaissance, where governments and other traditional centers of authority were merely competitors in a much broader spectrum of power and often far from the most significant competitors. Modern scholarship has been seriously distorted by what might be called a modernist fantasy of the state as the source and center of all power, but as that ideological premise of the modern state is deconstructed and scholars move out to examine the much more complex world of power in particular societies and cultures, exciting new perspectives are being opened on the past. This excitement has played an important role in revitalizing and reinvigorating even the study of government itself, as the first essay in this section by Edward Muir nicely demonstrates. Muir, known for his cultural studies of the organization of society through ritual activities and the breakdown of society in the face of violence, combines in this essay an excellent overview of the more traditional vision of government and the state with a newer cultural approach, in the process suggesting a host of interesting directions for new research. Contrasting the abstract theories of the state with the messy Renaissance realities of governance he quickly moves on to consider crucial questions about governments' actual ability to rule; the relationship between ritual and symbolisms of rule and ruling; the problematics of Renaissance states as unified spaces; the centrality of justice and order in formation of Renaissance states; the impact of court and patronage on states; and finally the symbolism of state. Using the Hapsburgs as an example, Muir shows how that great dysfunctional trilogy of the modern state – bureaucracy, taxes, and war – were already well in place in the Renaissance, undermining early attempts at state formation.

James Farr's essay follows Muir's lead, moving on from what might be seen as one of the most significant manifestations of Renaissance government's power, the law, to consider power dynamics that might be seen as largely escaping the authority of government, such as custom and honor. True to his complex studies of artisan honor and the relationship between law, honor, and sex in Renaissance France, Farr does not fall into such simple dichotomies. Rather, he sees law, custom, and honor as complex interrelated disciplining dynamics that articulated fields of power and control, deeply affecting Renaissance life. Farr also rejects as too teleological the traditional vision that sees written law triumphing over custom in the Renaissance and argues that honor is the missing link between the two and the key to understanding Renaissance discipline. "Everywhere in Renaissance Europe," he points out, "honor was a well-established, customary, and traditional regulatory process that had daily purchase on the people within it. It pervaded the very souls of men and women and regulated their everyday actions." In some ways Gregory Hanlon's essay on violence moves power back under the control of government. He outlines the strategies that he sees as central in Italian Renaissance governments' great long-term project of reducing the level of violence in society – the project that dominated the late Renaissance and state formation. True to the behaviorist vision developed in his important works on crime and violence in the Renaissance, however, Hanlon sees biology as ultimately more significant than government. He argues that for all the developments in governmental attempts to control violence, "magistrates were still confronted with Original Sin; that is, while rates of violence declined in ways we can measure, people (men, by far) continued to maim and murder their neighbors for reasons that appear to be universal and constitutive of human nature." While few other essays in this volume share this biological determinism it does suggest yet another way of seeing power in the Renaissance.

Robert Muchembled's essay, following the ground-breaking work of Norbert Elias, takes us to another fascinating and significant trinity of the time: courts, manners, and civility. Most noted perhaps for his own innovative volumes on Renaissance popular culture and the attacks on that culture at the end of the Renaissance, Muchembled introduces English-speaking readers to his new research on Renaissance courts and courtly ways. He goes beyond Elias to see courts and manners at their most significant as "cultural laboratories," where men learned to internalize discipline and order society via self-control: lessons that would slowly be incorporated – not in a linear fashion but in an ongoing give and take – into society and culture as the Renaissance ended and a modern era began. But even in Renaissance courts such changes were stoutly resisted by older codes of behavior that stressed male violence and a certain direct animality in a tight competitive space, where the will of the prince could literally be the law. Thus in Muchembled's nuanced vision such changes were hardly a triumphal march or a simple evolutionary civilizing process, but a complex set of negotiations that depended on courts, aristocracies, and manners.

Joanne Ferraro in her essay takes the discussion of Renaissance power to the locus where a person of the period would have turned first: to the family. According to the Renaissance ideal the family was the building block and primary sustainer of order and discipline. Ferraro, who has studied the family both in its political dimensions and from the perspective of marriage and the relationships between husbands and wives in ground-breaking studies based on archival material, here looks at the family both in its macro political and social dimensions and in its micro relationships of passions, loves, and conflict. The result is a thought-provoking essay that covers the traditional issues of family history, but also moves beyond them to suggest that we look more closely at the microdynamics of family relationships and their implications for Renaissance life, especially for women. Elissa Weaver follows in this vein, looking more closely at the way in which the cultural and social construction of gender differences disciplined and ordered Renaissance life. While Ferraro investigated the family using archival documents enriched by literature, Weaver looks at gender issues relying primarily upon Renaissance literature, backing this up with archival research. And as one might expect, given her path-breaking research into previously unknown works by Renaissance women, especially nuns, Weaver has an original perspective on the range of powers available to women. This places her squarely in the revisionist camp that sees women as having had a Renaissance in literature and life, albeit a modest one. But most notably these two essays are outstanding examples of how the newer research interests of the last generation have enriched our understanding of the complexity and range of discipline, order, and power in the Renaissance. The story can no longer be told in terms of high ideas and high politics carried out by a handful of men; such a story simply does not do justice to the richness of the Renaissance. More importantly, when looked at from the point of view of family and gender, whole new Renaissance worlds become visible.

In the last essay of this part John Martin tackles the controversial topic of identity and selfhood in the Renaissance. Some have argued that there was little sense of self or identity in the Renaissance, such concepts being in many ways what make modern individuals radically different from their premodern predecessors, who tended to see themselves as moments in a family tradition or part of much more significant corporate or spiritual groups. The idea that identity is a facet of modernity has generated much controversy (and interesting scholarship) and stands at the heart of the thesis advanced by Norbert Elias, and to a lesser extent by Muchembled in this volume, about how the beginning of the modern is predicated upon a change in the human psyche – a change that turns on the internalization of comportment and manners and a developing sense of an internalized self. Where the contest for power is fought out in a society and culture also depends on how the self that seeks power is located in society and conceived; thus in a way Martin's essay poses the ultimate question for power. With his studies on Renaissance heresy and popular religious beliefs, and a number of important essays on aspects of selfhood such as sincerity and honor, Martin brings to this essay experience both of a close reading of inquisitional materials from the archives and a wide-ranging reading in the more traditional intellectual history of the period. Crucially, in this essay, he makes a much needed qualification of the issues involved, pointing out that while one should not expect to find modern concepts of selfhood and individualism in other cultures and times, culturally specific senses of self are to be found in most societies and cultures. For the Renaissance, then, he sees three types of selfhood as being operative: a civic selfhood that builds out from the family to include local perceptions of community; a performative sense of self which was largely a product of the sixteenth century and tied to evolving courtly ideals and traditional concepts of honor; and a sense of a inner self – less in the modern sense of inner and more in the context of an inner opening to the spiritual world. Apparently radical, in many ways this is a subtle rereading of much of the traditional critique of ideas of modern selfhood. It shows from a Renaissance perspective how a Renaissance sense of self contributed to the way in which individuals constructed themselves, suggesting new ways of thinking about the relationship between self and power in the period.

The third part of the volume looks at the social and economic worlds of the Renaissance. As noted above, the Renaissance was a time of crucial social realignments, often underestimated because at the end of the period things in Europe seemed to look much as they had at the beginning, with society seemingly based upon an enduring three estates model: a clergy that prayed, a hereditary nobility that fought and largely dominated local society, and all the rest below. But, as pointed out above, this apparent continuity masked the presence of dynamic change and conflict across the social hierarchy. Matthew Vester, in his essay on the upper classes in the Renaissance, nicely brings out this complexity. Vester has worked on the nobility in Savoy and Piedmont, a kind of crossroads area in the late Renaissance, where Italian and French visions of nobility and the upper classes intersected and at times conflicted with interesting results. As a result his essay deals with the problematic relationship between new urban elites and older military aristocracies and the gradual building of a European aristocracy that would become the "old regime." Most notably, perhaps, he recasts the traditional theme of conflict between the growing nation-state and the local nobility and suggests that an emphasis on the rise of the territorial state with its teleological focus on modern political forms of centralization seriously misconstrues the complexity of the history of the upper classes in this period. He suggests persuasively that instead the nobility of the period should be seen much more as a European-wide collection of major families who lived in and dominated areas that did not fall neatly within state boundaries, and that the real conflicts of the age were much more about noble jurisdictions of a transregional type. As a result, this essay not only rethinks the way the upper classes were reformed in the Renaissance, it suggests some interesting ways to rethink the nature of power and government in the period.

James Amelang takes on the other side of the great Renaissance social divide in his essay on those below the upper classes. The seeming immobility and lack of distinction in the lower classes becomes in Amelang's accomplished hands a much more complex and rapidly changing phenomenon. Having worked on the world of artisans in Renaissance Spain and the development of the genre of autobiographical writing among the lower classes and especially artisans in the Renaissance, Amelang brings a wide-ranging familiarity with the lower classes to his essay. Thus he deals with traditional crucial themes like the conversion of the poor and the peasantry from integral parts of society to "outsiders" (at least for the category of poor defined as undeserving) and vile untrustworthy villains. This, along with the upsurge in vagrancy or people without a fixed place in society, radically changed the nature of life at the bottom of society and played a significant role in some of the darker aspects of the Renaissance that set it apart as a period. But when he turns to the social and cultural world of artisans Amelang is at his most original and suggestive and we get a fascinating look at a vibrant world that contributed much more to the Renaissance than has been traditionally recognized.

This theme returns from an economic perspective in Karl Appuhn's essay on the economic worlds of the Renaissance. Appuhn has worked on the economy of Renaissance Venice, especially on state control of the vital resources necessary for its shipbuilding industry, and the delicate balance between protecting natural resources and satisfying economic demands for raw materials to sustain economic growth. He brings a fresh perspective both to the changes in the agricultural sphere, which were crucial for sustaining the urban nature of Renaissance society, and to the economic strategies of urban society. Perhaps most notably he stresses new techniques and ways of organizing agriculture, trade, and urban production without falling into a simple technological determinism. He even brings a cultural dimension to economic history by arguing that quantification and more disciplined ways of organizing the economy and keeping records were crucial innovations, not just for the economic success of the period, but for the very nature of the period itself. John Marino's essay takes the economic innovations of the Renaissance onto a world stage. Most noted for his impressively detailed archival studies of the economy of southern Italy, Marino here demonstrates a much broader and even more creative synthetic vision that allows him to situate the voyages of discovery and the drive to open and dominate new markets around the world. Again, traditional themes like the shift from a Mediterranean focus of production and commerce to first a north Atlantic and then a world focus are nicely laid out. Then he traces how Italian and Iberian models and experience were translated and transformed gradually into the first global system of exchange, especially in regard to the powerful new drug-like stimulants of sugar and tobacco.

The next part of the volume examines the cultural worlds of the Renaissance, perhaps the area most associated with traditional ways of seeing the period. The range of subjects treated in this section and the adventurous approaches of the essayists who have contributed will further encourage the recent important trend of seeing Renaissance culture from a broad perspective. Right from the beginning of this part, with David Gentilcore's essay rethinking the concept of popular culture in the Renaissance, there is a fruitful move beyond the traditional emphasis on high culture. Gentilcore's recent publications on the magical and religious worlds of southern Italy in the period provide an interesting point of departure for an essay that attempts to rethink one of the most difficult issues in new cultural studies: the way the apparently varying cultures of different groups of people in society operate within a more general shared culture. For Gentilcore the answer lies in the concept of subcultures, the special cultures of groups within society who have their own customs, techniques, traditions, ways of speaking, etc., but still participate in the more general culture. So he considers subcultures defined by work, by rural life, by gender, by social distinctions, by living at the margins of licit society and does so without having to fall back on the older and perhaps oversimplistic vision of a sharp divide between high and low, popular and elite, or vernacular and Latin culture. This allows him to provide a nuanced picture of a central theme of the innovative and important work by scholars such as Peter Burke and Robert Muchembled in this area (the progressive attack on popular culture that marks so profoundly the end of the Renaissance), which he sees in terms of a much more complex series of intrusions of the dominant culture on specific subcultures.

Ingrid Rowland, in the second essay of this part, tackles the more traditional topic of high culture with a focus on humanism and how it formed and informed the intellectual life of the period. But true to her original work on humanism, she uses her classical training and new cultural perspectives to provide a new reading of humanism's significance without losing the richness of the great scholarly work that has been done in this area. Perhaps what makes this essay so interesting is the way in which Rowland sees Renaissance high culture as a set of practices and approaches that extended well beyond humanism, and rather than worshipping the great thoughts of great men she attempts to examine how such practices actually fit into the life of the Renaissance, again without losing sight of what was impressive, suggestive, and beautiful. The essay by R. Po-chia Hsia follows a path similar to the first two essays by examining how religion was lived in the Renaissance, examining it as a set of practices rather than merely as a set of ideas dominated by the elite of the Church. Hsia, noted for his micro and macro studies of religious experience and enthusiasm in the period, stresses in this essay a crucial point: that the boundaries between the spiritual world and the profane world were overwhelmed in the Renaissance by waves of popular piety and by a breakdown in the ideal of the clerical control of the spiritual – a breakdown that gave religious enthusiasm an explosive potential and a central place in the everyday life. Looking closely at four broad issues: the difference between spiritual styles in the Mediterranean and in northern Europe; conflicting visions of reform; the expression and repression of feminine spirituality; and the multiple eruptions of the divine in everyday life, he develops a thought-provoking and innovative vision of religious enthusiasm and conflict in an age that was anything but the secular.

Loren Partridge, in the fourth essay in this part, takes on the immense task of dealing with Renaissance art and to meet the challenge provides a more methodological perspective. Given the significant work he has done in the field his essay gains additional interest from the autobiographical approach he takes in discussing the ways in which Renaissance art historians have changed their ways of thinking about and seeing Renaissance art. Focusing on Italy, he lays out the parameters of the field and assesses the strengths and weaknesses of the various methods he sees as most significant. Partridge argues that the field has moved away from traditional interests in connoisseurship, style, and iconography towards a more contextual analysis, focusing on a range of social, economic, and cultural issues. Among these are: the function of art, the impact of patronage, the reception of artistic works, the social status of artists, the psychoanalytical analysis of art, the technical aspects of artistic production, and the relationship between gender, sex, and art. James Grantham Turner, in a playful essay on literature, stresses the playfulness of Renaissance literature itself – almost as if his essay in its form and aesthetics is designed to mirror to the reader the nature of Renaissance literature. Following on from his important publications on English Renaissance literature and the impact of sex, gender, and aesthetics on the literature of the period, this essay puts the perhaps most difficult question that one might pose: What will we define as Renaissance literature? After considering an evocative range of possibilities he suggests, "the typical Renaissance text is 'jocoserious,' cunningly poised between jest and earnest." One could say the same thing about this essay and in that tension between jest and earnest there are many suggestions for further research and many innovative ideas about Renaissance literature.

John Najemy's essay on Renaissance political thought is a compelling rethinking of the way ideas about government, ruling, and the state developed in the period. After his publications on the social and political life of Renaissance Florence based on massive archival work, and his newer publications on the thought of Machiavelli based on an especially sensitive reading of that difficult thinker, it will come as no surprise that this essay stresses the reciprocal relationship between political theory and political practice in the Renaissance. Building out from Italy and the republican and princely political ideologies that developed there, Najemy provides a powerful synthesis. It is noteworthy also, given the complaints of many (including myself) about the overemphasis on the centrality of Florence in Renaissance studies, that Najemy gives Florence a central place in his discussion and defends that placement impressively. But more importantly, in describing the development of the modern view of the state and political power, he provides numerous suggestions for rethinking this process and for re-examining the leading Renaissance figures who wrote on the subject. In the last essay of this part William Eamon tackles the immense topic of Renaissance science and medicine. He is noted for his magisterial study of Renaissance books of secrets and his many seminal articles on the impact of popular culture and anti-establishment thinkers on the development of science. Again, this essay is not an account of the triumph of great thinkers in the march towards modern science, but a much more complex tale of the conflicts and negotiations between different visions of the cosmos, nature, and medicine in the period, and the development of newer methodologies for trying to understand and manipulate them. Here culture, science, society are rethought from the bottom up. As with all the essays in this part the result is to reconfigure old heroes and the Renaissance itself, offering a series of new issues for consideration.

The last part of the book focuses on a theme that many of the earlier essays have already addressed in trying to break away from the overly triumphant traditional view of the period – the darker sides of the Renaissance. Actually the title is slightly misleading, because the concept "anti-worlds" articulates the attitude of the dominant culture of the Renaissance to places and peoples who were considered "other"; for many at the time, however, that view was highly problematic, especially those who lived in those other worlds. In theory these were separate worlds, but in fact in many ways these anti-worlds were deeply integrated into Renaissance society and culture, for better and for worse. The essay by Mary Lindemann that begins this part examines perhaps the most famous negatives of the Renaissance: the regular recurrence of the plague, the pervasiveness of disease in general, and the ubiquity of hunger. As a noted social historian of medicine who has written both in-depth archival studies of doctors, health policy, and poverty in Germany and an overview of medicine and health practice in early modern Europe, Lindemann deals both with the traditional issues surrounding the prevalence of disease and hunger and with the way in which these concepts were culturally constructed in the Renaissance. So, for example, she thoughtfully reviews the literature about what disease the plague actually was, even as she warns that attempting to identify it may well be a futile task given how rapidly bacilli (and viruses for that matter) can mutate over time. She then proceeds to ask more cultural questions about how the plague infected the imagination of people across the period. For Lindemann, hunger, disease, and plague had significant, direct material impacts on Renaissance life, in the classic modes of the history of medicine and social history, but they also were crucial cultural constructs. The way those constructs worked and fitted into Renaissance life were equally important, and they open up vast new vistas for study. Linda Woodbridge in turn, in her essay on Renaissance bogeymen and monsters, applies a similar cultural approach to the way people were defined as others and outside of society in this period. A noted expert on Shakespeare, Woodbridge has written on the way literature represents the poor and marginal figures of the Renaissance world, and has been innovative in her use of literature to study social practice and beliefs; this essay is a good example of her interdisciplinary approach. Here the underworld of the Renaissance comes to life and one gets another perspective on a process noted earlier in the essays on the social world of the Renaissance: the way in which the hierarchal structures of Renaissance society were as much constructed by exclusion as inclusion. The undeserving poor; the marginal at the bottom of society; the unreliable peasants of the countryside; the sexually perverse; "outsiders" such as Jews, thieves, con-men, charlatans, sodomites; even those who challenged gender norms – overly aggressive women and feminine men – all reappear here as various forms of monsters and bogeymen. And as monsters and bogeyman not only were they repressed formally; informally they were defined away, leaving the Renaissance safe in its dreams of itself.

Thomas Arnold, in his essay on war and violence, continues the consideration of areas of Renaissance life that in many ways were debarred from the ideals of the Renaissance, yet were deeply integrated into that life. Here, as in his important work on the history of Renaissance warfare, Arnold mixes traditional issues of military history with a deep cultural consideration of what warfare and violence meant to Renaissance society at both upper-class levels and more humble ones. Echoing the insights of Robert Muchembled's earlier essay about the predilection of the European nobility for aggression, Arnold stresses the way violent codes of behavior like the hunt not only prepared that nobility for violence but made it a central way of life, one that it is difficult for us to fully comprehend today. As he concludes, "For many noble participants, warfare was not something to be fought and won to allow a return to civilian life; rather warfare was life itself, formal campaigning providing just another murderous arena for the display of pride, courage, and skill at arms." And in fact the consideration of how violence was culturally constructed across the social spectrum and integrated deeply into Renaissance life offers a strikingly new perspective on the period. At the same time it supports Arnold's call for new forms of Renaissance military history that will return it to its deserved central place in our understanding of the period.

My essay on witchcraft and magic in the Renaissance attempts to stimulate rethinking on the subject by turning traditional approaches to the subject on their head – reversals of the established order being a noble Renaissance tradition. I have tried in this essay to take seriously the way witchcraft and magic were practiced in everyday culture – treating them not as simplistic fallacies of the uneducated but as complex ways of understanding the world – and in the process to show how deeply intertwined with and necessary they were to the everyday life of the age. Only then have I looked at them from the more traditional and truly frightening perspective of witch-hunts and the repressive capabilities of Renaissance society. With the example of the essays by Hsia and Gentilcore, it seems to me that understanding witchcraft and everyday magic as practices reveals just how present and permeable was the boundary between the spiritual and material worlds in Renaissance society. This was so even at the bottom, where many have postulated a populace mired in material conditions of life, incapable of considering spiritual matters. The ability of ordinary people to manipulate the spiritual gave them a range of powers generally overlooked and often negatively defined and repressed by the authorities. The final essay of the volume, by Ian Moulton, looks at the wide-ranging illicit worlds of the Renaissance, both as they were envisioned by repressive authorities and literature and as they actually functioned. Moulton's impressive first book on the erotic worlds and literature of early modern England, which often looks well beyond England to discuss the erotic worlds of the Renaissance, is nicely reflected in this essay. It moves out from England and the erotic to examine themes as diverse as sodomy and banking for their illicit dimensions in this period. Again Moulton is dealing with a crucial Renaissance construct, and another highly permeable and contested boundary – the boundary between the licit and the illicit. At the beginning of the period it was a boundary passed easily for pleasure and profit, but as the period progressed the illicit seems to have become not only more externally proscribed by institutions and customs, but also more internally restricted by conscience and guilt, a theme that echoes earlier essays. Moulton works into his illicit world the way in which early stimulants such as coffee and tobacco moved in and out of illicit status, suggesting once again the role that culture plays in constructing anti-worlds and conditioning Renaissance life in general.

My hope is that after reading these essays readers will come away from this volume with more questions than answers, with more things to think about than facts, with a sense of the Renaissance more as an exciting way of considering the past than as a period that they now know. For underlying our changing ways of looking at the Renaissance are profound changes in the ways of thinking about the past, which have developed over the course of the last century. Not only has the range of subjects increased exponentially as the number and range of the essays in this volume can still only suggest, but many of us are much less interested in piling up facts and knowledge. Rather, without giving up our desire to know and understand the past as best we can, we are also interested in the critical project of thinking analytically (and perhaps in an aesthetically pleasing and suggestive way as well) about how to understand the way humans live in time. Science's project *vis-à-vis* humanity (and it has been and remains a crucial one) has been to consider humanity outside of time, the unchanging and enduring patterns that can lend predictability to human actions. The humanist's project should focus – as Renaissance humanists once held – on the way in which humans live, change, and adapt, and what that means for human existence in terms of quality of life, success and, not to be overlooked, pleasure. It is my hope that these essays will contribute to rethinking the Renaissance and that larger project. So let me end this introduction with a typical Renaissance injunction: read, think, and play with our ideas, and applaud if you have enjoyed our performance!

PART I

The Course of Renaissance Events

CHAPTER ONE

The Italian Renaissance

GENE BRUCKER

The Burckhardtian Vision

In the vast panorama of European historiography, one book stands out for its success in defining a major epoch. *The Civilization of the Renaissance in Italy* was published in 1860 by an obscure Swiss historian, Jacob Burckhardt. For years, the book attracted little attention from scholars and lay readers; not until the early 1900s did it achieve the reputation that it has sustained for a century. Rare is the book or article on any aspect of the Italian Renaissance that does not cite Burckhardt's "essay." The English translation continues to sell thousands of copies annually; it is required reading for many college courses on the subject. More powerfully and persuasively than any other historical work, Burckhardt's masterpiece has shaped our sense of our own past, our perception of how our culture has developed over the centuries from its classical and Christian origins to the present.[1]

The Italian Renaissance marked, for Burckhardt, the beginning of the modern world; and Renaissance Italians were, in his memorable phrase, "the first-born among the sons of modern Europe." Thus, the Renaissance was a sharp, decisive, dramatic break with the medieval age that preceded it. That radical transformation occurred (so Burckhardt argued) in the course of the fourteenth century, though the seeds of this revolution had been sown earlier, in the second half of the thirteenth century. The medieval world, against which Burckhardt juxtaposed the Renaissance, was characterized by an agrarian economy, by a society that was hierarchical and feudal, by a political system that was dominated by kings with sacral power, and above all, by a culture that was profoundly and pervasively Christian and other-worldly. By contrast, the world of the Italian Renaissance described by Burckhardt was characterized by an economy that was mercantile and capitalist, by a society that was urbanized and individualistic, and by a culture that had rejected its Christian heritage for the lure of classical antiquity. Two concepts were fundamental to Burckhardt's vision of the Renaissance: secularism and individualism. By secularism, he meant a society and a culture that was firmly anchored in this world, in the here and now, rather than in the medieval focus on life after death. In one of the most famous passages in his book,

Burckhardt contrasted Renaissance individualism with the corporate and collective nature of the medieval mentality.

In the Middle Ages both sides of human consciousness – that which was turned within as that which was turned without – lay dreaming or half aware beneath a common veil. The veil was woven of faith, illusion, and childish prepossession, through which the world and history were seen clad in strange hues. Man was conscious of himself only as a member of a race, people, party, family, or corporation – only through some general category. In Italy this veil first melted into air; an *objective* treatment and consideration of the state and of all things of this world became possible. The subjective side at the same time asserted itself with corresponding emphasis; man became a spiritual individual and recognized himself as such.[2]

Burckhardt's view of the Renaissance, as a distinctive and revolutionary epoch in the history of western civilization, became and has largely remained, the authoritative interpretation: reflected in textbooks, in school and university curricula, in the media, and in the popular perception of the European past. Much has been written to explain the triumph of this historiographical scenario: the clarity and coherence of Burckhardt's analysis; its dramatic features (sharp divisions, revolutionary change); and its broad and comprehensive vision. Burckhardt sought to integrate all aspects of human experience into his conceptual scheme: to explain cultural change in the context of political, social, and economic phenomena. This attempt to write "total history" was very congenial to the nineteenth century. Equally attractive to that age was Burckhardt's emphasis upon "national" character as a fundamental source for the creation of a culture. "We must insist," Burckhardt wrote, "as one of the chief propositions of this book, that it was not the revival of antiquity alone, but its union with the genius of the Italian people, which achieved the conquest of the Western world."[3]

Every age creates its own image of the past to fit its particular needs and concerns. That Burckhardt's vision of the Renaissance, and more broadly his scheme of periodization, fitted neatly and comfortably into the values and concerns of late nineteenth-century European culture can be clearly demonstrated. But it does not explain the remarkable persistence and durability of the Burckhardtian vision into our century, with its series of convulsive revolutions – political, social, economic, and cultural – culminating in the traumatic events of recent years. Is that vision still fundamentally correct? Was Burckhardt a scholar of such brilliance, such phenomenal insight, such prescience, that he was able to create an historical perspective that was valid for all time? The answer to those questions must be negative. Burckhardt was a great historian, along with Ranke and Michelet one of the greatest produced by the nineteenth century. But (and this is an obvious point) his understanding was limited by the relative paucity and narrowness of his sources, which were largely literary, and by the lack of a solid scholarly edifice that has since been constructed by the labor of thousands.

A major theme in Burckhardt's interpretation, Italy's radical break with its medieval past, would find little support among scholars today, who instead would stress historical continuity. Change there was, to be sure, but more slowly and gradually, and more selectively (in terms of regions and social groups) than Burckhardt had suggested. The Swiss historian had also emphasized the significance of Italian political developments in the late thirteenth and fourteenth centuries. Specifically, he described the emergence of a new type of political ruler, the *signore* or despot, and the political structures crafted by those rulers ("the state as a work of art") as being a critical component in the formation of Italian Renaissance culture. Contemporary scholarship would place less emphasis on political influences and more on demographic, economic, and social patterns; for example, on the impact of the Black Death and on recurring epidemics of the plague; and on the emergence of new social elites and their systems of patronage.

Burckhardt's interpretation is also flawed, from our contemporary perspective, by its unarticulated premise (so basic to nineteenth-century historiography) that the only people who matter in history are kings and princes, popes and bishops, rich merchants, scholars, and artists. His analysis largely ignored the common people (the *popolo*) in the cities and peasants (*contadini*) in the countryside. These poor and illiterate Italians appear only rarely in Burckhardt's account, as participants or witnesses to processions; or in urban rebellions. They are nameless and faceless figures, who played no significant role in this world even though they constituted four-fifths of the population. Their rich culture, in its religious and secular dimensions, is only now being studied systematically, together with its links to elite or "high" culture. With respect to one very important group in this society, women, Burckhardt did have some opinions, but they were wrong. Generalizing from a few case studies of aristocratic women and from such books as Castiglione's *Courtier*, Burckhardt believed that Italian Renaissance women, at least upper-class women, had become emancipated. "We must keep before our minds," he wrote, "the fact that women stood on a footing of perfect equality with men."[4] The evidence contradicting that statement is conclusive and overwhelming; Italian women lived first under the total domination of the fathers or guardians, and then of their husbands.[5] Their condition was described pithily and poignantly by Nannina, the daughter of Lorenzo de' Medici, who wrote in a letter to her mother: "Whoever wishes to have control of his life should take care not to be born a woman."[6]

Burkhardt emphasized the secular, mundane concerns of Renaissance Italians, contrasting their preoccupation with the affairs of this world with the medieval preoccupation with the afterlife, with salvation and damnation. But the dichotomy that he formulated was much too sharp and rigid; it ignored the massive evidence of the secular concerns of medieval men: of feudalism, of chivalry, of courtly love; of money, markets, and trade; of war and conflict. And by stressing the paganism of the Italian Renaissance, Burckhardt ignored its deep and pervasive religiosity, displayed in its art and literature, its rituals and its traditions. The men and women of Renaissance Italy were as pious as their medieval forebears and as deeply concerned about their fate after death. Their testaments, their funerary chapels, their bequests to charity, their participation in liturgical ceremonies and religious processions, all testified to the power and relevance of their faith, which was a fundamental force in their lives.

The Burckhardtian concept of Renaissance individualism has been one of the most influential themes in his analysis. He believed that the unique historical conditions in thirteenth- and fourteenth-century Italy had fostered the creation of a new type of man: free and independent, detached from the traditional social and psychological bonds of kinship and solidarity; above all, self-conscious, acutely aware of himself and his world, and capable of ordering and controlling his life. Burckhardt's concept thus has a social and a psychological dimension. The social argument is most easily refuted. Historians of Italian Renaissance society have demonstrated the power and the persistence of family ties and obligations throughout these centuries. They have also shown how Italians sought protection and support by integrating themselves into patronage networks. They were as dependent upon the favor and help of their patrons as any medieval knight or cleric. Whatever their social condition – peasant, laborer, artisan, merchant, scholar – they were not free.

Contradicting the vision of Renaissance man joyfully breaking the traditional bonds and exulting in his liberty is the picture of the Florentine who desperately sought new sources of security and identity to replace those which had disappeared. He forged bonds of friendship and obligation with protectors and benefactors, who would defend him against his enemies and also against the burgeoning power of the state. Nor was the powerful citizen, the patron, really free. He too was enmeshed in a network of obligations and commitments which limited and controlled his freedom of action. He could not release himself from these obligations without incurring loss of social prestige and political influence. The social freedom of the Renaissance man postulated by Burckhardt is, in fifteenth-century Florence at least, a myth.[7]

Equally problematic is Burckhardt's claim for the psychological liberation of Renaissance men, and their heightened self-awareness. It is possible to find Renaissance authors and texts that suggest this liberation from traditional bonds and constraints, and the emergence of a new type of "Renaissance man": Pico della Mirandola's *Oration on the Dignity of Man* is a prime example, as is the career of the sculptor Benvenuto Cellini. But there is also much evidence to refute or to qualify this image: for example, Machiavelli's stress on the role of fortune in men's lives, and his depiction of men as "ungrateful, fickle, liars and deceivers, avoiders of danger, greedy for profit," who accept more easily the murder of their father than the loss of their property.[8]

The Context

The Italian Renaissance did not represent so radical a break with the medieval past; change was more gradual and more spotty, the mix of tradition and innovation more complex than the Swiss historian had imagined. Not only was Italian religious life still powerfully influenced by traditional customs and beliefs; so too was much of secular experience. The social order remained hierarchical; the divisions between elites and masses, between rich and poor were as great in the fifteenth as in the thirteenth century. The economic system, based on the exploitation of the countryside and of foreign markets, did not change significantly from Dante's time to that of Lorenzo de' Medici. For the vast majority of rural Italians – poor, illiterate, marginalized – there was no Renaissance. This description of the French peasantry in the eighteenth century neatly fits their Italian counterparts three hundred years earlier: "Along rutted lanes, paths through cornfields, and sheep tracks in the mountains, we meet...a multitude of weather-beaten figures, a spectacle of broken teeth, gnarled hands, rags, clogs, coarse woolen stockings and homespun cloaks."[9]

Not since the fourth century AD had the Italian peninsula enjoyed a modicum of peace and stability. The Renaissance centuries were no exception to that pattern. Conflict was endemic, involving city-states, feudal lordships, the Hohenstaufen and Angevin monarchs in the south, the papacy, and invading forces from across the Alps.

In the fourteenth century, bands of soldiers from wars in France and Germany filtered into Italy, pillaging, burning, and killing peasants and townsmen, and extorting ransom from weak city-states. Contributing to the destruction and disorder caused by these marauders were the population losses from famines and recurring visitations of the bubonic plague. Between the first scourge, the Black Death of 1348, and the 1420s, Italy's population had declined by one-third. In such crisis conditions, Italian regimes of every category were threatened by perils internal and external. These governments were built upon very shaky foundations. They lacked the patina of legitimacy enjoyed by the heads of sacralized monarchies in northern Europe, and they could never depend upon the solid allegiance of their subjects. The primary source of instability in the 200-odd city-states that dotted the Lombard-Veneto plain and the hilly zones of Tuscany and Umbria were the noble clans, the urban and rural aristocracies, which sought to dominate these towns and their hinterlands.

Burkhardt's focus on Renaissance individualism had persuaded him that the most dynamic elements in Italian politics and society in these centuries were the despots, the *signori*, who from the mid-1200s emerged as rulers of most communal regimes in northern and central Italy. He failed to see that the authority of these rulers was based on their families, and on the patronage networks which they had developed. Since the eleventh century, these clans had arisen from obscurity to establish their power in both city and countryside. These aristocratic families dominated Italian history throughout its medieval and Renaissance eras and beyond. Their names are ubiquitous in contemporary chronicles and histories: the Doria and Fieschi of Genoa; the Visconti and Della Torre of Milan; the Rossi of Parma; the Scaligeri of Verona; the Carrara of Padua; the Pepoli and Bentivoglio of Bologna. Even the history of a city with sturdy republican institutions and traditions like Florence was "in large measure the history of its principal families."[10]

The communal governments that emerged in the cities and towns of northern and central Italy did constitute a political order opposed to the hierarchical structures and the endemic violence and disorder so characteristic of feudal society. But these regimes, with their collective and egalitarian values, were systematically dismantled and overthrown by these aristocratic clans supported by their networks of clients and dependents. Machiavelli pithily described the process: "Men do injury through either fear or hate . . . Such injury produces more fear; fear seeks for defense; for defense partisans are obtained; from partisans arise parties in states; from parties their ruin."[11] In *Romeo and Juliet*, Shakespeare captured the essence of these bitter factional squabbles, which no prince or commune could ever fully suppress or control. The lords of Verona, members of the Scaligeri family, did manage to achieve a tenuous control of their city and surrounding district for a century before succumbing to the superior power of Giangaleazzo Visconti, lord of Milan, in 1387. A small number of these princely dynasties (the Visconti and Sforza of Milan; the Este of Ferrara; the Gonzaga of Mantua) did manage to govern their states for more than a few decades before being conquered by a more potent rival. Only Venice succeeded in creating a stable and durable polity which, though controlled by an oligarchic elite, did restrain factional violence and thwarted any effort by a single family or individual to dominate the city and its territory.[12]

The power and influence of these aristocratic families was based in part on their status and reputation and their penchant for violence, but also on their wealth. In the

Lombard plain and in the mountainous zones of the Apennines, where feudal values and institutions persisted, their resources derived in substantial part from their landed estates, and from rents and leases of lay and ecclesiastical property. In the coastal cities (Genoa, Pisa, Venice) and inland towns such as Asti, Piacenza, Florence, Lucca, and Siena, a larger portion of aristocratic wealth came from commerce, banking (including usurious loans), and industry. The quasi-monopoly of Italian merchants in the Mediterranean and northern European economies funneled vast sums into the coffers of these entrepreneurs. Florence's economy was one of the most dynamic and diversified of any Italian city. Its cloth industry provided a livelihood for some 10,000 inhabitants, of a total population in 1427 of 35,000. The most prosperous segment of the economy was banking and international commerce, from which derived the vast fortunes of families such as the Medici, Pazzi, Pitti, and Rucellai. One-fourth of the city's wealth (calculated in 1427 to exceed 10 million florins) was owned by just a hundred households. Cosimo de' Medici was Florence's wealthiest citizen in the mid-decades of the fifteenth century. His fortune, estimated at 150,000 florins, was greater than that of most European monarchs.[13]

This extraordinary concentration of capital in the possession of Italy's urban elites was the essential material foundation for Renaissance culture. As the dominant political force in cities large and small, they subsidized municipal buildings which remain today as symbols of civic pride. They also funded and embellished cathedrals, monasteries, friaries, and convents in the towns and countryside. They built imposing family palaces and endowed burial chapels in parish churches and in monastic foundations. Their motives for these massive expenditures were a mélange of the spiritual and the secular. The wealthy fifteenth-century Florentine merchant, Giovanni Rucellai, wrote that his ambitious building program (which included a family palace, a burial chapel and the façade of the Dominican church of S. Maria Novella) was inspired by his desire to honor God, his city, and himself.[14] In 1471 Lorenzo de' Medici calculated that since 1434, his family had spent some 663,000 florins for charity, buildings, and taxes. "I do not regret this," he wrote, "for though many would consider it better to have a part of that sum in their purse, I consider that it gave great honor to our [his family's] state, and I think the money was well expended and I am well pleased."[15]

The Cultural Revolution

In the restricted world of these Italian urban elites, significant changes did indeed occur in these centuries: in their culture, in their educational system, in their palaces and churches, and in their life-style. During the fourteenth century, there emerged a small but dedicated group of intellectuals who studied intensively the surviving literature of classical antiquity, and who claimed that the culture of the ancient world was far superior to their own, and worthy of emulation. These scholars, led by Petrarch (d. 1374) embarked upon an ambitious campaign to revive the study of the classics, to find copies of ancient writings that had been lost, and to enlarge the corpus of classical literature. Initially, that corpus was made up primarily of Latin authors, but later it included the writings of ancient Greek philosophers, scientists, and mathematicians, from both the classical and the Hellenistic eras. These scholars cultivated the discipline of rhetoric, the art of writing and speaking eloquently. They modeled their writing style upon the examples of the ancients. They tried to write moral treatises as Cicero had done, to write history as Livy had done, to write poetry as Vergil had done. As rhetoricians, they believed in the power of words to instruct, to educate, and to improve the quality of men's lives. Eventually they became known as "humanists" and their educational program was described as the *studia humanitatis*, or the humanities. They denigrated the disciplines that had been the foundation of medieval higher education: logic, natural philosophy, law, and theology. They sought to replace that curriculum, which they regarded as outmoded and irrelevant, with one based upon the writings of antiquity, which provided (so they argued) better training and guidance for living in this world.

As Erwin Panofsky has shown, this revival of interest and enthusiasm for the culture of the ancient world was not the first phenomenon of this kind; there had been earlier "renaissances" in the eighth and ninth and again in the twelfth century.[16] But this "renaissance" differed from its predecessors in several important ways. Unlike those earlier revivals, this Italian Renaissance was largely if not exclusively created by laymen and not by members of the clergy. These men found in the writings of the ancients a cluster of themes and topics that seemed particularly meaningful and significant for their own lives; for example, discussions by ancient historians of the rise and decline of states; the formation and maintenance of a civil society. They found too, in their reading of ancient texts, guidance on moral and ethical issues that seemed more pertinent and relevant than the counsel proffered by priests and theologians. As they became more aware of the range and breadth of inquiry by the ancients – their views about the human condition, about fundamental ethical problems, about the nature of the physical universe – they became ever more convinced of the relevance of this knowledge to their own age. They accepted their Christian heritage and its message of salvation, while believing that classical antiquity was a legitimate source of human knowledge and wisdom.

Lauro Martines has described Italian humanism as a "program for the ruling classes," by which he meant that this cultural movement was congenial to Italian ruling elites, whether in republics or in signorial regimes or in the papal curia.[17] These elites had only recently achieved power and status, and they employed humanists to justify and promote their rule and to glorify their achievements. And not only in Italy, but everywhere in Europe, new men were emerging to challenge the old elites, whether aristocratic or ecclesiastical. One can see this rising tide of new men at every social level and in every profession; for example, in the Roman papacy where in the fifteenth century a cluster of new men from new families were elected to the Holy See, several of them having humanist training.

The rise of humanism as a cultural movement was thus due in significant part to the perception of its relevance to contemporary concerns, and to its special attraction to newly emerging elites. Also contributing to humanism's ultimate triumph was the effectiveness of its propaganda in promoting its agenda through the rhetorical skills of its adherents and (as we would say today) their mastery of the media. Humanists utilized the newly invented printing press to establish a fixed canon of classical texts, and to make those texts more available to a wider audience at a much reduced cost. They also used the media to keep their opponents – the scholastic philosophers, the Aristoteleans, the theologians, and the lawyers – on the defensive, ridiculing their barbarous Latin style and their antiquated methodology. Anthony Grafton and Lisa Jardine have described the triumph of humanism and the establishment of Latin and Greek as the foundation of a new educational curriculum, which eventually displaced the old method of instruction, the so-called scholastic system, in European universities.[18] One can scarcely overemphasize the significance of this education revolution. The classics dominated the structure and content of European (and American) middle and higher education for four hundred years. Relics of that educational structure survive today in German *gymnasia*, in Italian *licei classici*, and in the classical curricula at Eton and Harrow, at Oxford and Cambridge. Not until the end of the nineteenth century were Latin and Greek abolished as required subjects in most American colleges and universities.

This educational revolution was the most significant consequence of the revival of antiquity in Renaissance Italy. It shaped the minds and values of generations of young Europeans, for it was widely adopted by Catholic, and particularly Jesuit, educators, and by most Protestant denominations (Lutheran, Calvinist, Anglican), to educate their clergy, and also by the laity. The cult of antiquity was also the major force in another revolution: in the plastic arts, where again Italy was the arena for a fundamental transformation of style and aesthetics. Art historians have traced the stages of that revolution, beginning around 1400 in Florence, with the innovations of Brunelleschi in architecture, Ghiberti and Donatello in sculpture, and Masaccio in painting. In fifteenth-century Italy, the combination of artistic talent, of wealthy patrons eager to hire that talent, and a new style based on antique models contributed to an explosion of creativity that still dazzles us, and which has rarely been equaled and never surpassed in the history of western civilization.

This classical style, based on mathematically defined proportions and emphasizing harmony and balance, spread from Italy across the Alps to every part of Europe, as far as Cracow and St. Petersburg; and across the ocean to America. Artists and their patrons accepted, as a fundamental truth, that this style developed by the Greeks and adopted by the Romans, was the ideal aesthetic form. Not until the nineteenth century did a few daring artists challenge that proposition and develop radically different styles in painting, sculpture, and architecture. The power, the tenacity, and the durability of classicism can be seen in the United States, where it became the model for the nation's capital in Washington, and for the buildings that were constructed there. The great majority of public buildings (state capitols, county courthouses, post offices, and libraries) erected in the nineteenth and early twentieth centuries, were built with columns, arches, and pediments.

This essay has defined the Renaissance as that strand in Italian and European culture that focused on recovering the literary and artistic heritage of antiquity. Its most powerful and most durable influences were in the realms of education and aesthetics, where it established standards that survived for more than 400 years. It did contribute to the promotion of secular concerns and values, by making available a large body of classical writing devoted to men living in the world, to their political, social, economic, and moral problems. The Renaissance produced political thinkers such as Machiavelli and historians such as Guicciardini, whose secular orientation was strongly influenced by their reading of classical authors. The discovery of ancient scientific texts, either lost or known only in fragments, by Euclid, Archimedes, Galen, Pliny, and Ptolemy contributed to the investigations and speculations that led ultimately to the revolutionary works of Copernicus, Vesalius, and Galileo. In yet another realm, that of religion, the influence of Renaissance humanism has been shown recently to be much greater than Burckhardt allowed. Scholars have pointed to the strong affinities between the Renaissance and the Reformation, both backward looking movements: the one to antiquity, the other to the early centuries of the Church. They have emphasized, too, this focus by reformers and humanists on the source of divine revelation in one case, and on human wisdom in the other. They have also noted the epistemological affinities between humanists and Protestant theologians, both of whom "distinguished between realms, between ultimate truths altogether inaccessible to man's intellect, and the knowledge that men needed to get along in this world, which turned out to be sufficient for his purposes."[19]

Maturity and Decline

Historians are in general agreement that the fifteenth century represented the mature phase, the apogee, of Italian Renaissance culture. After the crisis conditions of the late fourteenth century, the peninsula experienced a gradual recovery of its population and its economy, most notably in the decades after 1450. Italian politics became somewhat less chaotic, with the gradual formation of five powerful regional states: the republics of Venice and Florence, the signorial regime in Milan, the kingdom of Naples, and the Papal States. With varying degrees of success, each of these regimes developed larger and more intrusive bureaucracies, more exploitative fiscal systems, and more rational military structures. In 1454, these states formed a league which brought a limited measure of stability to Italian politics. The signatories agreed to seek peaceful resolutions to their disputes and to promote the idea of collective security. Pope Nicholas V (d. 1455) was the major advocate of the Italian League; he was motivated by the fear that "some Italian state . . . being desperate, might call the French or some other nation down into Italy and that the fire will spread so much that no one will be able to put it out."[20] The possibility of a foreign invasion, though often threatened, did not materialize until 1480, when a Turkish force temporarily occupied the city of Otranto on the Adriatic coast. In 1494, the French monarch, Charles VIII, led a large army across the Alps on his way to conquer the kingdom of Naples, thus initiating a process which led ultimately to the foreign domination of Italy.

Writing in the aftermath of the foreign invasions and "the calamities of Italy" which they had wrought, the Florentine historian, Francesco Guicciardini (d. 1540) described the state of the peninsula in the late fifteenth century as a terrestrial paradise. Not since the fall of the Roman Empire a thousand years before had Italy enjoyed such peace and prosperity. Guicciardini pointed to the large number of "very noble and very beautiful cities" and their talented inhabitants, "skilled in every discipline and in all of the arts."[21] To support his argument, Guicciardini could have compiled a catalogue of his Florentine contemporaries who had achieved distinction in their disciplines and *métiers*. Among these intellectual giants were the humanists Cristoforo Landino and Angelo Poliziano; the philosophers Joannes Argyropulos and Marsilio Ficino; the natural scientist Paolo Toscanelli; the poets Luigi Pulci and Lorenzo de' Medici. Guicciardini himself was just beginning his career as lawyer, diplomat, and historian, as was his younger friend and compatriot, Niccolò Machiavelli. While an earlier generation of renowned artists (the painters Masaccio, Uccello, Fra Angelico; the sculptors Donatello and Ghiberti; the architects Brunelleschi, Alberti, Michelozzo) had died, their successors continued the grand Florentine tradition begun by Giotto and Arnolfo di Cambio. Sometime before his death in 1494, the father of Raphael of Urbino, Giovanni Santi, made a list of the most famous painters of the fifteenth century. Of the twenty-five Italian artists in his corpus, thirteen were from Florence, of whom six (Ghirlandaio, Antonio and Piero Pollaiuolo, Botticelli, Leonardo da Vinci, Filippino Lippi) were still alive.[22] Missing from the list was Michelangelo Buonarroti, who in 1494 was just beginning his illustrious career as painter, sculptor, and architect: the supreme artist of the Italian Renaissance.

While writing his biography of Michelangelo, the sixteenth-century artist, Giorgio Vasari, speculated about the remarkable concentration of artist talent in Florence. "The Tuscan genius," he wrote, "has ever been raised high above all others, the men of that country displaying more zeal in study, and more constancy in labor, than any other people of Italy." In another passage, Vasari developed a sociological explanation for Florence's extraordinary achievement: "In that city men are driven on by three things: the first of these is disapproval, which many of them vent on many things and with much frequency, their genius never being content with mediocrity, but seeking what is good and beautiful . . . Secondly, industriousness in their daily lives, which means constantly drawing on their talent and judgment, and being shrewd and quick in their dealings, and knowing how to earn money . . . The third thing . . . is a quest for glory and honor, which is common to Florentines of all professions."[23] In recent historiography, there has developed a counter trend which has sought to minimize Florence's role and to promote the contributions of other cities: Venice, Milan, Rome, Ferrara, Mantua, Urbino.[24] But for many Renaissance scholars, Florence's cultural achievement remains unsurpassed. "There is about this city," a recent critic has written, "frequently morose, even harsh, a mystery of implosion, as if singular forces of intellect and feeling had been compelled into fruitful collision by the ring of hills, by a climate susceptible of white heat and bone-jarring cold. Genius and civic ferocity were intimately meshed . . . Out of catastrophes sprang energies that have, in essence, come close to defining Western civilization."[25]

Leonardo da Vinci (d. 1519) has often been perceived as the epitome of the Italian Renaissance. "Athletics, music, drawing, painting, sculpture, architecture, town planning, perspective, optics, astronomy, aviation; hydraulic, nautical, military, structural and mechanical engineering; anatomy, biology, zoology, botany, geology, geography, mathematics – the list of his interests is seemingly endless."[26] His confidence in his talents, his genius, was displayed in a letter that he sent to the Duke of Milan seeking employment: "I can carry out sculpture in marble, bronze or clay; and also I can paint whatever may be done as well as any other." He could build bridges, mortars, and cannons; he could blow up fortresses; he could construct war chariots that would disperse any enemy force. His skepticism about theoretical knowledge divorced from observation and experiment set him apart from his contemporaries and identified him as a prophetic advocate of the modern scientific method. "It seems to me that all sciences are vain and full of error that have not been tested by experience . . . that do not pass through any of the five senses . . . Experience does not feed investigators on dreams, but always proceeds from accurately determined first principles . . . as can be seen in the elements of mathematics founded on numbers and measures called arithmetic and geometry." One passage from Leonardo's notebooks is an eloquent testimonial of the curiosity and excitement, and also the fear and anxiety, experienced by this intrepid explorer of the unknown:

> Unable to resist my eager desire and wanting to see the great profusion of the various and strange shapes made by nature, and having wandered some distance among the rocks, I came to the entrance of a great cavern, in front of which I stood for some time . . . Bending my back into an arch, I rested my left hand on my knee and held my right hand over my eyebrows; often bending first one way and then the other, to see whether I could discover anything inside; and this being impossible by the deep darkness within, and having remained there for some time, two contrary emotions arose in me, fear and desire; fear of the threatening darkness, and desire to see whether there were any marvelous things within the cave . . . .[27]

Leonardo's professional career was profoundly affected by the invasions that transformed Italy into a permanent battleground for a half-century, from 1494 to 1559. When King Charles VIII and his army crossed the Alps, the Florentine artist was still employed by the king's ally, Lodovico Sforza. The French monarch did achieve his primary goal, the conquest of the kingdom of Naples, but was forced to retreat back across the Alps in the summer of 1495. In 1499, Charles's successor, Louis XII, launched an attack on Milan, occupying the duchy and imprisoning Lodovico Sforza. "The duke lost his state and his property," Leonardo commented, "and none of his works was completed for him." Having lost his patron, Leonardo traveled to Mantua, to Venice, and then to Florence in search of a stable environment. In 1502, he was hired as a military engineer by Cesare Borgia, son of Pope Alexander VI, who was then building a state in central Italy. When Cesare's state collapsed after his father's death in 1503, Leonardo returned to Florence but then moved back to Milan to serve the French rulers of the duchy. After the French were driven out of Milan by a Spanish army (1512), the peripatetic Leonardo traveled to Rome but received no support from Pope Julius II. He then returned to Milan and was invited by Louis XII to settle in France. He died in 1519 in a chateau in the Loire valley which the French monarch had given to him.

The depredations of these invading armies (French, Swiss, German, Spanish) and the Italian soldiery did enormous physical damage to the peninsula. Francesco Guicciardini wrote in the 1530s that in these "almost unremitting molestations of normal life," he "saw nothing but scenes of infinite slaughter, plunder and destruction of multitudes of towns and cities, attended with the licentiousness of soldiers no less destructive to friends than foes."[28] The single most devastating event in this orgy of destruction was the sack of Rome in 1527 by an imperial army, an undisciplined band of 20,000 German, Spanish, and Italian mercenaries, unpaid and poorly supplied with provisions. It has been estimated that, in the early days of the sack, 10,000 Romans were killed and another 10,000 fled into the countryside, where they were harassed by the local peasantry. Pope Clement VII and members of the Papal Curia took refuge in Castel San Angelo, where throughout the summer and autumn of 1527 they witnessed the carnage wrought by imperial troops, who did not abandon Rome until February 1528. The sack of Rome was a graphic demonstration of Italy's weakness and the failure of its political and military leadership. Machiavelli's pessimistic judgment about Italy's prospects for recovering her independence were shown to be accurate: "As for the unity of the Italians, you make me laugh; first, because there will never be any unity…And even if the leaders were united, that would not be enough, both because there are no armies here worth a penny, and because the tails are not united with the heads, nor will this nation ever respond to any accident that might occur."[29]

In 1559, France and Spain signed a peace treaty which ended their sixty-year struggle for control of the Italian peninsula. Hapsburg Spain was the victor in this conflict, having established its direct governance of the Milanese duchy and the kingdom of Naples (including Sicily), and its hegemony over a cluster of satellite states: the Medici grand duchy of Tuscany, Mantua, Ferrara, Genoa, Montferrat. Only the duchy of Savoy, the republic of Venice, and the Papal States survived as independent polities in this age of Spanish domination. During the last four decades of the sixteenth century, Italians experienced a rare interlude of peace and stability, during which the peninsula's population and economy revived, and the wartime damages to its infrastructure repaired. The most remarkable example of this recovery was the city of Rome. Devastated by the ravages of imperial troops, its population reduced to fewer than 10,000 souls, Rome slowly recovered under the leadership of its popes, from Paul III (1534–49) to Sixtus V (1585–90). Churches, monasteries, and palaces were rebuilt, while new construction (St. Peter's, the Farnese and Massimo palaces, the Villa Lante) provided livelihood for architects, artists, and laborers. By the late sixteenth century, Rome's population had grown to 100,000 and Sixtus V launched a massive campaign to restore the physical city: completing the dome of St. Peter's, building dozens of new roads and fountains, restoring and decorating the city's ecclesiastical buildings.

The two dominant powers in late sixteenth- and seventeenth-century Italy were the Spanish monarchy and the Roman papacy. Despite occasional disputes over their respective powers and jurisdictions, they forged an alliance to maintain their control over Italy's political and religious life. They were united in their commitment to repress political and religious dissent, and to monitor and regulate the lives of their subjects. The Spanish monarchy and their satellite states established large, expensive, and intrusive bureaucracies to enforce the will of their rulers. The Roman papacy created its own institutions, the Inquisition and the Index, to defend religious orthodoxy and to repress heresy. The list of prohibited books grew incrementally each year; it included not only the writings of Protestant theologians, but the works of Dante, Boccaccio, Lorenzo Valla, Savonarola, Erasmus, and Machiavelli. Among the Roman Inquisition's most celebrated victims were the Florentine aristocrat, Piero Carnesecchi and the Dominican friar, Giordano Bruno (executed); the philosopher Tommaso Campanella (imprisoned for 26 years); and the scientist Galileo, condemned for his support of the Copernican theory, and placed under house arrest. Interrogated about his depiction of the Last Supper, the Venetian painter Veronese was ordered (1573) "to improve and change his painting within a period of three months," or suffer penalties imposed by the inquisitors. Michelangelo was sharply criticized for painting nude human figures in his Last Judgment in the Sistine chapel. Pope Paul IV ordered the offending images to be covered by drapery.[30]

These episodes of repression and intolerance persuaded scholars such as Francesco De Sanctis and Benedetto Croce that the unholy alliance between Spain and the papacy was responsible for the degeneration of Italian culture from the mid-sixteenth to the end of the seventeenth century. In Croce's view, Italy "was bereft of all political life and national sentiment, freedom of thought was extinguished, culture impoverished, literature became mannered and ponderous, the figurative arts and architecture became extravagant and grotesque."[31] But recent scholarship has modified this harsh judgment on the impact of the efforts by Spanish and papal authorities to impose orthodoxy on cultural activity. In certain disciplines (theology, philosophy, history, literature), the loss of vitality and creativity was significant. The quality of Italian historical writing declined dramatically from the level established by Renaissance authors of the caliber of Leonardo Bruni, Flavio Biondo, Machiavelli, and Guicciardini. No historian of their skill and vision can been found among the hundreds of pedantic antiquarians who wrote laudatory accounts of their city's past, or in the case of some clerics, treatises justifying papal authority. But with the exception of cosmology, the natural sciences were largely exempt from regulations by censors and inquisitors. Croce's denigration of the plastic arts ignores the achievements of painters and sculptors, from Pontormo, Bronzino, Titian, Tintoretto, and Caravaggio in the sixteenth to Bernini, Borromini, and Pietro da Cortona in the seventeenth century. Throughout these years of "decadence" (Croce's term), migratory Italian scholars, poets, artists and musicians were spreading the knowledge and techniques of their disciplines to every part of Christian Europe, from Ireland and Scandinavia to the Slavic world.[32]

Italian authorities, secular and ecclesiastical, were not unique in their efforts to regulate and discipline behavior and belief. This impulse was Europe-wide in scope: a response to the chaos and turbulence produced by incessant warfare and the religious controversies of the Reformation. The Renaissance freedom to explore, to innovate, to challenge traditional values and institutions, had caused intense anxiety among European elites and their leaders. They yearned for a more stable political and social order, for religious uniformity and for a culture that reinforced authority.[33] This pervasive mood was brilliantly captured by the English poet, John Donne (d. 1631):

> And new philosophy calls all in doubt,
> The element of fire is quite put out;
> The sun is lost, and th'earth, and no man's wit
> Can well direct him where to look for it.
> And freely men confess that this world's spent,
> When in the planets and the firmament,
> They seek so many new...
> 'Tis all in pieces, all coherence gone;
> All just supply, and all relation....[34]

This tension between the drive for freedom and innovation, for the breach of barriers and boundaries, and the contrary impulse for order and stability, would be a permanent feature of European culture in the long and tortuous transition to "modernity."

NOTES

1   Brown, *The Renaissance*, pp. 2–3.
2   Burckhardt, *Civilization*, p. 143.
3   Ibid., p. 175.
4   Ibid., p. 389.
5   A central theme in Klapisch-Zuber, *Women, Family and Ritual*.
6   Kent et al., *A Florentine Patrician*, p. 66.
7   Brucker, *Renaissance Florence*, pp. 100–1.
8   Machiavelli, *The Prince*, p. 139.
9   McManners, *Church and Society*, I, p. 96.
10 Jones, "Florentine Families," p. 183.
11 Muir, "Civil Society," p. 381.
12 Ibid., p. 384.
13 De Roover, *Medici Bank*, p. 28.
14 Perosa, *Giovanni Rucellai*, p. 121.
15 Brucker, *Society*, p. 27.
16 Panofsky, "Renaissance," pp. 201–26.
17 Martines, *Power and Imagination*, ch. 11.
18 Grafton and Jardine, *Humanism*.
19 Bouwsma, *A Usable Past*, p. 228.
20 Furbini, *Quattrocento*, p. 167.
21 Guicciardini, *Storia d'Italia*, I, p. 2.
22 Baxandall, *Painting and Experience*, pp. 111–15.
23 Brucker, *Florence*, pp. 19–21.
24 Findlen et al., *Beyond Florence*.
25 Steiner, *The New Yorker*, pp. 76–7.
26 Hale, *Encyclopedia*, p. 183.
27 Richter, *Leonardo da Vinci*, p. 395.
28 Hale, *War*, p. 179.
29 Machiavelli, *Lettere*, p. 279.
30 Klein and Zerner, *Italian Art*, pp. 119, 122–4, 129–32.
31 Quoted by Julius Kirshner, in his introduction to Cochrane, *Italy 1530–1630*, p. 2.
32 Burke, *European Renaissance*, chs. 2, 3.
33 Bouwsma, *Waning*.
34 Donne, *Anatomy* (The First Anniversary, ll. 205–14).

REFERENCES

Baxandall, Michael, *Painting and Experience in Fifteenth Century Italy* (Oxford: Clarendon Press, 1972).
Bouwsma, William, *A Usable Past* (Berkeley: University of California Press, 1990).
——, *The Waning of the Renaissance* (New Haven: Yale University Press, 2001).
Brown, Alison, *The Renaissance*, 2nd edn. (London: Longman, 1999).
Brucker, Gene, *The Society of Renaissance Florence* (New York: Harper and Row, 1971).
——, *Renaissance Florence*, 2nd edn. (Berkeley: University of California Press, 1983).
——, *Florence: The Golden Age (1138–1737)* (Berkeley: University of California Press, 1998).
Burckhardt, Jacob, *The Civilization of the Renaissance in Italy* (New York: Harper, 1958).

Burke, Peter, *The European Renaissance: Centres and Peripheries* (Oxford: Blackwell Publishers, 1998).

Cochrane, Eric, *Italy 1530–1630* (London: Longman, 1988).

De Roover, Raymond, *The Rise and Decline of the Medici Bank, 1397–1494* (Cambridge, MA: Harvard University Press, 1963).

Donne, John, *An Anatomy of the World* (Cambridge: Printed for the Roxburghe Club, 1951).

Findlen, Paula, et al., eds., *Beyond Florence* (Palo Alto: Stanford University Press, forthcoming).

Furbini, Riccardo, *Quattrocento fiorentino* (Pisa: Pacini, 1996).

Grafton, Anthony and Jardine, Lisa, *From Humanism to Humanities: Education and the Liberal Arts in Fifteenth- and Sixteenth-Century Europe* (Cambridge, MA: Harvard University Press, 1986).

Guicciardini, Francesco, *Storia d'Italia*, 5 vols. (Bari: La Terza, 1929).

Hale, John, ed. *A Concise Encyclopedia of the Italian Renaissance* (New York: Oxford University Press, 1981).

——, *War and Society in Renaissance Europe, 1450–1620* (Baltimore: Johns Hopkins University Press, 1985).

Jones, Philip, "Florentine Families and Florentine Diaries in the Fourteenth Century," in *Studies in Italian Medieval History Presented to Miss E. M. Jamison*, ed. Philip Grierson (Rome: British School at Rome, 1956).

Kent, F. W., et al., *A Florentine Patrician and his Palace* (London: Warburg Institute, 1981).

Klapisch-Zuber, Christiane, *Women, Family and Ritual in Renaissance Italy* (Chicago: University of Chicago Press, 1985).

Klein, Robert and Zerner, Henri, *Italian Art 1500–1600* (Englewood Cliffs, NJ: Prentice Hall, 1966).

Machiavelli, Niccolò, *The Prince*, trans. Mark Musa (New York: St. Martin's Press, 1964).

——, *Lettere*, ed. Franco Gaeta (Milan: Feltrinelli, 1981).

McManners, John, *Church and Society in Eighteenth Century France*, 2 vols. (Oxford: Clarendon Press, 1999).

Martines, Lauro, *Power and Imagination: City States in Renaissance Italy* (New York: Knopf, 1975).

Muir, Edward, "The Sources of Civil Society in Italy," *Journal of Interdisciplinary History* 29 (1999).

Panofsky, Erwin, "Renaissance and Renascenses," *Kenyan Review* 6 (1944).

Perosa, Alessandro, ed., *Giovanni Rucellai ed il suo Zibaldone* (London: Warburg Institute, 1960).

Richter, Jean Paul, ed., *The Literary Works of Leonardo da Vinci* (London: Phaidon, 1970).

Steiner, George, *The New Yorker*, January 13, 1997, pp. 76–7.

FURTHER READING

Burke, Peter, *The Italian Renaissance* (Princeton: Princeton University Press, 1986).

Chambers, David, *The Imperial Age of Venice 1380–1580* (London: Thames and Hudson, 1970).

Graham-Dixon, Andrew, *Renaissance* (Berkeley: University of California Press, 1999).

Hale, John, *The Civilization of Europe in the Renaissance* (London: HarperCollins, 1993).

Hay, Denys, *The Italian Renaissance in its Historical Background* (Cambridge: Cambridge University Press, 1961).

——, *The Church in Italy in the Fifteenth Century* (Cambridge: Cambridge University Press, 1977).

Hay, Denys, and Law, John, *Italy in the Age of the Renaissance 1380–1530* (London: Longman, 1989).

Jones, Philip, *The Italian City-State* (Oxford: Clarendon Press, 1997).

Kent, F. W. and Simons, Patricia, eds., *Patronage, Art and Society in Renaissance Italy* (New York: Oxford University Press, 1987).

Trinkaus, Charles, *In Our Image and Likeness: Humanity and Divinity in Italian Humanist Thought*, 2 vols. (Chicago: University of Chicago Press, 1970).

Von Pastor, Ludwig, *History of the Popes*, 16 vols. (London and St. Louis: Herder, 1898–1953).

CHAPTER TWO

The European Renaissance

RANDOLPH STARN

How is it possible to think about the European Renaissance at the turn of this new century and millennium? There are good reasons, old and new, to begin point-blank with hard questions. The Renaissance was already in question as a kind of necromancer's trick in the fifteenth century. At one time or another it has served as a self-promoting professional gambit for backward-looking humanists, a shifty marker for the beginning of modern times, a trophy in triumphalist scenarios of Western Civilization. These days the idea of the Renaissance easily falls subject to the criticism that such ideas suppress the diversity of real historical experience and that modernity in any case means breaking with the past, not bringing it back. Meanwhile, "European" has come into terminological troubles of its own with the slippage of boundaries eastward since the end of the Cold War, the surfacing of regional and ethnic differences, and the blurring economic and cultural effects of globalization. What, if any, are the alternatives to dismissal, denial, or indifference in thinking about a European Renaissance?

The challenge is to admit the critiques where they are justified and to recognize that as a historical tag or a heuristic lever the idea of the Renaissance is not, after all, going to disappear anytime soon. Perhaps the most familiar response has been to downsize; that is, to reduce the Renaissance to a place, Italy, or to a movement, humanism, or to a micro-species of the mega-period of Early Modernity. This chapter takes a different tack by treating the European Renaissance not in the round as a period or in miniature as a discrete movement or moment, but as a process with complex thematic genealogies. As a kind of history, genealogy forms patterns that connect (its family trees) and works in and through time (its lineages), while also marking novelty and discontinuity: some new family connection and a new set of genes or a break in succession. History cast along these lines can add up and be cumulative without having a preordained plot or fixed goal. Although the whole of any genealogy is greater than its parts, it depends on the contingent multiplicity of quite different, if more or less parallel and occasionally overlapping, lines of descent. In a genealogical mode, then, it may be possible to think of the Renaissance without invoking a single view of the world or seeing in tunnel vision. So much the better that

this approach suits a culture often preoccupied with pedigrees for ideas and institutions as well as blood.[1]

Renewal, Revival, Renaissance

The concept of the Renaissance is itself a prime candidate for genealogical history.
The standard account runs from Petrarch's fourteenth-century anticipation and his
successors' pursuit of a literary and scholarly "revival of antiquity" to the extension of
the idea of renewal to an entire period of European history. As readers of this volume
will often be reminded, the periodic conception of the Renaissance would get its
canonical formulation by the nineteenth-century historian Jacob Burckhardt, establish the terms of a "Renaissance debate" in the twentieth century, and receive its
obituary, prematurely as it turns out, in recent times.[2] This seemingly expansive
history is actually quite limited, most obviously so in conjuring a historical period
out of a classical revival. Even at its most expansive, the notion of a Renaissance period
skews or flattens the rich complexity of history, not to mention, as medievalists are
always ready to remind us, slighting the achievements of the Middle Ages. To dismiss
the theme of renewal out of hand is not the only alternative, however, let alone the
good historian's solemn duty. There are too many variations on it for that. And this is
of course a point that the genealogy of ideas and ideals of renewal can make clear.

A privileged line of descent is discussed in some detail in the essay by Ingrid
Rowland and elsewhere in this volume. In a favorite metaphor the Moderns were
to the Ancients as dwarfs on the shoulders of giants. This image was glossed variously
to mean that the former were inferior to, dependent on, empowered by, or able to see
farther than the latter. One way or another, it revived and went beyond the figure of
speech used by a medieval grammarian and had anticipations in ancient Greek and
Roman writers themselves. Periodic returns to the ancients in European culture have
led historians to speak of "renascences" throughout the Middle Ages before a full-
fledged Renaissance from the fifteenth century on. There is plenty of evidence that
the later Renaissance drew on these precedents. To take just one small but clinching
example, virtually all the manuscripts of ancient authors discovered by humanist
scholars were copies by medieval scribes of works that would otherwise have been
lost. Even the classical Roman typefaces and italic script that are still with us today
derive from medieval models adapted to further uses in the fifteenth century.[3]

This already begins to link classicizing versions of renewal into wider contexts with
far-reaching ramifications that can be only hinted at here.[4] Some of these grew out of
popular culture and the experience and lore of nature's cycles of rebirth. Key biblical
references straddled the divide between popular and learned audiences. The Tree of
Jesse, the House of David's family tree from which Isaiah (11: 1–2) prophesied a
"branch shall grow" – the Messiah – was represented in manuscript illuminations, in
cathedral sculpture, and stained glass; the "born again" passages in the Gospels and
the call for spiritual regeneration in the epistles of St. Paul were read out in church
and commented upon by theologians. To the humble and the powerful alike the
Book of Revelations announced a millenarian scenario of punishing fall followed by
redemption in a Second Coming. At the highest institutional levels the coronation of
Charlemagne as emperor in 800 was touted as a restoration of the Roman Empire, a

propaganda coup that proved irresistible despite (or because of) wishful thinking. The casting of the Visigothic chieftain Vamba as the successor to King David and a New Charlemagne seems a quaintly ridiculous fiction; in the totalitarian ideologies of a Third Reich its twentieth-century variants turned grotesque and monstrous.[5]

Even in the barest of outlines, this complex of ideas and attitudes will not fit neatly into one period or kind of Renaissance. (Of course the fit is already a problem in more or less conventional accounts where the Renaissance begins in the fourteenth century in Italy and ends in the sixteenth, having just barely begun in France and England, not to mention Germany and Spain.) It is possible, however, to trace periodic twists and turns over time, and historically revealing to do so besides. In the fourteenth and fifteenth centuries, for example, the humanist program of going "back to the sources" (*ad fontes*) of classical culture paralleled the call "to return to the original form" (*ad formam primam reducere*) by councils of clerics and laymen convoked to unify and reform the divided Church "in head and members." The last quarter of the fifteenth century witnessed the more or less simultaneous outburst of astrological prediction and apocalyptic preaching, a clutch of miracles, a kind of People's Crusade led by the so-called Drummer of Niklashausen in southern Germany, and elegant Latin and Greek salutes to a new Golden Age in Florence and Rome. For a short time early in the sixteenth century a restoration of learning and a reform of religion were an indistinguishable couplet for scholars and churchmen on both sides of the Alps. With the hardening of divisions among and within the Roman Catholic Church and the new Protestant confessions, ideas of renewal tended to differentiate by religious affiliation, field of interest, or profession. Writing the lives of artists around the middle of the sixteenth century, Giorgio Vasari invented art history as a story of leading masters and a sequence of styles, and certainly formalized the idea of a *rinascita* in Italian art from Giotto in the fourteenth century to Michelangelo in the sixteenth. At the same time the Counter-Reformation Church, which commissioned Vasari's art for the Vatican, was in retreat from ideas of reform in religion as heretical. By then, visions of renewal had turned by and large either formal and routine in institutional incarnations, or suspect in enthusiasms felt at the margins of societies geared to conformity.

Among the early seventeenth-century proponents of a self-styled new philosophy and science, whose trinity was Francis Bacon, Descartes, and Galileo, the Ancients became young. Antiquity was one of the idols to be topped by the experience and reason deployed by the Moderns, who were the mature adults to the Ancients' children. Or so the manifestoes liked to say, prompting what became a dominant master narrative of modernity with ideas and ideologies of breakaway revolution in philosophy and science. Recent research has undermined this orthodoxy across the board to demonstrate both the durability and the productive potential of the Ancients. Humanist scholarship clearly was not gray and uniform, fecklessly antiquarian, abjectly servile to textual authority, or altogether cut off from the new intellectual currents. The motif of renewal was still a powerful cultural lens, not easily or abruptly relinquished. It was William Harvey, a founding father of a new science of medicine who crowed about "this age of ours which sees art and science gloriously rerisen after twelve centuries of swoon." Until the American and French revolutions the very idea of "revolution" meant turning back to some originary point, not a radical new departure. Copernicus's *On the Revolutions of the Celestial Spheres* (1543), the charter text of the new heliocentric cosmos, was revolutionary in this sense, a return to suggestions made by the Greeks and to the elegance of circular movement that had been corrupted by the tinkering of centuries trying to make observations fit the geocentric model. But metaphors of renewal had not prescribed literal regression or insisted on slavish imitation. Different degrees and different applications, and heated controversies about them, were part and parcel of its historical career. Indeed, the notion of a Renaissance practically invited heady assertions of progress and improvement and comparisons, and its greatest success would arguably be its own obsolescence.[6]

World-making

Whether the past and future seem near or far, or practically indistinguishable, depends on one's perspective or position. Since time and space are historical coefficients, we would expect tropes of renovation, restoration, and rebirth to have implications for configurations or reconfigurations of space. Burckhardt understood this with his usual good instincts for patterns and connections, but his formula for the Renaissance "discovery of world and man" made it seem as if "world" and "man" were there for the finding once medieval blinkers were lifted. A genealogy of travel and discovery belies this with any number of medieval forerunners – Marco Polo is only the most famous – and demonstrates besides that discovery is as often as not resisted, folded into the familiar, or distanced as alien and strange. To be found, the world had to be made, and this was hard material, intellectual, and cultural work.

As an incentive to the project of world-making, ideas about renewal in time also implied an ideal geography. The call to renew an institution, an idea, or a whole culture typically points to some exemplary place in past time as a model for the present. It is, on one hand, a summons to plot history in what would become the convention of three historical periods, Ancient, Medieval, and Modern. Seemingly neutral, this chronological scheme was originally value-laden, with the Middle Age cast as a time of regression between the beacon of antiquity and the resumption of progress in a modern age inaugurated by a Renaissance. On the other hand, the idea of renewal was projected in images of ancient places – say, Athens, Rome, or Jerusalem – that materialized the models and modeled goals for the future. The desire for close encounters with the past prompted in turn a heightened sense of its otherness. So, for example, in campaigning for a return to ancient texts and traditions humanist scholars set about reconstructing the cultural landscape that had produced them and in the end were obliged to acknowledge just how different and distant the Ancients were. Petrarch's imagined letters to ancient authors were at once knowingly intimate and poignantly cut off from them by his self-consciousness that he was writing from a world they never knew. In effect, antiquity was "invented" in the etymological sense of being "made" and "come upon," as a repertory of models to learn from and as a distant place to be seen in perspective. The fifteenth-century humanist virtuoso Leon Battista Alberti thematized this relationship quite literally when he presented a new theory of one-point pictorial perspective in his treatise *On Painting* and compared the accomplishments of contemporary Florentine artists favorably with their ancient counterparts. Even when their ideas were new, humanists sought validation by referring to an ancient elsewhere.

The logic of renovation, calling up the virtual reality of an exemplary past and an alternative world, was not a humanist monopoly. It operated in many different contexts. Genres that are thought of and actually were characteristically medieval had their later heyday long after the Middle Ages. This goes for grassroots appeals to the "good old days" – the community's law, the bounteous land of Cockaigne where tables groaned with food and drink, the reign of a benign old king denied a rightful inheritance – or legends of chivalric courts and heroes recycled for much later settings and purposes. Preachers and prophets looked back to different pasts and worlds to size up and counter the evils of later times that, so they charged, abounded in the centuries that posterity would see as cheerily "Renaissance." Contrary to another stereotype, medieval thinking was rich in cues on this-worldly contingency that would be picked up and elaborated on later as if they were early modern discoveries. In short, a similar logic did not necessarily produce the same effects. Model pasts and places could just as well relate to everyday existence as an escape or a discipline, as an ideal or an idyll, as a playful experiment or in deadly earnest.[7]

An imaginary library of the most influential books of the fifteenth and sixteenth centuries would be strong in recipes for world-making. Otherwise separated by topic, they would share the project of bringing exemplary alternatives to bear on the present. The list would include a genre named after Thomas More's book (1513–16) on the island society, simultaneously archaic and futuristic, of Utopia ("Nowhere"). Newly corrected and emended editions of classical and early Christian writers would line the shelves as a collective antiquity; they did so literally in the design of a sixteenth-century Italian humanist for a library where the ancient authors were to be bound in one color. The first modern classics in the vernacular languages appear as mirror-worlds or conduits to the ancient ones, a role that they still play in national literary histories of the Renaissance. Niccolò Machiavelli's letter of 1513 telling how he wrote the irreverent political analysis, *The Prince*, is emblematic of a program for bringing the ancients back to life in living languages. After spending the day killing time in exile, the ex-secretary of the Florentine Republic writes,

> I return to my house and go into my study. At the door I take off the clothes I have worn all day, mud spotted and dirty, and put on regal and courtly robes. Thus appropriately clothed, I enter into the ancient courts of ancient men, where, being lovingly received, I feed on the food which is mine alone and which I was born for; I am not ashamed to speak with them and to ask the reasons for their actions and they courteously answer me. For four hours I feel no boredom and forget every worry; I do not fear poverty and death does not terrify me.[8]

One quite literal case of world-making was so successful that we usually do not think of it as such. The New World was hardly new to the people who had lived there for thousands of years. It was Europe that had to be invented.[9] The physical geography of the continent could not be represented with much accuracy before the technical developments in surveying and geometrical projection in the sixteenth century. The first histories with Europe in the title appeared only around the middle of the sixteenth century, though without having the continental reach of the contemporary maps. For that even to be thinkable a mixed legacy of traditions had to be sorted through and transformed. The name "Europa" from the legendary princess abducted from Asia Minor to Crete by Jupiter in the form of a bull gave a dubious mythical lineage to a race "Europeans." The European provinces of the Roman Empire extended only to the Danube, the Rhine, and the south of Britain. Ptolemy, writing his *Geography* in Greek in Roman Egypt during the second century CE, centered the world as he knew it on the vastness of Asia, with Europe as a puny appendage. In a Judaeo-Christian counter to the scandal of the Europa myth, the sons of Noah after the Flood populated the three known parts of the world. Medieval world maps showed Africa, Asia, and Europe as a circle with Jerusalem in the middle; the symbolic geometry mattered, not relative shapes or sizes. These schemes wrote history large, as a providential progression since Creation, or local and episodic in tapestries of rulers, battles, or regimes, but it could not be written or made by "Europeans."

Europe as a whole and as a mosaic of differences – the concept and the reality were, as they still are, difficult to grasp. The Roman geographer Strabo had surveyed Europe as an entity of sorts with complementary climates, natural features, and forms of settlement. Clearer demarcations came irregularly and much later. The "rise" of Europe was in large part a function of regression and retreat: the collapse of the Roman Empire, and the Islamic and eventually Turkish conquests that reduced Christendom, with a few outposts, to European dimensions. Exploration from the continent's western margins in the fifteenth century was partly a consequence of implosion and relative isolation, and the triumphalist bragadoccio of the explorers was doubtless more intense for being a defensive cover. Borders remained fluid. (See the essays below by Linda Darling, Matthew Restall, and Edward Muir.) Eastern boundaries that are moving again in our own time were not fixed; national frontiers were unstable, when they were drawn at all. "Nation," the term for a chartered association, was hardly ever used before the seventeenth century to refer to all the inhabitants of a country, European or otherwise. National prejudices preceded and will surely survive the nation-state: people did not need to like one another to be Europeans – arguably to the contrary. One way or another, a story often foreshortened as the inevitable outcome of technological advances – compasses, plane tables, and sight rules – or of the political exigencies of state-building was far from inevitable or even predictable.

By 1623 Francis Bacon presumably assumed that his readers would not blink on being addressed as "we Europeans."[10] By then, a salute that would have been nearly incomprehensible a century and a half earlier may have seemed self-evident and natural, all the more so perhaps because it rallied, as if by nature, a collective "us" over and against a dispersed but distinct "them." Partly out of our experience of globalization, it is perhaps easier to appreciate how much shifting of mental furniture came with the reconfiguring of physical boundaries. Here again the ancient world worked doubly as a model and bridge for comparisons and as a gauge for the shock of the new. Denial by analogy or assimilation transformed the unfamiliar into the familiar: lush landscapes into a Greek Arcadia or an Earthly Paradise, disciplined strangers into noble savages or even good Romans, uncomprehended practices into barbarian or diabolical excesses. By a cruel paradox, acknowledgement and acceptance of radical difference could license more or less brutal forms of suppression or outright annihilation. Between the stereotypes and extremes, however, there were countless real-world variations, two-way exchanges, flashes of mutual recognition across cultural distances and differences. Today, critiques of Eurocentrism and shifting definitions of the meaning of Europe have undercut the received narratives of European history as the protagonist and norm of modern historical development. With this change in perspective both the parallels and the differences of non-European "early modernities" have come into focus: for example, the emergence of a public sphere of discussion and communication between official decree and private interest or the consolidation of collective identities in the Ottoman, Safavid, and Mogul Empires, in Japan under the Tokugawa, in Vietnam and even in Southeast Asia.[11] It is fitting that the scope of the early modern period should come up for discussion during a time when our own sense of boundaries is in flux.

The crowning achievement in traditional Age of Discovery scenarios, a Scientific Revolution in cosmology, is no less impressive as the ultimate demonstration of world-making. It is arguably more so in light of a fuller understanding on both sides of the so-called "science wars" (see below the essay by William Eamon) that nature, reason, and experience did not line up easily for the triumph of a new paradigm of rationalism and science. To the contrary, the main argument for the older version of the cosmos was that it was natural, reasonable, and authorized by long experience. The old model was commonsensical, orderly, and sanctioned by the consensus of ancient, Christian, and scholastic authorities: four elements (earth, water, air, fire), four basic qualities (heat, cold, moistness, dryness) and four medical humors (choleric, melancholic, phlegmatic, sanguine) within a universe bounded by the stars and centered on the earth, around which circled the planets, each with a corresponding set of influences. Phenomena high and low were classifiable, connected, and coherent in this creaky but accommodating form of Unified Theory.

It would only be surprising, then, if there were no carry-over from the old cosmic picture or if the new one were an unalloyed triumph of pure reason and science. Copernicus kept the planetary orbits circular while demoting the earth to a planet revolving the sun. The Danish astronomer Tycho Brahe measured astronomical motions with unprecedented accuracy but located the earth at or near the center of the universe; Kepler, who was essentially correct about the elliptical shape and variable speeds of planetary orbits, was a committed astrologer and mystic. The breakthrough experiments and observations of the new science were as likely staged in pursuit of patronage and prestige as in the disinterested pursuit of truth. Hypothetical guess-work about the autonomous reality of nature and the willful intervention of instruments to produce the desired results were not contradictions so much as prerequisites for an objectifying world picture. Surely this was a much more startling outcome than a Scientific Revolution that supposedly proved nature to be transcendent and absolutely independent of the world of our own making.[12]

Self-fashioning

The "Renaissance individual" is a stock character in studies of the Renaissance, virtually certain to appear in one form or another and just as likely to be dismissed by historians today as an impostor. Burckhardt put his chapters on "The Birth of the

Individual" at the beginning of the charter text of Renaissance studies, *The Civiliza-tion of the Renaissance in Italy*, and there he spun heady phrases around a newly "*objective* treatment . . . of all the things of this world" that, together with a "*subject-ive* side," replaced consciousness of oneself "only as a member of a race, people, party, family or corporation – only through some general category." The easy objec-tion is often made that webs of collective identity and obligation still mattered and that they were broken only later, if at all, by hardier and more relentless forms of individualism. The Calvinist elect, the Cartesian ego, and the capitalist entrepreneur are the usual suspects. But the proliferation of candidates only goes to show that, early or late, a prototypical Modern Individual did not spring forth all at once. Whether the self can be truly known, whether it is a spiritual substance, a material thing, a set of relationships, a luxury item, or common property, historical selves are circumstantial, acted out, and reflected upon in time. What we can say is that new senses of the self were under construction at about the same time as the new views of the world were taking shape.

"Self-fashioning" is by now a widely accepted term for a central dynamic in this process.[13] It originated in Renaissance literary studies but points to a pervasive cultural calculus of craft and craftiness, deliberate effort, and cool nonchalance. No doubt there were fashioned medieval selves and unfashioned early modern ones. As with other early modern genealogies, self-fashioning does not necessarily have abrupt beginnings and endings or uniform trajectories. (See the essay below by John Martin.) One trajectory moves on one side or another of the overlapping lines of temporal difference and spatial distance traced above. Other strands run through elaborate theories and practices defining and dividing the world according to roles people play; still others were intertwined in what has come to be called the "civilizing process." (See the essay below by Robert Muchembled.) The variants and offshoots can only be hinted at here.

Role-playing, to begin with, was a serious business in a world believed to be created in God's "image and likeness." A dominant medieval view held that humanity was the scribe, copyist, or glossator of the canonical authorities and that God was the Ultimate Author. Self-fashioning first shows up as a series of variations or mutations on simple forms of exemplar-copy thinking. Exemplary role-models proliferated beyond the medieval template of Three Estates praying (clergy), protecting (nobility), and produ-cing (everyone else) for the common good and ultimate salvation. The example of Saint and Scholar was too hard, that of Sinner too easy for most people on the road to salvation. Simple rosters of ideal types were complicated from the start by the idea that Creation was intricately abundant and then by the facts of human difference and social differentiation in increasingly complex societies. Systemic crises and abrupt upheavals in the fourteenth century further strained standards of behavior and markers of status and gave impetus to their being revamped or invented anew.

Ideas about doing one's very best or about striving for a place on the hierarchical ladder of things were one response from the fourteenth century on. A potent rationale for the first proposition came from the "modern" current of scholastic theology known as "nominalism" – from its characteristic doctrine that universal concepts such as justice, truth, and beauty or indeed the self were only names (*nomina* in Latin). Forms of university teaching developed in the Middle Ages turned out in this case, as in many others, to have critical, even emancipatory, potential. The prospect of rising to the angels or falling to the level of the beasts had a Platonic or Neoplatonic pedigree in the famous oration *On the Dignity of Man* (1486) by the humanist polymath and philosopher Giovanni Pico della Mirandola. These proposals for the realization of human potential had a darker side in the proximity of failure and the compulsion to perform without much assurance about the nature of the stage. Imputations of semblance and deception were common, even a kind of reality. One way or another, self-fashioning grew out of a preoccupation with models and types in antiquity, in nature, in the mind, or in a heaven of archetypes.

Down-to-earth versions were a major genre from 1400 to 1600. In this great age of how-to books there were guides for kings, saints, and sinners, for scholars and artists, for courtiers, secretaries, and diplomats. The best of these challenged easy formulas for success; all of them offered to make the most of a job description. Humanists and courtiers followed the best-known career paths. Teachers of the humanities, the *studia humanitatis* – definitions varied but usually included the teaching of grammar, poetry, rhetoric, history, and moral philosophy in Latin and Greek – held relatively low positions as undergraduate teachers in universities whose main mission was to offer graduate study and degrees in theology, medicine, or law. The narrow pedagogical niche expanded with a theory of education, a model product, and methods that worked. Humanists appropriated the justifications ancient teachers of rhetoric had used to promote themselves to Greek citizens and Roman senators: we cultivate the man in the boy, the well-rounded and humane person in the man, the master of eloquence in the public servant, the gentleman (rarely the lady) *and* the scholar. These claims reversed the priorities of the universities, eventually led to the invention of the grammar and classical high schools, and in spite of their high-mindedness, licensed teaching by rote, lists of favorite quotations, and systematic plagiarism from the classics. Celebrity teachers and scholars added luster and occasional notoriety to the more pedestrian routines, but it was everyday humanist pedagogy that produced a class of the initiated who, without being specialists or professionals, were linked by a common culture across otherwise unbridgeable differences in location, status, and class.[14] (See below the essay by Ingrid Rowland.)

Courtiers were supposed to have more than a smattering of humanist culture, at least in Italy, by the time that Baldassare Castiglione's *Book of the Courtier* was published in 1529. The book soon became a bestseller in several languages, but this was not a foregone conclusion. The old noble credentials of warrior prowess, blood line, and tenure in land, titles, and offices, idealized as they were in their medieval prime, had little to do with formal learning. Especially in northern Europe, crusty aristocrats still swore by the old values, but as the competition became stronger and the alternatives more alluring, the courtly ideal was recast. (See below the essay by Robert Muchembled.) Courtiers and court ladies recruited from different backgrounds came together in the charmed circle of Castiglione's dialogue as if to improvise codes of belonging that were more supple but hardly less exclusive than the old ones. Prowess could be exercised without a battlefield in physical grace and sallies of wit; graciousness had to be learned but acted out as if inbred and effortlessly natural; official functions were dressed up as sophisticated and skilled services. Aristocratic self-fashioning can be understood as a strategy for preserving social privilege, with the proviso that it also entailed a kind of submission: to a ruler, to social rules, to the disciplines dividing the person and the role that the strategy called for.[15]

In any case, the repertory of roles was not just for the real or a would-be elite; nor was it only gendered male. The Protestant principle that all believers were priests, each with a calling in the world, was a prescription for self-fashioning; the *Spiritual Exercises* of St. Ignatius Loyola, the founder of the Jesuit order, was a personal training manual for the Counter-Reformation, with a complete regimen of meditation and rules of conduct for disciplining the weaknesses of the spirit and the flesh. Far down the social ladder virtuoso self-fashioners left traces in the archives. In a large class of French judicial records otherwise anonymous people, men and women charged with serious crimes, crafted exculpatory tales seeking pardons from the king and his courts. Since they were effectively admitting guilt, their stories had to be good ones, all the more so in a culture of master storytellers of the likes of Boccaccio, Chaucer, and Marguerite of Navarre. Although illiterate himself, an enterprising peasant farmer living near Siena early in the fifteenth century recorded biographical details and business in the hired hands of notaries and secretaries. Women's options were severely curtailed by the prejudices, practices, and institutions of a patriarchal order. It has been argued that they became even more so, for example, with newly imposed restrictions on working women or the closing of religious orders and convents in Protestant countries. But recent research has also made a point of the agency and resourcefulness of women in confounding stereotypes, sometimes by actively appropriating and working through them.[16] (See below the essay by Elissa Weaver.)

Another branch in the historical genealogy of self-fashioning, what the historically-minded sociologist Norbert Elias called the "civilizing process," survives, however precariously, in prescriptions for minding our manners. Historians have expanded on the notion that beginning in the sixteenth century, school books, etiquette manuals, and physical and spiritual disciplines of all sorts enjoined and, far more surprising, actually succeeded to a remarkable extent in establishing norms of acceptably "civilized" behavior.[17] The impact of this gradual, unspectacular development was more profound than most historical events. Its unlikely manifesto was a little Latin manual called *On Civility in Children* (1530), a minor pedagogical treatise by the great humanist scholar and sometime teacher Erasmus of Rotterdam. Printed in 130 editions and translated into several languages, it was a hodgepodge drawn from different sources: the humanist treasury of ancient literature on education, but also compilations of precepts for the proper comportment of the religious, the so-called "mirrors of princes" for the education of rulers, instructions for knights, a rich legacy of proverbial lore and cautionary fables. Erasmus's innovation was not only to synthesize but also to maintain that good manners could be taught to children and accepted by everyone irrespective of age or social standing. His treatise comprised seven books of etiquette for practically everything, from bodily functions to gestures at church, behavior at banquets, public meetings, games, and amusements, and conduct in the bedchamber. The high embarrassment threshold measures how much room there was for improvement: throw food that you can't swallow somewhere but don't spit it out on the table; blow your nose on the napkin not in your hand or on your sleeve; don't crowd the people sharing your bed. A whole genre of civility books went on to elaborate and refine the rules. Manners that at first had to be learned eventually become a kind of second nature in an increasingly differentiated and complex society. Propriety in the eyes of others and in one's inner eye was a culmination and a revenge of self-fashioning.[18]

Transmission

The conventional picture of the Renaissance as a period unified by the Spirit of the Age and a top-down diffusion of culture has the paradoxical effect of freezing what were supposed to be epoch-making changes in an essentially still panorama. Current scholarship complicates and animates the picture with multiple and dynamic conjunctions of high and low culture, theoretical discourses and material practices, institutions and ideas. The old *Zeitgeist* painted charming views where there were buzzing currents and dense networks, genealogical filiations rather than static patterns.

Cultural transmission, before it can be mapped or diagrammed, begins of course with people. There is much research by now to show that people were routinely mobile at practically every social level in preindustrial societies that, except for the convulsions of nature, were once thought to be relatively immobile. The evidence goes beyond more or less professional classes of travelers – merchants, pilgrims, friars, soldiers, wandering scholars – to include craftsmen, laborers, and peasants. It ranges from countless laws against vagabonds and to a swelling genre of books and pamphlets on the profits and pleasures of travel. The agglomeration of diversely skilled populations in cities and towns, specialization for the market, and what has been called "the industrious revolution" whereby households work more for the income to consume than to be self-sufficient have all been taken to indicate steeper growth curves for expertise than for goods. By some recent accounts, Renaissance culture was the product of what amounted to an extended shopping spree in which cultural capital mattered more than the material thing. The emblematic peregrinations and personal encounters of cultural celebrities – the multiple residences of Petrarch and Erasmus; Copernicus and William Harvey studying astronomy and medicine in Padua; Leonardo da Vinci and Benvenuto Cellini summoned to the court of France; Montaigne and Dürer in Italy – have turned out to be more truly emblematic than we might have thought.[19]

Maps or diagrams of cultural exchange around 1500 would show an overall density, and centers and directions, that had not figured a century or more earlier.[20] The defining lines in the main traditions of Renaissance studies would show up of course – a distinctively Renaissance culture fanning out from Italy and, within Italy, from the cultural dynamos of Florence and, just beginning, of Rome. If anything, the signs of a far-reaching Italianization of culture would be more marked than they once were in a classicizing view of the Renaissance. Italianate styles practically everywhere; a New World discovered in spite of himself by the Genoese Columbus and named after the Florentine Amerigo Vespucci; French cuisine as an Italian import: for at least two hundred years Italy was the pace-setter that France had been in the Middle Ages and would be again before Britain and the United States took on this role in the nineteenth and twentieth centuries, respectively. Even so, cultural cartography should also make us wary of diffusion or dissemination models. Countering the image of a central source and emanating arrows of influence, it would show that sites of reception that should be passive according to the model were vital, dynamic, and discriminating. (See the essay below by Peter Burke.) Italy was a geographical expression and an occasional failed ideal for a madcap assemblage of republics, petty despotisms, a dynastic monarchy, and a theocracy; from time to time Antwerp and Amsterdam or

Prague and Cracow, not to mention Mantua and Urbino, were competing, not just consuming, centers in their own right. In any case, the big picture needs to be complicated if not necessarily undone by the micro-circuitry of sites and institutions as diverse as schools, courts, libraries, print shops, and not least important parish houses and military barracks.

The notion of "imagined communities" familiar to students of nationalism is useful here for suggesting how cultural transmission works without face-to-face connections.[21] New or revived textual genres fostered community of this sort: collections of letters in Latin and all the European vernaculars; geographical surveys and maps describing different countries and their inhabitants; the essay, the auto-biography, and the newsletter, which all became established forms in the sixteenth century; and the various kinds of how-to books already mentioned above. It does not demean spectacular achievements in the arts to see them serving similar functions. This is how patrons and artists mostly understood artistic production. Old justifica-tions for the Church – that images were the texts of the illiterate, memorable because vivid, effectively didactic for involving the emotions – were just as compelling for political propaganda and for advertising real or trumped-up distinction. There were international styles, from International Gothic to Mannerism in the sixteenth century and Baroque in the seventeenth, and there were artists and the relatively new figures of collectors and dealers working an international circuit. Another how-to book, Cesare Ripa's *Iconologia* (first edition 1603) was a dictionary, more copious than trustworthy, for the signs and symbols of a kind of esperanto of images. The exalted reward of a quite functional demand was a precipitous rise in the status, not to mention the pretensions, of the artist, from run-of-the-mill craftsman to intellectual, entrepreneur, and in Michelangelo's case, "divine" genius.[22]

Contemporary writers were often dazzled, as modern historians have been, by new tools and instruments and the mechanics of cultural transmission. The cannon was certainly one; without putting it this way, the early moderns knew at least as well as we do that military budgets produced invention as well as havoc, and that culture was delivered more often than one might like to admit from the end of a gun.[23] The printing press was a more respectable reference, though not, as we have been warned recently, in the form of technological determinism.[24] At least in theory, standarized production, wide dissemination, and fixed content were inherent in the medium. Unlike cultures beholden to manuscripts or oral communication, the texts of "print culture" were – again, in theory – reproducible in exactly the same form, and since texts were dependable, they could be compared, contested, and built upon, thus enabling the progressive improvement of knowledge. The radical argument for a Gutenberg revolution goes so far as to claim that Renaissance and Reformation not only spread on a flood of printer's ink but were enduring thanks to the production and reproduction of their canonical texts; that the propagation in print of national laws and languages was a cause of nationalism; that modern science became possible on the basis of phenomena and theories reliably recorded in print. Not surprisingly, practice was far less elegant than the argument. The vast majority of early printed works were perfectly traditional fare, the harvest of medieval manuscripts, not the harbinger of modern "print culture." As late as 1623, Shakespeare's first folio had 600 different typefaces, along with non-uniform spelling and punctuation, erratic divisions and arrangements, mispaging and irregular proofing. Far from being standardized or fixed by print, no two copies are identical. It has become increasingly clear that the supposedly inherent properties of printing were neither technologically determined nor mechanically delivered once and for all, and that the dependability and marketability of printed material had to be cultivated over generations. If there was "print revolution," it had as much to do with gradual developments – from editorial procedures to regulations for production, distribution, and advertising – that enhanced the cultural credit of print as with the printing press. Even that powerful engine of change had to operate through the complex lines of transmission.

Conclusion: Back to the Future

To rephrase the opening question, is it possible *not* to think of the Renaissance in European history? This chapter in a book such as this attests, after all, to the stubborn persistence of the thought. As a historical construct, the Renaissance is easy to dismiss but somehow hard to do without. Both the staying power and the ambivalence are practically congenital, bred into its long life as a testing ground and construction site for European historiography. The very idea of a European history with traditions going back to Greece and Rome was a Renaissance invention; the division by ancient, medieval, and modern periods was a corollary of the Renaissance idea that history could be plotted according to the rise and fall of secular culture from a distant past through new beginnings in a "modern" present. As a period or an age defined as such by some characteristic cultural cachet, the Renaissance is the original model for the Reformation, the Counter-Reformation, the Enlightenment, and a succession of smaller subdivisions (the "Victorian period" or even farther afield, the "progressive era"). In Clio's pantheon a historian of the Renaissance, Jacob Burckhardt, is the acknowledged founder of modern cultural history. In the more recent annals of the historical profession the Renaissance has occupied a pivotal position at the intersection of two important developments: the internationalization of European historiography and the contestation of triumphalist narratives of western civilization.

In short, some conception of the Renaissance is probably as unavoidable as ever in thinking about the history of Europe. Even in rejection its presuppositions cast long shadows. The by-now ritual criticisms that some allegedly Renaissance trait was actually a medieval one, or that the Renaissance was not for everybody, pay unintended tribute to the fact that the Renaissance sets the terms of the critique. The alternatives, moreover, are not at all foolproof. "Early modernity," encompassing great, not to say indeterminate, stretches of time and undogmatically juxtaposing time frames, is doubly slippery – accommodating but also treacherous. Seemingly neutral, it may actually recycle discredited teleologies of modernization – its inevitability, its progressive stages, its proof of western superiority – together with a priori conceptions of the modern and the traditional. In any case, the "early modern" label does nothing to call the old Whiggish notions of historical progress to account; if anything, it defers or actually defeats any obligation to think clearly about directions of change. There is of course the alternative of close-up specialization without much regard for sweeping interpretative categories. This is what most historians already do anyway. Yet there are risks in a historiography that deliberately gives up on the big picture. The results may be merely antiquarian and annalistic or, like the new ethnic republics and regionalisms, partisan and separatist. Besides, the unassuming mono-graph often assumes a great deal, including the overarching schemes of interpretation that are not supposed to matter.

The issue, then, is whether the Renaissance will be unavoidable like a barricade or a roadblock, or like a renewable resource for historical understanding. This chapter has suggested that the conception of the Renaissance as a historical period can be set aside – and that it ought to be in light of diminishing returns and actual liabilities in foisting illusions of consistency on the past. Rather than a period with definitive beginnings and endings and consistent content in between, the Renaissance can be (and occa-sionally has been) seen in terms of open-ended sets of practices and ideas to which specific groups and identifiable persons variously contributed or responded in differ-ent times and places. It would be in this sense an amalgam of diverse, sometimes converging, sometimes tangential initiatives, not a single time-bound culture. The alternatives to a narrative sequence by epochs and ages need not come down to the rather dispiriting choice between altogether plotless histories of Olde Europe or the kind of presentism that sees the past only in present-day terms.

Or so this chapter tries to suggest with a genealogical approach to the European Renaissance that allows for heterogeneity but also for connections and coherence. Genealogical history works discursively by pattern – for example,"trees" and their "branches" – and by indices of historical individuality such as names and dates. It figures structure, continuity, and succession as well as contingency, discontinuity, and deviation. The small-scale demonstration offered here maps some segments, so to say, in a genome of a European Renaissance, while also presenting an admittedly selective overview of some leitmotifs in recent historical scholarship on the Renaissance. In doing so, it also mirrors a mode of representing history in a culture that was intent on tracing elaborate ancestries for most things. A European genealogy of the genea-logical mode would probably show its most prolific growth of limbs and branches during the two centuries or so after 1400.

NOTES

1 Bizzocchi, *Genealogie incredibili*; Starn, "Who's Afraid."
2 Ferguson, *Renaissance*; for current discussion, see Findlen and Gouwens, "Persistence."
3 Panofsky, *Renaissance*.
4 Gerald Strauss, "Ideas of *Reformatio*," pp. 1–30.
5 The classic work that has prompted a large literature in turn is Cohn, *The Pursuit of the Millennium*.
6 Grafton, *Defenders*; the quotation is from William Harvey, cited by Hale, *Civilization of Europe*, p. 588.
7 Berger, *Second World*, pp. 3–40, is especially illuminating on this process, as is Hampton, *Writing from History*.
8 Letter to Francesco Vettori, 10 December 1513, in Machiavelli, *The Prince*, p. 5.
9 For an illuminating and richly documented account, see Hale, *Civilization of Europe*, chs. 1–4.
10 Quoted from the Latin version of Bacon's *The Advancement of Learning* by Hale, *Civilization of Europe*, p. 3.

11 See "Early Modernities," *Daedalus* 127: 3 (Summer 1998).
12 Shapin, *Scientific Revolution*; Latour, *Never Been Modern*.
13 Greenblatt, *Self-Fashioning*, first launched the term in English Renaissance literary studies.
14 Kraye, *Renaissance Humanism* contains excellent chapters by various scholars on all aspects of humanism.
15 Burke, *Courtier*.
16 Davis, *Fiction*; Balestracci, *Renaissance in the Fields*. Wiesner, *Women and Gender* is an excellent survey of recent research.
17 Elias, *Civilizing Process*; for the extension of the concept see Jacques Revel, "Uses of Civility," pp. 167–205.
18 See Arditi, *Manners* for long-term developments from the fourteenth to the eighteenth centuries.
19 Grafton and Blair, *Transmission of Culture*; Hale, *Civilization of Europe*, chs. 8–9; Jan de Vries, "Population," ch. 1.
20 Porter and Teich, *The Renaissance*.
21 Anderson, *Imagined Communities*.
22 The best overview, with a comparative discussion of artists and writers is in Hale, *Civilization of Europe*, ch. 6.
23 Cipolla, *Guns and Sails*.
24 Johns, *The Nature of the Book* makes the case against technological determinism and reviews debates over the "print revolution" in his detailed study.

REFERENCES

Anderson, Benedict, *Imagined Communities: Reflections on the Origin and Spread of Nationalism* (London: Verso, 1983).
Arditi, Jorge, *A Genealogy of Manners: Transformations of Social Relations in France and England from the Fourteenth to the Eighteenth Century* (Chicago: University of Chicago Press, 1998).
Balestracci, Duccio, *The Renaissance in the Fields: Family Memoirs of a Fifteenth-Century Tuscan Peasant*, trans. Paolo Squatriti and Betsy Merideth (University Park, PA: Pennsylvania State University Press, 1999).
Berger, Harry, *Second World and Green World: Studies in Renaissance Fiction-Making* (Berkeley: University of California Press, 1988).
Bizzocchi, Roberto, *Genealogie incredibili: Scritti di storia nell'Europa moderna* (Bologna: Il Mulino, 1995).
Burke, Peter, *The Fortunes of the Courtier: The European Reception of Castiglione's "Cortegiano"* (University Park, PA: Pennsylvania State University Press, 1995).
Cipolla, Carlo M., *Guns and Sails in the Early Phase of European Expansion, 1400–1700* (London: Collins, 1965).
Cohn, Norman, *The Pursuit of the Millennium* (New York: Harper, 1961).
Davis, Natalie Zemon, *Fiction in the Archives: Pardon Tales and their Tellers in Sixteenth-Century France* (Stanford: Stanford University Press, 1987).
de Vries, Jan, "The Population of Europe," in *Handbook of European History, 1400–1600*, vol. 1, ed. Thomas A. Brady Jr., Heiko A. Oberman, James D. Tracy (Grand Rapids, MI: Eerdmans,1996).
Early Modernities, Daedalus: Journal of the American Academy of Arts and Science 127/3 (Summer 1998).

Elias, Norbert, *The Civilizing Process*, I: *The History of Manners* [1939], trans. Edmund Jephcott (New York: Urizen Books, 1978).

Ferguson, Wallace K., *The Renaissance in Historical Thought: Five Centuries of Interpretation* (Cambridge, MA: Riverside Press, 1948).

Findlen, Paula and Gouwens, Kenneth, eds., "AHR Forum: The Persistence of the Renaissance," *American Historical Review* 103/1 (February 1998).

Grafton, Anthony, *Defenders of the Text: Traditions of Scholarship in an Age of Science* (Cambridge, MA: Harvard University Press, 1991).

Grafton, Anthony and Blair, Ann, eds., *The Transmission of Culture in Early Modern Europe* (Philadelphia: University of Pennsylvania Press, 1990).

Greenblatt, Stephen, *Renaissance Self-Fashioning: From More to Shakespeare* (Chicago: University of Chicago Press, 1980).

Hale, John, *The Civilization of Europe in the Renaissance* (London: HarperCollins, 1993).

Hampton, Timothy, *Writing from History: The Rhetoric of Exemplarity in Renaissance Literature* (Ithaca, NY: Cornell University Press, 1990).

Johns, Adrian, *The Nature of the Book: Print and Knowledge in the Making* (Chicago: University of Chicago Press, 1998).

Kraye, Jill, ed., *The Cambridge Companion to Renaissance Humanism* (Cambridge: Cambridge University Press, 1996).

Latour, Bruno, *We Have Never Been Modern*, trans. Catherine Porter (Cambridge, MA: Harvard University Press, 1993).

Machiavelli, Niccolò, *The Prince*, ed. Quentin Skinner, trans. Richard Price (Cambridge: Cambridge University Press, 1998).

Panofsky, Erwin, *Renaissance and Renascences in Western Art* (New York: Harper and Row, 1969).

Porter, Roy and Teich, Mikuláš, eds., *The Renaissance in National Context* (Cambridge: Cambridge University Press, 1992).

Revel, Jacques, "The Uses of Civility," in *A History of Private Life*, vol. III: *The Passions of the Renaissance*, ed. Roger Chartier, trans. Arthur Goldhammer (Cambridge, MA: Belknap Press, 1989).

Shapin, Steven, *The Scientific Revolution* (Chicago: University of Chicago Press, 1996).

Starn, Randolph, "Who's Afraid of the Renaissance?," in *The Present and Future of Medieval Studies*, ed. John Van Engen (South Bend, IN: University of Notre Dame Press, 1996).

Strauss, Gerald, "Ideas of *Reformatio* and *Renovatio* from the Middle Ages to the Reformation," in *Handbook of European History, 1400–1600*, vol. 2, ed. Thomas A. Brady Jr., Heiko A. Oberman, and James D. Tracy (Grand Rapids, MI: Eerdmans, 1996).

Wiesner, Merry, *Women and Gender in Early Modern Europe* (Cambridge: Cambridge University Press, 1993).

FURTHER READING

Cochrane, Eric and Kirshner, Julius, eds., *The Renaissance* (University of Chicago Readings in Western Civilization) (Chicago: University of Chicago Press, 1986).

Chapter Three

The Renaissance and the Middle East

Linda T. Darling

At one time the Middle East was in essence supposed to have caused the European Renaissance. The Ottoman conquest of Constantinople in 1453, it was said, forced Greek literati to flee with their favorite books to Italy where, earning their living as teachers of Greek, they sparked the rebirth of classical scholarship that we know as the Renaissance. Another popular narrative of the past maintained that the Ottoman conquests closed the routes of eastern trade, forcing the Europeans to discover the sea passages to India. In the "western civilization" view of the world, Europe's overseas discoveries and revival of learning were necessary elements in its modernization and eventual predominance.

We are now more impressed with the intellectual contributions of thirteenth- and fourteenth-century Muslim Spain to the revival of learning than with those of fifteenth-century Byzantine elites. Moreover, we realize that the Ottoman conquests and even the Portuguese arrival in India did not close off the spice trade through the Mediterranean. The scholarly pendulum has swung the other way, and our narratives of rebirth and discovery now ignore the Middle East. The Ottomans no longer have even the villain's part to play in the great drama of the growth of the modern world.[1] The Middle East appears to have been on a different historical track altogether, one that brought it to a destination far distant from the West's arrival point in modernity. One reason often cited for this divergence is that the Middle East never experienced a renaissance, a rebirth of learning which is seen as one of the main impulses for the series of changes we call modern. The cultural florescence of the late fifteenth century in Ottoman Istanbul and Timurid Central Asia was, in this view, not a rebirth of anything and had no modernizing consequences.

The original conception of the Renaissance had nothing to do with modernization; European writers of the period saw the revival of learning and culture as a sign of the return of a utopian age of gold. Its function as an agent of modernization was a later construct derived from the Enlightenment sense of the growth of knowledge as the motor of history. The twentieth-century turn from intellectual to socioeconomic history dethroned the Renaissance from its place as the principal engine of European modernization and replaced it with Europe's global discoveries and creation of an economic world system. Europe's rediscovery of its classical past and subsequent intellectual and artistic creativity were then seen to have had roots in the High Middle Ages and to have been much less sudden and original than formerly thought. The focus on exploration and colonization moved the period of inquiry into the sixteenth, seventeenth, and eighteenth centuries and generated interest in themes of political economy and social change for which the term "renaissance" seems inappropriate.

The concept of renaissance, however, retains its usefulness to designate a culture's creative rediscovery and reuse of its own distant past. In this sense, the experience of renaissance need not be confined to Europe nor to the fifteenth and sixteenth centuries. Some Europeanists are rediscovering connections between the Renaissance as rediscovery of the European past and European borrowings from places elsewhere on the globe.[2] Middle East scholars, however, still resist employing what has historically been such a Eurocentric paradigm. We are left with an image of fifteenth- and sixteenth-century Europeans importing the Middle East's cultural raw materials to manufacture newly powerful ideas and images, which were then resold to the unsuspecting orientals at the high price of increasing cultural backwardness. This essay argues against the idea that the Renaissance as such was a sufficiently unique phenomenon to have generated European geopolitical predominance, and for an attempt to uncover the effects of contemporaneous cultural florescence and political and economic expansion on Middle Eastern societies.

In the past, the term "renaissance" was used in connection with high-cultural developments under two Middle Eastern regimes, the Buyids (945–1055) and the Timurids (1370–1506). A re-examination of the dynamics of these two developments should help to restore a sense of this region as an active partner in worldwide cultural development and of the interconnectedness of the premodern world. Given the current state of research, this essay cannot hope to present a Middle Eastern counterpart to the vast scholarship on the European Renaissance, early modern popular culture, and social history. Moreover, the limits of space preclude the disaggregation of "Middle East" into its component regions and the discussion of variations in cultural dynamics across space, language, gender, or class. Instead, we will outline how the concept of renaissance can be used in the Middle Eastern context and then briefly address the cultural development of the Middle East in the age of the European Renaissance, focusing mainly on the Ottoman Empire.

The "Buyid Renaissance"

The concept of the fifteenth century as one of rebirth in Europe originally arose in contrast with the so-called Dark Ages. The fall of the Roman Empire did not eliminate learning and the arts, but it vastly reduced both their output and their impact, especially in the West, making the Renaissance appear as a quantum leap forward in cultural productivity. The trajectory of events was quite different in the Middle East, where there was no "fall of Rome." When the Roman Empire split in two in the fifth century, the Middle East was in the better-organized half. The shift of Byzantine literature from Latin into Greek had little effect on cultural productivity, although the decline of urbanization and of the old elite with its systems of education and patronage moved the creative focus from secular into religious literature. Interaction with the other major culture in the region, that of Sasanian Persia, increased at the same time and became, for a couple of centuries, the most important cultural interchange in Eurasia. Thus, the Arab invasion of the seventh century did not destroy a thriving Byzantine culture but inherited one in the process of change. The Muslim Arabs' new religious faith gave them the vision to form a new universal empire and high culture of their own, focused at first, like the Byzantine, on religion.

Islamic high culture was not independent of the achievements of its predecessors. By the mid-eighth century, the translation of classical literature into Arabic began. First to be translated were political literature and history, with the histories of Alexander the Great and the Persian kings taking the lead. In the ninth century Greek philosophy and science were copiously translated, often by way of Syriac. The ninth and tenth centuries have in fact been identified as the Islamic world's Renaissance, a "rebirth of the classical legacy and a general cultural revival" that took place well before similar events in Europe, a period that saw a "conscious attempt to retrieve the philosophical and scientific patrimony of antiquity" and the growth of a humanistic worldview.[3] The goals of this humanism were to revive the philosophical legacy of the Greeks for humanity's intellectual and ethical formation, to determine the relationship between philosophy and religion, and to acknowledge the common kinship of humanity across religious and cultural lines. Conquest of the Islamic capital by the Persian-speaking Buyid dynasty (945–1055) overturned the religious, political, and intellectual hierarchy of the Islamic empire and made space for further intellectual development based on non-Islamic sciences. Muslim scientists made new discoveries and new syntheses in fields opened up by the Greeks, such as philosophy, medicine, optics, mathematics, and astronomy.

Scholars have likened this "Buyid renaissance" to Europe's "twelfth-century renaissance" in that, in contrast to the later Italian Renaissance, its main accomplishments were in philosophy and science rather than the arts. This comparison betrays a thoroughly Eurocentric concept of the legacy of antiquity. While Greek and Roman poetry, drama, and essays remained untranslated and unappreciated in the Middle East, the region had another classical literary and artistic heritage on which to draw, that of Sasanian Persia. From this source came poetry, drama, entertainment, ethics, history, and practical information. Translation of Persian literature, first into Arabic and then into modern Persian, took place on much the same schedule as translation from the Greek. And just as the translation of Greek philosophical classics initiated a period of intense creativity culminating in the early eleventh century in the philosophical works of Ibn Sina (Avicenna), al-Biruni, and Miskawayh, so the translation of Persian classics simultanously inspired poets such as Firdausi, who in the early eleventh century created almost singlehandedly the primary imaginative world of the Middle East. His epic poem, the *Shahnama*, or the Book of Kings, retold from pre-Islamic sources the history of the Persian kings from the creation of the world to the rise of Islam. Another literary current fed from this source was the popular courtly genre of "mirrors for princes," whose greatest product was the *Book of Governance, or, Rules for Kings* by Nizam al-Mulk.[4]

In artistic terms, the ninth and tenth centuries saw a revival of pre-Islamic Persian architecture, which continued (as Roman architecture did in the West) to inspire the architecture of the Muslim East until today. Tombs and mosques, and later schools and caravanserais from Anatolia to India, displayed the influence of this revival.

Painting, ceramics, and metalwork were slower to change, but over the next two centuries the humanistic thrust of Buyid creativity found expression in these media. The philosophical and theological reconceptualization of the central place of the human being in the universe generated ideas about the individual as microcosm of creation and the development of the archetypal concept of the Perfect Man.[5] By the twelfth century, artists were using the human image to represent universal phenomena: stars, seasons, the known and unknown reaches of the earth, knowledge, virtue, and love.[6] The twelfth century also saw the rise of a new humanistic literary genre, the love story, in which love functioned as a generator of virtue; the most imitated example was Nizami Ganjavi's *Quintet* of romances.[7] Intellectual and emotional paths to perfectibility were conceived as meeting in the king, whose seated image was used to represent transcendent human potential. On both the physical and ethical planes artists, writers, and their publics sought to relate the order of the universe to human existence; analogous efforts were made by alchemists, astrologers, and magicians. The growth of educational institutions and the dissemination of philosophical and scientific literature fed the development of "renaissance men," capable of making contributions in several different fields.

Broadening the definition of the classical world beyond Greece and Rome thus permits us to see the Buyid accomplishment as a renaissance, a recovery of the culture of the past from its post-Roman obscurity, its incorporation as a building block for new scientific and aesthetic achievements, and the consequent development of a new worldview. In the Middle East, science and humanism did not become opposites but cooperated to generate a florescence of humanistic arts and sciences. This cultural florescence might have led on to greater things but for the interruption of urban culture and patronage by the Mongol conquest in the east. Its greatest monument remains the vital intellectual life of Muslim Spain, whose twelfth-century accomplishments, particularly the philosophy of Ibn Rushd (Averroes) and his contemporaries, but also the period's achievements in poetry and mystical theology, were a major source for Europe's "twelfth-century renaissance."[8]

The "Timurid Renaissance"

The better-known cultural florescence of the fifteenth century was, ironically, set in train by the Mongols. The Mongol conquest of 1258 did not bring down a great empire; in eliminating the Abbasid Caliphate it brought down only a symbol of unity. Over the previous three centuries, the Muslim world had been divided politically among warring dynasties, religiously into mutually intolerant sects, and culturally into two great language zones. While the eastern half of the region had developed a culture based on the Persian literary tradition, the western half maintained the Arabic-based culture; in both the Greek heritage formed a subordinate element. The Mongols, conquering the eastern portion, learned Persian and patronized Persian thought and literature even prior to their conversion to Islam. After converting, they stepped up their patronage of the civilizing arts, but the fragility of nomad political ties prevented them from building a stable and lasting polity. In the fourteenth century the Middle East again disintegrated into a patchwork of regional sultanates held together by the institutions and literatures of Islamic civilization.

Cultural trends initiated under the Mongols reached their highest development only in the fragmented post-Mongol period. Rulers of the Mongol successor state of the Jalayirids (1340–1410), though continually at war, became lovers, practitioners, or patrons of the arts. Centered on the former Mongol capital, they inherited the Mongols' artistic workshop, where manuscripts such as Firdausi's *Shahnama* and the world history of Rashid al-Din were copied and illuminated. The multiplication of artistic patronage in the fourteenth-century princely courts supported a growing number of poets, painters, and historians. Their output, oriented toward their dynastic patrons, was at first largely concerned with universalistic political and religious themes, but gradually it became more individualistic and personal. History-writing expanded its scope to encompass non-Middle Eastern and non-Muslim peoples such as the Mongols, Indians, Chinese, and Europeans. Poetry flourished, but although panegyrics were still composed, epics lost their popularity. The fourteenth century was instead the great age of Persian lyric poetry and the era of Persia's most outstanding lyricist, Hafiz (d. 1389).

During the fifteenth century the center of power in the Middle East migrated to eastern Iran and central Asia, the kingdom of the Timurids (1370–1506). Timurid Asia was divided into a number of principalities, among which leadership shifted from time to time; fighting continued but was nowhere so destructive as to halt cultural activity.[9] The Timurids and their contemporaries followed the same pattern of kingship as the Mongols and Jalayirids, combining military activity with artistic patronage to such great effect that the fifteenth century came to be known as the era of the Timurid renaissance, a match in glory (if not in transformative power) for the Italian Quattrocento.[10] More recently some Timurid scholars have abandoned that designation, for the reasons mentioned earlier, seeing the "Timurid florescence" as the swan song of a culture. Ottoman, Safavid, and Mughal historians, however, beg to differ; for them the Timurid florescence had a continuing development in the sixteenth century, producing cultural change in distant countries.

The Timurid florescence was not based, as the earlier renaissance of the Buyid period had been, directly on a classical revival but on a reworking of twelfth-century humanism. Timurid literature turned away from the classical models of the Buyid era to the later romances, lowering its standards in some eyes (both contemporary and modern) but broadening its appeal by employing a more colloquial style in Persian and by introducing the more widely-spoken Turkish as a literary and official language. The sheer number of poets and writers increased, thanks to the patronage of princes and wealthy urban landholders. Persian prose writers employed the simplified style to discuss history, Qur'anic exegesis, mysticism, and science. Although this period has not previously been famed for its scientific accomplishments, the study of previously ignored scientific manuscripts is causing a reappraisal of that conclusion. Samarqand had a working observatory where one of the Timurid princes added to the stock of astronomical observations, and Timurid scholars made important advances in mathematics. Moreover, it is now known that European scholars had access to Arabic scientific manuscripts of the twelfth to fourteenth centuries that anticipated the discoveries of scientists such as Copernicus and Harvey.[11]

The greatest cultural accomplishments of the Timurid age, however, were in the visual arts. Artistic production was intimately linked with Timurid political life; the dynasty supported a large corps of artists who created for it a striking visual style that was imitated by its dependents and successors. Architecturally, the main theme was continuity with the classical Persian style but on a new scale of size and gorgeousness. Larger buildings inspired an improved system of vaulting that allowed for clerestory lighting and a new sense of proportion and space. The building material was brick, and its extensive decoration generated advances in the use of ceramic and faience. Fabrics used for tents, carpets, and clothing were finely woven and highly decorated in a variety of techniques. But the most significant artistic development of the Timurid period was in painting, the creation of the Persian miniature.

Persian miniature painting developed in several cities of Iran and Central Asia, largely under the patronage of the minor princes and lesser dynasties that surrounded Timur's center of power. Born of the marriage of traditional Islamic manuscript illustration with Chinese painting styles imported during Mongol times, it emerged from the Mongols' manuscript workshops in the form of illustrations to Firdausi's *Shahnama*, which had become a cultural icon for the Mongol and Jalayirid rulers. The more typical style of miniature painting, however, developed in the context of the revival of the twelfth-century love stories and the new outpouring of romantic poetry under the Timurids.[12] Unlike Italian Renaissance art, which used the human body as a metaphor and vehicle for everything it wanted to say about the universe, miniature painting focused on the depiction of human emotion as its primary metaphor and vehicle. The colors and gestures, the relationships and situations portrayed, the architecture and natural life in the background all constituted pointers to emotional truths about the human condition. While Timurid artists were aware of perspective and capable of acute observation, they rejected perspectival realism in favor of a more abstract style that distanced the viewer from physical reality to focus on its emotional and spiritual aspects.[13]

To dismiss the Timurid florescence as not a renaissance may then be premature. True, it did not manifest a fascination with the past, although it grew out of such a fascination; nor can we connect it, as the European Renaissance was once connected, to a subsequent industrial revolution. But neither is it the case that what the Timurids wrought died with them; instead, it became the basis for new developments in the Ottoman, Safavid, and Mughal Empires. Further research into the intellectual achievements of the Timurid florescence and their consequences in the post-Timurid period is necessary before the real contributions of this movement can be accurately assessed. The Timurids, though far from Europe, were not isolated, and their cultural developments had consequences far distant from their place of origin. As a result of the Timurid breakup, a circulation of artists, manuscripts, and ideas took place among political centers both inside and outside the Islamic world. Timurid contacts with fifteenth-century Italy stimulated the creation of a literature of history and description introducing Europeans to the ideas and governing systems of the eastern lands. Commercial exchanges took place as well, as a result of alliances between Timurids and Italians, which had as one purpose to contain the expansion of the Ottomans.[14]

Ottomans and Renaissances

The West has an automatic tendency to see the Ottomans, the Italians' chief competitors for the eastern trade, as aliens on European soil. Like several of the European peoples, they had originated farther east in Asia, but by the fifteenth century they were nearly as much European as Asian and participated in the Renaissance world at least as fully as some other parts of Europe.[15] The Ottomans made their first conquests of European territory as mercenaries and allies of the Byzantines, and by the end of the fourteenth century it was clear that their center of gravity would be in Europe rather than in Asia: their capital and the largest and wealthiest portion of their empire were in Europe and over half their population was Christian (including the mothers of most of the sultans). Throughout the early modern period they were part of the pattern of European diplomatic and commercial alliances. Like other expanding states in the region, they made peace and war on terms favorable to their ambitions and secured the help of distant powers, such as the Venetians and French, against powers close at hand, the Serbs and Habsburgs. Their eradication of Crusader armies at Nicopolis (1396) and Varna (1444) did not "seal the Mediterranean" to trade and diplomacy, as was often alleged, although it certainly ended western European dreams of eastward expansion at Byzantine expense and turned Europe westward. The conquest of Constantinople in 1453 climaxed Ottoman replacement of the Byzantine Empire, and although a number of Greeks fled the city at its conquest, many others stayed on to become part of its cosmopolitan urban life and culture.

Mehmed the Conqueror (r. 1451–81) saw himself as a world-conqueror in the mold of Alexander the Great.[16] He was master of "the two lands" (Europe and Asia) and "the two seas" (the Mediterranean, or White, and the Black), a military champion, cultural connoisseur, and universal monarch. Europeans called Mehmed's Hungarian cannon founder a renegade, as if he had deserted his true heritage, but to Mehmed both East and West belonged equally to his domain. He created a genealogy tracing his birth to both the Byzantine and Seljuk royal houses. At the conquest of Constantinople, in defiance of the custom granting the conquerors three days of pillage, he stopped the looting after a single day to preserve the buildings and walls of the city. He added Byzantine leaders to his government and repeopled the city with groups drawn from all over the former Byzantine territory, making his new capital a microcosm of the empire.[17] His conquests sought to retrieve all the lands that had once been ruled from Constantinople; he even went so far as to invade Italy shortly before his death. At the same time, he considered himself the protector of the Christians and Jews of the empire as well as of the Muslims, giving both groups institutional recognition and permitting them to maintain their own laws and customs as well as to use the government-sponsored Muslim courts.

Although he spent most of his life on campaign, Mehmed devoted money and time to creating an imperial Ottoman culture. Ottoman architecture before his time has been described as "provincial Timurid," and early Ottoman literature consisted largely of translations into Turkish, imitations of great works of the past, and religious compositions. Mehmed, after conquering Constantinople, built himself a palace in the Byzantine style and another in the imperial Timurid style which translated into stone and plaster the arrangement of the royal tents on campaign.[18] Besides employing Byzantine and Anatolian writers and artists, he sought to lure the distant stars of east and west into his service. He built a great mosque in Istanbul surrounded by Islamic colleges offering high salaries to attract talented teachers from home and abroad, and he regularly assembled learned men at his court to debate important intellectual issues. To Persian poets in the Timurid and other eastern empires he sent lavish gifts but failed to induce any of them to move to his court.

His invitations to Italian Renaissance artists were more warmly received; Constanzo de Ferrara, Gentile Bellini, and a number of lesser lights spent time in the Ottoman domains, and it is possible that Leonardo da Vinci went there as well.[19] The Italian painters bequeathed to the Ottomans an interest in portraiture unique in the Muslim world at that time. Their erotic palace wall paintings (frescoes with nudes?) were destroyed by Mehmed's successor, and it used to be lamented that Ottoman painting was unaffected by the achievements of the Italian Renaissance, remaining a pale imitation of the more glorious Persian miniature style. Art historians, however, now see Ottoman art as combining Persian and Byzantine influences to originate a style that, while avoiding the creation of lifelike images that might arouse religious opposition, still moved toward realism and this-worldly concerns rather than the "otherworldly" directions taken by post-Timurid Persian art.[20]

At the same time fifteenth-century Ottoman astronomers were trained at the Timurid observatory, while religious scholars received their advanced education in Egypt. During the sixteenth century the direction of scholarly flow was reversed, and Timurid cultural achievements were disseminated through the Middle East to become the foundation for literary and artistic trends in the newly powerful states which would dominate the early modern landscape – the Ottoman, Safavid, and Mughal Empires. Wars and dynastic disruptions after 1500 also dispersed the Timurid poets and artists, some of whom ended up in the Ottoman domains. Their arrival coincided with the greatest period of Ottoman imperial expansion, and their talents were immediately employed in the embellishment of the regime, raising the level of Ottoman artistic expression both quantitatively and qualitatively and contributing to the aura of magnificence surrounding the Ottomans' greatest ruler, Süleyman (r. 1520–66). Also contributing to the formation of a new artistic vision were imports of Chinese porcelains and silks, European glass and metalwork, Indian gems, and Hungarian sculptures. Süleyman's reign saw the development of a classical Ottoman style, one that permeated urban society and (like the Tudor style in England) became characteristic of its creators to this day.

By around 1550, in architecture, ceramics, miniature painting, textiles, poetry, historical writing, and numerous other fields, Ottoman artists and their royal patrons defined a new aesthetic, neither Persian nor European though indebted to both and apparently satisfying Palladian requirements.[21] There is no room here to detail the many achievements of this cultural explosion, so we will focus on the most spectacular and visible one, the architecture of Sinan, the peasant boy and military engineer who in the second half of his life achieved the stature of a Shakespeare or a Michelangelo through the mosques he built for his imperial patrons. Merging Byzantine and Timurid precedents into a powerful synthesis, he created a new style of religious architecture that simultaneously expressed for Islam, as the Gothic cathedral did for Christianity, both temporal context and the highest spiritual aspirations. The centerpiece of his career, the Süleymaniye mosque in Istanbul, reflected Süleyman's status as the pre-eminent ruler of the Muslim world and his role as representative of Sunni Islam against the messianic claims of both Shi'ite Iran and Christian Europe. Its domes and fountain, the light of its windows and its columns of precious stone symbolically portrayed the empire's connection with heaven and thus the divine sanction of Süleyman's reign.[22]

The apocalyptic atmosphere of the sixteenth century (the tenth in Islam) affected the Middle East as well as Europe. To the east the messianic figure of Ismail Safavi initiated the Safavid regime (1501–1722) with the religious conversion of Iran to Shi'ism. To the West, Muslim reaction to the Spanish Reconquista took the form of prophecies of the end of history. At the center, Ottoman defeat of the Safavis and conquest of the Arab world gave the sultan a new status as World-Conqueror and Shadow of God on Earth, attributes with which Süleyman confidently confronted the world-conquering claims of the Habsburg ruler Charles V.[23] Süleyman's acquisition of magnificent ceremonial regalia made by Venetian goldsmiths and his advance toward the Habsburg capital of Vienna in 1532, during which the regalia were ostentatiously displayed to the view of the Austrian envoys, were his answer to Charles V's claim to the title of Caesar and the processions he had organized around his coronation as Holy Roman Emperor. Charles, however, refused the challenge, declining to engage the Ottomans in battle, and the following year he sued for peace.[24] The cultural competition between the two monarchs was an aspect of the geopolitical confrontation of the two empires, the great powers of the sixteenth century.

The "Age of Expansion"

The program for this volume puts a heavy stress on the consequences of the six-teenth-century explorations for European cultural and social life. The sixteenth century was an age of expansion in the Middle East as well as in Europe. The effects of this expansion on Middle Eastern cultures and identities are still unexplored, but it was clearly felt to be a continuation of the Mongol attempt at world conquest. While Mehmed the Conqueror had expanded the Ottoman Empire into Europe and Asia by land, his successor Bayezid II (r. 1481–1512) inaugurated a naval buildup and advanced westward by sea. Süleyman's stunning Ottoman naval victory at Prevesa in 1538 gave the Ottomans firm control of the eastern Mediterranean and moved the naval contest to the western end of that sea until the battle of Lepanto reopened competition in the eastern Mediterranean; in the same year the Ottomans' eastern fleet took Aden and menaced the Portuguese in India. Their southward expansion made the Red Sea and Persian Gulf their own, although neither they nor the Portuguese could gain a monopoly in the Indian Ocean. Likewise, their northward expansion put the Black Sea fully inside their territory, and they further proposed to dig a canal between the Don and Volga rivers that would have put Ottoman ships in the Caspian. Ottoman motivations for seafaring included control of commercial centers and trade revenues as well as acquisition of territory and enhancement of their imperial status.

On land as well, the Ottomans expanded in this "age of expansion." European historiography understandably emphasizes the frontier in Europe, which the troops of Süleyman advanced into Hungary and Romania, but during the sixteenth century the empire pushed outward in all directions, most of which were more profitable for the Ottomans than European conquest. Expansion to the south and conquest of the rich Mamluk Empire were the Ottoman response to the Mamluks' inability to control the Portuguese, who were making incursions into the Red Sea and attempting to monopolize the spice trade. Expansion westward in North Africa resulted from Ottoman aid to Muslims expelled from Spain and repulsion of Spanish advances along the coast. Expansion northward into Poland and the Caucasus countered Muscovite southward expansion and maintained Turkish control of the Black Sea trade routes. Most importantly, eastward expansion expressed the Ottoman mission to contain and if possible eliminate the "heretical" Safavis of Iran, and also to control the silk routes and the silk-producing region south of the Caspian Sea.

In this period Europe was a relative economic backwater, and only the import of precious metals from the New World enabled Europeans to participate in the Asian trade as equals.[25] The expanding economy of fifteenth-century Europe was jump-started by trade with a reconsolidated Middle East whose rulers' legitimacy rested in part on their protection of commercial and pilgrimage routes. The spice trade through Egypt was, of course, the most lucrative aspect of this trade; second in importance was the silk trade through the Ottoman Empire. As the Ottomans replaced the Byzantines in the Balkans and Asia Minor and the Mamluks in Syria and Egypt, they inherited these empires' trade connections with the Italian city-states. When the French and English entered the Mediterranean trade in the sixteenth century, they too became trading partners of the Ottomans. The Middle East was the first stage of Europe's global commercial expansion and its largest trading partner in the Renaissance era. It is difficult to pinpoint Europe's status in Middle Eastern trade, as we do not yet have overall figures for the Middle East's commerce, but European trade undoubtedly formed a much smaller percentage of the Middle East's total commerce than eastern trade did of Europe's. The Middle East had lucrative trades with China, Iran, India, Central Asia, Indonesia, and sub-Saharan Africa as well as with Europe, and its internal trade was immense and growing. It is not surprising that the Ottomans sometimes failed to make expected conquests on the European front or explore the Atlantic, as they found their eastern borders more important both politically and economically. Apart from the profits of the silk and spice trades, their responsibility for the defense of Islamic holy sites in Arabia and the Fertile Crescent gave a new importance to the eastern front.

Nor were the Ottomans the only expanding power in the Middle East at this time. The Safavis, after their defeat by the Ottomans at Chaldiran in 1514, had to give up their millenarian claims and their dream of conquering Anatolia. They did not, however, abandon conquest but turned toward the east and north, expanding into central Asia against the Uzbeks and becoming a conventional great power controlling a commercial empire that included both their own fabulous silk trade and the transit trade from Central Asia and China. In India the Mughals, after consolidating their hold on Delhi and the north, began a campaign to the south that brought most of the peninsula under their control and eventually brought them into confrontation with European powers that had established trading centers on the southern coasts. These expansions are less visible than those of Europe because they did not involve crossing the sea to reach the goal. India, of course, was already in the east, and even the Ottoman Empire had a "back door" into the Indian Ocean.

Instead of the age of "European expansion," this era should be rethought in terms of competing expansions and comparative advantages. Europe's eastern encounters were not actions upon colorful but passive victims but interactions with powerful, intelligent, and cultured partners. Historians of Iran draw attention to the commercial negotiations between Persian rulers and European merchants, in which the Europeans were clearly the suppliants and Persian control of the trade is plainly evident. Ottoman historians point out that the sixteenth-century capitulations were the benevolent grants of privileges by the "all-powerful" sultan to foreigners whom he wished to enlist as allies and subordinates. Meanwhile, Indian historians have done the most to explicate the real balance of forces between European naval power and Mughal state power and administration, giving it the name "contained conflict."[26] Throughout the sixteenth and seventeenth centuries this balance persisted, but although neither side could gain a permanent advantage in this period, their political and economic competition led to changes in both. Most obvious on the Middle Eastern side is the transformation of military technology; on the European side it is perhaps the centralization of administration that strikes the eye most forcefully.

Beyond these specifics, both sides had to come to terms with the fact that their contact and interaction would be increasingly intense and intimate, and it appears that one way of dealing with this increased contact was to thicken the imagined wall between them. This distancing seems to have begun on the European side. Middle Eastern monarchs readily employed Europeans as administrators, soldiers, and scientists, but the opposite was not the case. Not only did European monarchs not employ Muslims, they found Muslim employment of and rule over "Christians" irritating if not illegitimate. European descriptions of the Middle East speak admiringly of the order and centralization of the "oriental" monarchies, but they dwell less frequently and less admiringly on the diversity of their populations. They emphasize military preparedness and downplay tolerance and high-cultural achievements. Even when Europeans came to study Middle Eastern culture in earnest, the teaching and help they received from Middle Eastern scholars were largely erased from historical memory.[27]

In this context, the omission of the Middle East from the story of the Renaissance comes as no surprise. It is related, as both cause and effect, to a view of European modernization as unique – opposed to the historical movement of the rest of the globe – and self-generated – indebted only to its own past. In the process of questioning that view, revising the history of the Renaissance to include the Middle East is a necessary step. The Renaissance has long been considered a crucial point in differentiating "the West" from "the rest." This chapter is organized around a different story line, one that sees West and East not as eternal opposites but as members of a single world. What this story loses in drama it may gain in coherence. The revival of classical learning was not strictly a European occurrence, and even the European rebirth depended directly on Middle Eastern revivals. Neither was the period's cultural florescence unique on a world scale; the Middle East (and doubtless China) experienced comparable events whose inner dynamics we are just beginning to appreciate. The explorations and encounters of the Europeans also had their counterparts in the east, and European scientific endeavor and technological progress were part of a world-wide pattern of accomplishment and diffusion. The old view of the Renaissance as a strictly European affair deleted from the story some important elements of the intellectual and cultural transformation that went under that name, and it distorted our perception of the economic and geopolitical interconnections of the period. If those elements are restored, we may be able to see the European Renaissance as in some sense a global event.

NOTES

1   See, for example, Schwartz, *Implicit Understandings*, which omits the Middle East entirely, despite the fact that sixteenth-century publications on the Middle East far outnumbered those on the New World or China (Kafé, "Le mythe turc," p. 175). Note that when East and West are capitalized they refer to cultural entities; uncapitalized, they refer to geographical directions.

2   See Jardine and Brotton, *Global Interests*.

3   Kraemer, *Humanism*; Mez, *Renaissance of Islam*; on humanism see Makdisi, *Rise of Humanism*.

4   For translations of these works see Firdausi, *Epic of the Kings* and Nizam al-Mulk, *Book of Governance*.

5   On the cosmology of this period and humanity's place in it see Nasr, *Islamic Cosmological Doctrines*.

6   Pancarğlu, "A World Unto Himself"; the western notion of a complete ban on images in the culture of the Muslim world vastly oversimplifies the complex relationship between the avoidance of idolatry and the artistic depiction of the world.

7   There is no complete English translation of Nizami's *Quintet* (*Khamsah*), but see Chelkowski, *Mirror*; Clark, *The Iskandar nama*; Darab Khan, *Treasury of Mysteries*; Meisami, *The Haft Paykar*; Nizami Ganjavi, *Chosroes et Chirin*; Turner, *Laila and Majnun*.

8   On Spain see Fletcher, *Moorish Spain*, pp. 132–4, 147–53. For the science of the period see Jayyusi, *Legacy of Muslim Spain*, vol. 2, pp. 937–1058.

9   Grabar, "Persian Miniatures," p. 203.

10 For the comparison of Timurid Iran with Renaissance Italy see Yarshater, "The Persian Presence," p. 203; also Malik, "Muslims' Contribution"; Sadiq, "Iran dans la Renaissance."

11 Indeed, "the various collections of Arabic manuscripts still preserved in European libraries contain enough evidence to cast doubt on the autonomous nature of Renaissance science": Saliba, "Seeking Science."

12 Grabar and Blair, *Epic Images*; Soucek, "*Makhzan al-Asrār*."

13 Hillenbrand, "Space in Timurid Painting," pp. 92–5; see also Lentz and Lowry, *Princely Vision*; Robinson, *Persian Painting*, pp. 29–30, 38.

14 Brummett, *Ottoman Seapower*, pp. 21–6.

15 On Ottoman–French relations see Isom-Verhaaren, "Ottoman–French Interaction 1480–1580"; on the European understanding of the Middle East as "other" see Darling, "Rethinking Europe."

16 Inalcık, *The Ottoman Empire*, pp. 23–30; for the coincidence of Machiavelli's and Bodin's views of the Ottoman Empire with Mehmed's see Springborg, *Western Republicanism*; for the similar views of the Byzantine George Sphranzes and the Orthodox patriarch of Jerusalem see Hattox, "Mehmed the Conqueror."

17 Inalcık, "The Policy of Mehmed II"; Kritovoulos, *Mehmed the Conqueror*.

18 Necipoğlu, *Architecture*.

19 Atil, "Ottoman Miniature Painting"; Babinger, *Mehmed the Conqueror*, pp. 494–508; Jardine and Brotton, *Global Interests*, pp. 10, 120.

20 Grube, "Notes on Ottoman Painting," pp. 51–61.

21 Andrews, "Literary Art"; Atıl, *Süleymanname*; Goodwin, "Art and Creative Thinking"; Necipoğlu, "From International Timurid to Ottoman;" Rogers, "The Arts under Süleymân."
22 Necipoğlu, "The Süleymaniye Complex"; Shatton, *Sinan*; for a comparison of Ottoman domed roofs with those of Renaissance Italy see Tunçer, "Rönesans ve Klasik."
23 Fleischer, "Lawgiver as Messiah."
24 Necipoğlu, "Süleyman the Magnificent and the Representation of Power."
25 Frank, *ReOrient*, pp. 277–83.
26 Subrahmanyam, *Political Economy*, p. 7; see also Frank, *ReOrient*, chs. 2 and 4.
27 Tavakoli-Targhi, "Genesis Amnesia"; Goffman, *Britons*.

REFERENCES

Andrews, Walter G., "Literary Art of the Golden Age: The Age of Süleymân," in *Süleymân the Second and His Time*, ed. Halil Inalcık and Cemal Kafadar (Istanbul: Isis Press, 1993), pp. 353–68.

Atıl, Esin, "Ottoman Miniature Painting under Sultan Mehmed II," *Ars Orientalis* 9 (1973) pp. 103–20.

—— *Süleymanname: The Illustrated History of Süleyman the Magnificent* (Washington, DC: National Gallery of Art; New York: Harry N. Abrams, 1986).

Babinger, Franz, *Mehmed the Conqueror and His Time*, trans. Ralph Manheim, ed. William C. Hickman (Princeton: Princeton University Press, 1978).

Brummett, Palmira, *Ottoman Seapower and Levantine Diplomacy in the Age of Discovery* (Albany: State University of New York Press, 1994).

Chelkowski, Peter J., *Mirror of the Invisible World: Tales from the Khamsah of Nizami* (New York: Metropolitan Museum of Art, 1975).

Clark, H. Wilberforce, *The Iskandar nama, e bara, or, Book of Alexander the Great* (London: W. H. Allen, 1881).

Darab Khan, Gholam Hossain, *The Treasury of Mysteries* (London: A. Probsthain, 1945).

Darling, Linda T., "Rethinking Europe and the Islamic World in the Age of Exploration," *Journal of Early Modern History* 2 (1998), pp. 221–46.

Firdausi, *The Epic of the Kings*, trans. Reuben Levy (London: Routledge and Kegan Paul, 1967).

Fleischer, Cornell H., "The Lawgiver as Messiah: The Making of the Imperial Image in the Reign of Süleymân," in *Soliman le Magnifique et son temps*, ed. Gilles Veinstein (Paris: École des Hautes Études en Sciences Sociales, 1992), pp. 159–77.

Fletcher, Richard, *Moorish Spain* (Berkeley: University of California Press, 1992).

Frank, Andre Gunder, *ReOrient: Global Economy in the Asian Age* (Berkeley: University of California Press, 1998).

Goffman, Daniel, *Britons in the Ottoman Empire, 1642–1660* (Seattle: University of Washington Press, 1998).

Goodwin, Godfrey, "Art and Creative Thinking in the Reign of Süleymân the Lawgiver," in *Süleymân the Second and His Time*, ed. Halil Inalcık and Cemal Kafadar (Istanbul: Isis Press, 1993), pp. 295–316.

Grabar, Oleg, "Persian Miniatures: Illustrations or Paintings," in *The Persian Presence in the Islamic World*, ed. Richard G. Hovannisian and Georges Sabagh (Cambridge: Cambridge University Press, 1998).

Grabar, Oleg and Blair, Sheila, *Epic Images and Contemporary History: The Illustrations of the Great Mongol Shahnama* (Chicago: University of Chicago Press, 1980).

Grube, Ernst J., "Notes on Ottoman Painting in the 15th Century," in *Essays in Islamic Art and Architecture in Honor of Katharina Otto-Dorn*, ed. Abbas Daneshvari (Malibu, CA: Undena Publications, 1981).

Hattox, Ralph S., "Mehmed the Conqueror, the Patriarch of Jerusalem, and Mamluk Authority," *Studia Islamica* 90 (2000), pp. 105–17.

Hillenbrand, Robert, "The Uses of Space in Timurid Painting," in *Timurid Art and Culture: Iran and Central Asia in the Fifteenth Century*, ed. Lisa Golombek and Maria Subtelny (Leiden: E. J. Brill, 1992).

Inalcık, Halil, "The Policy of Mehmed II toward the Greek Population of Istanbul and the Byzantine Buildings of the City," *Dumbarton Oaks Papers* 23/24 (1969/70), pp. 231–49.

—— *The Ottoman Empire: The Classical Age, 1300–1600*, trans. Norman Itzkowitz and Colin Imber (London: Weidenfeld and Nicolson, 1973; repr. London: Orion Books/Phoenix, 1994).

Isom-Verhaaren, Christine, "Ottoman–French Interaction 1480–1580: A Sixteenth Century Encounter," Ph.D. dissertation, University of Chicago, 1997.

Jackson, Peter and Lockhart, Laurence, eds., *Cambridge History of Iran*, 7 vols. (Cambridge: Cambridge University Press, 1968–91).

Jardine, Lisa and Brotton, Jerry, *Global Interests: Renaissance Art between East and West* (London: Reaktion Books, 2000).

Jayyusi, Salma Khadra, ed., *The Legacy of Muslim Spain*, 2 vols. (Leiden: E. J. Brill, 1992).

Kafé, Esther, "Le mythe turc et son déclin dans les relations de voyage des européens de la Renaissance," *Oriens* 21/2 (1968–9), pp. 175.

Kraemer, Joel L., *Humanism in the Renaisance of Islam: The Cultural Revival during the Buyid Age* (Leiden: E. J. Brill, 1986; 2nd edn. 1992).

Kritovoulos, *History of Mehmed the Conqueror*, trans. Charles T. Riggs (Princeton: Princeton University Press, 1954).

Lentz, Thomas W. and Lowry, Glenn D., *Timur and the Princely Vision: Persian Art and Culture in the Fifteenth Century* (Los Angeles: Los Angeles County Museum of Art, 1989).

Makdisi, George, *The Rise of Humanism in Classical Islam and the Christian West: With Special Reference to Scholasticism* (Edinburgh: Edinburgh University Press, 1990).

Malik, Iftikhar Haider, "Muslims' Contribution in the European Renaissance," *Pakistan Journal of History and Culture* 3 (1982), pp. 92–101.

Meisami, Julie Scott, *The Haft Paykar: A Medieval Persian Romance* (Oxford: Oxford University Press, 1995).

Mez, Adam, *The Renaissance of Islam*, trans. Salahuddin Khuda Bukhsh and D. S. Margoliouth (London: Luzac, 1937).

Nasr, Seyyid Hossein, *An Introduction to Islamic Cosmological Doctrines* (Albany: State University of New York Press, 1993).

Necipoğlu, Gülrü, "The Süleymaniye Complex in Istanbul: An Interpretation," *Muqarnas* 3 (1985), pp. 92–117.

—— ,"Süleyman the Magnificent and the Representation of Power in the Context of Ottoman-Hapsburg-Papal Rivalry," *Art Bulletin* 71 (1989), pp. 401–27.

—— ,"From International Timurid to Ottoman: A Change of Taste in Sixteenth-Century Ceramic Tiles," *Muqarnas* 7 (1990), pp. 136–70.

—— *Architecture, Ceremonial, and Power: The Topkapı Palace in the Fifteenth and Sixteenth Centuries* (Cambridge, MA: MIT Press, 1991).

Nizam al-Mulk, *The Book of Governance: or, Rules for Kings*, trans. Hubert Darke (London: Routledge and Kegan Paul, 1978).

Nizami Ganjavi, *Le Roman de Chosroes et Chirin* (Paris: G. P. Maisonneuve et Larose, 1970).

Pancaroğlu, Oya, " 'A World Unto Himself': The Rise of a New Human Image in the Late Seljuk Period (1150–1250)," Ph.D. dissertation, Harvard University, 2000.

Robinson, B. W., *Fifteenth-Century Persian Painting: Problems and Issues* (New York: New York University Press, 1991).

Rogers, Michael, "The Arts under Süleymân the Magnificent," in *Süleymân the Second and His Time*, ed. Halil Inalcık and Cemal Kafadar (Istanbul: Isis Press, 1993), pp. 257–94.

Sadiq, Isa, "Le rôle de l'Iran dans la Renaissance," *Acta Iranica*, ser. 1, vol. 3 (1974), pp. 381–95.

Saliba, George, "Seeking Science from the Lands of Islam," in *Visions of Islam in Renaissance Europe*. http://www.columbia.edu/~gas1/project/visions/visions.html, November 20, 2000.

Schwartz, Stuart B., ed., *Implicit Understandings: Observing, Reporting, and Reflecting on the Encounters between Europeans and Other Peoples in the Early Modern Era* (Cambridge: Cambridge University Press, 1994).

Shatton, Arthur, *Sinan* (New York: Scribner, 1972).

Soucek, Priscilla, "The New York Public Library *Makhzan al-Asrār* and its Importance," *Ars Orientalis* 18 (1988), pp. 1–37.

Springborg, Patricia, *Western Republicanism and the Oriental Prince* (Austin: University of Texas Press, 1992).

Subrahmanyam, Sanjay, *The Political Economy of Commerce: Southern India, 1500–1650* (Cambridge: Cambridge University Press, 1990).

Tavakoli-Targhi, Mohamad, "Orientalism's Genesis Amnesia," *Comparative Studies of South Asia, Africa and the Middle East* 16/1 (1996), pp. 1–14.

Tunçer, O. Cezmi, "Rönesans ve Klasik Osmanlı Dönemi Dînî Yapılarda Kubbenin Amaç ve Uygulanış Açısından Karşılaştırılması," *Vakıflar Dergisi* 18 (1984), pp. 127–40.

Turner, Colin, *Laila and Majnun* (London: Blake, 1997).

Yarshatar, Ehsan, "The Persian Presence in the Islamic World," in *The Persian Presence in the Islamic World*, ed. Richard G. Hovannisian and Georges Sabagh (Cambridge: Cambridge University Press, 1998), pp. 4–125.

FURTHER READING

Hodgson, Marshall G. S., *The Venture of Islam: Conscience and History in a World Civilization*, 3 vols. (Chicago: University of Chicago Press, 1974).

Kunt, Metin and Woodhead, Christine, eds., *Süleyman the Magnificent and His Age: The Ottoman Empire in the Early Modern World* (London: Longman, 1995).

Labib, Subhi, "The Era of Süleyman the Magnificent: A Crisis of Orientation," *Saeculum* 29 (1978), pp. 269–82.

Runciman, Steven, *The Fall of Constantinople, 1453* (Cambridge: Cambridge University Press, 1965).

CHAPTER FOUR

The Renaissance World from the West: Spanish America and the "Real" Renaissance

MATTHEW RESTALL

At the heart of the Renaissance and its scholarship is the relationship between intellectual (re)innovation and physical reality. The former has usually been viewed as the driving force that changed the latter, a force given the face of fourteenth- and fifteenth-century Italian cultural and intellectual innovators and recyclers of the classic past. Privileged with this geographical and chronological primacy, these Italians and *their* Renaissance have persisted as *the* Renaissance, rendering as marginal or derivative the contributions of other Europeans and the development of other intellectual movements (or movements with major intellectual implications, such as the conquest of the Americas).

Yet there were other southern Europeans poised in the fifteenth century to participate fully in the great intellectual and cultural stock exchange of the Renaissance – to float ideas and see how they fared on the open market. This chapter is concerned in particular with the Castilians and their neighbors, who in the fifteenth century turned their Iberian kingdoms into Spain and then in the sixteenth century turned Spain into the largest empire the world had ever seen. My core argument is that these Spaniards, the native Americans they sought to rule, and the dynamic of interaction experienced by both groups, best embodied the Renaissance adage of Marsilio Ficino: "Nothing is incredible; nothing is impossible."[1] Put another way, the change in physical reality and its perception by Europeans effected by Spaniards and their New World subjects was the true driving force of the Renaissance; it was in Spanish America, therefore, that the "real" Renaissance was created.

This argument is presented through discussion of two topics. The first is urban planning: specifically, the attempts by Spaniards in the Americas to realize in street and structure a city ideal that was to some extent Renaissance in origin but which was also, I argue, heavily influenced by native American urban landscapes. The second topic is literacy, a phenomenon traditionally viewed by the Renaissance industry as a cornerstone of civilization, with the early-modern increase in literacy and literary production taken as one of the cornerstones of the Renaissance itself. I argue below that literacy in Spanish America – manifested in many forms and in many genres of literature, both in native writings and in foundational scholarship by Spanish clergy – produced a quality and quantity of literature that reflected, better than parallel developments in Europe, the Renaissance spirit of expanding possibilities.

The Best-planned City

Since the city was founded in our own time, there was opportunity to plan the whole thing from the start. Thus was it laid out with ruler and compass, with all the streets being carefully measured, and as a result, Santo Domingo is better planned than any city I have seen.[2]

In January 1542, Francisco de Montejo the younger founded what would become the capital of the colonial province of Yucatan (today part of Mexico), a city he named after the Spanish city of Mérida. The new city's layout, however, was not to imitate the medieval jumble of old Mérida. Instead it was to conform to an ideal, for which purpose Montejo had brought with him "a large sheet of paper upon which the city was drawn" (*un pergamino grande, donde traía dibujada la cuidad*).[3] As the city did not yet exist, this was presumably the model city plan that accompanied the conqueror's license and other such legal documentation that conquistadors were required to carry, and which Montejo the elder had acquired in Spain almost two decades earlier. What that plan contained is clear from the basic layout of Mérida's center, which consists of a square plaza from whose corners eight streets fan out to form the city's rectilinear grid. The initial city core was three blocks by three blocks, so that a ring of eight blocks surrounded the open plaza "block," but probably within a few years (as Spaniards "pacified" the Mayas of the surrounding region and began to settle in the new city) another ring of blocks was laid out, creating a five-by-five block grid. Each block was originally divided into four urban lots (see figure, (d) (e)).[4]

Neither the Montejos nor the Mérida they founded were unique. Spaniards arrived in the New World armed with plans on paper that reflected some deep-rooted and fairly specific notions as to what new colonial cities should look like. Historians have tended to assume that such notions originated entirely in Europe. Certainly, the idea of rectilinear urban planning has deep historical roots in the Mediterranean, going back to such prominent advocates of plazas and grids as the fifth-century BC Greek architect Hippodamus and the first-century BC Roman architect Vitruvius. Nevertheless, although a copy of Vitruvius's *De architectura* was in a Mexico City library at least as early as 1550, there is no evidence that his work or that of Renaissance Italians such as Alberti (who published a commentary on Vitruvius in 1485) directly influenced the Spaniards who planned colonial cities in the first few decades of the sixteenth century.[5]

Another possible Renaissance influence was Thomas More, whose *Utopia* was published first in 1516 in Latin and was thus accessible to educated Spaniards. Scholars have noted in particular the impact of More upon two prominent Spanish ecclesiastics in early-colonial Mexico: Juan de Zumárraga, the colony's first bishop, whose copy of a 1518 edition of *Utopia* is still extant; and Vasco de Quiroga, the founder of two putatively utopian village hospitals in Mexico and Michoacán in the 1530s. However, More's utopian towns simply "all look exactly alike" and are "all built on the same plan," which is "practically square."[6] This is an urban vision that reflects the Renaissance ideal of an ordered layout in outline only, and while More's widely read book may have contributed to the Spanish embrace of order as the first principle of city planning it could not have been a direct and detailed influence – especially not upon the Mexico City and other colonial settlements that Zumárraga and Quiroga saw constructed.

Potentially more relevant is the theme found in classical theories (by Vitruvius and others) and in classical cities of the importance of building well-ordered settlements in colonies – including the Iberian peninsula. However, although early-modern Spaniards were well aware of the Roman underpinnings to many of their cities (and Montejo even gave Mérida in Yucatan its name because the buildings of the Maya site upon which he founded the city reminded him of the Roman ruins of Mérida in Spain), Roman city grids had for long been buried under medieval layouts that followed the irregular and crowded settlement patterns of the Islamic *medina*. The Iberian city that would have been familiar to most Spanish colonists, as it was in effect their imperial capital, was Seville; its cathedral was built on the site of an earlier mosque in the *middle* of a would-be central plaza, thereby breaking up that space into several lesser spaces that could never compete as social foci with the major winding streets of the city. This side yard-plaza design can also be seen in Córdoba, where the most plaza-like space is the famous Patio de los Naranjos, which runs *alongside* the mosque-turned-cathedral known as the Mezquita.

Although Roman influences on early-sixteenth-century Spanish conquistadors seem therefore to be muted, there is evidence of a direct line of influence running to a specific Spanish American city. In late-medieval France, and in its Pyrenean neighbor, Navarre, a number of new towns were built along the lines of Roman colonial cities to impose or consolidate royal rule in peripheral areas. The urban plan of these towns, which feature central plazas and gridded streets and are usually called *bastides*, was also used by Castilians in 1491 to build the fortress town of Santa Fe, the headquarters of the *reconquista* campaign against the Muslim kingdom of Granada that culminated in Granada's capture on New Year's Day, 1492.

It was in Santa Fe, in April that year, that Christopher Columbus signed the *capitulaciones*, his agreement with Queen Isabel over his first voyage across the Atlantic. Santa Fe also appears to have been the model for the first city built by Spaniards in the Americas: Santo Domingo, on the Caribbean island of Hispaniola. Although Columbus and his brother Bartolomé built short-lived settlements on Hispaniola in 1492 and 1496, it was the Spanish colonial governor fray Nicolás de Ovando who in the following decade established Santo Domingo in its permanent site as a gridded city centered on a plaza. As in Córdoba and to some extent Seville, and as in the *bastide* model used in Santa Fe, Granada, the plaza was laid out as a side yard to the cathedral.[7]

The evidence above suggests that during the first generation of Spanish settlement in the Americas (1492 to the late 1510s), the Spanish sense of the ideal urban plan in a colonial setting was, loosely speaking, a Renaissance one, formed by a mix of classical, southern European, and southern Iberian influences. However, neither the Renaissance notion of gridded and centered urban order, nor the example of its first

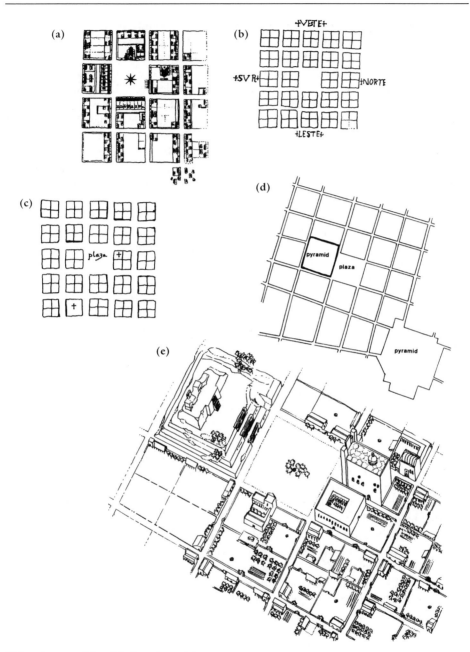

Urban layout of Spanish American cities:
(a) Perixá, Venezuela; (b) Mendoza, Mexico; (c) Caracas, Venezuela; (d) Mérida, Yucatan; and
(e) an aerial view of Mérida, Yucatan, ca. 1600

Sources: drawings by the author: (a) based on a drawing of 1751 reproduced in Vegas, *El Continente*, p. 69;
(b) based on the drawing in the foundation charter of 1563, reproduced in Kostof, *The City Assembled*,
p. 124; (c) based on a drawing of 1578 reproduced in Vegas, *El Continente*, p. 55; (d) based on Lindsay,
"Spanish Merida," Figure 3.1 and Restall, *The Maya World*, p. 32; and (e) based on Lindsay, "Spanish
Merida," Figure 3.2.

Spanish American application in Santo Domingo, are enough to explain the layout of
Spanish cities on the mainland from the 1520s on. Certainly, as one Spanish chronicler implied in the quotation that began this section, the American colonies were a
location better suited than Europe for turning the ideal city plan into bricks and
mortar. This was to some extent because colonial cities were being founded from
scratch and built from the ground up (such as Santo Domingo), or were constructed
upon native centers often ruined or damaged or demographically drastically reduced
(the native population of the Americas declined dramatically during the sixteenth
century).[8] But, more significantly, both the opportunity to build entirely new cities
and the experience of seeing and (re)building upon native cities did not simply give
expression to Renaissance urban ideals but profoundly influenced them. Not only
were native cities in Mesoamerica (and to a lesser extent in the Andes) the most
significant influence upon the development of Spanish urban planning ideas, but they
thereby heavily influenced Renaissance urban ideas in general. In other words, the
real Renaissance city was built in Spanish America because the experience of Spaniards
in the Americas helped create the image of that city.

The turning point to this development was 1517–21. The first two of these years
saw Spanish exploration along the Yucatec and Gulf coasts and thus the first siting of
Mesoamerican towns; the second two years (1519–21) saw the invasion of Mesoamerica in the form of the Cortés-led destruction of the Mexica (or Aztec) Empire.
The major native American cities encountered by Spaniards then and for decades to
follow were centered on rectilinear plazas formed by surrounding platforms, pyramids, and other monumental structures that were typically temples and the palaces of
the elite. Although this pattern occurred in the Andes, as the Spanish observed from
the 1530s onwards – in the Inca imperial capital of Cuzco, for example – it was
particularly well developed in Mesoamerica. The best known example of native urban
design is Tenochtitlán, the Mexica imperial capital upon which Mexico City was built.
Tenochtitlán was also one of the most fully developed examples of native urban
planning, partly for geographical reasons (its location on an island in a lake resulted
in canals being built in straight lines across the city, thus forming a grid for streets and
buildings) but also for cultural reasons (Venice's canals, after all, did not produce a
gridded city on that series of islands). In Mesoamerican culture, the city center was a
sacred space intended to reflect the order of the cosmos. Plazas were often oriented
towards the cardinal directions on a heliocentric east–west axis, while settlements
were located where water could be accessed and their pyramids conceived as sacred
echoes of nearby mountains (the term for town in the central Mexican language of
Nahuatl is *altepetl*, from *atl-tepetl*, meaning "water-mountain").

Spaniards were greatly impressed by this conception of space, especially the urban
orderliness that contrasted so strongly with European cities. In describing Tenochtitlán to the king of Spain, Cortés emphasized its order – its four equally wide "artifical
causeways," its "very wide and very straight main streets," its well-made bridges and
aqueducts, its many plazas, and so on – and its favorable comparison to Spanish cities,
being "as big as Seville or Córdoba" and centered on "a plaza twice as big as that of
Salamanca." In an oft-quoted passage the conquistador-chronicler Bernal Díaz
struggles to compare the Mexica capital with any European city, resorting instead
to medieval romantic fiction, so that the city and its neighbors, "great towns and
pyramids and buildings rising from the water, all made of stone, seemed like an

enchanted vision from the tale of Amadis. Indeed, some of our soldiers asked whether it was not all a dream." Like Cortés, Díaz gives a detailed description of Tenochtitlán that emphasizes its order, straight lines, symmetry, and the use of open spaces, especially its central plaza.[9]

Tenochtitlán was the first major site on the American mainland that Europeans explored, conquered, partially destroyed and then rebuilt. But other native settlements were seen by Spaniards in the years immediately before the discovery of Tenochtitlán, and in the decades after its fall Spaniards encountered hundreds of smaller sites in Mesoamerica that likewise featured a central plaza delineated by buildings that were religious, political, social, and economic in significance and function. Although virtually none of them were gridded beyond the central plaza as extensively as Tenochtitlán, larger sites often contained secondary plazas that reflected and reinforced the order at the core (the Maya city of Piedras Negras is a good example). Furthermore, the clusters of non-elite residential compounds that spread out from city centers were of less interest and concern to Spaniards; it was the native elite with whom Spaniards needed to deal, through the violence-inflected negotiations and accommodations of colonial imposition, and it was the urban centers with which Spaniards were most impressed and where they wished to place themselves – both physically and metaphorically.

A good example of this process is Tihó, one of a myriad of Maya sites with its characteristic central pyramid-bound plaza, and the Yucatec city upon which Spaniards founded the Mérida discussed above. Mérida's basic outline was the product of three influences. The first and second were deeply rooted but somewhat vague European ones and more recent and more specific Mexica ones. The third influence was Tihó, specifically the alignment of its plaza and the location of its two largest pyramidal structures (see figure, (e)). As a result, Mérida's plaza was overlaid on Tihó's, bound on the West side by its large principal pyramid, and oriented (as was typical of Maya settlements in Yucatan) roughly twelve degrees east of true north. The considerable size of the principal pyramid meant it was not torn down for almost a century, producing three features to the city center: the cathedral was built across the plaza from it, where a smaller Maya structure had been, rather than on the pyramid's base and site; while it remained standing, the pyramid blocked one of the central streets running out of the plaza; and its dimensions forced Spaniards to lay out oversized city blocks all down the West side. Furthermore, the location of two other pyramids in the southeast corner of Mérida's five-by-five grid, and the probable existence of raised Maya roads called *sacbeob* (literally "white roads") converging on those pyramids, likewise forced an irregularity onto the city plan as it evolved (see figure, (d) (e)).[10]

Mérida-Tiho is an example, then, of Spanish adaptation to Mesoamerican precedent. But it is also an example of how the Spanish experience of native urban patterns created a renaissance in Spanish urban concepts in the early sixteenth century. The date of Mérida's founding (1542) is significant not just because it came two decades after Mexico City began to be built over Tenochtitlán's outline, but also because it fell within the crucial decade of 1533–44, when some of the most important Spanish American cities were established: Santiago de Guatemala, Bogotá, Quito, Lima, Buenos Aires, and Santiago de Chile. During these same years, and in the decades that ensued, dozens more cities were founded by Spaniards in the Americas (see figure, (a) (b) (c)). The colonists tended, not surprisingly, to be blithely or deter-minedly unaware of native influences on any of their colony-building activities. The process whereby Spaniards and natives alike viewed their accommodations to each other through their own cultural lenses, dubbed "double mistaken identity" by one historian, applies very much to colonial city planning.[11] If the colonial endeavor was indeed, in the words of one sixteenth-century Spaniard, "to mix the world together and give to those strange lands the form of our own," the result involved far more mixing and far less Spanish form-giving than the colonists admitted.[12] (See the essay by Peter Burke below.) The new cities, strictly gridded and centered on large plazas bounded by the façades of important buildings, carry the post-Tenochtitlán influence of Mesoamerican city center planning far more clearly than they do the European influences of ancient Rome, fifteenth-century Italy, and the medieval *bastide*.[13]

Indeed, the flow of influence had begun to move east across the Atlantic by the late sixteenth century, when the Mesoamerica-inspired Spanish American city plan started to materialize in Spain itself. The two most obvious manifestations of this pattern are the layout of the new Spanish capital at Madrid, initiated by Philip II in 1561, and the 1573 Laws of the Indies, which included instructions on how colonial cities should be designed. The influence of the Mexica emphasis on pivot and symmetry in their capital's location and layout can even be seen in the choice of Madrid as capital, for "the town's only real claim to this particular honor lay in its geographical position as the mathematical center of Spain."[14] The emphasis in both the new Madrid and the 1573 laws on grids and large plazas (not as side yards but delineated by building façades, as was specifically mandated in 1573) has typically been taken by historians as evidence of the urban vision that Spaniards took *to* the Americas.[15] Hence the importance of chronology, for this was a vision taken *from* the Americas.[16]

Indeed the vision soon spread beyond Spain, and in the seventeenth and eighteenth centuries transformed European notions of how cities should be laid out. There is a contrast between Europe's pre-Tenochtitlán city plans, such as the new Italian plazas mentioned above, and later ones with their Spanish American-style plazas and grids. The fifteenth-century Italian plazas are each unique in shape, rather than uniformly square or rectangular; they lack the symmetry and relationship to a surrounding grid that can be seen in Madrid, in some of the new or redesigned seventeenth-century Scandinavian cities, in the new plazas built in Paris and London in the seventeenth century.

The so-called residential square is usually assumed, in accordance with the Italo-centrism of Renaissance studies, to have originated with such examples as the Sforza square begun in Vigevano in the 1490s (even though one such advocate admits it is an "imperfect specimen").[17] Yet the inclusion of a residential component in the central plaza is fundamental to its native American manifestation, particularly in Mesoamerica, and this component was strongly reinforced by the early Spanish colonists for the same reasons that churches were built on the ancient temple sites lining these plazas. Just as native nobles had once lived on such squares, so did conquistadors and their descendents; a good example is the Montejo palace built on Mérida's south side (see figure, (e)). This style of plaza – square-shaped, as much as possible creating a surrounding grid, and featuring elite housing – can be traced from early-sixteenth century Spanish America, to late sixteenth- and seventeenth-century Spain (good examples are *plazas mayores* in Valladolid and Madrid, the latter built in 1617–19). From Spain the form spread to other parts of Europe, beginning in 1587 with Ferdinando de' Medici's Piazza Grande in Livorno; later examples include Turin's Piazza Reale of 1621, London's Covent Garden (begun in 1631 by Inigo Jones), and the Parisian Place des Vosges (originally laid out in 1605–12 as the Place Royale), and the Place Vendôme (developed from 1685).

In the same century, having spread from Spanish America to Europe, the new planned plaza moved yet further east, appearing in Islamic cities such as Samarkand and Isfahan. Later, this plaza-grid model also spread back west to the Americas, in the form of English colonial cities such as Savannah and New Haven. The contrast between the earlier and later European styles can be seen in Boston, with its meandering seventeenth-century core and gridded nineteenth-century South End.[18]

The Oft-handled Quill

In many *pueblos* of Mexico the quill was handled as often as and perhaps better than in the villages of Castile or Europe in the same period.[19]

Just as Spaniards – and most of the scholars that have written of their imperial endeavors – saw the Americas as a blank slate upon which to lay out ideal cities, so did they see native Americans as a cultural slate that could be wiped clean and newly inscribed. Natives were seen as illiterate or effectively so, as they either lacked any writing tradition or had not developed an alphabet; the Franciscan Pedro de Gante, who first arrived in Mexico in 1524, told the king of Spain that the Aztecs were "people without writing, without letters, without written characters and without any kind of enlightenment."[20] Issues of literacy were viewed by Europeans largely in religious terms, as the Church in medieval Europe enjoyed a virtual monopoly on education and it was typically Spanish Franciscan friars and other churchmen who were concerned with matters of native literacy in the early-colonial Americas. Thus by bringing literacy to natives, Europeans were both civilizing barbarians and saving their souls.

However, the realities of both native and Spanish literacy were very different from this tidy image of the alphabet as a medium of salvation. There was, indeed, a flourishing of literacy and literary production in sixteenth-century Spanish America that rivals that of Europe during this time. One definition of a writing renaissance might be the proliferation of systems of literacy, the creation of new genres of text, the spread of new texts and the ideas therein, and a heightened sense of the importance of writing. Viewed through this definition, the "real" renaissance in writing was across the Atlantic.

My argument focuses on two topics, discussed briefly and in turn. The first is the nature of native literacy in the Americas in the period before the Spanish invasion and the decades during and immediately after it. The second topic is the nature of literary production by Spaniards in their American colonies, primarily regular clergymen (friars) in the sixteenth century.

Because Europeans were so concerned with classifying non-Europeans as one kind or another of barbarian or savage, and because they tended to lump native Americans together as "Indians," the vast majority of Europeans failed to appreciate both the vast diversity among native peoples and the complexity of native civilizations. Most natives lived within the two broad geographical and civilizational regions that we call Mesoamerica and the Andes, regions where two distinct systems of literacy had evolved many centuries before the arrival of Europeans.

Andeans had developed a unique form of literacy, the *quipu* system, that has for long been derided as non-literate and primitive because it used pieces of string rather than a set of written or carved symbols that conveyed language. In fact, the location of cords on strands or sticks, their colors, and the location of knots in the cords, combined to act as a complex mnemonic system for conveying information and knowledge; they encoded narratives not simply by listing raw ingredients, but by conveying relations of syntax between narrative elements. *Quipus* were thus effectively "written" when they were made and were later "read" as though they were a text.[21]

Perhaps less unique but more sophisticated were the four related writing systems of Mesoamerica: the Aztec, Mixtec, Zapotec, and Maya. The Aztec and Mixtec were more pictographic, the Zapotec and Maya systems more logosyllabic. Of these, the latter was the most complex, featuring some 800 symbols usually called hieroglyphs. Some 200–300 Maya hieroglyphs were in common use at any one time and place, most of them phonetic-syllabic in function; that is, each symbol or glyph represented a sound made up of a consonant and vowel. Maya hieroglyphic texts were aesthetically more attractive than European alphabetic texts while being no less elegant and equally capable of conveying anything the writer wished to communicate. Scribes, who were also painters (Maya culture recognized no distinction between the two), were members of the elite – in many cases royalty – but literacy was not confined to the elite; the Maya majority were in all likelihood semi-literate (and some scholars argue that most would have been more literate than that).[22]

The conventional wisdom on native literacy is that it was destroyed by the Spanish Conquest. The Mayas, typically the poster people for native literacy, are usually depicted as suffering the immolation of their hieroglyphic tradition in the bonfires set by fray Diego de Landa during his famous campaign against "idolatry" in the summer of 1562 in Yucatan; as evidence, scholars point to the fact that only four Maya books are extant today.[23]

In fact, native literacy and systems of writing survived far beyond the Conquest and deep into the colonial period, and in some cases into modern times. There are only four surviving Maya books because the climate in the Maya area is not conducive to the long-term survival of paper, because Spaniards continued to find and destroy hieroglyphic books for at least a century and a half after Landa's campaign of 1562, and because Mayas took to rewriting hieroglyphic works in alphabetic form (the best known examples are the "Books of Chilam Balam" in Yucatec Maya and the "Popol Vuh" in Quiché Maya). The significance here of the fact that Spanish priests continued to find works written in hieroglyphs (and in a combination of hieroglyphs and alphabetic letters) is that Mayas continued to produce such books; indeed, at least one of those four extant Maya hieroglyphic books was written *after* the Conquest.

In other regions of the large area dubbed New Spain by the invaders, Mesoamericans continued to produce manuscripts featuring pre-Columbian writing techniques. The Mesoamerican conception of writing and painting as aspects of a single medium of communication meant that alphabetic script was rapidly adopted as an accompaniment to pictorial text. From when the Spanish arrived in the 1520s, into the seventeenth century, Mixtec pictorial manuscripts were produced with glosses either in glyphs or in alphabetically written Mixtec, Nahuatl, or Chocho; Mixtec documents that are exclusively alphabetic survive only from the late-1560s.[24] Thus in sixteenth-century Oaxaca native peoples were producing texts that were pictorial, glyphic, and alphabetic, in local languages such as Mixtec and Zapotec and in the lingua franca of Nahuatl and Spanish – a veritable explosion of multifaceted literary expression.

Meanwhile, in the Andes, because Spaniards did not initially recognize the *quipu* as an effective medium of communication, let alone a writing system, sets of strings were neither banned nor destroyed until late in the sixteenth century. Even then, *quipus* tended to receive negative Spanish attention only in brief and irregular bursts following such perceived threats to the colonial order as the Taqui Onkoy movement of the 1560s. In the long run, the spread of alphabetic literacy meant that *quipus* were needed and used less, while their creators, *quipucamayocs*, became or were replaced by native community *escribanos* (notaries). But *quipus* continued to be created throughout the colonial period, while, arguably, their cultural significance was altered rather than diminished; *quipu* sets survive to this day as ornamental but powerful symbols of status rather than "texts" communicating specific information.

Not only did pre-Columbian forms of literacy survive the sixteenth century, but native societies took up alphabetic writing too, often with remarkable rapidity and effectiveness. Tens of thousands of documents written alphabetically in Mesoamerican languages during the Spanish colonial period are still extant in archives and collections in Mexico, North America, and Europe. This material, whose study has dramatically gathered pace in recent decades in part owing to the development of the New Philology school, is surely the merest tip of the iceberg of notarial production during these centuries. Most surviving manuscripts are in Nahuatl, but Mixtec and several Maya languages are well represented, and there are examples in Chocho, Cuicatec, Mixe, Otomí, Tarascan, Totonac, Zapotec, and other Mesoamerican tongues. While numerous genres are represented in these documents, most of them were corporate products – written by a native community notary and signed by the local elders – intended to defend community interests and thus reflecting the persistence of Mesoamerican literary traditions.

It is likely that literacy levels in Mesoamerica and the Andes were higher in early colonial times than before the Conquest. This was due in part to the dramatic demographic decline of the sixteenth century (leaving the literate as a higher percentage of the total population), in part to Spanish clerical efforts to alphabetize native nobles, in part to the devolution of native political authority from regional centers to the local level (where every village generated its own written records), and in part to the parallel persistence of native writing systems.[25]

Thus the long century following the Spanish invasion, from the early sixteenth to mid-seventeenth century, saw a florescence in native literacy in the Americas. Not only did pre-Columbian systems and techniques of writing survive, even while natives enthusiastically embraced alphabetic writing in native languages as well as in Spanish, but the Spanish emphasis on the importance of the written record reinforced the native sense of the utility and potency of literacy in Mesoamerica and (in a somewhat different sense) in the Andes. In turn, Spaniards increasingly came to see writing as a tool of empire as vital as the sword and compass. The latter two are famously depicted on the 1599 frontispiece to Vargas Machuca's *Milicia y descripción de las Indias* ("Soldiery and description of the Indies [i.e. the Americas]"), in which the author grips his cutlass with one hand and with the other holds a compass to a globe. By implication, the pen is the equally vital third tool, for it is the means whereby the Spanish captain has written his *descripción* and disseminated its motto, *A la espada y el compas, Mas y mas y mas y mas* ("To the sword and the compass, more and more and more and more").[26]

This acquisitive spirit presented Spaniards with more and more of a challenge in their efforts "to give to those strange lands the form of [their] own." Beyond the formidable tasks of imperial administration, profitable exploitation, and the logistics of supply and communication, this challenge was a dual one of description and dissemination.[27] At all stages of the Conquest, from early exploration to colonial consolidation, Spaniards struggled to describe what they saw and experienced, how they responded, why, and what others might do in their turn. In the process, they generated millions of manuscripts (anybody who suspects hyperbole here need only visit the General Archive of the Indies in Seville, created in colonial times to house these documents). By 1590 Joseph de Acosta could write that "the New World is no longer new, but old, as so much has been said and written about it."[28] Much of this documentation conformed to traditional genres of account, report, and petition, but others – through innovation and subsequent repetition – created new genres of literature and ultimately contributed to new disciplines of intellectual investigation. For having attempted to describe this new and different world, Spaniards sought to disseminate their interpretations and compilations (an old genre that saw a renaissance of its own in the Americas was the *recopilación*) to audiences ranging from the king to native New World parishioners.

Priests played a crucial role in this process. Indeed, the indigenous writing renaissance was paralleled by a related renaissance in literary production by colonial clergymen, mostly by the friars of the Franciscan order who in the wake of the Conquest had planted alphabetic literacy among Aztec, Maya, and other native nobles. At root, such friars were motivated by a dual ambition: to discover all they could about pre-Columbian native culture in order to destroy it and replace it with Christian "civilization"; but at the same time to detect and preserve what was laudable in native societies. Regardless of how we might judge such motives as far removed from those of modern scholars (and surely the friars' attitudes are closer to those of nineteenth- and early-twentieth-century scholars than we may care to believe), the clerics produced a remarkable and unprecedented body of ethnographic scholarship long before ethnography (or even anthropology) existed as a professional discipline.

Notable among these friars were the Dominicans Diego Durán and Bartolomé de las Casas (who has been called "perhaps the most monumental figure in the history of the Americas"),[29] and the Franciscans Toribio de Benavente (known as Motolinía), Gerónimo de Mendieta, Alonso de Molina, and Andrés de Olmos. This is just to name a handful from the sixteenth century whose work on central Mexico can be found in print today; dozens of other such ecclesiastics, in this and the succeeding centuries, toiled away at native languages and cultures in colonies ranging from New Mexico to Chile. I should like to mention in modest detail just two, both Franciscans who devoted their late-sixteenth century lives to a people and region within Mesoamerica: Bernardino de Sahagún; and Diego de Landa.

The best-known today of all the colonial scholar-friars, and no doubt deservedly so, is Sahagún. His twelve-volume study of central Mexican (or Nahua) culture and history, known as the Florentine Codex, exemplifies both forms of sixteenth-century literacy discussed here, as it was conceived and compiled by the Franciscan but executed over three decades by his noble Aztec informants and assistants – in both Spanish and Nahuatl, with copious illustrations in a hybrid Mesoamerican-European pictorial style. The result is an encyclopedic 2,500-page study of almost every imaginable aspect of Nahua culture, from religion and astronomy to rhetoric and gender relations. Its method and ambition make it a supremely Renaissance creation unequaled in early-modern European scholarship. Indeed, a recent study of Sahagún's work argues persuasively that the friar's medieval scholasticism was so compromised by Nahua culture – his intellectual tools and concerns forced to accommodate native ways of thinking and doing things – as to exemplify "the transition to modernity."[30] Admittedly, Sahagún follows Pliny's organizational categories much of the time, and his purpose is openly to garner "weapons at hand, in order to go out and meet" the devil. But he also adopts an extraordinarily modern approach to native culture, seeking to comprehend it on its own terms and through its own logic – above all through the logic of the Nahuatl language, lending his project an empirical and philological method and bent that was unprecedented in European intellectual history.[31]

In contrast, the ethnographic reputation of Landa rests on one slim volume, his *Relación de las cosas de Yucatán* or "Account of the Things of Yucatán," ostensibly written in Spain in 1566 after the Franciscan had spent a decade and a half studying the Mayas and working to convert them. Landa's fame rests partly on his brutal campaign against idolatry in the summer of 1562, in which four thousand Mayas were interrogated under torture, partly on the contrast between that campaign and the pastoral tone of his *Relación*, and partly on the importance of the book to Maya scholars since its rediscovery in the 1860s. Nevertheless, Landa's book, like the Florentine Codex, projects an ethnographic vision that gives it the feel of a work ahead of its time – an intellectual endeavor of foundational dimensions.

Close study of the *Relación* taken by scholars for well over a century to be a single, brief work, reveals it to be a late-colonial compilation of excerpts from several Landa manuscripts or from a far larger multi-volume work in the vein of the Florentine Codex. In my view, Landa's ambition to uncover and describe in dispassionate detail every aspect of Maya culture was even greater than has been assumed. This extended to an attempt to create a Rosetta stone for the reading of a writing system only very recently deciphered, that of the Maya hieroglyphs.[32] Landa's ambition, his unswerving commitment to the notions that thoroughness was a necessity and discovery a duty, allow us to reconcile his *Relación* (in whatever form it may originally have taken) with the violence he unleashed in the summer of 1562, and make him a larger-than-life Renaissance figure.[33]

Landa and Sahagún are "real" Renaissance figures, then, because their lifelong ambitions and their legacies on paper embody a set of Renaissance contradictions: the quest for knowledge for its own sake, and the quest to understand something in order to destroy it; the desire to create model, Christian communities, and the embrace of compromises that permitted native cultures to accommodate Spanish culture rather than be replaced by it; the interaction of medieval notions of scholasticism and religiosity, including millenarianism, with principles of investigation and pedagogy that were innovative and anticipated modernity; the recognition and celebration of the new, and the emphasis upon forcing the new into established frameworks of understanding. The Paduan philosopher Lazzaro Buonamico first articulated in 1539 a theme that would be repeated over and over by commentators from his day to the present, that the era's most notable achievements were "the invention of the printing press and the discovery of the new world; two things which I always thought could be compared, not only to Antiquity, but to immortality."[34] My argument has been that what was so momentous was the *combination* of these two phenomena (for printing press, read literature in all forms and systems), but with a twist. That twist assigns equal agency to native Americans and places emphasis on cultural interaction, for out of the New World encounter came a renaissance in both native and Spanish literary production – a writing (re)birth indeed.

A Singular Virtue

At one point, during the afternoon, I found myself chatting with three cardinals, one of whom, Cardinal Magalón, told me that my only fault was that I was a Spaniard.
    To this I replied, "With all due respect, your Holiness, that is my only virtue."[35]

The two topics discussed above, city planning and literacy, have been selected because they have a clear Renaissance relevance that does not require the kind of elaborate argument and copious citations that space would not permit here. They also combine both Spanish and native contributions in a way that is core to my assertion that only across the Atlantic could the "real" Renaissance be realized.

Other, trickier, topics are equally apposite, however, and I should like to conclude with a parting mention of a couple of them. The Spanish Inquisition, for example, has had its image denigrated in a Black-Legend tradition running from Las Casas to Monty Python as decidedly medieval and un-Renaissance (or even anti-Renaissance). This image may have much to do with the European witchcraze, the Iberian persecution of Jews, and the Catholic reformation in southern Europe. But it has little to do with the Spanish American manifestations of the Inquisition and the various ways in which the New World offered inquisitors an opportunity to explore all-too-Renaissance notions of social engineering. Inquisitors in the Americas were simply well-connected friars and secular priests. They seldom persecuted Jews or witches, and rarely employed violence after the initial Conquest decades; after 1570 jurisdiction over native peoples was removed from the Holy Office and placed with a new and separate body (the *Provisorato de Indios*, sometimes referred to as the "Indian Inquisition").

This left Inquisition officials to function more or less as social workers, resolving domestic disputes, investigating accusations of bigamy, adultery, homosexuality, blasphemy, and slander, attempting to police the clergy themselves, and in a myriad other ways trying to understand, categorize, and control human passions and unorthodox expression. The sum of all of this was a decidedly disorganized attempt to regulate social behavior, a sort of Spanish American version of Calvin's Geneva and

More's Utopia. The Inquisitors of the New World were thus far removed from the dungeons and devices of torture that adorned the Black Legend. Rather these were men working on the rough edge (it was not quite the cutting edge) of the applied social sciences, attempting in a very Renaissance fashion, that at times seems medieval and at times modern, to forge from seemingly incompatible ingredients a coherent, Christian, civic society. The Inquisition in Italy and other parts of Europe, likewise beginning in the late sixteenth century, also took on a less violent and broader social role.[36] The difference in Spanish America was the persistence of a multifaceted and dynamic cultural interaction, the same force that underpinned the development of city planning and literacy, but with an added component not discussed above, that of West African cultures.

This brings me to the final topic to be mentioned, which falls loosely into the category of race and gender. It really deserves book-length attention, but I shall try here to offer a tantalizing hint as to its relevance and potential by referring to a work of Spanish colonial literature that is increasingly well known and which suggests something of the complex nature of personal identity in Spanish America. That work is the autobiographical memoir of Catalina de Erauso, the Catalan woman who escaped from a convent before taking her final vows in order to pursue a conquistador's life dressed as a man in Spanish South America. On the one hand, such a quintessentially (even stereotypically) male existence was only available to a woman if disguised as a man; on the other hand, Erauso's male-female identity and other people's awareness of it is highly ambiguous in her account. In short, categories of gender – and my argument, if fully developed, would be that ethnoracial categories were comparable in their definition and treatment – were not nearly as clear and tangible as they might at first appear.[37] Nor were they as clearly defined as they appear to have been in Europe, which is why Erauso's adventures had to take place in the New World. Spanish American society, in other words, embraced and embodied paradoxical conceptions of the social and definitional boundaries between men and women and people of different ethnoracial backgrounds – these boundaries being sharply delineated and yet at the same time blurred and porous. In this sense, only in Spanish America was Erauso's life possible; only there, was nothing really impossible.

Indeed, in numerous ways the physical reality of the Spanish American colonies and the native cultures that persisted within them offered a New World of intellectual and conceptual possibilities. Manifestations of that reality ranged from the awesome urban landscape of Tenochtitlán to pages of hieroglyphs and bundles of *quipus* to the confusing multiplicity of ethnoracial types that began to develop before the dust had settled from the Spanish invasion. As complex and multifaceted as it was, the European Renaissance experience could not match its Spanish American counterpart. The latter, to be sure, was confusing and contradictory (which is partly why its Renaissance contribution has been ignored or understated); but – to borrow a twist from Catalina de Erauso – that may have been its greatest virtue.

NOTES

1   Quoted in Fuentes, *The Buried Mirror*, p. 84.

2   The Spanish chronicler Gonzalo Fernández de Oviedo y Valdés, writing in 1535 of Santo
    Domingo on the Caribbean island of Hispaniola (from his *Historia general y natural de las
    Indias*; see Fernández de Oviedo, *Natural History*, p. 11; also quoted in Low, *On the
    Plaza*, p. 98 and cited in Lindsay, "Spanish Merida," p. 72).

3   Cogolludo, *Historia de Yucatán*, vol. I, p. 271; also quoted in Rubio Mañé, *La Casa de
    Montejo*, p. 2, and in Lindsay, "Spanish Merida," p. 23.

4   Rubio Mañé, *La Casa de Montejo*, pp. 1–16; Restall, *The Maya World*, pp. 31–7; Lindsay,
    "Spanish Merida," pp. 39–61. For a brief account of the conquest of Yucatan, see Restall,
    Maya Conquistador, pp. 4–18, 26–8.

5   In addition to writing about urban grids, late-fifteenth-century Italians were also redesign-
    ing some of their cities on these principles; new rectangular plazas were built in Pienza in
    1462 and Vigevano in 1492, for example. Low, *On the Plaza*, pp. 86–9.

6   More, *Utopia*, pp. 70, 72.

7   Low, *On the Plaza*, pp. 89–90, 95–9; Kostof, *The City Shaped*, p. 109. The term *bastide* is
    from the medieval French verb *bastir*, "to build."

8   Franciscan millenarianism embodied the most extreme expression of the opportunities
    represented by new colonial cities; for example, Motolonía (whom I shall mention again
    below) saw Puebla, Mexico, as the new Jerusalem anticipated by St. John the Evangelist
    (Rabasa, *Inventing America*, p. 155).

9   Cortés, *Letters*, pp. 102–10; Díaz, *The Conquest*, p. 214, 216–41.

10 Lindsay, "Spanish Merida," pp. 58–71; Restall, *The Maya World*, pp. 31–7.

11 Lockhart, "Double Mistaken Identity."

12 Hernán Pérez de Oliva, quoted in Elliott, "A World United," p. 648.

13 Extant plans of twenty Spanish American cities, all built or expanded between 1561 and
    1598, show fourteen to be symmetrical, mostly square, and plaza-centered; Lindsay,
    "Spanish Merida," p. 52. Colonial Venezuelan city plans also illustrate well the Spanish
    American urban layout (see figure, (a) (c), for two examples); Vegas, *El Continente*.

14 In the words of Elliott, *Imperial Spain*, p. 254.

15 Low, *On the Plaza*, p. 85, cites fifteen works published between 1947 and 1982 contrib-
    uting to a "Eurocentric narrative of the evolution of this urban form" (i.e. Spanish
    American plaza-centered cities).

16 Spanish architectural historian Jesús Escobar has argued that not only Madrid's Plaza
    Mayor but other features of the city were strongly influenced by colonial cities and their
    native antecedents (Low, *On the Plaza*, p. 94). The 1573 Laws of the Indies, which
    reworked various laws from earlier in the century, has been described as "a genuine
    product of Renaissance thought. Its inspiration is ultimately...Vitruvius" (Kostof, *The
    City Shaped*, p. 114); I would argue that such a summary ignores the differences between
    Vitruvius and the 1573 laws and the ways in which native-inspired Spanish American cities
    explain many of those differences. The 1573 laws are ultimately inspired by the colonial
    experience and are a genuine Renaissance product in the sense that I am defining the
    "real" Renaissance in this essay.

17 Kostof, *The City Assembled*, p. 161.

18 Kostof, *The City Shaped*, pp. 46, 98–115; *The City Assembled*, pp. 161–3, 174. Northern
    Italian city planning in the fourteenth and fifteenth centuries still emphasized order and
    geometry, but each example represented a distinct expression of that order, with plazas
    evolving as L-shaped (e.g. the one along the Palazzo Vecchio in Florence), or rectangular
    with an important building in the middle (e.g. the Palazzo Pretorio in the plaza of San
    Giovanni Valdarno), or T-shaped (e.g. the two "Ideal City" oil panels probably painted in
    Urbino and Florence, ca. 1480–1500); Kemp, "The Mean and Measure," pp. 96–100,
    249–51. None of these Italian variations match the Spanish American model (see figure,
    (a)–(d)), or the non-Italian examples mentioned above. Even Alberti opposed strict grids

that made every city street straight; see the long quote in Kostof, *The City Shaped*, p. 70. Inigo Jones is a good example of an important early-modern European architect whose absorption of native American and Spanish American models has been ignored or understated by historians. The Place Vendôme varies the Spanish American model in that its streets enter the mid-point of the north and south façades, rather than the corners. An example of European urban grid reinforcement is the rebuilding and extension of Lisbon's lower town grid after the earthquake of 1755 (Kostof, *The City Assembled*, p. 248).

19 Gruzinski, *The Conquest*, p. 4.

20 Quoted by Hill Boone, *Stories in Red and Black*, p. 4. Hill Boone (pp. 4–5) cites more than a dozen sources, ranging from sixteenth-century Spaniards to prominent living scholars such as Jack Goody, who ignore or deny the Aztecs and other native Americans their literacy. Also see Coe, *Breaking the Maya Code*, pp. 18–26.

21 Urton, "From Knots to Narratives"; Cummins, "Representation," pp. 192–3; Salomon, "Testimonies," pp. 22–3.

22 Marcus, *Mesoamerican Writing Systems*; Coe, *Breaking the Maya Code*, pp. 262, 269–70; Miller, *Maya Art*, pp. 187–9, 197–206; Hill Boone, *Stories in Red and Black*.

23 Cummins, "Representation," p. 188, cites such mid-century authorities as George Kubler and Donald Robertson, but there is a more recent and subtle version of this perspective exemplified by the work of Enrique Florescano, Jorge Klor de Alva, and Walter Mignolo.

24 Terraciano, "Ñudzahui History," pp. 36–79.

25 Since 1976 the New Philologists have used native-language sources to reconstruct colonial Mesoamerican culture and society: Restall, "Heirs to the Hieroglyphs"; "A History of the New Philology."

26 Frontispiece reproduced in Elliott, "A World United," p. 647.

27 Two words used in a similar context by Elliott, *The Old Word and the New*, p. 18.

28 Quote in Rabasa, *Inventing America*, p. 210 (translation mine).

29 Rabasa, *Inventing America*, p. 164.

30 Browne, *Sahagún*.

31 Sahagún quote, translation mine, in Rabasa, *Inventing America*, p. 162.

32 Landa, *Yucatan*, p. 83; Coe, *Breaking the Code*, pp. 104–5.

33 Restall, *Maya Conquistador*, pp. 144–63. John Chuchiak and I are currently working on a new edition of the *Relación* from the manuscript in Madrid.

34 Quoted in Elliott, *The Old World and the New*, p. 10.

35 Erauso, *Lieutenant Nun*, p. 79.

36 Ruggiero, *Binding Passions*, p. 9.

37 For an elegant discussion of how gender and ethnoracial conceptions interacted in colonial Mexico, see Kellogg, "Depicting *Mestizaje*."

REFERENCES

Browne, Walden, *Sahagún and the Transition to Modernity* (Norman: University of Oklahoma Press, 2000).

Coe, Michael D., *Breaking the Maya Code*, rev. edn. (New York: Thames and Hudson, 1999).

Cogolludo, Fray Diego López de, *Historia de Yucatán* [1654] (Mexico City: Editorial Academia Literaria, 1957).

Cortés, Hernán, *Letters from Mexico*, trans. and ed. Anthony Pagden (New Haven: Yale University Press, 1986).

Cummins, Tom, "Representation in the Sixteenth Century and the Colonial Image of the Inca," in *Writing Without Words: Alternative Literacies in Mesoamerica and the Andes*, ed. Elizabeth Hill Boone and Walter D. Mignolo (Durham: Duke University Press, 1994).

Diaz, Bernal, *The Conquest of New Spain* (London: Penguin, 1963).

Elliott, J. H., *Imperial Spain, 1469–1716* (New York: Penguin, 1970).

——, *The Old World and the New, 1492–1650* (Cambridge: Cambridge University Press, 1970).

——, "A World United," in *Circa 1492: Art in the Age of Exploration*, ed. Jay A. Levenson (Washington and New Haven: National Gallery and Yale University Press, 1991).

Erauso, Catalina de, *Lieutenant Nun: Memoir of a Basque Transvestite in the New World*, trans. and ed. Michele and Gabriel Stepto (Boston: Beacon, 1996).

Fernández de Oviedo y Valdés, Gonzalo, *Natural History of the West Indies*, trans. and ed. Sterling Stoudemire (Chapel Hill: University of North Carolina Press, 1959).

Fuentes, Carlos, *The Buried Mirror: Reflections on Spain and the New World* (Boston: Houghton Mifflin, 1992).

Gruzinski, Serge, *The Conquest of Mexico: The Incorporation of Indian Societies into the Western World, 16th–18th Centuries* (Cambridge: Polity Press, 1993).

Hill Boone, Elizabeth, *Stories in Red and Black: Pictorial Histories of the Aztecs and Mixtecs* (Austin: University of Texas Press, 2000).

Kellogg, Susan, "Depicting *Mestizaje*: Gendered Images of Ethnorace in Colonial Mexican Texts," in *Journal of Women's History* 12/3 (autumn 2000).

Kemp, Martin, "The Mean and Measure of All Things," in *Circa 1492: Art in the Age of Exploration*, ed. Jay A. Levenson (Washington and New Haven: National Gallery and Yale University Press, 1991).

Kostof, Spiro, *The City Shaped: Urban Patterns and Meanings Through History* (Boston: Bulfinch, 1991).

——, *The City Assembled: The Elements of Urban Form Through History* (Boston: Bulfinch, 1992).

Landa, Fr. Diego de, *Yucatan Before and After the Conquest*, ed. William Gates (New York: Dover, 1978).

Lindsay, Mark C., "Spanish Merida: Overlaying the Maya City," Ph.D. dissertation, University of Florida, 1999.

Lockhart, James, "Double Mistaken Identity: Some Nahua Concepts in Postconquest Guise," in *Of Things of the Indies: Essays Old and New in Early Latin American History* (Stanford: Stanford University Press, 2000).

Low, Setha M., *On the Plaza: The Politics of Public Space and Culture* (Austin: University of Texas Press, 2000).

Marcus, Joyce, *Mesoamerican Writing Systems: Propaganda, Myth, and History in Four Ancient Civilizations* (Princeton: Princeton University Press, 1992).

Miller, Mary Ellen, *Maya Art and Architecture* (New York: Thames and Hudson, 1999).

More, Thomas, *Utopia* [1516] (New York: Penguin, 1961).

Rabasa, José, *Inventing America: Spanish Historiography and the Foundation of Eurocentrism* (Norman: University of Oklahoma Press, 1993).

Restall, Matthew, "Heirs to the Hieroglyphs: Indigenous Writing in Colonial Mesoamerica," *The Americas* 54/2 (October 1997).

——, *The Maya World: Yucatec Culture and Society, 1550–1850* (Stanford: Stanford University Press, 1997).

——, *Maya Conquistador* (Boston: Beacon, 1998).

——, "A History of the New Philology and the New Philology in History," *Desacatos* 2 (2001).

Rubio Mañé, Ignacio, *La Casa de Montejo* (Mexico City: Imprenta Universitaria, 1941).

Ruggiero, Guido, *Binding Passions: Tales of Magic, Marriage, and Power at the End of the Renaissance* (New York: Oxford University Press, 1993).

Salomon, Frank, "Testimonies: The Making and Reading of Native South American Historical Sources," in *Cambridge History of the Native Peoples of the Americas*, vol. III: *South America*, ed. Frank Salomon and Stuart Schwartz (New York: Cambridge University Press, 1999).

Terraciano, Kevin, "Ñudzahui History: Mixtec Writing and Culture in Colonial Oaxaca," Ph.D. dissertation, University of California, Los Angeles, 1994.

Urton, Gary, "From Knots to Narratives: Reconstructing the Art of Historical Record Keeping in the Andes," *Ethnohistory* 45/3 (summer 1998).

Vegas, Federico, et al., eds., *El Continente de Papel: Venezuela en el Archivo de Indias* (Caracas: Neumann, 1984).

CHAPTER FIVE

The Historical Geography of the Renaissance

PETER BURKE

This essay takes its point of departure from a simple assumption. To understand human productions, it is necessary to employ three kinds of analysis, which might be described as three dimensions: the chronological, the social, and the geographical. In the case of the Renaissance, the chronological approach is traditional. The social approach established itself in the 1930s and 1940s with the work of scholars such as Alfred von Martin (whose historical sociology of the Renaissance appeared in German in 1932), Martin Wackernagel, and Frederick Antal, the last two scholars both focusing attention on the artistic milieu of fifteenth-century Florence. The geographical approach, on the other hand, remains relatively neglected, a striking example of what has been described as the "devaluation of place" in social studies.[1] In the following pages, I shall try to compensate for this neglect by approaching the Renaissance from the point of view of a cultural geographer (more exactly, from what a cultural historian imagines to be the view of a cultural geographer), setting out a program – which it would take a large book to put into practice – and illustrating what may be learned from this approach.

Cultural Geography

The influence of place on culture is obvious enough, leading the German geographer Rudolf Haussherr to translate the art historian Heinrich Wölfflin's famous formula, "Not everything is possible at all times" into spatial terms: "Not everything is possible in all places" (*Nicht alles ist an allen Orten möglich*).[2] A more positive formulation of the strong links between culture and place, *Ortgebundenheit* as the Germans say, employs concepts such as the "culture area" or the "artistic region" (*Kulturkreis, Kulturraum, Kunstlandschaft*). Tuscany is an obvious example of such a region, but "region" in this sense may coincide with a nation (England, for example), or with a multilingual area (such as the Baltic area, the example discussed by a Polish art historian, the late Jan Bialostocki).[3] The essential point is, as the literary historian Franco Moretti puts it, "that geography is not an inert container, is not a box where cultural history 'happens,' but an active force."[4]

These concepts are easy, all too easy, to take for granted. If we use them, we need to be aware of the cultural baggage which they bring with them and the intellectual problems which they raise. They have often been associated with the idea of a *Volksgeist* or "national character" – explicitly so in the case of Nikolaus Pevsner's lectures on the "Englishness" of English art – and they have been linked on occasion to theories of racial determinism.[5] Viewing culture in terms of regions seems to deny agency (whether on the part of the artist or the patron). It also appears to assume cultural homogeneity at local level, ignoring conflicts between styles and the possibility for individuals to choose between them.

However, these criticisms apply only to the strong form of the theory, a geographical determinism. The idea of *Ortgebundenheit* need not be taken in this way, just as it need not be associated with the idea of national character. It is more illuminating to think in terms of local traditions, which are created by individuals and groups and constantly reshaped. If the historical and social dimensions are also kept in mind, concepts such as "culture area" can be extremely illuminating. We need to map time as well as space, to chart the flow of artifacts and ideas and to attempt to decide which groups in which regions were important in which respects at which moments. In what follows I shall privilege the geographical dimension without forgetting the other two.

Some geographical analyses are exemplary in this respect. Doreen Massey has argued, for example, that what we call the "local" should be viewed as the product of contacts with a wider world.[6] Alan Pred and other historical geographers have analysed place as process.[7] Renaissance Venice offers a spectacular illustration of these points, its unusual physical appearance owing something to its tradition of economic and political relations with Byzantium (most visible in the church of San Marco), and also with Islam. For example, the idea of the *fondaco*, a place in which to isolate foreigners, as well as its name (derived from *funduq*), come from the Muslim world.[8]

Two more distinctions are worth drawing at the start. In the first place, is one between the macrogeography of Italy or the Baltic and the microgeography of small but significant spaces such as courts, universities, workshops, and monasteries (the role of monasteries in the humanist movement, from Florence to Groningen, should not be forgotten).

In the second place, the geographical approach is not to be identified with diffusion, the spread of objects and ideas from the place in which they were originally produced. There is also a geography of production, since it is clear enough that Italians (and within Italy, Florentines) were responsible for far more than their fair share of the artifacts and ideas of the Renaissance, and we need to understand why this was the case.

These two processes are less easy to distinguish than one might think. On one side, "reception" is not purely passive. It is, at least on occasion, active and creative, a complex process of adaptation rather than a simple one of adoption. Whatever is new and comes from outside is first perceived in terms of local traditions and then employed by local people in local contexts. In the course of this process of "revision," the original model is transformed. Think, for example, what the Japanese, supremely creative imitators, have done with what they appropriated from China and from the West, "appropriated" not only in the sense of taking but also of making it their own. From the viewpoint of the donor culture the process is one of misinterpretation; from that of the receiver (insofar as the process is conscious) it is reinterpretation or adaptation.

On the other side, it may be illuminating to analyze innovation as creative adaptation, as "synergy" (in other words, new permutations or combinations of old information or ideas). After all, many inventions have been inspired by other inventions. A classic example is the derivation of the printing press from the wine press, and the classic discussion, that by Arthur Koestler. Discoveries too often depend on the drawing of analogies, as in the case of the "wave" theories of light, sound, economic booms, and so on. In other words, they are the result of cross-fertilization, of the perceptions of links between different phenomena which Koestler calls "bisociation."[9] If certain kinds of environment facilitate these processes, then we may speak of a "geography of innovation."

The Geography of Innovation

The British geographer Sir Peter Hall published a comparative study, *Cities in Civilization*, which is concerned with the question, "What makes a particular city at a particular time, suddenly become immensely creative, exceptionally innovative?"[10] Comparing and contrasting some twenty cities from ancient Athens to contemporary Los Angeles, he notes the importance of "chains" of innovation in particular places, which allow certain cities to act as "magnets" for talent and so become still more innovative. Nothing succeeds like success. Elsewhere, Hall makes the observation that "the geography of innovation shows considerable inertia: once it has taken root, innovation proves a resilient plant that may locally migrate, but proves difficult to destroy."[11] A fluid situation in which opportunities are more or less open crystallizes or congeals into a fixed pattern. The problem remains: how does the chain of innovation begin?

Surveying past theories, and rejecting Marxism because it "provides no real clue," Hall drew attention to the nineteenth-century French writer Hippolyte Taine's concept of the "creative milieu," but the inspiration for his book is a cluster of studies by Swedish geographers such as Torsten Hägerstrand and Gunnar Törnqvist which refine Taine's idea and take it further.[12] (Why the Swedes should be so important in this particular field remains an intriguing problem in the geography of geography.) Törnqvist, for example, notes the importance of information, especially the "non-routine" information which "requires direct personal contacts." Hence a creative milieu is one which facilitates such contacts by providing meeting-places. Törnqvist also emphasizes the importance of "structural instability," arguing that a milieu becomes particularly creative when cultural or social change has made old solutions irrelevant, thus forcing people to devise new ones.[13]

If these generalizations seem plausible, then we are in a position to argue that the Renaissance was a particularly creative period (in other words, one in which innovations took place more rapidly than they had done in the Middle Ages), precisely because the centers of power, wealth, and culture were located in cities, rather than in castles or manors in the countryside. This "turn to the city," as we may call it, made the examples of the urban civilizations of ancient Greece and Rome more relevant to more people than they had been in the past. In any case, cities encouraged creativity because the division of labor there was associated with a variety of skills and attitudes. The opportunity for people in different occupations to meet and exchange ideas led to cultural innovation.

Take the case of Renaissance Florence, for example. We know too little about the places in the city where individuals from different backgrounds most frequently met, but the testimony of the humanist Alberti to his regular conversations with the painter Masaccio, the sculptor Donatello, and the engineer-architect Brunelleschi shows how cross-fertilization could occur in the city. Florence also offers a vivid example of structural instability, especially so far as the political system was concerned. In one of his most famous metaphors, Dante compared Florence to a patient in bed, constantly changing position and never comfortable. The contrast between Florentine instability and Venetian political stability leads one to expect that, as turned out to be the case, Florence was a more creative milieu.

More difficult to explain is the way in which the Florentines established, by 1400 if not before, what might be called a "tradition of the new" in certain fields, notably the visual arts, the kind of chain-reaction which Hall identifies in all his creative cities. Perhaps Jacob Burckhardt was right, and competitive individualism is part of the answer (once again, a contrast between Florence and Venice, where the individual was subordinated to the group, seems appropriate). Ernst Gombrich's point about the "leaven of criticism" is also helpful here, his argument that the public tradition of criticizing the work of artists, a tradition which was particularly strong in Florence, kept them on their mettle.[14] The "magnet" effect was also important, since a number of leading "Florentine" artists and humanists, from Leonardo Bruni to Leonardo da Vinci, were actually born outside the city, usually in other parts of Tuscany.

Hall's focus on cities bridges the microgeography and macrogeography distinguished earlier in this chapter. By collecting so many different people in one place, cities encourage the division of labor. The increasing number of occupations is associated with a greater variety of attitudes or ways of viewing the world. The rise of different "occupational cultures," as we may call them, is in turn associated with the creation of different urban spaces with distinctive characteristics, religious zones centered on churches, a political zone around the town hall, an economic zone around the market, and so on. Venice offers a striking example of this functional specialization of space, with its economic center on the Rialto and its political center at the Doge's Palace and the neighbouring piazza. The meeting-places already mentioned allow the different occupational cultures to interact. Cities also act as the links between regions, cultural links no less than economic ones. In both cases the diffusion of innovations is a major urban function.

The Diffusion of the Renaissance

Diffusion is a concept which is taken less seriously than it used to be, but one which still has its value, especially if attention is given to the process of cultural selection on the part of the "receivers," in other words the adoption of some novelties from abroad and the resistance to others.[15] The diffusion of innovation, its movement outwards from a center to a periphery, especially since the Industrial Revolution, has attracted the attention of historians of technology. The Renaissance too may be examined from this point of view. An atlas of the Renaissance might include space-time maps of the diffusion of Doric, Ionic, and Corinthian capitals, for instance, or of equestrian monuments, of portraits, of classicizing epics, of humanist history. The movement was generally but not always from Italy to the rest of Europe, but the atlas would have to include the spread of the technique of oil painting from the Netherlands to Italy, and that of the printing press from Mainz along the Rhine and beyond.[16]

One might begin the story with diffusion within Italy itself. Italian history in this period is not so much one history as a cluster of regional histories, but the increasing interaction between regions is an important part of the story. Florence was a center from which many artists, scholars, and writers left to spread innovations elsewhere in the peninsula: Leonardo in Milan, Michelangelo in Rome, and so on. It is of course necessary to avoid a monocentric or "Florentinocentric" interpretation of the Renaissance and to recognize that Padua, Naples, and especially Rome were centers of innovation at some point – but the Florentine tradition of innovation was the most powerful.

Hence the value of the notions of "center" and "periphery" in the study of Italian art, for example.[17] If Florence or Rome were centers, major cities such as Milan or Venice might be described as "semiperipheries," relatively quick to note and to assimilate new trends, and then to pass them on to the periphery proper, to small towns and to the countryside. This sequence of diffusion was not an inevitable one: some artists and humanists wandered from place to place and sometimes settled down at least for a time in a small town or village. Piero della Francesca, for example, worked in and around his birthplace, Borgo San Sepolcro in Umbria, where some of his paintings may be seen to this day. All the same, the gradual movement of ideas and objects from city to small town to the countryside was probably the norm. (See the essay by Loren Partridge below.)

However, this chapter is essentially concerned with the next stage, which was the diffusion of innovation to other parts of Europe, and to some regions beyond it, especially the Americas. To discuss this process, it may be useful to distinguish the movement of people from the movement of artifacts.

Migration

It has been argued more than once that the movement of people rather than books is the crucial factor in the spread of new ideas, the "non-routine information," as Törnqvist puts it, which "requires direct personal contacts."[18] The warmth of personal encounters and the enthusiasm of individuals breaks down resistance to new ideas, while new techniques are most clearly demonstrated by practicing them rather than describing them. There was certainly no lack of people on the move in Europe at this time, including itinerant masons, artists, teachers, and students (their mobility encouraged by the fact that throughout Europe university teaching was conducted in a single language, Latin). As news of Italian innovations spread, foreign artists and scholars went to Rome or Florence to study (the French painter Jean Fouquet, for example, or the English theologian John Colet). There were also some major diasporas in this period, notably the Greek, the Flemish, and the Italian.[19]

It used to be thought that the Renaissance happened because the Turks captured Constantinople in 1453, an event which led to a flight of Christian scholars to Italy. This story is a myth, condensing a long process into a dramatic event, but it is certainly the case that the gradual advance of the Turks had encouraged a number of Byzantine scholars to move westwards from the end of the fourteenth century onwards, and that some of them played an important role in teaching Italian scholars ancient Greek. (See the earlier essay by Linda Darling.) The Greek colony in Venice was a particularly numerous one and members of this Greek community played an important role in the printing of ancient Greek texts by Aldus Manutius and others, setting the type and reading the proofs.[20]

The German diaspora must not be forgotten. Printing with movable type was not only invented in the German-speaking world but it was also spread by German printers. The first press in Rome was set up by two German clerics, Sweynheim and Pannartz, and the first press in Venice by the brothers Johann and Wendelin of Speyer. The first French press was set up by three German printers in the Sorbonne. The first printers in Spain were Germans, the leading firm being that of the Crombergers in Seville. German printing firms such as Koberger, Trechsel, and Gryphius were important in Lyons, a major printing center in the sixteenth century. The London printer "Wynkyn de Worde" was actually a German from Wörth in Alsace.[21]

The Flemish-Dutch diaspora was even more important in the history of the Renaissance. Indeed, in important respects the Netherlands was an alternative center of innovation to Italy. In music, the Netherlanders led Europe in the time of the Renaissance, although the break with the medieval polyphonic tradition did not take place till the end of the sixteenth century (and began in Italy). In painting, including the technique of oil painting, Netherlanders such as Jan van Eyck were innovators, and for this and other reasons considerable interest in Flemish art was shown in fifteenth-century Italy. The merchant from Lucca, Giovanni Arnolfini, who commissioned his wedding portrait from Jan van Eyck lived in Bruges, but a number of Flemish paintings were exported to Italy, as we shall see in a moment. Some Netherlanders made their careers in Italy, among them the musicians Josquin des Près and Heinrich Isaak and the painter Joos van Gent, who was invited to Urbino by the duke and worked for him in the 1470s.

Jan van Eyck visited Spain in 1428–9 and a Flemish influence on Spanish art is visible from that time onwards. However, Flemish painters and sculptors were active in many parts of Europe in the sixteenth century, including England but concentrating on Scandinavia and Eastern Europe (Bialostocki's "Baltic Area"). For example, Maximilian Colt (fl. 1595–1628), who came from Arras, settled in London, where he was active as a sculptor, his most famous works being the tomb of Queen Elizabeth in Westminster Abbey and the tomb of Robert Cecil Earl of Salisbury in the church of Hatfield in Hertfordshire. Willem Boy (ca. 1545–1628), a sculptor from Mechelen, worked at the court of King Gustav Vasa of Sweden and made the king's tomb in Uppsala cathedral. The sculptor Willem van den Blocke (ca. 1545–1628), also from Mechelen, worked for the kings of Poland and Sweden and settled in Gdansk (Danzig).

Many more places in the Baltic area (Güstrow, for example, Schwerin and Königsberg), and many more names, could be added to this list. Little is known of the reasons that led particular artists to leave the Netherlands, but it is likely that there was both a "push" and a "pull" factor in the situation. It was good to leave the Netherlands at a time of civil war, and Protestants from the South had all the more reason to leave at a time when the Catholic Church was being re-established with the aid of Spanish troops. Both London and Gdansk were known as environments in which a variety of forms of Christianity could be practiced. There is also the testimony of Ludovico Guicciardini, a Florentine living in the Low Countries, that a number of artists were "summoned with great salaries by princes."[22]

The most important of all the diasporas in the history of the European Renaissance was of course the Italian, whether the migrants were humanists or artists. Italian scholars were in demand as university teachers, particularly as teachers of rhetoric. A well-known example is that of the Sicilian Luca Marineo (ca. 1460–ca. 1533) at the university of Salamanca. Italians were also invited to a number of European courts to act as official historians, doubtless because they could write in what was becoming the fashionable classicizing style. Antonio Bonfini, for instance, was invited to Hungary by King Matthias Corvinus (r. 1458–90) to write a history of the country. Paulo Emili (ca. 1460–1529), who came from Verona, served three French kings as official historian. His history, *De rebus gestis Francorum*, was published posthumously in 1539. Luca Marineo was called to court in 1499 by the joint rulers Ferdinand and Isabella in order to write an official history of Spain. Some of these scholars left Italy for similar reasons to the Netherlanders. The Venetian Protestant Gian Michele Bruto (1517–92), for instance, went to Transylvania and Poland in the 1570s, a time when the cultural climate in both regions was one of religious toleration.

Italian artists also emigrated in considerable numbers, temporarily or permanently. On the "push" side, the number of sculptors and architects from the Ticino, a mountainous region with a tradition of emigration, deserves to be noted, while the prestige of Italian and especially Florentine artists abroad was the "pull" factor. For example, the introduction of an Italianate manner in Spanish painting took place in the 1470s when Rodrigo Borja, whose career in Rome had made him familiar with the new style, brought Italian painters to his native Valencia. Italian artists were still coming to Spain in the age of Philip II, who employed, among others, the sculptor Pompeo Leoni (ca. 1533–1608), and the painters Federico Zuccaro (ca. 1540–1609) and Pellegrino Tibaldi (1527–96), both of whom decorated the Escorial. King Francis I managed to entice Leonardo da Vinci to France, while it was for the palace of Francis at Fontainebleau that Rosso, Primaticcio, and Niccolò dell'Abbate all worked. The style of this "school of Fontainebleau" became exemplary in sixteenth-century France.

To the east of Europe, the courts of Buda, Moscow, Cracow, and Prague all attracted Italian artists. For example, Sigismund of Poland discovered the Italian style when he was living at the court of Buda. Franciscus Florentinus came to Cracow in 1502 at the king's invitation and was followed by Giovanni Maria Mosca, from Padua, and Bartolommeo Berecci, from Florence, all working on the building and decoration of the Wawel palace. Again, the architect Paolo Stella, from Lugano, was in Prague between 1538 and his death in 1552, and worked on the Belvedere there. Painters and sculptors were drawn to Prague during the reign of the art-loving

Emperor Rudolf II, among them the Milanese Giuseppe Arcimboldo (ca. 1527–93), famous for his fantastic portraits, and Adriaen de Vries, a Dutch sculptor (ca. 1545–1626), each of whom spent twenty-five years in central Europe.

The time-lag between capital cities and the provinces is worth noting. The style employed by painters in Fontainebleau in the 1530s could be found in (say) Tanlay in Burgundy in the 1560s. From Prague, Italian artists such as Baldassare Maggi, from the Ticino, moved to southern Bohemia. From Cracow, Italians took the new style to Vilnius in Lithuania (then part of the composite Polish-Lithuanian state) and to the new town of Zamosc, where from 1580 onwards Bernardo Morando, an architect from Padua, designed a town hall, an academy, a church, squares, and gates. From Zamosc the new style spread to L'viv. The European networks of cultural exchange at this period still await a full reconstruction, but it already looks as if we may adapt the concepts of the economic historian Immanuel Wallerstein and speak of a cultural "core" (Italy, especially Florence, and in some respects the southern Netherlands), a "semi-periphery," consisting of courts such as Buda and Cracow and mercantile cities such as Lyon and Gdansk, and a "periphery" (for example, Scotland, Sweden, and Muscovy).

The movement of artifacts

These networks of cultural exchange included artifacts as well as people, following established trade routes, sea routes such as Florence–Bruges or land routes such as Venice–Nuremberg, and responding to the cultural interests of the diaspora of Italian merchants, who often imported books and paintings from home, as well to the enthusiasms of local elites. The contrast between the Italianate architecture of France, closer to the model of Milan, and that of Germany, closer to that of Venice, is a reminder of the importance of trade routes in the history of the Renaissance, as in cultural history more generally. Although the export of images from Florence, Antwerp, and elsewhere may not have been of great economic importance, the cultural consequences were profound.

For example, the Portinari altarpiece by Hugo van der Goes (ca. 1440–82) was commissioned by the manager of the Bruges branch of the Medici Bank, Tommaso Portinari, for a church in Florence. Again, the Florentine artist Andrea Verrocchio, the teacher of Leonardo da Vinci, worked for King Matthias of Hungary without leaving his native city. The monument to Ture Bielke and Margaret Sture in the cathedral at Linköping was made by the Flemish sculptor Willem van den Blocke in his workshop in Gdansk and then transported to Sweden. The export of engravings, especially from Antwerp, was especially important because prints, unlike paintings, statues, and books, were cheap and light-weight and could therefore reach an exceptionally "wide" audience in both the social and the geographical senses of the term. In the sixteenth century, Antwerp prints, especially religious images and architectural designs, some of them exported by the famous printer Christophe Plantin, could be found in India, China, Japan, Mexico and Peru, where they encouraged local artists to adopt new forms and styles.[23]

In sixteenth-century Mexico, for instance, there was a veritable "invasion" of European images. Considerable numbers of paintings and engravings were imported.

Still more important (given what was said earlier about the influence of people relative to artifacts), missionaries and European painters taught indigenous artists to copy or to imitate images in the Renaissance style.[24] In China, following the arrival of the Italian Jesuit missionary Matteo Ricci in the late sixteenth century, the engravings illustrating the Antwerp edition of Jerónimo Nadal's *Gospel Stories* were particularly influential. It has even been argued that Chinese landscape painting, notably the representation of mountains, was transformed in response to these western images, although the term "imitation" is less appropriate than in the case of Mexico. The difference between the two regions is not difficult to understand since in China the missionaries relied on the goodwill of the local elites, while in Mexico they were supported by the Spanish imperial system and in a position to tell local artists what to do.[25]

It should not be assumed that the movement of forms and ideas was always one-way. Works of art from India, China, Japan, Mexico, Peru and many other places were brought back to Europe in the sixteenth century. They were displayed in cabinets of "curiosities" (in other words, private museums), and they awakened the interest of some artists, such as Albrecht Dürer, and some humanists, such as Paolo Giovio. Some of them played a role in the development of Renaissance art. It has been argued, for example, that the so-called "Manueline" style of Portuguese architecture and sculpture, which flourished in the early sixteenth century, incorporated and transformed motifs from India, as observed by Vasco da Gama and other mariners. A few borrowings from Aztec art, as represented by the treasures taken from Monte-zuma by the Spaniards and sent to Europe, can also be found, as in the case of some exotic birds in the loggia of the Vatican painted by Raphael and his collaborators. More speculatively, it might be suggested that the discovery of the New World and its vast expanses helped to change the ways in which space was imagined at this time. (See the essay above by Matthew Restall.)

The intellectual history of this period was shaped in part by the geography of the book. Before printing was invented, manuscripts were sent abroad by the Florentine dealer Vespasiano da Bisticci, to Spain, to Portugal, to England, and to Hungary. Needless to say the export trade in books became important in the age of print. For a time, in the 1470s, the Nuremberg printer Anton Koberger controlled the distribution of Italian books abroad, but as the trade grew it proved impossible to monopolize it. Among Italian printers, the products of Aldus Manutius of Venice, who specialized in small-format editions of the classics, were in particular demand abroad. Antwerp, Paris, Lyons, and Basel were particularly important centers of printing in this period, and many texts which we associate with the Renaissance, whether in Latin, Italian, or other vernaculars, came from the presses of those cities.[26]

In order to understand the effects of this international trade in books, we need to examine what was happening from the consumer's point of view, to see which Renaissance texts were present in public and private libraries in different parts of Europe, both humanist texts in Latin and works in Italian and other vernaculars.

As an example of the first category one might take the works of Lorenzo Valla, especially his *Elegantiae*, a text-book for students of classical Latin which spread much more widely in the Renaissance itself than his critique of the authenticity of the Donation of Constantine, which is better known today. The *Elegantiae* is known to have been present in at least thirty-six private libraries in Cambridge between 1537 and 1605, as well as appearing in surviving inventories of French and Spanish libraries of the time.[27]

In the case of the vernacular, we might examine the diffusion of three books which made the culture of the Italian Renaissance better known abroad. In the case of buildings, the key text is not the treatise on architecture by Andrea Palladio (now regarded as one of the greatest architects of the period), but the one by Sebastiano Serlio, which was translated wholly or partly into Dutch, German, French, Spanish, English, and Latin by 1611. The treatise can be found not only in the libraries of architects but also among the books of some French, German, and English nobles who were thinking of building houses for themselves and needed a pattern-book.

Again, although Vasari's *Lives of the Artists* was not translated during the Renaissance, it could be found in the libraries of artists (including El Greco, the Spanish architect Juan Herrera, and the Dutch painter Karel van Mander), as well as in those of scholars, from the French book collector Jean Groslier to the English antiquary John Selden.

An even greater success story than Serlio's, as far as publishing is concerned, is that of the fortune of the *Book of the Courtier* by Baldassare Castiglione, a dialogue discussing the ideal behavior of ladies and gentlemen at court, first published in Italian in 1528. By 1600 more than sixty Italian editions of the book had been published, and it had been translated into French, Spanish, Latin, German, English, and (freely adapted) Polish. By 1620, no fewer than 120 editions of the book had been published in different languages, suggesting that interest in Italian models of good behavior was considerably greater than interest in Italian art or even architecture.[28]

Studying the spread of grammar schools and colleges which followed the prescriptions of the humanists is another way of approaching the topography of the Renaissance. In the center and the semi-periphery, in Italy, the Netherlands, France, and England, for example, municipal initiatives were important in the founding of such institutions. On the periphery, the initiative was often taken by missionaries. A famous example is the college at Tlatelolco near Mexico city, founded in 1536 by the Franciscan bishop Juan de Zumárraga, which taught boys of noble Indian descent to speak and write classical Latin prose and verse.[29] In the later sixteenth century, Jesuit colleges spread ideas and practices associated with the Renaissance as well as the Counter-Reformation to eastern Europe, to Vilnius, for instance, to L'viv (Lwów) and to Kolozsvár (Cluj) in Transylvania.

It would of course be unwise to assume that ideas, forms, and practices "spread" like artifacts from one place to another while remaining unchanged. Even artifacts such as paintings and books changed in the sense of being located in different cultural contexts and understood in different ways from those in their place of origin. As they moved from region to region, ideas, forms and practices many of which had been "made in Italy" were adapted more or less successfully to local traditions. In that sense they were culturally "translated."

The Translation of Cultures

Like other innovations, the ones associated with the Renaissance often met with resistance of different kinds. Some frontiers acted as barriers, notably the religious frontiers with Islam and with the Orthodox world. The Alps slowed down communication between northern and southern Europe and made it more expensive, although they did not prevent it altogether. Languages and other local traditions were barriers to the spread of the Renaissance, barriers which were often crossed in some regions or domains but rarely in others.

For these reasons it is more realistic to speak of "reception" than "diffusion," of adaptation than of adoption, of transformation rather than transfer, of re-production rather than reproduction. Translation – from Latin and Greek, from Italian, and to a lesser extent from other vernaculars – played an important part in this process. The topography of translation has never been studied in a comparative manner – I hope to explore this territory in the near future – although a study of who translated what, when, where, and for whom might tell us a great deal about the process of cultural exchange. The metaphor of "cultural translation" is also useful here, since it reminds us of the importance of mediators and of the tension between faithfulness to the original and intelligibility or usefulness in a new context. This process of active reception both undermines and reinforces the idea of *Ortgebundenheit* with which this chapter began, illustrating the importance of place while at the same time denying geographical determinism.[30]

A useful concept for the analysis of the process of reception is that of the "ecotype," an idea which the Swedish folklorist Carl von Sydow – yet another Swede – borrowed from botany and adapted to the analysis of folktale variants. The point of the concept is to emphasize the collective rather than the individual transformation of an item which is borrowed, as well as the process of adaptation to the local environment. Bialostocki's concept of the "vernacular" makes a similar point, referring to local variants in architecture such as the so-called "Polish parapet," which transformed medieval battlements with the aid of Renaissance motifs such as volutes, masks, and vases, as in the case of the Cloth Hall of Cracow. Bialostocki later developed his argument into a positive assessment of artistic peripheries, noting that tradition had less weight there and that artists were therefore free to select elements from the artistic center and combine them as they pleased.[31] To what extent they appreciated that freedom it is hard to say: the argument about the great city as a "magnet" for talent, discussed above, suggests that given the choice, many artists preferred to work in the center. All the same, the suggestion that artistic conventions – like laws – were taken less seriously on the periphery is an illuminating one.

In the case of the Renaissance, architecture offers a particularly appropriate example of the formation of ecotypes, since it is a collective art and also one closely linked to everyday life, to the local climate, and to local materials. Designs intended for stone buildings in Italy might be carried out in brick or wood in other parts of Europe. Houses for patricians whose life-style was urban had to be adapted to the needs of rural nobilities.

The importance of ecotypes has been contested. The American art historian Thomas Kaufmann has criticized Bialostocki for his nationalist assumptions and places his own emphasis on the creation of an international style, comparing the deviations from classical standards in cities as far apart as Salamanca and L'viv. Both scholars have valuable points to make and distinctions doubtless need to be drawn. The concept of local variant, for instance, seems to work better in the case of architecture, the more collective art, than in that of painting or sculpture, where, as we have seen, artifacts might be made in one place and exported to another, though even here local "schools" may often be identified. The term "ecotype" is best used to refer to what happens in a place, not to the supposed nationality of the individuals involved in the process (for example, the Italian, German, and Polish craftsmen working together in Cracow). An international Renaissance style did emerge in this period, a hybrid style combining elements from the classical and the Gothic, the Italian and the Flemish, but in different regions the style developed characteristic inflections, or as Kaufmann puts it, "dialects of an international language."[32]

The term "dialect" brings us to language and literature, at a time when the international language, Latin, had to face increasing competition from a number of European vernaculars. Hybridization occurred here too. For example, English, French, Spanish, German, and other languages borrowed many words from Italian and phrases and even sentence structure from classical Latin. Again, poets, from Edmund Spenser to Luis Camões, both followed and tried to surpass ancient models, such as Vergil's *Aeneid*, as well as their Italian adaptations, such as Ariosto's *Orlando furioso* (itself a hybrid of classical epic and medieval romance). Spenser, for example, drew on "national" legends such as the story of King Arthur, while his vocabulary combined Latin forms with medieval terms which were archaic in his day. In his *Lusiads* (1572), the Portuguese poet Camões chose an epic hero from the recent past of his own country, the explorer Vasco da Gama.

In the case of humanism, viewed as a cluster or package of scholarly ideals and practices, ecotypes appear to have been less important. The attempt to reconstitute the literary and philosophical culture of ancient Rome was an international movement, encouraged after 1460 and especially after 1500 by the spreading use of identical printed copies of classical texts or scholarly commentaries. Even here, however, the concept of the local variant may still have its uses.[33] For example, in the sixteenth century, rival methods of interpreting Roman law were known respectively as the "Italian style" (*mos italicus*) and the "French style" (*mos gallicus*). In this case the difference was not so much macrogeographical, associated with national character, as microgeographical, linked to traditions in particular universities such as Pavia or Bourges, the academic equivalent of workshop-based "schools" of painters.[34]

Again, while the trilingual colleges of Europe taught in Latin, Greek, and Hebrew, the trilingual college of Tlatelolco taught in Latin, Spanish, and Nahuatl, a practical adaptation to the needs of local people, but also a significant divergence from a European model. If we look at humanism not so much in the traditional manner, as a system of ideas about philology, the dignity of man and so on, but – following the model of historians of science – as a set of cultural practices (collecting Roman coins, writing letters in classical Latin, teaching in grammar schools, and so on), local variations will appear even more significant than before.

Conclusion

This chapter has argued for the importance of a geographical analysis of Renaissance culture, alongside the better-known chronological and sociological analyses. It has distinguished diffusion from reception, micro-environments from macro-environments, centers from peripheries or semi-peripheries, and the movement of artifacts from the movement of people.

What might be called the "symbolic geography of the Renaissance" should also be taken into account. There were of course attempts to deny geography and to assert that Venice, for example, or Seville was a "New Rome," in the same way that the movement we call the "Renaissance" attempted to deny or defy chronology and to bring back the classical past. However, ancient Rome occupied a central place in the imagination of humanists and artists alike. They viewed it as a network of relics of classical antiquity such as the Colosseum, Pantheon, Capitol, and the Arch of Constantine, in parallel to the Christian network of holy places such as the seven churches of Rome which every pilgrim was supposed to visit.

Florence has been viewed in similar fashion for centuries by admirers of the Renaissance as the center or cradle of that movement, a network of places with their special associations and memories: the Duomo, Uffizi, the Piazza della Signoria, the Palazzo Pitti, Brunelleschi's Foundling Hospital, the church of San Lorenzo, the Medici Chapel, and so much more. It might be interesting to write a history of either Rome or Florence from this perspective, noting how different generations of visitors have foregrounded some places and "backgrounded" others. Seventeenth- and eighteenth-century travelers and their guides concentrated on the remains of the later Renaissance, for example, while twentieth-century tourists, like their guidebooks, begin with Brunelleschi, Masaccio, and Botticelli. The Brancacci Chapel, for example, once on the edge of mental maps of the Renaissance, has been moving steadily closer to the center in the course of the last hundred years or so. No account of the geography of the Renaissance can afford to neglect the geography of the mind, the geography of the imagination.

NOTES

1   The phrase comes from Agnew, "Devaluation."
2   Haussherr, "Kunstgeographie," p. 158.
3   Bialostocki, "Baltic Area."
4   Moretti, *Atlas*, 3.
5   Pevsner, *Englishness*, especially pp. 15–25. For the critique, Kaufmann, *Court*.
6   Massey, "Places."
7   Pred, *Place*.
8   Howard, *History, Venice*.
9   Koestler, *Act*, pp. 121–4.
10 Hall, *Cities*, esp. pp. 3–23, 279–88.
11 Hall and Preston, *Carrier Wave*, p. 260.
12 Hägestrand, *Innovation* and "Survival."
13 Törnqvist, "Creativity."
14 Gombrich, "Leaven."
15 McNeill, "Diffusion."
16 Hägerstrand, "Problems"; Moretti, *Atlas*.
17 Castelnuovo and Ginzburg, "Centre."

18   Törnqvist, "Creativity," p. 96; cf. Cipolla, "Diffusion"; Ziman, "Ideas."
19   Burke, "Hosts."
20   Burke, "Myth"; Burke, "Hosts."
21   Geldner, *Inkunabeldrucker.*
22   Jolly, "Netherlandish Sculptors."
23   Zerner, *Le stampe.*
24   Gruzinski, *Painting,* pp. 16ff.
25   Cahill, *Compelling Image,* pp. 86ff.
26   Febvre and Martin, *The Coming of the Book,* ch. 6.
27   Leedham-Green, *Inventories* (index, under "Valla").
28   Burke, *Courtier.*
29   Osorio Romero, *Enseñanza,* pp. xxii–xlv.
30   Hugill and Dickson, *Transfer.*
31   Bialostocki, *Art,* pp. 63–5, and "Values."
32   Kaufmann, "Italian Sculptors," pp. 52–7.
33   Sydow, "Geography"; Bialostocki, *Art*; Kaufmann, *Court.*
34   Kelley, *Foundations.*

REFERENCES

Agnew, John A., "The Devaluation of Place in Social Science," in John A. Agnew and James S. Duncan, *The Power of Place: Bringing Together Geography and Sociological Imaginations* (Boston: Unwin Hyman, 1989), pp. 9–29.

Bialostocki, Jan, *Art of the Renaissance in Eastern Europe* (Ithaca: Cornell University Press, 1976).

——, "The Baltic Area as an Artistic Region in the Sixteenth Century," *Hafnia* (1976), pp. 11–24.

——, "Some Values of Artistic Periphery," in *World Art: Themes of Unity and Diversity,* ed. Irving Lavin (University Park: Pennsylvania State University Press, 1986), vol. 1, pp. 49–58.

Burke, Peter, "Hosts and Guests: A General View of Minorities in the Cultural Life of Europe," in *Minorities in Western European Cities,* ed. Hugo Soly and Alfons K. L. Thijs (Brussels: Institut Historique Belge de Rome, 1995), pp. 43–54.

——, *The Fortunes of the Courtier* (Cambridge: Cambridge University Press, 1995).

——, "The Myth of 1453: Notes and Reflections," *Querdenken: Festschrift Hans Guggisberg,* ed. Michael Erbe et al. (Mannheim: Palatium Verlag, 1996), pp. 23–30.

Cahill, James F., *The Compelling Image: Nature and Style in Seventeenth-Century Chinese Painting* (Cambridge, MA: Harvard University Press, 1982).

Castelnuovo, Enrico and Ginzburg, Carlo, "Centre and Periphery," in *History of Italian Art,* ed. P. Burke (Cambridge: Polity Press, 1996).

Cipolla, Carlo M., "The Diffusion of Innovations in Early Modern Europe," *Comparative Studies in Society and History* 14 (1972), pp. 46–52.

Febvre, Lucien and Martin, Henri-Jean, *The Coming of the Book,* trans. David Gerard (London: NLB, 1976).

Geldner, Ferdinand, *Die deutsche Inkunabeldrucker,* 2 vols. (Stuttgart: A. Hiersemann, 1968–70).

Gombrich, Ernst H., "The Leaven of Criticism in Renaissance Art," in *The Heritage of Apelles* (Oxford: Phaidon, 1976), pp. 11–31.

Gruzinski, Serge, *Painting the Conquest: The Mexican Indians and the European Renaissance* (Paris: Flammarion, 1992).

Hägerstrand, Torsten, *Innovation Diffusion as a Social Process*, trans. Allan Pred (Chicago: University of Chicago Press, 1967).

——, "Survival and Arena," in *Human Activity and Time Geography*, ed. Tommy Carlstein, Don Parker, and Nigel Thrift (New York: Wiley, 1978).

——, "Some Unexplored Problems in the Modeling of Culture Transfer and Transformation," in *The Transfer and Transformation of Ideas and Material Culture*, ed. Peter J. Hugill and D. Bruce Dickson (College Station, TX: Texas A and M Press, 1988), pp. 217–32.

Hall, Peter Geoffrey, *Cities in Civilization* (London: Weidenfeld and Nicolson, 1998).

Hall, Peter Geoffrey and Preston, P., *The Carrier Wave: New IT and the Geography of Innovation, 1846–2003* (London: Unwin Hyman, 1988).

Haussherr, Renier, "Kunstgeographie: Aufgaben, Grenzen, Möglichkeiten," *Rheinische Vierteljahrblätter* 34 (1970), pp. 158–71.

Howard, Deborah, *The Architectural History of Venice* (New Haven: Yale University Press, 1980).

——, *Venice and the East: The Impact of the Islamic World on Venetian Architecture, 1100–1500* (New Haven: Yale University Press, 2000).

Hugill, Peter J. and Dickson, D. Bruce, eds., *The Transfer and Transformation of Ideas and Material Culture* (College Station, TX: Texas A and M Press, 1988).

Jolly, Anna, "Netherlandish Sculptors in Sixteenth-Century Northern Germany and their Patrons," *Simiolus* 27 (1999), pp. 119–43.

Kaufmann, Thomas DaCosta, *Court, Cloister and City: The Art and Culture of Central Europe, 1450–1800* (Chicago: University of Chicago Press, 1995).

——, "Italian Sculptors and Sculpture Outside of Italy," in *Reframing the Renaissance*, ed. Claire Farago (New Haven: Yale University Press, 1995), pp. 47–66.

Kelley, Donald R., *Foundations of Modern Historical Thought* (New York: Columbia University Press, 1970).

Koestler, Arthur, *The Act of Creation* (London: Hutchinson, 1969).

Leedham-Green, Elisabeth, *Books in Cambridge Inventories*, 2 vols. (Cambridge: Cambridge University Press, 1987).

McNeill, William H., "Diffusion in History," in *The Transfer and Transformation of Ideas and Material Culture*, ed. Peter J. Hugill and D. Bruce Dickson (College Station, TX: Texas A and M Press, 1988), pp. 75–90.

Massey, Doreen, "Places and their Pasts," *History Workshop Journal* 39 (1995), pp. 182–92.

Moretti, Franco, *Atlas of the European Novel 1800–1900* (London: Verso, 1998).

Osorio Romero, Ignazio, *La enseñanza del Latín a los Indios* (Mexico City: Centro de Estudios Clásicos, 1990).

Pevsner, Nikolaus, *The Englishness of English Art* (London: Architectural Press, 1956).

Pred, Allan Richard, *Place, Practice and Structure* (Cambridge: Polity Press, 1987).

Sydow, Carl Wilhelm von, "Geography and Folk-Tale Oicotypes," in *Selected Papers on Folklore* (Copenhagen: Rosenkilde and Bagger, 1948), pp. 44–69.

Törnqvist, Gunnar, "Creativity and the Renewal of Regional Life," in *Creativity and Context*, ed. Anne Buttimer (Lund: University of Lund, 1983), pp. 91–112.

Zerner, Henri, ed., *Le stampe e la diffusione delle immagini e degli stili* (Bologna: CLUEB, 1983).

Ziman, John, "Ideas move around inside People," in *Puzzles, Problems and Enigmas* (Cambridge: Cambridge University Press, 1981), pp. 259–72.

FURTHER READING

For an introduction to the topic, see Roy Porter and Mikulas Teich, eds, *The Renaissance in National Context*, (Cambridge: Cambridge University Press, 1991) and Peter Burke, *The European Renaissance* (Oxford: Blackwell Publishers, 1998). Relatively little has been written on the geography of humanism, but Anthony Goodman and Angus McKay, eds., *The Impact of Humanism on Western Europe* (London: Longman, 1990), offers a general survey. On the geography of the book, the best study remains that of Lucien Febvre and Henri-Jean Martin (1958) *The Coming of the Book*, English translation (London: NLB, 1976), especially chapter 6.

On painting, one might begin with the classic essay by Aby Warburg, "Flemish Art and the Florentine Early Renaissance" (1902), translated in *The Renewal of Classical Antiquity* (Los Angeles: Getty Research Institute, 1999), pp. 281–303, and then turn to Enrico Castelnuovo and Carlo Ginzburg (1979) "Centre and Periphery," in P. Burke, ed., *History of Italian Art* (Cambridge: Polity Press, 1996). The problem of local variants in architecture and sculpture has been studied most intensively in the case of eastern (or east-central) Europe, by Jan Bialostocki in "The Baltic Area as an Artistic Region in the Sixteenth Century," *Hafnia* (1976), pp. 11–24 and "Some Values of Artistic Periphery," in *World Art*, ed. Irving Lavin (University Park: Pennsylvania State University Press, 1986), vol. 1, pp. 49–58, and by Thomas DaCosta Kaufmann, "Italian Sculptors and Sculpture Outside of Italy," in Claire Farago, ed., *Reframing the Renaissance* (New Haven: Yale University Press, 1995), pp. 47–66. For the world outside Europe, see especially Serge Gruzinski, *Painting the Conquest: The Mexican Indians and the European Renaissance* (Paris: Flammarion, 1992) and *La Pensée métisse* (Paris: Fayard, 1999), and Valeri Fraser, "Architecture and Imperialism in Sixteenth-Century Spanish America," *Art History* 9 (1986), pp. 325–35, and *The Architecture of Conquest: Building in the Viceroyalty of Peru* (Cambridge: Cambridge University Press, 1990).

PART II

The Worlds and Ways of Power

CHAPTER SIX

Governments and Bureaucracies

Edward Muir

The Renaissance invented the idea of the state. The state, of course, manifests itself as an abstract idea in a way quite unlike the active presence of monarchs, councillors, and bureaucrats. An idea more powerful than any living person, the state evolved in the thinking of theorists from the early sixteenth century when Niccolò Machiavelli used the word "state" to mean something akin to estate or status, and the middle seventeenth when Thomas Hobbes and Samuel Pufendorf described the artificial person of the state as the true sovereign, an abstraction distinct from the natural person of the monarch or the corporate body of citizens or subjects. The power of the state rather than the power of the ruler became the true foundation of government, and rulers and subjects alike were obliged to be loyal to the state as the only legitimate source of law and coercive force. These theorists were struggling to gain analytical purchase on the elusive and volatile transformations, even revolutions, in government during their time.[1]

The invention of the idea of the state provided a new answer to an old question: What is government? In pondering the classical political texts, Machiavelli had offered two possible answers. The first depicted government as a principality – conceived as an extended household, managed by the ethic of the patriarchal family, an ethic embodied in the Roman law obligation to obey the paterfamilias. The prince's immediate family and distant relations, servants, retainers, friends, and allies constituted the princely court, which was imagined as if it were a large extended family. The father/prince commanded subjects and mediated disputes, marriage and reproduction were political acts, both men and women exercised defined political roles as befited their membership in a household, and the laws of inheritance implied if not guaranteed succession of rulers from father to son.

Machiavelli's second answer depicted government as a republic, which unlike the princely family was constituted exclusively by adult male householders with citizenship rights. In the Italian communal form, a republic required the election of officials and some level of citizen consent for major governmental decisions. As Hobbes later understood, a republic implied a contractual rather than hereditary foundation to government. Unlike princely families that followed the imperatives of reproductive biology, republics were knit together with the social capital of voluntary, male associations, a fact that made them inherently unstable. Republics had particular difficulty accounting for the public roles of mothers, sisters, and wives, let alone single women, whose political involvement was relegated to the private sphere. (See the essay below by John Najemy.)

Whether conceived of as a principality or a republic, governments during the Renaissance adhered to one of three possible institutional structures. First, there were city-states, found in Germany and Italy. During the fifteenth century Milan, Ferrara, and Mantua classified themselves as principalities; Venice, Florence, and Genoa as republics. The city-states survived as legal and territorial entities even when the forms of government changed, as happened briefly when Milan became the Ambrosian republic (1447–50) or when the Medici principality supplanted the Florentine republic after 1530. The city-states proved themselves exceedingly dynamic, especially in promoting and sustaining commerce. Since the eleventh century these nests of risk and enterprise had been stunningly successful, but by the sixteenth their days were numbered. Vulnerable to internal sedition and incapable of amassing the resources necessary to defend themselves against transalpine and Hapsburg aggression, most city-states were absorbed into larger political spheres of influence if not the direct rule of a foreign prince. Second, there were empires, most notably the German Empire with its complicated constitutional inheritance that limited the power of the emperor, and the Ottoman Empire, which was so effective at conquest. Both city-states and empires had been known since antiquity and had solid foundations in Roman law and classical political thought. In contrast to these venerable structures, the third possibility of feudal or national monarchy was relatively new. Feudal monarchies had evolved in England and France from the eleventh to thirteenth centuries through attempts of the kings to dominate their vassals, and in Spain in the fifteenth century through the reconquista and dynastic marriage. The national monarchies, all of which accepted the dynastic conception of government, proved during the sixteenth century their superior ability in comparison to city-states and empires to unify disparate groups around the monarch, to raise unprecedented sums of money to sustain aggressive dynastic policies, and to create the fledgling institutions of the bureaucratic state.[2]

This neat theoretical pattern of two forms of government (principalities and republics) and three institutional structures (city-states, empires, and national monarchies) masks innumerable anomalies and inconsistencies. Government during the sixteenth century was always a messy, even chaotic business. Venice, the most successful city-state and the doyen of republican political theory, was actually a city ruled by a tiny hereditary oligarchy that had conquered a far-flung empire. What was Switzerland? The confederation of free peasant republics and towns was certainly not a city-state, empire, or national monarchy, and yet it was resilient enough to stand up to the monolith of Hapsburg power and to rent out its citizen-soldiers to other European powers. The city-states of the German Empire, such as Augsburg and Nuremberg, steered a perilous independent course made possible by the emperors' financial dependence on them. The Baltic and North Sea cities of the old, quasi-independent Hanseatic League, which had never managed greater unity than a loose commercial alliance around the Code of Lübeck, found their commercial monopolies and political autonomy under assault from England, Holland, Scandinavia, the German princes, Poland-Lithuania, and the Russian tzar. Nevertheless, the surviving Hanseatic League cities, all of which were officially within various principalities and kingdoms, continued to call assemblies that performed certain governmental functions until 1669. And then there were pockets of people beyond the reach of any government across the steppe frontiers of Russia and Poland, beyond the Pale in Ireland, and along the pirate coast of Dalmatia.

The Papal State occupied a peculiarly anomalous position. In narrowly structural terms, the papacy was an elected monarchy, which had sovereign authority over a collection of cities in central Italy. But popes still exercised important extraterritorial authority throughout Latin Christianity. Canon law encompassed all kinds of cases involving the clergy, disputes about church property, pious donations, and priestly celibacy and morals. The law of the Church also touched upon many of the most vital concerns of the laity, including annulling marriages, legitimating bastards, prosecuting bigamy, protecting widows and orphans, and resolving inheritance disputes. The right of the papal consistory to issue dispensations gave it considerable power, especially over kings and aristocrats who wanted to marry a cousin, divorce a wife, legitimate a bastard, or annul a will. By the sixteenth century, the flood of legal business had transformed the Roman Curia into the most advanced, professional bureaucracy in Europe.

Most resistant to simple classification was the vast Polish-Lithuanian commonwealth. Loosely joined since 1336, the two principalities of Poland and Lithuania merged in the Union of Lublin (1569). The new entity was termed a republic (Rezeczpospolita) in which Poland supplied the king, but the Grand Duchy of Lithuania was an equal partner and retained its own laws, bureaucracy, and army. The most novel feature of the republic was how the nobles (szlachta) retained control of the Diet and elected the king, whom they treated as a kind of hired master of ceremonies. Throughout the Renaissance this unconventional government made Poland-Lithuania the dominant power in eastern Europe, but it defied classification and confounded even Polish political thinkers who squirmed to cram their singular constitution into the mold of neo-Roman republicanism.

The innovative idea of the state helped bridge the yawning gap between the classification schemes of political theory and the perplexing intricacy of actual Renaissance governments, but the art of governing remained less a matter of theory or even institutional routine than of the repeated assertion and representation of authority through iconography and especially public ceremonies and of face-to-face negotiations, often unequal negotiations, and sometimes coercive negotiations. No Renaissance government, no matter how august its claims, had the police or bureaucratic power to force consistent compliance with its decrees and decisions. As a result nearly all successful governments created the framework for continuous negotiations between rulers and subjects, the necessary haggling, bargaining, and intimidating through a network of personal, family, and client relationships that made day-to-day government possible. Perhaps only that most bureaucratic of kings, Philip II of Spain, possessed the strategic vision and financial resources to employ force simultaneously on several fronts and to govern almost entirely through a hierarchy of officials, but even he failed to achieve his strategic goals.

The Image of Government

Renaissance governments displayed an almost obsessive need to represent authority through emblems, seals, works of art, engraved or printed posters, public monuments, official histories, orations, and eulogies of deceased rulers. Although these lasting representations offer glimpses into the thinking of Renaissance rulers and officials, they were probably far less influential at the time than the more ephemeral representations of royal pageants, princely ceremonies, and civic rituals. These attempts to present government to courtiers, diplomats, subjects, and citizens, constituted the political media of the Renaissance. Besides managing impressions, many ceremonies, such as a coronation or swearing an oath, had a constitutive effect. Performed in the proper fashion they actuated the passage of a man or woman into rulership or officialdom.

Political ceremonies attempt to camouflage tensions, especially by representing more political harmony than may actually exist. The principle of harmony is necessary for any state, which to survive must transform diverse identities into a constructed singularity: Protestants and Catholics, Lyonnais and Parisians, Bretons and Provençals, Langue d'Oïl and Langue d'Oc, nobles and peasants, all became one as the subjects of the King of France. The obsession with representing harmony in public rituals made the European kingdoms and cities "theater states." The governors of these theater states were less masters of illusion or slippery fabricators of false images than directors of a drama that helped to constitute ruleship through the very act of representing it.[3]

Rituals also formulated a kind of ceremonial constitution of the state: ceremonies served both as a "model of" society, that is a representation of existing arrangements, and a "model for" society, a kind of instruction booklet for how the state ought to be put together. Rituals set apart the rulers of the state from others and defined the relationships among its constituent officials and subjects. Such rites "constitute" in the sense that their performance created a formal structure for the state in an era before written constitutions: "The state is invisible; it must be personified before it can be seen, symbolized before it can be loved, imagined before it can be conceived."[4]

The constitutive effect of governmental rituals can be seen in many ways. In medieval cities and kingdoms, the veneration of relics and icons had become the most potent model for social harmony. In Siena after 1308 all citizens processed past Duccio's famous Maestà, the central altarpiece in the cathedral, on the Virgin's feast days, especially the Assumption. Legislation made participation in the processions compulsory for all citizens of Siena and its subject towns, and everyone except for convicted criminals had to make offerings of candles. In effect, the very act of participating in processions in honor of the Madonna made one a subject of Siena.

Royal rituals of enactment tended to cluster around the most critical moment in monarchical regimes, especially the period of interregnum between one king and his or her successor, the period during which the questions of who was in power, and when did he or she take power, came to the fore. The interregnum ceremonies attempted to isolate the exact moment of the transfer of power, but a ceremonial performance always took time to arrange, especially if it was supposed to take place in a special location such as Rome, Rheims, Westminster, or Cracow. The problem of timing the transfer of power became the crucial ceremonial problem of enacted rites, and the period of the interregnum could be as fraught with dangers for the institution of monarchy as royal entries were for liberty of cities.

A cluster of enacting rites of passage framed interregna and made royal successions possible. The most important of these rites of passage were coronations and funerals. In the strictest cases, such as in Poland, before the rite of coronation, a king was not a king at all, just a king-in-waiting. In theory at least, only through a coronation could a mere man become a sacred king. The English word, "coronation," usually designated a variety of ceremonies associated with the ascension to authority of a new monarch in which the actual crowning may not necessarily have been the most important action. The ritual complex of the interregnum could include the predecessor's funeral, the new king's visit to the shrine of a patron saint, dressing the new monarch in regal attire, his anointment, blessing, crowning, oath taking, enthronement, entrance into the capital city, and first formal act of government, such as the lit de justice in France or addressing Parliament in England.

Despite the representations of harmony and enactment, Renaissance state rituals were virtually always performed within a social context of disharmony. The reality of disharmony presented the opportunity for ceremonial solutions. No monarch was more creative than Queen Elizabeth I in employing royal ceremonies to counter the persistent religious and political disharmony of the realm. Her calculatedly ambiguous actions at the moment of the elevation of the Host during her coronation allowed Protestants and Catholics alike to see what they wanted to see about her own religious commitments. Her ingenious use of the royal progress had her starring in a long-running, moving spectacle of her own fashioning, transforming herself into the adored object of her subjects as she bound them to her through self-display. Her successor James I avoided progresses for more private ceremonies that asserted the divine right of kings, and by failing to display his sacred body to his wanting subjects he undermined the royal sacrality he so ardently advocated in his long-winded treatises on kingship. All regimes, moreover, practiced rites of social exclusion against those deemed criminals, rebels, or even just dangerous nonconformists. Executions involved a public procession of the condemned who was often forced to conduct a formal penance. In Florence paintings of contumacious criminals were displayed on the exterior walls of the town jail as a form of public shaming. Nowhere were rituals designed to restore harmony in a broken body politic more forcefully elaborated than in the Spanish auto-da-fé.

Whether political rituals during the Renaissance exemplified an idealized harmony or countered very real disharmonies, they worked to constitute political ideas. The essential characteristic of political rituals is that they promote schematic thinking. Ritual performances produce schema or abstract formulas that organize the perceptions of the persons who have repeatedly witnessed them. Because they blur qualifications and discourage critical thinking, political rituals may be ambiguous in their precise meaning but direct in their emotional appeal. They seem to proclaim simple absolute truths. They encourage a single course of action. And they achieve these things by framing some images more prominently than others, focusing attention on certain objects, and enhancing some characteristics of a person and suppressing others. Rituals stimulate the senses in multiple ways through musical performances, artistic splendor, and sumptuous pomp. The attempt to create brilliant political spectacles in Renaissance Europe was not only an attempt to garner the attention of subjects but to make certain political ideas plausible and memorable. The combination of instruction in simplified ideas and an appeal to the emotions gave political rituals their power to influence. As David Kertzer puts it about political rituals in general, "our symbol system . . . is not a cage which locks us into a single view of the political world, but a melange of symbolic understandings by which we struggle, through a continuous series of negotiations, to assign meaning to events."[5] Political rituals were part of the art of governing and witnessing them one of the responsibilities of living under a government.

States as Unified Spaces

During the Renaissance most states remained more of a sphere of influence, a chain of jurisdictional authority, and a place of institutionalized negotiations than a delineated geographic space. During the Middle Ages the frontier between two kingdoms was typically the boundary between two villages that owed rents to different lords who were, in turn, vassals of different kings. The lands of France, of course, were a patchwork of jurisdictions divided between the kings of France and England, including some towns such as Rodez divided down the middle. There were boundaries between French and English jurisdictions but hardly a frontier line that could be plotted on a map. In some regions frontiers were not lines but broad bands of territory that was held in condominia by lords of different allegiances, or they were defensive zones, such as the Krajina that formed the Croatian border with Ottoman Bosnia. When Machiavelli thought strategically about borders he imagined a series of fortresses and mountain passes, not a line on a map, and he thought it foolish for a prince or republic to waste effort defending borders since enemies could easily bypass fortified positions to strike at the vital cities of the state. Even customs agents were more likely to be posted at a city's gates than along vaguely-defined borders. A feudal and jurisdictional rather than spatial conception of frontiers was especially pronounced along mountain frontiers, such as the Pyrenees between France and Spain or the Alps between the Italian states and their transalpine neighbors. In sixteenth-century Friuli numerous small enclaves of imperial jurisdictional authority dotted a landscape that was otherwise subject to Venice, a hazy border situation that entangled diplomats in simple matters of local law enforcement. Only with the extension of governmental authority through armed force and a legal bureaucracy did contended border zones gradually yield to frontier lines on a map.[6]

The conception of states with delineated geographical borders that can be sketched on a map was, nevertheless, invented during the Renaissance. Maps recording the geographical position of European frontiers began to appear in the fifteenth century, but their use escalated in the sixteenth, an era positively obsessed with mapping. The Tordesillas line separating Portuguese and Spanish spheres of control in the Americas became a common feature on sixteenth-century maps. Negotiators over the Anglo-French Treaty of Ardres in 1546 resorted to a map to resolve disputes. Various Italian governments concerned with the usurpation of the commons began to survey and map their own territories during the late sixteenth century, a project that heightened sensitivity to the precise location of borders. By 1602 the first map was printed showing the assumed borders of all the European states. But maps deceived as much as they revealed because European states were still not unified geographical entities, and the lines oversimplified the confused situation on the ground. (See the essay by Peter Burke above.)

During the Middle Ages it may have mattered little for most subjects whether they paid rents and taxes to one lord or another. During the Renaissance, however, the stakes of one political allegiance versus another became more costly because of the extension of the state's judicial authority, the government's ability to determine the religious affiliation of the entire state after the Reformation, and the enormous financial and personal costs of war. Nevertheless, the ultimate loyalties of subjects could be confused, convoluted, and contradictory. Did priests owe ultimate allegiance to the state or the Church? The answer to this question was particularly vexed in Catholic lands where they were subject to ecclesiastical rather than secular courts. To whom did an imperial notary owe allegiance since his patent to practice came from the emperor but he might actually live outside the empire's effective jurisdiction in northern Italy, Switzerland, Lorraine, or the Netherlands? These issues continued to complicate the reality of sovereign states throughout the *ancien régime*.

The penetration of royal justice into the hinterlands of the realm had long been the primary measure of the power of a state within its own dominions. The model of a centralized system of justice was the canon law of the Church, which from the twelfth century had employed Roman law principles to create an appellate judicial hierarchy. Perhaps the most persistent conflict of the Middle Ages dating back to the Investiture Controversy of the eleventh century had been over the balance between ecclesiastical and secular jurisdictions within the European kingdoms. The issue was far from dead in the Renaissance, as Henry VIII's dispute with Clement VII or the papal interdict against Venice of 1605–7 reveal. The papacy's use of Roman law deeply influenced secular governments. The supplanting of customary law with Roman law was usually correctly viewed by nobles as an assault on their privileges, by towns as a vehicle for reducing their liberties, and by peasants as an attack on their traditional freedoms. The spread of Roman law introduced standardized investigative and trial procedures, required judges to give written reasons for their decisions, introduced uniform judicial principles enforced by appellate courts, and greatly enhanced the power of university trained lawyers. Its introduction generated resistance against it, especially in France and Germany. But even where Roman law did not hold sway, as in England and Venice, the codification of laws and implementation of courts of appeal produced similar results. No legal innovation assisted centralization as much as appellate courts. In England and France appellate courts rested on twelfth- and thirteenth-century foundations. By the early sixteenth century nearly every German territorial prince had established a superior appeal court. Several Italian states set up itinerant courts of appeal. In Valladolid, Spain, the extension of royal justice increased the number of judicial appeals by 300 percent between 1500 and 1580.

The volume of judicial business soared during the sixteenth century as states attempted to extend the arm of the law into the most isolated corners of the dominion. Most governments could not fill the demand for justice they themselves had stimulated, but the backlog of cases in most jurisdictions need not be interpreted so much as a sign of governmental inefficiency as of the pent-up desire for justice. The very existence of an appellate process altered the balance of power within local communities by providing opportunities for judicial action against local tyrants. One of the most peculiar manifestations of extension of state power during the Renaissance might be the phenomenon of continuous litigation. Many suits took years to produce a verdict, only to spend many more years slogging through the labyrinth of appellate courts, some of which had overlapping jurisdictions. Only 12 percent of the cases at Valladolid, for example, were completed in a year or less. In the Veneto appellants could chose among several courts and if they were not pleased with the result could always move to an alternative court. Truly desperate litigants could sometimes switch jurisdictions entirely, especially within the complex layers of authority of the German Empire. But every case lost in the court system was not simply justice delayed or justice denied but a dispute that had been removed from quarrelsome communities and predatory feudal lords and placed in the more disinterested hands of the central government.

During the last half of the sixteenth century, Spanish Italy, Venice, the Papal States, and Scotland initiated campaigns to criminalize aristocratic violence. These governments forced disputants in vendettas to swear oaths of peace or face the confiscation of their property. The traditional means of conflict resolution among aristocrats, feuding and dueling, were either abolished or confined to carefully controlled venues, which dramatically reduced the levels of violence and forced combatants to recognize the superior authority of the government. The willingness of central governments to hear criminal complaints against provincial aristocrats was unevenly distributed but noticeable in northern Italy and England, in particular. The use of rural police hired by the central government in areas where justice had been exclusively in the hands of the feudal lord represented a tentative, yet revolutionary extension of state power. Lacking sufficient manpower to make arrests and prisons to hold criminals, most European governments had long relied on exile as a form of punishment. Exiles, however, became bandits, virtually licensed to commit crimes. Again during the late sixteenth century, several Italian states began sweeps of the countryside and mountains to root out the bandits. (See the essay by Gregory Hanlon below.)

Nothing made the geographical line between one state and another more meaningful to many common people than the religious ruptures of the sixteenth century. In medieval Europe divine or at least ecclesiastical sanction legitimated political rule, and the evocation of God's favor remained essential to every European leader. Not even the most cynical condottiere cum prince could survive for long without it. The religious divisions produced by the Reformation altered the terms of the alliance between Church and state, but not the necessity for it. In Protestant Europe monarchs still needed to represent divine sanction for their rule despite the fact that royal rituals derived from the Catholic liturgy, which had now been reformed or abandoned, and that the theory of secular monarchy borrowed heavily from the theory of the papal monarchy. If priests and bishops, for example, were no longer to be anointed with holy oil, what about kings? The first Protestant coronation in Denmark supplanted the mass with a Lutheran sermon, but the anointing and even the Latin coronation formula taken from the Roman mass were retained. Henry VIII solved the problem by simply having Parliament declare him the supreme head of the English Church, and although Protestant princes on the continent never went this far, they certainly proclaimed themselves God's vicars.

The success of the Reformation was fundamentally a political act, and many Protestant princes used the reformation of religion to assist the centralization of government. The Religious Peace of Augsburg (1555) provided the model for a solution to the confessional divisions produced by the Reformation. According to the principle of cuius regio, eius religio, each prince of Germany determined the confession to be followed by his subjects, and those who disagreed with him were obliged to emigrate elsewhere. Henry VIII in England, Christian III in Denmark, Gustav Vasa in Sweden, numerous German princes, Lutheran imperial cities, and the reformed cantons of Switzerland confiscated church property and seized independent ecclesiastical estates. Governments assumed the responsibilities of church finances, clerical appointments, public education, enforcement of morality, poor-relief, and hospitals, all of which had once been in ecclesiastical hands. The independent church courts, long a thorn in the side of jealous monarchs conscious of their authority, were integrated into the state court system. In Lutheran Germany pastors virtually became agents of the state, ultimately answerable to the prince and useful agents for disseminating his wishes to the people. The Reformation offered dramatic new opportunities for secular princes. Albrecht of Hohenzollern used the dissolution of the Prussian branch of the Teutonic Order to create a whole new principality for himself.

Catholic princes kept up with their Protestant cousins in employing ecclesiastical institutions to serve state power. The Spanish Inquisition operated under royal auspices, independent of the supervision of Rome. Other Catholic states either refused to accept the Roman Inquisition, such as France, or ensured that it served the political interests of the host government, such as Venice. The Wittelsbach Dukes of Bavaria wholeheartedly embraced the Catholic Reformation by becoming patrons of the Jesuits, implementing the decrees of the Council of Trent, and backing inquisitorial courts. Nevertheless, the Wittelsbachs profited from their dedication to the Catholic cause by taxing the Church, administering it through a council of lay lawyers, and placing members of cadet branches of the family in the most important bishoprics.

The Reformation profoundly threatened the first principle of political unity: "one law, one faith, one king." The discord produced when monarch and subjects avowed different faiths was too much for nearly all western European governments to bear. Mary Queen of Scots's refusal to accept the Scottish Reformation led to her deposition. Jesuit-educated Sigismund I lasted only eight years on the throne of Lutheran Sweden before he was deposed in favor of a Protestant uncle. The Catholic James II kept the throne of England for even less time. Except for a few small troubled principalities in Germany, hardly anyone thought it possible to allow more than one confession to coexist in the same state. Catholic Ireland, in fact, was the only place in western Europe where most of the subjects adhered to a faith different from the monarch's. Religious diversity was more sustainable in eastern Europe because of the very weakness of the state. The strength of the nobility in Hungary, for example, blocked systematic attempts by the central authority to enforce religious uniformity.

The problem, of course, with enforcing religious unity was the reality of religious divisions created by the Reformation. In some places in central Europe there were as many as three active confessions – Catholic, Lutheran, and Calvinist – and that did not even take account of the minor sects, such as the Anabaptists, or the communities of Jews. The alternative to religious unity would have been religious toleration, but hardly anyone in a position of authority was willing to advocate it. Calvin had expelled Sebastian Castellio from Geneva in 1544 for championing religious toleration, and Luther had been aggressively hostile to those who disagreed with him on seemingly minor theological points. After 1542 the Catholic Church was committed to exposing and punishing anyone who professed a different faith. Geneva and Rome became competing propaganda centers, each spewing out a flood of polemical tracts and specially-trained missionaries willing to risk their lives by going behind enemy lines to console their co-religionists and evangelize for converts. Wherever there were significant religious minorities within a state, a condition of anxious tension, omnipresent suspicion, and periodic hysteria was the best one could hope for. The worst possibility was civil war, of which the French Wars of Religion and the Dutch Revolt against Spain represent only the most dramatic and long-lasting examples.

The religious propaganda and civil wars of the late sixteenth century produced a new word to describe a personality type that may not have been entirely new but was certainly much more common – the fanatic. From its original reference to demon possession, the word "fanatic" mutated to refer to a person who expressed immoderate enthusiasm in religious matters, a person who pursued a supposedly divine mission to often violent ends. Fanatics from all sides of the religious divide engaged in grotesque massacres of their opponents, and fanatics initiated waves of political assassinations for ideological motives. The Massacre of St. Bartholomew's Day and other atrocities of the French Civil Wars revealed besides religious fanaticism substantial dollops of old-fashioned political cunning, but the political assassinations of Henri III, Henri IV, and William the Silent may be more indicative of the new kind of fanaticism. In each case the assassin carefully plotted his deed (for years in the case of William's assassin), relied on religious advisers to justify the murder, and was certain that killing the prince was a defensive act that would prevent even worse crimes against co-religionists. Unlike earlier assassins, none of these fanatic assassins hoped to achieve power for themselves or their faction, avenge a personal wrong, or redress injured honor. By cutting off the head of state, they acted on the belief that they possessed a superior understanding of God's will. One of the lasting results of the religious divisions of the sixteenth century was the potentially lethal mixture of ideology and political power.

The backwash from the Massacre of St. Bartholomew's Day also stimulated the systematic articulation of a Protestant theory of political revolution by François Hotman in *Francogallia* (1573) and Théodore de Bèze in *Right of Magistrates* (1579). They argued that since the authority of all magistrates, including even low-ranking nobles, came directly from God, the Protestant nobles had the right, even obligation, to resist a tyrannical Catholic king. During the same period Catholic moderates known as the "politiques" rejected the excesses of the Holy League and argued for an accommodation with the Protestants. Henri IV's resolution of the religious wars with the Edict of Nantes of 1598 allowed the Protestants to build a quasi-state within the state, giving them the right to have their own troops, church organization, and political autonomy within their walled towns, but they were banned from the royal court and the city of Paris. This singular compromise with the principle of state unity not only contributed to the Catholic animosity that led to Henri's own assassination but to a gnawing anxiety about subversion within the French state, an anxiety only relieved by the revocation of the edict under Louis XIV.

The sixteenth century witnessed the growth of political refugees of conscience. After the German Peasants' War of 1524–5 and the Münster Apocalypse of 1534–5, Anabaptists and other religious refugees sought to escape the coercive bonds of government altogether, to find a space where no prince could rule their lives. They found insecure sanctuaries in the Netherlands and Moravia, but the safest havens were in the tolerant East, especially Poland-Lithuania and Transylvania, where the central government was more a symbolic figment than an authoritative presence. After the Religious Peace of Augsburg the religious affiliation of the various German princes further conflated political loyalty with confessional adherence. All over Europe it began to matter a great deal exactly where the borders were. In the case of the persecuted religious minorities, successfully escaping across a frontier began to become a matter of life or death. (See the essay by R. Po-chia Hsia below.)

The Hapsburg Conundrum

Perhaps the supreme irony of Renaissance history is that the most powerful political entity, the far-flung Hapsburg dominions, exhibited virtually none of the characteristics of a unified state, a fact that cautions against overgeneralizing about Renaissance theories of the state. From their homelands in Austria, the Hapsburgs secured the imperial throne after 1438, but what the empire offered other than prestige depended far more than in France or England on the personal and military capacities of each emperor. The German Empire was the prime example of government by negotiation rather than bureaucratic norms as the emperor depended on the support of the 7 electors; 50 odd bishops and archbishops; 21 dukes, margraves, and landgraves; 88 independent abbots and assorted prelates of the Church; 178 counts and other sovereign lords; about 80 free imperial cities; and hundreds of free imperial knights. Emperor Charles V (1519–58) added to the Hapsburg dominions the Burgundian Netherlands and Spain with its rapidly accumulating colonies in the Americas and rich client states in Italy. After 1580, Spanish troops added Portugal to the Hapsburg collection with its thriving commercial empire stretching from Brazil and West Africa to Goa and the Moluccas.

The Hapsburg dynasty reintroduced the old recurring fantasy of universal monarchy that dated back to ancient Rome. Under the leadership of the sluggish Emperor Frederick III (1440–93) such dreams were farcical, and under Maximilian I (1493–1519) a diverting daydream, but under Charles V a nightmare for anyone in the path of Hapsburg ambition, most notably the encircled French. The task of realizing the dream of universal monarchy was complicated by the variegated, decentralized, sprawling German Empire that could only be governed through personal leadership and reliance on the aura of the imperial throne. Maximilian I had attempted to introduce constitutional and bureaucratic reforms to the empire, whose government was decidedly archaic in comparison to England, France, Burgundy, or the north Italian states. The reorganization of the 240 states within the empire into ten administrative circles for the keeping the public peace (*Landfriedenskreise*), and the creation of the Aulic Council as a court of appeal controlled by the emperor, largely failed due to the inherent weakness of the imperial throne in Maximilian's reign. Charles, however, had additional resources from outside Germany that gave him a formidable hand in negotiating with the imperial princes and cities. In opposition to him, Lutheranism furnished a counter-ideology that galvanized disparate elements within the empire. From the handful of cities and six princes who espoused Lutheranism in 1526, the movement grew to engage nearly two dozen princes twenty years later. The success of the Protestant alliance, the Schmalkaldic League, depended on external diversions of Charles's attention, such as the Ottoman siege of Vienna, and foreign support of the Lutherans, such as pensions from France. When Charles was freed from immediate threat from the Ottomans and French in 1544, he was able to crush the league. As formidable as it was, however, Hapsburg power relied on an ephemeral base of support that even Charles could not keep from crumbling. Renewed French interference within the empire led to war with the Protestant princes and Charles's dispirited withdrawal from public life in 1555.

What the Schmalkaldic League had been for Charles, the Dutch Revolt became for his successors. In 1548 Charles annexed the northern Dutch provinces that had been part of the empire to the southern Flemish and Walloon provinces he had inherited as the Duke of Burgundy. Charles's administrative amalgamation of the seventeen provinces meant that when Philip II became King of Spain all the Netherlands went along with the Spanish crown. With his characteristic bureaucratic mentality, Philip treated Dutch affairs as a management problem rather than a tender political sore spot, an attitude that subordinated the Low Countries to Spanish interests. Foreign rule irritated the Dutch who had long enjoyed ancient privileges, including the right to raise their own taxes and muster their own troops. Consolidating the Netherlands under the Spanish crown deprived the Dutch princes of the right to choose the official religion of their lands, which they would have enjoyed had the provinces remained in the empire where the Religious Peace of Augsburg was in force. Philip's rule-by-the-book attitude toward Protestants upset the delicate balance among Catholic, Lutheran, Calvinist, and Anabaptist communities, and Huguenot refugees from the French Wars of Religion heightened the anti-Catholic fanaticism of the local Calvinists.

After the Duke of Parma (regent 1578–92) subdued the southern provinces, Calvinist refugees flooded the seven northern provinces, which united and declared independence from Spain in 1581. The Netherlands' struggle for independence transformed the population of the northern provinces from mixed religions to staunch Calvinism, creating a confessionally grounded ideological foundation for the new republic. The Dutch ensnarement in the French Wars of Religion through the insistence of Huguenot refugees, and the Dutch reliance on England for much needed financial and moral support, created an international Protestant alliance; this separated European states into hostile ideological camps.

Philip II's failed strategy to contain the Dutch Revolt, manage foreign relations with England and Scotland, and to see through the Armada invasion of England is revealing not just of the Hapsburg conundrum but of the limits of government in the most powerful sixteenth-century state. As Geoffrey Parker has shown, Philip certainly possessed a plausible if flawed strategic vision. He attempted to manage his far-flung empire through the rational calculation of means and ends, one of the hallmarks of modern statecraft. No Renaissance prince had a greater appreciation for the norms and legalities of bureaucratic processes. No Renaissance prince better anticipated Weber's conception of how to govern a state. And yet, Philip failed. He failed, perhaps, precisely because he was too modern. Engulfed by an "information overload," neither he nor his ministers could possibly manage all the contingencies of such a grand enterprise as the Spanish circle of the Hapsburg dominions. Rather than the rigid legalities and sense of Providential mission that guided his decisions, Philip might have done better by ruling in a more old fashioned way through a process of negotiations with provincial and local elites, who were masters of the situation in their own territories.

Courts and Bureaucracies

Renaissance rulers had to rely on two basic kinds of institutions to enforce their will: courts and bureaucracies, both of which had important symbolic as well as practical functions. The escalation of court and bureaucratic positions for members of the nobility and even for highly skilled commoners grew dramatically during the Renaissance, a measure of the inflation of government business. In only forty years – from about 1480 to 1520 – for example, the French court more than doubled in size. In every princely regime the court constituted the center of political action, a centripetal force that drew persons of rank, talent, and wealth into the vortex around the prince and his family. The ability merely to be present at court symbolized political distinction and princely favor.

As Norbert Elias argued, the clockwork precision of court rituals and the self-consciousness demanded by courtly manners activated a "civilizing process" that made the regimentation and centralizing power of the modern state possible. The civilizing process integrated social control with self-control, producing not just a well-regulated society but well-regulated courtiers and subjects. The values codified in Baldessare Castiglione's *The Book of the Courtier* (published 1528) epitomized the distinctive rules of court society, which through social prestige spread outward geographically and downward socially from the princely courts. The ideal courtier not only exemplified the Renaissance ideals of civility but established a model for how to serve the prince effectively in whatever he may need. The male courtier must be adept at the military skills of handling horses, wielding a sword, and playing sports of all kinds. He should be able to draw (also a necessary military skill), dance, and play musical instruments. He should know Latin, Greek, and the modern languages. In this eclectic and flexible accumulation of broad-ranging skills, the courtier was the exact opposite of the narrowly-specialized professional. The courtier's contribution to government was solidified by following a code for social comportment that sustained him or her through the unpredictable vicissitudes of changeable fortune. By incorporating the twin values of *sprezzatura* (nonchalance) and *disinvoltura* (ease), the courtier erased the self in the service of the greater good of the prince. The ideal of personal detachment from the consequences of princely policy worked against the visceral aristocratic ethic of personal and family honor, which was one of the impediments of the spread of the abstract, rational state. The courtly ideal was far from universally practiced, but it contributed mightily to the notion of governing through moderate, unemotional deliberation. (See the essay below by Robert Muchembled.)

As a means of centralizing power, however, princely courts posed a dilemma because just as they generated the officials to carry the prince's will to the provinces, they brought the provinces' desires back to the prince. As courts became more important, local power masters were lured to the courts to advance their own interests. The supplicants for jobs and favors grew so much apace that some states had to institutionalize the very process of supplication, creating new opportunities for notaries and lawyers skilled at drafting appeals and for aristocratic patrons whose court contacts made them essential mediators. Sixteenth-century princes attempted to manage far more complex affairs than their grandfathers had even imagined, which made these harried sovereigns prey to their own relatives, chief ministers, and great nobles who had their own client networks to nurture. Clientage represented the most visible form of government by negotiation, but the task of managing clients threatened to overwhelm many sixteenth-century governments. Elizabeth I chose to isolate herself through regal aloofness and a peripatetic existence that kept the court on the move. Philip II protected himself with an encompassing wall of secretaries and a certain monastic seclusion from the bustle of the court, but even he was forced to show himself in court ceremonies to build political support. Others were far less successful in standing up to the strain: Ladislas II of Bohemia and Hungary, "King Okay" (d. 1516), apparently said yes to everyone, and at least twenty sixteenth-century German princes and princesses were confined or deposed owing to symptoms of serious mental disorder, in some cases driven to distraction by the pressures of court life. Emperor Rudolph II (1576–1612), either through philosophical genius but more likely through reoccurring lunacy, proved completely incapable of governing and soon after his election to the imperial throne moved his court from bustling Vienna to the lovely quiet of Prague in Bohemia. Fearful of noisy crowds and impetuous courtiers, standoffish toward foreign ambassadors who presented him with difficult decisions, paranoid about scheming relatives, and prone to wild emotional gyrations from deep depression to manic grandiosity, Rudolph was described by many contemporaries, who had their own reasons to underrate him, as hopelessly insane. Although Rudolph certainly suffered from moments of profound melancholy and irrational fears that may have had organic causes, he was probably unhinged by the Hapsburg conundrum of being the emperor, which trapped him between the glorious universal imperial ideal and the ignoble reality of unscrupulous relatives and petty rivalries.

The necessity to standardize and routinize the work of the court led to numerous innovations, some of lasting efficacy. Early in the sixteenth century the major European powers adopted the Italian model of resident ambassadors who were responsible for daily dispatches and regular reports on the political affairs of the host country. They produced mountains of paper delivered in bundles via regular couriers to the home court where the flow of information from numerous sources nearly drowned the prince in details. Everywhere the archiving of governmental records became a monumental task, and the amount of information gleaned revealed the astonishing capacity of Renaissance states to gather far more than could be analyzed by the few skilled bureaucrats and secretaries. In Spain, France, and England, a privy council of senior ministers attempted to digest information and advise the monarch, but these councils could be just as subject to division and rivalries as the court at large. In the republic of Venice, patricians who hoped for high political office began to specialize in certain territories or subjects requiring technical knowledge, but they seldom served in a single office long enough to capitalize on their expertise.

The alternative to the court was to rely on the bureaucracy, consisting of professionals who were masters of some specialized legal, military, or financial field. Despite
the inconclusive character of most sixteenth-century warfare, the size of armies and
fleets and the amount of time they spent in the field or at sea put Renaissance states
under crushing financial pressures. By 1552 Charles V was keeping in his pay three
times the number of soldiers than were needed for any single campaign. The number
of ships under sail, the necessity to construct new fortifications to defend against
artillery, the devastation of defeated cities, the escalating costs of mercenary army
contracts, and even the enormous growth in civic and peasant militias, all of which
needed training and weapons, drove up military costs. Levels of taxation from the
beginning to the middle of the sixteenth century increased three-, four-, even six-
fold. Although England avoided it, both France and Spain were bankrupt by costs of
war. Philip II repudiated his debts several times despite the breathtaking flow of silver
specie from the Americas. France and England continued to rely on their traditional
revenue-raising methods, which were in any event already more bureaucratic than in
any other kingdom of Europe. But after the middle of the sixteenth century their
methods had achieved as much as they could, and neither state found the means for
increasing the tax yield for more than a century. Resistance to the burden of taxation
prompted experiments in finding more efficient and equitable means for raising
revenues. Florence and Venice had employed tax censuses in the fifteenth century
to distribute the tax burden more rationally upon those best able to pay. During the
late sixteenth century the Dutch rebel state inaugurated a "financial revolution" that
took advantage of the commercial boom to finance the war of independence against
the Spanish. The failure to reform or revolutionize taxes elsewhere sometimes had
disastrous results. Overtaxation led to rebellion in France and the depopulation of the
countryside in Castile where desperate peasants gave up and flocked to the cities.
Russia, where taxes increased thirty-fold between the 1500s and the 1590s, produced
the most telling example of the self-defeating effects of overtaxation. As much as 90
percent of the farm land around Moscow and Novgorod was abandoned as a consequence of Ivan the Terrible's exactions. Countries that successfully created rational
and bureaucratic means for raising taxes, such as seventeenth-century Sweden,
quickly proved their ability to achieve major power status against their unreformed,
unbureaucratized rivals.

The costs of Renaissance military adventures stimulated bureaucratic development in
other directions as well. During the fifteenth and early sixteenth centuries the republic
of Venice, shocked by a series of expensive wars on land and sea, established what can
only be called environmental agencies: a water management bureau to regulate the
delicate ecology of the Venetian lagoon and mainland rivers and a forestry management office devoted to guaranteeing a consistent and predictable supply of high quality timbers for the fleet. Relying on practical technology from qualified experts and
the accumulation of quantifiable evidence such as censuses of trees, the Venetian
officials and bureaucrats generated elaborate long-term plans for the management of
resources. These agencies even exhibited some of the tendencies of modern state
bureaucracies by generating more data than analysis, and official inertia, which blinded
bureaucrats to the consequences of their own policies.

Sixteenth-century bureaucracies remained primitive by modern standards, especially
in their inability to develop statistical tools for the rational analysis of data. But in

another, perhaps less obvious sense, they were quite modern. All across western Europe, at least, governments created new offices with rudimentary bureaucracies to deal with perceived social problems, such as the rehabilitation of prostitutes, the protection of abused or badly married women, the feeding and housing of the indigent, the supply of cheap credit to the poor, the usurpation of common lands in the rural villages, and even the use of blasphemous language. Most of these new bureaucracies failed to solve the problem in a practical way, but their very establishment symbolized the more expansive social mission of Renaissance governments. They became the public embodiments of offical intentions, tokens of a wish if not an actual achievement.

Although the Renaissance invented the idea of the modern state, the actual Renaissance states were still far from recognizing the practical implications of the idea. As a peculiar combination of feudal, monarchic, imperial, and even republican structures, the Renaissance states were still overtly and explicitly governed in the interests of the prince or at best a small aristocratic or patrician class. Only through the bloody processes of religious division and controversy did European states begin to attach a distinctive ideology to patriotism, creating a sometimes messianic impetus behind political loyalty and making politics as much a matter of ideology as of personalities and actions. Some Renaissance states took important steps toward creating more rational, bureaucratic institutions, especially for the administration of justice and taxation, but in most government was a matter of personal negotiation, client networks, the distribution of favors, and the occasional use of brute force. Despite the apparent advantages of moving toward "modern" bureaucratic solutions, these solutions did not always work as well as more old-fashioned forms of personal government.

NOTES

1 Weber, *Economy*, vol. 1, p. 56; Skinner, *Foundations*, vol. 1, pp. ix–x; Skinner, *Liberty*, pp. 3–12.
2 These were, of course, national monarchies without "nationalism" in the modern sense. There is no clear consensus on the appropriate terminology to describe them. "Renaissance" monarchies may be the most widespread term, but the word does not tell us much about what was distinctive about these regimes, which had established a lasting institutional basis during the twelfth and thirteenth centuries. By the sixteenth century they had evolved beyond their primal medieval form in which the king was merely the highest ranking lord, but they had not yet cultivated an ideology of the "nation" as an imagined community to which the people owed their ultimate allegiance. See Anderson, *Imagined Communities*.
3 On the concept of the theater state, Geertz, *Negara*, p. 136.
4 Walzer, "Role of Symbolism," p. 194.
5 Kertzer, *Ritual*, p. 175.
6 Riley-Smith, *Atlas*, p. 7; Sahlins, *Boundaries*; Black, *Maps*, pp. 1–26.

REFERENCES

Anderson, Benedict, *Imagined Communities: Reflections on the Origin and Spread of Nationalism* (rev. edn., London: Verso, 1991).

Black, Jeremy, *Maps and History: Constructing Images of the Past* (New Haven: Yale University Press, 1997).

Geertz, Clifford, *Negara: The Theatre State in Nineteenth-Century Bali* (Princeton: Princeton University Press, 1980).

Kertzer, David I., *Ritual, Politics, and Power* (New Haven: Yale University Press, 1988).

Riley-Smith, Jonathan, *Atlas of the Crusades* (London: Times Books, 1991).

Sahlins, Peter, *Boundaries: The Making of France and Spain in the Pyrenees* (Berkeley: University of California Press, 1989).

Skinner, Quentin, *The Foundations of Modern Political Thought*, 2 vols. (Cambridge: Cambridge University Press, 1978).

——, *Liberty before Liberalism* (Cambridge: Cambridge University Press, 1998).

Walzer, Michael, "On the Role of Symbolism in Political Thought," *Political Science Quarterly* 82 (1967).

Weber, Max, *Economy and Society*, 3 vols., ed. Guenther Roth and Claus Wittich (New York: Bedminster Press, 1968).

FURTHER READING

Anderson, M. S., *The Origins of the Modern European State System, 1494–1618* (London: Longman, 1998).

Appuhn, Karl, "Inventing Nature: Forestry and State Power in Renaissance Venice," *Journal of Modern History* 72 (2000).

Davies, Norman, *God's Playground: A History of Poland*, rev. edn., 2 vols. (Oxford: Clarendon Press, 1982).

Elias, Norbert, *The Norbert Elias Reader: A Biographical Selection*, ed. Johan Goudsblom and Stephen Mennell (Oxford: Blackwell Publishers, 1998).

Ertman, Thomas, *The Birth of the Leviathan: Building States and Regimes in Medieval and Early Modern Europe* (Cambridge: Cambridge University Press, 1997).

Israel, Jonathan, *The Dutch Republic: Its Rise, Greatness, and Fall, 1477–1806* (Oxford: Clarendon Press, 1995).

Kantorowicz, Ernst H., *The King's Two Bodies: A Study in Medieval Political Theology* (Princeton: Princeton University Press, 1957).

Kirshner, Julius, ed., *The Origins of the State in Italy, 1300–1600* (Chicago: University of Chicago Press, 1995).

Midelfort, H. C. Erik, *Mad Princes of Renaissance Germany* (Charlottesville: University of Virginia Press, 1996).

Parker, Geoffrey, *The Grand Strategy of Philip II* (New Haven: Yale University Press, 1998).

Prodi, Paolo, *The Papal Prince: One Body and Two Souls: The Papal Monarchy in Early Modern Europe*, trans. Susan Haskins (Cambridge: Cambridge University Press, 1987).

Tracy, James D., *A Financial Revolution in the Habsburg Netherlands: "Renten" and "Renteniers" in the County of Holland, 1515–1566* (Berkeley: University of California Press, 1985).

CHAPTER SEVEN

Honor, Law, and Custom in Renaissance Europe

JAMES R. FARR

Shelves of research libraries are filled with books on the history of law and custom, many fewer on the history of honor. Yet, as this essay will suggest, all three are similar in that they are what the legal anthropologist Sally Falk Moore has called "regulatory processes," and can fruitfully be studied together especially during the period of the late Renaissance (1450–1650). The upheavals of that time prompted Europeans everywhere to try to impose an order upon a world that was seen as badly out of joint, and the regulatory processes of law, custom, and honor were called upon to impose order as never before.

A vast historiography points out that during the late Middle Ages and through the Renaissance, law and custom clashed, rivals over claims to adjudicate human affairs. The story usually told is one of the "triumph" of the written law of the emergent modern, territorial state and the vanquishing of particularistic, unwritten custom. There is some truth to this traditional if at times teleological narrative about the victorious march toward modernity of the "rule of law," but it rests upon a truncated notion of what law is. It also too narrowly assumes that written law and unwritten custom are the only competitive regulatory processes that held men and women in their grip. What is left out is another such process that arguably had more complete purchase upon the thoughts and actions of those men and women than either law or custom: honor. Honor, law, and custom can very fruitfully be studied together, and when they are, they can suggest to us how power, influence, and interest operated in the lives of the great as well as the ordinary. At times, honor, custom, and law worked independently of one another, at other times in competition, and still at other times in concord. To begin to appreciate the richness of these intertwining regulatory processes, let's begin with an illustration.

A French Illustration: The *Amende Honorable*

On Friday afternoon, May 8, 1643, Philippe Giroux, formerly one of seven presiding judges at the royal court of Parlement in Dijon, France, was tried and executed by decapitation for the murder of his first cousin. This is powerful testimony that the king's written law was visibly in force.[1] The execution, however, was not just an opaque statement about the power of the formal legal system, for just before meeting his fate, Giroux performed a judicial ritual that brought together in one symbolic act deeply held assumptions about law, custom, and honor. This ritual was the *amende honorable*, a particular kind of "fine" that reached back into a misty past of unwritten, rule-giving practices.

Immediately after hearing his sentence, Giroux began the march to the scaffold. The first stop in this lugubrious procession was every bit as significant as the last would be, for he halted between the columns of the porch of the courthouse and, as his death sentence explicitly commanded, he publicly performed the *amende honorable* before an enormous crowd of curious onlookers. Standing barefoot and dressed in an unadorned black doublet and clutching a four-pound taper in his bound hands, in a loud voice for all to hear, the condemned man begged forgiveness from God, King, Justice, and a wronged, earthly enemy. This degrading ritual Giroux dreaded more than death itself for "he feared," reported an eyewitness who kept an account of the execution, "losing honor even more than life; he was less sensitive to death than to this humiliating and dishonoring action." Indeed, immediately after performing the disgraceful ritual, he cried out: "Ah, my father! My son! My kin! My friends! What will you not suffer from this affront that will burst upon you all!"[2] The affront he was referring to was not just the impending execution, but the honor lost when he "paid" the *amende honorable*.

This ritual of medieval origin reached its peak of expression in France during the late Renaissance. It compressed into one symbolic performance fundamental and sometimes conflicting ideas about honor, law, and custom. During the Middle Ages the *amende honorable* can be found in custom, appearing in provincial and municipal customary laws, but never in formal royal edicts or decrees.[3] Indeed, the first mention of the *amende honorable* in formal royal legislation only comes in 1670 with Louis XIV's *Code criminel*. Jean Imbert, an early seventeenth-century jurist and author of a popular judicial handbook, confirmed in 1609 that the *amende honorable* was a "customary" penalty, and appears nowhere in "written [royal] law."[4]

Its late medieval form – the convict appearing bare-headed, barefoot, clad in a shirt and holding a taper and begging forgiveness "in a loud voice" for all to hear – remained constant through the late Renaissance. Only in the sixteenth century would the victims of the crime be extended from the wronged individual to include an almost holy trinity, God, king, and justice. Honor now was not only a possession of an ordinary individual, but of interest to God and king in seeing sacred justice applied.

Honor

Honorific rituals like the *amende honorable* were not confined to late Renaissance France, as Guido Ruggiero's work on fifteenth-century Venice attests.[5] Given the ubiquity of the notion of honor in Renaissance Europe, it should hardly be surprising that it should find expression in punishments. However, the reach of honor extended far beyond criminal law, and likely was appropriated by formal law precisely *because* it carried such extra-legal force. Everywhere in Renaissance Europe honor was

a well-established, customary, and traditional regulatory process that had *daily* purchase on the people living within it. It pervaded the very souls of men and women and
demanded that they conform to certain accepted standards of behavior and comportment. Legislation, in contrast, although equally a rule-giving system but one elaborated as official law and dictated by or in the name of a ruler, nowhere could boast such
pervasive purchase.

The Florentine humanist Leon Battista Alberti held honor as the supreme social
value, that which gave property and even life itself meaning. He would certainly have
agreed that "life without honor was a living death."[6] For Alberti,

> Honor is the most important thing in anyone's life. It is one thing without which no
> enterprise deserves praise or has real value. It is the ultimate source of all the splendor our
> work may have, the most beautiful and shining part of our life now and our life hereafter,
> the most lasting and eternal part ... Satisfying the standards of honor, we shall grow rich
> and well praised, admired, and esteemed among men. The man who scorns to hear or
> obey that sense of honor which seeks to advise and command him grows full of vice and
> will never be contented even if he is rich. Men will neither admire nor love him ... Fame
> and men's favor help us more than all the riches in the world."[7]

In his attention to the external, inter-personal quality of honor measured in terms of
social worth and standing, Alberti sounded a constant refrain in Renaissance notions
of honor. In 1607 the Englishman John Cleland wrote that "honor is not in his hand
who is honored but in the hearts and opinions of other men."[8] Robert Ashley, the
first man to pen a treatise explicitly on honor contended in 1597 that "honour ... ys a
certeine testemonie of vertue shining of yt self, geven of some man by the iudgement
of good men ... Honour ... ys not only in him as yf yt depended wholy of him, but
also in others, whoe must loue and commend that vertue in him which they seem
to allow of."[9] Indeed, even in the mid-eighteenth century and thus long after the
Renaissance, honor was a paramount possession held by the grace of judgment from
others. As one noted jurist wrote, "Of all the benefits of society, the most precious,
without question, is honor; it is the very soul and principle of social existence."[10]

Honor everywhere in the late Renaissance carried this meaning. It came to mean
much more, however. It is well known that the late Renaissance was a time of
dramatic demographic transformation. After the catastrophic century from 1350 to
1450, the population of Europe began to grow again. The encounter with new
worlds resulted in plunder and trade, which combined to increase the aggregate
wealth of Europe. Of course, not all Europeans benefited (tragically, many remained
snared in the inescapable net of poverty), but enough did to launch their families on
upward courses of social mobility. Such mobility seemed to challenge the natural
"truths" that hierarchy was God's intention and a stratified society of ranks his will. It
was during the late Renaissance that, paradoxically, the *idea* of social stratification and
hierarchical ossification was most explicitly articulated *and* when it was most challenged by demographic pressures. Honor was called upon to fix reality, to halt the
flux, and to do so it was encased in social, political, and even legal rituals (like doffing
of hats to superiors, rendering visible obeisance to kings, performing the *amende
honorable*). The function of these rituals was, in part, as with all ritual, to do just that –
to fix however momentarily the fluidity of social reality. Otherwise, all manner of
chaos and destruction would result.

Honor, then, increasingly became a prop to social and political order. Some commentators, like Ashley, wrote feverishly that the well-being of the polity rested upon honor. On the one hand, he contended, "the destruccion and overthrowe of a common wealthe [results from] . . . the want of regard to be had of honour and of shame." On the other,

> mens mynds are not easilie of themselves stirred upp to welldoing except some honour-
> able reward be proposed for good deeds, and some ignominious punishmentes for foule
> faultes and offences . . . Take honour out of vertuous action, magnanimitie will perish,
> fortitude, moderacion, and decencie will decay, the obseruance of laws and lawes them-
> selves will be neglected, offyces of honour despised, magistrates contemned, discordes
> arise among the citizens, and every one dare to do each foule and wicked deed.[11]

From Alberti to Ashley and beyond, Europeans assumed that honor was very much a possession, a "thing" as Alberti put it. As with any thing it could, indeed, must, circulate to have value, and like any commodity, it could be lost or stolen. Lost honor was "infamy," and to lose it – as Giroux did through the *amende honorable* – was worse than death. Honor's value was calculated in terms of "credit" and "debt," possession and loss. It was expressed through reputation, in what esteem others held you, and so to "discredit" someone by allegations of dishonorable behavior, raised doubt among the public. Since honor was possessed only if that "public" judged one worthy of it, and because honor was more dear than life itself, insults might have been rhetorical attempts at persuasion, but if made to stick were, quite literally, potentially deadly.

As society became increasingly stratified in the late Renaissance, a culture of dissociation took ever firmer hold. And not only was it society's elites who increas-ingly distanced themselves from social inferiors. We find the process of dissociation at all social levels and everywhere it was visualized by cultural markers of status which men and women at the time associated with possession of honor. Honor became society's measure of social standing in the increasingly visible hierarchy, and it enforced standards of accepted conduct and measured an individual's actions and worth against a norm recognized by peers, superiors, and inferiors. Duty and obliga-tion, revenge and redress against insult and humiliation, even vindication by violence, were all subsumed in an understanding of honor which relied on the notion that the social hierarchy was established by God and was mediated through signs and symbols by which the hierarchy could be "read." Clearly, then, if on one side of the coin of honor was status and hierarchy, on the other was discipline and subordination.

Until recently, those historians who wrote of honor assumed that it belonged only to the upper classes and to males. In this assumption they were misled by men like Ashley, who wrote that "honour is chiefly incident to those that are of a great and high spirite; and from them farthest removed which are base."[12] Ashley, however, was blinded by class and gender pretentions. Historians now know that honor was a value that permeated all of society and though a masculine construct, it also had feminine corollaries. (See the essays by Joanne Ferraro and Elissa Weaver below.) Attendant to honor were the feminine qualities of modesty and shame. Only men could possess honor, but they could lose it through actions of the women who, in this patriarchal culture, were theoretically under their control. A woman disrespectful of her father's or husband's control (evidenced primarily by sexual license) was deemed "immod-est" or "shameless," and brought dishonor upon the man.

Honor (for men) and shame (for women) were thought of as personal possessions and markers of status (for men) and obedience (for women). Honor and shame were imported into the formal law of polities (convicted female pimps, for instance, were often punished by public whipping and the forfeit of their shame which was an-nounced to everyone by signs worn on their heads reading "without shame"). It was the masculine quality of honor, however, that came to be a possession of the king (as in France) or the commune (as in fifteenth-century Venice) and of God. An import-ant assumption accompanied this importation of honor into the formal law of states: to disobey was to dishonor, to rob king, commune, or God of honor. Reparation for the "theft" was thus exacted in formal sentences, and "infamous" retribution (like the *amende honorable*) upon the criminal.

Law and Custom

Traditionally, historians of law have viewed the Renaissance (roughly 1300 to the mid-seventeenth century) as a time when formal law came increasingly to the fore as the fundamental ordering structure of the European polities. Its history has often been told in conjunction with that of the emergence of the modern state, and as the state grew in power, so too did the influence of law. Within this narrative (which has a vast historiography), one often finds a subplot of a competition between public, written law and private, unwritten custom. Everywhere (except in Great Britain), custom will eventually be vanquished in that it will lose its autonomy, and as civil law it will increasingly be subsumed under the universal power of the state.[13]

This story usually begins in the twelfth or thirteenth centuries with the growth of princely power, the rediscovery of Roman law, and the codification of canon law. These two bodies of written law comprise the *ius commune*, and emerged historically alongside and increasingly in competition with custom, often called the *ius proprium*. Both the *ius commune* and the *ius proprium* were rule-giving systems, the latter being "heterogeneous local juridical norms" and the former claiming universal sweep. The *ius commune* encompassed through Roman law a conception of and direction toward "founding and guaranteeing the commonweal and the terrestrial existence of struc-tures and persons," while canon law "was charged with creating the best conditions, in this world . . . to achieve salvation. Both regarded man in his terrestrial and juridical condition."[14] The *ius proprium*, in contrast, was particularistic by nature and emerged through practice and so had no textual base and no specific historical origin.

The conflict between the *ius commune* and the *ius proprium* is certainly an import-ant story to be told, and when stripped of teleology, a compelling one as far as it goes. We can find the dynamic everywhere in Europe over roughly the same period. Beginning in Italy in the fourteenth and fifteenth centuries, Bartolus of Sassoferato, his student and successor Baldus di Ubaldus, and the subsequent fifteenth-century commentators who wrote the *consiglia* which interpreted the meanings of Bartolism, all conceived of the legal system as a whole, as a universal structure comprised of both the *ius commune* and the *ius proprium*. This was subdivided into Roman law and canon law (the *ius commune*), and feudal law, laws of princes, statutes of cities, of rural

communities, of societies of nobles, of merchant and and artisanal guilds and fraternities, of monastic orders, of religious sodalities, and so on (the dizzyingly diverse
material of *ius proprium*). Bartolism as a whole maintained one very important assumption, however, and this was that in the case of gaps or silence in the *ius proprium*, the *ius*
commune was used as a supplementary source to render the law reasonable, systemic,
and rational.[15]

In Germany, Bartolism (there called the *mos itallicus*) took firmer hold than
anywhere outside of Italy. In 1495 the Imperial Chamber Court of the Holy
Roman Emperor declared that Roman law was to apply when customary laws were
either silent or in contradiction. More and more legal experts trained in Bartolism and
who knew and embraced Roman law (which was published in its entirety in Nuremberg between 1482 and 1504) were available to put this decree into practice, and
these legal professionals increasingly were employed by rulers of "emerging territorial, bureaucratic administrative state[s] [that] had appropriated the holistic aspect of
Roman Law." The opposition to Roman law was strong because such a princely
imposition was "profoundly unsettling to a traditional society so passionately conservative and so deeply entrenched in its localism as was Germany in the early sixteenth
century." [16] Such resistance rallied around the idea of custom, which was the same
everywhere in Europe: a bastion of traditional, immemorial legal practice erected on
the principles of popular consent and usage which defended ancient rights and
privileges. By the end of the Renaissance (the mid-seventeenth century), however,
local particularism fell to universalism as the law of the territorial state brought local
custom to heel.

The same story prevails in Spain. There provincial customs were called *fueros*, and
though these special juridical privileges will be used sporadically in various local and
municipal courts long after the Renaissance, the law of the king will erode their
autonomy. As early as the thirteenth century we find a king (Alphonso X) envisioning
a single, uniform, law code for his entire realm, who therefore ordered the compilation of the *siete partidas*, modeled after Justinian's *Corpus iuris civilis*. This initiative
toward regal legalism met resistance especially from the cities, whose municipal
privileges were bound up in the *fueros*. A compromise emerged in the fourteenth
century as the *partidas* were applied in royal courts, and local customs in rural and
municipal courts.

The conflict in Spain between local and royal legalism continued for centuries. In
1569 Philip II, mirroring French developments, published a collection of Castilian
royal laws and edicts, but still "it was not always clear royal law would triumph."[17] In
fact, in 1598 the jurist Castillo de Bobadilla could still write that "customs defeat the
[royal] statute and have more force than [written] law."[18] Ultimately, however, royal
law would defeat custom, largely because the *fueros* were rooted in a non-commercial,
pre-capitalist, rural world while royal law spoke directly to commercial and financial
matters and so better allowed for the adjudication of disputes of increasing contemporary concern. History (and capitalism) was on the side of legal regalism.[19]

With the advent of humanism and a textually-based historical perspective in the
fifteenth and sixteenth centuries, the universal pretentions of the *mos itallicus* and of
the *ius commune* came under attack everywhere in Europe, but most visibly in France.
French legal humanism historicized the *ius commune*, and as a result scrutinized it as a
historical text relevant only to a specific historical context. Practitioners of the *mos*

gallicus, as French legal humanism was called, like Jacques Cujas and Andrea Alciato, drew the important conclusion that the laws of the past could not be the laws of the present, and so no slavish universal application of the *ius commune* was appropriate to contemporary France. Such a position had two important ramifications. First, it opened the door to such anti-Romanist champions of custom as François Hotman, and second it fueled the movement to codify French customary laws.

For Hotman, the essence of custom was that it was immemorial and through continued use by the people it showed its continued relevance. As a body of rights and privileges rooted in the past, of no man's making and so not granted by any man, no customs could be annulled by a king. Hotman was joined in this stance by many late Renaissance jurists all across Europe: Pietro de Gregorio in Sicily, François Vranck in the Netherlands, Erik Sparre in Sweden, and above all, Edward Coke in England.

In France, Hotman's assumption that these usages of the people were interpreted by judges carried powerful constitutional implications, for according to this view the law-making function was not legislative in the sense that a prince was empowered to declare law, but rather judicial in that judges, as voices of the people, made law in the decisions they handed down. The judiciary, then, became viewed as a source of law equal in value to royal legislation, a controversial constitutional position of shared sovereignty dear to influential jurists such as Pierre Ayrault, Estienne Pasquier, and Antoine Loisel as well as to practicing judges.[20]

The historicizing of the *ius commune* had an impact on the codification movement, too. On the one hand, sixteenth-century jurists such as Charles Dumoulin championed the idea of a common custom (that there were common legal principles amid the bewildering diversity of provincial customs and that these could be sifted out and then generalized to all provinces). This was France's true common law. Roman law for Dumoulin was nothing more than "written reason." A century before Dumoulin, however, a royal ordinance called for the codification of the provincial customs throughout the kingdom. Provincial estates were to come to an agreement among themselves about what their customs were, to codify them, and to submit the written text to the king for review and approval. Of course, this was a political (royal) intrusion into the realm of custom, and one that was followed a century later by the royal initiative to "reform" the customs. Custom remained in the realm of private, civil law and although it could not be arbitrarily changed by royal legislation (as opposed to public and criminal which was more completely absorbed by the crown), it was henceforth placed under the authority of the king. Ultimately, the seventeenth-century movement of *reductio in unum* rang down the curtain on legal particularism. The royally-directed assault on legal particularism which sought to reduce the laws of France to a single, rational, written and uniform system culminated in Louis XIV's codes on civil, criminal, and commercial law which were published between 1667 and 1673.

The conflict between unwritten, particularistic custom and written, unified law was felt everywhere in Europe during the Renaissance, and nearly everywhere the story is the same: abstract rule of law championed by increasingly powerful monarchs and the emergence of the modern territorial state eventually triumph. There was one glaring exception to this European rule, and that, of course, is England. During the sixteenth and early seventeenth centuries, dominant jurists such as Edward Coke asserted that the only law that ever applied in England was "common law" (that is, customary law was never rivaled by the foreign *ius commune*), and, moreover, it was traceable to no original act of foundation. This carried a corollary of revolutionary implications, for proponents of common law argued that as the *only* law of the past common law was the only legitimate law of the present, and because there never had been a legislator in the past, there could be no legitimate one in the present. Therefore, the monarch's interference in England's legal system (by claiming to declare law as a legislator) could be resisted on constitutional grounds. The triumph of this idea in the English Revolution of 1688 charted a different course for Great Britain from the one followed by the rest of Europe.

The "Triumph" of Law?

Such, in broad strokes, is a picture of the legal history of Europe during the Renaissance. Custom (particularism) and law (universalism) compete, and as abstract notions of the rule of law become yoked to the emergence of the centralized, territorial state, law triumphs. Often this story has been told from the top down, or from the center (concentrated political power) to the periphery (fragmented, localized power bases), and most recent scholarship pays as much attention to resistance (the defense of custom) as imposition (legislation by a ruler). The *ius commune* then can be interpreted as a political tool seized by rulers to impose their interests, and the *ius proprium* (or customary law) as a tool appropriated by local powers to defend their local (usually material) interests to counter the incursion of rulers. The *ius proprium* applied mostly to the control and disposition of property, and so was a very appropriate law for subjects to invoke when monarchs claimed access to property (most notably in the form of taxation, in its modern form a Renaissance invention). This could and did entail thunderous conflicts over where private interest ended and the public good began which, in turn, had enormous and sometimes revolutionary constitutional results.

That this has been and continues to be an important and lively historiography, of course, needs no emphasis here.[21] In the best histories, the teleology of the "progressive" triumph of the modern state and the abstract rule of law has been jettisoned, and many historians are exploring the many ways in which the meanings of law have been interpreted, contested, and appropriated by individuals in the past to advance their ideological or material interests. These interests sometimes had constitutional impact, but many historians today are (usually tacitly) pursuing Michel Foucault's contention that interrelations throughout society are structured by continual and endless contests where people employ "microtechnologies of power." As a result, gazes have recently shifted away from high constitutional matters to the ways in which law is about power and how both pervade every social level. The modern state may have emerged from this chaotic, unplanned exercise of power and pursuit of interest, but it certainly was not the result of any master plan of progress. (See the essay by Edward Muir above.)

This approach to legal history coincides with developments in legal anthropology. As legal history has taken a cultural, interpretive turn, the anthropology of law has taken a historical one. Some of the recent and defining questions that anthropologists have asked are similar to ones put by historians. How does law act to legitimate particular ideological and asymmetrical power relations? How are power relationships transmitted through time? How does conflict (now taken to be a normal rather than pathological result of social interaction) develop among groups or between individuals that have different access to legal resources, and how does law (however understood by the various parties) resolve those disputes? Behind these questions sit key assumptions especially appropriate for Renaissance historians about what law is, and how it operates in society. Above all, the "command model of law" is inadequate because it views law as something imposed rather than used. Law should instead be understood as a simultaneously enabling and constraining.[22] In this process people use whatever legal resources are available to them. Access to resources within legal systems, moreover, is not equally open to all, for law itself (however understood) rises from particular historical negotiations among people whose positions in society are determined by relations of hierarchy and domination.

Within legal anthropology three approaches have taken hold which again can speak directly to Renaissance historians: interactional, discursive, and institutional. The interactional approach focuses on individuals and groups who appropriate laws and legal processes for their own ends. The discursive emphasis understands laws and legal systems as elements of a discourse, and thus law becomes part of a rhetoric of persuasion. The institutional approach emphasizes the ordering dimension of law in that law is viewed as preserving power asymmetries, and thus litigating individuals or groups represent specific interests and/or ideological positions.

Perhaps in the discipline of anthropology these approaches are divergent, but they need not, indeed should not, be for historians. Each of these approaches can be knit together if law is first understood as process rather than product. If we think of law in terms of use instead of imposition, then rules intentionally constructed to frame social order can only be a part of the story.[23]

Not only is a rule-centered approach to law reductionist, but it is also ahistorical, for law conceived as regulations enforceable by a government is not historically a universal one. Of course, historians of the unfolding relationship between law and custom have understood this very well. Custom during the Renaissance, after all, was precisely the law that was *not* dictated by government, but we must caution ourselves not to overly dichotomize law and custom. Indeed, there is a "constant struggle between deliberate rule-making and other more untamable activities and processes at work in the social aggregate, and these should be inspected together."[24]

This "constant struggle" is not just between "written law" (legislation) and unwritten customary law, for if we broaden our understanding of law to mean attempted, contested, but never complete regulatory processes, then honor can and should find a logical place alongside law and custom. People are always engaged in trying to fix or freeze social reality, and they do this by representing it as stable and possibly even immutable (during the Renaissance they called it "natural"). To "fix" in this way makes it possible to imagine social reality to be controllable and partly predictable, and this is in part what rituals and formalized symbolic repetitions (so central to the processes of honor) no less than explicit laws or customary practices are designed to do, to keep life from "slipping into the sea of indeterminacy." Yet despite all the attempts to crystallize the rules, and because of the competition between and among rule-giving or regulatory processes (like formal law, informal custom, and honor), there invariably remains a certain range of maneuver. Regulatory processes therefore can never be completely closed, but rather are continually refashioned.

Honor, Law, and Custom during the Late Renaissance

If we think of honor, law, and custom as alternative and sometimes competing processes intended to "fix" social reality, to freeze it in order to render it controllable, predictable, and intelligible, then historically they can and even should be studied together. Moreover, it was precisely during the late Renaissance that these three "regulatory processes" became more consciously pronounced, and more directly competed with one another. This is no historical accident, for it was just at this time that Europeans at least perceived that they were experiencing unprecedented upheaval. Many historians of the late Renaissance would agree that the flux of life then never seemed more chaotic, and for contemporaries never more in need of bringing to order. (See the essays of Linda Woodbridge, Gregory Hanlon, and Ian Moulton below.) Honor, law, and custom were all variously called into the breech as never before.

Europeans during the late Renaissance experienced a demographic surge, economic growth where wealth was distributed unequally, geographic and social mobility, religious upheaval where a unified Christendom was forever sundered, and political changes that realigned power in unprecedented ways. Poverty sometimes merged with religious fervor, spawning harrowing apocalyptic movements, like the one led by the German shepherd boy Hans Behem in Niklashausen in 1476 or more famously the German Peasant War spearheaded by the firebrand Protestant prophet Thomas Müntzer in 1525, both of whom also preached social revolution. Religious fervor and intolerance bred violence and war everywhere in Europe during this tumultuous century, notably first in Germany, and later in France.

The population began to grow again after 1450, roughly the time when new worlds were discovered and wealth flowed into Europe. Wealth was unequally distributed, of course, and along with growing riches for some came penury for many more. Wealth for the few created the means for upward mobility in terms of social status as families with newly acquired wealth purchased land and political office, both material resources that carried honor with them. Poverty for the many created mobility of a different kind – geographic. Agricultural productivity was relatively inelastic and so the increase in population pushed people off the farms, onto the roads, and into the cities. Many of these people were destitute, and their swelling numbers quickly outstripped society's traditional charitable mechanism for dealing with the poor, the Church. By the 1530s pauperization was viewed by people with property (and the leaders of the polities that represented their interests) as having reached crisis proportions, threatening the good order of town, duchy, principality, or kingdom. Throughout the sixteenth century the specter of social upheaval triggered in part by poverty loomed over Europe, and laws like the public welfare legislation in towns such as Lyons or Geneva or the Poor Law in Elizabethan England were fashioned to restore order, to "fix" the unprecedentedly mobile world that seemed to be racing out of control.

Honor, too, as we have seen, was called upon to order the world. Poverty was increasingly branded as a dishonorable social state, and conversely to own property carried honorable status. French men were proud of publicly declaring on the streets of their cities for all to hear, when their reputation had been called into question as a result of an argument, *Je suis un homme de bien!* This meant literally "I am a man of property!" but it also meant symbolically that "I am a man of honor." Honor and customary law (the *ius proprium*, as we have seen, was explicitly about the defense of private interest which almost exclusively addressed traditional rights to property) coincided as regulatory means to secure cherished and related social values – reputation and property.

Honor clearly was linked to the idea of social status, and possession of it declared one's place in the social hierarchy. Late Renaissance Europeans did not invent the idea of vertical social hierarchy, but they emphasized it and graded it more finely than ever before. Mobility created upheaval in social structures and threw into relief, and further refined, the regulatory ideologies – honor, custom, and law – that protected property and sustained social hierarchy. This was a time when social realignments were happening everywhere, and the anxiety about who was below and who was above prompted Europeans to redefine and reinvigorate social boundaries. (See the essays below by Matthew Vester and James Amelang.) Society became increasingly stratified, and one's place in the hierarchy was signaled by visible and verbal demonstrations – performances, actually – of honor.

Stratification between social levels was not the only area of social life that witnessed increased hierarchy. It more firmly seized gender relations, too. It was during the late Renaissance that the status of women in relation to men declined as patriarchy gained firmer hold. Women everywhere lost legal privileges they once held (to be mistresses in guilds, to control property in their own name, for example), and their behavior was ever more defined by the masculine construct of honor, property ever more the preserve of men. Women possessed no honor, only shame, and to breech the standards of modest behavior (usually by engaging in what patriarchal society increasingly defined as illicit sexual behavior) forfeited shame and dishonored the male (husband or father) who in principle was expected to control his women (wife or daughters). Discipline and purity became the operative words, and they were inseparably tied to a salient social value – honor. (See the essay below of Elissa Weaver.)

The late Renaissance was a time of political dislocation as well, and honor and law were once again invoked to restore an order perceived as lost. This story has often been told in the context of the triumph of monarchs, the rule of law, and the rise of the state, as rulers everywhere claimed sole sovereignty and so justified their legislation as being designed to bring order back from chaos. This story is not so much wrong as incomplete, and a fuller picture can be presented when we bring honor into it.

M. E. James, the most noted modern historian of honor during the Renaissance, situated the history of honor in a shift from a society whose values were rooted in the soil of chivalry and family lineage (feudalism) to one grounded in the humanistic virtues of stoicism and godliness (civil society).[25] As a result, by the seventeenth century the ideal role for a gentleman had changed from the Christian knight to the godly magistrate, and the notion of honor in public office came aggressively to the fore. James writes only of the English context, but some of his insights apply to all of Renaissance Europe. He certainly overdraws the completeness of the shift from feudal to civil society, for lineage even among magisterial families continued to be enormously important even in the seventeenth century (recall Giroux's cries about the dishonor the *amende honorable* will bring upon his family). Still, as magistrates everywhere came more and more to rise to the top of the social hierarchy, they brought with them a justification for their exalted social status and this justification rested upon their role as dispensers of justice, a political act. They came to see this task as a God-given privilege and charge. Their honor, in other words, was increasingly bound to their part in politics, specifically administering the law, and their view of honor and the law as the glue that held society together became the foundation of their judicial practice as well as the justification for their claim to high social rank.

Honor, law, and custom, then, can be viewed during the late Renaissance as alternative and even overlapping "regulatory processes" called upon to restructure a society and polities seen as badly out of joint. They could also conflict and compete, as the many histories of the relationship between law and custom have pointed out. Certainly this competition is a result of the upheavals of the late Renaissance which threw into relief these processes, and it certainly has a great deal to do with the gathering of power into the hands of the territorial ruler. The modern state *did* emerge and some of its power *is* rooted in a monopoly of the rule of law. Customary law was eventually subsumed under the aegis of the state as civil law, but what became of honor?

Legislation in the sixteenth and seventeenth centuries in France, as is well known, was only beginning to be codified and "rationalized" according to general principles, and though in theory its reach was total, in practice most people lived their daily lives well beyond its grasp. Most of the time honor and legislation coexisted without conflict. Sometimes, they even overlapped. At other times, however, their rivalry came into the open and contested for the men and women caught between them. That honor and formal law could be rival systems needs no further testimony than the words of Michel de Montaigne. In 1585 this former royal judge wrote: "There are two sets of laws, those of honor and those of justice, in many ways quite opposed." He added even more poignantly that "He who appeals to the laws to get satisfaction for an offense to his honor, dishonors himself."[26]

This rivalry between honor and formal law became increasingly evident during the late Renaissance because it was at this time that royal legislation was attached to the new concept of royal sovereignty, and sovereignty now defined (most famously by Jean Bodin in 1576) would brook no competition. The ensuing uneasy relationship between honor and formal law is well illustrated by the fate of the *amende honorable*. Recall that the *amende honorable* appears nowhere in written law (royal legislation), but during the sixteenth century it increasingly was evoked by royal judges so that, as the jurist Jean Imbert wrote in 1609, it had become "customary to inflict this penalty when the crime is against the authority and honor of God, king, the public welfare, or of the private party [that is, the plaintiff]."[27] In other words, judges rather than kings invoked the *amende honorable* and introduced God and king as wronged and dis-honored parties, now joining the plaintiff of medieval tradition.

Clearly, as countless judicial sentences show during the late Renaissance, the *amende honorable* had an important place in legal practice at least through 1700. How curious then that the *first* and *only* mention of the *amende honorable* in royal legislation occurs in the great criminal ordinance of 1670, and there it appears only in the ranking of punishments by severity. In this ranking it was held to be less severe than flogging, and far behind decapitation, hanging, or confinement in the king's galleys. In fact, it was held to be harsher than only one penalty, simple banishment, which was listed as the least severe punishment that the state could deliver for a capital offense.

The *lack* of attention to this punishment in royal legislation stands in sharp contrast to its prominent and severe place in judicial practice. Here in *arrêts*, or sentences, the *amende honorable* appears with regularity. Moreover, as Giroux's and others' reaction to being forced to undergo this dishonorable punishment shows, its severity was perceived by criminal and judge to be much more intense than legislation would seem to grant. Why such a difference in perception? Why, in other words, would judges and the condemned consider the *amende honorable* more severe than legislation would have it? Why was honor factored into judicial practice by means of the *amende honorable* much more prominently and importantly than in legislation?

The answer will not be found in the king or in the law, but in the judges' sense of self-, social, and professional esteem – their honor, in a word. Of course, conversely one would need to know why the king minimized the importance of honor in legislation. As noblemen, the judges shared with their king a staunch commitment to social hierarchy (which in the seventeenth century had reached its high-water mark in France and everywhere else in Europe) which was increasingly defined by visual demonstration, by performance. They knew in their *social* selves that honor and the law were important ingredients of the cement that held this system together, and served as a crucial bulwark against the forces of social upheaval that crashed about them and threatened the social order and their place within it. They also knew in their *judicial* selves that they, as administrators of the law and as dispensers of justice, were divinely appointed to protect, defend, and uphold, even restore that order. Indeed, their social status depended upon their juridical function and their choice of punishment of criminals reflected this.[28]

It is not by chance, therefore, that these judges tightly embraced the *amende honorable* just when France was plunged in the late Renaissance into a chaos that the Wars of Religion had unleashed. Nor is it by chance that this was just the time of unprecedented social mobility in France, which seemed to threaten the imagined traditional, stable social structure. Nor is it by chance that this coincides with an increase in the incidence of dueling by the nobility of the sword, this despite royal legislation outlawing it. In a sense, royal officialdom and the warrior nobility were *both* challenging their king by continuing to embrace that customary, regulatory process, that of honor.

So, what became of the *amende honorable*? And, more generally, did written law overwhelm honor as a regulatory process as it had customary law? By the eighteenth century the *amende honorable* fell into desuetude. Judges no longer invoked it as punishment, and legal commentators had even come to view it as an antiquated avatar leftover from a different past. As this ritual fell into disuse, however, honor was not conquered. It simply moved onto different ground. Unlike customary law, honor remained autonomous from the law of the state, and it continued for centuries – well beyond the Renaissance – to regulate human affairs.

NOTES

1   The trial proceedings can be found in the Archives Départementales de La Côte-d'Or, Series B, file 12175, and in the Bibliothèque Municipale de Dijon, manuscript 328.

2   Larme, *Relation*. In his dread of the *amende honorable* Giroux was far from singular. For other examples, see Du Rousseau de La Combe, *Traité*, p. 11; Muyart de Vouglans, *Instruction*, p. 823.
3   Lebigre and Leguai, *Histoire*, p. 127.
4   Imbert, *Pratique*, p. 764.
5   Ruggiero, *Boundaries*.
6   Kent, *Household*, p. 201.
7   Quoted in Kuehn, *Law*, pp. 135–6.
8   Quoted in Palmer, "That 'Insolent Liberty,'" p. 321.
9   Ashley, *Of Honour*, pp. 34, 52.
10   Muyart de Vouglans, *Instruction*, p. 412.
11   Ashley, *Of Honour*, pp. 28–30.
12   Ibid., p. 51.
13   Mazzacane, "Law," p. 63
14   Bellomo, *Legal Past*, p. 75.
15   Mazzacane, "Law," pp. 66–7.
16   Strauss, *Law*, pp. 112, 98.
17   Kagan, *Lawsuits*, p. 28.
18   Quoted by Kagan, *Lawsuits*, p. 28
19   Ibid., pp. 129–30.
20   Farr, "Paradox of Power."
21   Kirshner, "The State is 'Back In.'"
22   Starr and Collier, "Dialogues," p. 9.
23   Moore, *Law as Process*, pp. 1, 3.
24   Ibid., p. 29.
25   James, *English Politics*.
26   Montaigne, *Essays*, book 1, ch. 23.
27   Imbert, *Pratique*, p. 764.
28   Evans, *Rituals of Retribution*, pp. 53–4.

REFERENCES

Ashley, Robert, *Of Honour* (San Marino, CA: Huntington Library, 1947).
Bellomo, Manlio, *The Common Legal Past of Europe, 1000–1800* (Washington, DC: Catholic University of America Press, 1991).
Du Rousseau de la Combe, Guy, *Traité des matières criminelles* (Paris, 1757).
Evans, Richard J., *Rituals of Retribution: Capital Punishment in Germany from the Thirty Years War to 1945* (Oxford: Oxford University Press, 1995).
Farr, James R., "Parlementaires and the Paradox of Power: Sovereignty and Jurisprudence in Rapt Cases in Early Modern Burgundy," *European History Quarterly* 25/3 (1995), pp. 325–51.
Imbert, Jean, *La Pratique judiciaire* (Paris, 1609).
James, Mervyn E., *English Politics and the Concept of Honour, 1485–1642* (Oxford: Past and Present Society, 1978).
Kagan, Richard L., *Lawsuits and Litigants in Castile, 1500–1700* (Chapel Hill: University of North Carolina Press, 1981).
Kent, Francis William, *Household and Lineage in Renaissance Florence* (Princeton: Princeton University Press, 1977).

Kirshner, Julius, "Introduction: The State is 'Back In'," *Journal of Modern History* 67, supplement (1995).

Kuehn, Thomas, *Law, Family, and Women: Towards a Legal Anthropology of Renaissance Italy* (Chicago: University of Chicago Press, 1991).

Larme, Père, "Relation de la mort du Président Giroux," Bibliothèque Municipale de Dijon, Manuscript 328.

Lebigre, Arlette and Leguai, André, *Histoire du droit pénal* (Paris: Cujus, 1979).

Mazzacane, Aldo, "Law and Jurists in the Formation of the Modern State in Italy," in *The Origins of the State in Italy, 1300–1600*, ed. Julius Kirshner (Chicago: University of Chicago Press, 1995), pp. 62–73.

Montaigne, Michel de, *Essays* (1585).

Moore, Sally Falk, *Law as Process* (London: Routledge, 1978).

Muyart de Vouglans, François, *Instruction criminelle* (Paris, 1762).

Palmer, William, "That 'Insolent Liberty': Honor, Rites of Power, and Persuasion in Sixteenth-Century Ireland," *Renaissance Quarterly* 46/2 (1993), pp. 308–27.

Ruggiero, Guido, *The Boundaries of Eros: Sex Crimes and Sexuality in Renaissance Venice* (New York: Oxford University Press, 1985).

Starr, June and Collier, Jane F., "Introduction: Dialogues in Legal Anthropology," in *History and Power in the Study of Law: New Directions in Legal Anthropolgy*, ed. J. Starr and J. F. Collier (Ithaca, NY: Cornell University Press, 1989), pp. 1–28.

Strauss, Gerald, *Law, Resistance, and the State: The Opposition to Roman Law in Reformation Germany* (Princeton: Princeton University Press, 1986).

FURTHER READING

Cohen, Thomas, "Three Forms of Jeopardy: Honor, Pain, and Truth-Telling in a Sixteenth-Century Italian Courtroom," *Sixteenth Century Journal* 29/4 (1998) 975–98.

Cust, Richard, "Honour and Politics in Early Stuart England: The Case of Beaumont v. Hastings," *Past and Present* 149 (1995), pp. 57–94.

Farr, James R., *Hands of Honor: Artisans and Their World in Dijon, 1550–1650* (Ithaca: Cornell University Press, 1988).

——, *Authority and Sexuality in Early Modern Burgundy (1500–1730)* (New York: Oxford University Press, 1995).

Filhol, René, "The Codification of Customary Law in France in the Fifteenth and Sixteenth Centuries," in *Government in Reformation Europe, 1520–1560*, ed. Henry Cohn (London: Macmillan, 1971), pp. 265–83.

Fletcher, Anthony, "Honour, Reputation, and Local Office Holding in Elizabethan and Stuart England," in *Order and Disorder in Early Modern England*, ed. Anthony Fletcher and John Stevenson (Cambridge: Cambridge University Press, 1985), pp. 92–115.

Kelley, Donald R., " 'Second nature': The Idea of Custom in European Law, Society, and Culture," in *The Transmission of Culture in Early Modern Europe*, ed. Anthony Grafton and Ann Blair (Philadelphia: University of Pennsylvania Press, 1990), pp. 131–72.

Pennington, Kenneth, *The Prince and the Law, 1200–1600* (Berkeley: University of California Press, 1993).

Pocock, John G. A., *The Ancient Constitution and the Feudal Law* (Cambridge: Cambridge University Press, 1957).

Stewart, Frank Henderson, *Honor* (Chicago: University of Chicago Press, 1994).

CHAPTER EIGHT

Violence and its Control in the Late Renaissance: An Italian Model

GREGORY HANLON

Champions of progress are not always fair-minded in their criticisms. They disfigure and distort the present state of affairs in order to manufacture assent and mobilize action. Our image of Renaissance justice is still deformed by the well-meaning critiques of *philosophes* such as Muratori, Beccaria, and Filangieri, who advocated profound legal reforms. Italian *philosophes* castigated the amalgamation of the functions of policing, prosecution, and adjudication. Reformers decried the severity of statutory penalties and the arbitrary discretion of magistrates meting them out. They denounced the public corporal punishment that was inflicted upon offenders rather than allowing their humane reintegration into society. They condemned the judicial emphasis on extracting confessions from the accused, and especially the use of torture to obtain it. They distinguished between crime against real victims, and sin against God, ridiculing meanwhile the fear of magic and witchcraft. Writing in the more "policed" eighteenth century, they were far removed from the context in which the judicial institution had been created. By then, the tools fashioned to stem violence seemed barbaric in their ferocity, out of proportion to the threat.

We also lose sight of the progressive decline of violence in western civilization, the contours, extent, and duration of which are something of a mystery. From an "anomic" violence characterized by private war and vengeance, typical of the early Middle Ages, we have gradually come to accept state justice, dispensed by public magistrates, whose purpose is to deliver people from a never-ending cycle of retaliation.[1] This decline of violence over the sixteenth and seventeenth centuries shows how waxing state power, more efficient deployment of judicial resources, and consistent church policies to moralize individuals combined to check violent behavior. Although in many ways original, the Italian context fits conveniently into the European framework.

Political Offensive

In early medieval times, there was no substitute for the biblical exhortation, "an eye for an eye, a tooth for a tooth." In the face-to-face universe of village society, the threat of violence was always present. People understood the benefits of reciprocal altruism and the value of cooperation, according to norms maintained by male heads of households living together in close proximity. Being well integrated into the community was crucially important, for access to deliberative assemblies, to grazing lands, and charitable distributions was restricted to natives or long-term residents. Like favors, slights had to be measured and returned according to subtle accountancy practices. People behaved as "intuitive statisticians" (Pierre Karli), continually weighing the costs and benefits of aggressive behavior.[2]

Violence surged from two connected wellsprings, interest and honor, both rooted in the anthropological bedrock of Mediterranean sociability. Planted on specific pieces of soil by strong patrilocal bonds, and protected by kinship groups active to the third degree of descendance, families operated with tight cohesion and discipline. Widespread practices of cousin-marriage and high levels of endogamy tightened kinship groups even further. Village menfolk basked in the public acceptance of their peers, but they judged each other on their ability to provide for their families and to defend themselves from challenges. Cunning, courage, and risk-taking were all virtues. Any slur to the family's integrity or ambitions would be met with a predictable response of retaliation, for turning the other cheek to a challenge was a sign of contemptible weakness and stupidity. All members of the family benefited from this ethic of deterrence, and understood the necessity of standing together with their kinfolk. Not all reprisals entailed interpersonal violence. People could stop short of attacks on people by killing or maiming animals, by destroying crops or felling precious trees. Feuding was often the last stage of an escalation of reprisals between two families with conflicting interests. Potential revenge made people polite, but also watchful. People commonly feared mortal enemies against whose schemes they had to remain alert.

Much violence originated in the rowdy sociability of young males, irrespective of social class. The more frequent violence was, the more it was tolerated and the more the pretexts for it seemed trivial. Often a simple contradiction, the *mentita* was enough to spark bloodshed. Young men challenged in public were ready to swing out at acquaintances for reasons historians often find pointless, but they were acting with the same concern for their reputation as heads of families. This violence is all the more impressive when one remembers that drunkenness was rarer in Italy than in northern Europe, where bloodshed was often the consequence of tavern sociability. Apparently futile clashes like these could rend villages into feuding factions, unless the victim was an outsider, without compelling local alliances. Many individuals, however, had an interest in stifling feuds, and so mechanisms of arbitration, private compensation, or expulsion of the delinquents came into play.

This ethic of mutual deterrence made sense in the autonomous and small world of the village. When people moved away from their villages and the protection of their lords to the unfamiliar world of twelfth-century towns and cities, they often clustered in kin-districts and tight knots of compatriots replicating rural social structures. Cities magnified the occurrence of violent acts (if not their relative frequency proportional to the population) many times. Heads of families or factions fought over access to public office that opened avenues for influence and enrichment. When factions responded aggressively to affronts and exclusion, they upset the fragile equilibrium in the already fragmented urban space, and responded by erecting crenellated defensive towers and fortifying their residences.[3] Relatives and clients of powerful men were not usually innocent bystanders in these disputes and conflicts could quickly polarize large cities around the protagonists. Private justice and private compensation broke down in the urban world.

Citizens required security of life and property. In response to the paralysis of communal institutions through factional infighting and vendetta, Italian cities pioneered new judicial institutions and fashioned more stringent rules governing "fair" procedure. They developed by the thirteenth century a generic political structure designed to restore harmony in the city. Supreme magistrates called *podestà*, imported from outside and holding their tenure for a short time, presided over city institutions. Around the *podestà* appeared counselors trained in law, who advised on the punishment of powerful wrongdoers. As communal institutions stabilized around the fourteenth century, judges and rulers meted our harsher punishments. Italian universities elaborated an inquisitorial system of prosecution, based on Roman law, and honed first in the church courts. Increased procedural severity was not in itself a guarantee of dissuasion. Nevertheless, by the fifteenth century, Italian elites eschewed private, ad hoc justice and composition (that was still common in villages) in favor of codified procedure, interpreted by professional magistrates following set rules.

In Italy, generations of fighting between partisans of papal and imperial hegemony ultimately swept away any institutions providing an overarching framework of authority, like the French or English monarchies. Chronic instability and infighting resulted in the takeover of cities by "tyrants." The most successful of these lineages eventually became "dukes" in Milan, Mantua, Ferrara, and elsewhere. Elsewhere, apparent anarchy reigned. When weaker individuals could no longer look to communal institutions for justice, they would have to join a faction themselves. Faction rivalry transformed criminal acts into political incidents, judged according to the web of connections and protections the offenders enjoyed, and their future usefulness. Widespread desire for order and justice could only accelerate the drift towards princely governments, even if submission to a "tyrant" was not a conscious decision to promote law and order. An astute lord was seen to hold himself above factional infighting and guarantee impartial justice, where there was no realistic appeal to a king or an emperor for redress. The prince usually built a grim citadel on the city perimeter, submitting the citizens and transferring dangerous offenders to dungeons in these fortresses. Citadels were no mere symbols of domination, they were hated instruments of subjection. The Renaissance also witnessed the absorption of smaller communes by larger ones. Princes – and even republics such as Genoa, Florence, and Venice – emerged at the head of a conglomerate of separate communal entities, which considered themselves to be autonomous states of their own. When it submitted to a prince or a larger neighbor, each subject town made a separate pact to maximize its autonomy. While the emergence of the territorial state subjected to a *dominante* and prince resulted in the gradual chipping away of local autonomy, the medieval patrician institutions retained surprising longevity.

This gradual coalescence and subjection of towns centralized power in the hands of professional legal advisers receiving appeals from below in the sovereign's name. The prince claimed the administration of justice in the last resort, watching over city magistrates who frequently were patricians elected to these offices for limited terms. As the legal font of justice, the sovereign could suspend the law's application and judge exceptionally, while vetting judicial appointments. Magistrates summarized their trial proceedings for him, and explained the sentences they recommended. As a rule, any capital or corporal sentence or relegation to the galleys required the prince's signature. Cosimo I de' Medici (1537–74) was an archetype of these princes who administered justice with a firm hand. Ascending his Florentine throne soon after the imperial conquest, Cosimo gloried in his reputation for harshness against people who incited faction and vendetta. He produced a torrent of regulations with respect to public order, outlawing the carrying of daggers and swords in the city and clamping down on new, murderous firearms like the wheel-lock arquebuse.[4] Like princes elsewhere, he established a network of *bargelli* and squads of constables, called *sbirri*, in rural centers, who could arrest and try delinquents in the countryside. They did not so much prevent crime as take over the prosecution of dangerous offenders and remove them from their villages, where they would have benefited from various protections and complicities.

This was still "a society in which violence was an easy, and almost an acceptable method of solving problems."[5] The frequency of homicide, especially those committed by town notables with sordid material interests at stake, was appalling. Urban factions, articulated around noble clienteles, employed vagrants, soldiers, and hired hands as *bravi*, or contract killers. Noblemen in their villages could enlist scores of dependents to raid their enemies and defy the state.[6] In the Papal States, where judicial continuity was interrupted by each papal succession, faction members usually found a safe place in a cardinal's entourage, who backed them in their defiance of papal governors dispatched from Rome to keep order. Faction rivalry wracked provincial towns and district capitals in the Romagna, Umbria, and the Marches. Nevertheless, popes, princes, and patrician councils in the *dominante* gradually challenged aristocratic mores everywhere. Whereas the Emperor Charles V was too weak and distant to be harsh with noble delinquents in Sicily in the 1540s, Philip II intensified efforts against outlaws and their protectors after 1570. The energetic viceroy Osuna (governing 1600–10) overturned mild sentences and combed the archives to uncover suspicious leniency on the part of magistrates themselves.[7]

Authorities everywhere appeared overwhelmed by levels of violence at the end of the sixteenth century; whether this was a wave of heightened violence or the reflection of greater prosecutive initiative is an open question. In Mantua, Marzio Romani finds an oscillating annual average of around forty to sixty homicides per hundred thousand at the end of the sixteenth century, compared with the present-day average of fewer than two.[8] Giovanni Liva links the urban violence to poverty and war, but the late sixteenth century was generally a period of peace and high employment and no group appears as violent as the nobility, who lodged *bravi* in their palazzi, or hid them in villages. Noble patrons and relatives in state and church service intervened in their favor and so aristocratic crimes often went unpunished. Noble *prepotenza*, or bullying, has been little studied over the long term. In the countryside, all men tended to be heavily armed. The contemporary formation of peasant militias aggravated the generalized bloodletting. Village notables eagerly acquired the more efficient wheel-lock arquebuses and turned them on each other.

In the short term, the reinforcement of judicial power, and the establishment of repressive forces throughout the territorial state, inhibited private composition and reconciliation, and helped spread the disorder they sought to combat. Italy created more bandits after 1550 than any other country in western Europe. The greater emphasis on state justice must have added to the trend, by casting thousands of people outside the pale of legal society. The overly rigid repression of delinquency in Rome under Paul IV (1555–9) antagonized people of every social class. The end of the wars of Italy in 1559 then resulted in the layoff of thousands of violent men, led by poor aristocrats. When the papacy confiscated castles and feudal rights in central Italy in the 1570s, numerous noblemen resorted to banditry as a vengeance on the pontiff.[9] Osvaldo Raggio sees banditry outside the Papal States as the expression of an economic and social system founded on the competition of kin groups. Each of these explanations has much validity: all these factors played a part and interacted.[10]

A bandit was an escaped criminal subject to a *bando*, a decree moving him beyond the protection of the law. No specific crime made one a bandit, but most were convicted *in absentia* of extortion, aggressive theft, and murder. Bandits operated in tight little bands of a dozen or a score of individuals at most, frequently living in mountain zones, or in border villages and fiefs not subject to patrols by *sbirri*. They were ideal collaborators in smuggling contraband goods. When bandits were not employed by nobles to intimidate their enemies, nobles cared little what they did outside their estates. State justice was an abstract thing, and far away, so bandits could sneak back to their houses at night and no one would denounce them. Families dispatched someone to designated hideouts or drop-off points to leave clothes and shoes and bread for them. Bandits often depended upon solidarity between themselves and the local villagers. Lookouts would report on the movements of soldiers in the neighborhood; village militiamen might neglect to muster when the bell tolled to call them out; they might even seize some pretext to fight off the soldiers and free their prisoners, if they felt protected from above.

The state's increasingly ferocious legislation against bandits after 1550 was a sign of its weakness. Outlaws were assimilated to enemies of the state, against whom village militias and special forces were mobilized. Tuscan decrees instituted capital penalties for anyone who helped or even spoke to a bandit. Similar laws made relatives of bandits liable to pay victims compensation and to defray the costs of tracking them, inciting families to betray one of their own. Governments often assigned a "commissioner," who led a "cavalcade" of legal personnel and soldiers, to live off the culprit's neighbors or relatives until they were ready to talk. Nevertheless, when bandits enjoyed the support of their relatives, they were difficult to capture. Commissioners often preferred pacification to punishment, and brokered peace between village factions instead. The dispatch of autonomous commissioners to dampen local feuding and banditry was not everywhere successful. Similar officials operating in Sicily lived off the proceeds of fines and confiscations, with extortionate results. Stern measures designed to cut the bandits off from their rural support were accompanied by more expeditious methods of dispatching the ones they caught. Bandits were gradually denied the procedural controls and guarantees that the penal system allowed to others. Sixtus V hoped that planting their heads on public monuments would have a dissuasive effect. Apologists claimed that 5,000 bandits were executed in the five years before his death in 1590, but there were reputedly 27,000 more at liberty throughout central Italy. All the papal garrisons combined numbered only 5,000 men.

The disastrous harvests of the early 1590s – the worst in almost 300 years – gave fresh urgency to the problem by swelling bandit gangs with hungry peasants. Bands combined to prey on major axes of communication, and fought pitched battles with military escorts of merchant convoys. Bandit chiefs such as Duke Alfonso Piccolomini or the Abruzzi notable Marco Sciarra coalesced bands in order to storm sizeable towns. Rosario Villari described the bandit insurrection in the 1590s as a civil war of the countryside against the city.[11] Italian states mobilized regular army troops and cooperated on their mutual borders to prevent the outlaws from slipping away. More effective than the summary execution of suspects by the roadside was the practice of setting high prices on bandit heads, and granting pardons to outlaws who betrayed their companions. Grand Duke Ferdinand I of Tuscany placed 300 *scudi* on the head of leaders, a small fortune, given that 20 *scudi* was a typical annual income; the 50 *scudi* bounty on the rank and file was the equivalent of a good peasant dowry. By making sordid pacts with unsavory characters, district magistrates collected heads of bandits and their relatives. Piccolomini was soon seized by Tuscan troops in papal territory; Marco Sciarra was betrayed by his lieutenant in exchange for a dozen pardons and a sack of gold.

Improved harvests in the mid-1590s, and recruiting of papal and Tuscan armies for service in Hungary and Flanders absorbed most of the outlaws. Once the dynamic was reversed, generally after 1600, the state's new repressive apparatus operated with greater efficiency. The cities benefited first. Venice employed its patrician ambassadors or "rectors" to arbitrate disputes in subject cities, while the Council of Ten could arrest and spirit away to the capital city the most turbulent subjects. In Brescia, where one chronicler noted twenty-five major conflicts erupting in the city between 1599 and 1626, Venetian rectors decapitated nobles and swept away their *bravi*. They outlawed carrying firearms in 1608, in a city where this was the principal manufacture. Nobles gradually substituted for the ambush of their enemies the more honorable duel, which limited the pretext for revenge killings. Urban factionalism declined in the south too, as nobles adopted rules of intermarriage and alternating succession to town offices. The demographic decline of the aristocracy soon resulted in the shared heredity of offices among members of a small oligarchy.

"Gun control" gradually extended into the countryside, although offenders continued to defy the state in tight-knit mountain hamlets. Genoa's republican senate established a committee to extinguish rural banditry in 1651, whose mounting effectiveness rested on tight secrecy and the availability of its own troops. In the kingdom of Naples, Viceroy Del Carpio used absolutist arguments and illegal confinement on maverick noblemen who protected bandits in the remote Abruzzo region. A concerted military effort along the Papal-Neapolitan border broke the back of bandit resistance by the 1680s.[12] The state's resolve inaugurated an unprecedented era of civil peace throughout Italy.

Judicial Offensive

Desperate measures such as the ones described above have obscured the panoply of ordinary procedures followed by judges in order to acquit themselves of their functions. People had good reason to relinquish the duty of vengeance to the state, but would do so only if they could trust its officials to punish their aggressors. By the early sixteenth century, elected patrician magistrates sensitive to the political implications of specific crimes, were flanked by authoritative judges who worked from a "doctrine," acquired by study. We can appreciate their science not only from the books of conclusions judges published after years of judicial practice, but – even better – from the trial documents they produced. Judges had to apply the laws passed by princes and by legislative bodies operating under the sovereign authority. Magistrates consulted local statutes too, which contained a myriad of local exceptions.

Criminal archives in themselves are abundant, but can be deceiving if we assume they are an accurate reflection of total delinquency. The relation of the documents with the criminal reality they report is not a constant one and often reflect only the official response to an incident. To quote Mario Sbriccoli, criminal archives are ostensibly about crime, but they reveal the application of judicial process even better.[13] Judges were often at pains to document each stage of the trial, which they had to submit to superior authority for ratification. Whether or not they wished to elucidate the entire context of the misdeed they were investigating, their investigations often shed light on why people behaved as they did.

Italian judges were especially influential in the sixteenth and early seventeenth centuries, when the operating norms of "authorities" such as Giulio Claro (1525–75) and Prospero Farinacci (1554–1616) were widely adopted. The adoption of the inquisitorial procedure in continental Europe meant that procedural assumptions and opinions of leading judges, published in Latin, would soon be in the hands of colleagues elsewhere. One should not exaggerate the influence of Italian models on Europe, for countries with strong monarchies like France, England, and Castile developed their own, similar systems simultaneously, and Italian institutions could vary a great deal from one state to another. At the lowest jurisdiction, magistrates dispensed both criminal justice (governing the commission of a crime and attributing innocence and guilt) and civil law (determining who owed how much to whom). With the emergence of higher echelons, a specialization emerged and appeals courts multiplied on the model of the Roman Rota. Roman procedures substituted a single judge for a college of magistrates. Where pleading had once been oral, the use of written pleas developed, especially in civil law and on criminal appeal.

The lower-court criminal judge could either take action "ex officio," that is, inaugurate a case on his own authority, or else respond to a complaint carried forward by an accuser. In many places the community designated a public accuser who had to report every breach of the public peace to the magistrate, in order to circumvent the tendency to *omerta* or silence. Judges often began each criminal trial by imposing a truce on both parties, that sanctioned private retaliation with heavy fines. They then proceeded with an *informatio*, and summoned witnesses to come to testify in secret. This first phase ended with an indictment, a statement of complaint that mentioned the identity of the accused and the respective role for each, if there was more than one. Then the accused could be arrested, or summoned (if the crime was not grave) to respond to the accusation, again in secret. This inquisitorial procedure gave much initiative to the magistrate, who could collect proofs, hear testimony, issue summonses. There was much in the early modern process that depended upon private interests, however. Participants paid for each stage and the production of each legal document in a trial. Prisoners were expected to pay for their own arrest, transport, and incarceration, with rich detainees treated more deferentially than poor ones.

Accusers often used court proceedings to incite their adversary to make a private settlement, a process French historians call *infra-justice*, to which the magistrate was usually not averse.[14] If the crime was too serious to warrant a private settlement, the magistrate continued to seek evidence and proofs. The best proof was a confession. Flight was a form of confession, and permitted a rapid conclusion to the trial – but in all likelihood the culprit would never be punished. Most murderers escaped harsh punishment because Italy's political fragmentation made it possible to flee to a safe place. When the accused was in the hands of the magistrate, the latter did his best to convince the delinquent to tell the truth, or else trap him in a web of obvious lies and contradictions. The scribe meanwhile recorded the testimony, if not completely verbatim, then at least usually in the respondent's own terms. These documents are among the most immediate texts we have from the early modern era.

Torture could be used to extract a confession, if the judge had reason to believe that the person was guilty. Given that detective work was minimal, that people were legitimately afraid of the accused and his kin, and that forensic science was in its infancy, the use of torture looked appealing to princes, magistrates, and the general public too. It was not so much a form of punishment, as of interrogation, whose infliction dishonored the victim. In the sixteenth century it was widely used for crimes such as murder, rape, or aggravated theft. Its employ was closely regulated, limited to sessions of prescribed length, usually fractions of an hour, depending upon the age, sex, and physical condition of the suspect. In Italy it entailed tying the accused person's arms behind their back, then drawing them up toward the ceiling, a method called the *strappado*. The magistrate repeated his questions and the scribe scribbled the dialogue, distressed cries of pain included.[15] Any confession obtained under torture would have to be ratified later, however, and fit snugly with other evidence. If the magistrate could not extract what appeared to be the truth after three torture sessions, he had to release his prisoner. Torture was not as effective a method of interrogation as one might surmise, since most of its victims never provided a convincing story. It virtually disappeared in the eighteenth century, before legal reforms banned it.

Barring a confession, magistrates were forced to rely on evidence, in the form of physical proofs or solid testimony from sworn witnesses. The weight given to testimony varied with the credit-worthiness of individuals producing it, with rich people given more credit than the poor, men more than women, people of mature years to adolescents, local inhabitants more than outsiders. Through this testimony, the magistrate attempted to "reconstruct" the truth and arrive at conclusions.[16] Few crimes took place in a vacuum. The community was generally well informed of the issue at hand, *per pubblica voce e fame*, because most crimes were committed between social equals, where social interaction was most frequent.

A typical trial lasted one or two months, if the accused was apprehended early on. The proportion of acquittals could be close to 50 percent, if the magistrate followed the rules. A high acquittal rate reflected the magistrate's lack of evidence and his reasonable doubt. In other instances, the number of sentences rendered represents only a small portion of the number of procedures commenced, with cases dropped for lack of evidence, and others abandoned upon conclusion of a settlement out of court.

These settlements, or *paci* were commonplace instruments in the sixteenth century, ratified by notaries and inserted in their registers. The rapid rarifaction of such documents after 1600 needs to be explored, and may constitute strong evidence for the argument that Italians entrusted the state more readily to inflict revenge on their behalf.

In more serious crimes, the suspects were detained in prisons. These were not ordinarily places where one was sentenced as punishment, except in large cities. In most communities they were holding pens for the duration of the trial. Debtors and people suspected of fraudulent bankruptcy also languished there while their families raised funds to pay creditors. The consequences of prison confinement varied a great deal, depending upon the jurisdiction and the social status of the accused. Poorly kept prisons (this was not universal) were frequently fatal. Inmates deprived of money or connections could die of malnutrition, while everyone was exposed to fevers or typhus. Dangerous offenders and political prisoners were confined instead to fortress dungeons, such as the Castello Sant'Angelo in Rome.

In sentencing the convicted offender, magistrates enjoyed wide and increasing latitude. Statutory penalties inscribed into medieval municipal customs were gradually deemed too harsh to apply. Since the inquisitorial procedure was attentive not just to guilt or innocence, but also to determining exactly what had happened, magistrates paid consideration to the circumstances surrounding the crime: whether there was provocation or instigation, complicity or recidivism. They accounted for the age and social status of the offender and of the victim, and their credit in the community. There were many "qualities" to the crime that allowed the magistrate to arbitrarily select a sentence from a wide range of options. They consulted their textbooks, and picked from the opinions of famous magistrates the sentence that seemed best to fit the case at hand. Pecuniary fines were common for aggravated assault. Other times, they exiled culprits from the jurisdiction, or banished them to isolated malarial zones for a specific duration. Serious crimes warranting the death penalty might be punished instead with time chained to a galley bench, if the offender was male and able-bodied. Tribunals often sentenced men by the batch to that fate when a galley fleet was mobilizing.

The penalty decreed by the judge would not necessarily be applied. First, because perpetrators of serious crimes took refuge in nearby jurisdictions, and early extradition agreements between states applied principally to important criminals. As time lapsed, emotions dulled and repentant or impatient criminals went through official channels to obtain pardons. Clemency was applied either when the culprit showed some sign of being rehabilitated, or when he could find influential people ready to answer for him. Negotiations with the victim's family usually led to a reconciliation and a peace-making ceremony. When the culprit languished in prison awaiting execution, princes usually exercised their prerogative to show clemency. Unpremeditated murders were rarely punished with death even if the statutory sentence called for it. Granting pardons and exemptions in response to a petition was fundamental to the manner of governing in early modern Europe. Princes and judges, operating on a continuous scale of outrage, reserved the harshest demonstrations for the most incorrigible subjects, and showed mercy to the others. The more the crime was judged serious, and the more the accused had a record of recidivism, the more readily he was prosecuted and punished with a severe sentence.

There was a sharp sixteenth- and seventeenth-century drop in the number of capital executions, that testifies to a changing sensitivity towards capital punishment. Murderers and notorious thieves made up the great majority of the hangman's victims.[17] Capital punishment for sodomy was no longer inflicted in Florence, and while applied in Palermo until 1640, it disappeared suddenly thereafter. Gaming, blasphemy, and sexual deviancy that once occasioned harsh penalties became identified rather as deplorable private vices, that governments were disinclined to prosecute vigorously.[18] Probably, too, the drop in capital executions corresponds to a corresponding drop in homicides, but the connection has not yet been explored.

Where we have reasonably complete archives of prosecution for both secular and ecclesiastical courts, the evidence shows a sharp decline of violent crime after 1600, beginning with the upper classes. In Siena, nobles committed 30 percent of homicides prosecuted in 1600, 16 percent by mid-century and then only 8 percent by 1700, much closer to their proportion of the population.[19] Part of this decline reflects the decline of noble numbers in an era of economic contraction, but vigorous prosecution of noble delinquents had been a judicial emphasis since the time of Cosimo I, and Florentine magistrates and officials in Siena were free from clientele ties to the delinquents. In Brescia, a city rocked by the eruption of noble violence as late as the 1630s, those habits seemed passé by 1670 and ceased almost completely before the end of the century. Changing mores resulted in a substantial increase in the average life-span of Neapolitan noblemen once faction fighting, ambushes, and duels were no longer commonplace.

It is worth noting that the period after 1620 was marked by a sharp decline of manufactures, with mounting unemployment in the cities of north and central Italy. After 1630 the land market and grain prices collapsed, and Italy suffered a prolonged economic depression until well into the eighteenth century. The disciplining trend of Italian society was immune to the economic downturn, or rather, the effects of the depression were not enough to reverse the disciplinary process. Young aristocrats were ever more numerous in flocking to the court of the prince and seeking church benefices to stave off poverty and obscurity. Peasant expropriation resulted in the spread of *mezzadria* (sharecropping polyculture) over most of north-central Italy. While peasant incomes declined, the sharecropping institution ensured that hostile neighbors would move away from each other after a few seasons, thus cooling the friction arising from the proximity of men and livestock. The increasing submission of both noblemen and peasants to powerful employers and their insertion into an ever tighter hierarchy offset the effects of penury and misery.

The preceding exposition has emphasized the hierarchical, almost orderly system of basic and appeals jurisdictions emanating from the prince towards the rural parishes in his dominion. This simplicity would be entirely inaccurate, for early modern individuals belonged to specific corporations with their particular privileges. Italy was not original. Aristocrats were generally not subject to the lower courts at all, but rather their crimes were judged by superior magistrates from the outset. People belonging to artisanal or commercial corporations were subject to those courts if their minor offenses pitted them against other members. State tax agencies, such as the salt gabelles, investigated and judged cases against smugglers and their accomplices. Military courts judged offenses committed by soldiers, while the sentences of state judges against militiamen were subject to revision by militia leaders mindful of their privileges.

Italians also tolerated two medieval jurisdictions still powerful in the early modern era. Feudal jurisdictions were enclaves in the early modern state; the extent of immunity to state jurisdiction depended upon the feudal charter of foundation. In the kingdom of Naples and Sicily, feudal jurisdictions comprised the great majority – upwards of 90 percent of the communities, encompassing three-quarters of the population. Noblemen had purchased or acquired by royal favor the privilege of *mero et misto imperio*, the right to judge on appeal, even for capital offenses. This gave feudatories the power of life and death over their vassals. The royal government also depended upon feudal magistrates and their *sbirri* to intercept wrongdoers, and feudal lords maintained dungeons in their castles and palazzi.[20] Feudal lords were auxiliaries of the Spanish king's viceroy, but were not entitled to judge cases personally. Rather, they appointed magistrates who followed the same procedures as royal judges. Fines and confiscations that would normally devolve to the public treasury would enter the feudal revenues instead. The local judge generally required the consent of the local community (*università*) before assuming his function, and at the end of it he was subject to a review in which people could bring complaints of bias or denial of justice against him. The feudal lord was expected to retain another magistrate to review the trial transcript and judge more serious cases on appeal. The baron could mitigate the sentence if he judged it apropos.

In central and northern Italy, feudal jurisdictions were less numerous, and increasingly after 1600 their judges could no longer try serious crimes such as homicide or highway robbery, which devolved to state-appointed magistrates in the capital or some other city. Fief-holders themselves resided in capital cities. Court employment was much more lucrative for an aristocrat than the meager returns of fines and confiscations levied on peasants. From the rare research on feudal jurisdictions, it does not appear that lords abused their power. If abuse there was, it was likely in excessive lenience towards habitual offenders, and a corresponding denial of justice to the victim. Seigneurial pardon was a useful tool to cultivate good will and loyalty, which the lord needed if he wished to head off complaints his vassals could always direct towards the prince.[21]

Church immunities applied to all ecclesiastics, and Italy differed from other countries by the vigor with which the clergy defended its rights. Delinquent ecclesiastics answered to the bishop's court if they were secular clerics, and to the disciplinary institutions of their order if they were regular clerics. Church courts run by the diocesan vicar-general and the bishop routinely meted out excommunication against lay judges and subalternate personnel who interfered with their autonomy. Recruited among male bachelors of good family, the most violence-prone part of the general population, clerics appeared frequently in the annals of crime. About half the secular clergy was comprised of clerics in minor orders, not full-fledged priests entrusted with parishes or the care of souls. Integrated into family networks, with time on their hands, and subject to formal celibacy, their ecclesiastical career was not always voluntary, still less a calling. A history of crime that neglects the ecclesiastical courts is seriously deficient, given the number of delinquent priests they processed.[22] Diocesan vicars followed the same procedures as state judges; suspects were detained in prisons and paid for their own detention. These courts were less inclined to shed blood or apply corporal penalties to priests, so punished wrongdoers with exile, or deprivation of their benefice. Regular clerics could be confined to a cell –

the monastery cell was the prototype of the modern prison cell – for long periods of time. Chief among the church immunities was sanctuary, allowing criminal suspects refuge in church buildings. These rights were clarified by the bull Inter Alia (1591) authorizing church authorities to deliver dangerous criminals to state authorities under closely controlled conditions. The creation of a papal Congregation of the Jurisdiction in the 1620s further strengthened the Church's hand, as a separate administration in Rome scrutinized every perceived infraction of the rules, and pious Italian princes thought it wiser not to provoke controversy. The Church's rules on sanctuary were generally observed by Italian states until the eighteenth century.

Religious Offensive

Between the actions of state judges, backed by the prince, and church judges backed by the bishop, there was reasonable certitude by 1650 that wrongdoers would be punished. This meant that there would be fewer violent acts to begin with, and more confidence in the judiciary's management of them. But the emphasis on repression is not enough to explain the profound transformation of individual behavior. The legitimacy of the Church, like the state and the judiciary, hinged on its ability to guarantee the security of people both rich and poor. Priests had always been peace-makers. By imposing monogamy on everyone, the Catholic Church democratized the marriage bond and forced families to widen their horizons and enter into blood alliances with outsiders. While the Church did not eliminate cousin-marriages, it did exercise greater control over the process, requiring people to obtain prior dispensation from the bishop's court, which entailed an inquest, expenditure, and delay. The reform of the clergy itself was one of the goals of the Council of Trent, and the policies designed to control and improve local clerics put into place in the 1570s were applied constantly for two full centuries. I need not mention those designed to weed out ignorant or neglectful clerics; or those aiming to provide them with proper intellectual baggage; or to adhere to the requirements of canonical norms, such as celibacy. Counter-Reformation sensibility aimed at taming passions that tempted individuals and families, just as the prince sought to tame the passions of factions and communities to blend them into a single, subservient polity. Guido Ruggiero describes the trend as a move away from an exuberant Carnival nature to a dour, controlled Lenten climate. Moralists evoked neo-stoic strictures distinguishing correct and incorrect forms of passion. Perverse natural attractions needed to be yoked, tamed, or kept in bounds, by punishment on the one hand, and by self-control on the other.[23] Regular clerics were the instigators of the transformation, defining and implementing their own *disciplina*, a watchful repression exercised silently by each individual. Regular orders were also the first to tighten the norms: the Capuchins broke away from the most austere branch of the Franciscan order in the 1520s on the grounds they were too lax. Public opinion certainly applauded the prelacy's greater control over clerics, for their good behavior underlay social harmony. Priests rivaled judges as functionaries in their communities, writing marriage contracts and wills, formulating petitions, assessing taxes, healing the sick, pacifying disputes. Any clerical reform had an impact on other people. In the diocese of Siena, the bishops used church courts to reform clerical morals, and the most intense policing of them occurred around the mid-seventeenth century.

Moral reform of the rest of the population was an explicit aim of church leaders. By virtue of its sacraments, its compulsory attendance at mass, by the heavy Inquisition presence, Catholicism was a constraining religion designed to impose outward conformity. The Church obliged people to participate in church rites and to take Easter communion annually. Communion entailed prior confession, which required all individuals to bury their quarrels. One weapon the church hierarchy employed was stigmatization, subjecting the victim to a measure of exclusion, which could take different forms. A form more frequently applied in the seventeenth century was exclusion from communion, reserving absolution of grave sins to the bishop. Reintegration of the guilty party often took the form of a public ceremony that shamed the obdurate in the eyes of their neighbors. Bishops required parish priests to compile a list of non-pascalizers and to forward it to them to investigate the cause. In Mantua, Duke Guglielmo (r. 1560–87) also expected parish priests to draw his attention to such non-pascalizing, feuding individuals.[24] So sacramental institutions isolated people who placed their private rancour above societal restraints.

The Counter-Reformation promotion of devotional confraternities placed increasing emphasis on individual and collective prayer and soul-searching. The reinforcement of voluntary confraternity religion also brought individuals into social groups practicing solidarity and fraternity, eschewing disputes and litigation among the members. In the Piedmontese villages studied by Angelo Torre, confraternity religion, parish control over sacraments, and increased state control operated simultaneously.[25] The outcome of all these measures was a "virtuous circle" (Di Simplicio's term) of moral reform. Better-behaved and better-controlled priests raised expectations in each other and inspired lay persons to imitation. Priests then imposed stricter norms of behavior upon the rest of society.

Humanists contributed to the effort. Manuals for raising Christian children began to multiply after the 1470s. Erasmus of Rotterdam wished to inculcate into children the ponderation of the elderly he called *gravitas*. Erasmus's own works were proscribed by the Index, but Catholic writers in Italy elaborated versions inspired by them. Many such guidebooks to proper behavior were published like pamphlets, with detachable pages listing a few maxims. They guided a Christian deportment increasingly at odds with the agonistic honor ethic of old.[26] The school was an important place of socialization, and as educational institutions made great strides in sixteenth-century cities, so religious orders imposed this program on young males, the most turbulent category of the population. The multiplication of Jesuit colleges after 1545 marked the onset of a civilizing trend of great importance. There were almost 300 such colleges in Europe by 1600, and 669 in 1750, in addition to colleges of other orders inspired by their program, with on average several hundred students each.[27] Jesuits placed great emphasis on the monastic ideal of "modesty", which they drilled into their charges as the basis of good behavior. They exercised vigilance over body language day and night, without respite. The colleges stimulated a demand for literacy in the lower years and also provided catechism instruction and the inculcation of good manners. Piarist schools in Italian cities were created primarily from this religious wellspring, to teach catechism and to inculcate the "fear of God" into children.

Corporal punishments followed for the intractable. Individuals were thus brought up to control their passions better.

The growing contrast between the cities and their disciplining institutions, and the countryside, left to itself, came to appear untenable by the first decades of the seventeenth century, as levels of violent crime began to decline. The Counter-Reformation model of behavior was applied to the Catholic European countryside beginning in the seventeenth century, through the increased emphasis placed on confession. The confessional appears in Italian churches around the time of Trent (1545–63), and it was commonplace by 1600. Confession handbooks multiplied to help train ecclesiastics to hear confession, to judge the category and the gravity of individual sins, and to mete out the appropriate penance. Bishops examined priests repeatedly on their ability to administer confession and penance. The most prized confessors were friars, since people hesitated to confide their worst sins to parish clergy whose shortcomings they knew too well, and who knew them too well.[28] Capuchins appear active in Tuscany in the 1640s, having as one of their principal aims the extinguishing of hatred and vendetta. Missionary efforts redoubled force in the kingdom of Naples with Innico Caracciolo (during 1667–85), and then expanded again in the eighteenth century with the creation of the Redemptorist order. The religious message the missionaries bore was simplified, miraculistic, fearful, but they intended to inculcate individuals with a heightened conscience through their teachings – such as the cult of the Guardian Angel, a tool of self-surveillance. Their emphasis was on the duties of the Christian, on ethics, not doctrine. Missionaries were assisted locally by parish priests, who put themselves at the disposal of the monks to hear confession. Missionaries judged their results by the number and fervor of the full confessions they heard. They brought great pressure to bear on a small number of individuals who were public sinners. They excoriated vendetta and crimes of honor, and virtually obliged the obdurate to reform or leave. Notarial archives should reveal the impact of these campaigns by the number of pacification treaties they contain.

Conclusion

It is pointless to speak of changing "mentalities" in the evolution of violent behavior, for that concept is tautological and explains nothing at all. Deviance in its various forms obeys a curious rationality, albeit one with a short operant time-horizon, proper to delinquent individuals. The frequency of the deviant act is affected by any social change that modifies the benefits and disadvantages accruing to it. Princes, judges, priests, and the people they governed had good reasons for calling for more stringent controls, as Italians learned to identify with ever larger communities. By the late seventeenth century, reform efforts enjoyed considerable momentum. Absolutist princes imposed peace on factions and called nobles to their courts in the *dominante*. Magistrates applied the laws regularly and with increasing discretion in a rough pyramid of jurisdictions. Churchmen worked alongside the state to tame morals, and local notables often placed themselves at the service of the Inquisition and the ecclesiastical hierarchy to pressure delinquents to reform or leave.

Late seventeenth-century reformers were no longer preoccupied with violence, but with humanizing the judicial system and rendering it more efficient. State servants in

Florence under Cosimo III, under Victor Amedeus II in Turin, or clerical functionaries in the Rome of Innocent XI, wished to repress abuses in the system in order to
make it fairer to the accused, following guidelines of public utility. Simultaneously,
new guides on criminal and civil justice appeared in the vernacular, destined for larger
audiences. Demystification of the judicial process went hand in hand with the
emergence of a civil society that was itself the outcome of the great reforms. This
was not yet the Enlightenment era, which would soon repudiate the very instruments
that imposed the civilizing process, but the terminus of an inventive and pragmatic
reordering process beginning in the Renaissance. At the end of this *progress*, magistrates were still confronted with Original Sin; that is, while rates of violence declined
in ways we can measure, people (men, by far) continued to maim and murder their
neighbors for reasons that appear to be universal and constitutive of human nature.

How successful princes, magistrates, and priests were at curbing violence is still in
need of evidence. Crime statistics are certainly misleading; but they are indicative of
minima, which can then be compared to subsequent periods, when records are more
abundant and distortions more visible. Like crime statistics in our own time, they may
have been a good reflection of serious crime, which elicited the most outrage from
victims and bystanders alike. We urgently need more quantitative work on homicide
over the long duration, using all the sources available: not only archives of the
superior courts, but church court records, local courts, administrative correspondence, letters of remission, feudal courts, notarial peace treaties. A *nominative* body
count should be attentive whenever possible to the context of each case, the degree of
premeditation, the presence of weapons, the intervention of protectors, the means of
pacification, the sentence pronounced. With the body count, we need a map, for we
know that vendetta was not everywhere commonplace, even in the sixteenth century.
In addition, our knowledge of the frequency of capital punishment is still rudimentary. Until this work is undertaken, some of the most important features of modern
civilization will remain muddled in impressionistic speculation or mere hypothesis.

NOTES

1   Soman, "Deviance," pp. 3–28. I wish to thank Professor Soman for graciously reviewing
    this essay.
2   For the theory of accountancy, see Pierre Karli, *Aggression*, p. 176.
3   Zorzi, "Politique criminelle," pp. 91–110.
4   Guarini, "Produzione di leggi."
5   Davidson, "Local community."
6   Muir, *Mad Blood*.
7   Marrone, *Città*, pp. 55, 118.
8   Romani, "Criminalità" and Politi, *Aristocrazia*, p. 382.
9   Polverini Fosi, *Società violenta*, p. 48.
10 Raggio, *Faide*, p. 209.
11 Villari, *Rivolta antispagnola*, pp. 68–90.
12 Sabatini, "Fiscalità."
13 Sbriccoli, "Fonti giudiziarie"; see the response by Edoardo Grendi, "Risposta a Mario
    Sbriccoli."

14 Allegra, "Oltre"; Brackett, *Criminal Justice*, p. 90.
15 Cohen and Cohen, *Words and Deeds*, pp. 121–5.
16 Astarita, *Village Justice*, pp. 58–62.
17 Cutrera, *Cronologia*.
18 Zorzi, "Politique criminelle."
19 Di Simplicio, *Peccato*, see tables pp. 101, 130.
20 Labrot, *Quand l'histoire*, p. 101.
21 Doria, *Uomini*, pp. 241ff; Bobbioni, "Conflittualità"; the clemency of feudal justice appears clearly in the Tuscan fief of Montefollonico (1619–65), Archivio Comunale di Torrita 593–611 Criminale.
22 Di Simplicio, "Giustizia ecclesiastica."
23 Ruggiero, *Binding Passions*, pp. 8–14.
24 Romani, "Criminalità."
25 Torre, "Consumo" and "Politics."
26 Niccoli, *Seme*, pp. 117–32.
27 Faralli, "Missioni dei Gesuiti."
28 Mezzadri, "Missioni popolari."

REFERENCES

Allegra, Luciano, "Oltre le fonti criminale: Chieri nel '500'," *Quaderni Storici* 17 (1982).

Astarita, Tommaso, *Village Justice: Community, Family and Popular Culture in Early Modern Italy* (Baltimore: Johns Hopkins University Press, 1999).

Bobbioni, Maria Teresa, "Conflittualità e amministrazione della giustizia in un feudo padano tra la fine del '500 e il primo trentennio del '600," in *Persistenza feudale e autonomie comunitative in stati padani fra Cinque e Settecento*, ed. Giovanni Tocci (Bologna: CLUEB, 1988).

Brackett, John, *Criminal Justice and Crime in Late Renaissance Florence, 1537–1609* (Cambridge: Cambridge University Press, 1992).

Cohen, Thomas V. and Cohen, Elizabeth S., *Words and Deeds in Renaissance Rome: Trials before the Papal Magistrates* (Toronto: University of Toronto Press, 1993).

Cutrera, Antonio, *Cronologia dei giustiziati di Palermo, 1541–1891* (Palermo, 1917).

Davidson, Nicolaus S., "An Armed Band and the Local Community on the Venetian Terra Ferma in the Sixteenth Century," in *Bande armate, banditi, banditismo e repressione di giustizia negli stati europei di antico regime*, ed. Gherardo Ortalli (Rome: Jouvence, 1986).

Di Simplicio, Oscar, "La giustizia ecclesiastica e il processo di civilizzazione," *Bollettino Senese di Storia Patria* 97 (1990).

——, *Peccato, penitenza, perdono: Siena 1575–1800. La formazione della coscienza dell'Italia moderna* (Milan: Franco Angeli Storia, 1994).

Doria, Giorgio, *Uomini e terre di un borgo collinare, dal XVI al XVIII secolo* (Milan: A. Giuffrè, 1968).

Faralli, Carla, "Le missioni dei Gesuiti in Italia (sec. XVI–XVII): Problemi di una ricerca in corso," *Bolletino della società studi valdesi* 138 (1975).

Grendi, Edoardo, "Sulla 'storia criminale': risposta a Mario Sbriccoli," *Quaderni Storici* 73 (1990).

Guarini, Fasano, "Produzione di leggi e disciplinamento nella Toscana granducale tra Cinque e Seicento. Spunti di ricerca," in *Disciplina dell'anima, disciplina del corpo e disciplina della società tra medioevo ed età moderna*, ed. Paolo Prodi (Bologna: Il Mulino, 1994).

Karli, Pierre, *Animal and Human Aggression*, trans. S. M. Carmona and H. Whyte (Oxford: Oxford University Press, 1991).

Labrot, Gérard, *Quand l'histoire murmure: Villages et campagnes du royaume de Naples, XVe–XVIIIe siècles* (Rome: École Française de Rome, 1995).

Marrone, Giovanni, *Città, campagna e criminalità nella Sicilia moderna* (Palermo: Palumbo, 1955).

Mezzadri, Luigi, "Le missioni popolari dei lazzaristi nell'Umbria (1675–1797)," *Vincent de Paul: Actes du Colloque International d'Études Vincentiennes* (Rome: Edizioni Vincenziane, 1981).

Muir, Edward, *Mad Blood Stirring: Vendetta and Factions in Friuli during the Renaissance* (Baltimore: Johns Hopkins University Press, 1993).

Niccoli, Ottavia, *Il seme della violenza: Putti, fanciulli e mammoli nell'Italia tra '500 e '600* (Bari: Laterza, 1995).

Politi, Giorgio, *Aristocrazia e potere politico nella Cremona di Filippo II* (Milan: SugarCo, 1976).

Polverini Fosi, Irene, *La società violenta: Il banditismo nello stato pontificio nella seconda metà del Cinquecento* (Rome: Edizioni dell'Ateneo, 1985).

Raggio, Osvaldo, *Faide e parentele: Lo stato genovese visto dalla Fontanabona* (Turin: Einaudi, 1990).

Romani, Marzio, "Criminalità e giustizia nel ducato di Mantova alla fine del Cinquecento," *Rivista Storica Italiana* (1980).

Ruggiero, Guido, *Binding Passions: Tales of Magic, Marriage and Power at the End of the Renaissance* (New York: Oxford University Press, 1993).

Sabatini, Gaetano, "Fiscalità e banditismo in Abruzzo alla fine del Seicento," *Nuovo Rivista Storica* 79 (1995).

Sbriccoli, Mario, "Fonti giudiziarie e fonti giuridiche. Riflessione sulla fase attuale degli studi," *Studi Storici* 29 (1988).

Soman, Alfred, "Deviance and Criminal Justice in Western Europe, 1300–1800: An Essay in Structure", *Criminal Justice History* 1 (1980).

Torre, Angelo, "Il consumo di devozione: Rituali e potere nelle campagne piemontese nella prima metà del Settecento," *Quaderni Storici* 20 (1985).

——, "Politics Cloaked in Worship: State, Church and Local Power in Piedmont, 1570–1770," *Past and Present* 134 (1992).

Villari, Rosario, *La rivolta antispagnola a Napoli: Le origini (1585–1647)* (Bari: Laterza, 1964).

Zorzi, Andrea, "La politique criminelle en Italie (XIIIe–XVIIe siècles)," *Crime, Histoire et Sociétés* 2 (1998).

Chapter Nine

Manners, Courts, and Civility

Robert Muchembled

Translated by *Monique Zara*

The Italian Renaissance is associated more with towns and urban culture than with princely courts. Nevertheless, it played a fundamental role in the evolution of manners, courts, and civility in the western tradition. For paradoxically, the Italy of merchants, bankers, and humanists also produced the ideal model of the courtier and the theories of refined politeness that for centuries inspired what Norbert Elias called the "civilization of manners."[1] The court has been studied descriptively, but recent research has opened new vistas linking it to the origins of the modern state.[2] As historians' interest in ritual has grown so has their interest in the social and cultural meaning of polite behavior.[3] It is unlikely, however, that the development of behavioral norms can be interpreted as simply as Elias thought. His thesis stressed a general softening of mores in Europe: a "curialization of warriors" that took place at Versailles under Louis XIV.

Much earlier, however, Renaissance princely courts – virtually laboratories of modernity – had already started this process and at the court of Urbino in 1528 Castiglione gave form to a new courtly ideal in *The Courtier*. How did this work become such a great success, when at every turn it was contradicted by practice and reality? To answer we need to consider the underlying problem of violence, which was ubiquitous at court and beyond, as well as the methods used to obtain obedience, in a quasi-religious sense, to a prince whose figure was strikingly evoked at much the same time by Machiavelli.

From the 1520s on, this newly reinvented court was a crucible for these issues and provided a western model of spatial management and social hierarchy. Its language, its codes, and its values represented not so much a simple expression of politeness governing human relationships as a symbolic, ritualized system seeking to order the whole universe around an absolute center, the prince. The court was thus a privileged concentration of knowledge, *savoir-faire*, and power, whose behavioral norms then spread to other segments of upper-class society in the form of rules and proscriptions, of politeness and etiquette, which expressed the sacredness of western man and his specific position in a hierarchy of beings with the prince, like God in Nature, located at the pinnacle.

The Invention of the Court and Good Manners in the Quattrocento

The court, in the precise sense of the entourage of a sovereign or prince, existed well before the fifteenth century. It was not the privileged space of good manners, since its values were predominantly associated with war and virility, even if thirteenth-century courtly literature sought to soften the roughness of the knights. In Europe, two other traditions conveyed a more peaceful conception of relationships between human beings. The first drew upon medieval monastic traditions that emphasized the ideal of seeking the golden mean and controlling language, gestures, and dress. Introspection and self-control became the essential qualities of this monastic behavioral ideal, later emphasized by Erasmus, formerly also an Augustinian canon, in his *De civilitate* of 1530. The other tradition took root in the Italian towns of the thirteenth century in the form of numerous didactic works addressed not only to a public of clerics, but also written for notaries, judges, teachers, citizens, and women. These works provided advice on hygiene, household and civic behavior and integrated the heritage of classical culture, Arabic and Jewish traditions.[4] Like the clerical tradition, the urban tradition emphasized measure and equilibrium but adapted them to a public of fellow citizens. The humanists and the artists of the Renaissance, particularly those influenced by Neoplatonism, added to these traditions their vision of the dignity of man, the beauty and harmony of the body, and the importance of standing in an upright position, unlike animals – each reflecting the hand of God.

It would therefore be erroneous to believe that polite civility arose one day fully formed from the court culture of the Renaissance. Its advent had long been prepared in monasteries and to a greater degree in the towns of the two most urbanized regions in Europe, northern Italy and Dutch Burgundy, where the two reference texts of the new politeness were produced by Castiglione and Erasmus at virtually the same moment (1528 and 1530 respectively). Although both were in theory addressed to noble courtiers, they conveyed a lesson in civility that, as the word itself indicates (*civilitas* comes from *civilis*), drew much of its cohesiveness from the urban world. The brilliant courts of Italy and Burgundy in the fifteenth century in turn cannot be explained without referring to the urban world of the Renaissance. Italy alone had more than twenty cities with populations of at least 25,000 people whose vibrant economies – producing not only great wealth but also skilled workers, artists, and a range of cultural innovations – paved the way for the splendor of Renaissance courts. This was true even where cities were not particularly large, as was the case at Urbino, or when the Duke of Burgundy took his court to his castle at Hesdin. Conversely, Italians were surprised by the modest size and simplicity of the French court, which numbered approximately 270 people in 1480, much smaller than the court of Urbino. The French court grew to 500 to 600 individuals around 1520, but was still only approximately the size of the Mantuan court. Francis I dreamed of his court attaining a new splendor but it was only at the end of the sixteenth century that the French court equaled that of Rome, with around 2,000 members.[5]

The court was first of all a physical place, whether or not it was permanent, often a castle with a chapel. It was even more importantly an institution, a complex social organism that surrounded the prince on a continuous or occasional basis. According to Werner Paravicini, the court possessed five main functions from the standpoint of the prince: to organize daily life, to guarantee the safety of the prince, to impress rivals, to integrate the upper levels of society (including those members who were not present), to govern and to administrate.[6] Paravicini's historical approach links the court to the operation of the state and to the development of princely patronage, focusing on the way that traditional systems of clientele were articulated at court. A synthesis of research on this subject published in 1991, however, warned against the temptation of positing a universal model of courtly domestication of the nobility based on a linear vision of state centralization following Elias, given the marginal role of the Holy Roman Emperor's court, the disintegration of the courtly society in France during the Wars of Religion and the failure of courtly society in England in the years 1640–2.[7] This series of case studies, although it gives scant attention to Italy, demonstrates that "frequently the court was not able to integrate the political elites and assure their loyalty successfully." The court of the Duke of Burgundy seemed an example of integration, but Paravicini argues that this was largely a mythic vision and emphasizes the resemblance of this court to others of the time, its lack of integration, its limited size, and its lack of influence on the rest of Europe. This erudite study, however, leaves one with questions about the crucial developments of European courts: "the increasing distance between the ruler and those around him, the sacralization of the prince's person, the increase in court expenditure, and the development of a specific court culture."[8]

Two approaches now seem to divide the field. Numerous Anglo-American researchers as well as some European historians (primarily German and Belgian) work in an empirical tradition that produces microhistorical research, focusing on differences and details while still seeking a broader synthesis. In contrast, others have favored the macro perspective, although their views are less unified than their proponents claim. This second approach includes not only the sociologist Norbert Elias, but also representatives of the Centro Europa delle Corti, who have published dozens of volumes on the subject. "Much of this production has been the work of specialists in literature, not history, and has adopted a structuralist and interdisciplinary approach. Both their structuralism and their interdisciplinarity have drawn criticism from non-Italian scholars,"[9] largely because their analysis centers on the court as a theater or "structure-symbol, a form immutable in time." However, the micro and macro approaches need not be opposed in principle; rather they should mutually enrich each other by combining the analysis of detailed case studies with broader research involving comparisons with the rest of Europe, and possibly with similar phenomena in other civilizations and at other times.

Gregory Lubkin's study of the Milanese court of the 1470s ruled by Galeazzo Maria Sforza provides an excellent model of this marriage between microhistory and macrohistory.[10] The author describes with precision the nature of the Milanese court and its way of life. Yet he also underscores a broader historical transition from the 1460s, when "a prince was not yet obliged to maintain a splendid and highly formal court to earn the respect of others" to the 1470s, when "interests in court and household was growing rapidly, both within and between individual courts." At this later date, several princes requested that their peers provide them with details on their courts. Among them were Ferrante of Naples, Galeazzo himself (who in 1473 received a description of the court of Charles the Bold), and the king of England, Edward IV, whose *Black Book of the Household* was directly inspired by the Burgundian *Ordonnances de l'Hôtel* written by Olivier de la Marche in 1469. Avoiding a reductionist perspective as well as unfounded theorization, Lubkin tries to situate the Milanese court that he is analyzing in a larger context, both Italian and European. This court, invented by the duke, was located at the heart of a large city (70,000 people around 1550) without a strong municipal tradition. Rapidly it became "the greatest center of consumption of the dominion," the center of the state and the place *par excellence* "for bringing together disparate political, social and professional elements in the prince's presence." This integrating function was by no means limited to the nobility at court, for thousands of people not living there, large clienteles, and multiple networks of interests were involved as well. Town and court were intimately linked, as numerous courtiers rented or bought houses in Milan and contributed to the local economy. In turn, many servants of humble origins found in the court means for moving up socially.

As advocates of empirical history have asserted, the Milanese court reflected these economic and social realities. But it was also "a symbolic center," a space belonging to the prince who organized it according to an ideal model: "He sought to join Heaven and Earth, to link past and future." The sacralization of the prince and his space stood at the heart of the process of construction of the modern absolutist state, as can be seen with Galeazzo, who was hungry for a royal title and called for forms of language and gestures asserting his dignity as sovereign. But integration, an idea dear to macrohistorians, in the close quarters of the court where avoiding rivals was quite difficult, was necessarily associated with intense, often violent conflict. It was in Galeazzo's interest that his court be open and creative, rather than rigidly ruled by a prince trying to maintain peace between rivals. In sum, Elias's vision dangerously mistakes appearance for reality: the demarcation of a sacred space around the prince and the ordering of the courtiers around him, like the saints near God, belonged to the realm of the ideal. Manners and civility were part of this, but all were aware that these coins had a violent and conflicted reverse side.

In sum, the invention of the luxurious and integrative court constituted an unprecedented challenge for the sovereign as he concentrated around him not only signs of power, but also all the violence and human rivalries of an era when blood flowed freely. (See the essay by Thomas Arnold below.) Galeazzo was assassinated in church, on a day of religious celebration, at the very heart of the princely symbolism he had put in place. The court created in the last decades of the fifteenth century was the place *par excellence* of danger, where competitors and predators lay in wait without scruple for the least sign of weakness in prince or peer. In this space, in order to fulfill his political, social, and cultural role, the courtier also needed to invent new rules that eased the pressure; enabled him to put up a good front in a merciless world; and play his role toward the prince and the others at court. In the end these could not be warriors' rules, even courtly ones, since brutal competition was inscribed in that older culture. Thus, new courtly rules borrowed the idea of the golden mean from clerical and urban traditions, in order to produce a middle way: a culture of integration and self-restraint. But it seems that ideal of the courtier was really merely the new façade behind which the old human wolf lurked, hiding his dark ambitions and drives.

The Prince and the Courtier (around 1520)

En el medio està lo bueno.[11]

The early sixteenth century can be considered a pivotal moment in western history: the beginning of a new stage in the civilization of Europe. Emerging at the same time as the discovery of America and the flourishing of the Renaissance and humanism, courtly culture produced a complex synthesis that would provide the dominant model for several centuries; it would do this by adapting to change and promoting the integration of several social strata into the existing political, social and religious order. To understand the central issue here – how an individual conceived of and played out relationships with others – one must turn to the work of ethnologists and Erving Goffman.[12] In some societies, the group tightly controls norms and values, so that each individual becomes the conveyor of a code of honor that resides largely beyond that individual's being and interests. The tragedy of *Romeo and Juliet* reflects such a society well. In other societies, an individual's conscience has more importance and one's existence is more a matter of self-constraint. Clearly these two models do not exist as absolutes, rather some societies place more emphasis on one than the other. In my opinion, Renaissance Europe was primarily marked by the rule of shame, or in other words by a culture fundamentally based on honor socially evaluated. (See the essay by James Farr above.) And this was not limited to the nobility; every social group had its form of honor.[13] The crucial novelty appeared at the turn of the sixteenth century, particularly in Italian courts, with the construction of ideal codes of behavior that were much more internalized. There the courtier played out the first effective version of a practice of personal self-control, which had no real kinship with the honor-based value system of the nobility. Unlike Peter Burke,[14] I view this process not so much as a matter of language, a cultural factor in the narrow sense of the word, but rather as a new political and social ideal, a real cultural revolution.

Both Castiglione and Erasmus sought to educate princes (along with noble boys), as did Rabelais when he described the ideal world of the abbey of Thélème in *Gargantua* (1534). Too often, however, one forgets to link their humanistic reflections on princes with those of their famous contemporary, Machiavelli, and to the brutal realities of the time. Yet all these authors were pointing in the same direction: "by extending the principle of mediocritas to the realm of political behavior, the two authors, like Machiavelli and many others, come to embrace the same conception of the moral goal underlying the educational effort: the breeding of the rational prince." Castiglione's courtier, Erasmus's humanist, and Machiavelli's prince were the first important milestones on the road to a "new experience of individuation and the subjection of self" which led to "the constitutive hegemony of absolutism."[15] As early as 1513, Machiavelli abandoned all illusions concerning the civil liberties which he had ardently supported in Florence and converted to the myth of the prince as his hoped-for liberator of Italy. Fascinated by Cesare Borgia, with no illusions about the evil nature of men, he evoked the myth of the centaur Chiron, Achilles' teacher, and asserted that the prince must, like Chiron, be both a beast and a man. He must understand the use of force and law, as well as ruse, since the prince must "be a fox to recognize traps and a lion to frighten wolves" (*The Prince*, XVIII). Machiavelli did not know when he wrote that this ideal prince would be foreign, first Francis I, then Charles V. He understood, however, with rare sagacity, that the time of republics was past, in Italy as well as in the Netherlands. And he articulated a crucial vision of power: the sovereign must know how to display brutal realism, like an animal fighting to survive, as well as refined intelligence, like a man illuminated by humanism. His prince was both predator and liberator, a powerful and cunning being superior to others. He followed the path of the "golden mean" by mastering his passions in order to accomplish a superhuman undertaking. Castiglione made essentially the same points, merely dressing them up more pleasantly.

It seems a profound paradox that that same Italy associated with a powerful civic tradition would produce the theoretical definitions of absolutism and of the court that dominated Europe during the Old Regime. It becomes less paradoxical if one thinks of Italy at the turn of the sixteenth century as an intellectual and cultural laboratory for modernity, coming to grips with political defeat and foreign domination. This is, however, a relatively new and controversial way of seeing the period. Many historians have viewed the Italian courts of the sixteenth century as decadent, evoking the republican values of the "High Renaissance" that vanished with courts.[16] A more complex analysis of the formation of the modern state has recently reoriented research. This shift of focus also turns on a re-evaluation of the role of absolute monarchies in the political and cultural heritage of Europe.[17] It is in this context that Castiglione's *The Courtier* must be reread. Viewed in its time as a work teaching courtly manners and the art of conversation, it has been perceived as moralistic, a defense of the nobility, an escape from reality, a non-theoretical narrative of personal experience, a stoic handbook in a merciless world, etc.[18] All of which reflects the fact that the book was the complex product of an era of doubt. It underwent three successive stages of writing, the last between 1521 and 1524, which was directly tied to an affirmation of the absolute state, as much in France as in the areas where Charles V was attempting to impose new forms of power in his Spanish kingdoms and the Netherlands. Like Machiavelli, Castiglione, as ambassador to Spain, was well aware that the time of absolute princes had come. The Italian court nobility, who witnessed a disintegration of their world with the minor princes of Urbino as well as the powerful Sforzas of Milan being crushed by foreign "barbarians," had concerns that also showed in his revisions. Castiglione, then, was describing a world in its twilight, Urbino as it was before the turmoil, but also a world of the future: the monarchical court enlightened by humanism. The prince that he evoked was an absent figure, perhaps less because of the illness of the Duke of Urbino, than because the prince, like God, was a distant organizing principle of the universe.

The author has been accused of "élégant arrivisme" because he advocated "total submission to the good will of rulers."[19] While perhaps accurate, this description does not account for the extraordinary success of the work. Published in a mere 1,030 copies in Venice by Aldo Manuzio in 1528, a year before Castiglione's death, it eventually had sixty-two Italian editions and sixty translations.[20] Its greatest success was between 1528 and 1550, with fifty editions and translations, twenty-eight in the 1540s alone. Demand remained strong until 1590, then sharply declined in the seventeenth century. Its early success occurred as the tidal wave of Italian culture swept through Europe, especially France and Spain, at the same time as the "barbarians" dominated Italy and urban republican values were vanquished by the triumph of absolutism. The first French translation was published in 1537, for the use of a court that was eager for new things, but still coarse, brutal, and far from the model of Urbino. Erasmus's *De civilitate morum puerilium*, published in 1530, suggests that the nobles of the Netherlands, heirs to the luxurious Burgundian court, also needed instruction to refine their mores and behavior. It will take further study, however, to know what readers sought in *The Courtier*. Some commentators have asserted that the fourth book, which called for an absolute submission to the prince, was not well received, whereas the descriptions of conversations, word play, and jests were more popular. To what extent were non-Italian readers aware that the nobility that Castiglione described was not the same as their own? Numerous Italian aristocrats had only recently acquired status; the Sforzas, for example, were of peasant stock. Nonetheless, the civilization of the Renaissance and this newer nobility had a profound and durable influence on courts, bringing to them civic traditions, humanistic ideas, and an aesthetic perception linked to the fame of Italian art and artists. Castiglione proposed in fact a hybrid culture, a nobility attracted to intellectual issues, which could also appeal to the taste of wealthy citizens who admired the splendor of the court. It is doubtful, however, that other European societies, aside perhaps from the Netherlands, possessed such a social world.

The enthusiastic reception of *The Courtier* does not mean that it was understood as Castiglione intended. It might be hypothesized that first there was a phase of fascinated imitation of its seeming extreme refinement, much as the artists of the first French Renaissance affixed Italian artistic messages to traditional forms to "refine" them. In Italy itself, the extent of the diffusion of the book outside of courtly circles is revealed not only by the numerous copies printed but also by the switch from the heavy 1528 folio to the more manageable octavo format, followed by the appearance of paperback-like editions after 1549. The existence of sixty known foreign translations, produced from 1528 to 1619, also suggests that the book was extremely popular far beyond the court. The appearance of numerous imitations further evidences the work's popularity: 1,417 treatises addressed to gentlemen and 891 to their ladies were published in Europe before 1625. Peter Burke, in his study of the reception of Castiglione, divides Europe into three zones. In Italy, France, and Spain, the book experienced an early popularity; in England, Scandinavia, and central Europe it became fashionable at mid-century; and finally, the Moscovite dominions and the regions under Ottoman rule completely ignored it.[21] Generally speaking, this geographical divide reflected the area where the modern state developed as well as the impermeable border that isolated the Orthodox. It also reveals the less favorable reception of Castiglione's ideas in Protestant areas, especially where courts were weak, as in Scandinavia or in the northern Netherlands, which was in revolt against Philip II after 1568.

The best explanation for the widespread influence of Castiglione's work comes from the polysemy of the message, which could adapt to a great variety of situations, while conveying fundamental concepts. Crystallized around 1520, these concepts contained a certain *je ne sais quoi* that was profoundly seductive to the most dynamic elements of Renaissance Europe. Crucially these ideas seemed capable of resolving the basic contradiction between the economic, cultural, and intellectual growth based on towns and the dominance of social structures based on nobility and monarchy. The modernization of the state was impossible while maintaining the status quo, yet it was unthinkable to question the pre-eminence of the warrior nobility. Thus, the Italian experience was crucial: Italy had experienced urban republican life; suffered its failure at the hands of foreign conquerors; then sought a new approach, based upon the "golden mean." For Castiglione himself, "the courtier was an autonomous individual who was advised to speak frankly to his prince," a noble, without a doubt, but with an Italian twist, taking into account the specificity of a society where the prince was cultivated, civilized, urbanized, and polished by the urban and humanistic imprint of the Renaissance.[22] This political model was hardly exportable in this form, and the disaffection for the book after 1619, in particular in France when absolutism truly asserted itself, can be understood from this perspective.

As far as aesthetics are concerned, the work fascinated unrefined nobles, who felt inferior to their Italian peers and wished to learn their secrets, although they surely did not imagine that this refinement owed so much to a cultural universe quite foreign to their own. The individuals listed as owning the work were predominantly noble, sometimes patricians from large towns, who were well aware of their superiority and wished to adopt "a style of life which emphasize[d] their distinction from ordinary mortals."[23] They indeed found an explicit code of superiority in the figure of the courtier or of the *donna di palazzo*, his companion. This ideal was based on the idea of *gravità* (quiet dignity), *gentilezza* (a term associated with the service of ladies), honor, *vergogna* (shame), and *modestia* (modesty). It emphasized moderation and the golden mean, defined by the word *mediocrità*. Such an individual must demonstrate urbanity and elegance, and flee all that is *selvatico* (savage) and *contadinesco* (rustic). The humanistic concept that defined a human being as different from animals was at the heart of this ideal of moderation, discretion, and prudence, and implied a tight control of one's appearance, posture, and gestures to attain a *grazia* (grace) that culminated in the almost untranslatable notion of *sprezzatura*. This was not a matter of "casualness," although that term was sometimes used as a synonym by Castiglione, but an expression of the ability of the courtier to exert control over himself while expressing a calm self-confidence that marked his superiority.[24] This definition evoked a sort of sacred sphere surrounding the courtier, who was superior to others, accepting only his prince as superior. This perspective could only fascinate those who hoped to put it into practice.

In 1516, the pause in the Italian wars was interpreted by contemporaries as the possible beginning of a "golden age." Erasmus expressed such hopes, and even believed the conflict was over. This utopian dream was shared by many humanists, following the succession of young, brilliant, cultivated, and promising sovereigns to the thrones of the major monarchies. The drama of the rivalry of the Hapsburg and the Valois that would turn Europe into a battlefield for centuries, however, began to unfold in 1519, while Luther paved the way for a split in Christianity that would inflame the continent until the peace of 1648. Despite the fact that the 1520s are insufficiently studied, it is clear that it was a crucial decade, when the continent was ushered into a violent and intensely conflict-torn modernity. *The Courtier* of Castiglione can thus be viewed as a humanistic utopia, proposing an ideal prince who would bring a new golden age to a land laid waste by strife. This work represented one of the last attempts, along with those of Erasmus, Thomas More, and Rabelais, to try to prevent the shift toward violence that was occurring, an attempt based upon belief in the ability of man to assert himself at the center of a world created by a benevolent God. The prince was a giant, a Magnificent Gargantua, possessor of a divine spark, who placed his authority and his court at the heart of a system of relations where all men were marked by grace. This essential quality set men utterly apart from animals and placed them at the highest point on the Neoplatonist hierarchy of being, just below angels. This model was nevertheless adaptable to a much more mundane reality, precisely because it conveyed the idea of the intrinsic superiority of humans that could in turn provide a new justification for the brutal dominance of warriors.

From Civility to Politeness

The originality of Castiglione "lies in his first fully directing attention to the need to control one's own social space as a preliminary to controlling political space."[25] Although he was not the first to understand that the control of personal space was necessary at court, he skillfully showed that the ideas of distance and of visible forms of submission were crucial in defining the sacralization of the prince and of the symbolic expression of his power. Behaviorists have remarked that human beings are very competitive, but that they also know how to convey corporeal and verbal messages to appease enemies or rivals. Life in society always rests upon an equilibrium reached between these more or less contradictory tendencies. Regardless of its historical form, *savoir-vivre* can thus be defined as a "system that produces hierarchy within a system of reciprocity and exchange." Its purpose was to protect one from uncertainty and to channel violence, not by eliminating it (a utopian goal) but by dissimulating it under a rhetoric of civility.[26]

   With this perspective in mind, as noted earlier, the Italian courts of the Quattrocento were places that concentrated an extraordinary potential for competitive violence, requiring a ritualization of relations in an attempt to limit destructive explosions. Lubkin's Milanese court again provides a helpful example. Galeazzo viewed the members of his "household" as extensions "of his own person." Wearing "hose 'alla divisa' (one leg white and the other morello, a very dark red) was a sign of personal allegiance to the Sforza" and he reserved for himself the right to name those who might adopt this style of dress. Using descriptions of the court of Burgundy that he received in 1473, Galeazzo created a precise ritual to organize relations, as much with himself as between courtiers, in order to reinforce his princely dignity. Even language was enlisted in the cause. The world that associated with the duke was divided into an elaborate hierarchy of honorary titles and the personal pronouns *tu*, *voi*, and *lei* were carefully deployed to measure and stress the space that separated others from his dignity; in his correspondence, he used "the imperial plural" except when addressing persons of superior rank.

   In sum the Milanese court of the 1470s possessed a very hierarchical structure based on language, politeness, and good manners. One wrote to the duke addressing him as "Most illustrious and excellent Lord" and by humbly recommending oneself to him as the "Most Faithful servant of your Most Excellent and Illustrious Lordship." Some went as far as saying "true and sincere servant and slave of Your Excellency," or even occasionally, "your dog and slave."[27] Such a "style of humiliation," which some consider to reflect an oriental politeness, sought in this context to mark the total absence of aggressivity by those writing to the duke, and even more so by individuals who had the right to approach him closely and could thus easily do him harm. The sacralization of the space in which the sovereign moved, in particular that of the "invisible bubble" that surrounded his person, served both to mark his preeminence and to ritualize the least form of contact with him in order to preclude any potential violence.

Relations between courtiers were governed by an identical hierarchical principle, which created a precise protocol tempered by pleasant conduct. Under Galeazzo, "gracious words and appropriate gestures also contributed to affirming relationships." The usual form of marking respect between people who were not close was *toccare la mano* (to touch the hand), while "embraces and kisses were reserved for persons with a more intimate relationship."[28] It is likely that there also existed additional, subtler codes, although Lubkin does not discuss them. These codes depended on the social position of a given individual, on the favor of the duke, on gender, on the nature – official or less formal – of the circumstances, on a given tense situation. They especially depended on the use of space during ceremonies, since Galeazzo also sought to sacralize time by using "holidays as vehicles to symbolically affirm his role as a sovereign prince: the court furnished a context for bringing together disparate political, social and professional elements in the prince's presence."[29]

The Italian court, however, also forced its actors to negotiate constantly, both with each other and the prince, in order to keep their place and to assert their individuality on a very competitive stage. To avoid conflicts, courtiers needed to have a clear vision of their own personal space. To avoid appearing unmannerly, they needed to manipulate behavioral codes with dexterity in order to shine and constantly control their body and gestures. Not surprisingly then, their highly ritualized space was also the place where the self-evaluating gaze and the tight surveillance of self were invented. (See the essay below by John Martin.) Court civility was thus an intrinsically evolutionary culture. At its beginning, it was closer to the ideals of urban merchants, not only because it advocated extreme signs of submission to the sovereign, but also because it subordinated the profit from one's presence at court to a strict discipline more economic in nature than militaristic. The personal effort made to find a golden mean led to the slow accumulation of a symbolic capital whose profitability depended entirely on the constant favor of the prince.

The theme of the domestication of the nobility by the court is a historiographical commonplace. This phenomenon, however, was long in coming and far from the rule. It was largely absent in the Holy Roman Empire. In Poland, during the sixteenth century, the royal court exerted only a weak attraction, unlike the courts of the provincial magnates. Those courts, based on the Italian model, as was also the case in Hungary, attempted to "civilize" young nobles using the traditional framework of patron–client relationships.[30] Without seeking definitively to resolve this difficult problem of the domestication of the nobility, one can note that the penetration of the model of the court and civility occurred slowly, even in those countries that were most receptive to the Italian influence, like Valois France or Hapsburg Spain. Research on this theme, however, is still limited. The court of the Netherlands in the sixteenth century, the courts of Francis I and Henry II, as well as those of Charles V and Philip II in Spain, still have many secrets to reveal. Also, one must not forget the

English court; scholars have long debated about a "court and country" conflict there and have been skeptical about "the existence and effects of greater ritual and formality at court" in the seventeenth century.[31]

Even the French context has only been analyzed in general terms, especially from the perspective of civility.[32] Despite the wish of Francis I to create a brilliant and sumptuous court, reflected in his building of Fontainebleau, the court phenomenon only gained slowly momentum. In fact the physical setting changed more rapidly than the ways of thinking and behavior of the nobles. The appearance of great numbers of women at court was an early sign of change, despite the Estates General's unsuccessful attempt in 1576 to reduce spending by requesting that the ladies be sent home. This request was just one example of a strong resistance to what was viewed as Italian fashion. Under Henri II, *The Courtier*, available in French as early as 1537, seems to have had much less influence than tales of chivalry. The most famous of these tales, "Amadis de Gaule," was translated from Spanish and edited to comprise twelve volumes, from 1540 to 1546. The king and the nobles of his entourage enthusiastically identified with the adventures of war and love of a *chevalier gaulois*, whose culture was based on worthy deeds and honor and thus was quite distant from the world of humanists or refined Italian courtiers. French civility thus found its primary model in a modernized code of chivalry, somewhat crossbred with Italianisms (in fact, the translator of "Amadis," Nicolas Herberay des Essarts, owned Castiglione's book). The dominant codes of politeness drew their pompous formulations from this literary vein, whose popularity is evidenced by the publication of *Trésor des douze livres d'Amadis*, a collection of examples of *beau langage* to be imitated, around 1560.

Etiquette was in its infancy and mores still rough and even coarse; courtiers enjoyed scatological jokes and did not hesitate to amuse themselves by observing maids of honor through a crack in the wall. Appearances had changed more than reality, despite the emergence of somewhat more polite formulations and attitudes, probably because greater numbers of women at court required more restraint than previously. Indeed, "the man at court around the middle of the sixteenth century still retained a streak of violence," Edouard Bourciez asserted, shocked to find so much coarseness under the varnish of a recently developed politeness. In fact, the French court nobility was still profoundly rooted in a warrior culture of honor that caused it to be undisciplined and dangerous for the absolute king; conspiracies and episodes of defiance occurred regularly until the Fronde. The modest numbers of the second estate present at the king's side nevertheless represented the forefront of the evolution of mores in contrast to the rest of the nobility, who in the period 1540–59 not only rejected courtly manners, but also developed a model praising healthy rustic living.[33]

The real introduction of the Italian model occurred during the reign of Henri III (1574–89). The virulent criticism against Italianate affectation, the *Mignons* of the king, the imported dress, and the precious way of speaking attested to the difficulty of the graft and undoubtedly explain in part the execrable reputation of Henri III in the opinion of his contemporaries and historians. However, he was only attempting to follow Castiglione, or Galeazzo Maria Sforza, in creating a sacralized space for the prince that could provide a basis for absolutism and overcome noble factionalism. His court numbered roughly 6,000 people, but they only served for a quarter of the year, meaning that at any given time there were only 1,500 to 2,000 people present. As early as 1574, Henri III attempted to assert his royal dignity by surrounding his table with a barrier and by replacing the serving lackeys with noblemen. This attempt at sacralizing the prince and at demarcating a distance between him and others was poorly received by the nobles and townspeople, as was the title "Sa Majesté." After apparently abandoning these innovations, the king himself wrote a series of regulations, distributed in 1585, which revealed the vast distance between life at the French court and the Italian ideal. Henri stipulated that others must not get too close to him, read his dispatches before him or over his shoulder, wear a hat while speaking to him, and should present themselves properly dressed and not unbuttoned, etc. If a few courtiers did possess a translation of Castiglione, clearly very few attempted to practice its dictates.

The brilliant and luxurious court of Henri III was assuredly a social crucible, incorporating many Parisians, foreigners, and some provincial nobles. Yet it did not succeed in domesticating the nobility, because the overwhelming majority of them never went there and viewed it with animosity. French aristocratic culture remained strongly associated with notions of honor and with a disdain for intellectual matters, as well as viewing women in a decidedly uncourtly way. Unlike Urbino or Milan a century earlier, the prince in the French context alienated many nobles as well as the majority of Parisians by living in an artificial circle, cut off from the life of the country, and accused of producing affected mannerisms, incomprehensible jargon, laughable symbolism, and depraved mores. Instead of organizing a sacralized space for an absolute prince, the court remained a place where violence flourished, because the rituals that were supposed to control it were not accepted by the courtiers themselves. Brutally dispersed in 1589, the court was not reconstituted along Italian lines by Henri IV or Louis XIII.

Formal politeness nevertheless made some progress. A person with a superior rank was called Monseigneur and a peer was called Monsieur. Letters contained expressions of deference, in a style of humiliation reminiscent of the court of Galeazzo Maria Sforza. One wrote "Votre humble serviteur" toward high ranking individuals, "Votre obéissant serviteur" to someone superior, and "Votre bon serviteur" to a person of quality. However, at the beginning of the seventeenth century the court no longer set the tone. This role belonged to towns, especially Paris, where a public sphere was born, marked by a mundane politeness linked to the teachings of *The Courtier* and adapted to the urban world shaped by the Counter-Reformation. Reformed over the course of a generation in a dynamic urban society, the ideal defined by Castiglione reconnected with its urban roots and progressively conquered a nobility that slowly showed less reticence in intellectual matters, the liberal arts, and polite manners. Revised by Nicolas Faret in 1630, the urban model of the "honnête homme" of the time also taught "l'art de plaire à la cour." This new ideal led little by little to a synthesis in France between the town, the aristocracy, and the court. The curialization of the warriors dear to Norbert Elias thus only occurred after a phase of "urbanization" of a portion of the nobility under Louis XIII. Culture and civility needed to penetrate the world of the aristocracy in the crucible that was Paris, leading under Louis XIV to a domestication of warriors and to the symbolic agenda already in place in late fifteenth-century Milan.[34]

Nevertheless, civility was not completely linked to the court and absolutism. Good manners, which Erasmus taught in Latin, were diffused in the schools via Latin instruction using his works and those of his many imitators. Protestants also placed

Erasmus's precepts within their students' reach using vernacular translations. Civil behavior, in particular at the table or in relations between masters and students, became an academic ideal whose impact is still not clear. Schools, much like princely courts, were also places of close contact and tension. Students thus learned to keep their place as human beings and reject postures and movements resembling those of animals, as well as to manage conflicts with others, while avoiding symbolic personal injuries and loss of dignity. Christian humanism and Protestantism undoubtedly had different approaches to these general precepts, but research remains to be done on this subject.

The Italian peninsula also witnessed the publication in 1558 of a second important treatise on conduct at court, *Galateo* by Giovanni della Casa, followed in 1578 by a work intended for a broader public, *La civil conversasione* by Stefano Guazzo. Both were translated into French, English, and Latin. The former was also published in Spanish, perhaps because the author's insistence on the necessity of submission in order to succeed corresponded well to the evolution of an Iberian society more and more marked by noble hierarchy and the idea of "purity of blood." As a disillusioned courtier, Guazzo for his part offered his precepts to "all sorts of people, wherever they may live." The Counter-Reformation thus displaced the ideal behavior of the Court toward all good people without questioning the necessity of a strict social hierarchy. As with earlier forms of civility, the purpose of "civil conversation" was to "avoid extremes" and "seek the golden mean." However, for the first time, Guazzo used the word "politezza" in the sense of "polishing," correcting and improving individuals through cleanliness, proper speech, and good manners. Here, going beyond Peter Burke,[35] I would posit that we encounter a definite break with the humanistic model of Castiglione and Erasmus. The courtier was certain of man's greatness – at least if he was a humanist, wellborn, and better still, a prince. The emergence of politeness, which for Guazzo was linked to the "qualities of the soul," returned humans faced with an ineffable God to insignificance and a necessary humility. The tragic European culture that overthrew humanistic optimism after the middle of the century focused on man's fallen nature, penchant for sin, and an omnipresent diabolical temptation that focused on the body.[36]

Civility, then, slowly gave way to a universal pedagogy that focused on the development of moral values, with the saint as the ideal. The veiled monastic ideas present in the advice on moderation given to the courtier gradually replaced humanistic optimism, as the fear of sin became the driving force behind the surveillance of self and control of passions. Man did not, however, lose the divine spark that distinguished him from animals; it was retained, but was contingent on a total obedience to God. Politeness in the late Renaissance was dominated by the idea that man was a willing slave to God's impenetrable designs. If the civilization of manners continued to advance, it was due to its changing philosophy and objective, as would again be the case during its third great phase at Versailles under Louis XIV. Norbert Elias did not see that the Sun King was not the real initiator of this process, but rather the brilliant artificer of the synthesis between the utopian heritage of the Italian Renaissance courts and the tragic view of man conveyed by the Counter-Reformation. The equilibrium that Louis XIV finally achieved, mixing bourgeois and nobles at court, was more than social. It was above all symbolic – for he created a relatively peaceful myth of unity, far from both the excesses of humanistic optimism and the pessimism of the Counter-Reformation, and placed the lieutenant of God on Earth at the center of a classical system based on rigorous hierarchical principles, veiled by the graces of a radiant politeness.

Conclusion

Civility was not just a code of social relations; it was the base of European civilization, revealing a common perception of the human experience. Despite Europe's obvious cultural diversity and its virulent religious and political battles, it possessed in fact a hidden unity, a collective dynamic in the fifteenth and sixteenth centuries. This unity was based on the framing of violence with what can be called foundational myths, myths of civility and courtly behavior that went beyond religion to include all sacred spaces and relate to all activities of life. Castiglione's *Courtier* should be read as a social utopia centered on a myth that took shape at the right time. It incorporated disparate traditions, drawing on the monastic tradition and the civil mores of the great merchant towns. Castiglione went beyond these traditions, however, by creating a synthesis profoundly marked by humanism; such was his daydream of a "golden age" for the gentle rule of a prince enamored of beauty and knowledge, whose court was a fusion of harmony, good manners, and conversations as pleasant as they were learned. Reality fell far short of such a dream; yet ultimately the power of a myth lies in its ability to ignore and transform reality. *The Courtier* asserted that a utopia on Earth was possible, as Erasmus, Thomas More, and Rabelais also believed. For these humanists, man was at the center of creation, under the gaze of a benevolent God. Their prince possessed a superior sacred spark that enabled him to organize the world around him and to incite the individuals in his entourage to prove their humanity by rejecting all bestiality thanks to "civil conversation."

This cultural construct that appeared around 1470–1520 in Italy was humanistic and urban in nature, even if it was best expressed in princely courts. The disastrous political situation of the Italian peninsula only deepened the need for a hierarchical order and a sacralization of the minor local princes against barbaric foreigners who did not possess the secrets of this culture but had force on their side. Only Erasmus in 1530 provided a comparable model, based on the eminent dignity of man who must distinguish himself from animals by his words, his gestures, and his thoughts. The diffusion of both works closely followed the spread of the Renaissance culture across Europe and apparently culminated around 1550.

The situation changed dramatically at mid-century, with the religious and political fights that turned into the Wars of Religion. This marked the beginning of a period characterized by a tragic culture that defined man as weak and sinful, constantly threatened by the devil, under the fearsome gaze of a vengeful God, which lasted until about 1650. The symbolic grammar contained in *The Courtier* and in the humanists' books on civility readapted to this profound change in European civilization. The monastic strain of civility grew in importance. The self-control of a well-mannered individual referred less to exceptional dignity than to the fear of sin and the diabolical forces lurking in the body and omnipresent in the exterior world. It was in this context that the court of Henri III seemed scandalous and perverse, when, in fact, it was merely attempting to imitate the ideal of Castiglione. Civility continued its progress, but from then on, it conveyed the myth of the subjection of Christians to the unknowable will of a fearsome God. In France, it was this form that gained new momentum under Louis XIII, before definitively moving toward the virtues of court etiquette in the more peaceful, classical atmosphere of Louis XIV.

Civility was thus in fact more linked to the town than to the court, given its origins in the towns of Italy (and the Netherlands) as well as its French forms specific to the time of Louis XIII. One can define it as a sort of hidden grammar, eminently adaptable to different cultural forms. Its heart was constituted by a discourse of superiority producing clear hierarchies, whether in the name of a benevolent God and humanist Neoplatonic ideas or from the fear of a fearsome Creator, master of Satan and of men in a tragic era. It could thus adapt to numerous historical avatars. Civility for that matter continued in France in the eighteenth century through the politeness of the enlightened man, and in England through the progressive vision described by Peter Langford in *A Polite and Commercial People*,[37] only to wither, at least symbolically, under the blows of those promising equality in 1789.

NOTES

1   Elias, *Civilizing Process.*
2   Dean, "Courts," p. S136.
3   Muchembled, *Société policiée*; Arditi, *Manners.*
4   Romagnoli, *Ville*, pp. 58–9, 74–5, 78.
5   Burke, "L'homme," p. 146.
6   Paravicini, "Structure," pp. 1–2.
7   Asch and Birke, *Princes*, esp. the introduction by R. G. Asch, pp. 4, 37, as well as p. 156.
8   Ibid., pp. 25–8.
9   Dean, "Courts," pp. S138–9.
10   Lubkin, *Renaissance Court.*
11   Luis Milàn, *Cortesano*. Dedicated to Philip II, the book described the court of Ferdinand of Aragon, duke of Calabria and prince of Taranto.
12   Goffman, *Interaction Ritual.*
13   Muchembled, "Paroles d'inceste," pp. 9–16. Also by Muchembled, *L'Invention*, pp. 304–10.
14   Burke, "Langages," pp. 111–26.
15   Arditi, *Manners*, pp. 120–1.
16   Lauro Martines, *Power and Imagination*. H. G. Koenigberger and Erich Cochrane also develop similar arguments. See the update on this topic by Larner, "Courts," pp. 669–81. A reading of this work twenty years later reveals the recent accelerated pace and deeper nature of research on this theme.
17   Thanks in particular to the research project *Origins of the Modern State, XIIth–XVIIIth Centuries* conducted by the European Science Foundation, directed by Wim Blockmans and Jean-Philippe Genêt from 1989 to 1992. The results are currently being prepared for publication in several languages, in particular in English.
18   Larner, "Courts," p. 674.
19   Guidi, "Baldassar Castiglione." These ideas were again explored in his unpublished thesis, "Castiglione."
20   Burke, *Courtier*, pp. 41, 139.

21 Ibid., pp. 41, 82, 86, 156.
22 Ibid., p. 121.
23 Ibid., pp. 144–54.
24 Ibid., pp. 28–31.
25 Larner, "Courts," p. 676.
26 Rivière, *Rites*, pp. 146, 259.
27 Lubkin, *Renaissance Court*, pp. 129, 170–1.
28 Ibid., p. 171.
29 Ibid., pp. 251, 253–4.
30 Asch and Birke, *Princes*, pp. 4, 24, 156; Maczak, "Cour et l'espace," pp. 9–45. See also Prosperi, *Corte*, II, esp. p. 289.
31 Dean, "Courts," pp. S147–8.
32 Muchembled, *Société policiée*, pp. 23–76.
33 Smith, *Anti-Courtier*.
34 Muchembled, *Société policiée*, pp. 76–122.
35 Burke, "L'homme." pp. 68–9.
36 Muchembled, *Diable*, ch. iv, "Littérature satanique et culture tragique (1550–1650)."
37 Langford, *Polite and Commercial People*.

REFERENCES

Arditi, Jorge, *A Genealogy of Manners: Transformations of Social Relations in France and England from the Fourteenth to the Eighteenth Century* (Chicago: University of Chicago Press, 1998).

Asch, Ronald G. and Birke, Adolf M., eds., *Princes, Patronage and the Nobility: The Court at the Beginning of the Modern Age* (Oxford: Oxford University Press, 1991).

Burke, Peter, "L'homme de cour," in *L'Homme de la Renaissance*, ed. Eugenio Garin (Paris: Seuil, 1990).

——, *The Fortunes of the Courtier: The European Reception of Castiglione's "Cortegiano"* (Cambridge: Cambridge University Press, 1995).

——, "Les langages de la politesse," *Terrain* 33 (1999), pp. 111–26.

Dean, Trevor, "The Courts," in "The Origins of the State in Italy, 1300–1660," *Journal of Modern History*, supplement 67 (December 1995), pp. 136–51.

Elias, Norbert, *The Civilizing Process* [1939], 2 vols. (Oxford: Oxford University Press, 1981–2).

Goffman, Erving, *Interaction Ritual* (Garden City, NJ: Anchor Books, 1967).

Guidi, José, "Baldassar Castiglione et le pouvoir politique: du gentilhomme de cour au nonce pontifical," in *Les Écrivains et le pouvoir en Italie à l'époque de la Renaissance* (Paris: Université de la Sorbonne, 1973).

——, "Castiglione, mythe et réalité de la vie de cour," unpublished thesis, the Sorbonne, 1983.

Langford, Paul, *A Polite and Commercial People* (Oxford: Oxford University Press, 1989).

Larner, John, "Europe of the Courts," *Journal of Modern History* 55 (1983), pp. 669–81.

Lubkin, Gregory, *A Renaissance Court: Milan under Galeazzo Maria Sforza* (Berkeley: University of California Press, 1994).

Maczak, Antoni, "La cour et l'espace du pouvoir entre l'Italie du Pô et l'Europe du Centre-Est," in *La corte e lo spazio: Ferrara estense*, ed. Giuseppe Papagno and Amedeo Quondam (Rome: Bulzoni, 1982).

Martines, Lauro, *Power and Imagination: City States in Renaissance Italy* (New York: Knopf, 1979).

Milàn, Luis, *Il libro intitulado el Cortesano* (Valencia, 1561).

Muchembled, Robert, *L'Invention de l'homme moderne: Culture et sensibilities en France du XVe au XVIIIe siècle* (Paris: Hachette, 1994).

——, *La Société policiée: Politique et politesse en France du XVIe au XXe siècle* (Paris: Seuil, 1998).

——, "Paroles d'inceste: Les jeunes et l'honneur maternel en Artois aux XVe et XVIIe siècles," *Equinoxe, Revue des Sciences Humaines* 20 (1998).

——, *Une histoire du diable XIIe–XXe siècle* (Paris: Seuil, 2000).

Paravicini, Werner, "Structure et fonctionnement de la cour bourguignonne au XVe siècle," in *A la cour de Bourgogne: Le duc, son entourage, son train*, ed. Jean-Marie Cauchies (Turnhout: Brepols, 1998).

Prosperi, Adriano, ed., *La corte e il "Cortegiano," II: Un modello europeo* (Rome: Bulzoni, 1980).

Rivière, Claude, *Les Rites profanes* (Paris: PUF, 1995).

Romagnoli, Daniela, ed., *La Ville et la cour: Des bonnes et des mauvaises manières* (Paris: Fayard, 1995).

Smith, Pauline M., *The Anti-Courtier Trend in Sixteenth Century French Literature* (Geneva: Droz, 1966).

CHAPTER TEN

Family and Clan in the Renaissance World

JOANNE M. FERRARO

Family and clan were fundamental units of social organization in the Renaissance world. Dynamic rather than fixed structures, with overlapping chronological boundaries, these consanguineous and social networks continually changed during the transition from medieval to modern times, in response to fluctuating fortunes, to the aspirations accompanying social class, and to the intervention of church and state authorities. Europeans assumed family and clan to be universal models of social organization. During the Renaissance age of exploration, missionaries and settlers who reached the Americas exported their modes of living to the indigenous peoples they conquered, without regard for local custom. What began as a European phenomenon thus came to have broad social and moral resonance.

The absence of strong state structures gave authority to the medieval clan, a large network of non-coresident and coresident groups, linked by consanguineous and fictitious kinship as well as by alliance.[1] In a world challenged by violence and civil disorder, the corporate group provided people with solidarity, protection, and coercive force. The sworn associations of medieval Italy, like the kinship networks in the Scottish Highlands, the mountains of the Balkans, and the rural areas of Corfu and Corsica, assumed vital defensive and offensive functions. In the Italian cities clans dominated entire neighborhoods and played important roles in communal politics; in the countryside they lay claim to vast lands and feudal jurisdictions, holding monopolies of coercive force over rustics as well as hired retainers.

Clans underwent transformation between the thirteenth and sixteenth centuries.[2] In some regions these corporate groups persisted, but in others the horizontal networks of families with common names and ancestors divided into branches, and scattered throughout city and countryside. The lineages of the conjugal couple replaced emphasis on patrilineal groups, and the nuclear family became the main protagonist of Renaissance society and culture. It conferred identity and status, provided protection and livelihood, and brought membership to political councils, civic confraternities, guilds, rural factions, and more. In practical terms it was also a means of social placement and of capital accumulation. Humanist prescriptive literature gave the family central importance, characterizing it as the microcosm of society and a guarantor of social order.

Clans lost hegemony to the nuclear family for a variety of reasons. One was the influential power of the Catholic Church, whose marriage laws discouraged the establishment of kinship networks. Canon law opposed the faction-promoting endogamy practiced within clans. It weakened the cohesion of large kin groups by making four links the minimum for a marriage to be valid.[3] This law also prohibited marriages between godparents and godchildren, a practice within clans that had promoted artificial kinship. Further, the Church permitted partners to choose spouses independently of the will of the clan, a policy that subordinated the larger kinship network to the nuclear family.[4] The marital couple rather than lineage elders assumed the most prominent role in choosing partners for their children. Another practice advanced by the Church that weakened the clan was bilateral inheritance. Insistence on the endowment of daughters with shares of estates lessened the power of great lineages. As dowry levels throughout Renaissance Europe steadily increased, women gained more financial weight in marriage, both because they brought important resources to the union and because they passed them along to male and female offspring alike. Moreover, in consequence, as men with increasing wealth rose to positions of power, their mothers' natal families also grew in importance. Where wealth was bequeathed to both men and women – inheritance through diverging devolution – the lineage funds of the clan gave way to conjugal funds, and the importance of the larger kinship group diminished.

Other explanations for the decline of clans are tied to specific circumstances. In Florence it has been attributed to the anti-magnate legislation that wealthy businessmen levied on the nobility, and in Venice to the unchallenged hegemony of select noble families. Both cities were home to some of the richest and most powerful families that launched the commercial revolution and the new, civic Renaissance culture. Under their tutelage, city government and finance rose to new heights and gave prominence to the secular, nuclear family. In contrast, the inland cities of the Italian peninsula surrendered to family dynasts who established princely courts, raising their own families to positions of power that superseded that of any corporate group.

Traces of the clan still remained in the Renaissance world, side by side with the nuclear family. It clearly persisted in Corsica, the Scottish Highlands, and in some cities, like the Castilian center of Valladolid. But in other areas historians have not been able to agree on the respective importance of family and clan.[5] The Italian cities present specific difficulties. In Florence Richard Goldthwaite found that nuclear families conducted household and business arrangements throughout the fourteenth to sixteenth centuries. Yet Francis Kent demonstrated that Florentine families still exhibited a powerful sense of the larger kinship group, with family palaces clustered together in one parish, with families of the same surname being represented in government, and with notions of collective honor and collective shame. In contrast, Venetian patricians formed *fraterne*, whereby all brothers owned a family firm, living under one roof and using their palaces as bases of operations for their business activities. Kinship ties through the female line were as important as those through the patriline. For example, maternal uncles frequently advanced the political careers of young patricians. Moreover, Venetian councils excluded in-laws from participation when voting on issues involving individual patricians, expecting affinal collusion.[6] Like Venetian patricians, families in provincial Vicenza also stressed their horizontal connections with the wider kinship group formed through marriage and the female line.[7] Among Brescian elites, on the other hand, the family with bilateral kinship ties and the large clan co-existed. Some members of the urban ruling class had living arrangements resembling the Venetian *fraterne* and others were members of clans, who strove to see their relations represented in the city council as well as the feudal jurisdictions of the countryside.[8]

Clans continued to maintain primary positions in areas of the Renaissance world where the survival of feudal jurisdictions made them an important presence in city and countryside. They persisted in England, Scotland, Spain, and parts of France. Monarchs hoped to break clan solidarity in their efforts to build centralized states, but their intrusions on local elite families that had institutionalized patron–client ties were often thwarted. France provides a good example, where four noble dynasties and their respective clienteles in the last decades of the sixteenth century continually fueled the fires of civil war in order to dismantle or usurp the royal crown. The French case demonstrates that state development was not a smooth, linear process, but rather one of advancement, retreat, and sometimes dead ends. Nonetheless, the Atlantic monarchies made greater strides than the Holy Roman Emperors in this process. Only when royal bureaucracies obtained monopolies of coercive force, accumulating the massive tax resources that would finance canon and other new military technology, were the aspirations of noble dynasts held at bay. (See the essay above by Edward Muir.)

On the Italian peninsula clans remained prominent in the feudal territories of Piedmont, the Bresciano, the Friuli, the Papal States, parts of the south, and the islands.[9] Naples is a prime example. Ancient clans, steeped in military and feudal traditions, played a critical role in the political and economic life of the city and the kingdom as a whole.[10] Clans were linked to Naples and the surrounding villages by symbolic and reciprocal obligations. Within each group of individuals who could trace their origins to common ancestors were several lineages, associated with specific fiefs that remained in the patriline. Possession of a fief over many generations conferred status, power, and economic worth to the lineage. The behavior of Neapolitan aristocrats expressed a distinct clan consciousness that served the interests and traditions of the larger kinship group as a whole.

Sixteenth-century Friuli, on the northeast margin of the Venetian territorial state, was also fertile terrain for extended kinship networks. Several castellan lineages akin to clans in the Scottish mode dominated factions and waged wars among themselves. In this peripheral area of a loosely governed state, clan solidarity was both fluid and fragile, so much so that the dominant families relied on factions of non-consanguineous retainers to regulate tensions, build clientage with neighbors, and furnish some collective identity. The old Friulian families of prestige formed endogamous marriage alliances to ensure their social pre-eminence, even though the more exogamous families of lesser status were economically and politically ascendant. At the other end of the Venetian territorial state, bordering Lombardy, Brescian nobles formed similar configurations of feudal clans and factions, frequently turning city and countryside into theaters of war. However, neither the Friulian nor the Brescian clans were as cohesive as the *parentele* in Liguria, clans that provided an overarching structure for all political and economic relations.[11] The Genoese *albergo*, a formal association of families that accepted a common name, continued to behave like an extended family, with spheres of influence that extended far beyond the Italian peninsula. By the end of the fifteenth century Genoese merchants had founded large colonies in Lisbon, Bruges, and Antwerp; the Vanni, Gridetti, and Marchione families had founded the sugar economy in Madeira; and in sixteenth-century Seville Genoese families had organized the first links with the Americas.[12]

There is no uniform model of family or clan in the Renaissance world. The size, structure, behavior, and financial and social status of these kinship groups varied from region to region and changed in response to demographic, political, and economic pressures. Family and clan were shaped by the resources and constraints of their environments, and by standards and expectations linked to social class, honor, and gender. In principle, the clan prevailed in agrarian economies, where the state was weak and the Church did not regulate marriage, while the family flourished in urban societies, with hereditary or wealth-based social stratification. The wealthy made marriage contracts, emphasizing dowry and bilateral descent in urban lineages. Contract and dowry superseded religious ritual and gave way to a conjugal fund that made neither the Church nor the clan, but rather the marital couple the most important authority over family life.

Family Behavior and the Consolidation of Power

There were multiple centers of power in the Renaissance world. Royal and feudal dynasts, urban corporations, rural clans, and a variety of other patron–client networks competed for political and economic hegemony. The family unit was at the heart of each of them. In its capacity to guarantee the status quo for power-holders, it shaped the inner workings of state, regional, municipal, and rural configurations of power.

The strategies of urban oligarchs to enlarge and protect their spheres of influence furnish rich examples of the close connection between family behavior and the consolidation and exercise of power. Monographic study of ruling circles in Milan, Florence, Siena, Venice, Cremona, Genova, Lucca, Verona, as well as Rouen, Strasbourg, Barcelona, and the cities of Switzerland and south Germany reveals restricted numbers of families monopolizing wealth and the advantages of high office.[13] Few urban oligarchies in sixteenth-century Europe, save those in Barcelona or some of the Dutch and south German cities, conceded political rights to guild families or to other commoners.[14] The benefits of office-holding for urban oligarchs could only be equaled or surpassed by feudal privilege and jurisdictions or by the dynastic realms of Renaissance princes. In the northern Italian cities, for example, councillors supervised the funds of large enterprises such as the Monti di Pietà and hospitals; they designed fiscal and judicial systems; and they manipulated the systems of food provisioning to their own advantage. Their positions as office-holders were potentially so lucrative that they persistently excluded merchants, craftsmen, and most newcomers from their governing bodies, while their own careers in law or the notarial arts assumed inordinate importance.[15] Similarly, French cities were increasingly dominated by judicial elites that jealously guarded their privileges. Essential to the enterprise of state-building, lawyers and judges staffed most of the royal offices that were originally generated from the monarchy but transmitted through inheritance down the family line. Royal offices were family property that ensured prosperity and exclusive status.

Political consolidation was achieved through changes in family structure: biological attrition or expansion; cooptation into civic councils and professional corporations; the continuity of lineages; and the preservation of wealth over time. The strength of the domestic group hinged not only on its size and wealth, but also on the astute planning of marriage and kinship alliances.[16] Diverging devolution and bilateral wealth-conserving strategies were also important for maintaining hegemony over the *longue durée*,[17] and education in law or the notarial arts complimented and sustained positions in urban government.

It is important to examine the efforts of the elite family to protect and improve its status and conserve its wealth over time in further detail. First, reproduction was essential to the continuity of the lineage. It conferred the possibility of constructing both vertical and horizontal networks of power within and outside the family, and in instances where membership in an urban oligarchy was hereditary it also ensured the continuity of power. Second, because wealth was a fundamental requisite of power, financial strength over the *longue durée* was essential. It also bound the destinies of families joined by marriage alliance, giving domestic groups a cohesion and logic. Moreover, having heirs also necessitated practicing wealth conservation. Both mothers and fathers exerted a great deal of influence on the internal and external dynamics of the family in their efforts to maintain the social, economic, and political status that ensured their privileged positions in the Renaissance city.

The behavior of oligarchs in Brescia, a rich and vitally strategic city in the Venetian state, may be used as an example. Like many urban elite families in northern and central Italy, and in southern France, Brescians lived for at least part of their lives in complex households.[18] A function of wealth conservation, the complex household permitted the couple to economize on the costs of daily life; and it kept family patrimony intact for as long as possible.[19] Moreover, a large family living under the same roof was also a means of publicly representing its cohesion and power.

Brescian parents, like other elite couples, strove to prevent the dispersion of wealth among offspring. Although nuptial bonds were an indispensable political and social tool, the number of children who married impinged upon the economic equilibrium of the family. For this reason marriage was restricted according to financial means, even though both sons and daughters were ensured at least a share, if not the primary share, of their parents' property. Brescian fathers sometimes entailed their property to daughters as well as to sons. Entail, legally a deed of trust, made an heir the custodian of the property, with the obligation to hold it and then return it on his or her death. In some parts of Italy, like England, France and Spain, only the oldest son inherited the family estate, keeping the majority of wealth within the patriline.[20] Entail, coupled with primogeniture, guaranteed succession, counteracting the possibility that land be given as dowry or dower, or might be sold. It was an especially promising wealth conservation strategy when the prospects of earning large profits or circulating large sums of liquid capital were dim. In these circumstances entail prevented dispersion. Moreover, it sheltered patrimony from state confiscation.

Restricted marriage was another common wealth-conserving strategy. In Venice, for example, the *fraterna* limited marriage to one brother while other male siblings shared the family wealth and acted as an association.[21] Alternatively, unmarried siblings entered ecclesiastical institutions.[22] Few daughters were dowered to be married because of the expense involved. However, family honor was tied to female sexuality. Unmarried daughters, thus, were sheltered in convents. But daughters received a share of the inheritance as well, whether as dowry to marry or to enroll in a convent. In the first instance, women of economic substance played a significant role in the formation of the elites that ruled the Italian cities.

In the Italian cities, and similarly in Greece, Portugal, and Spain, where the conjugal fund was favored over patrilineal inheritance, wives and widows had an important impact on the elite marriage market.[23] Oligarchies practiced endogamy. Thus marriages were arranged to solidify social and political alliances. In order to make a valuable match, a substantial portion of the resources of the bride's natal family was earmarked for her dowry. Elite women thus received large dowries which in turn enriched their daughters' marriage possibilities. At the same time they often inherited substantial resources that they were free to dispose of as they liked. The combination of dowry and inheritance gave elite women the opportunity to have an impact on the matchmaking process by making contributions of substance to their daughters' dowries. Still further, wealth gave women the chance to effect a change in expectations about appropriate social and emotional behavior for men and women: the bequests and donations of wealthy women were oriented more toward affective ties with relatives rather than the traditional passing of wealth down the male line. Women in Venice, for example, chose to be generous to daughters, granddaughters, nieces, and other kinswomen because of personal regard and affection rather than loyalty or obligations to the lineage.[24]

Mothers and fathers, however, could not dower all daughters equally, especially because dowry levels steadily rose in Renaissance Europe.[25] This preoccupied civic leaders, who worried that inflated demands would ruin families and/or reduce nuptiality. Florentines created a municipal dowry fund in 1425 that remained central to marital strategy and public finance for over a century.[26] Meanwhile, moralists decried the ruinous dowry levels, advocating more social equality among marriage partners so as to arrest escalating costs. Yet the very parents who feared dowry costs were inflating them. Stanley Chojnacki has attributed inflation in Venice both to competition and to changes in women's attitudes: widows possessed of ever larger dowries increasingly dowered their female kin, fueling self-perpetuating upward pressure on dowries. It was not only women, however, who fueled dowry inflation. Fathers were also particularly keen on arranging marriages and enlarging dowries in order to elevate the political, social, and financial status of their families.

Not all European elites favored the conjugal fund, however, nor gave married women the right to bequeath their dowries to whomever they chose. Some protected the patrilineal fund at all costs. English law, for example, specifically reinforced the principle of primogeniture, so that women could not inherit the land earmarked for the patrilineal lineage, and in sixteenth-century France married women's rights to control their own wealth were increasingly curtailed.

Career strategies among urban oligarchs also helped to consolidate their power. Increasingly throughout the late Renaissance, in Italy, Spain, and France power holders abandoned activities associated with trade or crafts in favor of careers in law and the notarial arts. Making laws and enforcing legislation, designing tax systems, negotiating property transactions, and concluding marriage contracts were the very activities that endowed these families with a preponderance of power. Still more, the legal and notarial professions fit better with the new life-styles that these families had adapted for themselves. By the late sixteenth and early seventeenth centuries many had returned to emulating the life-styles of landowning aristocracies, even if they retained a distinctly urban social and cultural orientation. In contrast, their English and Dutch neighbors moved towards industrial capitalism. The progressive land-owning class in England strengthened its position in Parliament with the profits from commercial agriculture and global trade, while burghers in the Low Countries grew rich on transoceanic voyages and the establishment of centers of capital invest-ment. Whether by trade, capital investment, or commercial agriculture, by law, officeholding, rents or loans, family interests motivated wealth accumulation and the consolidation of power, making family behavior critical to our understanding of evolving systems of power in the Renaissance world.

Ordinary Families

The families of peasants and workers were subject to different constraints from those who ruled them. Far more concerned with subsistence or modest wealth accumulation than with social ascendency or political hegemony, their life-styles and behavior were in large part a response to demographic and economic circumstances. Marriage depended on whether a new family unit would have the means to subsist.

By the fifteenth century there were principally four household and family pat-terns, loosely divided into western, eastern, middle European, and Mediterranean regions.[27] The western model prevailed in regions stretching from France to the Baltic. Young people from the ordinary classes normally worked as servants until their early twenties. At that point, if they were able to establish their own households, they usually selected their own mates rather than having marriages arranged for them. Ten to 15 percent of the population never married, primarily because they did not have the financial means to do so. Men and women who did marry were usually in their mid- to late twenties. Marriage at this late age was a means of restricting the birth rate, as was offering children to monasteries or nunneries, a practice which first developed in southwest Asia and North Africa, reaching Europe in the Middle Ages as Christianity spread. Often parents whose offspring (or, if not, then nephews, nieces, younger cousins, neighbors, or friends) reached adulthood made a retire-ment contract with them. In areas where manor lords were few, they might divide their patrimony among their sons, staying with each son for a part of the year. In places where manor lords wanted to keep their holdings unified, they might turn over most of their holdings or use-rights to one son or son-in-law, retaining a small dwelling and garden plot, receiving food and other needs from the heir. The heirs who cared for older parents, in turn, would receive some assistance from their siblings.

The eastern model, found in Albania, Bulgaria, and northeast to European Russia, was very different. Unlike the northwest, new, independent households were not formed by marriage, but rather from the division of large existing family households (fission), or by combining small existing family households (fusion). Each hearth contained a core married couple in addition to other married couples. Marriages were arranged, and the typical age was mid- to late twenties for both sexes. Most people in these areas of the world married rather than becoming servants in others' households. In fact servants were scarce, except in the wealthiest families.

In the middle European model, which included central and southern France, parts of Italy, Austria and Germany, household structure was modeled on the stem family. Rather than a conjugal couple with co-resident, unmarried children, the household contained two co-residential married couples. Parents, for example, lived with married sons because opportunities for the latter to establish independent farms were not available. There was also some neolocality, fission, and fusion. Age at marriage was mid- to late twenties for women and men, and celibacy rates were high. People who did not marry became servants of the wealthy or worked for their married relations.

Mediterranean households in Greece, Italy, Spain, and Portugal also formed through the division of large households or the joining of smaller ones rather than starting a new household altogether. Marriage was arranged, with men marrying later than women, and 10 percent not marrying at all. Wealthy families relied on the assistance of servants, while those of more modest means distributed their work load among co-resident adult kin. In Spain and Portugal women came to marry later and less often, especially where emigration to the Americas was heaviest.

None of the household systems described above lend themselves to strict definition. A growing body of research shows highly variable household formations, even within the same geographical region. Peasants and workers in Renaissance Tuscany, for example, experienced a variety of living arrangements. Fewer than one-third of the male population in the countryside was financially able to set up hearths of their own.[28] Age at marriage for rural males was under 26; agricultural workers married around 22. Sons remained with their natal families even when married, with several generations living in one household. Married brothers lived in common, sharing the inheritance and jointly cultivating their land. Neolocality occurred only after age 40, but this was rare as long as the replacement rate for hearths remained low. The main consideration was whether a new household could be self-sustaining. Daughters married earlier than sons, around 18, leaving their natal families for their husbands' homes. Celibacy rates – 2 percent for rural women – were lower than elsewhere in western Europe. Extended families sometimes divided when their numbers exceeded their means of subsistence, but in general a high mortality rate combined with low fertility limited the sizes of their family groups. Because reproduction was slow, they chose to remain together and practice joint inheritance. In contrast, the urban centers of Tuscany presented a different family structure, linked to employment opportunities, degrees of wealth, and means of production. While the agrarian structure of Tuscan villages necessitated enlarging the family labor pool, in the cities, craftsmen and shopkeepers had to fend for themselves in a fluctuating market of supply and demand. Thus each generation divided. Financial means, as mentioned above, could also restrict marriage. Six per cent of women never married. Those who did, wed at around 18; men between 26 and 31. Wives, significantly younger than their husbands, generally experienced early widowhood. Gradually the practice of marrying young brides to much older grooms gave way to customs resembling northwestern Europe, where spouses were closer in age to one another.

The opportunities for marriage and children for ordinary people, therefore, depended to a great degree on the availability of resources to establish new households. A significant number of men and women did not marry at all, becoming servants or auxiliary members of the households of married kin.

The Family in the Age of Religious Reform

Several broad developments in Europe beginning in the sixteenth century weakened earlier family norms and behavior. Among them were the Protestant reforms, the resurgence of the Catholic Church, and the growth of the secular state. During the Reformation, Protestants advanced conceptual models of the family that challenged Catholic doctrine and canon law.[29] They denounced the celibate ideal that had accompanied religious vows, closing monastic institutions and elevating the status of husband and wife over that of monk and nun. This would clearly hinder the practice of restricted marriage, described above. Moreover, besides creating property, honor, and kinship, the reformers proclaimed marriage to be the normal place for sexuality and a cure for fornication. Protestants were thus encouraged to marry, and husbands and wives were urged to build companionate marriages, sharing responsibilities but still maintaining the hierarchy of wifely subordination to husbands. Protestant theologians also recognized failed marriage. While the Catholic Church upheld marriage as a sacramental bond that could never be broken, Protestants legalized divorce and remarriage. The possibility of marrying more than once, and of severing previous ties made the institution of the family far more complex under the new rules.

Responding to Protestant concerns as well as to the impulse of reform from within, the Catholic Church attempted to play a greater role in the regulation of marriage and sexuality. For centuries the Church had permitted the free expression of mutual consent between partners to be the only requisite for a valid marriage. Only medieval France had regularized the rites of marriage celebration, while in the rest of Europe a freedom of form had prevailed. However, while dowries and notarized contracts were only of secondary importance to the Church, they were still critical to the secular family. Therefore most parents wanted to play a prominent role in choosing the partners of their offspring, in order to guarantee the status of the lineage over time. Until the Council of Trent (1545–63) the Church had focused more on the sacrament of marriage, but afterwards it lay claim to the regulation of the contract as well.

This change was motivated by several factors. One was the flood of breach of promise suits that had inundated the medieval ecclesiastical courts. Another was the concern, both spiritual and temporal, for the honor of women who had been deflowered and abandoned. A third stemmed from the intense pressure from Spanish and French monarchs to arrest the flow of clandestine marriages that recalcitrant couples had concluded in order to avoid the arrangements their parents had made for them. Prelates at Trent hotly debated how to regulate marriage, and they disagreed over whether parental consent should be made a requirement of marrying. The result was the Tametsi decree, which insisted that the banns be published and that the couple pronounce their vows in the presence of the parish priest and several witnesses. Parental consent was not required, but clandestine marriage was strongly discouraged. Nonetheless, clandestine marriage was still valid, thus giving children more than just veto power over their parents' wishes. The Tametsi decree left free will intact, and a number of couples used the reform to have their arranged marriages annulled, arguing that they had been made without their consent.[30]

The family had more interest in protecting arranged marriage than did the Church, and by extension, so did the secular state. The French monarchy, in solidarity with the judicial nobility, put the requirement into law in 1556.[31] England followed in 1563. Disapproving parents were allowed to disinherit offspring who refused to marry partners of the parents' choice. Spain also advocated parental control of marriage but took less draconian measures, while the individual Italian regional states moved slowly and haphazardly toward regulation. Marriage was a social, political, and financial arrangement that helped guarantee the status of the lineage over time and that provided the social fabric of daily life. Most parents were unwilling to leave such an important step in the hands of their children. Nor were they willing to allow the Church absolute authority over the validity of the marriage contract. Thus, an ongoing tension existed between the state, which was essentially composed of conjugal families and represented their interests over ecclesiastical institutions, and the Church, whose ultimate claims of authority permitted children to marry in defiance of parental wishes.

The Catholic Church also made new efforts to discipline sexuality in the age of reform.[32] Its ideology was gender specific. Throughout the Middle Ages and well into the Renaissance, women were depicted as the physical and mental inferiors of men. Representing both virtue and vice, they provided a negative foil against which men could define themselves and justify male authority. Women's desires were held to be insatiable, thus requiring discipline. Moreover, with the spread of syphilis in Europe, disease began to be associated with women's sexual activities.[33] Catholic prelates advocated enclosure and purity as strategies for defending the faith and for protecting the family and the social order. Either the domestic enclosure of marriage or that of the convent were the recommended prophylactics to disorder and social instability.[34] Not all women were obliging, but those who disobeyed found themselves chastised by the community and often punished in both secular and ecclesiastical courts. Still, the sixteenth and seventeenth centuries witnessed a spirited literary debate among feminist writers such as Lucrezia Marinella and Moderata Fonte, who denounced arranged marriage and forced monacization.[35] The protests spilled over into the courts. At the Patriarchal Court in Venice women petitioned for annulments, claiming their parents had forced them into unwanted unions. Others demanded separations from abusive husbands. Clearly women had preferences of their own, which took into account love, physical attraction, and respect in addition to status and wealth accumulation.[36] (See the essay of Elissa Weaver below.)

The Family in a Globalizing World

Side by side with the religious reform movements, European exploration and colonization also led to sweeping changes in family patterns across the globe. Lisbon, Madrid, Paris, London, and Amsterdam became world cities after 1492, exporting European modes of living abroad. Portuguese colonization of the coasts of Africa and the Amazon Basin, Spanish hegemony from the Rio Grande to the Rio de la Plata and in the Caribbean; English, French, and Dutch commercial networks in Asia and the New World brought new models of family life to indigenous peoples. (See the essay of John Marino below.) Europeans often attempted to eradicate the cultural traditions that were dramatically different from their own. For example, the conquistadors found a variety of indigenous sexual mores, ranging from strict definitions of sexual morality in Aztec and Inca societies to looser definitions in many groups of Central and South America. Initially European men enjoyed cohabitation with indigenous women, either given by or taken from the conquered people. After 1530, however, when the Spanish and Portuguese crowns and the Catholic Church had secured control of the Americas, they attempted to enforce Christian behavior on the indigenous and settler populations.[37]

The first European conquerors and settlers exported the Mediterranean pattern of early marriage for women and later marriage for men, a practice foreign to the indigenous peoples and African slaves in the Americas.[38] Spanish and Portuguese women, persistently in short supply, almost always married men of European descent. While European men preferred early marriage to European women in order to secure the social and material properties of the patriline, some married Aztec and Inca aristocratic wives. Many also delayed marriage, taking concubines from among the indigenous women. Once married, men commonly maintained concubines, practicing a kind of informal polygyny. What is more, there were many consensual unions that were never formalized though the rites of marriage endorsed by the Church.

Race was a complex new variable that factored into family status, an important outcome of European colonization in the New World. The intimate unions between the European conquerors and indigenous women gradually produced a *mestizo* population. In Brazil the offspring of native peoples and African slaves who had been transported there by the Portuguese added a mulatto group to the mix. Spanish and Portuguese rulers organized these groups within a caste system, governed by Mediterranean concepts of family honor that were known from Portugal and Morocco to Greece, Turkey, Lebanon, and Iran.[39] Peoples of European descent sat at the top of the hierarchy. In Mexico the descendants of Aztec nobility came next, but elsewhere the offspring of Europeans and indigenous peoples stood on a second tier, above Euro-Africans. People of all three ancestries came next, then full-blooded indigenous peoples, then African-Indian, then Africans. European families of honor were separated from other mixed families that had been formed as a result of concubinage. Spaniards, as well as English, French, and Dutch masters in the Americas encouraged their slave populations to reproduce, although they frequently denied any legal validity to slave marriages.

Despite the consensual and non-consensual unions of Europeans and indigenous peoples, massive depopulation had quickly followed the arrival of the Spanish and the Portuguese in the Americas. In part this was the result of devastating epidemics and wars of conquest. Smallpox, measles, influenza, and possibly bubonic plague depopulated Mexico and Guatemala by 1520, paving the way for Cortez's victory in 1521. Syphilis followed closely on the heels of epidemic disease, bringing sterility and more deaths. But European intrusion on the family structures of indigenous peoples also contributed to the downward demographic spiral by affecting the birth rate. Indigenous peoples turned to infanticide and abortion, refusing to bring children into the world of their harsh conquerors and reacting negatively to the abrogation of their customs and beliefs. Some also practiced long lactation and abstinence when persuaded to renounce polygyny, again limiting births. They had been, unhappily, forced during the missionary experience to adapt to Spanish modes of life. They were corralled into missions, where the friars insisted they perform agricultural labor in order to be fed. In confinement, men and women were housed in separate quarters – again something new. With Christianity, indigenous peoples and African settlers were introduced to the concept that sex outside of formal marriage was sinful. Polygyny was gradually replaced by Christian marriage according to rites set down at the Council of Trent. Only those formally married by the Roman Catholic procedures that the friars introduced were permitted to cohabit. This too represented a dramatic change. For example, in northern California foragers had been used to making and unmaking and remaking marriages freely, and they found the new demands of the friars bewildering.[40]

The Spanish and Portuguese conquerors recognized the depopulation problem by 1560, but their response served more as a catalyst to this development rather than to arrest it. They imposed the formation of families patterned after Iberian models and following Iberian legal processes. Having the family as the basic social unit, they could hope to replicate their own cultural, legal, social, and economic societies in the New World. Again, indigenous peoples were confined to settlements to ensure a labor pool for mines and plantations. Friars wanted this as well in order to teach Christianity. African slaves were brought in to compensate for the loss of indigenous peoples and to make certain of a labor force. By 1600 the indigenous peoples in Spanish America averaged no more than two births per couple as opposed to the three to six prior to 1492.[41]

Several patterns of family life developed in the Americas; race and class helped produce difference. The Mediterranean concept of honor was the underlying basis for European patterns. It included providing for wife and children, keeping good kinship relations, protecting reputation for men and chastity for women. Spanish laws on marriage and property rights applied to Spaniards and to the members of the Aztec nobility with whom they had intermarried. (Aztecs had used dowry far less than the Spaniards did.) The wife of a Spaniard, whether European or Aztec, retained her dowry both for herself and her heirs. She succeeded to a deceased husband's property, unless it was entailed. A married woman needed her husband's permission for legal transactions. In contrast, among Indians and *mestizos* customary patterns of bride-wealth and neighborhood endogamy persisted. Land rights within the calpuli land corporations of the Aztec period might descend to children either patrilineally or bilaterally. Godparenthood was another important European practice introduced in Mexico. It served as a means of establishing ties between Indians and Spaniards, of acquiring protection and advancement, and of strengthening kinship and neighborhood ties.[42]

The end of the Renaissance thus brought reaction and repression to the freer forms of family life that had prevailed in the Americas as well as in the areas of Europe with less homogeneous populations. Women who did not fulfill prescribed gender roles, religious minorities, and non-Europeans were expected to conform to the ideal models of family. These models served the interests of expanding European states, reformed churches, and elites, which all focused on preserving hierarchies of race, gender, and class that protected their own strategies of wealth accumulation and power. Some nonconformists went unnoticed, but the less fortunate found themselves targeted and repressed by both secular and inquisitorial courts.

NOTES

1 Goody, *European Family*, p. 61.
2 Goldthwaite, *Private Wealth*; Kent, *Household and Lineage*; Chojnacki, "Patrician Women," pp. 176–203; Chojnacki, "Kinship Ties," pp. 240–70.
3 Quale, *Marriage Systems*, pp. 136–7.
4 Goody, *European Family*, pp. 61, 66–7.
5 Goldthwaite, *Private Wealth*; Kent, *Household and Lineage*; Davis, *Venetian Family*; Chojnacki, "Patrician Women" and "Kinship Ties"; Grendi, "Profilo storico"; Woolf, *Nobiltà piemontese*; Astarita, *Continuity*, pp. 160–1.
6 Chojnacki, " 'Most Serious Duty,' " pp. 146–7.
7 Grubb, *Provincial Families*, pp. 26–7.
8 Ferraro, *Family and Public Life*, pp. 51–71, 133–54.
9 Woolf, *Nobiltà piemontese*; Ferraro, *Family and Public Life*; Astarita, *Continuity*, pp. 76–8, 86.
10 Astarita, *Continuity*, pp. 9, 12, 21, 36.
11 Muir, *Mad Blood*, pp. 76–8; 86–8; Ferraro, *Family and Public Life*, pp. 133–54; Raggio, *Faide*, pp. 152–8. For Genoa see also Grendi, "Profilo storico, pp. 241–302. On Piedmont, Woolf, *Nobiltà piemontese*.
12 Braudel, "L'Italia fuori d'Italia," pp. 2139–41.
13 The historical literature for the Italian and European cities is compared in Ferraro, *Family and Public Life*, pp. 72–130, 222–7.
14 Amelang, *Honored Citizens*, pp. 217–21; for Flanders and Brabant see Koenigsberger and Mosse, *Europe in the Sixteenth Century*, p. 262; for Strasbourg and Ulm, Brady, *Turning Swiss*, p. 13.
15 The growing importance of a legal education for elite families was a trend characteristic of Europe as a whole. See the French case studied by Dewald, *Provincial Nobility*, pp. 15, 88, 102, 110, 309.
16 Ferraro, *Family and Public Life*, p. 72.
17 Quale, *Marriage Systems*, pp. 132–3, 181.
18 Barbagli, *Sotto lo stesso tetto*, pp. 142, 167, 170, 189–95.
19 See for example, Davis, *Venetian Family*, pp. 6–8.
20 Barbagli, *Sotto lo stesso tetto*, pp. 196, 199, 240–1.
21 For Venice, Davis, *Decline*, pp. 68–9; for Florence and Milan, Barbagli, *Sotto lo stesso tetto*, p. 199.
22 Sperling, *Convents*.
23 Chojnacki, "Dowries and Kinsmen," pp. 571–600; Ferraro, *Family and Public Life*, pp. 111–30.
24 Chojnacki, "Dowries and Kinsmen," pp. 571–600.
25 Grubb, *Provincial Families*, pp. 15–18; Amelang, *Honored Citizens*, p. 79.
26 Kirshner and Molho, "The Dowry Fund," pp. 403–38.
27 Hajnal, "Household Formation"; Laslett, "Family and Household"; Quale, *Families*, pp. 91–2, 133–4.
28 Herlihy and Klapisch-Zuber, *Tuscans*.
29 Ozment, *When Fathers Ruled*, pp. 2–9, 31.

30   Ferraro, *Marriage Wars*, pp. 69–103.
31   Hanley, "Social Sites," pp. 27–52.
32   Ruggiero, *Boundaries of Eros*, pp. 9–15.
33   Muir and Ruggiero, *Sex and Gender*, p. xi.
34   Perry, *Gender*, pp. 12, 53.
35   Labalme, "Venetian Women," pp. 81–109.
36   Ferraro, *Marriage Wars*, pp. 33–67.
37   Lavrin, *Sexuality and Marriage*, p. 3.
38   Quale, *Families*, p. 179.
39   Quale, *Marriage Systems*, pp. 272–5.
40   Ibid., pp. 180–1.
41   Ibid., p. 183.
42   Ibid., pp. 272–5.

REFERENCES

Amelang, James, *Honored Citizens of Barcelona: Patrician Culture and Class Relations, 1490–1714* (Princeton: Princeton University Press, 1986).

Astarita, Thomas, *The Continuity of Feudal Power: The Caracciolo di Brienza in Spanish Naples* (Cambridge: Cambridge University Press, 1992).

Barbagli, Mario, *Sotto lo stesso tetto. Mutamenti della famiglia in Italia dal XV al XX secolo* (Bologna: Il Mulino, 1984).

Brady, Thomas, *Turning Swiss: Cities and Empire, 1450–1550* (Cambridge: Cambridge University Press, 1985).

Braudel, Ferdinand, *The Mediterranean and the Mediterranean World in the Age of Philip II*, trans. Sian Reynolds (New York: Harper and Row, 1972).

Chojnacki, Stanley, "Patrician Women in Early Renaissance Venice," *Studies in the Renaissance* 21 (1974), pp. 176–203.

——, "Dowries and Kinsmen in Early Renaissance Venice," *Journal of Interdisciplinary History* 4 (1975), pp. 571–600.

——, "Kinship Ties and Young Patricians in Fifteenth-Century Venice," *Renaissance Quarterly* 38 (1985), pp. 240–70.

——, " 'The Most Serious Duty': Motherhood, Gender, and Patrician Culture in Renaissance Venice," in *Refiguring Woman: Perspectives on Gender and the Italian Renaissance*, ed. M. Migiel and J. Schiesari (Ithaca: Cornell University Press, 1991), pp. 133–54.

Davis, John C., *The Decline of the Venetian Nobility as a Ruling Class* (Baltimore: Johns Hopkins University Press, 1962).

——, *A Venetian Family and its Fortune, 1500–1900* (Philadelphia: American Philosophical Society, 1975).

Dewald, Jonathan, *The Formation of a Provincial Nobility: The Magistrates of the Parlement of Rouen, 1499–1610* (Princeton: Princeton University Press, 1980).

Ferraro, Joanne M., *Family and Public Life in Brescia, 1580–1650: The Foundations of Power in the Venetian State* (Cambridge: Cambridge University Press, 1993).

——, *Marriage Wars in Late Renaissance Venice* (New York: Oxford University Press, 2001).

Goldthwaite, Richard, *Private Wealth in Renaissance Florence: A Study of Four Families* (Princeton: Princeton University Press, 1968).

Goody, Jack, *The European Family: An Historico-Anthropological Essay* (Oxford: Blackwell Publishers, 2000).

Grendi, Edoardo, "Profilo storico degli Alberghi genovesi," *MEFRM* 87 (1975), pp. 241–302.

Grubb, James S., *Provincial Families of the Renaissance: Private and Public Life in the Veneto* (Baltimore: Johns Hopkins University Press, 1996).

Hajnal, J., "Two Kinds of Pre-industrial Household Formation Systems," in *Family Forms in Historic Europe*, ed. R. Wall, J. Robin, P. Laslett (Cambridge and New York: Cambridge University Press, 1983).

Hanley, Sarah, "Social Sites of Political Practice in France: Lawsuits, Civil Rights, and the Separation of Powers in Domestic and State Government, 1500–1800," *American Historical Review* 102 (1997), pp. 27–52.

Herlihy, David and Klapisch-Zuber, Christiane, *Tuscans and their Families: A Study of the Florentine Catasto of 1427* (New Haven: Yale University Press, 1985).

Kent, F. W., *Household and Lineage in Renaissance Florence: The Family Life of the Capponi, Ginori, and Rucellai* (Princeton: Princeton University Press, 1977).

Kirshner, Julius and Molho, Anthony, "The Dowry Fund and the Marriage Market in Early *Quattrocento* Florence," *Journal of Modern History* 50 (1978), pp. 403–38

Koenigsberger, Helmut G. and Mosse, George L., *Europe in the Sixteenth Century* (London: Longman, 1968).

Labalme, Patricia, "Venetian Women on Women: Three Early Modern Feminists," *Archivio veneto*, 5th ser. 117 (1981), pp. 81–109.

Laslett, Peter, "Family and Household as Work Group and Kin Group: Areas of Traditional Europe Compared," in *Family Forms in Historic Europe*, ed. R. Wall, J. Robin, and P. Laslett (Cambridge: Cambridge University Press, 1983).

Lavrin, Asunción, ed., *Sexuality and Marriage in Colonial Latin America* (Lincoln, NE: University of Nebraska Press, 1989).

Muir, Edward, *Mad Blood Stirring: Vendetta and Faction in Friuli during the Renaissance* (Baltimore: Johns Hopkins University Press, 1993).

Muir, Edward and Ruggiero, Guido, eds., *Sex and Gender in Historical Perspective* (Baltimore: Johns Hopkins University Press, 1990).

Ozment, Steven, *When Fathers Ruled: Family Life in Reformation Europe* (Cambridge, MA: Harvard University Press, 1983).

Perry, Mary E., *Gender and Disorder in Early Modern Seville* (Princeton: Princeton University Press, 1990).

Quale, Gladys Robina, *A History of Marriage Systems* (New York: Greenwood Press, 1988).

——, *Families in Context: A World History of Population* (New York: Greenwood Press, 1992).

Raggio, Osvaldo, *Faide e parentele. Lo stato genovese visto dalla Fontanabona* (Turin: Einaudi, 1990).

Ruggiero, Guido, *The Boundaries of Eros: Sex Crime and Sexuality in Renaissance Venice* (New York: Oxford University Press, 1985).

——, *Binding Passions: Tales of Magic, Marriage, and Power at the End of the Renaissance* (New York: Oxford University Press, 1993).

Sperling, Jutta, *Convents and the Body Politic in Late Renaissance Venice* (Chicago: University of Chicago Press, 1999).

Woolf, Stuart J., *Studi sulla nobiltà piemontese nell'epoca dell'assolutismo* (Turin: Einaudi, 1963).

CHAPTER ELEVEN

Gender

ELISSA B. WEAVER

...although rules of conduct for men are numerous, the moral formation of women can be imparted with very few precepts, since men are occupied both within the home and outside it, in public and in private, and for that reason lengthy volumes are required to explain the norms to be observed in their varied duties. A woman's only care is chastity; therefore when this has been thoroughly elucidated, she may be considered to have received sufficient instruction.[1]

> (Juan Luis Vives, *The Education of a Christian Woman*, 1523)

Ladies, who wish to live well,
Desirous to learn and to see,
On virtues and on books they dwell
Wedding learning to morality.[2]

> (Catherine des Roches, *Secondes oeuvres*, 1583, 1586)

"Gender is the social organization of sexual difference," as Joan Scott explains in her collection of essays on the subject. It is the way cultures and societies understand the relationships between men and women; always relative, this understanding varies "across cultures, social groups and time, since nothing about the body... determines univocally how social divisions will be shaped."[3] Gender roles are constructed from beliefs at the core of any culture, and one is taught by family, Church, and other communities to which one belongs, what according to one's sex and class is appropriate, what is not, and what brings honor or shame.

The Renaissance, especially the sixteenth and seventeenth centuries, was a time in which the appropriate behavior of men and women, what we call today their "gender roles," was a topic of widespread interest and the subject of a great deal of literature.[4] As many historians have noted, the period between 1500 and 1800 in Europe was characterized by polemics that signaled serious tensions in the sex-gender system. The causes were multiple and complex and must be sought in the dramatic social changes taking place, especially in the increased visibility of women in the growing cities, in changes in family structure, in new ways of organizing labor, in the production and dissemination of printed books, in greater literacy, in the philosophical revolution of Cartesianism, in scientific discoveries about the body and, perhaps, also through that mysterious mover, chance, in the appearance on the scene of famous, some powerful, women whose example upset received notions of gender difference (Elizabeth I of England and Isabella of Spain, most notably). How gender roles were conceived and debated, by whom, and what difference it may have had then and subsequently are the subjects of the following reflections.

To learn today how gender roles were understood in the Renaissance we look to their construction in language and in visual representations that come to us from the period, taking care to test the ideals expressed against the documentation we have of lived reality. We must also consider the gender of our witnesses, keeping in mind that the documents we have were for the most part written by men, who almost always saw the world in their own image and women as Other. Most of the literature assumes that men are the norm and, consequently, their roles need not be defined; it is only women to whom the restrictions and guidelines apply; all that is not specifically designated as the role of women is reserved for men. We must often assume, on the basis of what is allowed women, what is expected of men. Indeed, as Juan Luis Vives wrote in his influential comportment books for women, *De institutione feminae christianae* (cited above), it was too great a chore to outline rules of conduct for men, given their many and varied duties, and only a few precepts were necessary for the instruction of women.

It is also true that certain norms we find expressed in the rhetoric of the time, especially in comportment books and in sermons, represent little more than the desires of men. Carla Casagrande opens an essay on the medieval ideal of the *donna custodita* wondering how quietly the women who were enclosed in homes and convents accepted the precepts and advice of loquacious preachers, husbands, fathers, and spiritual directors.[5] Recent studies have documented the very vocal and some-times even physical protests of women religious against the strict confinement (enclosure) imposed on them by ecclesiastical authorities. Documents from the Vatican Archives studied by Craig Monson, for example, tell of nuns who fought ecclesiastical authorities attempting to impose reforms, in one case, hurling stones at the messenger who tried to deliver an order from the bishop.[6] One of the important lessons we have learned from recent studies of Renaissance Europe is just how much the ideal and the real diverged.

We will not find a clear set even of the ideals of masculine and feminine behavior that applied universally during the period we call the Renaissance. What was expected of individuals or classes of persons was determined by many factors: their economic and social conditions, whether they lived in city or country, northern or southern Europe, the political system that reigned, their religious beliefs and diverse occupations. There were also changes over time. Generalizations are risky, but we can begin with some very simple, broadly held notions about sex and gender that the societies of early modern Europe inherited from the medieval Catholic world, ideas based on readings of Scripture and on the philosophy and science of the ancients.

The Inherited Tradition

It was generally accepted that man's role was that of the provider, his realm the public world; whereas woman, his subservient and obedient helpmate, was to stay at home, watching over family and possessions. This hierarchical relationship was thought to have been natural: as God governed the world, the monarch his realm, so too the man his family. The honor of the family depended upon all of its members. A man's honor derived from his success in business and public life, and it was understood differently according to class. Merry Wiesner explains that loyalty and bravery brought honor to men of the upper classes, while for bourgeois and working-class men it was honesty, integrity, and good craftsmanship.[7] A woman's honor was always defined by chastity, which guaranteed the purity of blood lines, the certainty of legitimate inheritance, and thus a family's survival. Her chastity was ensured by silence and segregation.

These views and the social policies they fostered were justified by appeal to the Bible, especially Genesis 2 and 3 and the Epistles of St. Paul, 1 Timothy 2: 12–15, and 1 Corinthians 11: 3. Man was created before woman and was, therefore, in male rhetoric deemed the more noble being; woman, taken from his rib, was meant by this birth to be his helpmate and to be subservient to him. Eve was held responsible for the Fall, having succumbed to temptation and having led Adam to sin. The early Church Fathers wrote of the danger of women, the disruptiveness of their speech, their inability to control their passions. The Fathers taught the sinfulness of sex, which was to be tolerated only for procreation, exalted the virginal state, and fostered the cult of Mary, the sinless, virgin mother. The exponents of this culture were clerics, their rhetoric almost universally misogynist.

Humanists added to this picture of mankind and womankind the ideas of ancient philosophy and medicine: from Aristotle, the notion that man is the perfect, woman the imperfect creation of Nature, that the male imposes form on his offspring, the female only provides the material. Homologies in male and female sex organs gave rise to the belief that women's genitals were an internal, earlier stage in development of which men's external genitals were the perfection. This was not the only view, however: Galen had taught that each sex achieved its own perfection, though he maintained that male perfection was superior. The homological sex thesis was widely accepted, even long after contradictory evidence was discovered through scientific examinations. From the humeral theories of Galen and Hippocrates, the Renaissance inherited the belief that man's constitution was warm and dry, woman's cold and wet; heat was the source of strength, of mind and body, and, being larger and stronger, man was better suited to the active life and capable of greater reasoning. (See the essay of William Eamon below.) Since men tended to see the other sex as their opposite, they defined woman as weak and irrational, better suited to the private domain of the family; as their inferior, even in the domestic realm needing guidance and supervision. Because of man's greater strength and woman's frequent pregnancies and the cares of child-rearing, men were the providers and protectors of the family, women the custodians of its possessions and children and, through their chastity, of its integrity.

Leon Battista Alberti described the ideal woman and wife as silent, obedient, chaste, and enclosed. In his *Libri della famiglia* (*On the Family*, 1432–4), Book

III, by paraphrasing ancient philosophers (Aristotle and Xenophon, primarily), Alberti shows how little attitudes had changed over the centuries:

> the spirit of a man is much more robust that that of a woman, and it better withstands the onslaught of enemies; men are stronger and better suited to labor, they are more steadfast, and they can more honestly be permitted to travel to other lands buying and collecting fortune's goods. On the contrary women are almost all seen to be of a timid nature, soft, slow, and for this reason they can more usefully sit upon and watch over things. It almost seems that nature wished thus to provide for our livelihood, wanting men to bring things home and women to preserve them. Let the woman, enclosed within the home, defend the family's possessions and herself in peace, with fear, and suspicion. Let man defend his wife, his home, his family, and his country, not idly but actively.[8]

The enclosure of women was espoused by preachers, too, and other moralists in the late Middle Ages and throughout the Renaissance. In England in the late sixteenth century Edmund Tilney advised that the best way for a woman to keep a good name was for her never to leave her house, and this view continued to be repeated by others.[9]

The feminine ideal expressed by Alberti conforms in many respects to what we find in the letters of a prominent Florentine lady of the time, Alessandra Macinghi (1407–71), the wife of Filippo Strozzi. Writing to her exiled sons, she portrays her activities, limited to home, church, and convent, and concerned primarily with the family and household; her son-in-law handled all her relations with the political world. In her search for a wife for her eldest son, however, she makes clear that she would add personality to Alberti's recipe. As she looked over in church the young women of families of the appropriate social standing, in addition to their beauty and good reputation for honor and responsibility, she also considered aspects of their bearing and conversation that revealed intelligence and a pleasant personality. She sought a good companion for her son, a relationship, it would seem, not quite so hierarchical as Alberti envisioned.[10]

There were important exceptions to the model espoused by Alberti, and many examples of women entrusted with public responsibilities. In medieval feudal societies where family was the basis of the political structure, fathers ruled and handed down power and wealth through their sons; however, women could also represent the family in the absence or incapacity of a male family member and could be entrusted with temporary power to ensure continuity until another male family member was available. Women were also entitled to an inheritance in the form of a substantial dowry over which they exercised some control. The family's private affairs were public affairs. This continued to be the case for the land-based aristocracy throughout Europe in the Renaissance and subsequently, and the principle justified the rule of female regents and queens. The famous literary formulation of gender roles in this society is, of course, Baldassare Castiglione's *Il libro del cortegiano* (*The Book of the Courtier*, 1528).

Castiglione portrays court society of the early sixteenth century, whose norms differed from those of the mercantile cities. His courtier is an accomplished man of arms and letters, his lady a refined animator and moderator of court life for whom letters are befitting and important, however not at the same level of mastery as expected of the courtier. (See the essay by Robert Muchembled above.) Castiglione makes this abundantly clear by showing that the court ladies present at the discussions do not often contribute to them and complain when the debate employs arguments from ancient philosophy that they cannot follow: they are literate but not learned. The activities appropriate for men and women differ significantly. For Castiglione's spokesperson, Giuliano de' Medici, exercises that show men to be virile are vigorous and difficult, while those of court ladies should instead be slow and graceful. Beauty and chastity are expecially important for women, and the dress and speech of all should reflect dignity and grace. The elegant style and decorum recommended in all social encounters required that gentlemen and ladies keep to their own social class. While the primary occupation of the courtier is said to be military, it is his social behavior that interests the author, perhaps because Castiglione, himself primarily a diplomat, found social *savoir-faire* to be more important for the effective exercise of his duties.

Following the example of Castiglione's *Courtier*, many prescribed the responsibilities and appropriate conduct of the gentleman and the lady. Treatises defined the ideal gentleman or outlined the education that would produce him. From works such as Richard Brathwaite's *The English Gentleman* (1628) we learn that an English gentleman's appropriate masculinity, like the Italian courtier's, was based on family lineage, and upheld honorably through a display of personal courage in arms or sports. For the English gentry, however, Brathwaite also stressed the successful managing of one's estate or performance of one's military or government duties. The country gentleman of treatises, letters, elegies, and the like, often differs from the courtier also by placing less emphasis on cultural refinement, preferring action to contemplation. Brathwaite also wrote a treatise on *The English Gentlewoman* (1633), and the frontispiece illustrations of the two works show the gentleman and the gentlewoman in opposing settings: he is seen outdoors, with mountains, trees, sky, digging instruments, a ship; she is inside a windowless room, alone, occupied in domestic activities or reading devotional literature, except for two scenes, one in a garden, the other in heaven.[11]

In his memoirs the German Hans von Schweinichen (1552–1616), a member of the lesser nobility, shows how widely accepted were the courtly, chivalric virtues. However, Schweinichen's comportment was not so much formed by court society as it was by his Lutheran faith.[12] Unlike the Italian courtier and English gentleman, Schweinichen made himself out to be a "simple man," loyal, honest, and devout. He describes two phases of his maturing process: in the first, he learned not only the virtues but also the vices of court male society. He bonded with male friends by drinking, hunting, and having an interest in women; however, unlike his friends, he demonstrated considerable self-control and treated women with respect. Later, he shows his education and experience to have prepared him to work in his father's business with dedication. Hans von Schweinichen did not share the notion of virility exhibited by his companions, who drank excessively and were violent toward women. His was a somewhat different understanding of appropriate masculine behavior that existed alongside the dominant "virile" model, one in which religion, especially Protestantism, played an important role.

The conduct books for women continued to prescribe behavior with an emphasis on chastity and, following the medieval tradition, according to the social status of wife, widow, or virgin; a good example is Agostino Valerio's popular *Instituzione d'ogni stato lodevole delle donne christiane* (1575), the four parts of which, addressed to virgins, wives, widows, and *dimesse* (a variety of lay sister), were also reprinted separately. Rudolph Bell, in his study of "how-to" books in the Renaissance, notes that more were written for virgins and wives than for widows; Bell found nothing addressed to widowers, who remarried more often than widows.[13] For widows the advice was always not to remarry. Valiero was certain they would not want to make themselves again subject to the rule of a husband. The wealthy Roman widows studied by Carolyn Valone took to heart such good advice, which gave them economic power and freedom they had not had as wives, and they employed their wealth in artistic and architectural commissions.[14] Models of behavior for women were proposed, not only through treatises aimed at the different *stati*, but in Catholic areas also through biographies of female saints and of illustrious women. The model lives changed over time, reflecting changes in the Church's teaching and in society. Most of this literature was written for members of the bourgeoisie and aristocracy, since members of the lower classes, in large part, could not read; model saints' lives and biblical stories were instead conveyed to the illiterate in painted and printed images and through sermons.

In the social world of Renaissance cities, the modern family was emerging as the basic social unit, and its progressive separation from external society gave rise to an increasingly greater distinction between the public and the private realms. Laws were written that systematically excluded women from power, denying them property rights and confining them either to the home where they were subject to husbands or to convents and under the control of male ecclesiastical authorities. Such laws, however, varied from place to place. The difference between nearby cities could be striking: for example, in Florence women had to be represented legally by men, whereas in Pisa they could represent themselves in court.[15] There were generally more restrictions on the activities of women of the upper classes, while women of lower classes everywhere were allowed greater mobility, since, in contributing to the support of their families, they often had to work outside of the home. Like most generalizations, however, even this one regarding the confinement of upper-class women was not universally true, since it seems that in sixteenth- and seventeenth-century England, the social activities of women of the upper classes were expanding. Thomas Platter in 1599 wrote that women in England "have far more liberty than in other lands and know just how to make good use of it for they often stroll out or drive by coach in very gorgeous clothes and the men must put up with such ways and may not punish them for it," and one of the characters in Thomas Middleton's *A Mad World My Masters* claims that Englishmen are careless about their wives while the Italians keep them "under lock and key."[16] Marie de Gournay (*L'Égalité des hommes et des femmes* (1612) echoed the same sentiments, claiming that English and French women were free to socialize while Italian women were "shut up in dungeons" by their husbands.

The norms expressed in literary texts find corroboration in contemporary paintings and portraits. In Ghirlandaio's representations of the canonical moments in the life of the Virgin, women are shown in contemporary dress attending church services, wedding festivities, and at home reading devotional literature and assisting at births – occupying the gendered spaces Alberti and his contemporaries accorded them. In the portraiture of the sixteenth and seventeenth centuries men too are often shown at home, but it is in their studies, surrounded by symbols of their vocations and avocations, while women occupy less specific domestic spaces, often together with a child, sometimes with a book of devotional literature or poetry, the latter a change that attests to the increased access of women to literary culture already in the early years of the sixteenth century. Some women are portrayed with symbols of their domestic work; see, for instance, the beautiful portrait by Maerten Van Heemskerck of Anna Codde working at her spinning wheel (1529, Amsterdam, the Rijksmuseum). Such details, however, are fewer in the representation of women than in that of men. In sixteenth-century Italian portraiture women continued to be viewed through the perspective of the Petrarchan ideal. Interestingly, the self-portraits of women artists of the time depict the women with brush, palette, and easel, and often with musical instruments and other symbols of their culture (see, for example, the work of Sofonisba Anguissola, Artemisia Gentileschi, and Judith Leyster). Women artists, like contemporary men, obviously wanted to be known for their talents and cultural achievements. The depiction of women with books, especially canzonieri and anthologies of poetry, with musical instruments, or in the act of painting, points to the greater access of women in the sixteenth century to humanistic culture and, concomitantly, to a change in what was seen to be appropriate. Women throughout Europe were beginning to distinguish themselves in areas that had previously been the exclusive domain of men. Wives, sisters, and daughters trained in art and music, earlier thought to be exceptions, were becoming more common. Women of the patriciate, courtesans who frequented patrician circles, and also members of the prosperous middle classes were not only reading poetry but writing and publishing their verse as well. Clearly, by the early sixteenth century, the literary activity of women was becoming accepted, even considered admirable. The parameters of what was appropriately feminine were clearly expanding.

Different codes of behavior applied to the working classes, whose livelihood required that the sexes often mingled in public spaces. Women traded in the markets and ran retail establishments throughout the cities, though they rarely had occupations that required travel. Many northern European genre paintings show women working alongside men: see, for example, the fishmongers painted by Joachim Beuckelaer (1570), Franz Snyders (1618), or Emanuel De Witte (ca. 1672), Adriaen Van Ostade (1672), and others. Servant girls who migrated from the country to the cities in large numbers could be seen on errands in the streets and markets.[17] Women worked in many trades, though generally in positions of little prestige and low remuneration. If it was considered less than honorable in Italy, and probably in Spain and Portugal, as some scholars have suggested,[18] for women to work alongside men in the marketplace, archival sources for Italian cities in the fifteenth century indicate that it was nonetheless common. There is ample documentation for Italy and France that women were merchants, bankers, printers; they trained apprentices and managed properties.[19] In the late Middle Ages women could belong even to the major guilds; however, as early as the fifteenth century in some countries, later in others, they were progressively excluded, by law and custom.[20]

In Elizabethan England women were often outside of the home, and not only for work. They made up a large percentage of theater audiences as Shakespeare acknowledges, for instance in the epilogue to *As You Like It*.[21] Jean Howard argues that women, by attending public theater, became "consumers, critics, spectators, and spectacles" and, as such, were altering gender relations, transgressing "the physical and symbolic boundaries of the middle-class woman's domestic containment."[22] This would seem all the more significant because of what they were seeing on stage, a subject to which I shall return. Anthony Fletcher claims that in London, a "center for fashion and conspicuous consumption" in the sixteenth and seventeenth centuries, women were becoming more involved in an ever greater variety of social activities, and their increased visibility created a considerable anxiety about the gender order.[23]

That changes were threatening the patriarchal hierarchy would seem to be confirmed by the proliferation of normative literature throughout the Renaissance. It was not only that men and women sought through such reading to improve themselves, but also, and, I think, primarily, that those who commanded the power of the word (men of upper and upwardly mobile classes) sought to impose their views on others (women and other social inferiors), often with what they considered the best intentions, the preservation of important aspects of the social structure: the sex-gender system and class divisions. However, this attempt to impose control had within it the seeds of its undoing. To quote Jean Howard again, while the increase in women's literacy that followed the invention of printing allowed them to be "controlled and interpellated as good subjects of a patriarchal order," at the same time their "skills in reading and writing allowed some women access to some authorities (such as Scripture) and to some technologies (such as print), which allowed them to begin to rewrite their inscriptions within patriarchy."[24]

Books of advice to women and men on education or marriage were a popular genre among all religious groups. Those written by Protestants stressed husbandly authority and wifely obedience, even more than Catholic manuals, and more often also encouraged the sensual relationship between spouses; a Jewish manual, cited by Merry Wiesner, differs little from the others, except to recommend cheerfulness and emotional and physical responsiveness in a wife, along with obedience.[25] Most expressed traditional negative ideas about women, like Juan Luis Vives's *De institutione feminae christianae* (1523), even Erasmus's *Christiani matrimonii institutio* (1526), and Fray Luis de Leon's *La perfecta casada* (1583).

Vives and Erasmus believed in the spiritual but not the political equality of men and women. They were in favor of the education of upper-class women; however, they thought it should exclude subject matters they felt were inappropriate or unnecessary. For Erasmus, women who did not have to work should study Greek and Latin, while those who did should learn to read at least in the vernacular; a woman's moral education was to come from her husband. Vives favored an education for women based only on books that provided moral guidance and on learning the practical arts of spinning, weaving, and cooking. More important than learning in women, Vives, argued, were their chastity and obedience. His ideas on these matters were extremely severe and misogynistic: he felt rape was always a woman's fault and he would have women be obedient even to a violent husband. Vives had written at the request of Catherine of Aragon to provide guidance for her daughter Mary, but his advice was that a woman should study for her own benefit, not because she would teach others or speak publicly; her participation in public activities would be usurping a masculine role and show her to be unchaste. Both authors argued for the strict subservience of wives to their husbands, seeing this to be in accordance with the hierarchy ordained by God. Luis de Leon, a friar, who took the attributes for a "perfect wife" from the Book of Proverbs, like Vives and Erasmus, felt that her silent and subservient role was preordained. This belief was contested by others, especially women, whose participation in this genre, by introducing the view of the party in question, changed the discourse.

In Holland, Anna Maria van Schurman (1607–78) argued for a humanistic education for women, through the study especially of subjects that would make one a better Christian, including rhetoric, languages (especially Greek and Hebrew), history, metaphysics, and physics. She would not preclude the study of other subjects as well, even those with no practical application for women. In her treatise, the *Dissertatio, de ingenii muliebris* (*Whether a Christian Woman Should be Educated*, 1632), she makes it clear than many, perhaps especially women, no longer accepted the argument that the roles traditionally assigned to women were determined by nature. She wrote:

> they are apt to argue that pulling the needle and distaff is an ample enough school for women. I confess many have been thus persuaded, and those of today who are maliciously inclined agree with them in many cases. But we who seek the voice of reason, not of *received custom*, do not accept this rule of Lesbos. By what law, I ask, have these things become our law? Divine or human? They will never demonstrate that these limits by which we are forced into an order are ordained by fate or prescribed from heaven.[26] (italics mine)

Van Schurman was not the first, nor indeed the first woman, to understand that gender roles were socially constructed. Two centuries earlier Christine de Pizan (1407–71), perhaps the first woman to support herself and her family by her writing, understood that in doing so she had assumed a role considered the prerogative of men.

Christine de Pizan, the daughter of an Italian astrologer and physician at the French royal court, was educated by her father, despite the disapproval of her mother, and, when she married, even her husband supported her literary endeavors. However, both her father and husband soon died, leaving her alone to provide for her mother and children – and she did so through her writing. Proudly aware that she had assumed a role that tradition reserved for men, she created a myth of metamorphosis for herself. In the *Livre de la mutacion de Fortune* (1400–3) she described a dream in which she was on a ship and, suddenly realizing her husband had died, she threw away her wedding ring and was transformed:

> I found myself strong and courageous,
> And learned, to my great surprise,
> That I had truly turned into a man.
>
>   . . .
>
> That I'd become a true man was no fable,
> And to sail the ship I was now able.
> Fortune had taught me the art.[27]

Christine, by asserting that Fortune had taught her to assume a role normally considered appropriate only for men, claims that her feminine role was neither biologically determined nor heavenly ordained. This is not the commonplace of the "virile woman," she who "exceeds her sex," that men (Boccaccio, for example), in order not to give up their exclusive rights to literary, artistic, and political culture, had always attributed to accomplished, talented women. Christine's metamorphosis is an image that portrays an act of will by which she assumed the role of professional writer and provider of her family. She was not made by nature different from other women; she chose to behave differently. Christine did not envision a social revolution. She accepted the view that because nature had given women weaker bodies and the burdens of bearing and rearing children, they were meant to be subject to men; however, she defended her right to pen and parchment, and in nearly all of what she wrote she set out to correct the misogyny she found even in writers she loved.

Her early fame rested on the active part she played in the famous *querelle* of the *Roman de la rose*, in which she, along with others, objected to the mockery of women that characterized Jean de Meung's continuation of the famous allegorical poem. Christine also responded to Maltheolus' complaints about women and marriage in his *Lamentations*, by writing, in 1404, the first important treatise in defense of women, the *Livre de la cité des dames*. She objected that so many important writers, all male, said so much that was untrue about women; their arguments defied reason and experience. Her *Cité des dames* was the first important contribution to what would come to be called the *querelle des femmes*, a debate about the nature and role of women, and therefore also of men, which was especially lively in the sixteenth and seventeenth centuries.

Christine de Pizan's circumstances were unusual for the time. Most educated women lived in convents. While there is evidence as early as the thirteenth century that an increasing number of women owned books and could read in the vernacular language, few could write. Reading and writing were not taught together. As Merry Wiesner explains, teaching women to read but not write was the result not only of an economic decision (materials were expensive), but also of contemporary notions about the ideal woman. Reading would allow her to discover classical and Christian examples of proper female behavior in the work of great male authors, but writing would "enable her to express her own ideas, an ability which few thinkers regarded as important and some saw as threatening."[28] Some humanists, however, educated their daughters along with their sons in classical languages, literature, and philosophy, though public display of their learning brought with it the opposition of men and women alike. Their numbers were not great, but the literary achievements of Cassandra Fedele, Olimpia Morata, Laura Cereta, Isotta and Ginevra Nogarola, Caritas Pirkheimer, her sisters and their daughters, served to open the way toward the education of more women. The printing press allowed for the wide circulation of texts, many of which were translations, and made learning accessible to greater numbers of men and women. By the sixteenth century the numbers of educated women of the European aristocracy grew, as did those of women poets and writers of bourgeois extraction, such as the talented Lyonnaise poet Louise Labé.

Christine had argued that lack of education was all that kept women from equaling or exceeding men in learning, and the education of women became one of the important themes of the *querelle*. She had also argued for the important contributions women had made to society – to culture, to government, and to religion – and the subsequent debate, which was taken up throughout Europe and continued for nearly four centuries, illustrates changing attitudes to the role women could play in European society. By the late seventeenth century, the debate began to center on the contribution educated women could make to the common good, a central feature of the discussions during the Enlightenment period.

The pro-women arguments advanced in the *querelle*, by rejecting many limitations on the activities of women and claiming their right to greater participation in society, to an education which would prepare them to take on roles earlier considered the domain of men, even those of political leadership, show a growing awareness during the period that masculine and feminine roles could change with changing social conditions.

The Querelle des Femmes

The debate about the nature of women – their worth (often called "nobility"), their place in society – appeared in various literary forms, especially the treatise and the dialogue. This debate always included, if only implicitly, alongside claims about the nature of woman and her proper social roles, beliefs regarding the nature of man and his social functions and obligations (sometimes these became the subject of a separate treatise or book in defense or in condemnation of men). The arguments were always supported by catalogues of women (or men), modeled on Plutarch's *Mulierum virtutes* and especially Boccaccio's *De mulieribus claris*, taken from legend, ancient history, hagiography, and the contemporary world (often, the author's prospective patrons).

Throughout the fifteenth century texts in the tradition of Christine de Pizan's *Cité des dames* appeared in Spain, France, and Italy. Among the earliest contributions were Juan Rodríguez del Padrón's *Triunfo de las donas* (ca. 1400–50) and Martin Le Franc's *Le Champion des dames* (ca. 1440–2). Several treatises were written in the Po Valley courts of Ferrara, Mantua, and Milan and dedicated to prominent and powerful women of the ruling families. Some scholars feel it was a literary game, as it surely was in some instances, but a serious defense of women on the part of many authors cannot be entirely discounted. Men often presented both sides of the argument, accusations and defenses of women; in these cases we may suspect that it was for them primarily a game. Galeazzo Flavio Capra's *Antropologia* (1533) is a good example: it consists of a defense of men, a defense of women (first published as a separate text in 1525), and a third book critical of both. Baldassare Castiglione, in Book III of the *Courtier* entertains both sides of the argument, but the defense sustained by Giuliano de' Medici is presented more seriously than the accusations of the misogynists, and it is clear that the author's views are closer, if not identical, to those he expresses through Giuliano. However, as Valeria Finucci has shown, the defense is seriously undermined in Book II, where Castiglione makes women the brunt of many of the jokes offered as examples of clever speech.[29] Joan Kelly has pointed out that male authors often presented arguments for and against women, whereas women only defended their sex; Kelly has also observed that women, unlike men, participated in the debate as a direct response to the attacks of misogynists.[30]

One of the most influential treatises in the genre was Henricus Cornelius Agrippa's *De nobilitate et praecellentia foeminei sexus*, delivered first as a lecture at the University of Dôle in 1509 and published in 1529 with a dedication to Margaret of Austria.

The treatise was almost immediately translated into English, French, Italian, and German, and imitated repeatedly for two centuries. Agrippa, like Capra and Castiglione, offered examples of societies in which women's roles did not follow the theoretically universal patriarchal model. These authors and others, like Sir Thomas Elyot, who wrote a *Defense of Good Women* (1540), questioned the significance of sexual difference in determining social roles.

Ariosto's widely read chivalric poem, the *Orlando furioso* (1532), contains all the elements of the traditional defense of women: logical arguments, exempla, and more. His heroine Bradamante is presented as androgynous: she gains entrance to a fortress (the Rocca di Tristano) performing the feat of martial valor required of a knight and winning the beauty contest required of a lady. Although she is domesticated in the poem's final episodes, Bradamante's androgyny again shows that the sex-gender system is malleable. Ariosto's poem reflects the contemporary debate also by calling on women to defend themselves, to rewrite the history from which male authors have excluded them. His is less a prediction than an acknowledgment of the presence of women on the literary scene as writers as well as patrons and consumers, and it is no surprise that his appeal to women was soon answered. In Italy Moderata Fonte (Modesta da Pozzo), Lucrezia Marinella, and suor Arcangela Tarabotti, in France Marie de Gournay, in England Rachel Speght, in Spain María de Zayas, and many other women entered the debate. They responded promptly to the misogynist attacks that provided constant counterpoint to the defense tradition, reflecting the increased anxiety of men threatened with the greater public presence and prominence of women. Like Christine de Pizan, they argued strongly that all that kept women from successfully competing with men in intellectual endeavors was their inadequate education, and they proposed utopian feminine communities outside of the patriarchy where their worth could be defined. They mastered the rhetoric of their critics, both the reasoned defense and the invective. Arcangela Tarabotti offers a taste of the intelligence and wit of which they were capable in her response to the standard appeal to the authority of Aristotle as proof of the inferiority of women:

> Oh how much more it is with envious spite than sincere truth that you call woman an imperfect animal, while you, who have hair on your face, and beastly behavior as well as unseemly visage, imitate brute animals: and in order to become in every way an unreasoning creature like those to whom nature gave horns, you have worked hard to succeed in raising those hairs on your face, precisely in the form of horns, anxious to imprint above your mouth, if not on your head, a sign that distinguishes you as a perfect animal. (Arcangela Tarabotti, *La semplicità ingannata*, III)

Lucrezia Marinella expressed the hope for what we would call today a raising of women's consciousness: "if women, as I hope, wake themselves from the long sleep that oppresses them how meek and humble will those proud and ungrateful men become."[31]

Theater

In England the debate about gender roles also took place on the stage. Many have argued that the subject is implicit in the use of transvestite actors. I find more persuasive the argument that the practice of young boys playing feminine roles on the English stage was so much a part of accepted convention that it did not call attention to itself or create tension about gender, unless the author chose to do so as part of the play. I would argue that the same was the case in drama not only in England, but also in countries where women were allowed on stage, since plays there too were frequently put on by all male groups in boys' schools and acting confraternities, in some court and academy settings, and in private venues. Convent women, in their theatrical performances, played male and female parts, also without calling into question gender roles and established social hierarchies. However, all actors, male and female, must have tried to imagine the character they portrayed, and, when that character was of the opposite sex, as they sought to understand and correctly assume attitudes and movements, they had necessarily to consider sexual and gender differ-ence. One indication that this was true is that the Catholic Church found theatrical cross-dressing to be morally dangerous and insisted that convent women not adopt male attire and that Jesuit school plays not include female characters.

Theater, at least since Plautus wrote the *Menaechmi*, has made cross-dressing an important element of plot, but not every playwright has used it to make a statement about gender definition. Usually the gender identities of the male and female charac-ters are sorted out in the course of the action and all are either appropriately socialized in the end or they are sent away. Italian playwrights tended to use the occasions of cross-dressing for sexual double-entendres, for comic ends usually of the most obvious sort. Jokes that suggest homoerotic pleasures were commonplace, but, I would argue, not disruptive of a system in which homoeroticism was not a factor of gender definition.

Shakespeare, however, often called attention to the conventions he adopted in his plays, and transvestite actors and cross-dressed characters were no exceptions. The plays that have caused the most discussion and debate among critics for this reason are *Twelfth Night*, *The Merchant of Venice*, *Antony and Cleopatra*, and *As You Like It*. To take only one example, in *As You Like It* Rosalind, disguised as a man, imperson-ates a woman – herself – and in a way she knows Orlando would stereotypically imagine her. As Jean Howard puts it, Rosalind is "teaching her future mate how to get beyond certain ideologies of gender to more enabling ones."[32] Stephen Orgel argues that since Rosalind in masculine disguise is called Ganymede, Shakespeare's model for the scene must be a homosexual flirtation.[33] And, speaking in the play's epilogue, Rosalind reminds us she is played by a boy: "If I were a woman, I would kiss as many of you as have beards that pleased me." According to Orgel, she "undoes her gender," telling us that "the play has not represented an erotic and heterosexual reality at all."[34] There is considerable disagreement among critics about Shakespeare's meaning, but most agree that, as he exposes the conventions, he shows again and again that the origins of the gender system are human and not divine.

The most interesting cross-dressed figure in English comedy, however, is Moll Firth in Thomas Middleton and Thomas Dekker's *The Roaring Girl* (1608–11), whose male attire is not intended as a disguise but as a protest or resistance to patriarchy. Her dress is unconventional, but it is she who teaches a lesson to the others. She corresponds to the man-woman figure of the famous debate about women wearing men's clothes that around 1620 produced two pamphlets known as *Hic mulier* and *Haec vir*, the first critical, the second a defense of the practice, which not only confused the sexes but social classes as well. Women of different classes were cropping their hair and wearing men's clothes, a fashion that outraged James I, who ordered preachers to speak out against it. For James it showed that "the world is very much out of order."[35] Moll's action, like the behavior of the real woman on whom the character is based and the other cross-dressing women of the time, represents a challenge to social and sexual hierarchies. This is no longer simply a recognition that gender roles are contingent, but, in Jean Howard's words, a "utopian vision of social reform" of which women's oppression is central but part of a larger project.[36]

Religion

In organized religion, as in the family and secular society, gender has always been at the basis of institutional structure. Nowhere is the hierarchical relationship of male to female so rigid and so disadvantageous to women as in the Catholic Church. During the Renaissance the dramatic changes brought about by the Protestant Reformation and the Catholic Counter-Reformation created variations in gender relationships but never eliminated the disequilibrium.

The exclusively male hierarchy of the Catholic Church – from the Pope down to the last monk, friar, and country priest – has remained intact over the centuries. Women had limited power within that structure only by vowing perpetual virginity and leaving secular society for the convent. Women and men who entered religious life gained access to education (very different, however, for men and for women) that they would not have had in secular society, and they were free of the cares of family life, which for women, no longer subject to the dangers of childbirth, also meant longer lives. In convents abbesses, especially, could enjoy some spiritual and political power, and the indirect nature of male domination meant that it was possible for women, once they had renounced the secular world and inheritance rights, to acquire a measure of autonomy within convent walls. This was true before the Renaissance and remained so, even in the early post-Tridentine period when the limited freedom tertiaries had had to leave the convent and to have visitors there was severely restricted through the attempts to enforce enclosure.

In the fifteenth and early sixteenth century, women with local reputations of sanctity, renown for their visions and prophecies, the "living saints" studied by Gabriella Zarri, were frequently consulted by political leaders. The Church, however, by the 1530s, succeeded in keeping their numbers and influence down, silencing them or controlling them through their confessors, through whom their voices were filtered. The number of women canonized diminished during the sixteenth and seventeenth centuries, while the number of men increased. The women who achieved this distinction tended to be women religious, mystics and reformers. Two important examples are St. Maria Maddalena de' Pazzi and St. Teresa of Avila – women, especially St. Teresa, who achieved prominence through their faith but also their particular eloquence and clever strategies, and whose importance was felt beyond their convent walls and long after their death. (See the essay of R. Po-chia Hsia below.)

Many new religious orders sprang up throughout the sixteenth century, an important aspect of religious reform, some, most importantly the Jesuits and the Oratorians, opposing the founding of female branches. New women's orders were formed as well that went their separate ways; the best known example is the Ursulines, whose mission was to teach and to care for the poor. Their history, first of forced enclosure, but later of its relaxation, is indicative of the relationship of the Church hierarchy to women religious throughout the period: opposition, but failing that, eventual resignation and support. With the Ursulines and other congregations and orders that operated in the secular world, there was an expansion of the feminine role. But women's activism within the Church was always frowned upon. Some experiments were successful; others, such as that of the English recusant educator, Mary Ward, were eventually suppressed. First Ward's English Ladies were made to give up their missionary activities, finally their teaching as well, and Ward was imprisoned by the Inquisition.

The gender struggle of women with the masculine hierarchy of the Catholic Church took many forms, winning some successes and incurring many failures. It is clear that, while many women distinguished themselves, expressed agency (never autonomy) despite the odds, the period did not represent a Renaissance for women within the Catholic Church. However, the many repressive moves made by the Church during the period reveal that women were demanding more and that the threat was taken seriously.

The Church not only controlled the lives of women through local priests and confessors but also through powerful symbols of identity. As "brides," either secular brides or "brides of Christ," women were placed clearly in a dependent relationship with masculine authority, whereas members of male religious orders were empowered as "soldiers of Christ"; and these images were constantly reinforced through ritual and liturgy.[37] The post-Tridentine Church fostered the cult of Joseph, thereby detracting from the centrality of Mary in the representation of the Holy Family and strengthening the patriarchal model for the Christian family. Ann, the mother of Mary and another important feminine image, began to disappear from *sacre conversazioni* and Joseph came out of the background to represent the strong, protective father and husband. It is important to note that the idea of the Immaculate Conception, first proposed during the Counter-Reformation, though not confirmed as dogma until the nineteenth century, made Mary a less accessible symbol of womankind: born without original sin, she was an exception and not like other women.

An important question discussed by Natalie Zemon Davis in 1965 in her now classic study, *Society and Culture in Early Modern France*, was the extent to which the Protestant reform advanced the position of women within the family and in society. She concludes that in the relationship between the sexes the Protestant Reformation brought about a lessening of the distinction in female and male gender roles, by opening to women new forms of communication through religion (reading the Bible, singing in church together with men, teaching religion to children, proselytizing) and new places in which to act. She notes, however, that the loss of separate women's communities and religious identity that were available in Catholicism made women as individuals slightly more vulnerable to subjection.[38] Merry Wiesner argues that Protestant women had, in the early years of reform, enjoyed a phase in which their active participation was encouraged (proselytizing, preaching, martyrdom) but later, once the Reformation was established, there came a time of retrenchment, when they were more often obliged to express their convictions in a domestic setting.[39]

Women, and not only those of the elite classes, were empowered to speak and act in the name of their religion by both the Counter-Reformation and the Protestant Reformation. Natalie Davis cites, among others, the examples of the Catholic Marie le Jars de Gournay, who argued that it was only historical accident that Christ was born male, and the Protestant former nun, Marie Dentière, who preached conversion and who addressed to Marguerite of Navarre a defense of the right of women to publish their views on religious questions.[40] To these one could add many names of women from throughout Europe, such as the Quaker Margaret Fell Fox, who preached and who in 1669 published *Women Speaking Justified*, and the German Lutheran Anna Hoyer, who published satirical tracts in which she attacked the male clergy and urged mothers not to entrust the teaching of their children to churchmen.[41] Jewish women too benefited from this extraordinary moment in which participation in public life was opening up. Sara Copio Sullam, a well-to-do woman, living in the ghetto of early seventeenth-century Venice, presided over a literary salon frequented by members of the Venetian literary establishment and, in response to an attack from the Catholic prelate Baldassare Bonifaccio, published a pamphlet entitled *Manifesto* (1621) defending her belief in the immortality of the soul.

Many historians have noted that there was a general feeling of anxiety among men regarding the gender order in the sixteenth and seventeenth centuries in Europe that certainly in part was due to the new assertiveness of women. The reactions were many, some severe. We have seen that in response to a growing literature in praise of women and the appearance in print of works authored by women, there appeared strongly misogynist tracts, that the Catholic Church sought to assert stronger control over the many women religious through claustration, that successful experiments such as those of Mary Ward's English Ladies were suppressed, and that James I claimed the world was very much "out of order." Church and secular laws limited the rights of women in marriage, and working women were forced out of the more lucrative commercial activities by new restrictions on what jobs they were allowed to perform, the more prestigious and better paying jobs being reserved for men. These and many other political actions were taken to rein in the activities of women. The outspoken Venetian nun, Arcangela Tarabotti, who defended women and attacked fathers and brothers, the state and the Church for the practice of forced monachizations, saw much of her work to press during her lifetime, but her major work, the *La semplicità ingannata* (*Innocence Deceived*, earlier called *Paternal Tyranny*), published only in 1654, two years after her death, was soon put on Alexander VII's Index of Forbidden Books.

Anthony Fletcher, referring to the English situation, suggests that the assertiveness of women may have made men feel vulnerable, fearing that perhaps they were not living up to their understanding of appropriate masculinity, which they constructed to mean mastering themselves and those who were subject to them, a notion of masculinity that was much the same at the beginning of the period as it was at the end.[42] He argues, as I have in this essay, that the "overwhelmingly negative construction of womanhood" with which the Renaissance began changed over the course of the years between 1500 and 1800. While I do not believe that even in 1800 it was so positive throughout Europe as he claims it was in England, by the end of the Renaissance it was certainly changing in that direction. The reasons that have been proposed are many and complex. I suggested some of them at the beginning of this essay. I have sought to demonstrate, however, only that (1) at least by this period, if not before, and, as far as we can know from printed sources, beginning with Christine de Pizan, gender roles were understood to be culturally constructed and therefore changeable; (2) that gender roles, but especially those deemed appropriate for women, became the subject of discussion and debate that lasted for centuries; (3) that women's literacy increased during that period, albeit at a slower rate than men's, and that education began to seem appropriate for women and became more accessible to them; and finally (4), that women of the upper and middle classes began to participate more actively in the social and cultural life of the cities, though not in political life (or only indirectly), and, especially in Protestant areas, in the religious life of the community as well.

The filter of gender helps us to see the Renaissance in a new light. I believe it allows us to answer Joan Kelly's famous question with a qualified "yes": yes, there was a Renaissance for women as well as for men, but it began at the turn of the fifteenth century with Christine de Pizan, who saw that she could become "a man," that is, that she could rewrite the gender roles for women.[43] However, I have difficulty finding a date for the end of this "period" and would argue that the Renaissance for women must be seen as open-ended, and as yet not fully realized.

NOTES

1 Vives, *Education*, p. 47.
2 My adaptation of Ann Rosalind Jones's translation (*Currency of Eros*, p. 63).
3 Scott, *Gender*, p. 2.
4 By applying the concept of gender we distinguish the socially constructed notions of what is appropriately masculine and feminine behavior from the biological categories of male and female. While the term gender belongs to contemporary social theory, it is useful in historical analysis, since it allows us to examine forces at work in society that had not earlier been conceptualized.
5 Casagrande, "La donna custodita," p. 88.
6 Monson, *Disembodied Voices*, pp. 161–6.
7 Wiesner, *Women and Gender*, p. 34.
8 Alberti, *Della famiglia*, p. 217.
9 Howard, "Crossdressing," p. 424.
10 Strozzi, *Lettere*.
11 Sanders, *Gender and Literacy*, pp. 4–5.
12 Wunder, "Considerazioni," pp. 77–103.
13 Bell, *How To Do It*, pp. 265–7.
14 Valone, "Roman Matrons."
15 Cohn, "Women and Work," pp. 123–4.
16 Fletcher, *Gender*, pp. 3–4.
17 Hufton, *Prospect*, pp. 77–80.
18 Ibid., p. 70; Wiesner, *Women and Gender*, p. 100.

19 Davis, "City Women," pp. 95–6; Cohn, "Women and Work," p. 115.
20 Ibid.; Wiesner, *Women and Gender*, pp. 95–106.
21 See Gurr, *Playgoing*, pp. 56–64.
22 Howard, "Crossdressing," p. 440.
23 Fletcher, *Gender*, pp. 27–9.
24 Howard, "Crossdressing," pp. 427–8.
25 Wiesner, *Women and Gender*, p. 25.
26 van Schurman, *Whether a Christian Woman*, pp. 43–4.
27 Cited by Patrizia Caraffi, introduction to the French and Italian edition of Christine de
    Pizan's *La Cité des dames*.
28 Wiesner, *Women and Gender*, p. 123.
29 Finucci, *Lady Vanishes*, pp. 77–103.
30 Kelly, "Early Feminist Theory," pp. 66–7.
31 Marinella, *Nobility*, pp. 132–3.
32 Howard, "Crossdressing," p. 435.
33 Orgel, *Impersonations*, p. 43.
34 Ibid., pp. 50–1.
35 Rose, "Women in Men's Clothes," p. 371.
36 Howard, "Crossdressing," p. 438.
37 Zarri, "Gender" and *Recinti*, pp. 29–31 and 251–388.
38 Davis, "City Women," esp. p. 119.
39 Wiesner, *Women and Gender*, p. 188–9.
40 Davis, "City Women," pp. 108 and 118.
41 Wiesner, *Women and Gender*, p. 208.
42 Fletcher, *Gender*, Prologue and final chapter, especially pp. 411–12.
43 Kelly, "Did Women Have a Renaissance?"

REFERENCES

Alberti, Leon Battista, *I libri della famiglia*, ed. Cecil Grayson, in *Opere volgari*, vol. 1 (Bari: Laterza, 1960).

Bell, Rudolph M., *How To Do It: Guide to Good Living for Renaissance Italians* (Chicago: University of Chicago Press, 1999).

Casagrande, Carla, "La donna custodita," in *Storia delle donne in Occidente*, vol. 2: *Il Medioevo*, ed. Christiane Klapisch-Zuber (Bari: Laterza, 1990), pp. 88–128.

Cohn, Samuel K., Jr., "Women and Work in Renaissance Italy," in *Gender and Society in Renaissance Italy*, ed. Judith C. Brown and Robert C. Davis (London: Longman, 1998), pp. 107–26.

Davis, Natalie Zemon, "City Women and Religious Change," in *Society and Culture in Early Modern France* (Stanford: Stanford University Press, 1965).

Finucci, Valeria, *The Lady Vanishes: Subjectivity and Representation in Castiglione and Ariosto* (Stanford: Stanford University Press, 1992).

Fletcher, Anthony, *Gender, Sex and Subordination in England 1500–1800* (New Haven: Yale University Press, 1995).

Gurr, Andrew, *Playgoing in Shakespeare's London* (Cambridge: Cambridge University Press, 1987).

Howard, Jean, "Crossdressing, the Theatre, and Gender Struggle in Early Modern England," *Shakespeare Quarterly* 39/4 (1988), pp. 418–40.

Hufton, Olwen, *The Prospect Before Her: A History of Women in Western Europe*, I: *1500–1800* (London: HarperCollins, 1995).

Jones, Ann Rosalind, *The Currency of Eros: Women's Love Lyric in Europe, 1540–1620* (Bloomington, IN: Indiana University Press, 1990).

Kelly, Joan, "Did Women Have a Renaissance?," in *Women, History and Theory: The Essays* (Chicago: University of Chicago Press, 1984), pp. 19–49.

——, "Early Feminist Theory and the *querelle des femmes*, 1400–1789," in *Women, History and Theory: The Essays,* (Chicago: University of Chicago Press, 1984), pp. 65–109.

Marinella, Lucrezia, *The Nobility and Excellence of Women and the Defects and Vices of Men*, trans. and ed. Anne Dunhill (Chicago: University of Chicago Press, 1999).

Monson, Craig, *Disembodied Voices: Music and Culture in an Early Modern Italian Convent* (Berkeley: University of California Press, 1995).

Orgel, Stephen, *Impersonations: The Performance of Gender in Shakespeare's England* (Cambridge: Cambridge University Press, 1997).

Pizan, Christine de, *La Cité des dames,* ed. Earl Jeffrey Richards, published with the Italian translation: Christine de Pizan, *La città delle dame,* ed. Patrizia Caraffi (Milan: Luni Editrice, 1997).

Rose, Mary Beth, "Women in Men's Clothing: Apparel and Social Stability in *The Roaring Girl*," *English Literary Renaissance* 14 (1984), pp. 367–91.

Sanders, Eve, *Gender and Literacy on Stage in Early Modern England* (Cambridge: Cambridge University Press, 1998).

Schurman, Anna Maria van, *Whether a Christian Woman Should Be Educated* [1632], ed. and trans. Joyce L. Irwin (Chicago: University of Chicago Press, 1998).

Scott, Joan W., *Gender and the Politics of History* (New York: Columbia University Press, 1988).

Strozzi, Alessandra Macinghi, *Lettere di una gentildonna fiorentina del secolo XV ai figliuoli esuli,* ed. Cesare Guasti (Florence: G. C. Sansoni, 1877).

Tarabotti, Arcangela [pseud. Galerana Baratotti], *La semplicità ingannata* (Leiden, 1654).

Valone, Carolyn, "Roman Matrons as Patrons: Various Views of the Cloister Wall," in *The Crannied Wall: Women, Religion, and the Arts in Early Modern Europe,* ed. Craig Monson (Ann Arbor, MI: University of Michigan Press, 1992), pp. 49–72.

Vives, Juan Luis, *The Education of a Christian Woman, A Sixteenth-century Manual* [1523], ed. and trans. Charles Fantazzi (Chicago: University of Chicago Press, 2000).

——, *Women and Gender in Early Modern Europe* (Cambridge: Cambridge University Press, 1993).

Wunder, Heide, "Considerazioni sulla costruzione della virilità e dell'identità maschile nelle testimonianze della prima età moderna," in *Tempi e spazi di vita femminile tra medioevo ed età moderna,* ed. Silvana Seidel Menchi, Anne Jacobson Schutte, and Thomas Kuehn (Bologna: Il Mulino, 1999), pp. 77–103.

Zarri, Gabriella, "Gender, Religious Institutions and Social Discipline: The Reform of the Regulars," in *Gender and Society in Renaissance Italy,* ed. Judith C. Brown and Robert C. Davis (London: Longman, 1998), pp. 193–212.

——, *Recinti. Donne, clausura e matrimonio nella prima età moderna* (Bologna: Il Mulino, 2000).

FURTHER READING

Brown, Judith C. and Davis, Robert C. eds., *Gender and Society in Renaissance Italy* (London: Longman, 1998).

Dionisotti, Carlo, "La letteratura italiana all'epoca del Concilio di Trento," in *Geografia e storia* (Turin: Einaudi, 1967), pp. 227–54.

Hull, Suzanne, *Chaste, Silent and Obedient: English Books for Women 1475–1640* (San Marino, CA: Huntington Library, 1982).

Jordan, Constance, *Renaissance Feminism: Literary Texts and Political Models* (Ithaca: Cornell University Press, 1990).

Kelso, Ruth, *Doctrine of the English Gentleman in the Sixteenth Century* (Urbana: University of Illinois Press, 1929).

——, *Doctrine for the Lady of the Renaissance* (Urbana: University of Illinois Press, 1956; repr. 1978).

King, Margaret, *Women of the Renaissance* (Chicago: University of Chicago Press, 1991).

Laqueur, Thomas, *Making Sex: Body and Gender from the Greeks to Freud* (Cambridge, MA: Harvard University Press, 1990).

Maclean, Ian, *The Renaissance Notion of Woman: A Study in the Fortunes of Scholasticism and Medical Science in European Intellectual Life* (Cambridge: Cambridge University Press, 1980).

Turner, James Grantham, ed., *Sexuality and Gender in Early Modern Europe: Institutions, Texts, Images* (Cambridge: Cambridge University Press, 1993).

Wiesner, Merry, "Corpi separati. Le associazioni dei lavoranti nella Germania moderna," *Memoria* 27 (1989), pp. 44–67.

Woodbridge, Linda, *Women and the English Renaissance: Literature and the Nature of Womankind, 1540–1620* (Urbana: University of Illinois Press, 1986).

Zarri, Gabriella, *Le sante vive. Profezie di corte e devozione femminile tra '400 e '500* (Turin: Rosenberg and Sellier, 1990).

CHAPTER TWELVE

The Myth of Renaissance Individualism

JOHN JEFFRIES MARTIN

Images of Renaissance individuals – their portraits, their biographies, their letters, even their signatures – seem to us, now half a millennium later, importantly familiar. From the age of Petrarch and Giotto until that of Montaigne, Shakespeare, and Rembrandt (from about 1350 until about 1650), the individual appears to have emerged as a salient, well-defined force in western culture. Unlike their medieval ancestors, Renaissance men and women seem to have placed new value on the will and on agency, on expressiveness, prudence, and choice – and to have done so self-consciously and self-reflectively. Inevitably we feel that we recognize such individuals (or their robust, three-dimensional representations) as autonomous, self-contained, psychologically complex persons much like ourselves. They make a powerful impression, especially when the Renaissance is viewed (as it used to be) as the inauguration of modern western culture.

The "discovery of the individual" is such a central dimension of the popular understanding of the Renaissance that it would seem virtually heretical to challenge the notion that it was in Europe in this period that modern notions of personal identity first emerged. Yet no other single aspect of the Renaissance has been subject to attacks from so many different quarters. Medievalists have pointed to evidence for an interest in the individual in the eleventh and twelfth centuries, well before the age of Petrarch (1304–74). Cultural historians have attacked the elitism of the view that the Renaissance "discovered the individual," demonstrating quite clearly that claims about individualism have been based on a limited sampling of works drawn from high culture. Social historians have made compelling arguments for the decisiveness of communal, civic, and family structures in shaping notions of identity that they see as rooted in collective rather than individualistic contexts. Theorists have underscored the degree to which the very notion of the "individual" is suspect, viewing it as a cultural construction in the service of larger political and ideological interests that often had the paradoxical effect of hemming in individual autonomy through such factors as codes of civility or religious prohibitions and the increasing power of the state. Similarly, comparativists have questioned the notion of the individual as a uniquely western ideal.

But perhaps most devastating of all have been critiques that have argued that the very idea of the "discovery of the individual" is merely one component of a larger myth that portrayed the Renaissance as a major act in the drama of what we comfortably used to call the "history of western civilization."[1] Along with other major elements that make up the traditional stories we tell about the Renaissance – from the claim that it was this period that witnessed the emergence of capitalism and republicanism as well as realism, humanism, and secularism – the idea that the Renaissance was the period in which individualism first emerged from its previously dormant state and became a defining aspect of the modern western world is dubious at best. Historians are simply no longer able to offer such a neatly packaged history of the self, without recognizing that such a story, in the final analysis, itself served as a myth that both bolstered and explained a broad array of assumptions about individualism and identity throughout most of the nineteenth and twentieth centuries.

The rejection of liberal and teleological narratives of the self has not, however, resulted in a lessening of interest in this theme in Renaissance studies. If anything, the focus on this topic has expanded, and the perspectives on it have multiplied at an almost dizzying rate. Traditionally, historians and others had approached this theme from the vantage point of a few canonical autobiographies (those of Benvenuto Cellini, St. Theresa of Avila, Michel de Montaigne) or a few celebrated self-portraits (Albrecht Dürer, Raphael, Maarten van Heemskerck) that seemed to provide evidence for the development of modern forms of introspection, reflection, and individual expression. There was, furthermore, a corollary assumption that this development was related primarily to the emergence of humanism, a set of scholarly practices that – in their varied and often passionate efforts to interpret ancient and early Christian ideas and values – placed a new emphasis on context, contingency, and ultimately authorship in the explanation of texts and their meanings.

Today scholars are skeptical of this interpretative framework. On the one hand, it is no longer possible to view a few autobiographies as representative of a general trend. It is true that there was a veritable explosion of letter collections, diaries, memoirs, journals, *ricordanze, livres de famille, Hauschroniken* (many of which contain significant autobiographical elements) in late medieval and early modern Europe – as many as five hundred such texts in fifteenth-century Florence alone; and recent work has identified a plethora of autobiographies and other forms of personal documents or "ego-documents" in the sixteenth and early seventeenth centuries.[2] But regional variations render almost all generalizations suspect. While it was fashionable to keep *ricordanze* or *libri di famiglia* in fifteenth-century Florence, such works were rare in fifteenth-century Venice.[3] Ego-documents abounded in early modern England but were unusual across the North Sea in Holland. Even within the Netherlands, there were curious variations, with the inhabitants of the maritime provinces (Friesland, Zeeland, Holland) more likely to record aspects of their lives in journals and housebooks than their inland contemporaries.[4] Similarly baffling patterns emerged in the production of biographies, portraits, and self-portraits. Again, Florentine culture was rich in individual representations in each of these genres, but the popularity of each individual genre varied markedly from region to region, at times with paradoxical effects. Two of the most prolific portrait painters of the later Renaissance, for instance, were members of societies in which remarkably few autobiographical works were produced: Lorenzo Lotto of Venice (ca. 1480–1556) and Rembrandt van Rijn of Amsterdam (1606–69).

On the other hand, humanism played a less determining role in the development of such representations than has been generally assumed. This does not mean that humanists did not foster new perspectives that reinforced an interest in autobiography or self-portraiture. Rather it means that it is now possible to discern certain larger social, cultural, and political forces in the making of Renaissance identities. But the displacement of the role of humanism has not merely been a result of new scholarly researches. After the catastrophic expression of human cruelty in the century of the Holocaust, historians have lost confidence in narratives of a triumphant individualism. Moreover, with the collapse of traditional epistemologies and the development of postmodern thought, it has become increasingly difficult to view the self as anything but a "fiction," though this widely used term (through its emphasis on cultural and political forces) often has itself the unfortunate effect of eclipsing social and biological accounts of identity-formation.

In the wake of the collapse of traditional paradigms, scholars have begun to take a more particularistic approach, examining the diverse functions of a broad array of representations of the individual. What precise functions, for example, did portraits and self-portraits serve? What about humanist biographies and autobiographies, on the one hand, and spiritual biographies and autobiographies, on the other? Or how should we understand the relation of philosophical and theological discussions of the will to changing notions of the individual? Similarly how should we approach the relation of lay confession and other devotional practices to new notions of the self? What about the diaries, journals, and housebooks of Renaissance merchants and artisans? What about printing privileges and copyrights? Or contracts and changes in property law, inheritance laws, and marriage? Finally, what are we to make of the great silence that enshrouds most late medieval and early modern men and women? Should we assume that the absence of individualized representations for this great majority indicates an indifference to questions of identity? This last question is perhaps the most intractable, but nonetheless it is plain that it is no longer possible to tell the story of the Renaissance discovery of the self as a straightforward and heroic narrative that lays the foundations for the more "modern" forms of individualism seen as characteristic of the Enlightenment, the Romantic period, or even modern life generally.

Nevertheless, it is possible to distinguish three basic types of selfhood in Renaissance Europe. The first, which was the dominant type of the entire period, was what we might call the "communal" or "civic" self. In this context, group or collective identity was the defining characteristic of an individual's sense of his or her place in society, with the individual's family or lineage often serving as his or her primary point of reference. The second type, by contrast, which came to the fore quite suddenly in the early sixteenth century (though we find adumbrations of it in the late Middle Ages) was characterized by novel notions of the individual as an expressive, self-reflective subject, increasingly conscious about the need to assume different roles in different contexts – a notion that we might best describe as the "performative" or "prudential" self. But, in addition to these two fundamental types, scholars have in recent years begun to discover considerable evidence that points to a third species of selfhood, one that we might best call the "porous" or "open" self. Late medieval and early modern identities, that is, were often not constituted, as we might expect, of one

soul contained or neatly enclosed in one body. To the contrary, considerable evidence
– particularly though not exclusively at the level of popular culture – suggests that the
body was itself imagined as porous, open to strong influences from "spiritual" forces
(through witchcraft or possession) from the outside: a far cry, in short, from the
autonomous and self-contained individualist that is often assumed to have been a
defining characteristic of the self in this era. The typology I offer here makes no claim
that these species of selfhood were ever pure or exclusive; the "types" are offered
rather as a way of pointing to certain tendencies or tensions in Renaissance culture. In
fact, most individuals would have combined elements of all three types, though
frequently only one would be dominant. The goldsmith Benvenuto Cellini (1500–
71) certainly showed traits of each of these forms of selfhood. An incorrigible
braggart, he was an indefatigable performer in his friendships, his craft, and his
writing. At the same time he also celebrated his family, his guild, and his state. But
he also had a brush with demonic magic – during two heart-stopping necromancy
sessions led by a Sicilian priest in the Colosseum in Rome.[5] A student of the Renaissance, therefore, should not expect to find clearly defined notions of individualism.
Rather he or she should enter the study of the period recognizing that even such a
basic concept as the "category of the person" itself has a complex history, with
multiple possible representations, in an era that too often has born the burden of
serving as a precursor to our own.[6]

The Communal Self

Fifteenth-century Italian artists frequently portrayed individuals in their works. Nonetheless, their tendency was to offer such portraits in paintings that celebrated a
communal event, such as the consecration of a new parish, or made a didactic point
about the importance of faith, such as Masaccio's paintings in the Brancacci Chapel in
Florence. Even when individual portraits were produced in this period, they were
generally grouped with others from the same family, guild, or magistracy. Moreover,
at times little emphasis was placed on a likeness, with attention given to the type or the
social station of the person depicted crowding out attention to what we might call
"individuality." In fact, in the early age of printing, printers would often use the same
block or image of a human figure over and over again, now as a representation of one
personage, now as the representation of another – in one case actually representing the
German artist Albrecht Dürer (1471–1528) and the Flemish mathematician Gemma
Frisius (1508–55) with precisely the same features. And Dürer also, in perhaps his most
famous self-portrait, depicted himself not only as Dürer but also as Christ – a decision
that suggests his own notions of individual identity did not always differentiate the self
from the larger religious culture in which he was still absorbed and out of which he
drew his own power of expression and creativity. In such contexts, there is little
evidence that such portrayals were individualistic in the sense of either pointing to
psychological complexity or staking out claims to uniqueness. What mattered was the
collectivity or the station, with individual identity articulated in the context of something larger – one's family, one's faith, one's city.[7]

The striking interplay of the individual with the larger collectivity in Italian art in
this period is reflected as well in Florentine *ricordanze* or *libri di famiglia*. These texts

– which were often part account-books and part journals that recorded significant events in the lives of an individual, his family, and the city – also blurred the distinctions between a particular individual and the larger community of which he was a part. The individual was valued not as an isolated entity, that is, but rather as part of a larger whole – a whole that could be seen either as consisting of a merchant's or an artisan's lateral ties to his community or as reaching out over time and knitting together his lineage, with the journal itself passed from generation to generation. A similar pattern was evident in humanist biography, which drew on such classical or early Christian models as Plutarch (ca. 46–120), Suetonius (69–ca. 122), and St. Jerome (ca. 345–ca. 420). Lives of great men, whether ancient or contemporary, were published as collective biographies, a tradition that began in the fourteenth century with Petrarch's *De viris illustribus* and Boccaccio's *De casibus virorum illustrium* and *De mulieribus claris* and found important fifteenth-century parallels in Vespasiano da Bisticci's *Lives of Famous Men*, Platina's *Lives of the Popes*, and Enea Silvio Piccolomini's *On the Famous Men of his Day.* As in the case of late medieval portraiture, so in the case of biography, individual lives were conceived as part of a larger collectivity – of celebrated ancient men or women, of popes, of prominent Florentines, and so on.

Even the case of full-blown autobiography requires caution. As Anthony Grafton has observed, the authors of such texts did not go "to work with the characteristically modern notion in mind that their subject was a unique individual to whose every peculiarity they had to do justice."[8] The autobiography of the Milanese physician Girolamo Cardano (1501–76), for instance, was not only modeled on classical autobiography but also served as a case study of astrology. The work begins with his own geniture – his reading of the predictive configuration of the stars and planets at the moment of his birth – and then recounts in great detail his life experiences as a way of gauging the accuracy of astrological science. It is, in sum, a kind of retrospective horoscope.[9] Other "autobiographies" present comparable dilemmas. In his *Vita*, for example, Benvenuto Cellini claims to have dictated his story while working on his craft – a literary pose that, in fact, concealed how closely his work was modeled on Vasari's *Lives* and how it was written in part to enhance Cellini's own reputation.[10] But perhaps the best example of the complexity of "life-writing" in sixteenth-century Europe are the *Essays* of Michel de Montaigne (1533–92). This work, which takes Montaigne himself as its subject, is organized not as a narrative but as a series of "essays" on varied topics, from cannibals to coaches. Montaigne's identity is not that of a purposive, autonomous self but rather of a certain nature that Montaigne has set out to discover – a process in which the *Essays* themselves are deeply implicated. "I have no more made my book," Montaigne writes, "than my book has made me – a book consubstantial with its author, concerned with my own self, an integral part of my life; not concerned with some third-hand, extraneous purpose, like all other books."[11]

Although scholars in recent years have emphasized the cultural construction of the self in different historical periods, social and economic forces too deserve emphasis. In a famous essay, the French historian Marc Bloch drew a connection between individualism and agrarian regimes, noting that agricultural technologies and practices played a key role in shaping more collectivist outlooks among peasants in certain parts of Europe (those in which the long-furlong open field and the wheeled plough were the norm) and more "individualistic" outlooks in others (those where the irregular open field and the scratch plough dominated).[12] And it is undoubtedly the case that the commercial revolution of the eleventh and twelfth centuries, which initiated a process of urban growth and the gradual penetration of market forces into the countryside, encouraged a more individualist outlook. Largely because of their favored location, the cities and towns of the Italian peninsula played a precocious role in this economic revival. Yet even in England where urbanization was far less intense in the late Middle Ages than in Italy, agricultural practices combined with "a highly flexible social structure," may have led to certain forms of economic individualism as early as the twelfth and thirteenth centuries. Land, for example, was often held or alienated or inherited by individuals rather than the family or the group; and certain villagers, at least, showed remarkable independence in relation to their lords.[13]

By the thirteenth and fourteenth centuries these shifts had made an imprint on European culture. In the sphere of religion, for example, the stipulation by the Church that every Christian make his or her confession at least once a year (*omnis utriusque sexus* [1215]) undoubtedly fostered a sense of individuality. The growth of the mendicant orders, along with the rise of popular heresies, also contributed to and reflected this leavening of individualism. The ideas were equally felt in intellectual currents (in both scholasticism, especially among the nominalists) and in humanism. Both offered a new vocabulary that laid particular emphasis on the will, a theme that was perhaps most forcefully expressed in Pico della Mirandola's *Oration on the Dignity of Man* (1486) and that was reinforced both by humanist biography, especially in its emphasis on the exemplary life, and by the ideals of the civic life.[14]

Nonetheless, in the very late Middle Ages, from about 1350 to about 1500, bubonic plague – which first arrived in western Europe in the mid-fourteenth century but which would return with deadly force throughout the late medieval and the early modern period – appears to have been a galvanizing event in shaping a strong sense of communal selfhood. Already in 1348, when the Black Death first swept through Italy, Petrarch had turned inward to explore with a renewed intensity questions of his own identity and mortality – preoccupations that were most evident in his *Secretum*, a dialogue in which Petrarch offered his celebrated portrait of a fractured, melancholic self. Petrarch's concern with questions of interiority developed well before the fourteenth-century epidemics, as his early poetry and letters reveal. But the Black Death, which had carried off his beloved Laura, and its recurrence in the early 1360s rendered these questions all the more pressing. The recurrence must have been especially terrifying. It was in the midst of this calamity, which took the life of his son, that Petrarch offered his library to the city of Venice in "memory of himself."[15] And, indeed, Petrarch's concern with his own mortality was widely echoed in Europe at this time. Memorials at every level of society became increasingly common. Fearing the worst, men and women left wills instructing that burial chapels, paintings, sculptures, coats of arms, and inscriptions be made in their memories. In certain contexts, especially in Florence and Tuscany where painted or sculpted portraits were increasingly concerned with conveying a recognizable likeness of the individual so memorialized, scholars have often found evidence for the birth of individualism. Yet the evidence equally supports the notion that what was really decisive to such men and women was the commemoration through an individual memorial of the entire lineage.[16] Again, in the late medieval as well as in the early modern period, the tendency was for the individual to be depicted as part of a greater whole, and in

Italy, as a kind of communal or civic self, tied together with kinfolk and townsfolk in a web of interdependencies that make it difficult to speak of the Renaissance as an age of the "discovery of the individual." (See the essay above by Joanne Ferraro.)

The Performative Self

"Homines non nascuntur, sed finguntur – men are not born, but fashioned," the Dutch humanist Erasmus wrote in 1513 in his influential book of manners. In the same year, Machiavelli offered a similar argument in *The Prince*, a treatise that radically severed the ruler from a prescribed social role and stressed the importance of fictions in the shaping of a political power. It was no longer virtue but the appearance of virtue that mattered. Painted self-portraits in this decade (by Dürer, Raphael, Parmigianino) were equally self-reflective, underscoring the diversity of roles an individual might assume. In these works, the individual was represented not as a member of a larger group but as isolated, self-reflective, preoccupied with roles and decorum.[17] As Stephen Greenblatt has written, this was an age of "self-fashioning," adding that "perhaps the simplest observation we can make is that in the sixteenth century there appears to be an increased self-consciousness about the fashioning of the human identity as a manipulable, artful process."[18] Books of etiquette – Castiglione's *The Book of the Courtier* (1528), Giovanni della Casa's *Galateo* (1558), and Stefano Guazzo's *Civil Conversation* (1574) – reinforced this notion. Their readers were invited to reinvent themselves, play the proper role at the proper time. Portraiture seemed to dig deeper into the self than ever before. Lorenzo Lotto's many early sixteenth-century portraits give evidence of a psychological depth rare in the later Middle Ages. Self-reflection seemed to reach a new level of intensity in autobiographical writing also. Montaigne's *Essays* struggled self-consciously with issues of self-presentation. In the next century the Venetian rabbi Leone Modena (1571–1648) showed similar preoccupations in his autobiographical *Life of Judah*.[19] Women too articulated new roles for themselves, as works by such feminist authors as Lucrezia Marinella and Moderata Fonte make clear.[20] An individual's social role seemed less significant than the particular role he or she assumed. Autobiographies proliferated in this age – spiritual autobiographies, both Catholic and Protestant, often modeled on the increasingly popular *Confessions* of St. Augustine. Self-portraits too were legion, but with a new emphasis. In mid-seventeenth-century Holland Rembrandt's self-portraits betray a restless, protean quality as he cast himself in diverse roles.[21] At roughly the same time, the English poet John Donne (1572–1631), writing in the wake of the astronomical discoveries of Copernicus (1473–1543) and Galileo (1564–1642), captured something of the new individualism in his poetry:

> And new philosophy calls all in doubt
> ... all coherence gone;
> All just supply, and all relation:
> Prince, subject, father, son, are things forgot
> For every man alone thinks he hath got
> To be a phoenix, and that then can be
> None of that kind, of which he is, but he.
> (*The First Anniversary*, ll. 205–18)

None of this is to claim that notions of the communal self vanished. What we find in the early modern period is a set of fundamental tensions between the communal self – still probably the fundamental type for most Europeans – and the ideal of the performative or prudential self that seems to have become increasingly diffused in this age. The perdurance of the former type is clear in many forms: in the continuation of the practice of collective biographies, most famously perhaps in Giorgio Vasari's *Lives of the Artists* (1550; 2nd edn. 1568) and Karel van Mander's *Book of Painters* (1604); in the *ricordanze* tradition, with French and German merchants now keeping *livres de raison* or *Hauschroniken* that had much the same communal function that the house-books of their Florentine counterparts did a century or two earlier; and in portrait collections. Paolo Giovio (1483–1552) developed an extensive collection of portraits of famous military and political leaders for his *"musaeum"* at Como, a veritable *"templum virtutis"* (temple of virtue), as he called it, in which each portrait was accompanied by a brief biography or *elogium*.

The communal self was clearly the norm for most European peasants as well. There, even such basic categories as emotions (hate, envy, guilt) and memory appear to have played themselves out largely as functions of one's position in the social and power relations of village culture rather than as internal matters of conscience.[22] Nonetheless, certain forms of individuality do appear to have marked late medieval and early modern peasant culture. At least when an occasional source such as an inquisitorial register records the voices and identities of peasants in this era, individualizing traits can be quite striking, as in the case of the libidinous inhabitants of the southern French village of Montaillou in the early fourteenth century or the sixteenth-century case of the northern Italian miller Domenico Scandella, whose readings and opinionated harangues made him stand out as something of an eccentric among his fellow villagers in the Friuli.[23]

On the other hand, the performative or prudential self was not entirely new. In fifteenth-century Florence, for example, overlapping social networks had often led to the cultivation of what Ronald F. E. Weissman has called "the importance of being ambiguous." As Leon Battista Alberti put it in his famous treatise on the family – in language that is a striking anticipation of Machiavelli's – "How can anyone dream that mere simplicity and goodness will get him friends? ... The world is amply supplied with fraudulent, false, perfidious, bold, audacious, and rapacious men. Everything in the world is profoundly unsure. One has to be far-seeing in the face of frauds, traps and betrayals."[24] Other contemporary texts (memoirs, books of etiquette, and sermons) show how widespread the pressure to perform or "to manage impressions" had become. Yet even in the absence of a literature that articulated the need for prudence or that decried the duplicity of Renaissance men and women, conflicting social roles and tensions – between men and women, masters and servants, parents and children, lords and tenants, and so on – undoubtedly created some spaces in which people at all levels of Renaissance society were able to negotiate and, to some degree, protect their interests. As Stanley Chojnacki has observed, the way men and women "responded to the structural conditions of their ascribed identities and participated in the relationships associated with them were as important to the forging of personhood as the rules and expectations that cultural norms and authoritative institutions laid down for those roles."[25] The wives of patricians self-consciously and effectively carved out new social spaces for their daughters; artisans protected their social and economic interest by deliberately cultivating relations with fellow workers from their homelands; and, at the bottom of the social hierarchy, servants protected their dignity and honor through subtle and not so subtle acts of disobedience.[26] In short, social life alone was never entirely determining in the shaping of one's sense of self within the hierarchies of late medieval and early modern Europe.

Nonetheless, strategies of self-presentation reached a new level of intensity in the early sixteenth century. Once again, social and economic factors played a key role. For the first time, Europe saw the development of many large cities – Paris, London, Antwerp, Amsterdam – north of the Alps, with London's population, for example, racing from some 50,000 in the early 1500s to nearly 200,000 a century later. International commerce also intensified. Urbanization and trade clearly had the effect of bringing men and women into new forms of social relationships in which more traditional forms of identity based on familial or village life were less viable. New technologies played contributing roles. Some scholars have speculated, for example, that the development of the flat mirror in this period enabled a new sense of self, encouraging a kind of self-reflection and self-portraiture that had little precedent before the 1500s. One of Dürer's many self-portraits, in which he portrayed himself as a full-length nude, is one of the most striking artifacts of this new technology and constitutes on the visual plane something approaching the level of naturalism and honesty that Montaigne would attempt in his *Essays*. The introduction of the fork also shaped new sensitivities, at the very least facilitating the gradual shift from the medieval meal, at which men and women often ate from a common plate and used their hands, to the more individualized place settings of the early modern world and the use of utensils for the manipulation of many foods (viands in particular). But, in relation to new notions of the self, the new technology with the most far-reaching consequences was undoubtedly the printing press.

Introduced in Germany in the mid-fifteenth century, printing had become widely diffused throughout western Europe by the early sixteenth century. Books, which until then had to be copied out by hand and had circulated primarily among clerical elites, became accessible to a significant portion of the population. Literacy rates rose markedly, especially in the cities. In this context the diffusion of biographical writings, ancient and modern, provided new models for self-expression. And, indeed, this was the age not only of learned but also of popular autobiography – one historian has compiled a preliminary checklist of nearly one hundred artisan biographies from this period.[27] (See the essay by James Amelang below.) Printing also problematized the relationship of author to their texts. To be sure, there had been arguments about plagiarism in the late medieval period, but the question of printing privileges came to the fore in the sixteenth century, eventually resulting in the invention of copyright – laws that reinforced humanist notions of authorship. Early humanists had initiated the process of constructing notions of authorship as a function of individual voice or intention. The late Middle Ages is the first great age of attribution, as textual scholars developed editing strategies to determine whether or not a particular document was genuinely, say, Ciceronian or Augustinian. Printers – with their ability to reproduce texts mechanically, multiply copies at an unprecedented speed, and create new markets for books – found humanist notions of authorship useful as a means of introducing order and stability into the cross-currents of stolen, pirated, or altered texts that threatened the economic interests as well as the credibility of authors, publishers, and printers. And many writers seized on this new technology to bolster their reputations, with the result that publishing became another vehicle for the expression of the performative self. The first copyright laws were developed in Venice in the late fifteenth century, when the humanist Marcantonio Sabellico was granted an author's privilege in 1486 for his history of the city. These were followed by a plethora of royal privileges given to authors and publishers in sixteenth-century France and England, though the first modern copyright law, the Statute of Anne, did not go into effect until 1710, by which time the notion of the individual author had been naturalized as a universal, essential category.[28]

Yet two factors, in particular, were especially decisive in the development of the performative or prudential conception of the self: the rise of the court as a center of monarchial power and the religious turmoil of the Reformation, which now made religious identity an increasingly complex component of public and private life in the late Renaissance.

Courts had been important in the Middle Ages, but the early modern court was a new creature, with carefully scripted rituals and increasingly large gathering of courtiers and other hangers-on. (See the essay by Robert Muchembled above.) In a Europe that was still largely a patchwork of independent principalities, duchies, and bishoprics, there were hundreds of such courts on the continent, from the enormous Papal Curia in Rome to the much more modest, though nonetheless influential court of the Dukes of Urbino. In such contexts men and women came to find that the arts of prudence and self-reflection were necessary for survival. It was largely in this sphere that we find an emerging discourse of the problem of dissimulation. Castiglione's extremely popular *Book of the Courtier* might be seen as the script for the age. Courtiers grappled constantly with the questions of language, silence, decorum, and dissimulation. Life at court was studied and self-examined. One was expected to give the appearance of spontaneity but, in fact, be calculating at all times. In Castiglione's book, for instance, one of the interlocutors, the humanist Pietro Bembo states that one should never trust anyone, not even a dear friend, to the extent of "communicating without reservations all of one's thoughts to him," while the diplomat Federico Fregoso, the primary speaker of Book II, explicitly recommends "a certain studied dissimulation" in one's conversation.[29]

Religious factors were also crucial. The rise of Protestantism itself brought with it new conceptions of the individual. In particular, reformers such as Martin Luther (1483–1546) and John Calvin (1509–64) portrayed the human subject as fallen, as corrupted and sinful. There was also a new emphasis, especially among Calvinists, on sincerity – an ideal that clashed with courtly counsels of prudence. It is likely that the tensions between counsels of prudence and sincerity, moreover, played some role in the shaping of new notions of individual identity in the early modern period.[30] Such tensions were by no means exclusively Protestant. Cardano, for example, self-consciously struggled with the question of self-disclosure, at times counseling prudence or silence, at other times encouraging sincerity.[31] Moreover, Catholic reform placed greater emphasis on individual will. The Council of Trent aggressively reaffirmed in its decree *Tametsi* (1563) that both the bride and the groom were to give their consent to marriage – firmly rejecting the idea that such unions serve purely dynastic ends. And in the same era, confession became increasingly privatized, with the introduction of the confessional as a private place for the revelation of one's transgressions and concerns, a development that helped diffuse the practice of self-examination and a deeper sense of interiority in the period. Finally, the proliferation of new religious ideas and communities – from evangelical to Protestant to Anabaptist – shattered a previously unified sacred landscape, and made religious identity increasingly problematic. Protestants residing in Catholic lands both dissimulated their beliefs and simulated those of their Catholic neighbors – in a practice that has come to be known as *Nicodemismo* after the Gospel figure of Nicodemus, who had gone to Jesus "by night" to conceal his beliefs from his neighbors (John 3: 1–3). Catholics in Protestant lands did the same. Jews also often found it necessary to assume a Christian identity in one place and a Jewish identity in another, living life, like a "ship with two rudders," as Enriques Nuñes, a Portuguese Jew living in Venice, put it during his interrogation by the Inquisition in 1580.[32] Dilemmas of self-presentation even penetrated the countryside, at least this seems to have been the case in sixteenth-century Artigat, now famous as the home of the impostor Arnauld du Tihl, who assumed the role of Martin Guerre, taking his wife, raising his children, and tilling his fields until his deception was discovered some three years later.[33]

The Porous Self

Finally, recent studies, especially those concerned with the histories of *mentalités*, popular religion, magic, and folk culture, have unearthed curious fragments of a Renaissance culture defined in part at least by a view of the self that was anything but autonomous or self-contained – for a self, in short, that had little psychic or psychological integrity. Mystics, for example, made powerful arguments about the reality of divine immanence with the result that it was often difficult to discern the boundaries between their own selves and that of God. But, among the learned, it was especially among the Neoplatonists that we find examples of a porous self. To the Florentine Marsilio Ficino (1433–99), for instance, melancholia was not so much the state of an individual psyche as the result of a failure to make use of beneficial astral influences. Ficino's own influence was widespread. In the sixteenth century Cornelius Agrippa (1486–1535) in Germany, John Dee (1527–1608) in England, and Tommaso Campanella (1568–1639) in Italy were exponents of Hermeticism – a corpus of late antique magical doctrines that Ficino had done much to popularize – and their ideas did much to propagate the view that the self was in the grip of larger, cosmic forces.[34] There was also a widespread belief in the conjuring of spirits and the invocation of angels, practices that betrayed an underlying assumption that psychic forces were not to be understood on purely individualized grounds. In this context, moreover, witnesses asserted that they had seen spirits in the most bizarre forms: appearing disembodied in a crystal ball or in the well-preserved skull of a dead man, or even in the shape of an animal (usually a cat). As Cardano observed of demons, "they make some think they are entering their bodies," a view to which Cardano himself proved uncomfortably prone.[35]

It is, however, on the level of popular culture that the self appears to have been most porous, most labile. (See the essays by David Gentilcore and Guido Ruggiero below.) As Natalie Zemon Davis has pointed out, in the sixteenth century, "the line drawn around the self was not firmly closed," and she points to such widespread instances of possession by another's soul or subjection to the curse of a witch to underscore the porous or permeable nature of identity in this period.[36] Cases of possession were most frequent in convents, as the famous examples of the Devils of Loudun (1634) and the experience of the Venetian nun Cecilia Ferrazzi (1609–84) suggest.[37] Witchcraft too provides many examples of one person using a curse to influence another – one crucial aspect of what Guido Ruggiero has called "binding passions," and it is clear that these practices and beliefs were widespread in the Renaissance period.[38] Many early modern writers were skeptical of such claims, but they were often taken seriously. In 1566 the religious authorities in Picardy, as part of their anti-Huguenot propaganda, exorcized the 15-year-old girl Nicole Obry who was said to be possessed by as many as thirty demons. Her possession had begun, Nicole explained, when the devil, disguised as the ghost of her grandfather, had entered her body with the alleged goal of having his heirs say masses and undertake pilgrimages to speed his release from Purgatory. Nicole's own experience of being taken over by multiple beings was undoubtedly genuine and reflected a widespread belief in diabolical possession that endured throughout the early modern period. But not only were individual bodies open (at least in the views of many) to possession by the souls of others or to curses, it was equally possible for the spirit to leave the body altogether, at least so members of the Benandanti believed. As one peasant who belonged to this northern Italian agrarian fertility cult put it to the inquisitor, the body stayed behind while the spirit went forth to do battle for the crops, "and if by chance while we are out someone should come with a light and look for a long time at the body, the spirit would never re-enter it until there was no one left around to see it that night; and if the body, seeming to be dead, should be buried, the spirit would have to wander around the world until the hour fixed for that body to die."[39] We must understand Renaissance notions of identity on their own terms. Some Renaissance writers, artists, courtiers, and religious and political leaders may well have had a fairly well-articulated notion of an "individualist" self, but in many other respects, identity appears to have been fluid, protean, without the sharp lineaments of a centered, unitary self that we associate with Descartes's mid-seventeenth-century description of the self as an internal *res cogitans* – an internal thing doubting or thinking. Even if the anthropologist Clifford Geertz were correct in his observation that the "western" view of the individual privileges the "person as a bounded, unique, more or less integrated motivational and cognitive universe, a dynamic center of awareness, emotion, judgment, and action, organized into a distinctive whole," we would be hard put to find such "individuals" as the norm in the late medieval or early modern Europe.[40]

Conclusion

A narrative of an emerging individualism has given way, therefore, to a far more variegated history of the self in the late medieval and early modern periods. In the late Middle Ages and in much of the Renaissance, representations of individuals (biographies, *libri di famiglia*, portraits, and so on) were rarely expressions or celebrations of individuality. To the contrary, more often than not, they served to articulate something about one's group identity. With few exceptions, it is only in about 1500 that we begin to find the kind of self-consciousness and self-reflection that approximate what modern thinkers mean by "individualism." But even here we must exercise caution about generalizing this category. Such expressions were the exception, not the rule. Moreover, as many scholars have argued, even the most individualistic self was often more a function of social, cultural, and political factors than of will, choice, or agency. What is striking about this period is the perdurance of the communal self on the one hand and the fact that many Renaissance selves were not demarcated or neatly bounded in one clearly individuated body. To the contrary, the Renaissance body was often porous or permeable, at times under the influence of dual or multiple spirits or souls, at other times without a spirit at all – and yet somehow still vital, capable of animation.

In his celebrated book *The Civilization of the Renaissance in Italy* (1860), the Swiss historian Jacob Burckhardt argued that the "development of the individual" was a defining attribute of the period. The claim is tantalizing; late medieval Italy does indeed appear, as Burckhardt put it, "to swarm with individuality; the ban laid upon human personality was dissolved; and a thousand figures meet us each in its own special shape and dress."[41] But we must take great care here in assessing this argument. Only four years before Burckhardt published his now classic work, Alexis de Tocqueville made the opposite point. "That word 'individualism' which we have coined for our own requirements," Tocqueville wrote, "was unknown to our ancestors, for the good reason that in those days every individual necessarily belonged to a group and no one could regard himself as an isolated unit."[42] Increasingly, scholars are likely to side with Tocqueville. Burckhardt – it now seems clear – read nineteenth-century notions of individuality back into fourteenth- and fifteenth-century Italy. The Renaissance "discovery of the individual" turns out to be mostly myth.

NOTES

1   Bouwsma, "The Renaissance," along with Bouwsma's *aggiornamento*, *American Historical Review* 103 (1998), p. 115.
2   Cicchetti and Mordenti, *I libri de famiglia*; Pandimiglio, "Ricordanze"; Amelang, *Flight of Icarus*; and Dekker, "Egodocuments."
3   Grubb, "Memory and Identity."
4   Dekker, "Egodocuments," p. 64. For England, Mascuch, *Origins*.
5   Cellini, *Autobiography*, pp. 120–4.
6   Mauss, "Category."
7   Burke, "Renaissance, Individualism."
8   Grafton, *Cardano's Cosmos*, p. 181.
9   Cardano, *Book of My Life*; Grafton, *Cardano's Cosmos*, pp. 181–6.
10 Gardner, "*Homines non nascuntur.*"
11 Montaigne, *Essays*, p. 540.
12 Bloch, *French Rural History*, pp. 48–56.
13 Macfarlane, *Origins of English Individualism*, p. 197 especially.
14 Trinkaus, *In Our Image*; also Baron, *Crisis*.
15 Wilkins, *Petrarch*, p. 185.

16   Cohn, "Burckhardt Revisted."
17   Woods-Marsden, *Renaissance Self-Portraiture.*
18   Greenblatt, *Renaissance Self-Fashioning*, p. 2.
19   Modena, *Life of Judah.*
20   Cox, "Single Self."
21   Schama, *Rembrandt's Eyes*, 295–306.
22   Sabean, *Power in the Blood*, pp. 30–6.
23   Le Roy Ladurie, *Montaillou* and Ginzburg, *Cheese and the Worms.*
24   Cited in Weissman, "Being Ambiguous," p. 272.
25   Chojnacki, *Women and Men*, p. 23.
26   Chojnacki, *Women and Men*, pp. 178–89; Martin, *Venice's Hidden Enemies*, pp. 170–1;
     and Romano, *Housecraft and Statecraft*, pp. 207–22.
27   Amelang, "Checklist," in *Flight of Icarus*, pp. 253–350.
28   Rose, *Authors and Owners*, pp. 9–16 and 31–66.
29   Castiglione, *Cortegiano*, pp. 236 and 253.
30   Martin, "Inventing Sincerity."
31   Grafton, *Cardano's Cosmos*, p. 189.
32   Pullan, "Ship," p. 37.
33   Davis, *Return of Martin Guerre.*
34   Walker, *Spiritual and Divine Magic.*
35   Grafton, *Cardano's Cosmos*, p. 168, cf. p. 178.
36   Davis, "Boundaries."
37   Schutte, *Cecilia Ferrazzi.*
38   Ruggiero, *Binding Passions* and Thomas, *Religion and the Decline of Magic.*
39   Ginzburg, *Nightbattles*, p. 8.
40   Geertz, "Native's Point of View," p. 126.
41   Burckhardt, *Civilization of the Renaissance*, vol. I, p. 143.
42   de Tocqueville, *Old Regime*, p. 96.

REFERENCES

Amelang, James, *The Flight of Icarus: Artisan Autobiography in Early Modern Europe* (Stanford: Stanford University Press, 1998).

Bloch, Marc, *French Rural History: An Essay on its Basic Characteristics*, trans. Janet Sondheimer (Berkeley: University of California Press, 1966).

Bouwsma, William J., "The Renaissance and the Drama of Western History," *American Historical Review* 84 (1979), pp. 1–15.

Burckhardt, Jacob, *The Civilization of the Renaissance in Italy*, 2 vols., trans. S. G. C. Middlemore (New York: Harper, 1958).

Burke, Peter, "The Renaissance, Individualism, and the Portrait," *History of European Ideas* 21 (1995), pp. 393–400.

Cardan, Jerome (Cardano, Girolamo), *The Book of My Life*, trans. Jean Stoner (New York: E. P. Dutton, 1930).

Castiglione, Baldasar, *Il libro del cortegiano* (Turin: Unione tipografico, editrice torinese, 1964).

Cellini, Benvenuto, *The Autobiography*, trans. George Bull (Harmondsworth and New York: Penguin, 1985).

Chojnacki, Stanley, *Women and Men in Renaissance Venice: Twelve Essays on Patrician Society* (Baltimore: Johns Hopkins University Press, 2000).

Cicchetti, Angelo and Mordenti, Raul, *I libri di famiglia in Italia* (Rome: Edizioni di storia e letteratura, 1985).

Cohn, Samuel K., "Burckhardt Revisited from Social History," in *Language and Images of Renaissance Italy*, ed. Alison Brown (Oxford: Clarendon, 1995), pp. 217–34.

Cox, Virginia, "The Single Self: Feminist Thought and the Marriage Market in Early Modern Venice," *Renaissance Quarterly* 48 (1995), pp. 513–81.

Davis, Natalie Zemon, *The Return of Martin Guerre* (Cambridge, MA: Harvard University Press, 1983).

——, "Boundaries and the Sense of Self in Sixteenth-Century France," in Thomas C. Heller et al., eds., *Reconstructing Individualism: Autonomy, Individuality, and the Self in Western Thought*, ed. Thomas C. Heller, Morton Sosna, and David E. Wellbery (Stanford: Stanford University Press, 1986), pp. 53–63.

Dekker, Rudolf, "Egodocuments (Autobiographies, Diaries, Travel Journals) in the Netherlands, 1500–1814," *Dutch Crossing* 39 (1989), pp. 61–72.

de Tocqueville, Alexis, *The Old Regime and the French Revolution*, trans. Stuart Gilbert (Garden City, NY: Doubleday, 1955).

Gardner, Victoria C., "*Homines non nascuntur, sed finguntur*: Benvenuto Cellini's *Vita* and Self-Presentation of the Renaissance Artist," *Sixteenth Century Journal* 28 (1997), pp. 447–65.

Geertz, Clifford, "'From the Native's Point of View': On the Nature of Anthropological Understanding," in *Culture Theory: Essays on Mind, Self, and Emotion*, ed. Richard Shweder and Robert Levine (Cambridge: Cambridge University Press, 1984).

Ginzburg, Carlo, *The Cheese and the Worms: The Cosmos of a Sixteenth-Century Miller* (Baltimore: Johns Hopkins University Press, 1980).

——, *The Nightbattles: Witchcraft and Agrarian Cults in the Sixteenth and Seventeenth Centuries* (Baltimore: Johns Hopkins University Press, 1983).

Grafton, Anthony, *Cardano's Cosmos: The Worlds and Works of a Renaissance Astrologer* (Cambridge, MA: Harvard University Press, 1999).

Greenblatt, Stephen, *Renaissance Self-Fashioning: From More to Shakespeare* (Chicago: University of Chicago Press, 1980).

Grubb, James S., "Memory and Identity: Why Venetians Did Not Keep *Recordanze*," *Renaissance Studies* 8 (1994), pp. 375–87.

Le Roy Ladurie, Emmanuel, *Montaillou: village occitan de 1294 à 1324* (Paris: Gallimard, 1975).

Macfarlane, Alan, *The Origins of English Individualism: The Family, Property and Social Transition* (Cambridge: Cambridge University Press, 1978).

Martin, John Jeffries, *Venice's Hidden Enemies: Italian Heretics in a Renaissance City* (Berkeley: University of California Press, 1993).

——, "Inventing Sincerity, Refashioning Prudence: The Discovery of the Individual in Renaissance Europe," *American Historical Review* 102 (1997), pp. 1309–42.

Mascuch, Michael, *The Origins of the Individualist Self: Autobiography and Self-Identity in England* (Stanford: Stanford University Press, 1996).

Mauss, Marcel, "The Category of the Person," in *The Category of the Person*, ed. Michael Carrithers (Cambridge: Cambridge University Press, 1985).

Modena, Leone, *Life of Judah: The Autobiography of a Seventeenth-Century Venetian Rabbi*, ed. and trans. Mark R. Cohen (Princeton: Princeton University Press, 1988).

Montaigne, Michel de, *The Complete Essays* (Stanford: Stanford University Press, 1958).

Pandimiglio, Leonida, "Ricordanze e libro di famiglia: il manifestarsi di una nuova fonte," *Lettere italiane* 39 (1987), pp. 3–19.

Pullan, Brian, "'A Ship with Two Rudders': 'Righetto Marrano' and the Inquisition in Venice," *The Historical Journal* 20 (1977), pp. 25–58.

Romano, Dennis, *Housecraft and Statecraft: Domestic Service in Renaissance Venice, 1400–1600* (Baltimore: Johns Hopkins University Press, 1996).

Rose, Mark, *Authors and Owners: The Invention of Copyright* (Cambridge, MA: Harvard University Press, 1993).

Ruggiero, Guido, *Binding Passions: Tales of Magic, Marriage, and Power at the End of the Renaissance* (New York: Oxford University Press, 1993).

Sabean, David, *Power in the Blood: Popular Culture and Village Discourse in Early Modern Germany* (Cambridge: Cambridge University Press, 1984).

Schama, Simon, *Rembrandt's Eyes* (New York: Knopf, 1999).

Schutte, Anne Jacobson, *The Autobiography of an Aspiring Saint: Cecilia Ferrazzi* (Chicago: University of Chicago Press, 1996).

Thomas, Keith, *Religion and the Decline of Magic* (New York: Scribner, 1971).

Trinkaus, Charles, *In Our Image and Likeness: Humanity and Divinity in Italian Renaissance Thought*, 2 vols. (Chicago: University of Chicago Press, 1970).

Walker, D. P., *Spiritual and Demonic Magic from Ficino to Campanella* (London: Warburg Institute, 1958).

Weissman, Ronald F. E., "The Importance of Being Ambiguous: Social Relations, Individualism, and Identity in Renaissance Florence," in *Urban Life in the Renaissance*, ed. Susan Zimmerman and Ronald F. E. Weissman (Newark: University of Delaware Press, 1989), pp. 269–80.

Wilkins, Ernest Hatch, *Life of Petrarch* (Chicago: University of Chicago Press, 1961).

Woods-Marsden, Joanna, *Renaissance Self-Portraiture: The Visual Construction of Identity and the Social Status of the Artist* (New Haven: Yale University Press, 1998).

FURTHER READING

On Burckhardt's continuing influence, see William Kerrigan and Gordon Braden, *The Idea of the Renaissance* (Baltimore: Johns Hopkins University Press, 1989) and Keith Whitlock, ed., *The Renaissance in Europe: A Reader* (New Haven: Yale University Press, 2000). An excellent companion text to Burckhardt remains Johan Huizinga, *The Autumn of the Middle Ages*, trans. Rodney J. Payton and Ulrich Mammitzsch (Chicago: University of Chicago Press, 1996). For an introduction to the role of contemporary theory in the rethinking of Renaissance humanism, see Patricia Parker and David Quint, eds., *Literary Theory/Renaissance Texts* (Baltimore: Johns Hopkins University Press, 1986).

Peter Burke's "Representations of the Self from Petrarch to Descartes," in *Rewriting the Self: Histories from the Renaissance to the Present*, ed. Roy Porter (London: Routledge, 1997), pp. 17–28, provides a useful overview of many of the major themes in the recent historiography of Renaissance individualism. For a more ambitious approach, see Philippe Ariès and Georges Duby, eds., *A History of Private Life*, vols. II and III, trans. Arthur Goldhammer (Cambridge, MA: Harvard University Press, 1988–9).

On autobiography, see George Gusdorf, "Conditions and Limits of Autobiography," in *Autobiography: Essays Theoretical and Critical*, ed. James Olney (Princeton: Princeton University Press, 1980), pp. 28–49; Georg Misch, *Geschichte der Autobiographie*, 4 vols. (Bern: Francke, 1949–70); Karl Joachim Weintraub, *The Value of the Individual: Self and Circumstance in Autobiography* (Chicago: University of Chicago Press, 1978); and Thomas Mayer and D. R. Woolf, eds., *The Rhetorics of Life-Writing in Early Modern Europe* (Ann Arbor: University of Michigan Press, 1995).

On portraiture and self-portraiture, see Diane Owen-Hughes, "Representing the Family: Portraits and Purposes in Early Modern Italy," *Journal of Interdisciplinary History* 17 (1986), pp. 7–38; Joseph Leo Koerner, *The Moment of Self-Portraiture in German Renaissance Art* (Chicago: University of Chicago Press, 1993); and Peter Humfrey, *Lorenzo Lotto* (New Haven: Yale University Press, 1997).

For the social history of the self, see Marvin Becker, "Individualism in the Early Italian Renaissance: Burden and Blessing," *Studies in the Renaissance* 19 (1972), pp. 273–97; F. W. Kent, *Household and Lineage in Renaissance Florence: The Family Life of the Capponi, Ginori, and Rucellai* (Princeton: Princeton University Press, 1977); Lawrence Stone, *Family, Sex and Marriage in England* (New York: Harper and Row, 1979), esp. ch. VI: "The Growth of Affective Individualism"; Emmanuel Le Roy Ladurie, *The Beggar and the Professor: A Sixteenth-Century Family Saga*, trans. Arthur Goldhammer (Chicago: University of Chicago Press, 1997); Steven Ozment, *Magdalena and Balthasar: An Intimate Portrait of Life in Sixteenth-Century Europe* (New York: Simon and Schuster, 1986); and Barbara Diefendorf and Carla Hesse, eds., *Culture and Identity in Early Modern Europe: Essays in Honor of Natalie Zemon Davis* (Ann Arbor: University of Michigan Press, 1993).

PART III

Social and Economic Worlds

CHAPTER THIRTEEN

Social Hierarchies: The Upper Classes

MATTHEW VESTER

Introduction

Duke Emanuel Filibert of Savoy (1528–80) was the son of Charles III and Beatrice, a Portuguese princess. His father's sister was Louise de Savoie, mother of King Francis I and the most powerful woman in early sixteenth-century France. Beatrice of Portugal's sister Isabel was married to Emperor Charles V, whose son King Philip II of Spain was thus the Duke of Savoy's cousin. Emanuel Filibert spent much of his young adult life in his uncle's imperial suite in Germany, also visiting Spain and England, and was eventually named governor-general of the Netherlands. He married Margaret, sister of King Henri II of France, and their son Charles Emanuel in turn married a Spanish princess, Catherine, daughter of Philip II. The alpine lands over which Emanuel Filibert claimed dominion are today located in France, Italy, and Switzerland, and today, as in the sixteenth century, the inhabitants of those lands speak a variety of languages.

The cosmopolitan nature of Emanuel Filibert's family connections, career path, and jurisdictional reach was remarkable, but not unheard of, for a Renaissance noble. An international, or truly European, perspective on the Renaissance nobility has much to offer but must contend with old historiographic boundaries imposed by the analytical category of the nation-state. In this essay I would like to suggest that if we could see "the state" as a concept that during the Renaissance had only relative, not absolute, political importance, we would be rewarded with a richer and less anachronistic vision of the social position of the nobility and of noble self-perceptions. Viewing the nobility through the prism of territorial and family interests that were often transregional (indeed, European) clarifies the range of authorities that structured Renaissance society. It also helps us see nobles less as subjects and more as lords in their own right, with preconceptions that sprang from their desire to dominate, not merely from their interests in land, fortune, and offices in the service of the state.

Studies of the nobility have largely focused on its relationship to central authority and to the emergence of capitalism. These are important questions, but they tend to exaggerate the national character of the European nobility and shift attention away from the important questions of how, on a concrete level, nobles lived, interacted with members of other social groups, and understood their place in society. Drawing too close a connection between the political dominance of the nobility and their economic position is also problematic since the nobles had never totally dominated the European economy (and, as we shall see below, since nobles were not driven by a desire to maximize economic utility).

Ideas about nobility in Renaissance Europe were generally shared across the continent, in large part because of the common institutional heritage of Latin Christianity. Nobility was an "international" concept which reinforced the European character of the Renaissance elite's self-awareness, even after the seventeenth-century "rise of the nation-state." Scholars agree that "national identity mattered relatively little to men and women who might have familial attachments throughout Europe." Nobles "moved easily across national boundaries, quickly acquiring land and influence in the new setting. Linguistic and cultural differences posed few problems."[1] While there were important differences between nobles in different parts of Europe, these differences tended to correspond to regional rather than national boundaries (urban Mediterranean nobles vs. a rural nobility in northwestern Europe, etc.). (See the essay by Peter Burke above.) An important area of future research on the Renaissance nobility thus should be the structure and impact of contacts between nobles from different parts of Europe.

This essay will combine an overview of recent scholarship on the Renaissance nobility with suggestions for new research possibilities in five areas. First it will examine how nobility has been defined on a normative level during the Renaissance, pointing particularly to the pan-European nature of such definitions. Next it will historicize the problem of noble domination during the Renaissance in order to consider how the practice of lordship affected the social position and mentality of the nobility. The topic of how the relationship between nobles and rulers, or between lordship and sovereignty, played itself out in a variety of European contexts will then be addressed, followed by a look at how these problems were experienced by nobles and urban elites in Renaissance Italy. Finally, the essay will consider the problem of social divisions and solidarities, both within the nobility and between social classes. In each section I hope to show how relatively more attention to family and territorial interests and relatively less to the impact of the "rise of the state" on the nobility might benefit future research.

Defining Nobility on a Normative Level

Renaissance debates over how to define nobility took place largely in the context of a common European heritage rooted in classical thought and Christian ideals. While some parts of Europe witnessed the construction of specific intellectual arguments in favor of one position or another, most positions had an impact across the continent. Discussions about what it meant to be noble were also generally full of contradictions.

Two of the early contributors in the western tradition to literature on nobility were the ancient Greeks Xenophon and Aristotle, both of whom made important statements about social hierarchy but also about meritocracy. Xenophon's *Life of Cyrus* was widely available during the Renaissance, and anticipated many later contradictions in the discussions of nobility. His account of Cyrus' youth and kingly career depict the great Persian king deftly combining "courtly" manners and sophistication with "warrior noble" instincts. Although Cyrus was said to embody "inborn nobleness and superiority" to other Persians, Cyrus inspired his soldiers by insisting that through hard work they could "possess those qualities which are thought to be peculiar to what we call 'the better classes'." In order to maintain his dominion over the recently conquered Assyrians – men whom Cyrus knew to be "true warriors, who carried arms... confident, as he could plainly see, of their own power to rule" – Cyrus resolved to shower kindness and honors upon them, thereby binding his former foes to himself. Xenophon observed that those whom Cyrus honored were themselves held in high esteem and were sought out by others who rushed to please them.[2] These themes – courtly nobility, feudal militarism, hereditary nobility versus meritocracy, and the use of favors and patronage by sovereigns to create ties of loyalty – all figured centrally in the imagination and practice of Renaissance nobility.

The Aristotelian tradition was also both an important part of the mental set through which Renaissance Europeans thought about nobility, and another source of contradictions. Aristotle taught that the goal of the household was to become autonomous, and that this self-sufficiency created the conditions which permitted the male head of the household to live virtuously, in accordance with reason. Those able to attain such self-sufficiency and virtue deserved to receive honor and possessions in accordance with their superiority. This kind of social hierarchy obviously appealed to later European nobles seeking to justify their positions, and inspired the search for the political autonomy that colored their mental preoccupations. On the other hand Aristotelian virtue does not appear to be hereditary but instead linked to material conditions. Furthermore, Aristotle was unwilling to make any absolute claims about the position of the "best men" in society in the ideal political constitution, arguing instead that "rulers and ruled are in one way the same and in another different" (*Politics*, VII). He also taught that the best form of constitution for a given place at a given time varied according to local conditions.

After the disintegration of the Roman Empire, contradictory normative discussions of nobility reappeared when new structures of domination were elaborated during the twelfth century. In reaction to the honor claims of the landed military nobility, whose status was based on feats of arms and ties of vassalage to kings and emperors, other elites began to stake a claim for their own nobility. Ernst Kantorowicz showed how, with the explosion of scientific jurisprudence during the late twelfth century, doctors of the law began to assert the right to be called *domini*, lords, and also portrayed themselves as *milites legum*, knights of the laws.[3] The fourteenth-century jurist Cynus de Pistoia argued that merit (read: scholarship) ennobled a man more than descent from a noble lineage. Such arguments were reiterated during the fifteenth and sixteenth centuries by Guy Pape, Barthélemy de Chasseneux, Jean de Montholon, and André Tiraqueau. By 1600 or so these views on the nobility of magistrates were widely accepted, in part because many landed nobles, especially in Mediterranean regions, had also long appreciated the utility of a legal education.

In Renaissance Italy, ideas of noble civic virtue were developed in the context of communal government in Florence, in direct opposition to theories of virtue being celebrated in the princely court of Milan. Cesare Mozzarelli has shown how the identification by Matteo Palmieri (*Della vita civile*, ca. 1435) of human virtue with civic virtue gave way by the late fifteenth century to a vision elaborated by Platina. According to this, citizens position themselves hierarchically with respect to the most virtuous citizen, the *optimo cive* (Lorenzo de' Medici). Castiglione's *Il cortegiano* and its courtly virtue was the final step by which the urban patriciate could pursue the ideal of noble virtue in a changed political environment. For Mozzarelli, Castiglione opens (but never resolves) a debate over whether nobility is inherited or acquired through virtuous acts.[4] This debate is related to a normative conflict surrounding nobility – a conflict reaching back to Xenophon and ever-present during the Renaissance – between the courtly ideal (à la Castiglione) and the traditional life-style of feuding knights. (See the essay by Robert Muchembled above.)

By 1550 or so, the court rather than the warrior host had become the key locus of noble culture, although (echoing a theme first elaborated in the twelfth century by John of Salisbury) not everyone appreciated court life. Natural philosophers and moralists during the sixteenth century sometimes saw the court as an evil, dangerous place where one might catch a "court disease" (*morbus aulicus*). This mindset saw brilliant people (such as outstanding princes) as likely to be melancholic, and court life destroyed the tranquility of mind essential for the well-being of such individuals.

During the sixteenth century, just as the tensions between different kinds of nobility (feudal-military, civic, magisterial, courtly, etc.) and between lordship and sovereignty (to be discussed below) were coming to a head, an "imaginative re-feudalization"[5] was taking place in the literary sphere, through the wild success of chivalric romances such as *Amadis of Gaul, Orlando furioso*, and the like. This chivalric turn was reinforced by the invention of a number of new knightly orders during the Renaissance: in France, the Orders of St. Michael and the Holy Spirit; in Burgundy, the Order of the Golden Fleece; in Savoy the Order of the Annunciation, etc. Yet chivalric noble ideals were themselves at odds with certain Christian principles: on a basic level Christianity was radically egalitarian, and some Christian writers (both Catholic and Protestant) were uncomfortable with the notion of status distinctions rooted in violence. The ethic of humility central to Christianity and the growing insistence by rulers on political allegiance regardless of religious concerns further widened the gap between the demands of Christ and those of chivalry.

In the late nineteenth and early twentieth centuries, cultural historians began to rethink the meaning and function of the nobility during the Renaissance. For Burckhardt, the Italian Renaissance took place largely because the social divisions that prevented cultural dynamism in northern Europe were absent from Italy. Johan Huizinga, in *The Autumn of the Middle Ages*, came to an opposite conclusion: that the Renaissance pursuit of ideal beauty was a legacy of French knightly culture. The divergence of these viewpoints embodies the contradictions about nobility that affected all Europeans: "being noble" during the Renaissance was at the same time a way of thinking nostalgically about the past (from a European perspective, this nostalgia must have been powerfully affected by the rapid disintegration of the *Corpus Christianorum* during the sixteenth century), an aesthetic response to the miseries of the present (this was Huizinga's view), and an energetic way of positioning one's family for success in the future.

In each of these areas though, noble status depended on one's actions, reputation, and the memory of those actions and reputation. This concept was also common to the various normative definitions of nobility discussed in this section; even the nobility of one whose claims were based on heredity could be called into question owing to a failure to reiterate this status continually, through actions. Key indicators of nobility included having a body marred by battle scars, marrying nobly, giving gifts liberally, carrying a sword, exercising the right to hunt, enjoying the right of first instance in higher judicial fora, being beheaded rather than hanged, wearing special clothes, displaying a coat of arms, and being exempt from taxation and other dues. When noble status was determined by actions, reputation, and memory, nobility itself was a discontinuous state demanding constant reiteration. Keeping this in mind helps makes sense of the practices of lordship described in the next section.

Historicizing Noble Domination

The social position of the nobility during the Renaissance was closely tied to the practice of lordship. The way in which nobles thought of themselves was conditioned by the concrete forms of feudal domination exercised by those nobles. Lordship and its impact on noble self-perceptions operated within boundaries that were family-defined, regional, and transnational.

There is a long tradition of scholarship attentive to the dangers of projecting the nation-state into the past in order to explain political life, and concerned with preserving a sense of the "otherness" of the political environment in Renaissance Europe. Otto Brunner and Bartolomé Clavero have described an environment in which the boundaries between the kind of authority exercised by the nobility and the kind of authority asserted by territorial sovereigns were far from clear. The authority exercised by the noble lord was not private and subordinate to "the state," but was grounded in a sense of right and an obligation to protect one's dominion and those within it. Such rights and obligations were all-encompassing, and could not be limited to the lord's "private" activities in his lands: they were fully political. (See the essay by Edward Muir above.)

Noble political action – such as feuds between noble houses – should be analyzed within this historicized context of lordship, not as a form of uncontrolled behavior displayed by an irrational warrior elite. For Brunner, a noble feud, even with the emperor, was perceived by the participants as a just war, and followed well-established procedures. The feud was the chief mechanism by which nobles exercised their right and obligation to defend themselves and their dependents; it was the basic expression of their political capacity. Historians have begun to try to make sense of the political activity of Renaissance nobles by assessing such activity in light of "a culture of feud," and by exploring the relationship between feuds and the emergence of new claims of sovereign territorial authority.

Just as there was no legal distinction between war and feud, the utility of the distinction between "Spanish nobles," "French nobles," etc. must be questioned, since each lord was really a state unto himself. Clavero's legal anthropological approach uncovers a system of norms governing political action during the Renaissance long before modern states began to try to regulate public activity through laws. This scholarship shows that prior to the eighteenth century in Europe a *peculiar mentalidad* governed the way people thought of "persons" and "states": just as the king was thought to have two bodies and different family members were thought of as one lineage-person, so might a single person holding several different lordships be conceptualized as several persons, according to the formula *tot personae quot feuda*.

Late medieval jurists identified a variety of kinds of lordship, possession, dominion, and authority: efforts to make sense of Renaissance nobles' political actions should take into account the complex legal and customary environment in which those nobles interacted. Medieval and Renaissance legal scholars inherited a set of authority-related concepts dating from the Roman Empire: *imperium*, which was the highest form of public power; *iurisdictio*, which was related, but not of the same magnitude; and *merum imperium*, which was the abstraction of the highest general powers of jurisdiction. During the Middle Ages jurists sought to elaborate this Roman conceptual foundation in a way that reflected changing conditions, in particular the fact that a variety of lords (including lower ones) and territorial rulers exercised apparently unlimited power over their subjects, despite the fact that they did not technically hold *imperium*. Even the jurists admitted that full jurisdiction was exercised in a variety of juridical orders. In the words of the late thirteenth-century *Coutumes de Beauvoisis*, "chascun barons est souverains en sa baronnie."[6]

By the time of the Renaissance, jurists distinguished between special feudal law and the natural jurisdiction of the king, but argued that when the two were in conflict, the alternative that more clearly advanced the *publicam utilitatem* was to be preferred. During the sixteenth century, scholars began to dissect the relationship between *iurisdictio* and *imperium* in order to develop a conceptual system that corresponded to contemporary conditions. This led to more distinctions (between *merum* and *mixtum imperium*, for example), and eventually to the work of Charles Loyseau, the early seventeenth-century theorist of absolutism who differentiated "the king's 'public lordship' (*seigneurie publique*), the state, from 'private lordship' (*seigneurie privée*), landed property." Still, Jean Bodin, also portrayed as a theorist of absolutism, refused to consider " 'sovereignty' and 'seigneury' . . . as two fundamentally different things; for him sovereignty was nothing but 'supreme power' (*suprema potestas*)."[7]

Thus, during the Renaissance, the notion that the authority exercised by the nobility was "private" while that exercised by the sovereign was "public" was not widely accepted. In a number of ways Renaissance lords continued to assert a kind of authority that did not admit such a distinction. It was not obvious to subjects of Renaissance sovereigns that the authority of their noble provincial governors was distinct from sovereign royal authority. Nobles on their lands were seen as much more than simple landed proprietors; they were believed to hold special economic and political power.

Such power was exercised by Renaissance nobles as members of houses, not as isolated individuals. The importance of the family in the political calculations of noble lords seems obvious, but surprisingly few recent historians have explored in depth the way in which family interests structured the political interactions between nobles, sovereigns, and other power actors during the Renaissance. Family interests were not limited by national boundaries, and marriage alliances could lead to the construction of noble houses that were truly international in scope. Jacques de Savoie, Duke of Genevois-Nemours, provides a modest example. Jacques had connections by birth and marriage to a number of sovereign European houses: Savoy, Lorraine, Este, and Valois. His case also illustrates the fact that the interests of the house often embodied contradictions; Jacques was the head of a cadet branch of the Savoyard dynasty and as such had goals which frequently brought him into conflict with the head of the ruling branch, his cousin Emanuel Filibert. While family was really the relevant political unit for the Renaissance nobility, intrafamily relationships were not always cooperative. In this regard, the findings of historians of the nobility reinforce the work of scholars of urban elites during the Renaissance.

A central element of nobles' self-perception, and one that grew out of their practice of lordship, was their sense of honor. Historians of the French religious wars, following the lead of Kristen Neuschel, who sees "the motives for nobles' political behavior within a warrior culture that was still materially and psychologically independent of the state," have urged scholars to take chivalric values more seriously in their interpretations of noble culture. A seventeenth-century treatise on duels linked noble honor to the service of the sovereign: "The honor of a gentilhomme is inseparably united with the public honor, the usefulness of his Majesty's service and the good of his State" (P. Boyssat, *Recherche sur les duels*, 1610). Here also, though, were contradictions: Ed Muir has drawn attention to the "double-binds" caused by conflicting honor demands placed on nobles trying to defend their patrimonies, respond honorably to vendetta challenges, adopt courtly manners, and respect new state-sponsored criminal statutes. In fact, these contradictions affected rulers themselves, who as nobles were subject to the same honor code that required actions prohibited by their own law![8]

Protecting and maximizing their realm of lordship was a fundamental motivating force for noble political action. Honor emphasized competitive assertiveness, especially in realms where honor positions were not clearly defined, as was the case in much of Renaissance territorial politics. (See the essay by James Farr above.) Even the lesser noble "held power that rendered him as autonomous, proportionately, as the greatest noble," and the heads of all noble houses were obsessed with protecting even minor privileges.[9] For Renaissance nobles, the importance of increasing one's grandeur and prestige, through means which guaranteed their own autonomy if possible, was self-evident. This drive for political self-sufficiency, a key Renaissance legacy of the Aristotelian tradition, also placed nobles in a variety of convoluted roles. The case of Charles de Gonzague-Nevers is instructive in showing how princely nobles dealt with such complexity. When faced with the choice of greater revenues and political stability in the service of another, or risking fortunes and offices in order to protect his own sovereign claims and autonomy, this early seventeenth-century noble chose the latter.

Renaissance nobles such as Gonzague-Nevers asserted their autonomy on a European playing field, and did not hesitate to pursue advantages and make alliances with other nobles and sovereigns from multiple European regions. European nobles formed international connections through kinship, marriage, and service ties, and these links were mediated by an institutional structure that included courts, ecclesiastical bodies, educational establishments, and military service. As far as I am aware, the function of such institutions as communication nodes in a cultural network of European nobility has been unexplored.

Jonathan Dewald has identified the rise of a modern, "capitalistic" form of property as the key shift affecting the European nobility between 1300 and 1800 or so. When this new kind of land tenure replaced lordship, it created a new structure for social relations and radically altered the political preconceptions of nobles and their subjects. According to Dewald, when this began to happen, "rather than influence over men, direct and indirect, landowners increasingly wanted only money from their properties.... Those who wanted to exercise political power did so within state institutions."[10] Much research is needed to shed light on the precise timing and nature of this shift, and to clarify the complicated relationship between lordship and sovereignty that continued to complicate European politics long after the Renaissance. Gerhard Oestreich reminded us that well into the seventeenth century

> there existed a plurality of rights and authorities at different levels which were not dependent on or delegated by the central authority. Only in theory was there such a thing as "centralization."...In reality monarchic authority had only a partial influence on what came to be known as the provincial level and hardly any, or none at all, in local government.[11]

European Nobles and Territorial Politics

Nobles were key targets of the efforts by the most prestigious and powerful members of their own class – sovereign territorial rulers – to consolidate their authority and protect themselves against potential usurpers. Most scholarship on the Renaissance nobility has characterized this conflict as one between central states and their nobilities. It might, however, be more productive to think of this struggle as a series of transregional or European disputes among noble houses, each interested in maximizing jurisdiction.

The Renaissance "state" itself followed a lordship/household model; indeed, in some ways the feudal overlord monopolized authority over his domain to a greater degree than the sovereign did over his! Thus it was difficult to distinguish the "court" from the "state" in most Renaissance principalities, and the fact that family members (or high officials) of many dynasties held their own courts – separate from the sovereign's – complicated matters more.

Local and regional political relations (which were often "international") continued to form the basis of noble power throughout the Renaissance. Antoni Maczak has suggested that the dichotomy center/locality be replaced with the notion of extensive versus particular power structures, the latter permitting a better appreciation of the territorial interests of the nobility during the Renaissance. The practical authority of Renaissance nobles, rooted in the possession of castles, large caches of weapons, and influence over bandit networks that controlled major trade routes, expressed itself territorially in ways that disregarded "national" boundaries but were reinforced by local institutional environments.

In 1561 the Venetian ambassador to the court of Savoy identified four "first nobles of Piedmont" and noted that the duke of Savoy

> uses these lords only to listen to their opinions, and when occasionally he learns that one of them dissents from his own view, he makes and executes his decision without telling them. Such lords are a great help to His Excellency, especially when it is necessary to require the country to accept some tax or provide some subsidy to the prince, because these lords are like heads of factions, and hold great authority in the places where they reside.[12]

Rulers sought to tie great nobles such as these to themselves through the distribution of honors and patronage, and through the prestige of their courts. Historians of Renaissance France have disagreed over how precisely to characterize the emotional, material, and political links between nobles involved in social interactions. General agreement exists, however, that rulers wanted to turn the great nobles of the realm into their clients through the distribution of favors, pensions, and offices, thus co-opting the provincial patronage systems of these great nobles into royal service. Over the course of the late Renaissance "was established," to cite Arlette Jouanna, "bit by bit, a pyramidal system in which all of the threads led to the king." Jouanna emphasizes that this process was not designed to slight the nobility, but rather to maintain positive, albeit altered, relations with nobles. Jouanna also points out that in order to facilitate this process, the crown had a vested interest in doing away with the principle of hereditary nobility, in order to confirm royal control over nobles.[13] Scholars have documented this centralization of patronage, or "spider-web" model, throughout Europe during the Renaissance, in the Spanish realms, in England, the Netherlands, Muscovy, and elsewhere.

Another major historiographic theme pioneered by Georges Pagès in the 1930s, and then revived by Perry Anderson and others in the 1970s, is that the end of the Renaissance saw the creation of an absolutism that was based on an alliance between sovereigns and their aristocracies. This "absolutist compromise" (to use Dewald's term) between rulers and nobles granted extensive local (especially fiscal) authority to nobles in return for their obedience to the ruler. While this development heralded the denouement of certain lordly cultural attitudes and political claims, it also created a new kind of cultural and political position for the nobility in society. Still, the "absolutist compromise" was problematic for rulers, especially since the favors and autonomy granted to local nobles by rulers increased their local authority and sphere of action. Jouanna's assessment that "the [French] peasant uprisings of the 1590s ...managed to persuade the nobles that strong royal power capable of mastering social disorders was in their interest"[14] also points to assumptions implied by the "compromise" thesis that need further examination: was the king relying on the local authority of the nobility in order to spread his reach across the realm as a whole, or were local nobles trying to tap into royal power in order to apply it to problems too difficult for them to solve? Further, this "compromise" was uneven, and more often than not, resistance by local nobles or their peasants, or by both, was the norm.

The contradictions of the "absolutist compromise" also haunt the spider-web patronage theory. Scholars have pointed to the need for patronage models to incorporate more precisely the phenomenon of service to multiple patrons in the context of nobles pursuing independent strategies. Maczak argued that the prince was only able "to gain a monopoly of opportunities for social and economic advancement among the nobility as well as other ambitious groups," once "the aristocracy's regional power bases had been destroyed and the other nobles somehow deprived of their independence." The obvious problem here is that the very utility of centralizing patronage is that it permits the ruler to become the indirect beneficiary of pre-existing political networks. If the process of centralization destroys those same networks, the entire exercise becomes futile. Edoardo Grendi critiqued the model from a different perspective: the patronage model presents itself as the sole or dominant source of personal influence, without engaging in "a concrete reconstruction of personal roles in the context of the community."[15]

The useful spider-web and absolutist compromise models could be profitably refined and explicated through a focused examination of how they interacted with older cultural and political patterns of lordly domination. This will inevitably focus attention on how the conflict between the noble as lord and the noble as client expressed itself concretely on the local level. Luciano Allegra, in his study of credit relations in the Piedmontese town of Chieri, found that the integration of Chieresi nobles into the Savoyard court in Turin (15–20 km away) changed the town's political environment. Nobles left town, but Chieresi merchants and moneylenders found a new market in the nearby capital.[16] The last section of this article will look more carefully at how relations between nobles, sovereigns, and other social groups played themselves out locally. First, though, having provided an international context for the Renaissance nobility, it would be useful to examine how some of the themes explored so far can be identified in the experience of the Italian nobility of the Renaissance.

The Italian Nobility

There were significant similarities and connections between nobles in Italy and those elsewhere in Europe. There were also regional differences throughout Italy, and family interests that were European in scope.

In Italy, as elsewhere in Europe, the upper classes were composed both of feudal aristocracies and of urban patriciates; recent studies "underscore the variety of arrangements possible in the course of the constant dialectic between centrifugal [medieval and feudal] and centripetal [modern and largely urban] forces at work on the Italian scene during the late mediaeval and early modern centuries."[17] During the Renaissance, nobles across Europe began to spend more time in cities, constructing urban residences and aristocratic neighborhoods in which aesthetic concerns, comfort, and privacy outweighed defensive considerations. This was especially true in Italy, in many parts of which the urban presence of the nobility had long been significant. But during the fifteenth century in Florence, patricians began building new palaces that traded public loggia for private interior courtyards, thereby expressing the increasing hierarchization of society that accompanied the consolidation of Medici authority. Between the fifteenth and seventeenth centuries, urban patricians in Genoa, Ferrara, Bologna, and other cities also asserted their pre-eminence, both through architectural projects and through leadership in confraternal organizations.

There were also important landed nobilities in Italy. Tommaso Astarita has described this group in the kingdom of Naples, showing that during the late Renaissance in their feudal lands the Caracciolo Brienza continued to exercise traditional rights, collecting non-landed revenues and tithes, protecting common lands for their peasants, and interacting with their subjects in contexts unmarked by large markets or "the domination of village life by local closed oligarchies." Old feudal nobilities were also well established in Piedmont, Lombardy, Friuli, and Liguria.

In Italy, as elsewhere, there were debates over the relationship between virtue and nobility. Especially after 1550, Italians felt the need to define the concept of nobility and identify the duties of such a group. Some (Girolamo Muzio, *Il Gentilhuomo*,

1575), argued for a nobility of civil and scholarly virtue, while others (such as the Ferrarese courtiers Annibale Romei and Alessandro Sardo), emphasized magnificence, strength, wealth, and splendor, and only after these prudence, justice, and temperance. Sardo, like the Monferrino Stefano Guazzo, posited the hereditary nature of nobility, but also warned that a noble family did lose its nobility as a result of the ignoble actions of certain of its members. Most Italian commentators accepted Tiraqueau's view that commercial activity was not incompatible with nobility, an idea that proved particularly attractive to mercantile Italian elites. Thus the oligarchs of the republic of Lucca began to style themselves *nobiles viri*, and in 1568 a young Lucchese author named Pompeo Rocchi declared in a tract that "the strongest and the best reproduce themselves; so is one led to believe...that gentlemen born of desirably honorable persons, are also valorous themselves." Such arguments did not sit well with (ostensibly) republican Lucca, and before too long another Lucchese named Nicolao Granucci responded with a violently anti-noble invective.[18]

In Italy, as elsewhere, noble classes were reconstituted as a result of their interaction with sovereign princes. However, this process unfolded in parts of Italy in ways that differed from developments in other European regions. One can identify two stages for this: a fifteenth-century process during which rulers and dominant cities extended their dominion over provincial towns and constructed ties with influential, but not yet dominant, social groups. These ties often eventually led to the replacement of the previous sets of ruling elites with new groups that favored, and were favored by, the dominant city or ruler. These developments have been well documented for the Po valley, including the lands of the Visconti, Sforza, Este, and Gonzaga, and for the Florentine dominions in Tuscany.

The second stage came about during the late sixteenth and seventeenth centuries when urban aristocrats began to invest heavily in land and feudal tenures, adopting the life-styles of old landed nobles. Historians have referred to these developments as "refeudalization," a theme that has attracted much scholarly debate: over whether there had ever been a "defeudalization," over the relationship of this process with the emergence of regional states, and over the precise role of merchant families (and merchant mentalities) in such events. Recent work tends to show that the peasantry in Italy, as in other parts of Europe, did not always view "refeudalization" negatively, and that peasants often saw nobles as their protectors against exploitation by dominant cities, the prince, or other wealthy commoners.

Solidarities and Divisions among Renaissance Nobles

While Renaissance nobles were at pains to distinguish themselves from wealthy members of middling classes, they were also frequently divided among themselves along other lines. It is not clear whether nobles thought of horizontal divisions as more fundamental than various vertical ones. Recent scholarship convincingly demonstrates that the class position of the nobles was not seriously threatened by economic crisis between the fifteenth and seventeenth centuries, though it is clear that economic change drove a continual recomposition of the ruling group during the Renaissance. It also seems clear that "national" divisions were not very important for most Renaissance nobles.

Nobles on the whole proved flexible and capable of adapting advantageously to changing economic conditions; this has been demonstrated for Tuscan, French, Neapolitan, and other nobles, though the Castilian nobility might provide an exception to the rule. Indeed, great nobles were themselves important sources of credit for cash-strapped Renaissance princes; their investment in state debt gave them an additional incentive in supporting the ruling dynasty. The side of the ledger that proved most problematic was spending, especially as courtly demands required increasing sophistication in dress, table, and stable. It would be a mistake, however, to discount such spending patterns as irrational, just as it would be wrong to blame aristocrats for not adopting more efficient management methods on their lands, since political imperatives such as autonomy, honor, and reciprocity motivated Renaissance nobles far more than profit.

Economic conjunctures conditioned noble strategies and sometimes changed the composition of the elite. Some scholarship has shown how the phenomenon of the nobility or urban elites "closing ranks" to upwardly mobile groups occurred at different times in different areas, depending on local conditions. This happened in Venice during the fourteenth century, in England and in the kingdom of Naples during the sixteenth, in Catalonia during the sixteenth and seventeenth, and in France during the seventeenth.

Still, most recent historians hesitate to identify the interests of power elites with class interests, either of nobles or bourgeois, preferring to direct attention to "the complexity of the networks of social relationships within which people find their lives woven."[19] Scholars increasingly depict a nobility that rarely formed a smoothly unified social group, but that was divided within – and tied to non-nobles – in a number of ways. Noble houses such as the Guise constructed spheres of influence by including actors from a variety of social levels. In Spain "there was a whole network of communal ties and horizontal links within village communities and Hermandades, as well as between them" and "the exercise of authority was by no means a monopoly of the upper classes."[20] In early seventeenth-century France town magistrates were faced with fractured communities and disputes among themselves, a situation that became even more explosive when local nobles led portions of the citizenry in factional revolts. Minister-favorites in the service of sovereigns were frequently the targets of harsh criticisms from aristocrats and the high clergy, and figures such as Richelieu took delight in despoiling the members of their own class whenever possible.

Gender and generational differences structured other divisions between European nobles. The court was perhaps the only early modern political venue in which women were intimately involved. Not only did this create a sexually-charged atmosphere at court, as Jonathan Dewald has observed, it also provided women with varied means by which to broker or dispense patronage. Some have argued (less convincingly, in my view) that Renaissance noblewomen played important roles in military matters also. Factions in the court of Elizabeth I of England were divided between young and old. Noble sons were faced with the honorable challenge to outdo their own fathers; these " 'house traditions' . . . were all the more cumbersome the higher placed one's family was in the hierarchy of nobility."[21] Such intergenerational tension also affected the ruling house of Urbino, and various members of the Venetian nobility during the late sixteenth century.

The Renaissance nobility of Europe was also divided along religious lines. Six-teenth-century nobles were often quicker to accept religious innovation than other groups, up to one-third of French nobles converting to Calvinism by 1560. This may be in part due to the fact that local lords were believed to be responsible for providing their subjects with good pastors and preachers, though villagers sometimes disputed noble prerogatives in this regard. This raises two other important issues which have not been explicitly addressed, as far as I am aware: (1) the international character of the assumptions surrounding noble religious values and practices; and (2) the function of particular churches and religious orders as networks through which concepts and practices of nobility spread across Europe.

Hints have been made in preceding pages of how spatial and historical-geographic characteristics created different environments and thus different social roles for Renaissance nobles. (See the essay by Peter Burke above.) If Mediterranean nobles exhibited certain particularities, so did nobles from mountain regions (the Alps, the Apennines, the Jura, the Cévennes, much of Iberia, Scotland, etc.) where nobles were presented alternately as victims or instigators of bandit activity. In some mountain areas, such as the Savoyard lands, mountain nobles continued to exert considerable authority. On the other hand, "communes rarely dismantled lordly authority as completely as they did" in alpine areas such as the Grisons.[22] Although in the Grisons lordship was reduced to a private property matter, this did not prevent peasant leagues themselves from adopting feudal ideology as a tool for exercising authority over their own subject territories.

Not readily apparent in the scholarly literature are examples of groups of nobles distinguishing themselves from others on the basis of nationality. It seems likely that the literature has not explored the theme of nation-based differences between nobles simply because such differences were not perceived by contemporaries and were thus not recorded. This is speculation that remains to be verified. More important, and in a general sense, this orientation to the European nobility of the Renaissance makes it clear that much work – especially that which does not take old historiographic boundaries (formed by preconceptions of national difference, of the centrality of the state, or even of class barriers) for granted – remains to be done on the inter-national and local nature of the aristocracy.

NOTES

Thanks to Claude Bellini, Salvatore Busetta, Peter Kahn, and Guido Ruggiero for their assistance and suggestions.

1 Dewald, *European Nobility*, p. 135.
2 Xenophon, *Education of Cyrus*, pp. 12, 26, 28, 260–2.
3 Kantorowicz, "Kingship," pp. 151–3.
4 Mozzarelli, "Aristocrazia e borghesia," pp. 332, 336, 340–1.
5 Yates, *Astraea*, pp. 23, 108.
6 Cited in Calasso, *Glossatori*, p. 122.
7 Brunner, *Land and Lordship*, pp. 202–3.

8   Neuschel, *Word of Honor*, p. 16; Boyssat cited in Schalk, *From Valor*, p. 169; Muir, "Double Binds."
9   Jouanna, *Devoir de révolte*, p. 70; Eurich, *Economics of Power*, p. 7.
10 Dewald, *European Nobility*, pp. 70, 73–4.
11 Oestreich, "Structure," p. 263.
12 Andrea Boldù, "Relazione," in Firpo, *Relazioni*, vol. 11, p. 42.
13 Jouanna, *Devoir de révolte*, pp. 69–70, 77–8, 84–5, 87–8, 90, 111–13, 246, 397.
14 Ibid., p. 202.
15 Maczak, "Aristocratic Household," p. 319; Grendi, "Il sistema politico," p. 120.
16 Allegra, *Città verticale*, pp. 168, 179–80.
17 Molho, "Patronage," pp. 237–8.
18 These works are cited in Berengo, *Nobili e mercanti*, pp. 252–63.
19 Dolan, "Artisans," p. 175.
20 Nicolas et al., "Monarchic State," p. 75.
21 Jouanna, *Devoir de révolte*, pp. 47–8.
22 Head, *Early Modern Democracy*, pp. 11–12, 18, 32–3.

REFERENCES

Allegra, Luciano, *La città verticale: usurai, mercanti e tessitori nella Chieri del Cinquecento* (Milan: Franco Angeli, 1987).
Berengo, Marino, *Nobili e mercanti nella Lucca del Cinquecento* (Turin: Einaudi, 1965).
Brunner, Otto, *Land and Lordship: Structures of Governance in Medieval Austria*, trans. Howard Kaminsky and James Van Horn Melton (Philadelphia: University of Pennsylvania Press, 1992).
Calasso, Francesco, *I glossatori e la teoria della sovranità. Studio di diritto comune pubblico* (Milan: Giuffrè, 1951).
Dewald, Jonathan, *The European Nobility, 1400–1800* (Cambridge: Cambridge University Press, 1996).
Dolan, Claire, "The Artisans of Aix-en-Provence in the Sixteenth Century: A Micro-Analysis of Social Relationships," in *Cities and Social Change in Early Modern France*, ed. Philip Benedict (London: Unwin Hyman, 1989).
Eurich, S. Amanda, *The Economics of Power: The Private Finances of the House of Foix-Navarre-Albret during the Religious Wars* (Kirksville, MO: Sixteenth Century Texts and Studies, 1994).
Firpo, Luigi, ed., *Relazioni di ambasciatori veneti al senato*, vol. II: *Savoia (1496–1797)* (Turin: Bottega d'Erasmo, 1983).
Grendi, Edoardo, "Il sistema politico di una comunità ligure: Cervo fra Cinquecento e Seicento," *Quaderni storici* 46 (1981), pp. 92–129.
Head, Randolph C., *Early Modern Democracy in the Grisons: Social Order and Political Language in a Swiss Mountain Canton, 1470–1620* (Cambridge: Cambridge University Press, 1995).
Jouanna, Arlette, *Le Devoir de révolte. La noblesse française et la gestation de l'état moderne (1559–1661)* (Paris: Fayard, 1989).
Kantorowicz, Ernst H., "Kingship under the Impact of Jurisprudence," in *Selected Studies*, ed. Ernst H. Kantorowicz (Locust Valley, NY: J. J. Augustin, 1965).
Maczak, Antoni, "From Aristocratic Household to Princely Court: Restructuring Patronage in the Sixteenth and Seventeenth Centuries," in *Princes, Patronage and the Nobility: The Court at the Beginning of the Modern Age, c.1450–1650*, ed. Ronald G. Asch and Adolf M. Birke (Oxford: Oxford University Press, 1991).

Molho, Anthony, "Patronage and the State in Early Modern Italy," in *Klientelsysteme im Europa der Frühen Neuzeit*, ed. Antoni Maczak (Schriften des Historischen Kollegs, Herausgegeben von der Stuftung Historisches Kolleg, Kolloquien) (Munich: R. Oldenbourg Verlag, 1988).

Mozzarelli, Cesare, "Aristocrazia e borghesia nell'Europa moderna," in *Storia d'Europa*, vol. 4, ed. Maurice Aymard (Turin: Einaudi, 1995).

Muir, Edward, "The Double Binds of Manly Revenge in Renaissance Italy," in *Gender Rhetorics: Postures of Dominance and Submission in History*, ed. Richard C. Trexler (Binghamton, NY: Medieval & Renaissance Texts & Studies, 1994).

Neuschel, Kristen B., *Word of Honor: Interpreting Noble Culture in Sixteenth-Century France* (Ithaca, NY: Cornell University Press, 1989).

Nicolas, Jean, Baruque, Julio Valdón, and Vilfan, Sergij, "The Monarchic State and Resistance in Spain, France, and the Old Provinces of the Habsburgs, 1400–1800," in *Resistance, Representation, and Community*, ed. Peter Blickle (Oxford: Clarendon Press, 1997).

Oestreich, Gerhard, "The Structure of the Absolute State" [1964], in *Neostoicism and the Early Modern State*, ed. B. Oestreich and H. G. Koenigsberger (Cambridge: Cambridge University Press, 1982).

Schalk, Ellery, *From Valor to Pedigree: Ideas of Nobility in France in the Sixteenth and Seventeenth Centuries* (Princeton: Princeton University Press, 1986).

Xenophon, *The Education of Cyrus*, trans. Henry Graham Dakyns (London, 1914).

Yates, Frances A., *Astraea: The Imperial Theme in the Sixteenth Century* (London: Routledge and Kegan Paul, 1975).

FURTHER READING

Anderson, Perry, *Lineages of the Absolutist State* (London: Verso, 1974).

Arriaza, Armand, "Adam's Noble Children: An Early Modern Theorist's Concept of Human Nobility," *Journal of the History of Ideas* 55/3 (1994), pp. 385–404.

Astarita, Tommaso, *The Continuity of Feudal Power: The Caracciolo di Brienza in Spanish Naples* (Cambridge: Cambridge University Press, 1992).

Blockmans, Wim, "Patronage, Brokerage and Corruption as Symptoms of Incipient State Formation in the Burgundian-Habsburg Netherlands," in *Klientelsysteme im Europa der Frühen Neuzeit*, ed. Antoni Maczak (Schriften des Historischen Kollegs, Herausgegeben von der Stiftung Historisches Kolleg, Kolloquien) (Munich: R. Oldenbourg Verlag, 1988).

Bohanan, Donna, *Old and New Nobility in Aix-en-Provence 1600–1695: Portrait of an Urban Elite* (Baton Rouge: Louisiana State University Press, 1992).

Carroll, Stuart, *Noble Power during the French Wars of Religion: The Guise Affinity and the Catholic Cause in Normandy* (Cambridge: Cambridge University Press, 1998).

Connell, William J. and Zorzi, Andrea, eds., *Florentine Tuscany: Structures and Practices of Power* (Cambridge: Cambridge University Press, 2000).

Descimon, Robert, "The Birth of the Nobility of the Robe: Dignity versus Privilege in the Parlement of Paris, 1500–1700," in *Changing Identities in Early Modern France*, ed. Michael Wolfe (Durham, NC: Duke University Press, 1997).

Gilmore, Myron, *Argument from Roman Law in Political Thought 1200–1600* (New York: Russell and Russell, 1967).

James, Mervyn, *English Politics and the Concept of Honour 1485–1642* (Oxford: The Past and Present Society, 1978).

Kollmann, Nancy Shields, *By Honor Bound: State and Society in Early Modern Russia* (Ithaca, NY: Cornell University Press, 1999).

Major, J. Russell, *From Renaissance Monarchy to Absolute Monarchy: French Kings, Nobles, and Estates* (Baltimore: Johns Hopkins University Press, 1994).

Midelfort, H. C. Erik, *Mad Princes of Renaissance Germany* (Charlottesville: University Press of Virginia, 1994).

Nader, Helen, *Liberty in Absolutist Spain: The Habsburg Sale of Towns, 1516–1700* (Baltimore: Johns Hopkins University Press, 1990).

Parrott, David, "A 'Prince Souverain' and the French Crown: Charles de Nevers, 1580–1637," in *Royal and Republican Sovereignty in Early Modern Europe: Essays in Memory of Ragnhild Hatton*, ed. Robert Oresko, G. C. Gibbs, and H. M. Scott (Cambridge: Cambridge University Press, 1997).

Romano, Dennis, *Patricians and Popolani: The Social Foundations of the Venetian Renaissance State* (Baltimore: Johns Hopkins University Press, 1987).

Simons, Patricia, "Alert and Erect: Masculinity in Some Italian Renaissance Portraits of Fathers and Sons," in *Gender Rhetorics. Postures of Dominance and Submission in History*, ed. Richard C. Trexler (Binghamton, NY: Medieval & Renaissance Texts & Studies, 1994).

Zmora, Hillay, *State and Nobility in Early Modern Germany: The Knightly Feud in Franconia, 1440–1567* (Cambridge: Cambridge University Press, 1997).

CHAPTER FOURTEEN

Social Hierarchies: The Lower Classes

JAMES S. AMELANG

Did the lower classes have a Renaissance? Did the revival of classical learning that transformed the lives of so many among the educated and powerful affect in any real way men and women working in the fields, or laboring in the shops lining the streets of Renaissance cities? Exactly who had a Renaissance is a persistent question. Answering this question not only focuses attention on the close interaction of social and cultural experiences. By interrogating the categories used to describe these experiences, it also opens for inspection the fracture-lines within a profoundly hierarchical order. The most prominent social border in Renaissance Europe separated high from low, the handful of lords and prominent citizens from the inferior and dependent masses. One useful starting-point, then, would be to inquire exactly how these masses – the "people," in the strict sense of the term – were identified, and how their social position was interpreted from both without and within.

Shifting Perspectives on the Poor

The popular classes of Renaissance Europe were much discussed by their betters, and some of these opinions have reached us in written form. One of the more striking features of this discourse is the imprecision with which the lower classes were defined. The principal source of socio-lexical confusion was the habit of relegating all those beneath the elite to a single, amorphous category. Catch-all designations such as the "people," "commoners," or "lower orders" wound up dredging in their nets all men and women outside the reduced circle of the socially and economically privileged. The advantage of such an approach was its simplicity, as it reduced social differentiation to one all-important boundary, the line between upper and lower levels. Its principal drawback, however, was its tendency to hide from view an imposing reality: the enormous complexity of roles, ranks, and spaces among those who lived and worked underneath the elite.

Recognizing this complexity meant acknowledging, first, that the lower classes had an internal hierarchy of their own. This placed merchants and yeomen farmers at the top, craftsmen and tenant farmers in the middle, and workers, urban as well as rural, toward the bottom. Nuanced use of the term "people" itself often involved such recognition. When the Neapolitan scholar Giulio Cesare Capaccio published his *Il forastiero* (1634), a lengthy dialogue on the history of his adopted city, he subdivided its *popolo* into three separate groups: landlords, civil magistrates, and merchants. He also took pains to separate these respectable if juridically subordinate citizens from the *plebe*, the truly lower part of the lower orders: "the dregs of the republic, given to sedition, to revolutions, [and] to condemning to failure laws, customs, and obedience to superiors." Another text from the same time and place similarly distinguished among the plebs (vagabonds and those without trades), the "people" – merchants, artisans, and shopkeepers – and *cittadini*, honorable commoners who resembled the nobility in their ability to live off rents.[1] The crucial nuance in both works is the distinction between people and plebs. It had deep roots in classical, and especially Roman history, and not surprisingly, it cropped up in many places. It informed social commentary within political and legal thought on the one hand, and more prosaic forms of administrative documentation, such as censuses and tax rolls, on the other. Even architectural texts and blueprints for ideal cities replicated the basic distinction between the upper and lower reaches within the broader category of popular classes. Hence the care the fifteenth-century theorist Filarete took to differentiate the housing of simple artisans from the dwellings of the *popolari*, or merchants, in the plans for his utopian Sforzinda – a pattern that would be duplicated less than a century later by Sebastiano Serlio in book VI of his widely-read treatise on architecture.[2]

Despite its use throughout Europe as a social label, the composition of the "people" was far from fixed. The specific groups that fell on one side or the other of the divide it marked differed according to time, place, and the vagaries of local social and political relations. Even within Italy itself, usage varied from one city to another. What Capaccio referred to in Naples as a *popolo* was known in Renaissance Florence more specifically as the *popolo grasso*, a clear elite among the commoners. The same system of classification recognized the existence of a *popolo minuto*, or middling sort perched between the upper crust among the commoners and the plebs underneath. In Venice, however, the *popolari* was a single group which included the plebeians. In the words of Donato Giannotti, a visiting Florentine writing in the 1520s, "these are persons who engage in the lowest trades in order to earn a living. They have no rank in the city." Giannotti went on to rank this group beneath the *cittadini*, a sort of "more honorable" middle class which in Florence would doubtless have formed part of the *popolo*.[3]

Drawing on this notably slippery contemporary discourse, and rendering due homage to the intricacies of social and linguistic taxonomies, this essay approaches the lower classes as an unstable amalgam that included independent farmers, lesser tradesmen, and master artisans at the upper end, along with all those further below them on the social scale. One can begin to penetrate this nether world by focusing on the material and symbolic bases of the internal distinctions within this social group, distinctions which crucially shaped its broader identity. The most important of these, that differentiating plebs from *popolo*, contrasted long-term poverty with owning property and belonging to guilds. House-holding and membership in corporations were more often than not the consequences as well as the outward signs of diverse types of access to a wide range of resources. As will be seen, they served as a flexible basis for inclusion in circumscribed but significant circles of social, economic, and political decision-making.

It is thus necessary to keep in mind how varied were the lived experiences and expectations of the members of the lower classes – as much so, if not more, than the variation that marked life in the elite. Pronounced differences in individual and family trajectories found concrete expression in diet, dress, housing, and other measures of standards of living. It would be an obvious mistake automatically to identify the popular classes with poverty; simply put, while virtually all the poor in early modern society belonged to the people, not all of the people were poor. Still, there is no denying that, at least in the eyes of the elite, the defining characteristic of the lower orders was poverty. As a result, it occupied the center of upper-class perceptions of the rest of society.

Since "the poor will never cease out of the land," Christians and Jews were enjoined to open wide their hands to help the needy, whom they were to call their brothers (Deuteronomy 15: 11). And help they did, through impressive mechanisms of solidarity, formal as well as informal. The Renaissance period witnessed an out-pouring of efforts to alleviate poverty. These ranged from individual acts of charity, which left abundant documentary traces in the form of testamentary bequests, to the creation of large-scale institutions, such as the foundling hospitals that began to flourish toward the close of the later Middle Ages. In some Italian cities municipal law even brought together these different types of initiatives. All testators in fourteenth-century Siena, for example, were obliged to contribute to the Hospital of Santa Maria della Scala, the *opera* or building fund of the cathedral, and to the archbishop, thus assuring ongoing support of key institutions charged with the welfare, spiritual as well as physical, of all local inhabitants.[4]

In terms of daily practice, Renaissance-era attitudes and policies toward the poor showed strong continuity with the medieval past. Yet a longer-term perspective reveals the beginnings during this period of a fundamental shift in understanding poverty, and in the actions undertaken to relieve it. Earlier generations of historians habitually credited this change to the Reformation, and to Lutherans and Calvinists who defended a "Protestant ethic" of belief in the dignity of labor and in divine recognition of success in earthly pursuits. Such an ethic militated against the indolence of the poor, especially when it was voluntary, a vice the poor shared, in the eyes of Reformers, with the Catholic regular clergy. More recently, the drift toward more modern notions of responsibility and work has been shifted backward in time, toward events and initiatives of the fourteenth and fifteenth centuries. The unprecedented demands on society posed above all by the recurrent cycles of epidemics that began with the Black Death of the mid-fourteenth century led not only to new policies toward the poor, who were increasingly seen as carriers of contagion within and between cities.[5] They also helped put in motion a largely novel vision of the poor themselves in Catholic as well as Protestant Europe, one that would eventually convert them from central members of local communities, to distrusted and feared inhabitants of their margins. (See the essay below by Mary Lindemann.)

This transformation of centuries-old frameworks of belief and action took place almost exclusively within the civic sphere – so much so, in fact, that one could perhaps refer to this change as an urbanization of poverty, as it was converted from a life-destiny into a problem requiring solutions. The forging of a new image of the poor in the cities contrasted with notable inertia in elite views of the lower orders in the countryside. The dominant motif in such views was ambivalence. On the whole, the increasingly educated urban ruling classes continued to despise peasants as ignorant and treacherous rustics, little better than the animals with whom they lived in squalor. At the same time, they regarded the rural lower classes as both needy and needed poor, whose patient, exemplary suffering not only brought them closer to God, but also provided the basic goods and services on which the rest of society depended.[6] This two-sided representation of the rural lower classes changed little during the Renaissance era. If anything, and despite the intense demographic and economic interaction between the urban and rural spheres, the cultural gap widened between followers of a humanist movement deeply committed to the classical ideal of *urbanitas,* and a countryside seen as ever more isolated from the loci of educational and cultural attainments.

In the cities themselves, new attitudes and behavior toward the poor drew on, and nourished in turn, a new discourse, one that laid the foundations for novel means of categorizing and disciplining the more dependent members of society.[7] Two innovations were of particular importance. The first was related to the perceived scale of the problem. Almost all those who wrote about the poor took for granted that their ranks and range of mobility were on the rise. Ironically, the first stirrings of recognition of the new dimensions of the question of poverty dated to the fifteenth century, when overall living standards were by and large improving for those farmers and workers who managed to survive the plague. However, the great outpouring of texts, especially of a theoretical and theological nature, took place in the sixteenth century, when conditions visibly worsened. Needless to say, it is impossible to measure the number of poor in this era, much less to follow closely their fates. However, there can be little question that the intersection of strong demographic growth with certain economic trends – enclosures and rising land rents in the countryside, declining real wages in the cities – induced ever greater numbers of impoverished peasants and workers to migrate from the country to towns, or from one city to another.[8] The result was an unprecedented sense of urgency, and of the need to take practical and, if necessary, harsh measures to combat what were increasingly seen as problems of vagrancy and vagabondage. (See the essay below by Linda Woodbridge.)

The second change involved new ways of understanding and depicting the poor as a group. The ambivalence of traditional attitudes toward the peasantry began to dissolve in urban settings, where the impoverished were increasingly relegated to the margins inhabited by the disorderly and distrusted. Paupers and beggars were consigned along with lepers and the incurably ill (including syphilitics after the 1490s), the insane, criminals, gypsies, prostitutes, and Jews and others belonging to religious and ethnic minorities, to a single, generic category of what would eventually be called the "dangerous classes." Civic officials, however, retained and even deepened their emphasis on the long-standing distinction between insiders and outsiders, separating the deserving poor from the growing mass of undeserving vagabonds and undesirables. The former were regarded as reformable members of local society and thus worthy of ameliorative measures, while the latter were condemned to confinement, public punishment, or expulsion by their lack of local roots or identity.

The new perception of the poor – simultaneously aggregative and discriminating, and ever more detached from traditional frameworks of interpretation, especially regarding the virtue of alms-giving – informed the wide range of experiments in poor relief essayed throughout Europe during the sixteenth century. Many of these new departures involved changes in legislation, including the radical measure in some cities of prohibiting street begging.[9] Others led to administrative changes, including the centralization of the widely dispersed hospices and hospitals of the Middle Ages and the creation of altogether new institutions. These ranged from large-scale, omnibus pesthouses and central hospitals, such as those in Florence and Milan, to combinations of indoor and outdoor relief with vocational training, as in the workhouses of Amsterdam and Nuremberg.[10] Firm institutional support for the poor also came from the parishes, which assumed especially prominent roles in northern Europe. In many if not most Catholic cities, the bulk of charitable activity remained in private hands. While *monti*, or communal pawnshops, were promoted as means of providing the poor with much-needed credit during periods of special hardship, most relief took place either through individual bequests, or through the initiatives of confraternities and other voluntary associations of laymen and women devoted to mutual aid and to limited assistance to non-members.[11] Private and public measures became closely intertwined approaches, as various groups and families among the elites competed to exert patronage over the diverse institutions founded to deal with the sick and the needy. By assuming the role of benefactors they not only opened up for themselves new avenues of social promotion, but also strengthened their ties with client families recruited among their servants, neighbors, vassals, and other dependents. The overall effort brought a chaotic but at times surprisingly broad level of both informal and institutional coverage, one that members of the lower classes learned to take advantage of and even manipulate in their own strategic pursuit of greater security.[12]

While vertical relations of patronage never closed the gap between rich and poor, they did much to assuage the unpredictability of daily existence that took such a harsh toll in the lives and fortunes of the the disadvantaged. All the same, one should resist the temptation, if there is one, to read these relations in overly sentimental terms. The powerful and privileged did not hesitate to respond with force, or even to mete out savage violence to those who failed to meet their expectations regarding hierarchy and deference. This lesson was learned all too well by a nameless Tuscan peasant who was murdered for having offended two Roman noblemen, the Bishop of Ancona and his son, the Abbot of San Galgano. In 1542 these clerics hired some ruffians to carry out an act of vengeance. The confession of one of the henchmen makes clear how violence of this sort was meant to serve as warnings to others: "it is true that the bishop said to us that he would have wished us not to kill them, but rather disfigure and lame them, cut off their ears and hands, or the arms, so that people could see it and know it, but the abbot said that he wanted us to kill them, and if we couldn't kill them, to burn their houses."[13] Public authorities could do little to limit even such extreme cases of instrumental violence. While the Renaissance period saw a decline in factional disputes within cities, individual members of the privileged classes still behaved with virtual impunity toward their inferiors in the countryside. Aristocratic violence was not effectively curbed until the "civilizing process" of the second half of the early modern era transformed the territorial nobility into an urban ruling class increasingly dependent on monarchical favor and forced to share power with the servants of the state.[14] (See the essays above by Robert Muchembled and Gregory Hanlon.)

Vox Populi

Humanists throughout Europe were divided over the advisability of extending to the people any educational opportunities beyond the rudiments of devotion and training for trade. The majority clearly preferred to limit formal instruction to members of the elite, the only members of society equipped with the *otium* or leisure permitting the full enjoyment of the benefits, spiritual and material, of learned culture. Rather than wait for their betters to provide them with education, however, many members of the popular classes strove to create their own opportunities. To be sure, much of the stimulus responsible for the "educational revolution" of the sixteenth century – the notable expansion in the numbers of persons enrolled in all levels of schooling – stemmed from the desire of old as well as new elites to equip themselves with the new learning, increasingly regarded not only as a sign of social distinction, but also as an avenue to employment in the expanding lay and ecclesiastic bureaucracies. Yet a substantial part of the growing demand for literacy and schooling came from below, from those from the lower and middling classes who looked to education above all as a pathway to social and economic improvement.

One result of this pattern, not to say program, of mobility through study was a collective increase in popular literacy. No way exists at present to chart the exact chronology and contours of this change. However, the available evidence – which derives largely from indirect measures such as the ownership of books and other forms of writing, including accounts, notarial documents, and family chronicles – points to a slow but perceptible expansion in the number of craftsmen, peasants, and workers who were able to read and write. Once again, clear internal differences marked the experience of the popular orders. Lower-class literacy never confined itself strictly to the urban sphere.[15] Still, it flourished there much more extensively than in rural settings, thanks not only to the greater weight of commerce and services in cities, but also to the broader supply there of educational opportunities. Access to and demand for the basic skills of literacy and numeracy also varied considerably by occupation. Owing in part to their sedentary nature, certain trades, such as weaving or shoemaking, won a precocious reputation for high levels of familiarity with the written word. Above all, popular literacy regularly followed lines of gender. While an unquestionable increase occurred in the number of women who could read, female literacy lagged far behind that of men throughout the period, especially in the countryside, where opportunities for either formal or informal schooling for girls were few and far between.

If the long-term cultural impact of the Renaissance within the lower classes revealed itself in their growing ability to participate in the expanding written and print culture of the period, arguably the most visible, short-run change was the consolidation of a new social type: the artist, writer, scientist, and even scholar of popular origins. One influential study has estimated that almost one-fifth of the "creative elite" of the Italian Renaissance were the sons of artisans or shopkeepers.[16] The sixteenth century in particular saw a blossoming of writers from popular backgrounds, ranging from Pietro Aretino and Giambattista Gelli in Italy, to Hans Sachs (the "Meistersinger of Nuremberg") in Germany, Joan Timoneda in Spain, and Thomas Deloney, John Taylor, and Ben Jonson, among others, in England. Lower-class scientists included not only iconic figures such as Leonardo, but also a wide range of specialists employed at more middling levels. One particularly intriguing example involved a pair of royal cosmographers in France, André Thevet and his associate François de Belleforest; an even more famous cluster in Paris formed around the ceramicist Bernard Palissy and the surgeon Ambroise Paré, and included by extension Louise Bourgeois, a midwife whose husband had studied with Paré.[17] Historians and other scholars also contributed to the roster of popular writers. The indefatigable chandler turned chronicler John Stow was merely one member of a larger circle around Ralph Holinshed whose ambitious publishing efforts made popular perspectives available to a wider audience.[18]

The rise of talented individuals from peasant or artisan backgrounds into higher social and cultural standing did not in itself constitute an entirely new phenomenon. Such patterns of promotion had important precedents in the Middle Ages, and especially in long-standing practices of recruitment for the clergy. The key innovation lay elsewhere, in the public recognition of such lowly origins, and in the ties that many of these individuals chose to maintain with the popular world of their birth. The outcome was the consolidation of an essentially new figure, the learned artisan or curious peasant who won, precisely because of his practical labors and familiarity with nature, a certain respectable berth within elite culture, especially in its more Baconian reaches.[19] Popular expertise extended to non-technical subjects as well. The shoe-maker-philosopher Gelli, for example, played a prominent role in the *Accademia fiorentina*, founded in 1541. Interestingly, Gelli was not the only plebeian figure in this scholarly world; his fellow shoemaker Michele Capri also joined this sodality, while the rival and eventually more famous academy of the Crusca was founded by his bitter enemy Anton Francesco Grazzini, an apothecary. Gelli himself was widely respected as an expert on the history of the Tuscan tongue, despite his eccentric views on its Aramaic origins, and on Florentine writers from the Middle Ages. His lectures on Dante and Petrarch formed part of a broader campaign to extend learning beyond the elite through the translation of Latin works into the vernacular, along the lines of similar efforts in defense of popular knowledge and values in other spheres.[20]

Without doubt religion acted as the greatest motivation to expressiveness among the lower classes. Gelli himself indulged in relatively little direct social or political commentary, beyond assertions of the dignity of manual labor. However, his religious views contained stronger stuff, and he was widely suspected of harboring Protestant sympathies. The same could be said of a fellow artisan author, Alessandro Caravia. In his *Sogno del Caravia*, published in 1541, the Venetian goldsmith not only openly praised Martin Luther. He also recounted a burlesque tale of a dream in which a buffoon, Zanpolo, journeyed to hell, where he teamed up with a devil named Farfarello to lampoon clerical greed and corruption and the ostentation of wealthy laymen. Not surprisingly, Caravia's text, with its evangelical emphasis on a simple faith shorn of non-essentials such as purgatory and the intercession of the saints, belonged to the handful of books that inspired the heretical miller from Friuli Domenico Scandella, nicknamed Menocchio, the main character of Carlo Ginzburg's *The Cheese and the Worms*.

In retrospect, it seems ironic that the sixteenth-century peasant best known to modern readers struck his betters as having ideas too extravagant to be readily comprehended, even by experienced judges of the Inquisition. For years on end Menocchio subjected his fellow villagers to an endless torrent of opinions. Some of these, such as his anticlericalism, hostility to the pomp and ceremony of the Church and to the use of

Latin in the liturgy, or the denial of the virginity of Mary, echoed standard Protestant positions, and may have derived from direct contact with the Anabaptists active in this corner of Italy. Others, however, were much more idiosyncratic, and had their origins in Menocchio's own patient struggling with books that ranged from a translation of the Koran to Boccaccio's *Decameron*. His efforts at hammering out a worldview of his own produced a tolerant and rationalist sort of pantheism that contained a highly unusual creation myth: according to the miller, in the beginning was chaos, and from this "a mass formed – just as cheese is made out of milk – and worms appeared in it, and these were the angels."[21] Menocchio's recasting of Genesis was merely the tip of an iceberg of heterodox opinion, some of quite striking originality. The Counter-Reformation Church saw it as a serious enough threat to warrant not one but two trials, the second of which led to his execution in 1600.

Thanks to the printing press, contemporaries could – for a while, at least – imagine for themselves the voices of a Gelli or Caravia. The tale of the hapless Menocchio shows how heterodox opinions could reach smaller circles through conversation, in this case with the neighbors who stoically put up with his harangues for years before they were denounced (by someone outside the village) to the Inquisition. Other voices from among the lower orders resounded in equally firm fashion. Arduino Ariguzzi, the architect who built a new model for the church of San Petronio in Bologna in 1514, indignantly complained that the church had never been finished because "people of all sorts, priests, monks, artisans, farmers, schoolmasters, bailiffs, harness-makers, spindle-makers, porters, and even water-carriers behave like architects and voice their opinions." Some seventy-five years later, a tailor named Carlo Carazzi openly challenged Ariguzzi's successor, the architect Francesco Morandi, accusing him of miscalculating the height of the church's vaults through his ignorance of Gothic construction techniques. Local opinion heavily favored Carazzi, and only papal intervention brought this dispute to a (temporary) end.[22]

Public disputes – in this case, over local styles, proper taste, and sound decorum – evinced no unanimity in popular opinion. Gelli and the Bolognese tradesmen took stands as cultural conservatives, defending vernacular traditions in the face of the universalizing classicism of the elite. Yet one could easily cite other cases – the published writings of Bernard Palissy, for instance – in which popular writers proposed more innovative and cosmopolitan options than those defended by their social superiors. Advocacy of this sort also extended to more directly social and political questions. To be sure, the early generations of popular writers included relatively few Hesiods, poets who wrote from first-hand knowledge of the works and days of the suffering poor. Yet some did take on the mantle of spokesmen for the lower orders. One such person was the Bolognese surgeon Leonardo Fioravanti, who won an international reputation for his Leonardian defense of experience over theoretical knowledge, and for his Paracelsus-like attacks on learned physicians and the monopolies they and other academics held over formal education and entry into the professions. His example inspired even more radical figures, such as Costantino Saccardino, a libertine clown, healer, and converted Jew executed in Bologna in 1622 for having led a small group of followers in a series of nighttime desecrations of religious images. "The dovecote has opened its eyes" was a phrase the clown adapted from Fioravanti, who had optimistically argued that the invention of printing would allow the people to see through the lies physicians and others from the elite invented to enrich themselves at the expense of others. Saccardino and others hoped for a similar awakening in the religious and political sphere, one in which the popular classes would throw off the yoke of custom, such as belief in hell, which allowed "the princes" to rule over them.[23] (See the essay below by William Eamon.)

Greater union of opinion existed on the freedom of opinions, and on the right to be heard in public as well as private. In many instances this notion of entitlement drew on a sense of personal achievement, one that often followed success in professional and cultural endeavors, and in individual and family mobility. Yet such claims also had broader, more social origins. Lower-class expressiveness derived from collective political experience and long-standing traditions of self-governance both within and beyond the city walls.

Subjects and Citizens

Religious expectations, particularly those which emphasized the rights and responsibilities of membership in communities of belief, nourished popular insistence on having a voice. That insistence also arose from daily practice outside the spiritual realm, in participation in various communal and corporate bodies. More numerous and complex in urban as opposed to rural settings, such bodies were far from absent within the countryside. In fact, in some parts of Europe the rural popular classes enjoyed a much greater say over their own destinies than did their civic counterparts. In villages throughout Europe, peasant householders gathered to decide such vital matters as the election of representatives, the use of common lands and resources, and the distribution of taxes. Some of these assemblies possessed extra-local scope, as in the parliamentary estates of certain German territorial states, or the peasant leagues of Graubünden (the Grisons) in Switzerland, which were widely recognized as having achieved extraordinary levels of plebeian self-government.[24]

Such meetings continued veteran traditions of communal self-governance that had long since disappeared in the vast majority of cities. The Renaissance era witnessed a visible decline in popular involvement in the institutions of civic power. Italian cities in particular took the lead in a recomposition of elite hegemony that either left all mechanisms of formal governance in patrician hands, as in the precocious *serrata* or closing-off of the Venetian nobility in 1297, or confined lower-class participation in public matters to the lowest echelons of municipal office.[25] As a result, popular politics became preoccupied with decision-making in local "micro-institutions," or took place in venues completely removed from the formal instances of power.

Yet the range and overall importance of these institutions should not be underestimated. In many cities, neighborhoods served as the entry level of municipal government. Known as *gonfaloni* in Florence, *rioni* in Rome, or *sestieri* in Venice, these councils oversaw a wide range of administrative functions. In some cities, they were charged with distribution of the tax burden, and even with (limited) electoral responsibilities. Their equivalent in the religious sphere was the parish or, more specifically, the vestry or parish council. In much of Europe fundamental control over the basic territorial institution of religious life lay in hands of the parishioners themselves, who took charge of maintaining church buildings, organizing and carrying out charitable and liturgical services, and even in some areas – the city of Venice, for example

– electing the resident clergy and their assistants. Yet the best-known popular institutions were the guild and its close cousin, the devotional confraternity. While often
subjected to oversight by civic or royal governments, these corporations were largely
run by their members, who chose their officers by election or rotation. Both guilds
and religious brotherhoods combined multiple functions, ranging from the organization of local economic and spiritual activities to mutual assistance and even charity
toward non-members. Along with the neighborhoods, guilds also served as the basis
for urban militias, often the only force available for routine protection of order
(through the night watch) as well as for the defense of the city against external attack.

There is no reason to idealize any of these institutions. They were often hothouses
of misgovernment and corruption. Moreover, effective control by small oligarchies
was often the rule; thus, in the case of many parishes, participation by all congregants
gave way to "select" vestries, rule over which was formally reserved to more "substantial" tax-payers.[26] All the same, while such micro-institutions rarely functioned as
schools in democracy, they did provide many members of the lower classes an
apprenticeship in citizenship, and permitted a wide range of (invariably male) heads
of households to exercise a substantial degree of control over their own daily lives.
Neighborhoods, parishes, and corporations also provided a fulcrum from which
leverage could be sought in higher levels of power. Through petitions, promises of
electoral support and other client services, and even more direct forms of collective
expression, the lower classes used such bodies to exert pressure in local politics, thus
converting voice into influence. (See the essay above by Edward Muir.)

Popular politics also had recourse to the street. Despite the risks involved, the real
or threatened use of force always loomed as an alternative to maneuvering through
institutional channels. Many circumstances led to lower-class uprisings. Tax increases,
such as those the city of Florence imposed on the Tuscan countryside in the century
following the Black Death, met with (ultimately successful) resistance from the peasant communities of the neighboring highlands.[27] Triggers of revolt in cities included
shortages or abrupt rises in the price of staples, and mismanagement and corruption
in civic government, as in Agen in 1514, when protest by the *pauvre peuple* against
the elite's misuse of public funds finally had to be suppressed by troops brought in
from outside.[28] At times disputes over work conditions escalated into broader economic and social conflicts, as in the *Ciompi* rebellion in Florence. In 1378 the city's
textile workers armed themselves and forced the creation of a guild that challenged
the hegemony of their employers, grouped in the Wool Guild (*Arte della lana*).
Struggle over control of this industry led smaller, independent masters to ally themselves with the craft oligarchy, thus bringing to an end this short-lived experiment in
specifically working-class organization.[29]

For all its uniqueness, the *Ciompi* revolt drew upon deeply-rooted patterns of lower-
class political action, most strikingly the often highly ritualized nature of popular
appropriation of public power and space. The carnival-like character of such events,
which included the inversion of standard hierarchies of status and wealth, was exemplified by the momentary pillaging of clerical property that took place in Rome during the
Vacant See, or period immediately after the death of a pope. "The *popolo* is the master"
at such moments, shouted a mob gathered in the Piazza Navona, and their temporary
sway rarely met with challenges.[30] The ritual tradition of street politics fostered
participation by a wider cast of characters, in both class and gender terms – participa-

tion which extended to times of revolt. Popular involvement in institutional politics was limited to men, and more often than not to the organized and propertied members of the lower order, that is, guildsmen and wealthier, more respectable heads of households. When social and political action burst the bonds of traditional institutions, such as during bread riots, women and the poor played much more prominent roles, often with the tacit complicity of those higher up in social and gender hierarchies.

Finally, even though in most cases the scope of lower-class action remained strictly local, popular mobilization could easily impinge on elite politics. This intrusion was especially in evidence on those occasions in which revolt threatened to give way to revolution.[31] While the vast majority of violent popular uprisings proved to be episodic or quickly extinguished outbursts, on more than one occasion lower-class violence seriously threatened the structures of power. The German Peasants' War of the mid-1520s combined widespread peasant discontent toward the seigneurial regime with popular enthusiasm for religious reform to produce a heady if unsuccessful challenge to lordship in secular as well as religious spheres. Urban craftsmen figured prominently in the other major dispute of the 1520s, the *Comunero* and *Germania* revolts in Castile and Valencia respectively. Discontent over the policies (and higher taxes) of the new king Charles V, and frustration with crown inaction in the face of aristocratic disorder and factionalism sparked these uprisings, in which the popular classes were joined by many members of the civic gentry, especially in Castile.

Spiritual issues came to the fore again in the second half of the sixteenth century, when lower-class political and religious militancy loomed large on both sides of the confessional divide. Popular Protestantism provided much of the backbone of the Dutch Revolt against Spain; as one of William of Orange's representatives wrote, "our regime finds most support . . . in the *gemeente* [commoners], and it is therefore necessary that we comply with their wishes."[32] A similar lower-class protagonism marked the Catholic League formed in Paris and other French cities toward the end of the Wars of Religion.[33] Finally, popular political mobilization played a role in each of the "six revolutions" of the mid-seventeenth century, from the Catalan and Portuguese revolts of 1640 to the 1647 uprisings in Naples and Sicily, the English Civil Wars, and the Fronde. The lower classes came closest to taking power in Naples where, under the short-lived leadership of the fisherman Masaniello, lower- and middle-class discontents met to form a government whose aims were initially reform-ist. However, the revolt's eventual radicalization, especially after Masaniello was assassinated and armed crowds of *lazzari* or the unemployed poor began to take vengeance on the nobility, led to the reconquest of the city by local aristocrats in alliance with the Spanish crown.[34]

Seen from a long-term perspective, one can easily understand why even the most absolutist of kings did not hesitate to recognize the significance of popular grievances. Lower-class violence did not in itself suffice to topple thrones. Yet when combined with elite disaffection, it posed the gravest possible threat to political and social stability. As the Count-Duke of Olivares wrote king Philip IV in a memorandum of 1624, "it is always important to pay attention to the voice of the people."[35] Rulers at all levels ignored this warning to their peril.

In retrospect, it seems clear that the Renaissance – just like the later Reformation – raised hopes for collective liberation. Humanism preached the moral reinvention of mankind through intellectual development and the refinement of sensibility according to ancient models. Yet according to its adepts, the new ideal of humanity, such as it was, could only be fully cultivated in the upper reaches of society. Despite notable exceptions, it failed by and large to penetrate downward, to the daily lives of men – and especially women – at lower levels. Above all, it failed to reform contemporary society and the polity to the extent that it promised to transform individuals. As Menocchio told his judges, "My mind was lofty and wished for a New World and way of life."[36] For him and countless others, this hope was to remain unfulfilled.

By the 1640s, as the winds of revolution blew across the continent, the Renaissance was a distant memory. Classical ideals could still inspire political action among the people, as in the bygone times of Cola di Rienzo, the self-styled tribune of the plebs whose violent death in 1354 dashed the hopes of learned sympathizers such as Petrarch. Indeed, it would not be farfetched to speak of a "popular humanism," in the sense of specifically popular response to the challenges the humanist movement posed.[37] However, evocations of ancient traditions of justice and liberty had to compete with other reborn visions, ranging from millennial traditions of lower-class radicalism to the ages-old biblicism brought to new life by religious reform movements of the preceding century. Shortly after crowds in the streets of Naples likened the Spanish viceroy to Pharaoh, contemporary Englishmen condemned their king to death as the Old Testament's "man of blood" whose tyranny had defiled the land. Masaniello himself was acclaimed as a new Moses, and compared to David, or the fisherman Peter.[38] A man of humble origins and means, he too sought a New World and way of life, beginning in the very market square among whose inhabitants he found his most fervent political support. He proposed to remove the vendors' stalls and call it the *Piazza del popolo*. Depending on the way one looks at it, it was either a new, or very old name.

NOTES

I am grateful to Lou Rose and Guido Ruggiero for their comments on and suggestions for improving this essay.

1   Both cited in Benigno, *Specchi*, p. 253.
2   Ackerman and Rosenfeld, "Social Stratification."
3   Cited in Pullan, *Rich and Poor*, p. 99.
4   Cohn, *Cult*, p. 12.
5   Carmichael, *Plague*.
6   Freedman, *Images*.
7   One excellent recent overview is Robert Jütte's *Poverty and Deviance*.
8   For a summary of the growing economic difficulties of both rural and urban lower classes during the "long" sixteenth century, see Rowlands, "Conditions of Life."
9   Detailed study of the memorable debate that began with the 1526 *De subventione pauperum* of the Valencian humanist Joan Lluís Vives can be found in Martz, *Poverty and Welfare*, especially pp. 7–91.
10   Harrington, "Escape."
11   The best studied case remains that of the *Scuole Grandi* of Venice, analyzed in Pullan, *Rich and Poor*.

12 See Cavallo, *Charity and Power*, for a highly revealing analysis of poor relief in Turin.

13 Cohen and Cohen, *Words and Deeds*, p. 38.

14 Muir, "Sources of Civil Society."

15 Balestracci, *Renaissance in Fields*, p. xxi. General remarks on the evolution of popular literacy are in Houston, *Literacy*, pp. 131–4, and Grendler, *Schooling*, pp. 47 and 102–8.

16 Burke, *Tradition and Innovation*, pp. 54–61.

17 Lestringant, *Mapping*; Egmond and Mason, *Mammoth*, pp. 107–28; and more generally, Amelang, *Flight of Icarus*.

18 Patterson, *Reading*.

19 Rossi, *Philosophy*, especially pp. 1–62.

20 For a thorough biographical study, see De Gaetano, *Giambattista Gelli*.

21 Ginzburg, *Cheese and the Worms*, p. 6. Menocchio's reading of Caravia is discussed on pp. 22–6. For more on Caravia and his circle of heretical artisans, see Martin, *Venice's Hidden Enemies*, especially pp. 156–8.

22 Cited in Miller, *Renaissance Bologna*, pp. 158–9, and Wittkower, *Gothic vs. Classic*, pp. 66–78.

23 Eamon, "Rules of Life," and Ginzburg and Ferrari, "Dovecote."

24 Jean Bodin wrote that it was "the most popular, and most popularly governed of any Commonweale that is" (cited in Head, *Early Modern Democracy*, p. 248). See Blickle, *Obedient Germans?*, for a forceful exposition of the political dimension of peasant communalism in the German-speaking lands of medieval and early modern Europe.

25 Details in Berengo, *Europa delle città*, pp. 201–12. See pp. 171–224 for broader aspects of civic politics from the later Middle Ages through the sixteenth century.

26 At the time of Archbishop Laud's survey in 1638, 59 of London's 109 vestries were select (Griffiths, "Secrecy and Authority," p. 948).

27 Cohn, *Creating*.

28 Berengo, *Europa delle città*, p. 89.

29 Stella, *Révolte des Ciompi*.

30 Cohen and Cohen, *Words and Deeds*, p. 77; background in Nussdorfer, *Civic Politics*, pp. 228–53.

31 Two recent overviews with differing interpretative emphases are Te Brake, *Shaping History*, and Benigno, *Specchi*.

32 Cited in Parker, *Dutch Revolt*, p. 184. Not surprisingly, in 1577 Orange reversed Charles V's policy of repression toward guild cities such as Ghent by restoring its privileges and recognizing the local hegemony of its newly-organized working-class militia and artisan-led committee of government.

33 Crouzet, *Guerriers de Dieu*.

34 See Benigno, *Specchi*, pp. 199–285 for a thoughtful summary.

35 Cited in Elliott, *Richelieu and Olivares*, p. 45.

36 Ginzburg, *Cheese and the Worms*, p. 13.

37 Much remains to be studied in this regard; for one point of departure, see Peter Burke's "Learned Culture."

38 Hill, *English Bible*, pp. 324–31, and Benigno, *Specchi*, pp. 264–5.

REFERENCES

Ackerman, James S. and Rosenfeld, M. N., "Social Stratification in Renaissance Urban Planning," in *Urban Life in the Renaissance*, ed. S. Zimmerman and R. F. E. Weissman (Newark, DE: University of Delaware Press, 1989), pp. 21–49.

Amelang, James, *The Fight of Icarus: Artisan Autobiography in Early Modern Europe* (Stanford: Stanford University Press, 1998).

Balestracci, Duccio, *The Renaissance in the Fields: Family Memoirs of a Fifteenth-Century Tuscan Peasant*, trans. P. Squatriti and B. Merideth (University Park, PA: Pennsylvania State University Press, 1999).

Benigno, Fancesco, *Specchi della rivoluzione: Conflitto e identità politica nell'Europa moderna* (Rome: Donzelli, 1999).

Berengo, Marino, *L'Europa delle città: Il volto della società urbana europea tra medioevo ed età moderna* (Turin: Einaudi, 1999).

Blickle, Peter, *Obedient Germans? A Rebuttal: A New View of German History*, trans. Thomas A. Brady, Jr. (Charlottesville, VA: University of Virginia Press, 1997).

Burke, Peter, *Tradition and Innovation in Renaissance Italy: A Sociological Approach* (London: Fontana, 1974).

——, "Learned Culture and Popular Culture in Renaissance Italy," in *Varieties of Cultural History* (Oxford: Polity Press, 1997), pp. 124–35.

Carmichael, Ann G., *Plague and the Poor in Renaissance Florence* (Cambridge: Cambridge University Press, 1986).

Cavallo, Sandra, *Charity and Power in Early Modern Italy: Benefactors and Their Motives in Turin, 1541–1789* (Cambridge: Cambridge University Press, 1995).

Cohen, Thomas V. and Cohen, Elizabeth S., *Words and Deeds in Renaissance Rome: Trials before the Papal Magistrates* (Toronto: University of Toronto Press, 1993).

Cohn, Samuel K. Jr., *The Cult of Remembrance and the Black Death: Six Renaissance Cities in Central Italy* (Baltimore: Johns Hopkins University Press, 1992).

——, *Creating the Florentine State: Peasants and Rebellion, 1348–1434* (Cambridge: Cambridge University Press, 1999).

Crouzet, Denis, *Les Guerriers de Dieu. La violence au temps des troubles de religion, vers 1525 – vers 1610*, 2 vols. (Seyssel: Camp Vallon, 1990).

De Gaetano, Armand, *Giambattista Gelli and the Florentine Academy: The Rebellion Against Latin* (Florence: Olschki, 1976).

Eamon, William, "'With the Rules of Life and an Enema': Leonardo Fioravanti's Medical Primitivism," in *Renaissance and Revolution: Humanists, Scholars, Craftsmen and Natural Philosophers in Early Modern Europe*, ed. J. V. Field and F. A. J. L. James (Cambridge: Cambridge University Press, 1993), pp. 29–44.

Egmond, Florika and Mason, P., *The Mammoth and the Mouse: Microhistory and Morphology* (Baltimore: Johns Hopkins University Press, 1997).

Elliott, John H., *Richelieu and Olivares* (Cambridge: Cambridge University Press, 1984).

Freedman, Paul, *Images of the Medieval Peasant* (Stanford: Stanford University Press, 1999).

Ginzburg, Carlo, *The Cheese and the Worms: The Cosmos of a Sixteenth-Century Miller*, trans. J. and A. Tedeschi (Harmondsworth, NY: Penguin, 1982).

Ginzburg, Carlo and Ferrari, M., "The Dovecote has Opened its Eyes," in *Microhistory and the Lost People of Europe*, ed. E. Muir and G. Ruggiero, trans. E. Branch (Baltimore: Johns Hopkins University Press, 1991), pp. 11–19.

Grendler, Paul F., *Schooling in Renaissance Italy: Literacy and Learning, 1300–1600* (Baltimore: Johns Hopkins University Press, 1989).

Griffiths, Paul, "Secrecy and Authority in Late Sixteenth- and Seventeenth-Century London," *The Historical Journal* 40 (1997), pp. 925–51.

Harrington, J. F., "Escape from the Great Confinement: The Genealogy of a German Workhouse," *Journal of Modern History* 71 (1999), pp. 308–45.

Head, R. C., *Early Modern Democracy in the Grisons: Social Order and Political Language in a Swiss Mountain Canton, 1470–1620* (Cambridge Cambridge University Press, 1995).

Hill, Christopher, *The English Bible and the Seventeenth-Century Revolution* (London: Allen Lane, 1994).

Houston, Robert A., *Literacy in Early Modern Europe: Culture and Education, 1500–1800* (London: Longman, 1988).

Jütte, Robert, *Poverty and Deviance in Early Modern Europe* (Cambridge: Cambridge University Press, 1994).

Lestringant, Frank, *Mapping the Renaissance World: The Geographical Imagination in the Age of Discovery*, trans. D. Fausett (Berkeley: University of California Press, 1994).

Martin, John, *Venice's Hidden Enemies: Italian Heretics in a Renaissance City* (Berkeley: University of California, 1993).

Martz, Linda, *Poverty and Welfare in Habsburg Spain: The Example of Toledo* (Cambridge: Cambridge University Press, 1983).

Miller, Naomi, *Renaissance Bologna: A Study in Architectural Form and Content* (New York: P. Lang, 1989).

Muir, Edward, "The Sources of Civil Society in Italy," *Journal of Interdisciplinary History* 29 (1999), pp. 379–406.

Nussdorfer, Lauri, *Civic Politics in the Rome of Urban VIII* (Princeton: Princeton University Press, 1992).

Parker, Geoffrey, *The Dutch Revolt* (Harmondsworth: Penguin, 1988 rev. edn.).

Patterson, Annabel, *Reading Holinshed's Chronicles* (Chicago: University of Chicago Press, 1994).

Pullan, Brian, *Rich and Poor in Renaissance Venice: The Social Institutions of a Catholic State, to 1620* (Cambridge, MA: Harvard University Press, 1971).

Rossi, Paolo, *Philosophy, Technology and the Arts in the Early Modern Era*, trans. S. Attanasio, ed. B. Nelson (New York: Harper and Row, 1970).

Rowlands, A., "The Conditions of Life for the Masses," in *Early Modern Europe: An Oxford History*, ed. E. Cameron (Oxford: Oxford University Press, 1999), pp. 31–62.

Stella, Alessandro, *La Révolte des Ciompi: Les hommes, les lieux, le travail* (Paris: Éditions de l'École des hautes études en sciences sociales, 1993).

Te Brake, Wayne, *Shaping History: Ordinary People in European Politics, 1500–1700* (Berkeley: University of California Press, 1998).

Wittkower, Rudolf, *Gothic vs. Classic: Architectural Projects in Seventeenth-Century Italy* (New York: G. Braziller, 1974).

FURTHER READING

Barry, Jonathan and Brooks, C., eds., *The Middling Sort of People: Culture, Society and Politics in England, 1550–1800* (New York: St. Martin's Press, 1994).

Beik, William, *Urban Protest in Seventeenth-Century France: The Culture of Retribution* (Cambridge: Cambridge University Press, 1997).

Blickle, Peter, "The Popular Reformation," in *Handbook of European History, 1400–1600. Late Middle Ages, Renaissance, and Reformation*, ed. Thomas A. Brady Jr., Heiko A. Oberman, and James D. Tracy. (New York: E. J. Brill, 1994), vol. 2, pp. 161–92.

Brucker, Gene, "The Florentine *Popolo minuto* and its Political Role, 1340–1450," in *Violence and Civil Disorder in Italian Cities, 1200–1500*, ed. Lauro Martines (Berkeley: University of California Press, 1972), pp. 155–83.

Burke, Peter, *Popular Culture in Early Modern Europe* (New York: New York University Press, 1978).

Burke, Peter, *The Historical Anthropology of Early Modern Italy: Essays on Perception and Communication* (Cambridge: Cambridge University Press, 1987).

Cohn, Samuel K., Jr., *The Laboring Classes of Renaissance Florence* (New York: Academic Press, 1980).

Davis, Natalie Z., *Society and Culture in Early Modern France* (Stanford: Stanford University Press, 1975).

Davis, Robert, *The War of the Fists: Popular Culture and Public Violence in Late Renaissance Venice* (New York: Oxford University Press, 1994).

Geremek, Bronislaw, *Poverty: A History*, trans. A. Kolokowska (Oxford: Blackwell Publishers, 1994).

Leinwand, Theodore, "Shakespeare and the Middling Sort," *Shakespeare Quarterly* 44 (1993), pp. 284–303.

Lindley, Keith, *Popular Politics and Religion in Civil War London* (Aldershot: Scholar Press, 1997).

Pullan, Brian, "Plague and Perceptions of the Poor in Early Modern Italy," in *Epidemics and Ideas: Essays on the Historical Perception of Pestilence*, ed. T. Ranger and P. Slack (Cambridge: Cambridge University Press, 1992), pp. 101–24.

Romano, Dennis, *Patricians and Popolani: The Social Foundations of the Venetian Renaissance State* (Baltimore: Johns Hopkins University Press, 1987).

Thompson, E. P., *Customs in Common: Studies in Traditional Popular Culture* (New York: New Press, 1991).

Trexler, Richard C., "Neighbours and Comrades: The Revolutionaries of Florence, 1378," *Social Analysis* 14 (1983), pp. 53–106.

Van Deursen, Arie T., *Plain Lives in a Golden Age: Popular Culture, Religion and Society in Seventeenth-Century Holland* (Cambridge: Cambridge University Press, 1991).

Villari, Rosario, *The Revolt of Naples*, trans. J. Newell and J. A. Marino (Cambridge: Polity Press, 1993).

Chapter Fifteen

Tools for the Development of the European Economy

Karl Appuhn

In 1338 Alberto Calli, a wealthy Venetian, signed a profit-sharing contract known as a *colleganza* or *commenda* with his son-in-law, Giovanni Loredan. Calli lent Loredan the sum of six ducats, which Loredan was to use to buy and sell commodities of his choosing during a voyage to Delhi.[1] Losses would be written off against Calli's investment, but eventual profits would be divided according to a formula agreed upon in advance by the two partners. Calli was not Loredan's only partner. Loredan would have been acting as agent for several other investors, each of whom would have negotiated a separate agreement with him. He was also accompanied on the voyage by five other Venetian noblemen, including his brother Paolo, each of whom were acting as agents for other investors under the terms of agreements similar to the one between himself and Calli. Giovanni Loredan never saw Delhi, dying en route, but his brother assumed his obligations and completed the journey. After Paolo returned to Venice and liquidated the commodities he had purchased with his dead brother's capital, Alberto Calli sued Giovanni's heirs to obtain his share of the profits. Despite winning his case, he was no doubt disappointed when he did not even double his initial investment in what had been projected to be a highly profitable undertaking.

The voyage of the Loredan brothers is one of the most popular anecdotes employed by historians to illustrate the emergence of a global economy during the Renaissance. Certainly the brothers' adventures in India were dramatic, as were many similar journeys undertaken by Italian merchants overseas in the three centuries leading up to the voyages of Columbus, and the remarkably successful expansion of Europeans to other parts of the globe. Yet it is important to remember that such voyages would have been unthinkable without the support of countless silent partners like Alberto Calli. His material investment in the Loredan brothers' journey, and any number of more mundane journeys throughout Italy, Europe, and the Mediterranean basin, was not simply a matter of handing money to an agent. It was predicated upon a whole host of institutional and business arrangements, many of them based on quantitative techniques, which were relatively new in fourteenth-century Italy, and almost unheard of in other parts of Europe. By the late fifteenth century, Italian business techniques and quantitative skills had spread to the rest of the continent, in the process transforming the European economy from a collection of isolated regional systems into something resembling an integrated whole. Eventually, the Italian tools and concepts that had helped create the Renaissance economy were themselves replaced by further innovations in economic thought and practice, which had their origins in northern Europe during the seventeenth and eighteenth centuries.

The Italian techniques and concepts that contributed to the development of the Renaissance economy are the same ones that stood behind the voyage of the Loredan brothers. They included merchant banks that could issue letters of credit; contracting mechanisms, such as the *colleganza*, which controlled the risk factors associated with trading expeditions; and local manufacturing industries based on an increasingly sophisticated division of labor, which produced high-quality goods, especially textiles, worth trading in other markets. Equally important to the emergence of the new European economy, if less specifically Italian, were an agrarian sector capable of producing a wide variety of commodities that could be exported to other markets, as well as supporting the needs of urban industries and populations; and the development of states that could enforce rules and exercise some measure of control over the growing economy. Seen from this perspective, the journey to Delhi is as much about what was happening inside Europe as it is about the world beyond the Mediterranean basin. Thus while the development of a world economy was very much a reality during the Renaissance, Europe's participation in it should not be taken for granted, depending as it did on the existence of completely new systems of production, exchange, and consumption based on completely knew conceptual and practical mechanisms of trade.

The Context of the Renaissance Economic Expansion: Urban Growth

The growth and development of the European economy during the Renaissance must be understood within the context of widespread and significant urbanization that would start in Italy and spread to other areas of the continent. Beginning in the late eleventh century, Europe was in the initial stages of a long period of significant population growth that would last until the middle of the fourteenth century. The growth of towns was one of the most visible and dramatic features of this high medieval population expansion. Urban growth was most pronounced in areas that were already urbanized, which by medieval standards meant about 8 percent of the total population living in towns (except in Italy where that figure reached as high as 17 percent). The towns themselves were also of limited size. In northern Italy, the Rhineland, and the Low Countries, a handful of major towns achieved populations of over 40,000, while only a select few major centers, such as Venice, achieved populations in excess of 100,000.[2] These three areas accounted for most of the urban growth before the middle of the seventeenth century, when towns began to proliferate in areas that had remained rural throughout the Renaissance.

Beginning with the arrival of the plague in Italy in 1348, Europe experienced a period of dramatic population decline with a mortality rate that averaged around 30 percent of the total population in most areas, and was as high as 50 percent in the most densely populated urban centers. (See the essay by Mary Lindemann below.) After the catastrophic events of the fourteenth century Europe's demographic history entered a period of slow growth, characterized by occasional local and regional outbreaks of plague (the last major episode occurring in 1715), which caused episodic declines throughout the continent. Except in rare cases, populations did not return to pre-plague levels until at least the 1570s, after which Europe experienced slow growth that eventually plateaued in the seventeenth century before another take-off, even more dramatic than that of the High Middle Ages, occurred in the late eighteenth century.

Within this broad pattern of population growth and urbanization, there exist regional trends that are also important to consider. While the population expansion of the High Middle Ages was a continent-wide phenomenon, sixteenth- and seven-teenth-century growth tended to favor northern Europe, with the rapid expansion of French, German, and English towns, while the Mediterranean region stagnated or even declined.[3] This pattern reflects broad environmental and agricultural conditions which prevented, with few exceptions, southern Europe from keeping pace with northern European growth. It also serves as a convenient guide for the long-term trajectory of the economy in Renaissance Europe, which had its roots in the Medi-terranean region, especially northern Italy, but whose center would eventually shift to the Atlantic before being superseded by the beginnings of a recognizably modern capitalist economy in England and Holland.

Finally, local trends also played a crucial role in this pattern of development. Despite the overall rise in urban populations during the entire period from 1100 to 1350, and again from 1570 to about 1660, mortality rates in the cities, even in non-plague years, remained exceptionally high, especially among the laboring classes. While upper-class urban dwellers enjoyed relatively clean living conditions, good diets, and long lives, the vast majority of the urban population lived in tight, disease-infested quarters, ate poorly, and lived relatively short lives. Nearly one half of all those born in towns never reached the age of 20, so the population of towns and cities was maintained and expanded only through the constant influx of rural emigrants, who replenished the labor supply and rid the countryside of excess population. (See the essay by James Amelang above.) This is not an insignificant consideration, especially within the context of the increasing regional differentiation that was beginning to manifest itself. Northern Europe's relatively higher growth was, in part, fueled by the expansion of agricultural production, which in turn allowed rural areas, to put it crudely, to produce sufficient numbers of people to sustain urban expansion. Prior to the modern agricultural revolution of the eighteenth century, southern Europe faced limits on its potential for agrarian growth which to some degree dictated that it would inevitably fall behind northern Europe in terms of both agricultural productivity and urban growth.

The Rural Economy: Food Production and the Rationalization of Nature

Food production

The history of agrarian growth mirrors that of the urban expansion it helped stimu-late. The agricultural revolution of the High Middle Ages had its origins in the most densely populated areas of the Mediterranean region, quickly spread to the rest of the continent, and eventually gave way to a modern system of agricultural production that originated in northern Europe during the eighteenth century. The high medieval agricultural revolution was the product of both climatic and technological changes that boosted the productivity of the entire agrarian sector. The population growth of the twelfth and thirteenth centuries was accompanied by a continent-wide climatic shift, or optimum, that brought warmer temperatures to Europe. Warmer conditions extended the growing season, creating larger, and sometimes multiple harvests, especially of grain staples. Moreover, technological advances such as the moldboard plow, the use of nitrogen-fixing crops in a three-field rotation, which eliminated fallow, and the integration of stock-keeping and agriculture through manuring, made land that was under cultivation far more productive than it had ever been before. Finally, the expansion of arable through the clearing and cultivation of marginal lands, or lands that had lapsed into disuse since antiquity, helped boost agricultural production and drive the overall pattern of population growth.

Like the high medieval population growth, the increases in agrarian food production were most pronounced in those areas where the bases for more intensive agriculture already existed. These were, of course, the same regions where urban growth was most pronounced: Italy, the Rhineland, and the Low Countries. Northern and central Italian agricultural expansion, in particular, was greatly aided by the recovery of an antique agricultural legacy. On a practical level this meant the restoration of ancient Roman irrigation systems that had fallen into disuse and disrepair. On a more abstract level, Italian humanists revived a significant classical corpus on agronomy.[4] The practical and theoretical knowledge that emerged from these activities quickly spread to other areas, where equally dramatic increases in productivity manifested themselves. Land owners, both lay and ecclesiastical, took an ever increasing interest in improving agricultural yields for profit, and by the sixteenth century, extensive new irrigation systems were being built, and the techniques and technologies of the high medieval agrarian revolution were being applied and improved upon. Thus the medieval agricultural revolution is probably best seen as a long-term process, extending well into the sixteenth century, and leading eventually to the growth of completely new urban centers and their inclusion in regional and continental trade networks.

This is not to say that the new agricultural economy was an unqualified success. Overall rates of food production fluctuated a great deal from year to year and decade to decade, because they were very vulnerable to climatic shifts, as well as the ill effects of war and plague, making agrarian production a leading indicator for European demographic history. The 1348 plague arrived on the continent about fifty years after the end of the long climatic optimum. This had resulted in lower average temperatures and a shorter growing season, the effects of which had been manifesting themselves in decreasing agrarian production and periodic famines since the last decade of the thirteenth century. Thus the epidemics hit a population already weakened by a food supply that had suddenly become stretched to its limits after a long period when it had managed to stay ahead of demographic growth.

While urban statistics are most often cited to convey the dramatic effects of the plague, rural areas were not exempt, and agrarian productivity proved to be highly susceptible to episodes of population decline. Because gains in agrarian productivity were heavily dependent upon the availability of a fairly flexible labor force that could be put to work on a wide variety of seasonal tasks, plague episodes could be particularly devastating in rural areas. Seasonal labor was obviously crucial for the successful conduct of the harvest, but several other "off-season" activities also drew on the same pool of rural labor. Timber harvesting, for example, which tended to take place at the beginning of the rainy season when the newly sown fields lay largely untended, required a significant amount of labor power. Rural labor was also crucial to the success of reclamation projects and the construction of irrigation networks. Much of this labor was harnessed through forms of taxation in kind such as the corvée in France, or the *angaria* in Italy, but by the sixteenth century wage labor was increasingly important in the rural context.[5] Thus as the pool of available short-term wage labor in rural areas fluctuated because of plague, famine, or emigration to urban areas, so too did the productivity of the entire agrarian sector. This meant that throughout the Renaissance period, the amount of acreage under production tended to fluctuate in rhythm with demographic expansion and contraction.

In addition to environmental and epidemic factors, the increasing military activity of European states played a role in curbing the expansion of agrarian productivity, beginning in the fourteenth century and extending through the eighteenth. The fact that Europe experienced almost constant warfare throughout the Renaissance cannot be ignored in any discussion of food production. (See the essay by Thomas Arnold below.) In France during the Hundred Years War (1337–1453), Italy during the Italian Wars (1494–1538), and Germany during the Thirty Years War (1618–48), as well as in countless other conflicts, small and large, all across the continent, crop yields fell dramatically, sometimes for several decades at a time, as marauding armies pillaged crops and stores, brought disease to vulnerable populations, and appropriated the best livestock for use as food and draft animals for supply trains.[6] It did not matter if the armies belonged to friend or foe. In the absence of reliable techniques of food preservation and extensive logistical networks, armies had little choice but to pillage the area they happened to be in if they wished to keep the field.

As a consequence of these broader factors, a new pattern of land use developed during the Renaissance. In place of the steady expansion of arable that had accompanied the high medieval period, a pattern of periodic expansion and contraction developed. Marginal lands were brought into service during periods of population growth, only to be abandoned again whenever signs of decline became pronounced. This pattern is significant, because it reflects the fact that despite many Renaissance technical innovations, such as cross furrowing, the more extensive use of nitrogen-fixing forage crops such as alfalfa, as well as the limited introduction of New World plants, the relationship between the acreage under cultivation and food production was largely static. Only in the eighteenth century would this relationship change in a significant way, when the modern agricultural revolution brought new agricultural technologies and the widespread introduction of new crops, both of which were capable of increasing yields per acre to a degree that would have been unthinkable a century earlier.

In addition to this pattern of local activity, the Renaissance also saw a slow, but inexorable change in the distribution of agrarian wealth across the continent as, beginning in the sixteenth century, northern European agriculture began to outpace that of the Mediterranean region in overall productivity and, to a lesser extent, in technical innovation. The reasons for this difference are still debated, but historians of agriculture have tended to look at patterns of land-tenure for the answers. This approach has led to the conclusion that northern Europe prospered because, despite the persistence of traditional techniques, the large-scale consolidation of rural property, beginning in the sixteenth century and accelerating throughout the seventeenth, provided the basis for modern factory farming in the eighteenth. By contrast southern Europe is seen to have faltered because of the persistence of small-scale farming and traditional forms of land-tenure and taxation which appear to have hampered growth.

The narrow focus on land-tenure, however, ignores several factors that were at least as important to the ability of rural areas to sustain growth.[7] These include access to trade networks, availability of wage labor, prolonged periods of peace, sustained demand from urban areas, and, most important of all, environmental conditions. Regardless of regional variations in plot size and land tenure patterns, the Renaissance system of expanding production through periodic expansions of arable ultimately favored northern Europe. Because the technical limitations of Renaissance agriculture dictated that the best way to expand production was to expand acreage, northern Europe had, on average, a greater potential for growth than the Mediterranean region. Italy, and the rest of the Mediterranean basin had been host to significant urban populations for far longer than the North. These urban populations had done irreparable damage to marginal lands, especially in antiquity, making them ultimately unsuitable for agriculture.[8] Moreover, the remaining areas that might be brought under cultivation tended to contain very low quality soil. An ever-decreasing margin of return on the expansion of arable, therefore, would always be more pronounced in the Mediterranean region.

In northern Europe these conditions did not hold, as there had been little permanent damage done to marginal lands before the eleventh century. This meant that the potential acreage available for the expansion of arable was far greater and of better quality, allowing for more expansion at better returns.

One way of measuring the practical limits of Renaissance agriculture to expand production in the Mediterranean area is to compare the relative rates of deforestation with those found in northern Europe. In central and southern Italy, much of the forest cover had already been removed in antiquity, and the subsequent erosion, especially in the Apennine Mountains, rendered those areas forever unproductive. In northern Italy, where most of the forest cover survived into the twelfth century, the value of timber as a resource meant that governments tended to take measures to preserve the total wooded area in their territory.[9] Italian states, therefore, had few options when it came to creating new arable. Given the state of agriculture at the time, this placed very real practical limits on population growth.

In northern Europe, by contrast, deforestation was widespread and dramatic. Beginning in the thirteenth century, and proceeding fairly consistently into the modern era, vast areas were put to the plough to support towns old and new. By the seventeenth century, as new areas were rapidly being opened up for cultivation, northern Europeans also began to experiment more extensively than their southern European counterparts. This represents a reversal of the situation that had held sway from the eleventh through the sixteenth century, when Mediterranean, and especially Italian agriculture had clearly been the leader in innovation. But the willingness to experiment with new crops and technologies that distinguished northern and southern Europe by the seventeenth century cannot be seen simply as a function of northern ingenuity or southern stagnation. It must also be seen as a function of the fact that southern European agriculture was on more tenuous ecological footing by that period, and could no longer afford to risk predictable crop yields for potentially risky experimentation.

The rationalization of nature

The obvious limits of Renaissance agriculture and the slow decline of southern European food production have tended to convey the image of a static rural society standing in stark contrast to the vital and dynamic world of the cities. This has meant that any discussion of the Renaissance economy has tended to privilege the urban over the rural to the extent that the urban economy might appear to have prospered despite the backwardness of the countryside. This is unfortunate, since the urban economy could not have functioned without the support of the rural, and the notion that little of interest occurred in the countryside is ultimately false.

In addition to the revival of classical agronomy, and the increasing interest in experimenting with garden plots and new plants, the rural world of the Renaissance saw developments that bear a remarkable resemblance to what was happening in the urban economy. Despite the dramatic regional variations in land-tenure and taxation patterns, land owners and states all across the continent began to take an active interest in the land that went well beyond what they might extract from it.

The sixteenth and seventeenth centuries saw a proliferation of manuals such as the Venetian Alvise Cornaro's *On the Sober Life* – which went through at least a dozen editions – offering advice to property owners on how to maximize crop yields and profits. New ideas about land management were applied with equal enthusiasm on large estates in the North and small farms in the South. States also became increasingly interested in understanding what the rural hinterland looked like, both for fiscal purposes and to better regulate land-use. State control over rural areas required the development of rational tools and procedures for surveying the countryside. These included topographic maps, cadastral surveys of farms and forests, land surveys to establish firm property lines, and regular inspections by government officials.[10] All of these efforts at state control helped bind the rural economy more tightly to the urban centers and regional trade networks. More than any other feature of the agrarian economy of the Renaissance, the development of conceptual tools offering a rationalized view of nature and landscape laid the foundation for the eighteenth-century agrarian revolution.

The Urban Economy: The Division of Labor and Rational Mechanisms of Exchange

The guild system and the division of labor

It was within the broader context of an increasingly sophisticated agrarian economy and dramatic demographic fluctuation, that the urban economy of the Renaissance took shape. Not surprisingly, developments in the urban economy follow closely trends in the agrarian economy and the continent-wide pattern of demographic. A period of expansion in the twelfth and thirteenth centuries when Italy was the clear innovator, was followed by a period of crisis and uncertainty during which Italian expertise and techniques spread to the rest of Europe, until, by the mid-seventeenth century, not only economic power, but also innovation had shifted definitively to northern Europe.

As the urban centers of the Low Countries, Rhineland, and northern Italy grew during the High Middle Ages, urban industries began to assume far greater import- ance than they ever had in the past. Local industries – based almost entirely in small, decentralized workshops – drew on the growing urban labor pool to produce and sell an increasing variety of goods. Increased production in turn necessitated institutional mechanisms to control economic activity and provide reliable access to wider markets. Medieval regimes, which were based largely on the control and distribution of agra- rian wealth, were poorly placed to deal with the new economic challenges facing urban residents. Thus control of sometimes entirely new industries devolved, at first, to local entities: town administrators and, far more often, to trade and craft guilds.

The guild system, which continued to control many aspects of Europe's urban economy until the Industrial Revolution, constituted an extremely powerful political, social, and economic force during the urban growth of the twelfth and thirteenth centuries. Guilds served several related functions within the system of small workshop manufactures. Such a system was vulnerable to a number of potential vicissitudes, including uneven quality of output, wage disparities, and the monopoly of knowledge by one workshop, or group of workshops, to the detriment of others. Guilds acted to curb such practices by regulating the wage and labor markets within individual trades, regulating competition in the marketplace through price controls, monitoring the quality of output from individual workshops in an effort to promote uniform stand- ards of production, and even acting as arbiters of disputes between workers and masters, or between workshops.

Such practices have often been characterized as collusive and exploitative, especially of labor, but absent a state with the power to enforce labor and manufacturing standards from above, the guilds performed a much needed function within a growing manufacturing economy.[11] Moreover, although the system clearly favored the master craftsmen who owned the workshops and controlled the wages, there was more room for maneuver on the part of the workers than might at first appear, especially after the demographic crisis of the fourteenth century opened up what has sometimes been referred to as "the golden age of labor." Subsequently, the guild system remained relatively open and effective until the middle of the sixteenth century, as wages levels remained relatively high, the number and variety of guilds – and therefore jobs – grew. During this period the state also emerged as a counter- weight to the power of the masters. By the beginning of the seventeenth century, however, increasing competition on the European and world markets, especially from cheaper, lower-quality goods that were increasingly being manufactured outside of the guild workshops, had begun to take its toll, after which the guild system and the labor market went into decline.

Most of the urban labor force – as much as 65 percent – was employed in the production and distribution of food, clothing, and shelter for the local market.

During the high medieval expansion, when agricultural production and urban populations were steadily rising, local demand drove economic growth, with production for external markets constituting the smallest component of the urban economy. Most of the export trade was in specialized crafts. Among these, textiles – wool and cotton, with silk becoming increasingly important by the fifteenth century – held the place of honor as the medieval and Renaissance commodities par excellence.

Textiles were the engine of the medieval and Renaissance economy, because their manufacture involved not only local workshops, but long-distance trade in raw materials as well. Woolen cloth produced in England, for example, was finished in Florence. The industry also required some hard-to-find raw materials, especially dyestuffs, which drove some of the earliest trading ventures outside the Mediterranean. Alum, for example, which was the most sought-after chemical binding agent for high quality dyes, could not be found in Europe until the discovery of the deposits at Tolfa in the Papal States in the fifteenth century.

Besides textiles, finished metal, wood, glass, and leather products were gaining importance. But social and economic mobility were severely limited in the twelfth and thirteenth centuries, and per capita income, and therefore the demand for specialized goods, remained fairly static, as most people had to spend their entire income, such as it was, on necessities.

In this climate of fixed opportunities, guilds tended to act to keep the limited amount of circulating capital in the hands of the masters. Thus wage earners remained pinned at the bottom of the ladder, often only slightly above the level of the indigent poor, and the guilds limited access to the ranks of the masters as much as possible. In the expanding economy of the twelfth and thirteenth centuries this was a tenable strategy, as wage levels could keep the workers above the poverty line and the masters firmly in control of the wealth and the workshops without running the risk of bankruptcy or revolt. But as the agrarian economy began to slow in the last decade of the thirteenth century, the urban economy followed suit. At this point the guild system, and the urban economy, faced a crisis, with ever increasing levels of poverty in the cities, ever decreasing levels of capital flowing to the workshops, and often violent episodes of worker discontent.

The fourteenth-century crisis served to break this deadlock in a number of ways. The plague had a far greater effect on the lower classes, and mortality rates among the upper classes were significantly lower. The result was a significant redistribution of wealth in the cities. While precise figures are hard to come by, it seems that prior to the plague the top 10 percent controlled about 50 or 60 percent of the total wealth in the cities, with the rest distributed downwards to the remaining 90 percent of the population.[12] But the high mortality rates among the lower classes meant that that wealth was now distributed among fewer people. Moreover, skilled labor became harder to find and consequently commanded higher wages – as much as triple pre-plague levels – and the guilds were forced to accommodate a far greater degree of upward mobility than they had in the twelfth and thirteenth centuries.

The alarming increase in poverty levels that preceded the plague had also begun to capture the attention of governments all across Europe. The Grand Ordnance of 1351 in France, the Statute of Labourers of the same year in England, and similar laws in other parts of the continent imposed minimum wage levels for workers, and attempted to regulate working conditions; in Aragon, for example, the length of the working day was fixed by law in 1350 – with mixed results.[13] The result was that after the fourteenth-century crisis, European states took an ever increasing role in regulating the economy, something that, with the exception of commercial republics such as Venice and Florence, they had done little of during the economic expansion of the twelfth and thirteenth centuries. Ultimately, this tended to work to the advantage of urban industries that were increasingly reliant on regional and international trade, because the state tended to overrule the parochial concerns that drove town and guild regulations in favor of regulations aimed at benefiting an entire sector of the economy.

The increasing attention of the state combined with the redistribution of wealth that had favored the wage-earning classes, forced the guilds to adapt themselves to new realities. This should not suggest, however, that the guilds relinquished their control over economic activity. Despite the continuing state attempts to regulate prices and wages, as well as the increased leverage of skilled wage laborers, Renaissance guilds still kept a tight grip on most aspects of industry, especially those relating to controlling manufacturing processes and quality control.

Guild workshops were also the locus of a great deal of technological innovation during the Renaissance, when manufacturing technology experienced significant, if limited technical improvements that allowed for greater production of finished goods. Many of these technologies had applications in the textile industry. Throwing machines for silk, for example, sped up manufacture and helped make Venetian silks the most sought after in Europe. Likewise, Venetian dyeing techniques, which guaranteed uniformity and richness of color, helped make the silk guild and the silk sector highly profitable.[14] Most industrial technology, however, relied on either water or animal power, and just as with agrarian technology, this imposed an upper limit on productivity, which would only be exceeded in the eighteenth and nineteenth centuries with the introduction of steam energy. Thus a seventeenth-century throwing machine, while perhaps slightly more durable and reliable than a fifteenth- or sixteenth-century example, was recognizably the same technology, and was incapable of delivering significant gains in productivity.

Despite the limited productive gains achieved through new technologies, the heart of the guild system remained the workshop. Within the workshop there was a clear division of labor whose sophistication depended largely on the complexity of the particular manufacturing activity in question. Workshops where high quality luxury goods, such as finished gold, were produced, required a great deal of skill on the part of the artisan. Consequently, in such manufacturing activities, there was no division of labor in the modern sense. The workshop was run by a master, who had a small number of apprentices and journeymen working under him, each of whom, in theory at least, aspired to become a master one day. In practice, very few became masters, but even those who did not constituted a highly skilled labor pool, not to mention a significant financial investment on the part of the master. Not only was their training expensive and time-consuming, but they usually lived as members of his household, working, eating, and sleeping under his roof. Each one was competent in a wide range of skills, and the ones who were offered the opportunity to become masters would have to demonstrate those skills by producing a masterwork to be evaluated by the guild leadership. If the work passed muster, the journeyman would ascend to the level of master and have the opportunity to set up a shop of his own and take apprentices.

In industries with more complex production processes, such as textiles, a more sophisticated division of labor often existed. Wool production, for example, required at least five separate stages: carding, spinning, weaving, fulling, and dyeing. Each process would have its own set of skilled labor, and sometimes a separate guild, but there were usually at least two distinct processes taking place under a single roof. Thus each process would have its own set of dedicated workers. These workers remained relatively skilled, but the process of production was broken down into component parts to speed up and rationalize production. Nonetheless, even very successful workshops remained tiny by modern standards, with even the largest having no more than a dozen employees at a time. Thus even when rationalized through a clear division of labor, this form of industrial organization faced very real limits on productivity.

Some larger industries provide an exception to this pattern of Renaissance manufacturing. Building and mining, for example, required a large pool of relatively unskilled labor, which could either be wage or forced. These activities, however, bear a greater resemblance to agriculture, especially because of the presence of forced labor, and so must be considered separately from the workshop industries of the guilds. Nonetheless, these industries were subject to a process of rationalization during the Renaissance that is important in light of later developments in labor organization. Workers in these sectors were increasingly trained in specific, repetitive tasks rather than the entire process of production, as was the case in the guild workshops.

The most famous Renaissance example of rationalized industrial organization was the Venetian Arsenal, where the republic built and maintained a huge fleet of commercial and war vessels. The Arsenal had originally resembled a series of extremely large workshops working side by side. Each aspect of shipbuilding had its own guild, with highly skilled masters training journeymen and apprentices in the nuances of their craft. During the sixteenth century, however, the labor force in the Arsenal was reorganized, with a handful of skilled masters supervising an increasingly unskilled labor force. Unlike the workshop system, each worker was assigned a very specific task to perform: driving nails, caulking planks, or mounting fittings, for example. Unlike guild workers, they were trained to perform a single task for the duration of their employment, and there was no possibility of their becoming masters themselves.[15] This highly rationalized model of labor organization that prefigures in many ways the advances of the Industrial Revolution, allowed the Arsenal to turn out a complete galley in the time it took King Henri III of France to eat his dinner during a visit to the complex in 1574. It remained, however, a highly visible exception in the workshop world of the Renaissance.

By the seventeenth century the guild system was clearly in decline. The productive limits of the workshop system were increasingly unable to cope with the growing hunger for consumer goods that was sweeping Europe.[16] While historians disagree as to whether the increased demand was related to the birth of a consumer economy or a conservative investment strategy in a period of economic recession, the effects on the workshop system were widely felt – especially as the middle class began to imitate upper-class tastes on a wider scale. Guild workshops produced goods of extremely high quality, but they sold them at equally high prices, trapped as they were by fairly fixed costs for materials and expensive skilled labor. The salaries of workers were protected by guild statutes, and monitored by the state. Moreover, guild statutes imposed minimum quality standards that also served to keep prices high. Generally speaking, the guilds proved unwilling to consider adjusting to new realities by producing lower quality goods at bargain prices by employing unskilled labor and cutting the costs of materials.[17]

The limits of the workshop proved to be a particular problem in Italy, where states tended to favor and protect guild systems of production; this contributed to Italian industries losing ground to their northern European competitors, who used low-skilled, cheap labor to undersell high quality Italian textiles and other goods. This was usually accomplished through a putting-out system in which work was doled out to individual workers, often women in depressed rural areas, who were paid a low piece rate. Eventually, in the eighteenth century, this system would give way to large workshops on the model of the Venetian Arsenal, employing semi-skilled labor supervised by a single skilled master.

This new form of labor organization would become one of the bases of the advances on productivity that would be achieved during the Industrial Revolution, and would largely doom the guild system to extinction. By the beginning of the seventeenth century, the golden age of Renaissance labor was truly over. The new unskilled and semi-skilled workers enjoyed few of the protections that the guild workers had enjoyed. Wage levels dropped significantly, and the purchasing power of the laboring classes was a fraction of what it had been in the late fifteenth century, when wage levels peaked;[18] wage laborers once again found themselves in the same situation as their pre-plague counterparts: pinned at the bottom of an increasingly rigid social hierarchy with little or no prospect of social or economic advancement, just barely above the level of the indigent poor. Thus breaking the productivity limits of the Renaissance economy came at a hefty price for many urban dwellers.

Rationalizing exchange

Improved processes of production were by themselves inadequate to sustain the growth of the Renaissance economy. Equally important was the development of rational systems of exchange without which reliable ways of trading the products of the new agrarian and urban economies would have been unthinkable. Before the twelfth century, Europe's economy consisted mainly of isolated barter systems based on towns and their immediate hinterlands. During the twelfth- and thirteenth-century expansion, these local economies became bound together by a European-wide system of annual fairs, such as the famous Champagne fairs in France. These fairs brought the foreign market directly to the producers in the person of buyers who would then exchange the goods at subsequent fairs in other locations.

By connecting local manufacturers to wider trading networks, the fairs helped stimulate the growth of local economies during the High Middle Ages. The growth of local economies also stimulated, and was stimulated by, the development of a monetary economy, which gradually replaced local barter systems.[19] By the thirteenth century local metal currencies (paper money was not used in Renaissance Europe) that permitted both local exchange and long-distance trade were sprouting up all over the continent. The coins used in local markets tended to be made of increasingly debased silver, while high quality gold coinage was reserved for large transactions between merchants or governments. As the number and quality of local currencies grew, a system of exchange rates was developed to help merchants trade in different markets, in turn providing new avenues for profit through currency speculation.

After the fourteenth-century crisis the fairs began to give way to regular trade routes, plied by individual merchants as well as large merchant companies. Merchant companies, which were usually family concerns, would establish permanent representatives in major towns to monitor the local market and act as brokers on behalf of the travelling members of the company. Representatives of Italian concerns installed themselves throughout the major trading centers of the Mediterranean basin and northern Europe, and could even be found as far afield as Timbuktu. In addition to merchant companies, there were also state-controlled trade routes, such as the Spanish and Venetian maritime convoys, which bound together all the merchants making for a specific port under the protection of the government. The trade routes offered many advantages over the fair system. They gave local manufacturers uninterrupted access to external trade networks, and allowed merchants to speculate on, and take advantage of, market fluctuations and price differentials in ways that had not been possible before.

Both the medieval fairs and the Renaissance trade routes relied on Italian techniques of banking, credit, accounting, and contracting. Large merchant banks constituted the backbone of the emerging European trade system. While banks had existed in Europe since antiquity, the Italian merchant banks of the High Middle Ages were unlike anything that had come before, because they were based on commercial credit rather than agrarian wealth.[20] The banks performed a series of crucial functions, including issuing credit, transferring funds between branches in different cities through bills of exchange (thus obviating the need to risk transporting hard currency over long distances), and negotiating exchange rates between the bewildering number of local currencies. These services opened up new opportunities for investment and participation in commerce that had never existed before. Resident merchants in cities such as Venice or Antwerp could now invest their capital in distant markets without actually having to travel there themselves. Thus the banks brought new capital into the European market and contributed to the larger pattern of economic expansion.

Like the high medieval guilds, the merchant banks relied upon economic growth to hide organizational flaws. Merchant banks were mostly family concerns, with a board of partners resident in one city holding all the assets and liabilities of the enterprise, including foreign branches. The three most important banks of the thirteenth century were all Florentine, belonging to the Peruzzi, Acciaiuoli, and Bardi clans. The Peruzzi bank maintained fifteen separate branches in Europe and the Mediterranean, all managed by family members. Concentrating the assets and liabilities of the bank in the hands of a small group of partners worked well during the long economic expansion of the twelfth and thirteenth centuries, since default rates were relatively low, and easily covered by the profits on other investments. Indeed, loans to governments, who were among the least trustworthy borrowers, were often simply a way to gain access to other markets where the losses might be recouped. So, for example, Italian bankers floated large loans to the English crown in the thirteenth century knowing full well that the king would default, but hoping to make huge profits by speculating on the exchange rates between English and Italian currencies through the transactions.[21]

Such risky practices proved fatal during the long economic slowdown of the early fourteenth century, which hit the Florentine banks particularly hard. In 1345 all three of the big Florentine houses went bankrupt, as the collapsing European economy and the liability of the partners left them badly vulnerable to a run on deposits by investors looking for safer places to put their money.

The merchant banks that emerged from the fourteenth-century crisis were smaller, but more organizationally sound than their pre-plague counterparts. The fifteenth-century Italian banks spread their liability by setting up each branch as an independent entity. This prevented the kind of calamity that had befallen the thirteenth-century banks, because the failure of a single branch would no longer set off a chain-reaction capable of toppling the entire organization. Fifteenth-century banks, such as the Medici bank of Florence or the Borromei bank of Milan, also invested in a broader range of activities than the medieval banks, ranging from insurance, to tax-farming, to currency speculation.

In the early sixteenth century Italy began to rapidly lose its pre-eminence in European banking, as a number of large German banking families – the Fuggers, Hochstetters, Welsers, and Imhofs among others – rose to prominence. The German bankers were modeled on the Italian banks, although there were some important differences. The German banks were possessed of a stronger central organization than their Italian counterparts, which allowed for somewhat quicker decision-making during crises. The German banks also benefited from the general northward shift in the European economy. The decline in the agrarian sector and the plateauing of the Mediterranean carrying trade coincided with the rise of Atlantic ports, primarily Antwerp, in which the German banks had invested heavily. The Fuggers in particular also enjoyed imperial monopolies on silver mining in Tyrolia, but the rise of extractive industries in northern Europe lifted all the banks with it.

In addition to the big merchant banks, local deposit banks began to play an important role in the Renaissance economy. By the fifteenth century local deposit banks had become common, with Venice the clear industry leader. Local deposit banks provided a wider range of services for individual customers than the big merchant banks. One of their main services was to allow local merchants to settle transactions through the bank without having to have hard currency on hand. They also permitted individuals to earn interest on long-term deposits that would be invested in trade and other commercial activities.

Investing deposited funds was possible because the local banks created bank money, or *monete di banco*, as it was known in the fifteenth century. Bank money was one of the most important innovations of the Renaissance banking system, and remains a key feature of modern banking. Because so much business was conducted through ledger transactions, bankers could keep only a fractional reserve of their total deposits on hand, investing the rest in various commercial enterprises. The first record of bank money dates to 1321 in Venice, and by the fifteenth century it had become common practice throughout Europe. Bank money stimulated the economy by introducing more capital into circulation. It also left the banks vulnerable to the sort of runs on deposits that had wiped out the fourteenth-century merchant banks. Panics were common, especially because the carrying trade in which the bankers often invested was itself quite risky, and the rate of bank failures was extremely high.[22]

The risks associated with deposit banks and the practice of creating bank money led to the intervention of the state, and the development of public banks. Public banks managed the public debt, consolidated tax surpluses, and even accepted deposits from private citizens. The main purpose of the public banks was to stabilize the volatile banking sector by providing a depository that would not be subject to the vicissitudes of sudden panics and runs. Therefore, public banks were not permitted to create bank money, nor could they engage in speculative investment. The first public bank was established in Barcelona in 1401, and by the end of seventeenth century there were at least twenty-five spread across the continent, as nearly every European state had taken an active interest in exerting some measure of control over the economy and the public debt.

While banks were the most visible avenue through which larger numbers of people participated in the economy, individuals and institutions also began to invest directly in commercial activities, especially after the collapse of the medieval economy in the fourteenth century. As trade routes multiplied, and merchants ventured further and further from their home bases in search of commodities to trade, reliable contracting mechanisms became crucial to the success of any venture. Because timely information about distant markets was impossible to come by, given that any communication could take several weeks, even months, to travel between distant trading centers, the network of resident and traveling agents was the only reliable way to transact business. But the investors and resident merchants who remained behind in the home port had to be certain that they were receiving a fair return on their investment. In other words, they had to be sure that their agents were giving them accurate reports about market conditions in distant towns, and that there was no collusion on the part of the agents, or the agents and the resident merchants overseas, to defraud them of their fair share of the profits.

The family structure of many merchant companies, as well as informal controls such as the reputation of individual agents, provided some means of minimizing the risk of fraud, but they were not sufficient guarantee for investors who were neither members of the clan, nor familiar with all the available agents. Thus contracting mechanisms designed to encourage accurate reporting on the part of agents and discourage collusion were developed and refined throughout the Renaissance.[23] The three basic contract types developed in Italy were *prestiti marittimi* (sea loans), *cambi marittimi* (sea exchanges), and *colleganze* (profit sharing). As these techniques spread to other regions of Europe, they took on new names – Hanseatic partnerships, for example, were known as *sendeve*, *vera societas*, and *contraposito* – but the essential features remained those of their Italian models.

The first two contract types offered the investor fixed return on his investment, regardless of the success or failure of the voyage, with the difference being that the sea exchange paid out in a different currency from that originally invested, thus adding the opportunity for currency speculation. In both cases, the agent assumed all the risks of the venture, but also stood to profit more if the voyage offered a better return than the contract stipulated. The profit-sharing contract, on the other hand, offered the investor the opportunity to share the risks, but also any unanticipated profits with the agent. A variation of the *colleganza* involved the pooling of resources by a large group of investors, some of whom would undertake the voyage while the rest stayed at home.

Contract selection depended upon a host of factors, including the reputation of the agent, the reliability of the route, the availability of verifiable information against which to check agent reports; the distance to be traveled, and the type of commodities involved in the exchange. Generally speaking, the riskier the voyage, the more likely a debt contract, such as a sea loan, would be used, regardless of the distance involved.[24] This insured the investor against the fact that agent's reports were unverifiable, and secured the investment from the loss of cargo or market fluctuations by guaranteeing a return of some kind. Secure routes, and the availability of reliable information on market conditions at the destination port encouraged the use of risk-sharing contracts, such as the *colleganza*, especially among informed investors who knew what rate of return they ought to expect from such a voyage and could verify the reports of their agents. War and plague tended to disrupt information flows, and thus conditioned contract selection. Informed investors either reverted to debt contracts, regardless of the distance involved, or employed a pooling contract, which had the advantages of the *colleganza*, with the added insurance that if one agent died the other members of the party could fulfill his contracts.

The development and diffusion of rational mechanisms of exchange, including banking and contracting mechanisms, were crucial to the development of both the European and world economies, because such mechanisms offered reasonably secure channels for individuals to invest their money in commercial enterprises. This meant that far more capital was invested in trade than had been the case in the twelfth and thirteenth centuries, when the merchants who traveled the circuit of fairs also provided the bulk of the capital, and opportunities to raise outside money were rare. The opportunity for individuals and institutions to invest, either through the banks or trading contracts, without being actively involved in commerce, was, therefore, one of the key features of the Renaissance economy. It contributed significantly to the volume of trade, and provided the key link between local systems of agrarian and workshop production, and broader trade networks.

What was Renaissance about the Renaissance Economy?

The Renaissance economy that emerged from the fourteenth-century crisis, and dominated European economic concepts and practices until the middle of the seventeenth century, presents the modern viewer with a curious mix of archaic and novel practices. The European economy in the period 1350–1650 was largely built on refinements of agrarian, manufacturing, banking, and technological systems that had their origins in the period of peak medieval prosperity in the twelfth and thirteenth centuries. But Renaissance merchants, bankers, manufacturers, and farmers put these medieval tools to new and unanticipated uses in the quest for larger markets and higher profits. So despite the archaic nature of many of the features of the Renaissance economy, its spirit seems to belong to the modern age. This can lead to interpretive problems that have more to do with our own dilemmas than they do with the way Renaissance merchants, manufacturers, and farmers saw their world.

One way to approach this problem is to look at what was distinctive about the Renaissance economy when compared to the medieval world that preceded it, as well as the modern capitalist system that followed. One might begin by noting that all of the mechanisms that made the Renaissance economy possible – banking, credit, a monetary economy, and sophisticated contracting instruments – required a fairly literate, and more importantly, numerate society. Literacy rates in urban areas were relatively high for the period, and anyone involved in the daily transactions of the economy, from the workshop masters on up, could at least do simple sums and read account ledgers. Indeed, if there is one element that ties together all the components of the Renaissance economy – rural and urban, agrarian, carrying, and manufacturing – it is numeracy.

Numeracy lay at the heart of the European economy in the Renaissance, and it also was the basis of the Renaissance impulse to rationalize the world that sets the period from 1350 to 1650 apart from the apparently similar medieval system upon which it was founded.[25] The quantitative tools that were developed in the commercial context spread to other realms of thought, especially public administration, and led to the increasingly widespread use of numbers to make sense of the territory and people under the control of the state. The Florentine Catasto of 1427, which quantified and registered real property owned by residents of Florence, is only the most famous example of what became common practice for European states. By the end of the sixteenth century, European governments were routinely using quantitative surveys to track and tax both urban and rural property; measure populations; catalogue resources such as timber or grain; and draw up boundaries ranging from national borders to local property lines.

Most of the core elements of the Renaissance economy – guilds, workshops, traditional land-tenure arrangements, forced labor – began to disappear during the seventeenth and eighteenth centuries, when the Renaissance economy went into decline and commercial capitalism began its rise to dominance in northern Europe and the world. Some Renaissance practices, such as the division of labor in large industrial enterprises such as the Venetian Arsenal survived, albeit in an altered form, but numeracy and the fascination with quantitative reasoning not only survived, it prospered. Numeracy was the springboard for the emergence of the modern economic system, since without it there could have been no joint-stock companies, stock exchanges, not to mention the navigation and maritime technology necessary for the Atlantic economy to stretch out to ports and markets on the far side of the world. Consequently just as the practices of the workshop, the bank, and the field were the most important bequest of the High Middle Ages to the Renaissance, the numerate approach to economic organization is the thread that links the Renaissance economy to the modern one.

Even so, the persistence of quantitative thought ought not to be turned into a prime mover. While the numerate approach to understanding the world is clearly the most modern feature of the Renaissance economy, there are also important differences between the quantitative reasoning of the Renaissance, and our own undeniable love of numbers and statistics. Even the most comprehensive state surveys, investment schemes, or bank transactions of the Renaissance used their new numerate knowledge in extremely rudimentary ways. Mathematics was relatively unsophisticated – in the sixteenth century quadratic and cubic equations were still not universally known – which limited the potential uses to which quantitative knowledge could be put. Thus while the data being collected were undoubtedly impressive, the uses to which they were put were ultimately quite simple. Renaissance merchants and bureaucrats were concerned with totals and subtotals, not regressions and projections. Numbers were tools, but they were far from the totalizing language they would become in the modern world. The modern approach to quantitative reasoning is at least as much a product of the quantitative and probabilistic revolutions of the eighteenth century as it is a Renaissance holdover.[26] Just like Alberto Calli and Giovanni Loredan, who signed a medieval contract to finance a Renaissance enterprise, we are caught between looking forward and backwards every time we use numbers to understand the world.

NOTES

1   Lopez, "European Merchants."
2   Cipolla, *Before the Industrial Revolution*, pp. 3–5; de Vries, "Population," pp. 15–16.
3   de Vries, "Population," pp. 11–15.
4   Ambrosoli, *Wild and the Sown*.
5   Brenner, "Agrarian Roots."
6   Hale, *War and Society*, pp. 179–231.
7   Hoffman, *Traditional Society*, pp. 143–92.
8   Meiggs, *Trees and Timber*, pp. 151–2, 181.
9   Appuhn, "Inventing Nature," and Kjaergaard, *Danish Revolution*, pp. 9–32; 256–60.
10   Marino, "Administrative Mapping."
11   Epstein, *Wage Labor*, pp. 102–54.
12   Cipolla, *Before the Industrial Revolution*, pp. 7–22.
13   Epstein, *Wage Labor*, pp. 232–48.
14   Molà, *Silk Industry*.
15   Davis, *Shipbuilders*, pp. 10–82.
16   Goldthwaite, *Demand for Art*, pp. 212–42.
17   Rapp, *Industry*, pp. 107–70.
18   Cipolla, *Before the Industrial Revolution*, pp. 198–208.
19   Lane and Mueller, *Money and Banking*, and Kaye, *Economy and Nature*, pp. 15–36.
20   Lopez, "Dawn."
21   Prestwich, "Italian Merchants."
22   Mueller, *Venetian Money Market*.
23   Lopez, *Commercial Revolution*; Greif, "Reputations and Coalitions."
24   Williamson, "Design of Agency Relations."
25   Crosby, *Measure of Reality*, and Baxandall, *Painting and Experience*.
26   Frangsmayr et al., *Quantifying Spirit*.

REFERENCES

Ambrosoli, Mauro, *The Wild and the Sown: Botany and Agriculture in Western Europe, 1350–1850*, trans. Mary McCann Salvatorelli (Cambridge: Cambridge University Press, 1997).
Appuhn, Karl, "Inventing Nature: Forests, Forestry and State Power in Renaissance Venice," *Journal of Modern History* 72 (2000), pp. 861–89.
Baxandall, Michael, *Painting and Experience in Fifteenth-Century Italy: A Primer in the Social History of Pictorial Style* (Oxford: Oxford University Press, 1988).

Brenner, Robert, "The Agrarian Roots of European Capitalism," in *The Brenner Debate: Agrarian Class Structure and Economic Development in Pre-Industrial Europe*, ed. T. H. Aston and C. H. E. Philpin (Cambridge: Cambridge University Press, 1985), pp. 213–327.

Buisseret, David, *Monarchs, Ministers and Maps: The Emergence of Cartography as a Tool of Government in Early Modern Europe* (Chicago: University of Chicago Press, 1992).

Cipolla, Carlo M., *Before the Industrial Revolution: European Society and Economy 1000–1700* (New York: W. W. Norton, 1994).

Crosby, Alfred, *The Measure of Reality: Quantification and Western Society, 1250–1600* (Cambridge: Cambridge University Press, 1997).

Davis, Robert C., *Shipbuilders of the Venetian Arsenal: Workers and Workplace in the Preindustrial City* (Baltimore: Johns Hopkins University Press, 1992).

de Vries, Jan, "The Population of Europe," in *Handbook of European History, 1400–1600: Late Middle Ages, Renaissance and Reformation*, 2 vols., ed. Thomas A. Brady Jr., Heiko A. Oberman, and James D. Tracy (Leiden: E. J. Brill, 1994–5), vol. I.

Epstein, Steven A., *Wage Labor and Guilds in Medieval Europe* (Chapel Hill: University of North Carolina Press, 1991).

Frangsmayr, Tore, Heilbron, J. L., and Rider, Robin E., *The Quantifying Spirit of the Eighteenth Century* (Berkeley: University of California Press, 1990).

Goldthwaite, Richard A., *Wealth and the Demand for Art in Italy, 1300–1600* (Baltimore: Johns Hopkins University Press, 1993).

Greif, Avner, "Reputations and Coalitions in Medieval Trade: Evidence on the Maghribi Traders," *Journal of Economic History* 49 (1989), pp. 857–82.

Hale, John R., *War and Society in Renaissance Europe, 1450–1620* (Leicester: Leicester University Press, 1985).

Hoffman, Philip T., *Growth in a Traditional Society: The French Countryside 1450–1815* (Princeton: Princeton University Press, 1996).

Kaye, Joel, *Economy and Nature in the Fourteenth Century: Money, Market Exchange and the Emergence of Scientific Thought* (Cambridge: Cambridge University Press, 1998).

Kjaergaard, Thorkild, *The Danish Revolution, 1500–1800*, trans. David Hohen (Cambridge: Cambridge University Press, 1994).

Lane, Frederic C. and Mueller, Reinhold, *Money and Banking in Medieval and Renaissance Venice: Coins and Moneys of Account* (Baltimore: Johns Hopkins University Press, 1985).

Lopez, Robert S., "European Merchants in the Medieval Indies: Evidence of Commercial Documents," *Journal of Economic History* 3 (1943), pp. 164–84.

——, *The Commercial Revolution of the Middle Ages, 950–1350* (Cambridge: Cambridge University Press, 1976).

——, "The Dawn of Medieval Banking," in *The Dawn of Modern Banking*, Center for Medieval and Renaissance Studies, University of California (New Haven: Yale University Press, 1979).

Marino, John, "Administrative Mapping in the Italian States," in *Monarchs, Ministers and Maps: The Emergence of Cartography as a Tool of Government in Early Modern Europe*, ed. David Buisseret (Chicago: University of Chicago Press, 1992), pp. 5–25.

Meiggs, Russell, *Trees and Timber in the Ancient Mediterranean World* (Oxford: Clarendon Press, 1982).

Molà, Luca, *The Silk Industry in Renaissance Venice* (Baltimore: Johns Hopkins University Press, 1999).

Mueller, Reinhold, *The Venetian Money Market: Banks, Panics and the Public Debt, 1200–1500* (Baltimore: Johns Hopkins University Press, 1997).

Prestwich, Michael, "Italian Merchants in Late Thirteenth- and Early Fourteenth-Century England," in *The Dawn of Modern Banking*, Center for Medieval and Renaissance Studies, University of California (New Haven: Yale University Press, 1979).

Rapp, Richard T., *Industry and Economic Decline in Seventeenth-Century Venice* (Cambridge, MA: Harvard University Press, 1976).
Williamson, Dean V., "The Design of Agency Relations: Four Essays on Contract Theory, Applications, and Experimentation," Ph.D. dissertation, California Institute of Technology, 1999.

FURTHER READING

Braudel, Fernand, *The Mediterranean and the Mediterranean World in the Age of Philip II*, 2 vols., trans. Sian Reynolds (Berkeley: University of California Press, 1995).
De Roover, Raymond, *The Rise and Decline of the Medici Bank, 1397–1494* (New York: W. W. Norton, 1966).
Duplessis, Robert S., *Transitions to Capitalism in Early Modern Europe* (Cambridge: Cambridge University Press, 1997).
Kedar, Benjamin, *Merchants in Crisis: Genoese and Venetian Men of Affairs and the Fourteenth-Century Depression* (New Haven: Yale University Press, 1976).
Kruger, Lorenz, et al., *The Probabilistic Revolution*, (Cambridge, MA: MIT Press, 1987).
Mackenney, Richard, *Tradesmen and Traders: The World of the Guilds in Venice and Europe, c.1250–c.1650* (London: Croom Helm, 1987).
Marino, John, *Pastoral Economics in the Kingdom of Naples* (Baltimore: Johns Hopkins University Press, 1988).
Miskimin, Harry A., *The Economy of Early Renaissance Europe, 1300–1460* (Cambridge: Cambridge University Press, 1975).
——, *The Economy of Later Renaissance Europe, 1460–1600* (Cambridge: Cambridge University Press, 1977).

CHAPTER SIXTEEN

Economic Encounters and the First Stages of a World Economy

JOHN A. MARINO

In 1291, two Genoese brothers (Ugolino and Vadino Vivaldi) set out "for India by way of the Ocean," presumably an Atlantic circumnavigation of Africa, never to return.[1] Later in November of that same year 1291, Jaime II of Aragon and Sancho IV of Castile partitioned Morocco into spheres of influence as part of their Reconquest ambitions.[2] Four years later in 1295, two Venetian brothers (Niccolò and Maffeo Polo) with Niccolò's son Marco returned to Venice after a twenty-four-year journey to the court of the Great Khan in China.[3] Such early enterprises found culmination two centuries later in the earth-shattering voyages of Columbus and Vasco da Gama in 1492 and 1498 and in the division of the New World by Spain and Portugal in the 1494 Treaty of Tordesillas. Such exploits in and out of the Mediterranean basin exemplified medieval commercial practices and political experiences, from the eleventh-century rise of the city to the late fifteenth-century emergence of strong centralized states.

During the Renaissance, new maritime contacts with Africa and Asia, the unexpected "discovery" and concerted "invasion" of America, and the establishment of European overseas empires resulted from two main causes: the late-medieval entrepreneurial quest to quench growing consumer demand, and the support of and competition between newly reconstituted monarchies and their bureaucratized states. By the end of the increased economic activity, price inflation, and overseas expansion associated with the "long sixteenth century" (1450–1650), the pre-eminence of the Italian-led Mediterranean world had given way to a new dynamic center in northwestern Europe. English goods and shipping displaced Italian in the Mediterranean itself, Dutch merchants replaced the Portuguese in Asia, and American Indian forced labor (later African slave labor) in the New World was used to extract the silver and refine the sugar that would fuel growth and forge the first stages of a world economy.

Towns, Trade, and Trading Networks in Late Medieval Europe

Long-term demographic movements – a pluri-secular, double wave pattern of rise/decline/stagnation from 1000 to 1450 and rise/relative decline/take-off from 1450 to 1650 – help to explain the trajectory of late medieval and Renaissance economic growth and expansion. The dynamic story of economic expansion outside Europe revolves around what happened inside Europe: the growth of medieval towns to comprise about 7 or 8 percent of the population between the year 1000 and the early fourteenth century. The fourteenth-century crisis, including the 1348 plague and its subsequent recurrences and consequences, reduced Europe's population by about one-third to 52 million people by 1400, where it remained stagnated at that low level through most of the fifteenth century. Slow population growth from the second half of the fifteenth and early sixteenth century only returned European population to its pre-plague level by the 1570s. The end of the long population expansion by the mid-seventeenth century was unlike the sharp and universal decline of the fourteenth century, but instead varied in intensity across Europe, with sharp divergence between northern and southern Europe in population growth profile and in pattern of settlement in large urban centers.[4] This demographic framework mirrored the shift in political and economic power from the Mediterranean to northwest Europe and the three so-called revolutions – urban, commercial, and price – that lie behind European emergence as a dominant player in the world economy by the end of the Renaissance.

The urban context

Towns welcomed immigrants from the countryside because high mortality rates, with half the population never reaching 20 years of age, meant that equally high birth rates could barely maintain stable population levels. To feed their burgeoning immigrant populations, towns also sought to reap agricultural surpluses by controlling their rural hinterland.

The core of the city's dynamism was its division of labor and wage-earning workforce, which produced goods and services in response to consumer demand for food, clothing, and shelter, these items accounting for about 98 percent of private expenditures. Merchants, who were not only specialists in the distribution of goods but also often provided the capital and procured the labor needed in manufacturing, were instrumental in the process of turning independent craftsmen into dependent employees through credit and indebtedness, and by developing the "domestic" or "putting-out" system among seasonally underemployed agricultural laborers, especially women, who worked in their own homes at piece-rates. Skewing at the top and the bottom of the social and economic pyramid (with the richest 10 percent controlling one-half the wealth and the bottom 60 percent only 5 to 20 percent) meant that the wealthy few held sway and commanded the expansion of luxury markets, that the middling sort were relatively few, and that a large number of the poor could suffer during conjunctural downturns and join the ranks of the hard-core poor or "beggars."

The commercial context

Markets and exchange grew with the wealth and diversity of the city. As it drew in people and raw materials from the countryside, the city re-exported finished manufactured goods (especially textiles), promoted organizational and technological in-novations, and developed trading networks near and far.[5]

Late medieval and early modern merchants and bankers, who were indistinguish-able one from another, controlled production and distribution, capital and credit. Whether northern Italians from the late twelfth century or southern Germans from the late fifteenth to mid-sixteenth centuries, the merchant bankers' need for the efficient exchange and transfer of goods, money, credit, and news required a range of new business techniques that created the fundamental instruments of modern banking and commerce. Italians developed the two most important financial innov-ations in the twelfth and thirteenth centuries: deposit-and-transfer banking (keeping a fraction of deposits in reserve while lending out the majority of funds) and foreign-exchange or bill-of-exchange banking (a credit or transfer letter that employed a principal/agent system to deliver or remit funds). A whole range of business and accounting mechanisms followed: modern dating, the introduction of Arabic nu-merals (originally Indic), double-entry bookkeeping, the check, the endorsement, insurance, commerce manuals, partnership contracts, joint stock companies, the stock exchange, and the central bank. Business and commerce not only infused money into the economy, but also fostered the spread of literacy, expertise in mathematics, and entrepreneurial skills.

Medieval Europe's economic development and the early commercial and financial leadership of Italians in it must be seen in the broader context of a 60-day "world-economy" (the maximum time needed to hold long-distance trading circuits to-gether),[6] in which western Europe remained a marginal outlier to the two larger, well-developed circuits of exchange in the Middle East and Asia that dominated international trade.[7] In the thirteenth century, the three evolving western European nodes of exchange around the textile producing region of Flanders, around the industrial communes of northern Italy, and at the meeting ground of northern and southern Europeans in the Champagne Fairs to the southeast of Paris were slowly forming into a more integrated, single trading circuit. From the European peripheral circuit, Venice and Genoa especially operated in a trans-Mediterranean subsystem that linked them to the Middle East circuit. There they found themselves in contact with three extended trading subsystems: in western Asia (from Constantinople and the Black Sea to China, depending on the Mongol unification of central Asia and conquests in China); in the Levant (from the Palestinian coast to Baghdad, joining the central Asian caravan route or going south to the Persian Gulf and Indian Ocean); and in Egypt (from Alexandria, Cairo, and Mamluk Egypt via the Red Sea to the Indian Ocean). The powerhouse of this early world economy was the Asian circuit, which was centered in the Indian Ocean and shared by Persians and Arabs in the West, Indians of Islamic faith on the West coast of the subcontinent and of Hindu and Buddhist culture on the east coast, and Chinese in the east between Java and China.

Four Italian maritime communes – Genoa, Pisa, Amalfi, and Venice – vied for power in this medieval trans-Mediterranean trading circuit centered on Constantin-ople and the Islamic Middle East from the ninth and tenth centuries. By the thir-teenth century the commercial, banking, and manufacturing quadrilateral around Venice, Milan, Genoa, and Florence led the way in reaping the profits from price differentials in long-distance trade. Spices for the aristocratic luxury market and more mundane Syrian cotton for cheap, light fabrics were the most important imports from the Levant. In addition, the Italian cities brought raw materials from around the Mediterranean for industrial transformation and re-export as luxury goods – silk and woolen cloth, leather, furs, and glass; or they imported more humdrum commodities for local consumption: salt, wine, fish, cheese, butter, oil, flax, common dyes, non-precious metals, timber, and grain. The widening disparity between rich and poor from war-inspired, debasement-induced, population-loss inflations meant that the high-return luxury markets drove this trade to precocious heights, but at the same time, that demand was relatively inelastic and open to competitors once new products, wider markets, and lower prices took hold in the sixteenth and seventeenth centuries.

Rivalries in the eastern and western Mediterranean shaped the history of the rise and fall of these early European trading empires.[8] In the eastern Mediterranean, the island city of Venice acquired an overseas empire that included large colonial holdings on the Italian mainland, the Dalmatian coast, Corfu, Crete, Cyprus, and a strong role in Constantinople. With the fall of the Venetian-dominated Latin Kingdom of Constantinople (1204–61), the Genoese were able to move in decisively as slave traders and provide slaves from central Asia and the Caucasus for Mamluk military manpower needs in Egypt.[9] The Venetians and Genoese fought a series of inconclusive wars for over a century between 1257 and 1384; but, by managing to survive intact and tie their eastern trade to the Egyptian/Red Sea route to Asia, the Venetians won the long duel. The Genoese were never able to gain the same kind of state-centered control in their eastern Mediterranean and Black Sea strongholds at Pera, Kaffa, Tana, Chios, Cyprus, and Egypt as enjoyed by the Venetians, and Genoa's eastern trade declined to only 20 to 25 percent of that of Venice. The Genoese, for their part, suffered from internal demographic decline and civil strife, with some thirteen urban uprisings between 1413 and 1453, external wars especially the Hundred Years War (1337–1453), and intense foreign competition that disrupted their more important western trade. Because its small population base generated low local demand and few natural resources, the Genoese were not able to compete as a manufacturing center in the production and marketing of textiles (silk, cotton, and woolen cloth) with its western Mediterranean rivals Florence, Milan, Lyon, and Barcelona. With its eastern trade shrinking, its western trade in jeopardy, and less and less able to carry on an independent foreign policy (buffeted as it was between the Aragonese, the Milanese, and the French in the second half of the fifteenth century), Genoa turned more to its skills in banking and finance. In switching sides from France to Spain in 1528 during the Italian Wars, the Genoese gave Charles V a decisive naval advantage; and later from 1557 to 1627, the Genoese served as exclusive bankers to the Spanish empire in Europe and the New World.

In the northern European trading circuit that extended from the Low Countries through the Baltic and North Seas down the rivers of central and eastern Europe, Lübeck merchants took the lead from the mid-twelfth century. The Hanseatic League had become a formal association of towns by 1370 and eventually included as many as one hundred. The post-plague foundation grew out of four regional town-leagues: in the western Baltic led by Lübeck, Hamburg, and Bremen; in the eastern Baltic by Riga; in Prussia by Danzig and the Teutonic Order; and along the Rhine by Cologne. The Hanse exported primarily high-bulk, low-valued foodstuffs and raw materials (rye, barley, forest products, naval stores, copper, and iron) as well as Baltic high-value goods (beer, salt, and herring), and a few luxury items (furs, amber, and wax) from as far east as Novgorod and as far north as Bergen, to London and Bruges in exchange for woolen cloth and silver. As incursions into the German Hanse towns by Holland-Zeeland and English merchants challenged the Hanse monopoly and protectionism, Bruges and Ghent in the Low Countries and later Antwerp through the Brabant Fairs established Flanders as the urbanized center of the northern European trading circuit. In Flanders industrial production flourished and foreign products were transshipped: English woolens (which were dyed and dressed in the Flemish towns), south German metals and Rhineland products, and after 1500 Portuguese-Asian spices. The growth of the Antwerp market into a world market by the end of the fifteenth century gave way after the Dutch Revolt to Amsterdam; from the last third of the sixteenth century, Amsterdam, at the head of the century's most productive agricultural sector and booming industrial towns, became Europe's greatest staple market and financial center.

Economic cycles, conjunctures, and change

The path to northwest Europe's hegemony in the first stages of a global world economy was far from inevitable. Instead of a direct line of succession from Venice to Antwerp to Genoa to Amsterdam, we must understand the contingencies and discontinuities, the overlapping and intertwining of multiple nodes or the polynuclear clustering of commercial circuits in late medieval Europe.

Even before the plague of 1348, population pressures mounted as agricultural yields declined, little new arable land was available for new planting, rents increased, real wages fell, and famines became more common. Military expenses from increased warfare taxed already hard-pressed citizens, increased the public debt, and caused the English monarchy to default on its loans, which bankrupted the Florentine banking houses in the 1340s. After the plague, the decline of the Mongol Empire in central Asia and closure of the land routes to Asia, the rise of the Ottoman Turks in the eastern Mediterranean, the social dislocations that concentrated greater wealth in fewer hands, the decreased labor supply that led to peasants' and artisans' rebellions, the abandonment of hundreds of depopulated villages and the scurrying of displaced rural people to the towns, all contributed to a reconfiguration of internal power relations within the towns and of international relations between towns and states, to a reorganization of production and the profile of demand, and to a rethinking of values, confidence, and priorities.

Europe's internal restructuring as a consequence of the century-long crisis of the fourteenth century set the terms for development in the next economic cycle, which began in the third quarter of the fifteenth century. Despite the setbacks, the Hanseatic League expanded; German towns with large quantities of newly mined silver, such as Nuremberg and Augsburg, became financial centers; Portugal embarked on its explorations and expansion; and the Italian states, because of the absence of intruding foreigners, were free to establish new political and economic relationships. Agricultural productivity increased with the abandonment of marginal lands, income redistribution allowed for large expenditures from the new super-rich, workers' real salaries increased, and living conditions improved. Finally, an era of New Monarchies ruling over large, centralized states in England, France, and Iberia ushered in new economies of scale in both military affairs and commercial endeavors. (See the essays above by Edward Muir and below by Thomas Arnold.)

The sixteenth-century inflation that extended up to the 1640s, the so-called European price revolution, is, thus, really another name for economic growth and expansion. Monetary forces (the central European silver-mining boom from the mid-1520s, Portuguese imports of African gold, currency debasements, and the exponential increase in private and public credit) played an important role in this five- or six-fold price rise long before American silver shipments after 1570 greatly increased the European money supply. Demographic growth also played its part in the story, since prices rose because rising demand from the increased population and the increased money supply far exceeded real national income or the aggregate output of goods and services.[10] As a consequence, Holland and England gained with the relative decline of the Italian and south German, Spanish, and Antwerp markets.

Three new technologies of Chinese origin – the compass, gunpowder, and printing – transformed trade and transport in the sixteenth century as a new "world economy" (an *expanded* 60-day world) was established. From the thirteenth through the fifteenth centuries, technological changes in shipping, navigation, and armaments created the large, heavily-armed, full-rigged carrack as the dominating long-distance tool at the center of European trade, expansion, and empire. Ship design and production, through shipyard division of labor, sail and hull changes to allow exploitation of following or contrary winds in open ocean or coastal waters, improvements in instrumental or mathematical reckoning with the magnetic compass, water clock, astrolabe, portolan or naval chart, trigonometric tables, and sternpost rudder, and finally, artillery and gunpowder already developed in land and siege warfare, all contributed to the European maritime reconnaissance. Likewise, print culture – with the adaptation of Chinese technology for the appearance of paper in the thirteenth century, water mills to pulp rags into paper, and printing and moveable type by the mid-fifteenth century – so formative for the intellectual culture of the Renaissance, Reformation, and scientific revolution, found new markets: travel literature, accounts of overseas adventures, maps and atlases.[11] At the same time it facilitated business practices by greatly aiding the dissemination of news and information. "Asia in the making of modern Europe" is no exaggeration.[12]

How to explain European growth and innovation, its rise from marginal participation in the Asian-centered "world-economy," and how to determine whether the agrarian or urban sector led the transformation, has attracted serious attention, from Adam Smith (market expansion and the division of labor) and Karl Marx (specific economic, political, and legal changes creating new relationships between owners/controllers of the means of production and workers) up to the late twentieth century. The 1950s had the Sweezy/Dobb's debates on the "transition from feudalism to capitalism," the 1970s–80s Wallerstein–Brenner–Mendels/Kriedte models on world-systems, class structure, or proto-industrialization, and the 1990s research on consumption, women's work, and work experience as well as Asia-oriented comparisons and reformulations.[13] Very simply, if one assumes an evolving and expanding system rather than a cyclical or static one before the Industrial Revolution (1780–1850), the fifteenth/sixteenth-century growth cycle (1450/70–1620/50) can be seen as the first phase of a process that accelerated during the second phase (1620/50–1780/ 1800). During the first phase, which corresponds to the Renaissance in Italy and its spread beyond, there is general consensus that the Europeans narrowed the gap between themselves and Asia, but that from about 1600 to 1800 a rough parity existed among a number of "gunpowder empires" across Eurasia, from the English, Dutch, French, Portuguese, and Spanish in the West to the Ottoman Turks, Safavid Persians, Mughul Indians, Ming and Ch'ing Chinese, and Tokagawa Japanese. How the Europeans did it – whether through some endogenous advantages and absence of impediments or through some exogenous colonial extraction – has been hotly contested in two basic Eurocentric models. These emphasize either the quantitative benefits of available resources garnered through demography, ecology, and overseas accumulation (Jones) or the qualitative transformation of new mechanisms for accumulation through the emergence of efficient markets and property rights and of strong firms and institutions, either through class struggle (Brenner) or coercion and collusion (Wallerstein).[14] Whatever the line of argument one follows, the variables in the mix – land, labor, and capital – remain the same; but what unit led the transformation – the state, private enterprises, regions, or world-systems – is at issue. An alternative tradition from Max Weber's thesis on ideology, culture, or religion to explain the origins of capitalist mentalities seems much less viable today in light of what we now know about Europe's long economic gestation period, the similarities rather than the differences between Catholics and Protestants in trade, and the details of capitalist accumulation and market mechanisms in Asia.

The crisis or end point of this first phase of economic encounters and expansion in the world economy, the so-called "seventeenth-century crisis," is now understood to be a period (roughly 1620–80) of reconfiguration and consolidation. Ruinous wars, faltering public finances and overextended credit, failures and famines in agriculture, inflationary pressures from bullion flows, and cheaper goods from abroad led to an economic slowdown for Spain and Italy by the 1590s. With the independence of the United Provinces in 1609, the economic crisis of 1619–22 after a decade of uncertainty, and then the devastation of Germany in the Thirty Years War (1618– 48), the Mediterranean states experienced a relative decline *vis-à-vis* their former inordinate success and earlier economic dominance over the states of northwest Europe.

Contact, Conquest, and Colonization

The political-economic ties between Italy and Iberia long preceded the Spanish "conquest" of Italy in the sixteenth century, the subsequent Genoese "century" of financing the Spanish Empire, and the Mediterranean's relative decline in the seventeenth century. The late medieval/Renaissance story of the Iberian–Italian rise is grounded in commercial capital, African gold, the slave trade, the Reconquest of Muslim Iberia and the rim of Africa, exploration, exploitation, and exportation from the Mediterranean to the Atlantic world and beyond. The success of the two Iberian trade routes – Spanish to America and Portuguese to Asia – led to a conflation of the medieval trading circuits in the Mediterranean and the Hanse with a new, truly global world economy forming around the Low Countries at Antwerp.

Iberian–Italian models and experience

By the end of the thirteenth century, Aragonese conquests extended to an island empire of Majorca (1229), Ibiza (1235), Sicily (1282), Malta and Gozo (1283), Djerba and Kerkennah (1284–6), Minorca (1287), Sardinia (1290s), and in 1311 out to Athens with aspirations for Jerusalem: a stepping-stone network of maritime outposts that would serve as a model for later Atlantic expansion. At the same time, the Aragonese also expanded south to Valencia and Murcia to incorporate a Mediterranean land empire thought to be richer even than its Catalan homeland. Also during the thirteenth century, the Castilian Reconquest gained an Atlantic-facing empire that increased the Crown's territories by 50 percent as it metabolized Cordova and Seville and colonized Andalusia. In 1251 the Genoese were given commercial privileges and their own quarter in Seville, which would grow into the main entrepôt of the Genoese diaspora and Genoa's entry to the Atlantic. Genoese capital, commercialization, and experience with the establishment of a network of centers of production and exchange put the Genoese in competition and cooperation with the Catalans, Castilians, and Portuguese for the riches of North Africa. Wool and woolens dominated the early trade of the western Mediterranean, with gold, iron, saffron, pitch, canvas, and leather also important. Gold, above all, was the high-value commodity sought in the towns along the Maghrib coast, the northern terminus of Saharan caravans to the source of gold in the West African interior. Lured by gold, Mediterranean merchants seeking to secure a base at the other end of the Saharan gold road ventured into the Atlantic in the late thirteenth and early fourteenth centuries, where they reached the Canary Islands by the 1330s.

Bounded by the Azores in the north and the Canaries in the south, by the western island archipelagoes and by the Iberian and African coasts in the east, was a new zone of exploration, a kind of "middle sea" or "Atlantic Mediterranean." It became the focus for a new round of navigational experimentation and colonial expansion through the early fifteenth century. Portugal, which like Castile had grown dramatically (some 70 percent) during the thirteenth-century Reconquest, joined the competition with a pre-1339 joint Portuguese-Italian enterprise, the first chronicled expedition to the Canaries. With its political unification under the Aviz dynasty, independence from Castile in 1385, and fortified with an English alliance in 1386, Portugal exported wine, olive oil, citrus fruits, cork, salt, and salted fish to England and Flanders. In the first half of the fifteenth century under the mistakenly lauded Infante Dom Henrique, expanding trade and experiments in ship design led to Portuguese settlement in the Madeira Islands and the Azores, but also to failure in their primary objectives, conquest of the Canaries and the quest for the gold source in West Africa. From the 1440s, gold (17 metric tons shipped between 1470 and 1500 with another 19 tons by 1550), slaves (some 150,000 Africans sold into European slavery between 1450 and 1500), sugar, *malaguetta* pepper, and ivory dominated the Portuguese trade with West Africa and the Atlantic islands. A foreign commercial/industrial/financial elite who made the colonial economy possible – Genoese in Madeira and the Canaries, Flemish in the Azores – acted as middlemen between the Portuguese colonial island society's aristocratic lords and settler peasants. From the 1460s with the development of the Cape Verde Islands (and later in the 1490s on the islands of the Gulf of Guinea), the Genoese–Portuguese enterprise introduced a new model of colonial power, the slave-based plantation economy that linked slave traders and sugar planters in the importation of black slaves from West Africa for work in sugar production. Gold, slaves, and sugar were the motives and the motor of the Genoese-financed, Portuguese-controlled imperial expansion.

During the first half of the fifteenth century, the Aragonese Empire reached its greatest extent with Alfonso of Aragon's 1443 conquest of the Kingdom of Naples, which despite its loss on the division of Alfonso's states among his heirs, later provided the justification for the Catholic Kings Ferdinand and Isabella to invade Italy in defense of their Neapolitan Aragonese cousins. The Genoese Christopher Columbus sailed as a pirate in 1472–3 in the service of René of Anjou, the Angevin pretender who contested Aragonese kingship in Naples. In the following year, Columbus's Genoese roots took him to Chios in the eastern Mediterranean, but by 1474 he was fighting with the Portuguese against the Genoese off Cape St. Vincent, became a resident of Porto Santo in the Portuguese Madeira Islands in 1480, and visited São Jorge de Mina (Elmina), the Portuguese fort on the Gold Coast (Ghana) in 1483. Columbus unsuccessfully presented his proposed western voyage to the Portuguese king in 1484, later received similar rejection from the Catholic kings in Castile, and again was turned down by the Portuguese who lost interest after rounding the southern tip of Africa in 1488. With their Reconquest of Granada complete in January 1492, the Castilians finally commissioned Columbus that same month in order to catch up with their Portuguese rivals in gold and trade as part of their ongoing strategy for conquest of the Canaries (1478–96). Indeed, Columbus's letter on his return (February 15th, 1493) emphasized the hoped for commercial rewards: gold, slaves, spices, cotton, mastic, rhubarb, cinnamon and "a thousand other valuable things."[15]

Castilian arms soon established a series of Portuguese-like settlements as stepping-stones to wider conquest: Santo Domingo on Haiti (1496), Panama (1509) on to Nicaragua, Cuba (1511), Mexico (1519) on to Guatemala, the Yucatan, and Honduras, Peru (1534) on to Ecuador, Columbia, and Chile. But the real prize came as colonial settlement brought regular trade, with nearly a hundred ships sailing annually from Spain in the 1520s and increasing to twice that number of ships and four times the carrying capacity (because of larger ships) by the late sixteenth century.

From Vasco da Gama's 1497–9 voyage, meanwhile, the Portuguese realized their ambition to reach Calicut, the greatest spice market in the Indian Ocean, for pepper (85 percent of Asian exports to Lisbon in the first half of the sixteenth century), ginger (6 percent), cinnamon (2 percent), and other spices: nutmeg, cloves, and mace (6 percent).[16] Not content to share the Asian trade with other merchants, the Portuguese sought to create a monopoly through military force to exclude the Mamluk, Gujurati, Turkish middlemen and above all the Venetians from these profits – as much as 90 to 150 percent on pepper! A string of forts controlled trade along the coast of East Africa at Sofala (1505), along the western coast of India at Cochin (1503) and Goa (1510), at Malacca in the eastern straights (1511), at Hormuz in the Persian Gulf (1515), in Ceylon at Colombo (1518), and on Ternate in the Moluccas (1522). Aden in 1513 at the entrance to the Red Sea and the Venetian spice route through Ottoman Egypt was the only setback, so that later by mid-century the Venetians had recovered more than half of the European spice trade. Between 1500 and 1635, the Portuguese Cape route between Asia and Europe sent about seven ships of 400 to 2,000 tons annually from Lisbon to India and four in return.

On the second voyage to India in 1500, Pedro Álvares Cabral's thirteen-ship mission (ten ships outfitted by the king, three by Portuguese noblemen–Italian financier companies) sighted Brazil. Initially Brazil remained a small part of the early Portuguese enterprise by exporting the red dye-wood brazilwood, but it began to be colonized by Portuguese Atlantic islands settlers in response to French competition in the 1530s. The new colonists established a fast-growing, slave-labor, sugar-plantation economy, with the first sugar mill in 1533. The sensational story of sugar, like that of the quest for gold and spices, reveals how the first global world economy brought Europe, Africa, and America together as unequal partners in an interlocking system.

Exchange in the first global world economy

Sugar, although known in ancient and medieval times, did not become a European staple until its intensive production in the New World linked it with the newly introduced crops of coffee, tea, and chocolate – bitter drugs enhanced by sugar – as well as with the related imports of rum, molasses, and syrup.[17] In Brazil sugar production rose four-fold between the 1560s and 1610, when African slave labor (between 10,000 to 15,000 slaves brought in annually) was exploited in some 130 sugar plantations and 210 mills. When England entered sugar production in the West Indies in the 1640s, British sugar consumption grew exponentially. Although British population barely doubled by the end of the early modern period, sugar consumption grew twenty-five-fold between1650 and 1800, far more rapidly than the use of bread, meat, and dairy products.

The rise of sugar is part of the tragic story of what later in the eighteenth century developed into two well-known triangular trade networks: Britain shipped finished goods to Africa for slaves to be sold in the Americas where tropical commodities – especially sugar – were sent back to the mother country; and similarly, New England rum went to Africa for slaves sent to the West Indies where molasses to make rum was shipped back up to New England. The sharp juxtaposition of black Africans sold into Caribbean slavery to produce sugar and European free laborers working in mines and factories hooked on sugar-infused drugs for empty calories and cheap pleasure points to a well-nourished capitalist class reaping the profits of agro-industrial enterprise built on the back of human exploitation. Before 1700 over a million and a half African slaves had been brought to America; and by the slave trade's nineteenth-century abolition, some 12 million African slaves had been shipped to the Americas and 14 million east to Islam. While still a luxury at the end of the sixteenth century, sugar (like tobacco by the end of the seventeenth century) had been produced and exported by the Portuguese in a slave-plantation system that would serve as a forerunner to the triangular trade and a model to the Spanish, French, Dutch, and English.

Tobacco, introduced to Europe in the 1560s, was also initially a luxury good, whose market grew chiefly from its purported therapeutic powers and mutated from a cure-all to an all-consuming addiction.[18] When the price of tobacco plummeted 97 percent from 3 shillings to a penny per pound in the 1630s owing to increased supply, cheap tobacco was on its way to mass consumption. Slavery would take root in the Chesapeake in the 1660s and Virginia would become a slave society based on race by the 1680s and 1690s.

New World sugar and tobacco production and their slave-labor system fueled the expanding Atlantic economy, but silver and gold were the most valuable New World exports and the first global market commodities. The Americas provided 85 percent of the world's silver and 70 percent of its gold from 1493 to 1800. By 1650 some 181 tons of gold had been exported from the Indies in an uneven flow (the vast majority in the first half of the sixteenth century), and almost 90 times that amount of silver, 16,000 tons (with exports becoming more important after the great discovery at Potosí (Bolivia) in 1545 and at Zacatecas (Mexico) in 1546). With the discovery of mercury mines in Peru, the new mercury amalgamation method of refining silver caused silver production to triple after 1573 and then double again in the late 1580s. In 1611 Potosí's boom-town population of 160,000 inhabitants was the largest in the Americas. Simultaneously, a direct route linked Spanish America to Asia in the 1560s; Manilla was founded in 1571 and a convoy of "Manilla galleons" made annual voyages between Acapulco and Manilla. Throughout the seventeenth century, more than 50 tons of silver annually was exchanged via the Pacific route for Chinese silks and luxury goods. Bullion flows – American silver to Europe in support of Spain's Genoese creditors and its imperial wars as well as American silver to Asia and Asian gold to Europe – were primary drivers of the first world economy from the 1540s to the 1640s.[19] Divergent bimetallic ratios (the cheap production and ship-ment of American silver for sale at a higher price in China) rather than the oft-repeated erroneous explanation of a European trade deficit *vis-à-vis* Asia determined the silver bullion flows. Europe, then, was one axis in a four-cornered, not just a triangular trade, with arenas in Africa, America, and Asia.

During the early stages of the global world economy, non-bullion goods from the New World fell into two categories: high-value commodities (wine, oil, sugar, and later tobacco) and bulky, low-priced industrial raw materials (hides, Mexican cochin-eal – a red dye from insects, indigo – a blue vegetable dye, and exotic woods). Among these goods, only cochineal, native woods, and tobacco were indigenous New World products. Over time, other American contributions to the Columbian exchange would prove to be extremely valuable: potatoes, sweet potatoes, maize, chile peppers, tomatoes, cacao (chocolate), cassava, cinchona trees for quinine, peanuts, kidney and lima beans, pineapples, avocadoes, and papayas. Spanish colonial goods were intended to support, not compete with, the home economy, which in return sent finished products such as wine, liquor, textiles, and manufactured goods from Spain.

The circle of the Columbian exchange was completed by three Old World move-ments into the Americas: the devastation of disease, the immigration of people (both settlers and slaves), and the problematic conversion to Christianity. Hispaniola (Haiti), the site of Columbus's first large base, had an estimated population of 3.7 million in 1496, but only 250 native Americans still alive in 1540. Mexico, which may have had a pre-Conquest population between 20 and 25 million in 1519, had only one million Indians a century later in 1608; Peru's probable population of 9 million in 1520 had fallen to less than 700,000 Indians by 1620. Endemic European diseases, smallpox and measles above all, found no immunities among the native people, almost eradicated the Indian population; and a depopulated Americas made it easier for conquest and colonization. Migrants to Spanish America, 90 percent Castilian, numbered about 450,000 people between 1506 and 1650.[20] By 1650, the Spanish colonies had about half a million people who could pass as Spaniards, an equal number of acknowledged mixed blood, and nearly as many Africans living with the remaining 2 million Indians. Portuguese emigration to Brazil, Africa, the Atlantic islands and Asia from 1500 to 1640 has been estimated to be about 600,000 migrants, with about 100,000 to 150,000 residents overseas in the late sixteenth century, but only a very small number, about 15,000, resident in Asia by 1600.[21] Escape from poverty, the call to command, status, or service were among the motives that led these voluntary migrants to leave their old society or to be attracted by the prospects of the new. Without question, the supply of labor was the central problem of the colonial economy, and solutions ranged from forced labor of the natives on a model inherited from the indigenous societies themselves to the importation of African slaves, a monopoly in Spanish America controlled by the Portuguese on and off from 1573 to 1676.

Finally, Christian conversion in Asia and America was directly tied to the world economy. The Jesuit mission in China and Japan, financed in the last quarter of the sixteenth century by its participation in the silk trade from China on the annual "black ships" from Goa via Macao to Japan, may be the most famous Asian example. In the Americas, although complicity in Spanish-Conquest cruelties and colonial policies of Indian forced labor or slavery may have been the majority position, the Dominicans were the first to denounce and condemn native exploitation on Hispaniola in 1511.[22] The result of disease, migration, and proselytism in the Americas was the destruction of its people and the creation of a new complex, multiracial society.

Colonial systems in theory and practice

Two models of colonial administration emerged from the late Middle Ages: a Venetian statist model with colonial settlements and local government control, and a Genoese trading-post/entrepôt model with strong military coercion through strings of forts. In practice, these simplistic models often became mixed forms, depending on time and place. In Asia, the Portuguese fortress model was implemented differently west of India and east of Malacca. Later in the Americas, the settlement model would have significant variants between Spanish and English according to their laws and customs of possession.[23] The Spanish arrived with the native population at its height, and because the Spanish saw their mission as commercial and religious, the Spanish Conquest aimed to rule the natives, control their labor, and Christianize them. The English, on the other hand, arrived over a century later in less densely populated areas, and they were interested in a territorial conquest to gain land for themselves, their commercial enterprises, and against their European rivals.

The fifteenth-century Portuguese expansion around Africa saw three permutations of the Venetian and Genoese models: in North Africa, a network of control fortresses that held trade together by military force in a constant state of war that was later applied in the western Indian Ocean; on the Atlantic islands, an agrarian territorial colonization and settlement that was later exported to the sugar, slave-plantation economy of Brazil; and in Guinea, a coastal network with a more commercial and peaceful profile and less territorial occupation, settlement, or direct control of the means of production that was later employed east of Malacca.[24] Portuguese imperial ideology also changed over time so that the early sixteenth-century crown monopoly ("monarchic capitalism") and a messianic crusading impulse both gave way by the 1580s to the king's disengagement from commerce in favor of trading *fidalgos*, and German-Italian consortia of mercantile capitalist middlemen. Portuguese New Christians (Jews and crypto-Jews) also played significant roles in imperial trade and later in the rise of Amsterdam. By the end of the sixteenth century, the Portuguese Empire, then under Philip II (who rejected the idea of moving his capital from Castile to Lisbon), showed increased interest in creating territorial holdings in Asia.

Spanish imperial practice in the Americas followed the statist model and was grounded in territorial rule in the viceroyalty of New Spain (Mexico) and the viceroyalty of Peru with about 200 colonial municipalities exercising administrative and legal control. Direct authority over the native people was exercised through two institutions. Under the *encomienda*, a method of providing a pension/reward for royal service first developed in the Canary Islands, Indian villages were "entrusted" to Spanish settlers, who protected and oversaw the Christianization of Indians in exchange for their labor and tribute. The *repartimiento* used forced Indian labor due to the Crown in private enterprises deemed essential for the public good, and eventually, after 1609, used such Indian forced labor for the mines and public works. From the beginning, private enterprise and royal concessions controlled Spanish colonial commerce, although the king took his royal fifth off the top. Hotly contested by circles within the Spanish court, the theory of universal monarchy and legal claims to the American imperium were vexed issues that had profound implications for conquest and settlement; but, whatever the moral conclusions or victories enacted as in the 1542 New Laws providing for Indian protection and rights, practice trumped theory, as the pressure for Indian labor and American bullion only increased over time.[25]

Extra-legal trade (unregistered production or unregistered remittances of treasure) probably amounted to 10 percent above registered trade. Smuggling such as that of Potosí silver brought down from the Andes to Atlantic ports and exchanged for smuggled African slaves would not have been unusual. Privateering was a common threat to the Spanish and Portuguese monopolies. Englishmen such as Drake and Hawkins ranged from the Guinea coast to Brazil and the Caribbean, the Dutch attacked Portuguese bases in the Moluccas, Amboina, and the Banda Islands, Piet Heyn captured the Spanish silver fleet in 1628, the French temporarily established themselves in Rio de Janeiro from 1555 to 1560 and in Florida from 1562 to 1565, and in the Huguenot republic of La Rochelle also engaged in privateering. These exploits presaged the northwestern European powers' entrance into overseas empire in the Mediterranean, Asia, and the Americas.

Dutch maritime superiority rested on their newly developed all-purpose cargo ship, the flute, a fully-rigged carrack without cannon, a much faster, more maneuverable, smaller-crewed ship built for trade, while the English entered international competition with joint stock trading companies, which pioneered a new kind of colonialism that accumulated vast capital resources and operated on strict commercial rationality. English new draperies – cheap, coarse, light semi-worsted fabrics – conquered textile markets in Spain, Italy, and the Levant, which paved the way for English take-over of the Mediterranean carrying trade. English success in the Mediterranean spurred interest in founding the English East India Company (1600) to break into the spice trade, while the Dutch, who had been disrupting the Portuguese Asia monopoly since 1595, unified a number of different Dutch companies in their own East India Company (VOC) in 1602. The Dutch set up a trading base in Java in 1619, gained exclusive trading rights in Japan, occupied Formosa, captured the Ceylon coast, took Malacca in 1641, and with the English replaced the Portuguese in Asia (except in Goa and Macao).

In the Americas, the Dutch and French established trading stations, while the English followed the colonial settlement model. The French founded forts in Nova Scotia and finally at Quebec in 1608, a small foothold for trade in furs. The Dutch set up trading posts at Albany in 1624 and New Amsterdam the following year, but the small trading colony was taken over by the English in 1664 and renamed New York. By the mid-seventeenth century, the French settlements had about 300 inhabitants; to the south in the Hudson valley, the Dutch numbered about 4,000. In Brazil, the Dutch could not hold their captured Portuguese territory in the northeastern sugar-producing areas (1624–54), but they took and held Elmina in 1637 for a slaving base on the Guinea coast. From 1623, the Dutch along with the French and English were able to seize islands in the West Indies to compete with the Portuguese in the triangular trade of European goods for African slaves for sugar back to Europe. The English settlements were established by chartered commercial companies on three models: the first permanent settlement in Virginia in 1607 by a joint stock company financed by merchants for exportation of New World products; proprietary colonies such as Maryland (1633) and the West Indies (1630s) by court favorites who made grants of land in exchange for cash or rent from settlers who came to farm their own land; and the Massachusetts Bay Company by religious foundations such as the Plymouth colony of radical Protestants (1620), who likewise came to settle and farm their own land. By 1650 the English colonies were a small foothold of 42,000 whites and 1,100 blacks in comparison to the vast empire of Spanish America, but they were poised to take off in the second phase of the world economy, from the 1660s, with Caribbean sugar, Virginia tobacco, spices from India, and intra-Asian commerce leading the way.

Renaissance colonial practice and its rationalizing ideology should not pass without comment. An ethnocentric comparative ethnology denigrated new peoples and cultures as inferior,[26] and such European preconceptions and prejudices determined policies imposed through force and fear. (See the essays of Matthew Restall and Linda Darling above.) Yet misunderstanding cannot excuse the militant regimes that were enforced.

Nor can the end results of the first stages of the world economy justify the means of their establishment. While Adam Smith may have been correct in his 1776 judgment that, "the discovery of America, and that of a passage to the East Indies by the Cape of Good Hope, are the two greatest and most important events recorded in the history of mankind,"[27] the still contested inequalities between the First and Third Worlds leave the pursuit of justice and the problem of an uncertain impact open-ended. In economic terms, the value of growth and complexity (is bigger better; and what are its limits?), the meaning of affluence (is there an equilibrium between needs and wants?), and the importance of incentives, competition, and taste (how do we understand production, distribution, and consumption?) must all be re-examined. In socio-political terms, the problem of inequality highlights the tension between individuals and the community, vying castes or classes, and the monarchy and society. In religious terms, the embarrassment of riches may have been the Dutch Protestant motive; but much earlier, in the medieval economic expansion, Franciscan poverty and the indictment of riches created equally ambivalent mentalities. Wealth derived from trade, religious scruples over usury or the "just price," the scapegoating of Jews, and the contradiction of forced conversions or forced labor had to be debated and rationalized. And philosophy was closely tied to religion, so that as old cosmographic certainties were disproved and the diffusionism of biblical stories such as the expulsion from the Garden of Eden or Noah's universal flood were questioned, the nature of the American Indians, the degeneration or progress of civilization, the existence of a universal natural law or only relativist principles had to be addressed. Utopian dreams of the Terrestrial Paradise and of a new Arcadia had to give way to the bitter realities of New World peoples and colonial exploitation. The ambiguities and responsibilities of imperium are a Renaissance legacy.

Most descriptions of the origins of the modern world economy carry with them an ideological commitment or policy implications, for the problems of our time are never far from view. Steve Stern's quincentenary essay "Paradigms of Conquest," welcomes such ethical engagement, because this "darker side of the Renaissance" – slavery, colonization, and world hegemony – was forged, as much as Machiavelli's politics, in the crucible of power and struggle.[28] European dominance in the first stages of the world economy during the economic cycle of 1450–1650 grew out of the late medieval crisis of agricultural productivity, urban demography, the division of labor, the rise of the centralized state, commercial and financial capitalism, and resulted in the seventeenth-century divergence between northern and southern Europe. Competition for the control of land, labor, and capital drove the Renaissance European states to contact and conquests in Africa, America, and Asia, with the janus-face of empire: "expansion abroad, security of property at home; plunderers, slavers and extortioners abroad, law-abiding businessmen at home."[29] The imposition of European market mechanisms and mentalities on subject peoples was much more than the comparative advantage of transaction costs, market-driven growth, ecological constraints, or colonial extraction. The first stages of a world economy also embodied the range of Renaissance dilemmas and divisions; it was as much a result of fortune as force, as much about the past as the future, and reveals as much about ourselves as about others.

NOTES

1   Epstein, *Genoa*, pp. 181–2.
2   Fernández-Armesto, *Before Columbus*, pp. 127–8.
3   Larner, *Marco Polo*, pp. 31–43.
4   Jan de Vries, "Population," in Brady et al., *Handbook* I, pp. 13–15.
5   John H. Munro, "Patterns of Trade, Money, and Credit," in Brady et al., *Handbook* I, pp. 147–95.

6 Wallerstein, *The Modern World-System*, I, pp. 16–17.
7 Abu-Lughod, *Before European Hegemony*, pp. 32–8.
8 Kedar, *Merchants in Crisis*, p. 76.
9 Epstein, *Genoa*, pp. 101–2, 267–70, 281–3.
10 Munro, "Patterns of Trade, Money, and Credit," in Brady et al., *Handbook* I, pp. 172–5.
11 Rudolf Hirsch, "Printed Reports on the Early Discoveries and Their Reception," in Chiappelli, *First Images*, II, pp. 537–58.
12 Lach, *Asia*.
13 Duplessis, *Transitions*, pp. 3–13.
14 Pomeranz, *The Great Divergence*, pp. 3–27. See Jones, *European Miracle* and Wallerstein, *Modern World-System*.
15 Jane, *Selected Documents*, no. 65, pp. 2–19.
16 Sanjay Subrahmanyam and Luís Filipe F. R. Thomaz, "Evolution of Empire: The Portuguese in the Indian Ocean during the Sixteenth Century," in Tracy, *Political Economy*, p. 309.
17 Mintz, *Sweetness and Power*, pp. 57–73, 197.
18 Earl J. Hamilton, "What the New World Gave the Economy of the Old," in Chiappelli, *First Images*, II, p. 862.
19 Ward Barrett, "World Bullion Flows, 1450–1800," in Tracy, *Rise of Merchant Empires*, pp. 224–54.
20 Magnus Mörner, "Spanish Migration to the New World prior to 1810: A Report on the State of Research," in Chiappelli, *First Images*, II, pp. 737–82.
21 Sanjay Subrahmanyam and Luís Filipe F. R. Thomaz, "Evolution of Empire," in Tracy, *Political Economy*, p. 318.
22 Hanke, *Spanish Struggle* and Pagden, *Fall of Natural Man*.
23 Seed, *Ceremonies of Possession*.
24 Sanjay Subrahmanyam and Luís Filipe F. R. Thomaz, "Evolution of Empire," in Tracy, *Political Economy*, pp. 298–305 and José Jobson de Andrade Arruda, "Colonies as Mercantile Investments: The Luso-Brazilian Empire, 1500–1808," in ibid., pp. 360–73.
25 Pagden, *Lords of All the World*, pp. 47–73.
26 Pagden, *Fall of Natural Man*.
27 Elliott, *Old World*, p. 1, quotes Adam Smith, *Wealth of Nations*, ii, p. 141.
28 Stern, "Paradigms of Conquest" and Mignolo, *Darker Side*.
29 Thomas A. Brady Jr., "The Rise of Merchant Empires, 1400–1700: A European Counterpoint," in Tracy, *Political Economy*, p. 160.

REFERENCES

Abu-Lughod, Janet L., *Before European Hegemony: The World System AD 1250–1360* (New York: Oxford University Press, 1989).

Brady, Thomas A. Jr., Oberman, Heiko A., and Tracy, James D., *Handbook of European History 1400–1600: Late Middle Ages, Renaissance and Reformation*, 2 vols. (New York: E. J. Brill, 1994–5).

Chiappelli, Fredi, ed., *First Images of America*, 2 vols. (Berkeley: University of California Press, 1976).

Duplessis, Robert S., *Transitions to Capitalism in Early Modern Europe* (Cambridge: Cambridge University Press, 1997).

Elliott, John H., *The Old World and the New, 1492–1650* (Cambridge: Cambridge University Press, 1970).

Epstein, Steven A., *Genoa and the Genoese 958–1528* (Chapel Hill: University of North Carolina Press, 1996).

Fernández-Armesto, Felipe, *Before Columbus: Exploration and Colonization from the Mediterranean to the Atlantic, 1229–1492* (Philadelphia: University of Pennsylvania Press, 1987).

Hanke, Lewis, *The Spanish Struggle for Justice in the Conquest of America* (Boston: Little, Brown, 1965).

Jane, Cecil, ed., *Selected Documents Illustrating the Four Voyages of Columbus*, 2nd. ser., nos. 65 and 70 (London: Hakluyt Society, 1930–2).

Jones, E. L., *The European Miracle: Environments, Economies and Geopolitics in the History of Europe and Asia*, 2nd edn. (Cambridge: Cambridge University Press, 1987).

Kedar, Benjamin Z., *Merchants in Crisis: Genoa and Venetian Men of Affairs and the Fourteenth-Century Depression* (New Haven: Yale University Press, 1976).

Lach, Donald, *Asia in the Making of Europe*, 3 vols. (Chicago: University of Chicago Press, 1965).

Larner, John, *Marco Polo and the Discovery of the World* (New Haven: Yale University Press, 1999).

Mignolo, Walter D., *The Darker Side of the Renaissance: Literacy, Territoriality, and Colonialization* (Ann Arbor: University of Michigan Press, 1995).

Mintz, Sidney W., *Sweetness and Power: The Place of Sugar in Modern History* (New York: Elizabeth Sifton Books–Viking Penguin, 1985).

Pagden, Anthony, *The Fall of Natural Man: The American Indian and the Origins of Comparative Ethnology* (Cambridge: Cambridge University Press, 1982).

——, *Lords of All the World: Ideologies of Empire in Spain, Britain and France c.1500–c.1800* (New Haven: Yale University Press, 1995).

Pomeranz, Kenneth, *The Great Divergence: Europe, China, and the Making of the Modern World Economy* (Princeton: Princeton University Press, 2000).

Seed, Patricia, *Ceremonies of Possession in Europe's Conquest of the New World, 1492–1640* (Cambridge: Cambridge University Press, 1995).

Stern, Steve J., "Paradigms of Conquest: History, Historiography and Politics," *Journal of Latin American Studies* 24, Supplement (1992), pp. 1–34.

Tracy, James D., ed., *The Rise of Merchant Empires: Long-Distance Trade in the Early Modern World, 1350–1750* (Cambridge: Cambridge University Press, 1990).

——, *The Political Economy of Merchant Empires* (Cambridge: Cambridge University Press, 1991).

Wallerstein, Immanuel, *The Modern World-System*, vols. 1–2 (New York: Academic Press, 1974–80).

FURTHER READING

Chaudhuri, K. N., *Trade and Civilisation in the Indian Ocean: An Economic History from the Rise of Islam to 1750* (Cambridge: Cambridge University Press, 1985).

——, *Asia Before Europe. Economy and Civilisation of the Indian Ocean from the Rise of Islam to 1750* (Cambridge: Cambridge University Press, 1990).

Cipolla, Carlo M., *Before the Industrial Revolution: European Society and Economy 1000–1700*, 3rd edn. (New York: Norton, 1994).

Crosby, Alfred W., *The Columbian Exchange, Biological and Cultural Consequences of 1492* (Westport, CT: Greenwood Press, 1972).

Davis, Ralph, *The Rise of the Atlantic Economies* (Ithaca, NY: Cornell University Press, 1973).

PART IV

Cultural Worlds

CHAPTER SEVENTEEN

The Subcultures of the Renaissance World

DAVID C. GENTILCORE

Introduction: Ways of Understanding Culture

From Peter Burke's milestone work on popular culture to the more recent decon-struction of the subject, the last decades of the twentieth century saw a plethora of studies which sought, albeit in very different ways, to describe "the social creativity of the so-called inarticulate."[1] Culture – popular or otherwise – was certainly no mono-lith in the period covered by this volume. In sociological parlance, it could be seg-mented or stratified in different ways. Somewhere at the center was a "shared" or "dominant" culture, in which the various groups making up society participated, or to which they reacted, depending on the circumstance. Social structure was thus intim-ately related to culture, though not in a determinant fashion. But how to depict these "segments" and "reactions"? How to describe their relationship to the larger whole? I have opted for the culture-subculture model as a means of structuring this essay. The model underscores the crucial role played by the social sciences in the historical study of everyday culture. If "culture" allows people to make sense of the world and their actions, then "subculture" reflects a perceived sense of self-sufficiency, even isolation, from the rest of society and culture by a specific group. Such a group shares an organized set of social meanings related to the main culture. The culture-subculture approach enables us to refer to these wider sub-groupings within a broader culture, while preserving other kinds of sociocultural divisions – geographical, linguistic, economic, religious, ethnic – which had clear meaning for those who experienced them. Subculture models posit either societies made up entirely of overlapping subcul-tures, or consisting of a single dominant culture with a few isolated variants.[2] My view of the Renaissance world, as surveyed in the following pages, contains features of both, with strong, pronounced subcultures shaped by an increasingly forceful and intrusive dominant culture. It is during the centuries covered by this volume that the dominant culture became just that. Ironically, perhaps, it is this process that also provides historians of the period with such rich archival material.

Subcultures become most evident to the historian in their contacts or clashes with the dominant culture; reconstructing what they shared with the latter is often more difficult. As for the dominant culture, it was neither unified nor monolithic, but is represented in this essay in many different forms and guises. The culture-subculture model allows us to understand the processes of cultural differentiation, modification, domination or subordination that characterize the Renaissance world. It also puts the stress firmly on the individual, within an environment that is pluralistic and fluid. Subcultures were as much a question of how people perceived themselves as how they were perceived by others. We can explore how men and women imparted value to their world – or to the plurality of worlds any given individual might inhabit. To adopt Steve Rappaport's formulation, these are the "worlds within worlds" that constituted Renaissance society. We can reconstruct the ways in which group members developed fellow-feeling and kept their distance from others, through a system of mental attitudes and patterns of thinking, perceiving, and acting – Pierre Bourdieu's "habitus." The model also serves as a means of imposing some kind of order on the fascinating, though at times bewildering, variety of recent work included under the labels "popular," "oral," and "everyday" culture.

The Rural World

The most dominant subculture in Renaissance society was that of the agricultural world. By anyone's guess, peasantries made up something like three-quarters of the European population. Peasants have too often been categorized as not really part of the cultural world at all. They have been seen as silent, timeless, bound to the unchanging cycles of nature. This, in contrast to the cultural, creative activities of even the most wretched artisans in the towns. Anglo-Saxon historiography in par-ticular has tended to regard peasant culture as residual, locating it either "under-neath" or on the periphery of the dominant culture. Piero Camporesi, borrowing from Russian literary theorists such as Mikhail Bakhtin and Vladimir Propp, seems to invert this perception. In his 1981 contribution to Einaudi's *Storia d'Italia*, Cam-poresi identified in agrarian culture the original, archaic culture of Europe, the substratum upon which all culture rested. For Camporesi the "agrarian cultural paradigm" was coherent, original and autonomous; it served as a fertile reservoir from which medieval popular culture drew its structure, motifs, and figures. He criticized Burke for regarding popular culture as the culture of the towns, which engulfed the countryside as part of their territory and exported their culture to it. Rather, it was the country that predominated over the town, with its ways of thinking, imagining, and communicating.

We may chafe at Camporesi's rosy picture of the later Middle Ages. We may reject the fact that, for all Camporesi's sympathy with peasant culture, he still seems to regard it as passive and submissive, rather than as a fluid entity capable of acting and reacting to suit its own needs and circumstances. Despite all this, it does bring into relief the neglect of rural culture by English-speaking scholars. Research has focused on the socioeconomic characteristics of Europe's peasantries. This, at least, has the virtue of reminding us of the difficulty in defining who was a peasant. While some scholars have had little difficulty in identifying an ideal peasant "type" for the purposes of historical study, definitions have usually striven to be open-ended so as to account for the wide variety. Historians seem agreed with the anthropologists that peasants constituted a "part society." That is to say, peasant communities were not autonomous – either politically, economically, or culturally – but a part of the wider society. Nevertheless they could be relatively coherent on a cultural level, by shaping cultural imports to suit their own needs. Research has rightly focused on the nature of the relationship with the wider society – in terms of power relations, or the social, economic, and cultural links that existed and defined peasant life.

The "peasant village" has been the focus of research. Historians of Golden Age Spain, much like the playwrights of the period, have cherished the egalitarian image of the village council, where "citizens" met at the ringing of the church bells to take decisions affecting the life of the village. In reality, village life was not nearly as democratic as depicted. As early as the late thirteenth century Spanish lords had succeeded in binding peasants to the soil or in exacting arbitrary and oppressive dues. Moreover, the closer we look, the more difficult finding compact, self-enclosed peasant communities becomes. In large swathes of southern Europe, one cannot think of the rural world as separate from the urban environment. Most small towns were outgrown villages, essentially agrarian towns, with close links to other similar communities. Southern European peasants, for instance, were the first commuters, traveling long distances from their town or village before dawn, to their scattered patchwork of fields, and then back again after nightfall.

The tendency has been to emphasize peasant traditionalism and immobility, at the expense of adaptability and change. Peasants remained closely subject to the constraints of the natural environment. As a result, it has often been suggested, they tended to undergo history rather than act it. Certain continuities in ritual behavior might be used in support of this notion of an unchanging peasant mentality. However, when we look at religious belief and practice, we find that villages were part of a shared identity expressed in local religion. According to William Christian, individual communities, large and small, took vows to build a shrine to a certain saint, keep collective fasts, and give charity; but they did this according to a common pattern. Urban and rural worlds met in the religious feasts that formed part of the liturgical cycle of most towns. Rural areas were dotted with sacred spaces, sites imbued with sacred power, as were the towns. Country and town dwellers alike privileged certain occasions of the year, like Easter or St. John's Eve, as especially powerful, and certain events in life as particularly meaningful, singling them out as rites of passage, such as the churching of women. These ritual moments were part of a shared culture. If these persisted, even in the wake of confessionalization, it was because they "met a perceived religious need, and reflected a consistent attitude towards a world".[3] This was not for want of trying on the part of the reformed ecclesiastical authorities. For example, inhabitants of "fringe" areas in Catholic Europe underwent missionary activity, to bring them into line with Counter-Reformation orthodoxy. The point is that these continuities may be just as important to the historian as signs of change and adaptation.

While looking for signs of peasant immobility and passivity, historians were also more concerned with uncovering evidence of peasant hardship and exploitation than with developments within rural society itself. Where once peasant attachment to their plots of land was seen as a given, we now see that, in certain circumstances, peasants could willingly and knowingly enter the land market. Women especially might engage in what has been called "proto-industry," such as taking in spinning to do at home for town-based merchants. Peasants might put off marriage as a way of regulating population growth. And they might revolt.

Breaches in the everyday, paradoxically, allow us to penetrate into the partly closed world of the European peasantries. Anthropology has proved helpful here. By studying the kinds of peasants involved in revolts, the experiences and expectations which influenced them, their behavior during them, and the models used by them to master conflict it is possible systematically to work out peasant attitudes. Large-scale peasant uprisings occurred in Iberia, France, England, and Germany. As the largest and perhaps best organized mass peasant movement in this period, the German Peasants' War of 1525 has attracted considerable scholarly attention. Peter Blickle has seen the regional revolts which made it up as a full-scale political revolution against seigneurial and state authority, derived from the evangelical teachings of Luther and Zwingli. The events point to the strength of the peasants' communal traditions and their ability to achieve, however temporarily, religious, political, and economic goals.

Smaller, more localized uprisings have their historical uses, too. The model for the close analysis of a single rebellion remains Emmanuel Le Roy Ladurie's study of the 1580 events in and around the town of Romans, southeast of Lyons. What most excited the author was the way social conflict existed at different levels and was expressed in different ways. In the historical analysis, the action of a minor insurrection may prove less illuminating than the way the parties involved sought to negotiate their respective positions. As Thomas Cohen has pointed out in his study of a small village uprising in 1558, this could be done from positions of weakness as well as strength. The peasant community's weakness became its strength, in this "calculus of jeopardy."[4] Cohen's work reveals that peasants could be shrewd, hard-nosed negotiators with the "outside," "literate" world – with which they were in close contact, it turns out. Moreover, peasant notions of a communal past were not confined to distorted visions of a distant age. The narrative of past events – what James Fentress and Chris Wickham have called "social memory" – allows us a way of studying how oral culture "worked." This is true even when viewed through the prism of written testimony. Cohen's short study of the mountain village of Rocca Sinibalda, following seigneurial depredations of the mid-sixteenth century, reveals the villagers to have a sense of time, as history.[5] The villagers' accounts were rooted in the village topography and structures, which formed their "memory theater." In the same way, as Ann Carmichael has suggested, in community memories of plague epidemics it might be physical artifacts that provided tangible evidence of a previous plague.

If large-scale peasant rebellions did not occur in Italy, it may have been because peasants had other ways of expressing their grievances. On the day-to-day level all peasants might resort to various forms of trickery: mock ignorance or passive disobedience. But they were also adept at using the existing legal and political channels. Finally, there were illegitimate responses, like social banditry. On state frontiers, as in the mountains between Genoa and France, "banditry" persisted because of its close association with smuggling. These bandit groups, it turns out, were usually organized networks of real and fictive kin, probably set up during the later Middle Ages. They straddled political borders and pooled skills and resources to engage in what they considered to be mountain trade. They formed networks, with their own internal hierarchies, which structured their members' lives, gave rise to intermarriage and feuding, but which were also used to settle disputes between members and with the outside world. Their identity was constructed in response to state offensives during the later sixteenth century, which labeled the mountain trade in which these groups engaged as smuggling. In this case, the subculture has become a counter-culture: in conflict with society at large. Beggars and thieves were likewise suspected by contemporaries of forming a counter-culture, an underworld – though an urban one – with its own organization, rituals, and jargon. Real thieves and beggars were probably more prosaic. (See the essay below by Linda Woodbridge and the essay above by Gregory Hanlon.)

Peasant communities were neither closed nor homogeneous. "Peasant" villages were themselves complex societies, with their own elites. Indeed the study of village communities reveals the difficulties inherent in determining the boundaries of subcultures. The village tavern-keeper, the miller, the schoolmaster were essentially different from the others. Larger villages would have had a limited range of craftsmen (coopers, cartwrights, saddlers, blacksmiths), notaries, medical practitioners. Every rural community had its herder: someone charged with looking after the villagers' sheep, pigs, or cattle. Shepherd culture could indeed be quite distinctive, in areas where pastoralism was widespread. Shepherds might have their own residential and work patterns, their own festivities, associations, and dress. Add to this the fact that shepherds were often rejected by the rest of society, as men without fixed abode (for much of the year) often were, to say nothing of their close connection to animals (themselves seen as somewhat mysterious), and we have the makings of a distinctive subculture.

The rural world was evidently much more complex than this brief discussion has so far allowed. From a religious standpoint, a Christian peasant community might find itself next door to a Muslim one, as in Valencia (see below). The reality of confessionalization meant that Catholics and Protestants might live alongside one another, not merely village to village but also house to house. Whole Alpine valleys might be inhabited by Protestant groups, like the Waldensians of Savoy, their self-governing villages forming a kind of rural ghetto. From an occupational standpoint, in a few parts of Europe mining was the main occupation of rural inhabitants after agriculture. Miners might make up their own villages, often in agriculturally marginal areas, far from towns. The iron ore miners at Rancié in the French Pyrenees, for instance, regarded themselves as a single extended family. As this brief survey suggests, the rural world was far from unchanging and undifferentiated. It might be as pluralistic and as integrated into the wider culture as the world of the towns.

"National" and Religious Subcultures

Then as now, ethnicity and religion often seem to be inseparable. They are also obvious instances of subcultures seeking to co-exist within a larger, in this case, "host" culture. The varying cultural processes of assimilation, appropriation, and rejection are at their most historically visible. This is true of both endogenous (home-grown) and exogenous (imported) subcultures. One group that arrived in Europe during this period, and yet remained on the margins of European society throughout, is the Gypsies. If ever there was an understudied group, this is the one. Certainly, historians face a lack of direct primary sources. But this objection has been raised with regard to virtually every grouping discussed in this survey, and the obstacles have been, at least partially, overcome. We know much more about European reactions to Gypsies than the Gypsies themselves, as Bronislaw Geremek has pointed out. At first they were welcomed as pilgrims, apparently obliged to wander for a specific period by the Pope to expiate their supposed apostasy to Islam while in "Egypt." But as they remained nomadic, legislation against them became stricter in the course of the sixteenth century. Both state and Church aimed for the forced acculturation of Gypsies; failing that, expulsion, which only served to reinforce their nomadism and marginality. In Spain, Gypsies were widely suspected of blasphemy, irreligion, and magical practices. However, they rarely came before the Inquisition, owing – Maria Sánchez Ortega has suggested – to a combination of their impenetrable language, culture, and mobility. In some cases Gypsies did abandon their nomadic way of life, settling in towns and taking up trades, yet the details of this process remain unclear.

If we know little about the culture of the Gypsies during this period, we know considerably more about another group of "aliens within": the Jews.[6] As with the Gypsies, it is easier to gauge the attitudes of the wider community towards them than to ascertain how they viewed themselves. It is suggestive, however, that when western European Jews depicted themselves in art – such as when they illuminated Hebrew manuscripts to show scenes from Jewish life – they resembled the Christians around them. Of course, one would not expect Jews to depict themselves with the canonical hats, yellow or red badges, and hooked noses of the Christian stereotype; but, apart from the use of religious objects like prayer shawls, Jews seem to have seen themselves as largely indistinguishable from their Christian contemporaries.

Enforced segregation meant that many Jewish communities were internally self-governing, responsible for tax-collecting, education, and so on. They might have a fully articulated social structure, as in Spain before the definitive expulsion of 1492; they might form their own "estate," with its own rights and rules set down in legislation, as in the Commonwealth of Poland-Lithuania after 1400; they might function similarly to Christian guilds, with considerable self-governance but subjected to the authority of the city council, as in the Holy Roman Empire from the sixteenth century. As such, Jewish communities provide a fascinating test-case for the study of subcultures in all their ramifications, including issues like variety within the subculture and relations with the dominant culture.

Subcultures can have internal subdivisions and this was true of Venetian Jews. Venice's eventual two ghettos were a microcosm of European Jewry. In 1589 the Venetian Senate recognized three main "nations" of Jews in the city: the "Germans," who were by this time effectively Italian, the "Ponentines," who came from Spain, Portugal, or the Low Countries, and the "Levantines," from the eastern Mediterranean. This could give rise to conflict, for example between existing inhabitants and Sephardic immigrants. Their very differences – in origins, dress, and language – led to a certain degree of integration. Thus Jews in Venice and elsewhere in northern Italy tended to use Italian as their lingua franca.

Were Jews any different from other ethnic groups? After all, most larger European cities had their foreign quarters, their "nations." But whereas these groups bound together voluntarily for mutual protection or economic convenience, the Jews were confined by compulsion. This enforced segregation is best understood in the context of a society that thought in terms of "estates" or "orders," with each having a well-defined place and role. The ongoing attempt to define and regulate this ordered view of the world, by both Church and state, was a characterizing feature of the Renaissance world (a process to which we shall return in the conclusion of this essay). Jews could be accommodated in a Christian community so long as they were manifestly in it but not of it.

Evidence of contacts, friendships, and partnerships across the religious divide suggest a different reality. It could affect devotional practices on both sides, in which case the communities might come in for much opprobrium for tolerating the "contamination." As Elliott Horowitz discovered, when the rabbi and Talmudic scholar Obadiah of Bertinoro visited Palermo in 1487, he was scandalized to find himself venerated by his co-religionaries almost "as a Catholic holy man," common people competing for fragments of his clothing as a relic. Our best evidence of the daily lived experience of Jews and their relations with the wider society comes from court records of the time. Thomas Cohen has studied a single Roman criminal case from 1551, prompting him to ask, How did the Jews of Rome experience the ambiguities of their position? To what extent did they feel themselves a world apart, and to what extent members of a larger Roman world?[7] During the Jewish festival of Purim – which the accused Roman Jews referred to as "the week of our carnival" – a group of them were able to pass themselves off as the city's night watch and, in the true swaggering fashion of the Roman *sbirri* (constabulary), cheat and badger a poor rope-maker. Cohen sees the minor prank on trial as evidence of how, at least at special times and under special conditions, Roman Jewry could treat its Christian neighbors as subject with them to a common morality. There is a sense of belonging to a shared community. At the same time, the accused Jews, while in the cells, communicated to one another using Hebrew words so as not to be understood by their jailors. They continued to belong to two worlds, possessing a dual identity.

The most systematic study of such documents has been conducted by Brian Pullan in his work on Jews in Venice. If the tendency has been to focus on groups, his contribution is fundamental in allowing us to appreciate how individual men and women made cultural choices. This is most evident in the case of those known disparagingly as Marranos: converted Jews, and their descendants, suspected of practicing Judaism in secret while remaining Christian on the surface. Persecution was sometimes the result. Rather than seeking to generalize about Marrano behavior, Pullan finds it more useful to pinpoint and describe a range of individual experiences. He focuses especially on those who opted for the path of ambiguity and vacillation, presenting the cases of ten different individuals accused of crypto-Judaism before the Venetian Inquisition. Renaissance society disliked and feared what it could not classify. The same could be said of another group: the many European Christians who converted – some quite freely – to Islam in north Africa or the Near East. For Europeans they were simply "renegades" (indeed the origin of the word). Those who chose to return to Catholic Europe were subjected to investigation and faced a bureaucratic ritual of reconversion. For our purposes, both of these sorts of accounts – involving converted Jews, on the one hand, and Christians, on the other – bring to the fore the importance of subculture(s) in the individual's search for identity within a wider society composed of worlds within worlds. They are invariably tales of temporizing and hesitation, of repentance and relapse, of long voyages of exploration (both within the individual and across the world). They emphasize the confusion inherent in individual life choices, and the way people could inhabit several worlds at once, bridging separate cultures, even acting as mediators between them.

In addition to converts to Islam, Europe had its own endogenous Muslim population. Historians of Spain have likewise made use of the records of repression to explore Muslim society and culture. After their forced conversion to Catholicism by the 1520s, and prior to their expulsion after 1611, the degree to which they managed to maintain their literary culture, language, use of the Koran, and so on, varied a great deal. It was almost complete in Valencia, where their communities – segregated in small rural hamlets – remained largely intact. There was little mixing with the dominant society of the towns or Catholic villages. In Aragon, they lived alongside Spanish Christians. Their religion remained intact, but in much else they were acculturated into the dominant Christian culture. There had been cultural syncretism here even before conversion, facilitated by economic integration (among artisans and merchants) and high literacy. At the other end of the spectrum we have the communities of Castile. Displaced and reduced to the status of serfs, their culture underwent disintegration. The once vibrant tradition of Islamic medicine, which had formed its own medical subculture in medieval Spain, faced the same cultural disintegration as the rest of Morisco culture under the onslaught of Counter-Reformation attitudes. Moriscos – as Spains's converted Muslims and their descendants were known – nevertheless sought to adapt as best they could. When the authorities forbade the circumcision of newborn infants in an attempt to put an end to the Muslim practice, Morisco communities responded simply by delaying the age of circumcision, rendering the legislation ineffective. A loophole in the law became a means of reinforcing group identity. In the process, once again, a subculture became a counter-culture. That is, it expressed not only difference and distinction, but active opposition to the dominant culture.

The question of cultural assimilation, of changing identity and conflict over the course of several generations is also relevant to the "national" minorities that were a common feature of Europe's cities and towns. The "nations" present in a town had a recognized status. The reactions of these exogenous cultures to new, dominant host cultures – as a result of which they became subcultures – could vary according to local circumstances. These could cause it to harden, soften, or otherwise modify their identity over the generations. What mechanisms served to "insulate" the group, in the sense of enabling its members to resist assimilation, at least for a time? Group identity was clearly strengthened when nationality and occupation coincided – especially when the product of the latter was much in demand. Of all urban immigrants, silk workers – such as those from Lucca during the fourteenth century – seem to have displayed the greatest internal cohesion in terms of provenance, social status, and residential distribution within host cities. The phenomenon of migration in the Renaissance world has been studied more by economic than cultural historians. Looking at the Italian *Nationi* present in Antwerp, Paola Subacchi has suggested the existence of two patterns of migration. Merchants involved in long-distance trade and financial activities tended to have a circular migration pattern. They did not settle permanently anywhere and returned to their home city – Genoa, Lucca, Florence, Milan – from time to time. By contrast, the migration of the skilled and semi-skilled workforce led to a sedentary exercise of the trade or craft. These artisans settled close to the premises in which they worked; they might marry locally and tended to integrate into the life of the host city. At the same time they maintained the friend-ship, kinship, and patronage networks based on their regional origin in Italy.[8] Italian immigration to France exhibited the same mixture of integration into, indeed success within, the host society and the maintenance of ties to the place of origin and with compatriots in the adopted town.

Internal disputes within the host society could force the national subculture to examine its allegiances and take up sides. In the French city of Rouen the forty mostly Castilian families who arrived in the years 1480–1540 assimilated quickly and com-pletely. During the Religious Wars they rejected Catholic Spain for Protestant Rouen, even when they did not abandon their Catholicism (though some did this too). The example of Spanish communities abroad also points to the fact that strange things can happen within the subculture, unknown in the land of origin (where it is the host culture). The adaptation of the subculture may presage what is to come. In a study of the Spanish confraternity of the Most Holy Redeemer in Rome, Thomas Dandelet has shown how the Spaniards in sixteenth-century Rome were also part of a process of nation building. In their practices of collective representation, national self-constitution and imagining, the smaller Iberian "nations" present in the city began to merge. In the fifteenth century the Castilians, Aragonese, and Portuguese each had their own pilgrimage churches in the city and they had functioned as separate groups. By 1580 the "natione di Spagna" was composed of Galicians, Castilians, Catalans, Andalusians, and Portuguese. It had its single confraternity, which brought the disparate groups together. Nevertheless identity continued to function on several different levels. When the wealthy Portuguese merchant Antonia Fonseca died, the beneficiaries of his will included a mixture of Roman, "Spanish," and Portuguese churches and charitable institutions. At the same time, Rome was also home to working-class Spaniards. They were present in all the city's districts and practiced a wide variety of trades. This reiterates the main theme of this section: the possibility that individuals might inhabit more than one subculture at once, in this case those of ethnic group and occupation, or move from one to another at different points in their lives.

The Subcultures of Work

Work-related migration undoubtedly contributed to a sense of group identity. The centrality of work in a person's life prompts the question of whether occupation alone could give rise to subcultures. Trade guilds might help give craftsmen, artisans, and shopkeepers a common culture. This meant a large part of a city's population: one-fifth of Amsterdam's population belonged to a craft, and one-third of Dijon's, while 70 percent of Venice's population consisted of artisans and their families. All a town's guilds would come together at certain times of the year, to mark important dates in the festive calendar of the town. At the same time, artisan culture could splinter, both vertically and horizontally. On the one hand, a town's master artisans, regardless of trade, might perform similar social and economic functions, transcending guild boundaries and self-consciously distinguishing themselves from other groups, such as journeymen. On the other hand, each craft can be said to have had its own culture, in the sense of possessing its own particular craft-related skills and traditions. These would be transmitted orally within the shop, passed down from master to apprentice as closely guarded secrets. Guild prerogatives, jurisdictions, customs, and specializations were written into their statutes. As this suggests, it was not an exclusively oral world. Orality mixed with literacy. This intermingling is most evident in the "notarial culture" of Italy and the rest of Mediterranean Europe. Artisans, who may not have been able to write, nevertheless made frequent use of notaries to record their proceedings, exchanges, accounts, and membership lists. They – like the inhabitants of rural villages discussed above – were aware of the power of collective organization and a legal system based on Roman law. Furthermore, some artisans were numerous, prosperous, and literate enough to become self-consciously distinct, like silk weavers. For them, the workshop could become the place where the latest Protestant ideas were read out and discussed.

Occupational subcultures were probably at their strongest and most cohesive in some highly specialized and cyclical industries where skills were kept within closely knit kin networks: Alpine mining, iron-making, shipbuilding, high quality masonry. Migration, as we have just seen, might be another factor in reinforcing cultural boundaries. A third factor was the tendency of artisans, in town, to live and work in the same area, in clustering patterns. In Bologna, silk workers lived in what was virtually an "industrial district," under the watchful eye of the authorities. Robert Davis has used the expression "company town" to describe the community of shipbuilders and their families of the Venetian Arsenal. The Arsenal brought together the members of various guilds associated with shipbuilding. The *arsenalotti*, as the workers and community were known, became self-conscious of themselves as a worker group with their own traditions, privileges, and status within the larger society. Their community, which surrounded the Arsenal, was relatively isolated and self-sufficient, to the extent that it formed an urban village. But in order to gauge just how typical such a workers' subculture was, Davis admits, we need to know more about other worker communities – in shipyards, foundries, mining, and other large-scale, state-run manufactories.

The difficulty in gauging the significance of occupational subcultures lies in trying to understand the place that the practice of a trade had in an individual's life, and the role of different spheres of belonging: gender, age, geographic origin, religion, and so on. Guild membership was probably never an individual's total identity. Nor did the guilds necessarily bring together all those involved in the same craft. They had long ago ceased being egalitarian associations of masters. Guilds thus increasingly differentiated, rather than united, the world of work. This is evident in the increasing restrictions against women, the numerous demarcation disputes between different aspects of the same trade, and the hierarchical structure within guilds. In some parts of Europe, journeymen – most of whom would never become masters – formed their own associations. These organized religious activities and provided assistance to members. As a result of their own mobility as workers, they eventually forged bonds that transcended local communities. In France these networks of wandering journeymen were known as *campagnonnages*. The set networks around the country that journeymen could follow in search of work may have helped create a national journeyman subculture.

Other groups on the fringes of settled life add further dimensions to the pluralistic culture of the Renaissance world. The sailors' subculture has been perhaps the most studied. This may be out of proportion to their relative numbers, but it does serve to reinforce the increasing importance of transoceanic commerce from the mid-sixteenth century. Sailors had a dual identity, straddling the land and the sea. Mariners from places as diverse as Seville, Amsterdam, London, or Genoa shared certain common cultural denominators. People who spent many months away from their homes necessarily had a perception of the family and neighborly ties different from that of non-sailors. They could escape the rules and norms of that little world on land. But evidence also suggests that society aboard ship tended to be a microcosm of society ashore, with its complex hierarchies and distinctions. The seamen's subculture gave shape to, and was shaped by, their everyday lives aboard. It was fluid, in the sense that its members could come and go. The same could be said of soldiers, as the work of Frank Tallett has shown. One would expect the element of subculture to be most pronounced among companies of mercenaries. For instance, the Swiss mercenary companies, so much a part of battles in this period, achieved a well-developed corporate sense of identity. They were self-governing and egalitarian, and acquired the reputation of forcing battle against an employer's wishes in order to profit from the spoils (a necessary supplement to their pay), or, conversely, of holding back when they were not paid. Like the everyday life of sailors, the soldiers' subculture was formed out of adversity and risk. Both groups were known for their profanity and irreligion; devotion was a matter of obtaining sacred protection in the face of specific situations. The soldier's mental world was evident in their jargon, composed of technical terms, curses, and patter, with words drawn from a variety of European languages. The latter element was indicative of the internationalism of the professional soldier. Whether this ever reached the linguistic status of a separate patois, comprehensible only among the community of military men, is, however, debatable.

The Subculture of Women

The occupational subcultures outlined above all had some degree of gender segregation. This could vary a great deal even within occupations. In small, family-run mines, for instance, women might have a central role, whereas the place of women in large-scale mining enterprises, involving wage labor, was far more complex and peripheral. Gender relations were sustained and shaped by culture, just as culture was shaped by gender. (See the essay by Elissa Weaver above.) In this penultimate section I would like to reformulate Joan Kelly's landmark query – did women have a Renaissance?[9] – and ask if women had a subculture.

There is no doubting the predominance of patriarchal and misogynistic notions during this period. Gender lines were more boldly drawn during the Renaissance and in the wake of the Reformations, with both positive and negative ramifications for women. As has been shown for Counter-Reformation Seville, women and men were supposed to operate within separate "spheres." However, research has found that if women were subordinate to men, it was subordination of a limited kind.[10] Patriarchal prescriptions were modified by negotiation and accommodation, as the study of daily lived experience has revealed. The contribution of women to the maintenance of health and the treatment of illness continued, although it was increasingly marginalized. In the Renaissance world, as in most societies, women ran many or most of the key moments of the life cycle, especially birth and death. The wife was also manager of the household and was responsible for the health of its members. (See the essays by Mary Lindemann and Guido Ruggiero below.) Moreover, by helping her husband or by taking on paid work of her own – however menial and badly paid, and even if done at home, alongside other domestic burdens – a woman might achieve a measure of independence.

Certain situations might result in a matriarchal exercise of authority and control. This could serve to reduce – just as it might increase – the formation of a distinct female subculture. In port towns, the wives of sailors and high-seas fishermen might have to support their families for months, even years on end, while husbands were away at sea. In the coastal villages of northern Portugal this role extended to the merchandising of the catch and the ownership of ships. In one Portuguese fishing community in 1580 almost all the bakers, grocers, oven-keepers, sardine-counters, and salt-measurers were women. Whole Alpine villages were likewise emptied of their male populations by seasonal migration, leaving the women in charge of day-to-day affairs. When their menfolk failed to return, their widows became household heads in name too. Indeed in any European town most of the women listed as household heads or as having an occupation would have been widows. In Florence, women household heads engaged in a wide variety of economic activities. Some widows had the chance to carry on the trades of their deceased artisan husbands. We should not make too much of the supposed freedom of widows as heads of households, however. Their mere presence in society was fraught with difficulty and ambiguity. Any woman living alone was suspect, but a solitary widow was a threat to the honor of not one family but two. Remarriage was seldom an option – certainly much less of one for women than for men. Moreover, for most widows, trying to make ends meet was the first priority.

There were other types of female-centered household. In some communities, two or three poor, single women might choose to live together in all-female families. So did prostitutes, especially in large cities where they tended to be concentrated in a particular district. This was a "female territory," a world dominated by women, providing them with some scope for social and psychological maneuver. However, in her study of prostitutes in fifteenth- and sixteenth-century Rome, Elizabeth Cohen found them to be rather more integrated into the neighborhoods in which they lived, but with little by way of male kin. Roman prostitutes lived alone, with other prostitutes, with their children, with other working women, with their mothers. Finally, the nunnery may also have provided the setting for a female subculture, but one that was increasingly mediated by men.

The behavior of women diverged from prescribed patterns outside closed walls too. This is where evidence for a female subculture is strongest. The possibility has been articulated most clearly by Bernard Capp, who has studied how ordinary women could create their own social networks and social space. Most women had supportive networks of female relations, friends, and neighbors. Women's lives were never tied wholly to the home; their lives revolved equally around the street, the well, the marketplace, the washing-place, the bread oven. Rural women had their winter evening spinning bees and *veillées*, largely (though by no means exclusively) female networks facilitating shared work and social exchanges. Women had their own work songs, to accompany spinning, the grinding of grain, the gathering of olives. When it came to giving birth, they were invariably assisted by the midwife, along with a small group of other local women. Daily social interaction fostered "female public opinion," gossip and insult being powerful weapons in face-to-face societies where reputation was a highly valued commodity. Women often took part in riots over grain or bread prices, enclosures, common rights, and so on. Women's social memory was distinctive too. Despite their role in riot and demonstration, it tended to be less "public" than that of men, more oriented around the home and neighborhood. There was, to return to Capp, "a semi-separate female domain, a subculture which existed uneasily and at times almost invisibly alongside the dominant, masculine culture of the age."[11] Given the numbers involved, it might be more apt to refer to it as a "complementary" culture. In any case, like all subcultures, its boundaries were fluid; individuals occupied more than one according to circumstance and need. Nor did it apply equally to all levels of society. Some women, like those of high social status, seem to participate in the female subculture hardly at all, while Morisco women in Aragon might be said to inhabit several subcultural groupings. They carried out their domestic routines inside houses which were physically separate from the Old Christian parts of mixed villages, and often connected with each other in one gigantic labyrinth. At the same time, they interacted with Christian women at various public places. This example serves to remind us of the complexity of the cultural experience in the Renaissance world.

Patterns of Change

The Renaissance world was a society of orders, estates, and categories. From an anthropological perspective, the roles, status, and place of all individuals in this complex society were delineated by "symbolic lines and boundaries" which brought "order into experience."[12] Religious difference was sometimes tolerated, but became increasingly the object of persecution during the sixteenth century. Otherwise, groupings were generally tolerated as long as they stuck to their allotted and officially sanctioned place within the dominant society. The processes whereby these limits and boundaries were established, reinforced, redrawn, or allowed to fade was a defining characteristic of social and cultural relations in the Renaissance world. At the same time, subcultural boundaries were never set in stone; rather, they were in a constant state of flux. We can only explore the nuances of such cultural borrowing if we look at culture as a whole, as I have attempted to do in this chapter.

However, by exploring popular, everyday, and oral culture from the standpoint of the culture-subculture model there are many legitimate topics that have had to be neglected. Nothing has been said about youth, for instance. Despite rich evidence of youth socialization and interaction, even insubordination, there does not seem to have been a youth subculture in the way we might see it today. Nor have I had much to say about sexuality. And while it could be argued that the gay experience today constitutes a subculture, the same could not be said for Renaissance practices. These, Michael Rocke has argued, tended to be part of the fabric of mainstream male life. Sexuality could certainly have extensive cultural implications – not least the increasingly moralizing attempt by the dominant culture to regulate it during our period. And, like other sociocultural factors – such as age, gender, religion, rank – it might even form the basis of significant cultural elements. But in order to amount to a subculture there had to be some systematically interrelated set of social and cultural factors, rather than just one. These had to include structural factors in some way, culminating in the existence of the "group." The latter might vary from actual organization or corporate status, to a looser sense of common identity and belonging.

Such factors are at their most apparent in the group's place *vis-à-vis* the host or dominant culture. Subcultures were not created equal. While the Spanish "nation" in Rome was influential and well connected, bolstered by its close links with the powerful home country, Gypsies enjoyed no such support. At the level of the individual, some people – like sailors and soldiers – might choose their subculture, or their time and place in it; others had it more or less thrust upon them, as in the case of those belonging to religious minorities. The different subcultures explored in this survey were engendered by, or came into contact with, different faces of the dominant culture. Economic and power relations could lead to the formation and continuation of a subculture (peasants, artisans), as could acts of civic or religious repression (Gypsies, Jews, Moriscos). Enforced marginality could engender a sense of common purpose among the marginalized. As mentioned at the outset, this was the period when the dominant culture became so. The plural "dominant cultures" might be more appropriate, however, given the variety in the dominant culture throughout Europe. Nor is it always clear where the dominant culture ends and a subculture begins. Certain elements of the dominant culture could even be analyzed in subcultural terms. The Society of Jesus is one such group. Whether we choose to interpret the wider movement in terms of the "reform of popular culture,"[13] the "civilizing process,"[14] or "social disciplining,"[15] the culture-subculture dynamic comes down to a question of power, its distribution, and exercise. This was not a wholly effective or unitary process, nor was any one group able completely to control cultural processes. But a dominant culture did emerge. The groupings explored above reacted in a variety of ways to it, some accepting or acquiescing, others rejecting and resisting. I have sought to survey how historians have depicted the processes, differentiation, and subordination inherent in some of this, even when they have not been specifically concerned with exploring subcultures. If I have said little about the dominant cultures in this essay it is because they would merit a study of their own. They are aptly described, in various guises, elsewhere in this volume.

NOTES

1 Burke, *Popular Culture*; Harris, *Popular Culture*; Davis, *Society and Culture*, p. 122.
2 Clarke, "Sub-culture."
3 Scribner, "Impact," p. 326.
4 Cohen, "A Long Day."
5 Cohen, "Social Memory."
6 Bonfil, "Aliens Within."
7 Cohen, "Mysterious Coil of Rope."

8   Paola Subacchi, "Italians in Antwerp in the Second Half of the Sixteenth Century," in Soly and Thijs, *Minorities.*

9   Kelly, "Women."

10 Amussen, "Gendering of Popular Culture."

11 Capp, "Separate Domains," p. 139.

12 Douglas, *Natural Symbols*, p. 50.

13 Burke, *Popular Culture*, pp. 207–18.

14 Elias, *Civilizing Process*, pp. 443–543.

15 Schilling, "Confessional Europe"; Hsia, *Social Discipline.*

REFERENCES

Amussen, Susan, "The Gendering of Popular Culture in Early Modern England," in *Popular Culture in England, c.1500–1850*, ed. Tim Harris (London: Macmillan, 1995) pp. 48–68.

Bonfil, Robert, "Aliens Within: The Jews and Anti-Judaism," in *Handbook of European History, 1400–1600*, 2 vols., ed. Thomas A. Brady, Heiko Oberman, James D. Tracy (Leiden: E. J. Brill, 1994–5), vol. 1, pp. 263–302.

Burke, Peter, *Popular Culture in Early Modern Europe* (Aldershot: Scolar Press, 1994).

Capp, Bernard, "Separate Domains? Women and Authority in Early Modern England," in *The Experience of Authority in Early Modern England*, ed. P. Griffiths, A. Fox, and S. Hindle, (New York: St. Martin's Press, 1996), pp. 117–45.

Clarke, Michael, "On the Concept of 'Sub-Culture'," *British Journal of Sociology* 25 (1974), pp. 428–41.

Cohen, Thomas, "The Case of the Mysterious Coil of Rope: Street Life and Jewish Persona in Rome in the Middle of the Sixteenth Century," *Sixteenth Century Journal* 19 (1988), pp. 209–21.

——, "A Long Day in Monte Rotondo: The Politics of Jeopardy in a Village Uprising (1558)," *Comparative Studies in Society and History* 33 (1991), pp. 639–68.

——, "Social Memory as Festive Therapy in Village Politics," *Histoire sociale: Social History* 24 (1992), pp. 291–309.

Davis, Natalie Z., *Society and Culture in Early Modern France* (Stanford: Stanford University Press, 1975).

Douglas, Mary, *Natural Symbols: Explorations in Cosmology* (London: Barrie and Rockcliff, 1970).

Elias, Norbert, *The Civilizing Process*, I: *The History of Manners*, II: *State Formation and Civilization*, trans. E. Jephcott (Oxford: Blackwell Publishers, 1994).

Harris, Tim, ed., *Popular Culture in England, c.1500–1850* (London: Macmillan, 1995).

Hsia, R. Po-Chia, *Social Discipline in the Reformation: Central Europe, 1550–1750* (London: Routledge, 1989).

Kelly, Joan, "Did Women Have a Renaissance?," in *Women, History, and Theory: The Essays of Joan Kelly* (Chicago: University of Chicago Press, 1984), pp. 19–50.

Schilling, Heinz, "Confessional Europe", in *Handbook of European History, 1400–1600*, 2 vols., ed. Thomas A. Brady, Heiko A. Oberman, and James D. Tracy (Leiden: E. J. Brill, 1994–5), vol. 2, pp. 641–81.

Scribner, Robert, "The Impact of the Reformation on Daily Life," in *Mensch und Objekt in Mittelalter und in der frühen Neuzeit: Leben-Alltag-Kultur* (Vienna: Verlag der Österreichischen Akademie der Wissenschaften, 1990), pp. 315–43.

Soly, Hugo and Thijs, Alfons, eds., *Minorities in Western European Cities (Sixteenth–Twentieth Centuries)* (Rome: Institut historique belge de Rome, 1995).

FURTHER READING

Ankarloo, Bengt and Henningson, Gustav, eds., *Early Modern Witchcraft: Centres and Peripheries* (Oxford: Clarendon Press, 1990).

Briggs, Robin, *Communities of Belief: Cultural and Social Tension in Early Modern France* (Oxford: Clarendon Press, 1989).

Brown, Judith and Davis, Robert, eds., *Gender and Society in Renaissance Italy* (London: Longman, 1998).

Christian, William, *Local Religion in Sixteenth-Century Spain* (Princeton: Princeton University Press, 1981).

Cruz, Anne J. and Perry, M. E., eds., *Culture and Control in Counter-Reformation Spain* (Minneapolis: University of Minnesota Press, 1992).

Farr, James, *Hands of Honor: Artisans and Their World in Dijon, 1550–1650* (Ithaca: Cornell University Press, 1988).

Fentress, James and Wickham, Chris, *Social Memory* (Oxford: Blackwell Publishers, 1992).

Gentilcore, David, *From Bishop to Witch: The System of the Sacred in Early Modern Terra d'Otranto* (Manchester: Manchester University Press, 1992).

——, " 'Adapt Yourselves to the People's Capabilities': Missionary Strategies, Methods and Impact in the Kingdom of Naples, 1600–1800," *Journal of Ecclesiastical History* 45 (1994), pp. 269–96.

——, *Healers and Healing in Early Modern Italy* (Manchester: Manchester University Press, 1998).

Ginzburg, Carlo, *The Night Battles: Witchcraft and Agrarian Cults in the Sixteenth and Seventeenth Centuries*, trans. J. and A. Tedeschi (Baltimore: Johns Hopkins University Press, 1983).

Goubert, Pierre, *The French Peasantry in the Seventeenth Century*, trans. I. Patterson (Cambridge: Cambridge University Press, 1986).

Kaplan, Stephen, ed., *Understanding Popular Culture: Europe from the Middle Ages to the Present* (Berlin: Mouton, 1984).

Klapisch-Zuber, Christiane, *Women, Family, and Ritual in Renaissance Italy*, trans. L. Cochrane (Chicago: University of Chicago Press, 1985).

Mackenney, Richard, *Tradesmen and Traders: The World of the Guilds in Venice and Europe* (London: Croom Helm, 1987).

Medick, Hans, "Village Spinning Bees: Sexual Culture and Free Time among Rural Youth in Early Modern Germany," in *Interest and Emotion: Essays on the Study of Family and Kinship*, ed. H. Medick and D. Sabean (Cambridge: Cambridge University Press, 1984), pp. 317–39.

Muchembled, Robert, *Popular Culture and Elite Culture in France, 1400–1750*, trans. L. Cochrane (Baton Rouge, LA: Louisiana State University Press, 1985).

Naphy, William and Roberts, Penelope, eds., *Fear in Early Modern Society* (Manchester: Manchester University Press, 1997).

Pumfrey, Stephen, Rossi, Paolo, and Slawinski, Maurice, eds., *Science, Culture and Popular Belief in Renaissance Europe* (Manchester: Manchester University Press, 1991).

Rappaport, Steve, *Worlds within Worlds: Structures of Life in Sixteenth-Century London* (Cambridge: Cambridge University Press, 1989).

Rocke, Michael, *Forbidden Friendships: Homosexuality and Male Culture in Renaissance Florence* (New York: Oxford University Press, 1996).

Safley, Thomas and Rosenband, Leonard, eds., *The Workplace before the Factory: Artisans and Proletarians, 1500–1800* (Ithaca, NY: Cornell University Press, 1993).

Scott, Tom, ed., *The Peasantries of Europe from the Fourteenth to the Eighteenth Centuries* (London: Longman, 1998).

Scribner, Robert W., *Popular Culture and Popular Movements in Reformation Germany* (London: Ronceverte, 1987).

——, "Is a History of Popular Culture Possible?," *History of European Ideas* 10 (1989), pp. 175–91.

Truant, Cynthia, *Rites of Labor: Brotherhoods of Campagnonnage in Old and New Regime France* (Ithaca, NY: Cornell University Press, 1994).

Wilson, Adrian, "The Ceremony of Childbirth and its Interpretation," in *Women as Mothers in Pre-industrial England: Essays in Memory of Dorothy McLaren*, ed. V. Fildes (London: Routledge, 1990), pp. 68–107.

CHAPTER EIGHTEEN

High Culture

INGRID D. ROWLAND

The period we know as the Renaissance marked the transition between the feudal society of the Middle Ages and the modern nation-state, between the scholastic Latin culture of medieval universities and the vernacular national cultures of their modern counterparts, between courtly chivalry and nationalist neoclassicism; in short, its high culture, and a high culture there definitely was, developed in an atmosphere of constant and challenging flux. Renaissance high culture's chief driving force was a movement to revive ancient Latin language and aesthetics, what contemporaries called "humane studies" (*studia humanitatis*) and later scholars have called humanism; its chief seedbed of development was the city, and its chief participants were not just the landed aristocracy who had ruled the medieval world, but also, and importantly, the sharp-witted, well-traveled urbanites who gradually garnered influence and authority from Italy to the Baltic to the distant shores of the New World. And like many a progressive movement before and since, the humanist movement began first with a penetrating look at what had gone before.

Humanism

The word "humanism" does not occur before the early nineteenth century. The Italian word *umanista*, however, sprang up at the same time that scholars began to identify the study of grammar, rhetoric, poetry, history, moral philosophy, and politics as *studia humanitatis*, "humane studies" or liberal arts, in the belief that such a course of instruction would provide particularly useful training for participation in civic life. From the outset, the *studia humanitatis* served a dual role in Renaissance society. As a distinctive educational plan, "humane studies" were instrumental in cementing ideas of citizenship, of human progress, of national and personal identity, of a precise sense of placement in time, space, and history. But the means by which *umanisti* arrived at these innovative achievements was, ironically, a self-conscious attempt to revive the past.

The past that especially concerned Renaissance humanists was the past of the ancient Greco-Roman world, and probably for good reason. The problems faced by these great trading powers of the ancient Mediterranean often suggested analogies with the problems facing the cosmopolitan cities of the same regions in the thirteenth and fourteenth century: how to balance the turning of a profit with the living of a moral life, how to balance wealth and taste, how to parlay wealth into influence and status, what to read, how to deal with foreign cultures. By the thirteenth century, such ancient arts as the writing of letters (*ars dictaminis*), eloquent public speech, and the governing of small city-states had acquired what seemed to people of the time a fresh new relevance to their own situations, most conspicuously, perhaps, in Italy, situated as it was in the center of the Mediterranean and exposed to a cornucopia of influences from the countries with which it was compelled to deal as a result. Italian merchants had established trading colonies on the coasts of North Africa and Dalmatia, on the islands of Crete and Samothrace, in Asia Minor. Against this favorable urban and cosmopolitan background, however, the humanist movement was effectively given its recognizable shape by the efforts of a single writer, a man of prodigious imagination and energy, Petrarch (Francesco Petrarca, 1304–74). Born in Arezzo to an exiled Florentine notary, Petrarch spent most of the first half of his life in Provence, where his father and he both worked at the papal court, which had been transferred to Avignon for political reasons and would not return to Rome until the 1420s. At 16, however, he was sent by his father to study law at the University of Bologna, and there he would stay for six years, reading ancient authors such as Cicero and Vergil rather than the ponderous legal texts that were supposed to occupy his attention. What distinguished Petrarch from his contemporaries and from slightly earlier writers like Dante (1265–1321) was the single-minded intensity of his engagement with the ancients, pursued first with the enthusiasm of a rebellious student, and then with the zeal of a genuine vocation. If Dante's *Inferno* had already featured the ancient Roman poet Vergil as his guide to the underworld and presented a moving series of dialogues between the Italian poet and the long-dead Roman he so admired, Petrarch's sense of connection with ancient authors compelled him to address them still more personally, actually writing them letters, in which he sent his greetings as a grateful reader and lamented with disarming urgency the fact that such friends as Cicero could not share his own joy in his Christian faith. Petrarch's sensitivity to the ancient world was no less physical than imaginative: he visited Rome and wrote vividly about how it felt to stand amid the ruins of the Forum, which by the fourteenth century had acquired the unglamorous name of "Campo Vaccino" – the "cow pasture." In Rome and everywhere else he traveled among the former domains of the Roman Empire, he collected ancient coins and other physical relics as lovingly as he gathered together manuscript texts of his beloved authors. His broad-ranging imaginative ability, his voracious reading, the sheer magnitude of his own writings, and their quality, exerted an immediate effect on his contemporaries. He was, quite simply, the most exciting writer of his age.

Petrarch's acute sensitivity to literary style prompted him to emulate the Latin of the ancient authors rather than the very different Latin of his own day – the Latin of the law books that so repelled him as a university student. Everyday spoken Latin, mingled with local dialects in every corner of the vast Roman Empire, had long ago developed into the variety of local vernaculars that we now identify as the Romance languages. At the same time, however, the more stable Latin of scholars, lawyers, doctors, and bureaucrats had also created new words to meet new situations, and invented new forms of poetry, based on stress and rhythm rather than, as in the ancient world, on the length of vowels. Petrarch maintained that these changes to the Latin language had largely come about because of the barbarian invasions that began to destroy the Roman Empire in the fifth century of the Christian era: events like the sack of Rome by Alaric and the Visigoths in 410, and the overthrow of the Emperor Romulus Augustulus in 476. In order to restore Latin to its pristine splendor, therefore, Petrarch began to examine surviving monuments and literary texts in hopes of retrieving the essence of ancient Rome.

Like most writers, Petrarch was also an avid reader, a book lover who collected manuscripts of ancient texts and lingered over them with loving care, striving to model his own writing on what he most admired in the "excellent ancients." Reflecting his own contemporaries' interest in the art of letter-writing, he took their techniques of correspondence still further by writing directly to the illustrious figures of antiquity in a language that they might have recognized had they lived to read the messages of their fourteenth-century friend. He trained himself for this mission on what he could read of ancient letter-writers like Cicero, Seneca, or Pliny the Younger. But Petrarch also read other kinds of ancient writing no less eagerly: the reluctant lawyer happily pored over technical treatises such as the *Ten Books on Architecture* composed for the Emperor Augustus by the Roman architect Vitruvius, filling the margins of his manuscripts with copious notes; these marginalia, in turn, were so prized by Petrarch's admirers that they, too, were frequently copied along with the ancient texts. At the same time, very much a man of his own era, Petrarch infused new enthusiasm into the medieval tradition of courtly love-poetry in his *Canzoniere*, "Songbook," a collection of 365 vernacular poems, mostly sonnets, devoted to his beloved. Like ancient Roman poets who invented appropriate names for the women to whom they addressed their poetry, Petrarch called his lady "Laura" to evoke the image of the laurel tree, sacred plant of Apollo, the ancient Greco-Roman god of music and poetry. Thus even Petrarch's most contemporary, idiomatic achievement always connected him back to the ancient origins of his art. Both in the *Canzoniere* and in his letters to the ancients, Petrarch seemed to reveal his own most personal thoughts and feelings with striking honesty; this was yet another of his innovations. Yet he did so with magnificent control: his sonnets, with their strict rhymes, intentionally spare vocabulary and repeated images, look simple on the surface, but, as generations of imitators and emulators were to discover, that simplicity was the result of painstaking care, subjected to Petrarch's rare responsiveness to the sounds and meaning of language. Because ancient poets considered epic the highest expression of a writer's genius, Petrarch drafted an epic of his own, *Africa*. Composed in the style and meter of ancient Roman heroic verse, echoing the words and rhythms of writers such as Vergil, Statius, and Lucan, Petrarch's *Africa* focused on the exploits of the great Roman general Scipio, conqueror of Carthage – and, significantly, a hero of the Roman Republic rather than the Empire. The merchant society of the late Middle Ages had spawned a whole series of city-states in which republican ideals more accurately reflected the desires of the citizens than a remote, tax-hungry monarchy.

What Petrarch's achievements sparked in contemporary readers, especially Italians, was a new awareness of the passage of eras and civilizations; the poignant longing for ancient Rome's majestic architecture and expressive literature became a mood that was both widely shared and regarded as eminently desirable. At the same time, however, this nostalgia created a sense of challenge: Petrarch's own prodigious efforts to write like the ancients suggested that the enterprise was feasible; at the same time, of course, he inspired not only the quest to write in a renewed and improved Latin, but also in a vivid vernacular. Furthermore, in certain respects, the humanist movement always regarded the present as entirely superior to the past. Unlike the ancients, Petrarch and his admirers gloried in the joys promised them by their Christian faith; when Petrarch called his crucifix his "chief delight," he was probably telling the truth, or at least hoping to. The quick-witted urbanites of the fourteenth century also enjoyed the advances of technology: navigating by the magnetic compass, calculating with Hindu-Arabic numerals, they had no intention of renouncing these conveniences any more than their religion.

As a result, Petrarch's younger contemporaries, such as Giovanni Boccaccio (1313–1375), combined veneration for the ancients with a contemporary agenda to create a vibrant literature in Latin and vernacular alike; famous above all for his *Decameron* of 1353, a vernacular storybook set just outside Florence during the Black Death of 1348, Boccaccio (who like Petrarch gave up the study of law for literature) also wrote a vernacular romance about the goddess Diana and her nymphs, set just outside Florence (*Ninfale fiesolano*), two short mythological verse romances, again in vernacular (*Filocolo* and *Teseide*), as well as sober Latin works such as his *Genealogy of the Pagan Gods* (written 1350–60, published 1373) and, in a lighter vein, a *History of Famous Women* (1362). His scholarly stature was also established in vernacular; he lectured in Florence on Dante, and in 1373 produced a commentary on the *Inferno*. Boccaccio was one of the first authors to take note of a trend that would become increasingly important with the invention of printing: both his *Decameron* and his *History of Famous Women* aimed specifically at female readers, the latter, indeed, at women learned in humanistic Latin.

In the continuation of these literary developments, the city of Florence, as one of the most wealthy and populous in fourteenth-century Europe, was to play a crucial role. It was here that Petrarch's literary and emotional reach toward the ancient past swiftly found kindred spirits among the shrewd merchants, guildsmen, and government officials who ran the Tuscan city according to the same set of civic ideals that Cicero had once enunciated for the Roman Republic. The merchant communities of Florence, Siena, Pisa, Padua, Venice, and many smaller Italian city-states had found for some time that the conditions and societal values about which Cicero wrote in the first century before the Christian era bore significant similarities to their own lives. With patriotic exaggeration, they likened the papacy to the Roman Empire and themselves to the more rough-and-ready, sternly virtuous republican Rome that had preceded the days of imperial decadence (and eventually to the Etruscans, whose league of twelve independent city-states and distinctive culture had preceded Roman rule). Roman authors provided these humanists with an ample repertory of complaints against the corrupting influence of luxury on what had once been a stern – and tiny – nation of farmers, herdsmen, and matrons who spun and wove with ceaseless industry. Tellingly, *ordo*, the Latin word for "order," derived (like its English cognate) from the row of warp threads the Roman *materfamilias* laid out on the family loom; social order and social fabric were almost literally one and the same.

What the humanist movement contributed to this already strong late medieval civic sentiment was a sense of style, the idea that Cicero's thoughts were best expressed with Cicero's words and Cicero's grammar rather than by using the precise, modern, legalistic Latin that had developed throughout the Middle Ages to meet the changing needs of European society. Members of the early fifteenth-century Florentine city council like Poggio Bracciolini (1380–1459) and Leonardo Bruni (1369–1444) collected manuscripts of ancient authors as eagerly as Petrarch had before them, and like him, they strove to model not only their conduct, but also their literary style, their choice of literary genre, and even their handwriting on those of the ancients. They adopted the form of their capital letters from ancient Roman inscriptions, and imitated what they thought was true Roman script for the lower-case letters. In fact, however, they copied a hand, Caroline minuscule, that had been devised in the age of Charlemagne (the eighth and ninth centuries). The humanists' carefully individuated letters stood in stark contrast to the flowing cursive scripts favored, for convenience, by merchants and notaries, and when typographers in Italy began to design their fonts in the mid-fifteenth century, they chose to imitate humanist script; our own roman and italic type faces are both the direct result of those early predilections. (So are our distinctions between upper- and lower-case letters, our spacing between words, and our punctuation marks; ancient Roman texts were written entirely in capital letters without divisions between words.)

By 1427, the city constitution of Florence had been rewritten so that its language would imitate the style of Cicero. Shortly thereafter, Chancellor Leonardo Bruni composed a history of the city in Latin as classical as he could make it. Always, however, the move to collect ancient texts, purify Latin of its medieval accretions, and adopt a style of living that approximated the elegance of the ancient Romans coexisted with tendencies that we might regard as more progressive. Most humanists continued as fervently practicing Christians, and continued to nurture an equally abiding interest in contemporary vernacular literature. Their culture, like that of ancient Rome itself, was multilingual. The common bond of humanism seems, if anything, to have fortified their interest in the varieties of contemporary vernacular culture.

If Florence was an important seedbed of humanism, it was certainly not the only city to recognize and put into effect what was far more than a republican literary movement. The Kingdom of Naples, first under the French Angevin dynasty and then under Aragonese rule, hosted pioneering humanists such as Giovanni Boccaccio in the fourteenth century, and Lorenzo Valla (1406–57) and Giovanni Gioviano Pontano (1426–1503) in the fifteenth. By the end of the fifteenth century, however, the most coveted venue for humanists had become papal Rome, the capital of an extensive secular state as well as the Catholic Church, replete with its own tax collectors and mercenary armies. Eventually the humanist outlook would extend its enthusiasms to every corner of cosmopolitan Europe and far beyond, irrespective of nationality or governmental system: Johannes (1488–1544) and Olaus (1490–1557) Magnus of Uppsala in Sweden, King Matthias Corvinus (1443–90) in Hungary, the itinerant Conrad Celtis (1459–1508) in Nuremberg, Ingolstadt, Cracow, and Vienna, would all transform the definitions of barbarian and Roman so that they and their ancestors could be included among the forces of civilization. Still, the phrase that this community of like-minded scholars, readers, and writers used to describe itself was tellingly egalitarian: *res publica litterarum*, the Republic of Letters.

Although its adherents included heads of state, soldiers, and noblewomen, the Republic of Letters effectively began as a movement among professional writers, who dedicated their work to aristocratic patrons but themselves came from a variety of backgrounds: Petrarch, as mentioned above, was the son of a notary, that is, of a literate professional, and in this he was fairly typical. Often these enterprising souls came from ambiguous positions in society: Leon Battista Alberti (1404–72), Giulio Pomponio Leto (1428–97), and Erasmus (d. 1536) were all illegitimate sons, Alberti of a Florentine merchant, Leto of a Calabrian prince, and Erasmus of a physician's daughter whose lover subsequently entered the monastery. Lorenzo Valla, author of a refined book *The Elegance of Latin*, was thoroughly plebeian, a fact he tried to hide through his feats of erudition; so was Coluccio Salutati, the historian and Chancellor of Florence. The professions taken up by humanists varied as widely as their origins and personalities: Marsilio Ficino (1433–99) was a physician and a philosopher, Pietro Bembo (1470–1547) a Venetian aristocrat and failed politician; both, above all, were prodigious writers. Alessandro Farnese (1468–1549) was a landed noble from the Papal States who became cardinal when his sister became the mistress of Pope Alexander VI Borgia (1431–1503), but he had been trained in humane letters at the University of Rome and remained a humanist despite his lofty position; he was elected Pope in 1534 as Paul III. No matter the range of professions practiced by humanists, however, it was the self-made authors who consistently set the pace and standards for cultural attainment.

High culture in the Renaissance was significantly defined by the closest possible adherence to classical standards of style, and usually the most expert arbiters of such standards were in fact practicing humanists rather than landed nobles in the traditional mold, who were often too busy administering their states, leading armies, or carrying out diplomatic missions. Federico da Montefeltro (1416–92), the learned Duke of Urbino, amassed a library of parchment manuscripts that are still impressive to look at, but not necessarily as impeccably edited and copied as the well-thrashed, unattractive paper volumes used by working humanists in Rome like Pomponio Leto, Angelo Colocci (1474–1549) or Tommaso Inghirami (1470–1516). Rulers were not always superficial in their interests, however; Federico da Montefeltro had his beautiful books read to him daily; Cosimo de' Medici (1389–1464) and his grandson Lorenzo Il Magnifico (1449–92) threw themselves into humanist study as well as patronage of first-rate scholars such as Ficino (1433–99) and Angelo Poliziano (1444–94); a century later, Henry VIII (1491–1547) and his daughter Elizabeth I (1533–1603) of England took pleasure in dazzling their interlocutors with their erudition in ancient and contemporary languages.

In the fields of rhetoric, literature, art, architecture, and behavior in particular, the existence of evident standards by which to compare contemporary achievements with the work of the ancients led to what might almost be termed an archaeological appreciation of ancient ways. But the standards set by the ancients exerted powerful influence in music and technology as well, where today the resemblance between ancient works and their Renaissance counterparts may seem particularly far-fetched; most of our own contemporaries would never mistake an opera by Monteverdi (1567–1643) for a Greek tragedy, nor see the utility of an ancient manual of war for the age of gunpowder. But humanism was not only a search for concrete facts of ancient life; it was also a search for systems, what Machiavelli (1469–1527), among many others, called *modi e ordini,* "methods and orders": ways of doing things and the sequence in which they are done.

The classical aesthetic system to which the humanists and their contemporaries looked for guidance was rooted in ancient rhetoric. Rhetoric provided the basic training that educated Greeks (including citizens of the expansive Hellenistic world created after the conquests of Alexander the Great), and subsequently Romans, shared as essential preparation for participation in civic life. Formal training in rhetoric was minutely systematic, and it was designed above all to create persuasive public speakers. Instruction therefore included honing such arts as currying favor with the audience (*captatio benivolentiae*), glossing over weak arguments, and unabashed appeal to the emotions through the deft use of dramatic changes in the voice, graceful gestures, and direct personal appeals (*apostrophe*). Rhetorical questions provided yet another effective technique for driving away boredom and winning over the audience.

Just as importantly, however, classical rhetoric emphasized the need for a coherent underlying structure (arrangement, Greek *taxis,* Latin *dispositio*) whether for an individual argument in the public arena or for an entire legal case, whose final summation might go on for six or seven hours – all, ideally, delivered from memory. As the ultimate development of that coherent structure, rhetoric also placed great importance on ornament. (The word "decoration" derived from the same word as "decorum" and meant imparting a final polish through appropriate expression.) The training, moreover, worked. The orators of the ancient Greco-Roman world were phenomenally successful lawyers and leaders. But then most of the rules invoked by ancient rhetoricians – coherent organization, clarity of argument, clear pronunciation, delivery from memory, appropriateness – operate just as effectively today. They were practical rules for any age.

The same technical terms applied by ancient rhetoricians to the art of public speaking were adopted by ancient writers on the other arts to establish similar criteria for quality. Aristotle's *Poetics* defined the persuasive power of Greek tragedy as the ability to strike "pity and fear" into the audience, a remarkably analytical assessment of what had been primarily a religious ritual. The Roman architect Vitruvius called for buildings to exhibit "firmness, utility, and concision" – they could almost be speeches. The ancient Roman poet Horace expressed this interconnection of the arts, or at least of ancient thinking about the arts, in a line of poetry that quickly became a cliché among humanists (and has remained a cliché among scholars who write on the Renaissance): "ut pictura poesis" ("poetry is like painting"). Coherent structure or design (*dispositio* again) applied to laying out the basic framework of buildings, statues, or musical compositions no less than speeches, and as with speeches refined ornament crowned each design's development, so that, if successful, the result moved the emotions, and, ultimately, persuaded. Effects analogous to those of a successful speech were thus demanded of successful paintings, sculptures, and buildings: indeed, in theory, rhetorical criteria defined the success of works in these other media. The development of humanism in the fifteenth century thus revived not only a set of standards for elegant Latin, but at the same time learned from the ancients to apply these same standards for composition and evaluation to a whole range of creative activities.

Another crucial element in the classical rhetorical system served as the basic guideline in developing a speech or a design from *dispositio* to final ornament. This was the concept that the Greeks called *genos* and the Romans *genus*; in both languages the word meant "family" or "clan," and its closest English equivalent is probably "kind," with that word's double sense of classification and of kinship. Like members of a human family, the members of a rhetorical family displayed both shared characteristics and individual quirks; the concept of *genus*, or more precisely, the practice of composition by *genus*, allowed for creative variety within certain definite boundaries. *Genera* (this was the Latin plural) were as ubiquitous and as varied as the whole world of human creativity. They included: epic and lyric genera ("genres") of poetry; Doric, Ionic, and Corinthian genera ("orders") of columns; Dorian, Lydian, and Phrygian genera ("modes") of music; high, medium, and low genera ("styles") of rhetoric. It was *genus* that defined standards of appropriateness for proportional systems in art, scales in music, sentence structure in speeches, ornament in every creative work. It was at once a remarkably strict and remarkably open idea. Combining two genera to create a third, however, could breed either brilliant inventions, like the Corinthian column, or monsters; there was no certain means to distinguish one from the other beforehand. For that matter, there was no fixed standard for distinguishing good taste from bad except by discovering how effectively a work persuaded – whatever persuasion might be. Generic composition therefore gave humanistic culture a tool that was both suggestive and almost perfectly ambiguous; to that very ambiguity it probably owed its long success.

Ancient rhetoricians, and, by extension, dramatists, painters, and sculptors often judged persuasiveness by a specific criterion: truth to nature, whether nature in its actual state or nature distilled to some idealized essence. The great Greek painter Zeuxis reportedly portrayed grapes of such realistically juicy appearance that birds pecked at them. Indeed, persuading the animals, as Orpheus did with his lyre, seems to have served ancient critics as supreme evidence of successful human creativity: truth to nature proven by nature's own testimony. When called upon to paint a picture of Aphrodite, the great Zeuxis asked that a series of beautiful youths and maidens be paraded before him so that he could take the best of each of their features and combine them himself into something more beautiful still – nature's quirks ironed out to create the image of divinity. Similarly, the sculptor Praxiteles carved a marble Aphrodite so voluptuous that men hurled themselves upon the statue and were rebuffed by cold marble in place of warm flesh. In an endlessly repeating chorus, ancient and Renaissance writers on the arts were to praise statues or paintings as "seemingly about to speak," "lifelike," "almost breathing." Again, the criterion for success was wonderfully suggestive – and totally imprecise.

By the same reasoning, truth to nature served as touchstone for the quality of architectural form: Vitruvius, in a profoundly influential passage of his *Ten Books on Architecture*, traced the classical column types to the human body in all its variety: Doric to the robust body of a young man, Ionic to a matron, Corinthian to a slender maiden. Extrapolating in the same vein in the early sixteenth century, the painter Raphael, in a famous letter to Pope Leo X, gave the Gothic pointed arch qualified praise because it derived, so he said, from the interlacing of the branches of trees in the forest. Another passage from Vitruvius denounced the wall-painting of his own generation (circa 25 BCE) as hopelessly decadent precisely because it deviated from nature, portraying strange creatures and impossibly delicate architectural fantasies. Like their ancient Roman predecessors, Renaissance artists read his fulminations –

and ignored them; these painted fantasies persuaded everyone but Vitruvian purists through the sheer delight of beholding them.

Proportion served as another crucial component of the classical aesthetic system, based again, initially, on rhetorical principles. Both the capacity of human lungs and the human attention span put definite quantitative limits on the length of spoken phrases and the structure of comprehensible arguments. In the same way, ancient architects measured states and buildings alike by the scale of the human body. The proportion of breadth to height in a true classical column fell within a comparatively narrow range, whereas Romanesque or Gothic columns exhibited infinite freedom to become slender or stumpy. Vitruvius' outcry against contemporary painting stressed its violations of proportion alongside its failure to imitate nature, two sides of the same deficiency.

Humanist critics sought to impose much the same discipline on the arts as their classical predecessors, although precise ideas of what such discipline might entail changed constantly. Certain subtleties of architectural proportion, for example, were taken for granted by ancient architects. No two moldings had the same dimensions or degree of projection; instead, every piece of a complex architectural design had its own shape, size, and three-dimensional relief. This system of individualization, however, had not been worked out coherently by Renaissance architects until the early sixteenth century, which meant that fifteenth-century architecture in the classical tradition actually employed a far greater variety of forms and proportional systems than did the work of the sixteenth century, but subjected these forms to less complicated rules of scale and placement.

The vocabulary and syntax of Latin underwent a similar process of refinement throughout the Renaissance, culminating in the movement known as Ciceronianism. When early humanists looked at contemporary Latin with its apparatus of precise but cumbersome legal and theological terms they identified these new words as one of the reasons that the language had declined from the glory days of Cicero's eloquence. They were not unreasonable to think so; the objects of their scorn included the language of bureaucracy, pedantry, and legal punctilio as well as more picturesque additions to the post-antique lexicon like "nun" and "pizza." By purging their own vocabularies of non-classical words, humanists hoped to attain greater elegance, but in so doing they also created difficulties for themselves, especially in describing contemporary phenomena such as the Christian Church, whose basic terms were transformed by the most radical Ciceronians into ancient equivalents that existed long before Jesus. The College of Cardinals became the "Sacred Senate"; nuns were "Vestal Virgins," psalms were "oracles," communion was "sacrifice," the Pope was "Jupiter the Thunderer" or that ancient Roman priest called Pontifex Maximus ("supreme bridge-builder"). Furthermore, however cumbersome medieval Latin may have been, its legal terms, like the apparatus of scholastic theology, commanded pinpoint precision; humanist Latin achieved beauty and emotional immediacy at the price of a certain lack of clarity.

The combination of humanist attention to the specifics of ancient texts and the classical aesthetic system's evocation of nature encouraged the tendency to scrutinize nature with the same analytical attention as manuscripts and monuments, treating the observation of details as attention to nature's equivalent of ornament. In many respects, antiquity and nature served the same purpose: they were both absolute sources of validation for aesthetic choices. And if humanists frequently came from professional rather than aristocratic backgrounds, so did such experts in the vagaries of nature as artists, metallurgists, surgeons, and military architects. They might not be humanists proper – Leonardo da Vinci (1452–1519) and the architect Donato Bramante (1444–1514) famously considered themselves illiterate for their lack of proficiency in Latin – but they often carried out humanist aesthetic ideals and a humanist's mission of active exploration.

Furthermore, despite its close attention to the past for aesthetic clues, Renaissance humanism and the culture it engendered continued to live in a technological present. Filippo Brunelleschi's design for the dome of Florence Cathedral may have been based on his observation of the Pantheon in Rome, but its shape was very different, and distinctively its own. Like Petrarch, Brunelleschi was the son of a Florentine notary, but he became a member of the goldsmiths' guild rather than a humanist. His friend and rival Leon Battista Alberti, on the other hand, established his reputation as a humanist long before making his own forays into the practice of architecture. And as a writer Alberti took Brunelleschi's clever invention of one-point perspective and described it for the reading public in his own, not Brunelleschi's, words in the treatise called "On Painting" (1427). Alberti's opportunism was not unusual among his colleagues. For the most part, humanists, no matter how piercing their nostalgia for the ancient world, encouraged technological innovation. When printing was invented in the mid-fifteenth century, humanists often took the lead in exploiting the new medium, and certainly dominated the higher reaches of publishing. The Venetian humanist Pietro Bembo, rigid in his criteria for good Latin and vernacular, worked closely with the printer Aldus Manutius on designing typefaces for print and even invented the semicolon; his training as a humanist allowed him to identify a syntactic unit in Latin that needed effective punctuation, and in the absence of the proper symbol he made one up.

Like the ancient educational system on which it was based, humanism could open the way to native talent, as indeed rhetoric had for Cicero and poetry did for Horace and Vergil. Distinctively, however, the Renaissance encouraged similar developments in vernacular literature and in the arts. Partnerships like those of Brunelleschi and Alberti, Pietro Bembo and Aldus Manutius (1449/50–1515), Raphael (1483–1520) and Angelo Colocci, and, in the late sixteenth century, the architect Andrea Palladio (1508–80) and the humanist Daniele Barbaro (1514–70), continually crossed the boundaries between the arts, between social strata, between humanists and non-humanists. And because humanistic Latin was an artificially recreated language, it was also international and universal. Learned patrons demanded not only learned literature, but also learned works of art, learned banquets, learned table settings. Collaboration was the only way to achieve these goals, and it infused humanist culture with conviviality. Works of art such as Botticelli's panel paintings for the Medici in Florence, or Raphael's frescoes for the apartments of popes Julius II and Leo X in the Vatican Palace (painted 1508–20) were executed with the help of humanists who provided an actual program, or at least a set of ideas. In the case of the frescoes on the walls of the Sistine Chapel, executed by a team of artists including Botticelli, Perugino, Ghirlandaio, Luca Signorelli, and Cosimo Rosselli in 1481–3, the provider of the program was probably none other than Pope Sixtus IV himself.

If humanism gave much to Renaissance culture, it also exacted its price. Increasing codification of aesthetic standards could lead to the outlandish jargon of radical Ciceronianism, or simply to the florid emptiness of diplomatic speeches, to the flat imitation of classical motifs in art or architecture, or, in the hands of a Bramante, a Raphael, or a Michelangelo (1475–1564), to their thorough, exhilarating rethinking. The most vocal arbiter of literary elegance in sixteenth-century Italy, the Venetian aristocrat Pietro Bembo, emphasized style over content, and a narrow definition of style at that: in Latin, he advised imitating Cicero for prose, Vergil for poetry; in Italian, Dante and Petrarch. The effect on Italian literature was a powerful guideline, but it was also a noose. Not surprisingly, northern writers like Erasmus rushed in to fill the vacuum with individual Latin styles that had real heft and bite – but then Erasmus, unlike Bembo, also had a good deal to say.

Universities, Schools, and Academies

Because humanism originated as an outlook rather than a professional curriculum, its relationship with that uniquely medieval institution, the university, was not initially a consistent one. In fact, the first important schools for humanists provided instruction at a more elementary level. The grammarians Guarino of Verona (1370–1460) and Gasparino Barzizza (1360–1431) taught Latin and Greek according to humanistic principles at various levels and in various places in northern Italy during their long careers, but significantly, it was to young students. To the same seminal effect, Manuel Chrysoloras in Florence (d. 1415) and Demetrius Chalcondylas in Milan and Florence taught elementary Greek. Children at the highest levels of the aristocracy continued to be instructed by private tutors: Lionello d'Este was tutored by Guarino da Verona, the sons of Lorenzo de' Medici (including the future Pope Leo X) by Angelo Poliziano. Girls almost always learned Latin and Greek at home; examples range from Nigella Laeta, a pupil of her father, Pomponio Leto, Professor of Rhetoric at the University of Rome, to rulers such as Isabella and Beatrice d'Este, Lady Jane Grey, and Elizabeth I. Humanists somewhat lower down the social ladder were often tutored privately as well; the nobles Angelo Colocci of Iesi and Pietro Bembo of Venice were both leading humanists in their own day without benefit of university education.

Church schools could also impart humanistic learning, like the orphanage of Santa Maria in Aquiro in Rome, founded by the humanist Blosio Palladio in the mid-sixteenth century; so did the city-run schools like those at which the sixteenth-century humanists Pacifico Massimi and Andrea Fulvio taught to earn their rather meager livings. A thriving population of humanists depended, indeed, on a thriving system of education at every stage before the university level. When Rome's humanists hoped to establish a Greek Academy on the model of their highly successful Roman Academy in the second decade of the sixteenth century, they discovered that a "gymnasium" geared to teach elementary Greek was a better idea.

Still, it is no accident that Petrarch, the first humanist, studied at the University of Bologna, an institution developed initially (in 1088) to train lawyers, but from 1316 onward also engaged in teaching what were called *artes*, the arts: rhetoric, logic, philosophy, grammar, dialectic, astronomy, and, importantly in Bologna, the *ars notaria*, the art of drawing up contracts, an indispensable skill in the developing merchant economies of central Italy. Bologna is the place where Petrarch (and after him, Leon Battista Alberti) learned to be such a careful reader and writer; indeed, it was his own training in grammar and rhetoric that fine-tuned his sensitivity to the differences between the literature of his own day and the Latin of antiquity. By 1420, encouraged by the growth of humanist emphasis on ancient languages, the University of Bologna had added a professorship in Greek, and in 1460, a professorship of Hebrew. Other institutions throughout Europe followed much the same pattern.

Although the right to confer university degrees was normally conferred to an institution "ex privilegio" by the Pope or the Holy Roman Emperor, a breakaway group of students from the University of Bologna had already established an entirely independent university at Padua in 1222, and the tendency toward free universities would continue. At Padua the students themselves created what would eventually become one of the world's great universities. In city-states, local rulers often took over the dispensing of privileges, as did Elector Frederick the Wise of Saxony when he founded the University of Wittenberg in 1502, and Archduke Albrecht VI of Upper Austria to charter the University of Freiburg in 1457. Louis the Rich, Duke of Bavaria, founded the University of Ingolstadt in 1472, but he drew on a papal privilege of Pius II, dating from 1458. A humanist Pope like Eugenius IV could ensure that university curricula were humanist-inspired from the outset, as he did with the University of Poitiers in 1431. With the University of Rome, originally founded in 1303, Eugenius reorganized the university's structure and finances – for many years the University of Rome would derive its income from a tax on wine! – and in the process also encouraged it to take an explicitly humanist direction. The later a university was founded, the more likely it was to reflect humanist concerns, as with Louvain (1425) and Leiden (1575), an institution that was not only humanist, but Protestant. And sometimes a university's motives clashed with one another; the first rector of the University of Freiburg, Matthaeus Hümmel, announced in his inaugural address that "Scholarship has built itself a house," but Archduke Albrecht VI had rather different ideas; he had chartered the university to prepare young men for careers in the Church!

Institutions such as the Universities of Paris, Naples, and Oxford continued to retain their close identification with scholasticism well into the Renaissance. In the cases of Paris and Naples, both of which had played host in the fourteenth century to the massive presence, physical, intellectual, and bibliographic, of Thomas Aquinas, this enduring connection with the past was understandable; scholasticism had provided these establishments with their original reputation, as was also true of Oxford. The Universities of Salerno and Padua, on the other hand, were renowned for their medical schools and therefore prided themselves primarily on their professional training rather than the nurturing of literature. Nor was university education restricted to the independently chartered foundations mentioned so far. The monastic orders of the Franciscans and Dominicans, and, in the sixteenth century, the Jesuits, continued to grant their own higher degrees; in Naples, in fact, the city university shared quarters with the Dominican College within the massive warren of the convent of San Domenico. Private colleges could also be founded by cardinals (the Collegio Capranica in Rome, established by Cardinal Domenico Capranica in the fifteenth century; Christ Church in Oxford, established by Cardinal Wolsey in the sixteenth), by bishops (Corpus Christi College in Oxford, by Richard Fox, Bishop of Winchester, 1517), or by wealthy individuals, like John Caius of Cambridge, a physician who obtained a new charter and sweeping reorganization for his alma mater, Gonville College, in 1557. In some of these schools, like Rome and Poitiers, humanists would thrive; in some, like Paris, they would meet stout opposition; in some, like the legal and medical schools, humanism was a matter of personal choice. On occasion, however, as with Eugenius IV, the monarchs who exercised the real power to grant privileges might also intervene in the university curriculum; in 1536, Henry VIII banned the teaching of scholastic philosophy at Cambridge, an open encouragement to the development of humane letters – humanism.

There was one university, however, where the humanist revival of antiquity took on greater, or at least more picturesque, urgency than anywhere else in the world: the University of Rome in the late fifteenth century. In 1467, Giulio Pomponio Leto, the illegitimate son of a Calabrian prince, took up the chair of rhetoric at what was called the *Studium Urbis* (Rome was the *urbs* or city that needed no further specification) and joined forces with his colleague in the chair of grammar, Giovanni Sulpizio da Veroli, to mount a massive effort to recover ancient Rome's bygone glories. They had a unique resource at their disposal: the ruins of the city itself. Not only did Leto encourage the usual humanistic activities of collecting manuscripts and subjecting their texts to minute examination, he also encouraged his students to focus the same kind of piercing scrutiny on the city's ancient monuments, especially the elegant inscriptions in Greek and Latin that could be found above and below ground in varying states of repair. A small, shy man with a pronounced stutter, Leto was also a spellbinding teacher, his bright black eyes burning with enthusiasm for his subject. His students imitated not only his scholarly methods, but even his handwriting, and like him they filled the margins of their books with notes gathered in the course of study and first-hand observation of ancient artifacts.

Leto devoted his own scholarly career to improving the understanding of Roman history, working to extract fact from fiction in the great ancient historians Livy and Tacitus as well as the gossipy tales of later Roman emperors gathered in a collection of writers known as the *Scriptores Historiae Augustae* ("Writers of Imperial History"). Both he and his colleague Sulpizio pored over the *Ten Books of Architecture* penned by the architect and catapult technician Vitruvius for the Emperor Augustus (ca. 25 BCE). In 1486 Sulpizio prepared an edition of Vitruvius for the printing press, begging his readers to send in corrections; like most of his fellow humanists, he realized that their great joint project of classical revival could never be the work of a single person. At nearly the same time, their eager students pressed them to do more than study and write about the glories of ancient Rome; the students wanted action, and they got it. Sulpizio, Vitruvius in hand, guided the reconstruction of an outdoor theater near an open piazza (and execution ground) with the incongruously lovely name of Campo de' Fiori, the "Field of Flowers," and there, in 1486 or 1488, the students mounted the first production of an ancient Roman play to have been seen for centuries, if not a millennium. They chose a tragedy of Seneca that focused on the unrequited love of the Greek queen Phaedra for her stepson Hippolytus (they called this play *Hippolytus*, modern classicists call it *Phaedra*). The production made use of the local buildings as well; dressed as Queen Phaedra, the 16-year-old prodigy Tommaso Inghirami emoted in Latin from a real tower, and then descended to the stage itself to meet one of the occupational hazards of amateur theater: a piece of the scenery collapsed. As the students hauled the fallen set back into place, Tommaso Inghirami held forth undaunted in extemporized Latin, and stole the show. He went on to become librarian of the Vatican Library, a canon of St. Peter's Basilica, and a sharp investor in real estate, who managed a troupe of professional actors – and he never shook off the nickname "Phaedra" for the rest of his life. Tommaso Inghirami also excelled in the very subject that Pomponio Leto was officially charged to teach: rhetoric. His resonant voice could be heard from one end of Rome's huge medieval basilicas to the other, and as a result a significant part of his career also involved delivering speeches for the Pope. The students, meanwhile, went on to create other productions in Latin, until theatrical performances in Latin became a beloved feature of Roman cultural life.

Where ancient Rome did not exist, it had to be recreated entirely through the imagination, and that is what the Holy Roman Emperor Frederick III did when he crowned the poet Conrad Celtis with laurel in Nuremberg in 1487. The ceremony recalled Petrarch's crowning with laurel on the Capitoline Hill in Rome, a ritual that Pomponio Leto had subsequently revived in a more republican spirit among his colleagues and students, with characteristic brio. But the flexibility of the humanist movement meant that in effect, any hill could become another Capitoline through the magic of Latin verse; and so in faraway Germany, Conrad Celtis, too, dared to boast the title of Poet Laureate.

Pomponio Leto's students at the University of Rome were not the only group of humanists to gather in the city; he shared his antiquarian enthusiasms with equal gusto among his fellow professors and other like-minded humanists employed at the papal court, creating a group known as the Roman Academy. Similar gatherings, inspired by the convivial settings of so many works of ancient literature, from Plato's *Symposium* to Athenaeus' *Sophists at Dinner* (*Deipnosophistae*) to Cicero's *Tusculan Disputations*, were convened everywhere that ancient literature captured its readers' imaginations. In fifteenth-century Florence, gatherings centered around Cosimo de' Medici and Bernardo Rucellai, whose "Orti Oricellari" – "Rucellai Gardens" – became a favorite setting for learned discussions and performances of poetry set to music; humanists took Vergil at his word when he claimed to sing "of arms and the man" in the first line of his *Aeneid*. A manuscript in the Bavarian State Library commemorates a similar gathering of 1493 in a Regensburg Gasthaus; wherever wine and Latin were brought together, humanist partygoers could feel themselves transported to Mount Parnassus.

Sometimes, as with Leto's Roman Academy, the rules for membership in these humanist clubs were fairly strict: aspiring members were required to demonstrate their competence in Latin by reciting one of their own compositions, and if successful were rewarded by a laurel crown; at the same time they took on a new name by which they would be identified during all academy proceedings. Leto himself adopted three names like an ancient Roman: Julius, his praenomen or given name, Pomponius, his family name, and a third, personal descriptive name known as the cognomen: his own, Laetus, meant "happy," and, from all we can tell, accurately described his personality. His young protégé Angelo Colocci (or "Angelus Colotius") took the cognomen "Bassus," presumably for his short stature. Their histrionic friend Tommaso "Phaedra" Inghirami exerted Herculean efforts to be identified as "Phaedrus," like the comely young man who figures so prominently in Plato's dialogues *Phaedrus* and *Symposium*, but Queen "Fedra" he remained to friends, public, and, above all, to his own family, where the names "Fedra" and "Tommaso Fedra" passed down the generations among Inghirami boys and girls.

In Naples, Giovanni Gioviano Pontano established his own Academy on lines similar to those of Leto's, with which he maintained close contacts. They met in his elegant classical chapel or on the wooded slopes of Mount Posillipo, looking across the Bay of Naples to Vesuvius. In Rome and Naples alike, the Neapolitan humanist Jacopo Sannazaro became known as Actius Sincerus, and the Catalan poet Benedetto Gareth changed his Hebrew-derived given names to the Greek "Charitaeus" – "belonging to the Graces."

Pomponio Leto's Roman Academy fulfilled many of the same purposes as a guild for humanists (indeed medieval professionals like notaries and physicians joined guilds as eagerly as craftsmen), and for that very reason the organization was regarded with more than a little suspicion by Pope Paul II, who made a brutal attempt to suppress it in 1468. Arrests, imprisonment, and interrogation by torture failed to yield any information of substance about allegations of sodomy, pagan rites, or plots to assassinate the Pope, and gradually the humanists of the Academy were set free again; the Pope needed his learned staff. In a pattern that would obtain for many other humanist academies from Naples to Nuremberg, Pope Paul's successor, Pope Sixtus IV (reigned 1471–83), chartered the Roman Academy under his own sponsorship as a Catholic religious sodality, and greatly expanded the papal bureaucracy to provide still more humanists with jobs. To Pope Sixtus, a Franciscan scholar of distinction and a clever politician, humanism was a means to make papal Rome a showcase to the civilized world, just as the Florentine companions of the Orti Oricellari and the Platonist followers of Marsilio Ficino brought beauty and distinction to Medicean Florence. In the Kingdom of Naples, Giovanni Gioviano Pontano's Academy served many of the same purposes: honing the skills of humanists through practice, providing "pastime with good company" (as Henry VIII would term it), encouraging the collaborations that provided the lifeblood of the humanist movement, and bringing glory to the city lucky enough to play host to their achievements, grand or antic.

With increasing frequency, academies of every sort became a lively feature of Renaissance society. The combination of humanist examination of language and the growth of academies as a social phenomenon produced a curious new hybrid in mid-sixteenth-century Florence: the Accademia della Crusca (the Academy of the Kernel), devoted to the study and purification, not of Latin, but of Tuscan vernacular. In true humanist fashion, the members of the Crusca traced Florentine vernacular to Etruscan, not Latin roots; in true humanist fashion, they subjected new words to exacting analysis before approving them as legitimately Tuscan. In due time, the erstwhile inhabitants of what ancient Rome called "Transalpine Gaul" would establish their own Accademia della Crusca – the Académie de France, which, like the Crusca, still carries out its active mission today, valiantly battling to expunge every foreign taint from the pure French language. On the same model (and with the same ancestry of guilds and religious confraternities), the Accademia di San Luca in Rome (named after Saint Luke, who was believed to have painted the first portrait of the Virgin Mary with the Christ Child) established standards for painting, as the Roman Accademia dei Lincei and the Florentine Accademia del Cimento would later do for science. In this way as in so many others, the universal high culture of the Renaissance set the stage for the developing nation-states of Europe, and for the ways of thinking that brought on the eighteenth-century Enlightenment.

Conclusions

The high culture of the European Renaissance spoke a common language, Latin, as well as a bevy of vernaculars. Its common grounding in the legacy of ancient Greece and Rome produced acute sensitivity to individual variations of language and culture, but also a common repertory of well-loved literary works, myths, stories, visual and metaphorical images. Its roots in classical rhetoric created a common set of aesthetic standards that applied the same criteria and the same terms to speaking, writing, building, painting, musical composition, sculpture, and city planning. The development of printing in the fifteenth and sixteenth centuries ensured the spread of this broadly shared high culture across the globe and throughout the social structure. For this very universality, the Renaissance combination of classicism and innovation can be seen as a distinct, coherent phenomenon.

In an age torn by political and religious strife, the shared store of values and knowledge that defined high culture served as an attractive force bringing people together; the ancient myths, with their gossiping, philandering gods and fallible heroes made it possible to tell universal truths about human nature without harm or slander to the living. Classical rhetoric's emphasis on the persuasive powers of beautiful form and elegant behavior was widely believed to have created all that was civilized about civil society, and perhaps it did. Certainly high culture gave a wide variety of people common subjects to discuss and shared protocols by which to conduct their conversations. When political structures often tended toward local tyranny or centralized monarchy, or both, high culture created the idea of a republic of letters, a domain in which, by definition, the individual voice counted in the public forum.

Although the specific definition of every one of its canons was constantly subjected to vigorous, sometimes virulent debate, although the rigor of its aesthetic standards sometimes seems more like rigor mortis, the shared high culture of the Renaissance was really a creation of remarkable flexibility and remarkable durability, a universal vision with ample room for individual variation whose legacy still survives in contemporary hopes for global cooperation and communication.

FURTHER READING

Grafton, Anthony, *Defenders of the Text: the Traditions of Scholarship in an Age of Science, 1450–1800* (Cambridge, MA: Harvard University Press, 1991).

——, ed., *Rome Reborn: The Vatican Library and Renaissance Culture* (Washington DC: Library of Congress, 1993).

Grafton, Anthony and Jardine, Lisa, *From Humanism to the Humanities: The Institutionalizing of the Liberal Arts in Fifteenth- and Sixteenth-Century Europe* (Cambridge, MA: Harvard University Press, 1986).

Grendler, Paul F., *Schooling in Renaissance Italy: Literacy and Learning, 1300–1600* (Baltimore: Johns Hopkins University Press, 1989).

Hankins, James, ed., *Renaissance Civic Humanism: Reappraisals and Reflections* (Cambridge: Cambridge University Press, 2000).

Kraye, Jill, ed., *The Cambridge Companion to Renaissance Humanism* (Cambridge: Cambridge University Press, 1996).

Rabil, Albert, Jr., ed., *Renaissance Humanism: Foundations, Forms, and Legacy* (Philadelphia: University of Pennsylvania Press, 1988).

CHAPTER NINETEEN

Religious Cultures (Spirituality, Reform, High and Low)

R. PO-CHIA HSIA

The characteristics of religious history in the Renaissance can be succinctly stated: an enthusiastic, spontaneous, and heterogeneous manifestation of popular piety accompanied the crisis in the authority of the Church. In fact, this formulation can be further refined to read that an effervescent popular piety represented both the result and the cause of the crisis in ecclesiastical authority. Two parallel histories, two concurrent developments: official and popular religions evolved in close dialectic tandem. If we imagine "Religion" and "Society" to be two distinct threads, the Renaissance may be thought of as a period in which the two were interwoven into the fabric of Christianity. One can even argue that the Protestant Reformation and the Tridentine Catholicism of the sixteenth century represented reactions to desegregate the profane and the sacred, which were so inextricably mixed up in Renaissance Europe.

Boundaries, of course, had existed in the medieval West: between the clergy and the laity, between the holy and everyday, between men and women, between Christians and non-Christians, and between the orthodox and heretics. It is my argument that during the Renaissance these boundaries were submerged both by the leaks in the dam of ecclesiastical authority and by the waves of popular piety that flooded the banks of official approbation. The chronological outline of that history is well known; the Great Schism, the Lollard movement in England, the Hussite Revolution in Bohemia, the Conciliar Movement, and the Renaissance papacy – well known themes in conventional church history – represented rather the visible icebergs of stronger undercurrents. In probing these deeper currents of spirituality, I propose to examine four themes in this essay. They deal with (1) the geographical differences between northern and Mediterranean Europe in spiritual styles; (2) the conflicting reform impulses that alternately threatened and strengthened the authority of the Roman Church, in particular that of the papacy; (3) the expression and suppression of feminine spirituality between the thirteenth and sixteenth centuries; and (4) the multiple manifestations of the eruption of the divine in the religious cultures of the Renaissance.

In his study of sanctity in western Christendom in the late Middle Ages, André Vauchez proposes two types of saints: the non-Mediterranean model focused on "the suffering of a leader," exemplified by kings, queens, princes, and bishops, anchored in the aristocratic ethos of heroism, and a Mediterranean model of "the suffering of the poor," exemplified by ascetic holy men and women, who labored among the urban poor. These contrasting models of aristocratic versus bourgeois sanctity also reflected a chronological shift from northern to southern Europe. Whereas saints in the eleventh and twelfth centuries hailed from many countries of Latin Christendom, by the fourteenth and fifteenth centuries they came predominantly from France and Italy. The majority of French saints canonized by the Avignon papacy were, in fact, natives of Provence, a region heavily influenced by Italian spirituality, which accentuated even more the dominant position of Italy in the history of sanctity. Between 1198 and 1431, the period studied by Vauchez, 25 percent of all saints recognized by the papacy were Italians; and more than 50 percent of all saints who had a local cult – whether canonically recognized or not – were of Italian origin.[1] No other country came close. The preponderance of Italians was especially striking because in the same period no saints from the Iberian peninsula, northern Germany, and the Low Countries received papal approbation.

While differing in details, the longer-term study of sanctity (1000–1700) by Donald Weinstein and Rudolph Bell also comes to the same conclusion. This north/south contrast is best illustrated by an analysis of saints' birthplaces. While Italian saints comprised 20.3 percent of all saints of the eleventh century, their percentage rose in the twelfth century to 22.9, in the thirteenth to 49.7, in the fourteenth to 69, only to fall slightly in the fifteenth century to 63.8. For saints born in the Holy Roman Empire, by contrast, their numbers diminished from 25 percent in the eleventh, to 17.6 percent in the twelfth, 13.8 percent in the thirteenth, 6.5 percent in the fourteenth, and only 4.8 percent in the fifteenth century.[2]

The hegemonic position of the Mediterranean in Latin Christendom marked the transition from an international Church of the High Middle Ages to one marked by southern French domination in the fourteenth and Italian preponderance after the resolution of the Great Schism. With the re-establishment of the papal seat in Rome, Italians came to comprise the overwhelming majority of popes. Between the pontificates of Martin V (1417) and Paul III (1534), only the Dutchman Adrian VI came from northern Europe. Of the fifteen popes, twelve were Italian, two were Catalans – the Borgias Calixtus III and Alexander VI had spent long years in the Papal Curia before their election – and one Dutch. Not only did the papacy and Papal Curia become predominantly Italian during the fifteenth century, these institutions evolved to represent the interests of the dominant social classes of central and northern Italian cities. Again, papal origins tell the story. The Piccolomini of Siena, the Della Rovere of Savona, and the Medici of Florence each supplied two popes. Altogether, there were 5 Tuscans, 3 Ligurians, 2 Venetians, and 2 Romans among the popes of the Renaissance, all from the urban nobility and patriciate. A similar trend characterized the cardinalate. In the 1447 conclave that elected Nicholas V, 11 of the 18 cardinals were Italians; in the 1458 conclave that elected Pius II, they were 9 out of 18. Thereafter, the proportion of Italian cardinals only increased, from 27 out of 38 in the 1503 conclave that elected Julius II, to 18 out of 25 in the 1513 conclave that elected Leo X, and 34 out of 39 in the 1523 conclave that elected Clement VII.[3] Lower down in the ladder of success of the Papal Curia, the noble and middle classes of Italian cities also claimed the lion's share of the lucrative posts in the expanding papal government. In the period 1471 to 1526 studied by Peter Partner, for example, Italians comprised 60 percent of all papal chancery officials, a reversal of the Avignonese period when 70 percent of all curialists were French.[4] The substitution of Italian for non-Italian officials in the papal bureaucracy and the growth of a clerical office-purchasing class among the Italian notables was a process largely completed by 1500 and would remain in place throughout the early modern period.

This fundamental transformation in the character of the Roman Catholic Church had a pervasive and crucial impact in the history of spirituality in western Christianity. Reflecting the cultural hegemony of the Renaissance in Italy, the Italianization of the Church focused discussions of church reform on Rome and the papacy. Increasingly, religious dissent and criticisms of ecclesiastical corruption assumed an anti-Italian, anti-Roman, and anti-papal stridency; and the north/south divide was further sharpened by the currents of anti-Roman dissent in northern Europe that resulted in the Lollard movement in England, the Hussite Revolution in Bohemia, and the Protestant Reformation in the Holy Roman Empire.

Castigated as the new Babylon by many, Rome remained nevertheless the envisioned New Jerusalem for others. The anti-Roman partisans of reform had a long genealogy that dated back to the Ghibelline imperialist party of the eleventh century; over the course of the late Middle Ages, they would include the radical wing of the Franciscan movement in Italy as well as dissenters north of the Alps. The Florentine Dominican reformer and prophet Girolamo Savonarola and the Dutch humanist Desiderius Erasmus were among the many who saw Rome as the center of paganism, sin, and corruption.

The recovery of papal prestige after the failure of the conciliar movement led to a reinvigorated and politically significant papacy, a cause for both celebration and condemnation. From the mid-fifteenth century onward, the Roman Jubilee, proclaimed by the popes and celebrated every twenty-five years, transformed the Holy City into the most important pilgrimage site of western Christendom. The introduction of printing further promoted the influx of pilgrims: the best-known guidebook for pilgrims, the *Indulgentiae ecclesiarum urbis*, included forty-four Latin editions between 1475 and 1523, in addition to twenty German, Italian, French, Spanish, and Flemish editions. With its numerous holy sites of Mary, Christ, the apostles, and martyrs, Rome represented a gateway to salvation. Papal panegyrists proclaimed the city to be the center of the celestial kingdom on earth; Rome was the "City of God," the new, holy Jerusalem, lauded by the Fifth Lateran Council in 1512.

The increased emphasis on indulgences and pilgrimages enhanced the papacy's spiritual powers and augmented the sacred character of the city of Rome. The number of "reserved sins" under direct papal jurisdiction and absolution increased, as did the papal coffers, for absolution came at a price. As pontiff and prince, the popes expanded their secular dominions and incomes, even while their spiritual incomes from outside of the Papal States declined, owing to the appropriation of ecclesiastical properties by secular rulers. The papacy grew into a body with two souls, one secular, the other spiritual, to use the expression of Paolo Prodi.[5] During the pontificate of Julius II, the fusion of secular and spiritual powers permeated Roman humanist rhetoric. Addressing the Fifth Lateran Council, Cristoforo Marcello praised Julius II as "shepherd (pastor), physician (medicus), governor (gubernator), cultivator (cultor) – in short, another God on earth."[6] The hyperbole of the Pope as Moses and Caesar did not save Julius II from the savage satire of Erasmus, who lambasted him in his play, *Julius Exclusus*, which had the warrior-pope being rejected from heaven by an outraged St. Peter.

For many critics of the Church, the hoped-for reform implied not the destruction of Rome and the papacy but its cleansing. They included highly placed curialists in Rome, men such as the Franciscan Giorgio Benigno Salviati (1448–1520), the General of the Augustinian Hermits Egidio of Viterbo (1469–1532), and the Spanish cardinal Bernardino López de Carvajal (1456–1523). Influenced by the prophetic work *Apocalypsis Nova*, attributed to Amadeus of Portugal, a Franciscan hermit of the late fifteenth century, this current of reform was inspired by millenarian prophecies in the figure of the Last World Emperor and an Angelic Pope. Sympathetic to Girolamo Savonarola, the Florentine Dominican prophet condemned by Alexander VI, these sympathizers within the Church played a role in the reform movements undertaken by the various mendicant orders that resulted in the foundation of Observant congregations. These men pinned their hopes successively on Leo X, Clement VII, and Paul III for church reform; they saw Emperor Charles V as the Last World Emperor, an instrument of God's chastisement of ecclesiastical corruption; and they interpreted the war against the Turks, the Lutheran dissent, and the discovery of the Americas as signs of the impending millennium.

In fact, the desire for church reform was strongly felt among the ranks of the clergy, especially in the mendicant orders; indeed, Salviati, Egidio of Viterbo, and Savonarola represented members of the Franciscan, Augustinian, and Dominican Observant movements. The fifteenth century was a period of reinvigoration and renewal among the mendicant orders, especially in the towns of central and northern Italy. Attracted by their strict observance of religious rules, their asceticism and charity, the urban populace of Italian cities and the lay ruling classes lent ready support. Between 1420 and 1517, the number of Observant communities in Italy rose from 30 to 1,260.[7] By 1442, for example, the Observant Franciscans had more than 200 convents and 4,000 friars in Italy and boasted famous popular preachers such as Bernardino of Siena and Giovanni da Capistrano. Attacking the corruption of the powerful and the usury of the Jews, the Observant Franciscans sponsored the establishment of funds of charity, the Monti di Pietà, which lent money to the poor at low interest. The first Monti was established in 1462 in Perugia, followed by others in Orvieto and Gubbio. In the wake of the ritual murder accusation against the Jews of Trent in 1475, the Observant Franciscans, who vigorously promoted the cult of the alleged child martyr Simon of Trent, gained further momentum in their anti-Jewish and anti-usury campaign, which led to the official recognition of the Monti di Pietà by the Lateran Council in 1515.

Famous popular preachers also came from the other mendicant orders. Vicente Ferrer, a Spanish Dominican, exerted a strong influence on the Italian mendicant preachers. His order produced a number of fierce reformers, the most famous of whom was Savonarola. The famous Dominican convent San Marco in Florence, the venue of Savonarola's sermons and demise, was taken over by the Observant movement in 1436, with the support of Cosimo de' Medici. Many Observant Dominicans were known for their piety and especially for their role as spiritual advisers and hagiographers of holy women: Raymond of Capua (confessor of St. Catherine of Siena), Battista Carioni (confessor of Countess Lodovica Torelli), Niccolò Alessi and

Serafino Razzi (hagiographers of St. Caterina de' Ricci) were some of the most prominent names. The large number of holy women or beatae following the Third Rule of St. Dominic, which we will discuss in more detail later, also testified to the spiritual vibrancy of the Observant movement.

In addition to their famous General, Egidio of Viterbo, the Augustinian Observant movement exerted a strong influence in the Holy Roman Empire through the congregations associated with the vigorous Windesheim Chapter. Promoters of a renewed Augustinian theology in the fifteenth century, a number of important theologians emerged from their ranks, the last of whom was Martin Luther.

While the mendicant reformers could be harshly critical of corruption in the Church, they pinned their hopes on institutional renewal. Other critics and reformers, both lay and cleric, came to question the very legitimacy of the sacerdotal order. They ranged from a controversial movement that stayed within the Church, such as the "Modern Devotion," to outright opponents of the Roman Church such as the Lollards and Hussites. Uniting these various voices of dissent was a fundamental anti-clericalism that reflected a growing tension between the laity and clergy in the late Middle Ages.

The life and work of Geert Grote (1340–84), a patrician from Deventer in the Low Countries, spiritual father of the Modern Devotion, and founder of the Brethren of Common Life, exemplified the ambivalent tensions between acceptable spiritual reform and dissent. A deacon in the Church, Grote converted to a rigorous spirituality at the age of 34, preaching the apostolic life and turning his father's house into a hospice for poor women. Rejecting repeatedly ordination to the priesthood, Grote severely criticized the corruption of the secular clergy. Following his footsteps of charity and spiritual asceticism, the Brethren of Common Life established congregations of clerics and laity who refused to take religious vows or to assume the status of a religious order. By blurring all distinctions between clergy and laity, the Brethren elicited sharp criticisms in the 1390s when the movement first emerged, especially from the mendicant orders. Gerard Zerbolt of Zutphen, an outspoken defender of the Brethren, praised their virtuous life, lived in protest against priestly arrogance. Preaching and writing in the vernacular, the Brethren of Common Life produced an important spiritual literature in Middle Dutch. Thomas à Kempis, the author of *The Imitation of Christ*, the best-known spiritual work of the late Middle Ages, came from this milieu, as did Erasmus, the great humanist of the early sixteenth century.[8]

Criticism from the laity touched a raw nerve with the clergy, for the latter's legal status and economic privileges often rendered them targets of popular resentment. Local and regional studies seem to indicate that the Church substantially increased its property holdings during the fifteenth century. In San Gimignano in Tuscany, the landed wealth of religious institutions increased from 12 percent of all taxable property in 1315 to 25.7 percent in 1419 and 28.8 percent in 1475; in Florence the increase was from 13.5 percent in 1427 to 23.2 percent in 1498.[9] Criticism of an ever more wealthy and corrupt Church constituted a refrain in the Lollard and Hussite movement. Where religious dissent succeeded in establishing a political presence, as in Hussite Bohemia, the Roman Church found 80 percent of its property expropriated.[10] In a land where the higher clergy siphoned off one-third of the country's entire yield of land rents, anti-clerical resentment persisted even after the establishment of Utraquist Church. The persistent lay criticism of the civil dominion of the clergy would later carry over to the Protestant Reformation.

The period from ca. 1300 to 1530 was a remarkable time for female spirituality. Tommaso Buzio, an Oratorian priest at the end of the sixteenth century marveled that there existed "so many women in a single time and province, adorned with such gifts of divine inspiration . . . as in this our Italy alone," adding that since the era of Constantine there had never been such a potent concentration of female sanctity in one time and place.[11] The statistics support Buzio's observations: of the forty-four Italians beatified between 1494 and 1559, twenty-one of them were women.[12] Vauchez speaks of a "feminization of sanctity" after the thirteenth century: among saints from the mendicant orders in the period 1198–1431, 21.4 percent were women; among the laity who were beatified in the same period, 58.5 percent were women.[13] The feminization and laicization of sanctity, therefore, went hand-in-hand. The pyramid of female sanctity broadened from an apex of elite holy nuns to a large base of lay holy women, known only in their local communities.

Compared to the well-known female mystics and saints of the High Middle Ages – St. Hildegard of Bingen, St. Bridget of Sweden, etc. – women of the Renaissance could choose more paths to sanctity. Conjugal chastity represented an alternative model to cloistered virginity; and women in different stages of their life cycle found an open though difficult path to spiritual recognition. St. Catherine of Genoa (1447–1510) of the noble Fieschi family and daughter of a viceroy of Naples, trapped in an unhappy marriage when she was betrothed in 1463 at the age of 16 to a 13-year old husband began to have visions of Christ's passion. Ten years after their marriage, Catherine convinced her husband that he should convert to a life of conjugal chastity; and Catherine acquired her saintly reputation in twenty years of charitable work in the hospitals of Genoa.[14] Francesca Ponziani, daughter of a prominent Roman patrician family, acquired the "odor of sanctity" during her lifetime as a wife and mother; a female community inspired by her attracted mainly women of the nobility, who sought to establish a non-cloistered spiritual community of laywomen.[15]

The female saint in tertiary orders is particularly interesting. St. Catherine of Siena was naturally the model. These charismatic girls and young women, with their privileged access to the divine through their visions and prayers, became potentially dangerous sources of ambivalent power. The suspicion of diabolic inspiration was never far from the minds of the male ecclesiastical hierarchy. It was a testimony to the spiritual powers of these women that the friars assigned to supervise and survey as confessors often succumbed to the charisma of their charges. The Franciscan and Dominican Observants were especially active in promoting the holy women of their Third Orders. Through the printing press and sermons, the Dominicans promoted these beatae – Catherine of Siena, Colomba of Rieti, Veronica of Binasco, Angela Merici, Caterina de' Ricci, Lucia Broccadelli of Narni – and made them exemplars of Renaissance female sanctity.

The expansion of female sanctity between 1300 and 1530 accompanied the institutional crisis of the Church; St. Catherine of Siena, for example, made her mark during the Great Schism. During the political and social crisis of the Italian Wars (1494–1559), many holy women stepped into the spiritual vacuum evacuated by a failure of political and ecclesiastical leadership. In addition to their austere and pious lives, many beatae attracted attention because of their prophecies during the uncertain years of war. Lucia Broccadelli of Narni (1476–1544), reputed to be a "living saint" by virtue of her stigmata and prophecies, was carried off to Ferrara on the orders of Duke Ercole I d'Este to act as his political adviser. In cities filled with refugees from the war, these women were social workers, teachers, prophets, and charismatic leaders. Through fasting, frequent communion, ecstasies, and stigmata, they acquired the reputation of sanctity and provided living exemplars and consolation to a society afflicted by the scourge of God. Immensely popular between 1490 and 1530, these women followed the example of St. Catherine of Siena. Defined by the religious, political, and social roles in the cities of Italy, they contributed to and satisfied to some extent the longed-for reform of the Church.

The Italian beatae exerted a strong influence in Spain as well. The Dominican tertiary Maria Piedrahita (de Santo Domingo) used her mystical and prophetic gifts to promote a more rigorous reform of the Dominican houses in Spain. Devoted to Savonarola, Maria admired the Italian beata Lucia Broccadelli of Narni. Maria became a protégé of the Duke of Alba, who established a large convent for her and her followers. Among them was the friar Antonio de la Peña, who lobbied for Maria's canonization and in 1511 translated St. Catherine of Siena's "Life" and her letters into Castilian. The genealogy of Spanish holy women survived the 1530s crisis of the Inquisition campaign against the alumbrados, alleged heretical mystics in several Spanish convents. In the person of St. Teresa of Avila in the late sixteenth century and Maria de Agreda in the seventeenth, the legacy of the beatae would continue, albeit under much stricter male ecclesiastical control.

In the land of "the St. Catherines," to use Gabrielle Zarri's formulation, an adverse wind was blowing against female sanctity. With the cessation of intense warfare after 1530, the political role of female prophets waned. Although the social crisis in the Italian cities persisted, female spiritual leadership was increasingly seen as inappropriate. In the 1520s and 1530s, new religious orders emerged in northern Italy to help those most vulnerable in urban societies, impoverished women and children. While both men and women were involved in these spiritual and charitable initiatives, female charismatic leaders came increasingly under ecclesiastical censorship. Paola Antonia Negri, a founder of the Angelic Sisters in Milan, a "divine mother" to her followers and her confessor, was disciplined by the Church and deprived of her leadership; her followers were cloistered and regulated by a Church more anxious than ever about alternative sources of authority after the outbreak of the Protestant challenge. The mood of spiritual reform heightened the anxiety about female sexuality. (See the essay of Elissa Weaver above.) A saying of the sixteenth century associated feminine spirituality with female sexuality: "Whore in the summer, procuress in autumn, and beata in winter," a saying that reflected as much popular prejudice as the harsh reality of female poverty in the cities.

If female sanctity declined in Italy after 1530, women in northern Europe were losing their influence much earlier. The thirteenth century in the Holy Roman Empire, for example, witnessed the height of female monastic spirituality and a widespread feminine movement of piety known as the beguine movement. Living communally in houses under their own names, pious women of the urban middle classes of different age groups shared their economic resources while pursuing an exemplary life of virtue, without submitting to the rules of monastic enclosure. Herbert Grundmann describes this feminine spirituality as the most significant development of the High Middle Ages. As in the cities of central and northern Italy, female spirituality in northern Europe concentrated in the most urbanized regions: along the cities of the Rhine from Basel to Cologne, and throughout the Low Countries, especially in the southern Netherlands. The beguinages, the communal houses of these holy women, were dotted throughout the towns of Ypres, Ghent, Antwerp, Louvain, Amsterdam, Cologne, Mainz, Frankfurt, Strasbourg, Freiburg, Konstanz, and Basel, just to name the more prominent centers. In 1350, there were 1,170 beguines in Cologne living in 169 beguinages, forming 3.34 percent of the urban population; in Basel, the 350–400 beguines comprised 3.5 percent of the population in 1400.[16]

The beguinages represented an urban middle-class response to the socially exclusive convents for women of the nobility. While the urban patriciate predominated in the early history of the beguinages, the status of the beguines declined in social prestige after 1330 as a result of heightened ecclesiastical hostility. Suspicion was never far from the minds of male clerics, who disliked these independent female institutions that blurred the boundaries of clergy and laity. Dominican inquisitors carried out repeated investigations of beguinages: 1405 in Basel, 1406 in Mainz, 1409 in Konstanz, 1430/8 in Freiburg, 1457 in Frankfurt and Strasbourg, and 1458 in Mainz. By the 1360s, owing to the economic retrenchment after the demographic collapse and greater ecclesiastical hostility, the beguinages had reached their greatest extent of growth. The gradual and slow decline, more accentuated after 1400, was accompanied by the subjection of most of these independent beguinages under male ecclesiastical authority as they were placed under the Third Rule of the mendicant orders. With the concomitant decline in the economic role of women in the guilds of German cities during the late fourteenth and fifteenth centuries, the movement of feminine spirituality in northern Europe had passed its climax long before the decline of the beatae in Italy and Spain. It was also in the Germanic lands of the north that the witch, counter-figure to the holy woman, made its first appearance – in the mid-fifteenth century in the highlands of Switzerland and southern Germany.

In Rome, St. Thomas of Aquinas was the most honored theologian because of his emphasis on the harmony of nature and God and his triumphalist view of the destiny of the Church. At the papal university, the Sapienza, the Dominicans Thomas Torquemada, Gaetano Cajetan, and Sylvester Prierias were professors of theology; and on the feast day of St. Thomas in the Dominican Church of S. Maria sopra Minerva, the entire college of cardinals attended to show their respect. The Thomist harmony of God and Nature, optimistically formulated in the thirteenth century, built on the foundation of reason and ecclesiastical authority, was however subjected to repeated inundations of the supernatural in the fourteenth and fifteenth centuries. Some challenges were intellectual: Neoplatonism, Christian cabala, and humanist theology presented other interpretive systems to Thomism. Another danger came from East: the advance of the Ottoman Turks again raised the banner of Islam as a challenge to Latin Christendom. Still other developments unsettled the Aristotelian-Christian synthesis: the deep undercurrent of eschatological prophecies would rise to storm level with the crisis of the late medieval Church.

In the 1457 feast of St. Thomas at the Dominican Church in Rome, Laurenzo Valla delivered a laudation, "Encomion sancti Thomae," that was to be the last work of the famous humanist. In this speech, Valla opposed philosophy (the works of Aristotle and the scholastics) to theology, the Word of God. Criticizing the scholastics for adulterating the pure Word of God with pagan Greek philosophy, Valla advocated a return to the Scriptures, whose truth would be revealed by a close textual study in the original languages. This "humanist theology," as Charles Trinkaus called it, animated in fact the work of Italian humanists from Petrarch to Marsilio Ficino. (See the essay of Ingrid Rowland above.) If Valla directly challenged the authority of scholastic theology by appealing to the Bible, others circumvented the theologians by rediscovering the philosophy of Plato and his followers. Stimulated by the arrival of Byzantine refugee scholars and Greek manuscripts in Italy after the fall of Constantinople in 1453, the Neoplatonic movement in Italy centered on the circle around the Florentine priest Marsilio Ficino, who was supported by the Medici family. In their devotion to an esoteric and hidden philosophy, the Neoplatonists, through numerological and magical studies, hoped to discover divine wisdom encoded in the ancient texts. A young protégé of Ficino, the nobleman Pico della Mirandola, went further; by studying Hebrew and the mystical texts of the Jewish Kabbala, Pico hoped to discover the highest truths hidden in the scriptural texts and thereby harmonize Christianity, Greek philosophy, and Judaism. Pico's friendship with learned Jews aroused the suspicion of the Church; and the attempt to create a Christian cabala encountered censorship and inquisitorial investigation, as the German humanist Johannes Reuchlin, influenced by Pico, would discover in the 1510s.

The fervor of a few Christian intellectuals in turn had an impact on Jewish thought, as exemplified by the Italian rabbi Leone Ebreo's attempt to syncretize pagan philosophy, Renaissance humanism, and Jewish thought in the early sixteenth century.[17] These attempts at Christian-Jewish rapprochement, undertaken tentatively by a handful of intellectuals, tinged with the hopes and anxieties of conversion, generally met with suspicion and hostility on the part of the Church. The attitude of the ecclesiastical authority reflected rather the popular Christian attitude toward Jews: the maintenance of a strict boundary between the two faiths, and an unremitting pressure for Jewish conversion. While officially opposed to forced conversion, the papacy was powerless to stop the forced conversions of Jews in Castile and Aragon after 1391; it did not criticize the waves of expulsion of Jews from German cities throughout the fifteenth and early sixteenth centuries, nor did it condemn the ritual murder and host desecration accusations against the Jewish communities of central Europe and northern Italy. In the notorious case of Simon of Trent in 1475, Sixtus IV played an ambivalent role, which stopped short of condemnation. All in all, the ecclesiastical and spiritual center had little control over the expressions of spirituality and sanctity at the local level, even when sanctity was achieved by means of alleged martyrdom and religious violence.

In response to the exuberant growth of piety and sanctity, the Church limited the number of recognized saints to a handful of spiritual elites. But even these saints seemed to present a threat to the boundaries of ecclesiastical control. The saints of the Renaissance stood out in contrast to those of the High Middle Ages and the post-Tridentine Church: first, the proportion of clergymen (the saintly bishop was a model in the High Middle Ages and in Counter-Reformation Catholicism) declined in relation to women and the laity; and secondly, Renaissance saints seemed to manifest superhuman virtues in their capacity to fast, suffer, levitate, fly, and bleed. By no means limited to female saints, the sanctity of mysticism acquired a feminine aura in that it approached divinity and revelation directly through self-mortification, meditation, trances, visions, and passion, obviating the institutions of grace established by the Church.

Saints were never alone. The hermit, ascetic, mystic, and holy men and women communicated their sanctity through gestures and words to neighbors, family, strangers, and fellow religious. Stigmata, trances, extreme bodily mortification were meant to be exhibited, for the saints represented merely the instruments of God. Through their deeds and words, God communicated his will to the faithful, in addition to the teachings and sacraments of the Church. Ecclesiastical authority and mystical eruptions existed in a dialectical tension. By reserving the right to distinguish between divine and diabolical visions, the Church tried to contain and control the many expressions of spiritual charisma. In times of crisis, as in the period of the Hussite Revolution and the Italian Wars, charisma could strengthen the authority of the Church. During periods of institutional renewal, as in the decades preceding and following the Council of Trent, ecclesiastical self-confidence led to greater repression of alternative sources of charismatic spiritual leadership.

The difficulties of the Church in controlling lay and popular spirituality reflected the enormous appetite for the divine in the period from the Black Death to the Reformation. The natural order – and God's representation in that order, the Church – seemed unable to satisfy the growing hunger among the faithful for holiness. For one, the harmony between God and nature seemed shattered by the recurring plagues, warfare, and the ever-menacing threat of the Turks. For another, the authority of the Church was compromised by its internal crisis and its claims to worldly dominion.

The appetite for the divine showed itself in the need to feel, touch, and experience the beyond, the supernatural, of which the mysticism we have discussed above was but one expression. Everywhere there were signs of spiritual hunger. The faithful longed to hear God's Word, whether from the pulpit or from the city square, whether it be an explication of a biblical text or a prophecy calling for repentance and threatening imminent divine punishment. There was an explosion of preaching in the fifteenth century. In addition to itinerant preachers and famous mendicant preachers on circuit-tours, the clergy delivered more and longer sermons. With the printing press, sermons and preaching handbooks circulated widely; between 1460 and 1500 in France alone, over 5,000 volumes of sermons appeared in print.[18] The best-known preachers such as Geiler von Kaysersberg, preacher at the cathedral of Strasbourg, also became renowned authors with the publication of their sermons. Many cities endowed preacherships in order that their citizens could regularly dine on the Word of God. In other urban communities, such as Florence, the tradition of civic preaching by the Dominicans dated back to the mid-thirteenth century; and it was from the pulpit that Savonarola served the Florentines their homiletic feasts of repentance and conversion.[19] To quote the words of Bernardino of Siena, one of the most popular preachers of his day, addressed to his audience: "There is less peril for your soul in not hearing mass than in not hearing the sermon. Tell me, how could you believe in the holy sacrament of the altar but for the holy preaching you have heard?"[20]

Anchored in the liturgical context and grounded in biblical texts, preaching only became potentially subversive when it responded to extraordinary events and expressed itself in the prophetic mode. In 1472, a hermit with a long beard by the name of William of Morano preached throughout Rome and prophesied many dire future events. He was arrested and beaten, his cross confiscated, but his warning echoed in the chronicles and popular memory of the Roman populace, who heard many more prophets of doom preaching in the Campo de' Fiori and other public spaces of their city.[21] William the Hermit was followed by another who looked like St. Paul; in 1485 it was the turn of a Franciscan hermit who rode astride a steer carrying an image of the crucifix. An unknown ballad singer in 1511 evoked the popular mood in Rome: "An ancient hermit with long beard and hair, goes crying through Rome "peace, peace"; then whenever he wishes he goes away invisible and many believe firmly that he is Elijah."[22] The flood of prophecies and preaching surrounding the Council of Pisa (1511–13) and the Fifth Lateran Council (1512–17) subsided only for a few years, when the Sack of Rome by imperial troops in 1527 unleashed another flood of prophetic and homiletic doom. Transcending the boundary between high and low, the prophetic and eschatological themes were echoed from street preachers to the aisles of the Church Councils. Words of doom heralded the immediate presence of the divine, that of divine wrath specifically, a sign of the corruption of the times.

As if words were insufficient to make known his anger, God sent other portents to warn his people. The eruption of the divine was manifest in the many supernatural prodigies reported between the last decades of the fourteenth and the first decades of the sixteenth century: floods, storms, comets, fire, and unnatural shapes in the heavens, and the monstrous births of humans and animals. The first deformed creature to attain notoriety in Renaissance Italy was the so-called Pope-Ass, allegedly found on the banks of the Tiber after the disastrous winter flood of 1495. Widely interpreted as a portent of God's anger with the pontificate of Alexander VI, the Pope-Ass story reached its widest circulation in the Protestant anti-papal propaganda of the 1520s. Another famous monster in Italy, the so-called "Monster of Ravenna" of 1512, said to be the offspring of a monk and nun, served in the propaganda against Julius II before it too was appropriated by the followers of Luther in their anti-clerical satire.[23]

Fully conscious of the danger of popular prophecies, the Fifth Lateran Council prohibited and limited the foretelling of future events. In a bull of 1514, it condemned the use of incantations and divinations to foretell the future; in 1516, the Council forbade clerics to predict the specific advent of the Antichrist or the Day of Last Judgment. Unable and unwilling to ban all divine eruptions in the natural order, the Council fathers issued decrees to ensure maximum ecclesiastical control over revelations and prophecies.[24]

The prohibitions decreed by the Fifth Lateran Council hardly dampened the spirit of prophecy. In a letter sent to the newly elected Pope Leo X in 1513, the anonymous prophet predicted great changes because of the conjunction of Saturn, specifying that "this change will take place in the religion of men, so that one sect will destroy another." After predicting the destruction of the Turks, the letter prophesies that in 1519 and 1520 there would be a great disturbance in the Church, from which a general reformation would commence.[25] There were other prophecies that rang true.

Take the prophecies of the Florentine layman Francesco da Meleto, for example. Having studied the Bible and mathematics, he predicted the year 1517 as the beginning of the long-hoped-for church reform, a renovation that would commence with the conversion of the Jews and end with the destruction of the Turks in 1536.[26]

Prophecies and prodigies were not limited to Italy. One of the most popular prophetic works was the *Prognostication of Johannes Lichtenberger*, a German astrologer who published his findings in 1488. Lichtenberger's prophecy of a great flood that would cleanse the sins of the world and herald a new age of renovation reflected the great excitement with natural and supernatural prodigies in northern Europe. Reprinted in 1526, Lichtenberger's prognostications were retroactively interpreted as true divinations predicting the evangelical reform movement. The tradition of prophecy declined in Italy after the 1530s but remained strong in Protestant Germany, as unnatural births and astronomical portents found widespread dissemination from Protestant pulpits and broadsheets, at least into the mid-sixteenth century.

The Word made flesh was made very real in the popular piety of Renaissance Europe through a broad spectrum of visual images. Of the 2,033 Italian paintings from the period 1420–1539 surveyed by Peter Burke, 87 percent had a religious theme; of these half depicted the Virgin Mary, one-quarter that of Christ, and the rest represented saints.[27] The theme of Madonna and Child, graced by the brushes of the great masters, was also popular in the mass-produced woodcut broadsheets that became available with the advent of the printing presses. With the feminization and laicization of spirituality, it was not surprising that Marian devotion reached a new intensity during the fifteenth century, when the rosary and the doctrine of the Immaculate Conception were introduced, the first by the Dominicans and the latter by the Franciscans. Another favorite theme in visual imagery was the Holy Family representing the infant Jesus in an extended family, with his parents (Mary and Joseph) and grandparents (Anne and Joachim); others depicted the child Jesus riding a hobby-horse, while Joseph practiced his carpentry; still others showed the Virgin surrounded by female friends and relatives. Widely disseminated in the Holy Roman Empire and the Low Countries, these woodcuts reflected the fundamental desire of the laity to find sanctity in kinship and ordinary family life, in the immediacy of their own material world and flesh.[28]

Conversely, the representation of evil also focused on the real pain and suffering of humanity. Every drop of blood on the crucified Christ in the Passion painted by Martin Grünewald (Isenheim Altarpiece, 1510–15) expressed the excruciating pain of a redemption of humankind thanks to the incarnation of the Word. Reflections on the passion of Christ became the focus of a spirituality that found expression not only in Kempis's *Imitatio Christi*, but also in the countless stations of the Cross erected in churches and roadways throughout Christendom.

The Passion of Christ intensified the imaginings of the bodily punishment of sinners. Between the High Middle Ages and the Renaissance, as Jerome Baschet has argued, the visual depiction of hell changed from one of devouring monsters to the dominant theme of individuals suffering bodily torture.[29] As artists sought to remind the faithful of the sins of the flesh, they turned to the actual judicial torture and executions of their world to remind their viewers of that mirror image of torture and execution: the crucifixion of Christ that redeemed all human flesh. Not for nothing was Simon of Trent, the best-known child martyr of alleged Jewish ritual murders, represented in the image of the Child Jesus and the crucified Christ. The Christian appetite for divine flesh, exemplified by the fervor for frequent communion among the spiritual elite, reflected in turn the cannibalistic impulses attributed to the diabolical Jews.[30]

By making the holy visible, tangible, and attainable, it was as if the Renaissance tried to overcome death itself. The bequests from testators in Tuscan cities in the fourteenth century showed a significant shift in pious endowments towards preserving the memory of the testator and the longevity of the lineage. Those who were about to die were busily making arrangements to ensure their remembrance among the living.[31]

All of this contradicts the idea that late medieval Christianity was a religion of fear, or that the clergy was engaged primarily in a campaign of culpabilization. Sin and fear notwithstanding, as Jerome Baschat argues, the Church cared above all for the salvation of souls. The path to heaven was marked by a broad array of doctrines and devotional practices; and on that voyage, the pilgrim came well equipped with vernacular prayer books, endowment masses, indulgences, sacraments, sermons, confraternities, amulets, popular magic, and learned doctrines. All doomsayers and critics of the Church notwithstanding, Renaissance religious culture represented a time of hope. The Jews and Muslims, identified by the Spanish humanist Martin Martinex de Ampies as followers of the Antichrist in his *Libellus de Antichristo* (1496), were after all defeated, subjugated, and expelled from the triumphant land of Christian reconquista.[32] And was not the discovery of the Americas another sign of the triumph of Christianity? In sending twelve Franciscan missionaries to assist in Hernan Cortez's military conquest in 1523, Francisco de Quiñones, general of the Spanish friars minor, believed his order was completing the Gospel's conquest of the world in preparation for the Second Coming of Christ. The return to an apostolic time of evangelization signified not so much the end of time, which it was, but a return to a golden age of the Gospels. In the person of Charles V and the Spanish Empire, these optimistic millenarian hopes would find the imagined instruments for the ultimate fulfillment of the religious dreams of the Renaissance.

NOTES

1 Vauchez, *La Sainteté*, p. 323.
2 Calculations based on Weinstein and Bell, *Saints and Society*, p. 167.
3 Stinger, *Renaissance*, pp. 94–5.
4 Partner, *Pope's Men*, pp. 7, 12.
5 Prodi, *Papal Prince*.
6 Stinger, *Renaissance*, pp. 152–3.
7 Traeger, *Renaissance und Religion*, p. 37.
8 On the Devotio Moderna, see Post, *Modern Devotion* and John van Engen, "Late Medieval Anticlericalism: The Case of the New Devout," in Dykema and Oberman, *Anticlericalism*, pp. 19–52.
9 Pullan, *Early Renaissance Italy*, pp. 325–6.

10   Frantisek Smahel, "The Hussite Critique of the Clergy's Civil Dominion," in Dykema and Oberman, *Anticlericalism*, pp. 83–90.
11   Zarri, "Living Saints," p. 222.
12   Ibid.
13   Vauchez, *Les Laïcs*, pp. 189–91.
14   Kenneth Jorgensen, " 'Love Conquers All': The Conversion, Asceticism and Altruism of St. Caterina of Genoa," in Monfasani and Musto, *Renaissance Society*, pp. 87–106.
15   Anna Esposito, "St. Francesca and the Female Religious Communities of Fifteenth-Century Rome," in Bornstein and Rusconi, *Women*, pp. 197–218.
16   Schmitt, *Mort d'une hérésie*, pp. 39–40.
17   Riccardo Scrivano, "Platonic and Cabalistic elements in the Hebrew Culture of Renaissance Italy: Leone Ebreo and his Dialoghi d'amore," in Eisenbichler and Publiese, *Ficino*, pp. 123–39.
18   Taylor, *Soldiers of Christ*.
19   See the contributions by Daniel R. Lesnick and Ronald Weissman in Verdon and Henderson, *Christianity and the Renaissance*, pp. 208–28, 250–71.
20   Pullan, *Early Renaissance Italy*, p. 333.
21   See Ottavia Niccolo, "High and Low Prophetic Culture in Rome at the Beginning of the Sixteenth Century," in Reeves, *Prophetic Rome*, p. 205.
22   Ibid.
23   See R. Po-chia Hsia, "A Time for Monsters: The Eruption of the Divine in the 16th Century," in Landes and Knoppers, *Monstrous Bodies* and Ottavia Niccolo, "High and Low Prophetic Culture in Rome at the Beginning of the Sixteenth Century," in Reeves, *Prophetic Rome*.
24   Nelson H. Minnich, "Prophecy and the Fifth Lateran Council (1512–1517)," in Reeves, *Prophetic Rome*, pp. 63–88.
25   Aldo Landi, "Prophecy at the Time of the Council of Pisa (1511–1513)," in Reeves, *Prophetic Rome*, pp. 53–62.
26   Nelson H. Minnich, "Prophecy and the Fifth Lateran Council (1512–1517)," in Reeves, *Prophetic Rome*.
27   Peter Burke, *Culture and Society*.
28   Hsia, "Die Sakralisierung," pp. 57–75.
29   Baschet, *Les Justices*, p. 580ff.
30   Hsia, *Trent 1475*.
31   Cohn, *Cult of Remembrance*.
32   Adriano Prosperi, "New Heaven and New Earth: Prophecy and Propaganda at the Time of the Discovery and Conquest of the Americas," in Reeves, *Prophetic Rome*, pp. 279–304.

REFERENCES

Baschet, Jérôme, *Les Justices de l'au-delà. Les représentations de l'enfer en France et en Italie (XIIe–Xve siècle)* (Rome: École Française de Rome, 1993).
Bornstein, Daniel and Rusconi, Roberto, eds., *Women and Religion in Medieval and Renaissance Italy* (Chicago: University of Chicago Press, 1996).
Burke, Peter, *Culture and Society in Renaissance Italy* (New York: Scribners, 1972).
Cohn, Samuel K., *The Cult of Remembrance and the Black Death: Six Renaissance Cities in Central Italy* (Baltimore: Johns Hopkins University Press, 1992).

Dykema, Peter A. and Oberman, Heiko A., eds., *Anticlericalism in Late Medieval and Early Modern Europe* (Leiden: E. J. Brill, 1993).

Eisenbichler, Konrad and Publiese, Olga Zorzi, eds., *Ficino and Renaissance Neoplatonism* (Ottawa: Dovehouse Editions, 1986).

Hsia, R. Po-chia, *Trent 1475: Stories of a Ritual Murder Trial* (New Haven: Yale University Press, 1988).

——,"Die Sakralisierung der Gesellschaft. Blutfrömmigkeit und Verehrung der Heiligen Familie in der Reformation," in *Kommunalisierung und Christianisierung Voraussetzungen und Folgen der Reformation 1400–1600* (*Zeitschrift für Historische Forschung*, Beiheft 9, 1989), pp. 57–75.

Landes, Joan and Knoppers, Laura, eds., *Monstrous Bodies/Political Monstrosities in Early Modern Europe* (forthcoming).

Monfasani, John and Musto, Ronald G., eds., *Renaissance Society and Culture: Essays in Honor of Eugene F. Rice* (New York: Italica Press, 1991).

Partner, Peter, *The Pope's Men: The Papal Civil Service in the Renaissance* (Oxford: Clarendon Press, 1990).

Post, R. R., *The Modern Devotion* (Leiden: Brill, 1968).

Prodi, Paolo, *The Papal Prince: One Body and Two Souls. The Papal Monarchy in Early Modern Europe* (Cambridge: Cambridge University Press, 1987).

Pullan, Brian, *A History of Early Renaissance Italy* (London: Allen Lane, 1973).

Reeves, Majorie, ed., *Prophetic Rome in the High Renaissance Period* (Oxford: Clarendon Press, 1992).

Schmitt, Jean-Claude, *Mort d'une hérésie. L'Église et les clercs face aux béguines et aux béghards du Rhin supérior du XIVe au XVe siècle* (Paris: Mouton, 1978).

Stinger, Charles L., *The Renaissance in Rome* (Bloomington, IN: Indiana University Press, 1985).

Taylor, Larissa, *Soldiers of Christ: Preaching in Late Medieval and Reformation France* (New York: Oxford University Press, 1992).

Traeger, Jörg, *Renaissance und Religion. Die Kunst des Glaubens im Zeitalter Raphaels* (Munich: C. Beck, 1997).

Vauchez, André, *La Sainteté en Occident aux derniers siècles du moyen âge* (Rome: École française de Rome, 1981). English translation: *Sainthood in the Later Middle Ages* (Cambridge: Cambridge University Press, 1997).

——, *Les Laïcs au moyen âge. Pratiques et expériences religieuses* (Paris: Cerf, 1987). English translation: *Laity in the Middle Ages: Religious Beliefs and Devotional Practices* (South Bend, IN: University of Notre Dame Press, 1993).

Verdon, Timothy and Henderson, John, eds., *Christianity and the Renaissance: Image and Religious Imagination in the Quattrocento* (Syracuse, NY: Syracuse University Press, 1990).

Weinstein, Donald and Bell, Rudolph M., *Saints and Society: The Two Worlds of Western Christendom, 1000–1700* (Chicago: University of Chicago Press, 1982).

Zarri, Gabrielle, "Living Saints: A Typology of Female Sanctity in the Early Sixteenth Century," in *Women and Religion in Medieval and Renaissance Italy*, ed. Daniel Bornstein and Roberto Rusconi (Chicago: University of Chicago Press, 1996), pp. 219–303.

FURTHER READING

D'Amico, John F., *Renaissance Humanism in Papal Rome: Humanists and Churchmen on the Eve of the Reformation* (Baltimore: Johns Hopkins University Press, 1983).

Hale, John, *The Civilization of Europe in the Renaissance* (New York: Atheneum, 1994).

Kelly, Kathleen Coyne, ed., *Menacing Virgins: Representing Virginity in the Middle Ages and Renaissance* (Newark, DE: University of Delaware Press, 2000).

O'Malley, John, ed., *Humanity and Divinity in Renaissance and Reformation* (Leiden: E. J. Brill, 1993).

Trinkaus, Charles, *In Our Image and Likeness: Humanity and Divinity in Italian Humanist Thought*, 2 vols. (Chicago: University of Chicago Press, 1970).

—— *The Scope of Renaissance Humanism* (Ann Arbor: University of Michigan Press, 1983).

CHAPTER TWENTY

Art

LOREN PARTRIDGE

With no previous training in the field I began studying art history at Harvard in the early 1960s. English had been my undergraduate major at Yale where New Criticism still reigned supreme, an approach focusing exclusively on close critical readings of individual texts treated as self-sufficient verbal constructions with no reference to their cultural context. I gravitated quite naturally, therefore, to Sydney Freedberg who concentrated solely on the visual characteristic of Italian Renaissance painting through connoisseurship and stylistic analysis. James Ackerman, however, with whom I also studied, approached Italian Renaissance architecture much more in terms of function and cultural context without ignoring questions of style. As a student I also read Erwin Panofsky's erudite iconographical studies with admiration and awe, but was taught to believe, however incorrectly, that most of what was essential about works of art could be gleaned simply by close looking. These disciplinary methods of connoisseurship, style, and iconography in which my generation was trained continue to impact on the field today, although their limitations are far more clearly recognized. But they have gradually lost ground to contextual approaches previously anticipated in part by Ackerman, which have transformed the study and teaching of Renaissance art.

Connoisseurship

In his 1550 and much enlarged 1568 edition of the *Lives of the Artists* Giorgio Vasari initiated the study of Italian Renaissance art history. He chronicled the great flowering and regional diversity of Italian Renaissance art through artists' biographies in which he enumerated at length each artist's corpus of works more or less in chronological order. Beginning at the turn of the twentieth century, when the method of connoisseurship began to reach full stride, these biographies provided the foundation for the work of all connoisseurs of Italian Renaissance art, the most famous of whom was Bernard Berenson. By sustained exposure to the originals, constant comparing of photographs, and much intuition these connoisseurs developed the expertise to distinguish one artist's hand from another and over time accomplished the monumental and fundamental task of attributing a name and date to most of the many thousands of works of individual artists that constitute our heritage. Working in collaboration with dealers, Berenson also helped to guide the formation of some of the major private collections of Renaissance art in the United States, now mostly in public museums. Over the years the efforts of connoisseurs have been supported and refined by the hundreds of monographs and catalogues raisonnés on individual artists or regional schools as well as by the catalogues of museums and private collections, usually compiled by museum researchers and curators in collaboration with connoisseurs. Even though the corpus of Renaissance art is essentially fixed, with few works remaining to be discovered, there is still considerable disagreement about the attribution and dating of a body of unsigned or undated works, especially drawings, prints, and works of minor masters. Connoisseurship, therefore, will continue to serve a useful purpose. Furthermore, those working in museums and auction houses in daily contact with artworks are required to develop and maintain a keen "eye."

For art historians working in academic settings, a degree of connoisseurship will always be expected, but is no longer a central concern. In spite of Giovanni Morelli's early efforts to make connoisseurship objective in his *Italian Painters* (London, 1900), the perceived distinguishing marks of an individual hand are often too subtle or varied to be clearly isolated, and a priori standards or financial interests can cloud judgments. All too often card houses of attribution and dating have tumbled, blown down by a lucky archival find or lack of consensus. Further, judgments made in the name of artistic quality, beauty, and genius – often nothing more than a connoisseur's subjective projections – have rightly become problematic with the advent of post-structural analysis unsympathetic toward such universalizing notions. Nevertheless, monographs on individual artists – for which connoisseurship remains an essential ingredient – continue to be produced in great numbers however dated the form. As long as monographs address more than pure connoisseurship, as most recent examples do, they will continue to be important far into the future.

The subjectivism of connoisseurship, especially in painting, has also been mitigated by technological developments that have been adapted by conservators to their laboratories. X-radiography, the investigative technique of longest standing, penetrates an object often to reveal *pentimenti* or changes under the paint surface as well as certain peculiarities of the support, such as its technique of manufacture or its fragmentary state resulting from later cutting. The fluoresce produced by ultraviolet light can assist in distinguishing varnish layers and later over-painting, while at the other end of the light spectrum infrared reflectography often renders a paint surface transparent, to reveal much of an artist's preparatory work, especially work involving charcoal pounce patterns or carbon under-drawing. Certain varieties of wood used in panel paintings and sculpture can be quite accurately dated by dendrochronology, the comparative study of growth rings. Although it is rarely practiced except in extreme cases where the destruction of the work seems imminent, it is possible to separate and remove the smooth outer plaster layer (*intonaco*) of paintings frescoed on walls or ceilings from the underlying rough plaster (*arriccio*), thus exposing any sinopia or charcoal under-drawing. A much more common and non-invasive procedure used for frescoes involves tracing overlapping plaster patches of successive days of fresco work (*giornate*) to show the direction and duration of the work's execution. Scanning electron microscopy accurately analyzes the chemical properties of minute samples of pigment, and the magnification of tiny cross-sections of paint layers often reveals techniques of execution peculiar to a particular artist or workshop. Although expensive to do, organic materials are sometimes dated by the measurement of radioactive carbon 14 deterioration. Thermoluminescence is commonly used for dating ceramic objects. And in rare circumstances magnetic resonance imaging can be a useful tool for subsurface examination of certain three-dimensional objects. All of these investigative methods facilitate judgments about authenticity, authorship, genesis of design, and dating, as well as aid in the reconstruction of scattered fragments of previously whole objects.

But the main work of conservators – arresting deterioration from insects, moisture, or pollutants, stabilizing supports and surfaces, removing discolored varnish, grime, and later over-painting, and judiciously reconstructing lacunae with removable pigments – not only preserves our heritage, but restores the integrity and legibility of works of art to states approximating, within reasonable limits, the moment of their completion. The restored state can often be crucial in evaluating authorship, style, and sometimes even subject matter and patronage.

Removal of any element of an art object results in an irretrievable loss of part of its history, but, with few exceptions, what is gained by returning a work as closely as possible to its original state, in my view, far exceeds in value the loss. In any case, any number of important scholarly contributions – including modern museum exhibitions with their attendant catalogues and conferences – have demonstrated that a much closer cooperation between conservators, curators, and art historians will be essential in the future.

Stylistic Analysis

In combination with his artists' biographies, Vasari laid out a compelling stylistic history of Italian Renaissance art based on a biological model of three ages: birth (age of Giotto), adolescence (age of Masaccio), and full maturity (age of Leonardo, Michelangelo, and Raphael). He believed that the third age continued as the *bella maniera* of his own day, thus avoiding the decline into old age and senility implied by his model. Renaissance style for Vasari grew toward an ever more convincing naturalism learned from the direct study of nature as well as from the transcriptions by previous masters, including classical masters. At the same time, this naturalism was structured ever more rigorously on the principles of classical order and harmony in architecture, anatomy, and narrative. Once full maturity was reached in the third age, according to Vasari, artists were able to transcend both nature and order to achieve a surpassing ideal beauty, a *bella maniera*, which simultaneously displayed the unique mind and hand of each individual artist.

Up until fairly recently, a large part of Renaissance art historical scholarly energy has been devoted to refining and expanding Vasari's stylistic periods. Vasari's first age has been subdivided into Byzantine (late thirteenth century), Gothic (fourteenth century), International Gothic (late fourteenth, early fifteenth centuries), and early Renaissance (fifteenth century). Within the early Renaissance various sub-styles have been detected including the scientific, poetic, proto-Mannerist, and archaeological (e.g., Pollaiuolo, Botticelli, Piero di Cosimo, and Ripanda respectively). Scholars still accept Vasari's third age as the High Renaissance, but make distinctions between the Roman, Florentine, and Venetian versions; some have also identified elements of evolution toward the Baroque or devolution into the "crisis" of Mannerism. The post-High Renaissance style which Vasari was unable or unwilling to recognize – pejoratively termed Mannerism by later seventeenth-century critics for being what they saw as mannered, formulaic, and stylized – has been re-evaluated, rehabilitated, and dissected into a first (experimental) and a second (more elegant) generation *maniera* (for example, Rosso vs. Salviati). As a parallel to the Counter-Reformation, the austere style of the later Renaissance has often been termed "counter *maniera*," although "anti-Mannerism" (sometimes "classicizing *maniera*"), "proto-Baroque," and *arte sacra* or *arte senza tempo* have also been applied to certain stylistic currents within this period. These terms do say something about general developments and serve as useful guideposts in teaching. But all such broad designations explain little of interest about any individual work of art, and typically treat naturalism and classicism as objective, normative, and unproblematic criteria not related to any cultural context. However, only when Renaissance styles, sources, and influences – especially the reception of classical motifs, forms, and subjects – are linked to broader cultural issues, such as the relationship between classicism and political power, Mannerism and court culture, or landscape and pastoral poetry, can they meaningfully enlighten essential processes of Renaissance image-making.

Iconographical Analysis

The third traditional methodological mainstay of the field became widespread beginning in the 1930s with the wave of German scholars who fled Germany with the rise of Nazism. Pre-eminent among these art historians were Ernst Gombrich and Edgar Wind who emigrated to England and Erwin Panofsky who moved to the United States. These scholars – trained or influenced by the Hamburg scholar Aby Warburg – transformed the field from aesthetic evaluation and appreciation, often with a strong undercurrent of moral instruction, to one that was rigorously intellectual and professional. They did so by teaching ways of unlocking the symbolic meaning of images, primarily by linking them to textual sources drawn mostly from mythography, theology, and philosophy. By tracing the evolution, revival, and transformation of texts and images across time from classical antiquity to the Renaissance they developed an erudite form of cultural history, which Panofsky termed *iconology*. For about two decades iconography/iconology not only influenced other fields, but also placed art history – especially Italian and Northern Renaissance art history – at the forefront of humanistic studies.

Even at its best, as a powerful form of cultural history, however, iconography tends to be more enlightening about broad intellectual and visual traditions than in the interpretation of specific works of art. Furthermore, in the hands of the less skilled and learned followers of Panofsky, Wind, and Gombrich, the study of iconography has all too often been reduced to a sterile exercise with texts privileged over images and images reduced to mere pictograms. Symbolic problems become puzzles solved by unearthing a specific text or visual source to provide the one and only answer. The interpretation of the subject matter and symbols of Renaissance art, of course, remains an important and necessary part of any analysis, and will certainly continue to constitute a fundamental element of research. But such work will have to illuminate specific works and their unique circumstances as well as be informed by a post-structuralist recognition that any visual language is unstable, indeterminate, and multivalent, and that texts are not transparent, but themselves imbedded in complex, contingent historical discourses.

Contextual Analysis

If the connoisseurship, style, and iconography in which I was first trained are no longer the dominant methods of Renaissance art historical studies, what has taken their place? The answer is a many-faceted contextual approach that seeks to understand artists and artworks in terms of the cultural conventions, constraints, and contexts that shaped the outlook of both artists and audience alike. Michael Baxandall pioneered this method of research in his 1972 *Painting and Experience in Fifteenth-Century Italy*, by exploring incunabula for early Renaissance social practices that shaped what he aptly calls the Renaissance "period eye." A manual on practical mathematics, for example, which taught merchants to quickly estimate the contents of a container by barrel gauging, could help explain the appeal of Piero della Francesca's highly geometrical painted forms. Treatises on preaching or on dance could illuminate certain gestures and postures in painted narratives. Or an essay on equestrian art might help account for the proportions or gait of a painted or sculpted horse. The implications of Baxandall's work have been far-reaching, stimulating many varieties of contextual approaches.

Function

One such approach is to study a work of art from the perspective of its function, its practical, ritualistic, or liturgical purpose in society. A painting viewed as an altarpiece rather than as a milestone in an artist's stylistic development, for example, requires studying its form and content in relationship to religious doctrines, rituals, and forms of piety. Studying the entire genre of altarpieces functionally rather than merely aesthetically highlights the dialectic between changes in altarpiece design – from an iconic to a perspectival form, say, or from the contemplative *sacra conversazione* to the dramatic narrative type – and changes in doctrine, liturgy, and piety over long periods of time, as from the early Renaissance to the Counter-Reformation. Beyond altarpieces, Renaissance churches and their entire range of ecclesiastical furnishings deserve further study from a functional point of view.

In terms of secular architecture, the High Renaissance palaces of Rome have been researched with great acumen and intelligence by Christoph Frommel, who examined their component parts – courtyards, reception rooms, chapels, bedrooms, baths, and so on – and systematically surveyed each part within the group of palaces as a whole. The composite picture that emerges is of labyrinthine, multifaceted fabrics that contained and constructed the elaborate hierarchical life in noble courts. But in spite of Frommel's work and numerous monographs on individual palaces, we still know far too little about Renaissance domestic residences for the full range of social and economic classes, and how they functioned in terms of family life and urban rituals.

With regard to palace decoration, my colleague in early modern history, Randolph Starn, and I have studied a few selected palace state rooms according to their function in our 1992 *Arts of Power*. Starting with the premise that a hall of state was designed to display and exercise power, we studied how its fresco decoration staged the processional axis to the dais, depicted the sources of authority and legitimacy claimed by the sovereign, and constructed the regime's affirmation of strength, wealth, and triumph. Studying halls of state across time and space revealed how various regimes, whether communal, seignorial, or autocratic, produced different visual schemes and programs reflective of their different functions and ideologies. But there still remain hundreds of palace state rooms that await further study from a functional point of view.

Patronage

The study of patronage has been a long-standing area of investigation. Understood from the broadest perspective, patronage concerns wealth and demand. In his 1993 *Wealth and the Demand for Art in Italy 1300–1600*, the economic historian Richard Goldthwaite undertook just such a global study of the accumulation of surplus wealth that made consumption possible among Italian nobles and merchants, as well as the cultural forces behind the expansion of religious institutions and secular palaces that fueled the demand for art. However, he discussed no specific commissions or individual works of art.

Traditionally, individual patrons have been understood as the person or institution that paid for a work of art. But more contemporary studies have focused on the patron as an agent of a particular ideology and how that ideology inflects the form and content of the art commissioned. Patrons, therefore, are studied in terms of family and kinship, education and training, occupational obligations, economic ties, political allegiances, institutional affiliations, religious or philosophical thought – in short, all that establishes a patron's sense of identity and claims to worth, status, and power. Eve Borsook and Johannes Offerhaus's 1981 *Francesco Sassetti and Ghirlandaio at Santa Trinita, Florence*, for example, provides a wealth of information about the patron's triumphs and tragedies, classical erudition, business interests, civic patriotism, political associations, religious beliefs, and artistic taste.

Or, to take two examples of institutional patronage, Rona Goffen in her 1986 *Piety and Patronage in Renaissance Venice* has greatly enhanced our understanding of both the theological implications of the subject matter and the theatrical style of representation of Titian's great high altarpiece of the *Assumption of the Virgin* at the Frari in Venice by her study of the doctrinal beliefs and civic connections of the conventual Franciscan order for which it was painted. Similarly, in her 1988 *Venetian Narrative Painting in the Age of Carpaccio* Patricia Brown studied the membership, administrative structure, rituals, and rivalries of Venetian confraternities as a key for interpreting the sumptuous decoration they commissioned for their meeting halls.

Art collecting represents another aspect of patronage. Research into the kinds and range of materials collected, their organization and classification, and the decoration of the sites where collections were stored and displayed – studies, galleries, and sculpture courts – offers important insights into Renaissance cosmology, constitution of human knowledge, constructions of political power, and in some cases the impact of the New World upon the Old. Since there are still large numbers of influential Renaissance patrons, both institutional and individual, who have never been systematically or thoroughly studied, patronage will no doubt continue to be a valued area of research.

Audience and reception

The audience for, and the reception of, a work of art also involves patronage, for a work is always at some level addressed to the patron. But the audience is usually more extensive than the patron and the reception of the work continues long after the work's completion. While Baccio Bandinelli's sculpture *Hercules and Cacus* in the Florentine Piazza della Signoria, for example, was addressed to its patrons, Pope Clement VII and Duke Alessandro I de' Medici, the citizenry of Florence constituted its principal audience. Only by examining the clash of ideologies in this politically charged civic center – the dynastic, ducal, autocratic aspirations of the Medici on one hand, and a range of the republican, oligarchic, patrician, plebeian, and mercantile interests of their detractors on the other – does the significance of the work come into sharp focus. Furthermore, Cellini's famous verbal attack on the work recorded in his autobiography – part of his effort to dislodge Bandinelli and insinuate himself as a favorite of the Medicean court – dramatically demonstrates how an artwork's reception can shape taste and even forestall an understanding of its considerable artistic achievement, even up to the present day.

Michelangelo's *Last Judgment* in the Sistine Chapel serves as another classic case of the importance of a negative reception. Pietro Aretino initiated an attack on the fresco without even having seen it. He was piqued because Michelangelo both rejected his unsolicited program for the work's iconography and failed to pay for his advice with a work of art. Religious zealots picked up the critique for very different reasons. Stung by Protestant attacks on Catholic art, these critics objected to Michelangelo's breaks with iconographical tradition, especially the figures' nudity (even if theologically justified), and the inclusion of non-scriptural subject matter – Charon and Minos – from Dante and mythology. Even though the fresco's patron, Pope Paul III, and its audience, the *capella papalis*, were among the most sophisticated in Europe and appear to have initially received the work with nothing short of enthusiasm, the uproar surrounding the work at the height of Counter-Reformation prudery and fundamentalism nearly resulted in its destruction immediately after Michelangelo's death. The work was saved only by the compromise of covering with drapery the most offensive nudity.

Studying the audience and reception of works of art runs the risk of falling into the trap of positing a universal, monolithic audience or an idealized, undifferentiated reception. Only with many and varied voices in the historical record, and only if each voice's gender, class, political allegiances, and religious ideology can be determined, does the approach yield satisfactory results.

Status of artists

The audience of any work of art in the first instance is, of course, always the artist. As already noted, the artist's biography is the oldest form of Renaissance art history. The information featured in Vasari on the education, training, and social status of Renaissance artists has been much expanded by modern scholars. In a detailed comparison of artists working for communes within the guilds with those working for courts outside the guild structure, Martin Warnke has shown in his 1992 *The Court Artist* that service at court was the major means for artists to improve pay, working conditions, security, and prestige. Studies of Renaissance art theory, written for the most part by artists themselves, have shown how the arts came to be viewed as liberal rather than mechanical by drawing on classical notions of the *paragone* (comparisons of the arts) and the equation of visual and verbal rhetoric. The social historian Peter Burke has demonstrated in *The Italian Renaissance*, however, that almost no artist had sufficient education or class status to truly qualify as a practitioner of the liberal arts. Studies of artists' tombs, burial rites, and self-portraiture have further clarified the rise of artists' status. By means of the administrative structure, statutes, educational programs, and sponsored artistic projects of the new art academies that arose in the later sixteenth century, first in Florence then in Rome, Bologna, and elsewhere, artists gained independence, tax relief, status, and unity by finally breaking the guilds' hold on artistic training, standards, prices, and competition. In the process, however, artists were transformed into courtiers subservient to the needs of authoritarian princely regimes, especially for their (often ephemeral) multimedia extravaganzas celebrating important dynastic events such as births, marriages, investitures, and deaths. Further work is needed in all aspects of the artists' reality, including critical editions of theoretical texts and contextual analyses of the texts themselves, such as the work of Paul Barolsky, Patricia Rubin, and Robert Williams on Giorgio Vasari and Patricia Reilly on Alessandro Allori.

Psychoanalytic approaches

Ostensibly a psychoanalytic or psychobiographical approach stands to provide insightful takes on individual artists. But attempts to date have not been promising. Myths and legends about artists' collective psychological makeup – artists as precocious child prodigies, autodidacts, melancholic loners, tricksters, magicians, the godlike, and so on – were recurrent and widespread throughout history and certainly conditioned Renaissance artists' conceptions of themselves, as Ernst Kris and Otto Kurz have shown in *Legend, Myth, and Magic in the Image of the Artist*. But we will never be privy enough to essential details of the early childhood of any Renaissance artists, in my view, to make a Freudian analysis convincing. However, the mechanisms of personality and gender formation identified by Freud and his followers may well be useful tools in explaining male rivalries among Renaissance artists, such as those between Brunelleschi and Ghiberti, Michelangelo and Raphael, or Bandinelli and Michelangelo. Lacan's insights into the perceptual constitution of selfhood might explain aspects of one-point perspective. A rigorous, systematic, and convincing study of Renaissance perspective and perception, in any case, has yet to be published.

Production

Artistic production, another major area of investigation, can be approached from a variety of angles. One can research the manufacture of individual objects, such as the methods of carpentry and joinery used in an altarpiece or the genesis of a particular altarpiece design, work facilitated by the scientific techniques of conservators discussed above and by the study of preparatory drawings. Preparatory drawings also instruct about the structure and procedures of Renaissance workshops. In the early Renaissance, for example, a master often maintained model drawing books filled with a stock of finished motifs, including classical designs, to train apprentices and assist his own designing. Latter drawings and documentary evidence demonstrate that some Renaissance workshops were much more extensive, headed by an artist-in-chief such as Raphael, Taddeo Zuccari, or Giorgio Vasari, who produced literally volumes of original compositions for large and complicated programs, often drawn at high speed with vigorous pen or brush strokes. They also indicate that the scale of the projects and their tight deadlines often necessitated leaving to assistants the production of *modelli* or full-scale cartoons, as well as certain details, such as topographical backgrounds or portrait heads. This division of labor usually extended to the execution of the work as well. Such a hierarchical structure with the artist/impresario at the top directing a corps of specialized assistants tells us that workshops not only mirrored the regimes they served, but elevated the status of artist-in-chief to quasi princely status, as he consulted with humanist advisers and commanded vast resources of men and supplies as might a military commander-in-chief.

Archival records are particularly rich, and often untapped sources, for understanding large-scale projects, especially architectural commissions, which were built over long periods and employed large quantities of men and materials. They tell us much about the economics of construction, the organization of the labor force, and methods of supply. For example, drawing on surprisingly abundant documentary evidence William Wallace in his 1994 *Michelangelo at San Lorenzo* has exploded Michelangelo's self-constructed image as the purely liberal artist-autodidact, loner, melancholic and divine genius, untainted by contract with workshops of mere craftsmen. Michelangelo not only traveled repeatedly between Florence and Carrara to select and to help quarry the necessary marble, but also employed and efficiently managed a large group of quarrymen and transporters at Carrara, and stonecutters and masons in Florence, all the while keeping a tight reign on his budget. While evidence of Michelangelo's intelligence and colossal energy emerges clearly, this study also dramatically illustrates how he channeled his entrepreneurial efforts though the traditional building practices of the mechanical arts.

With regard to Renaissance altarpieces, a clear picture of their methods of construction, expenses and payments, and importance in export and import trade over a relatively long period has been offered for the first time by Peter Humfrey in his 1993 *The Altarpiece in Renaissance Venice*. Similarly, Evelyn Lincoln's 2000 study, *The Invention of the Italian Renaissance Printmaker*, illuminates the new career of printmaker (including a woman printmaker), the techniques of production and uses for prints, and the enabling economic conditions and constraints of the print trade. Many more such studies based on wide-ranging gathering of statistical, archival, and visual information remain to be written on all genres of art.

Feminism and gender studies

Feminism and gender studies have shaped the interpretation of Italian Renaissance art more profoundly than any of the other recent contextual approaches, especially regarding images of women, including the female nude, and art made by, addressed to, or patronized by women. Once considered as marginal, for example, painted wedding chests, furniture and wainscot painting, and birth trays – all used in palace bridal chambers and addressed to both spouses for their instruction – have been effectively studied by Cristelle Baskins and others. They have revealed a range of anxieties surrounding marriage and family life such as sexuality (virginity, chastity, fidelity, adultery, lust, rape, homosexuality, and lesbianism), power (obedience, dominance, subservience, rebellion, dependence, independence, strength, weakness, potence, impotence), age (older husbands, younger wives), children (birth, death, legitimacy, illegitimacy, rearing, inheritance), in-laws (dowries, counter-dowries, and social, political, and economic status), religion (piety, impiety, carnal love, spiritual love), and, since marriages were often viewed as the microcosm of the state, community (patriotism or sedition, peace or violence, civilization or savagery). Mark Wigley has also usefully analyzed the domestic architecture where these objects were housed, in terms of gender.

Patricia Simons has shown how portraits of women, commissioned mostly by men, indicate family wealth, rank, virtue, and dynastic continuity while reflecting and constructing the largely marginal roles – decorative and procreative – that women were expected to play within a patriarchal society. They could also, as Elizabeth Cropper believes, visually connote the Petrarchan struggle between erotic desire and poetic triumph, passion and possession, matter and spirit. Similarly, with regard to the Mona Lisa, Mary Garrard has demonstrated convincingly that for Leonardo, women embodied the dynamic, natural forces of the cosmos, both creative and destructive, across space and time. Since the ultimate aim of the artist according to Renaissance art theory – the depiction simultaneously of natural truth and ideal beauty – was often metaphorized as a beautiful woman, images of women, especially nude or lightly draped women, often came in the sixteenth century to signify artistic creativity and prowess, as Rona Goffen has argued in her 1997 *Titian's Women*.

In religious imagery Margaret Miles has studied the Virgin with one bare breast in the context of anxiety over the food supply and the power of women to nourish. Within the political arena women often served as allegories of the state, especially in Siena (the Virgin), Florence (Flora), and Venice (Venus) and were thus commonly represented as sites of civic piety, prosperity, and domination, the later usually in the context of rape or violence toward women.

Although women patrons appear not to have been numerous in the Renaissance, Catherine King has usefully surveyed the topic in her 1998 *Renaissance Women Patrons*. Stefanie Solum has recently shown not only how a woman's commission can be decisively different from a man's, but also result in a major artistic innovation. In "Lucrezia's Saint: The Child Baptist and Medici Redemption in Fifteenth-Century Florence" (Ph.D. dissertation, University of California at Berkeley, 2001), she has convincingly demonstrated that the mid-fifteenth century invention of an entirely new and extremely popular subject, the youthful John the Baptist, stemmed from the spiritual writings and patronage of Lucrezia Tornabuoni, wife of Piero de' Medici.

Male sexuality constitutes another area of recent research. The overt display of Christ's sexual organ, according to Leo Steinberg in his *Sexuality of Christ*, has theological connotations signifying his humanity and redemptive sacrifice. And studies on homosexuality, a topic quite ignored until recently, have also begun to emerge, most notably in the 1986 *Ganymede in the Renaissance* by James Saslow.

Renaissance Art Outside of Italy

Beginning in the late fifteenth and continuing throughout the sixteenth century, the influence of Italian Renaissance art, especially in architecture, was pervasive throughout western and eastern Europe, as far as Portugal and Spain to the West, Hungary, Poland, and Russia to the east, and Scandinavia to the north. Missionary activity of the Catholic Church carried Renaissance styles to the New World and the Far East. Within Europe the agents of transmission were multiple. The invasions of Italy that began in 1494 awakened transalpine sovereigns, especially the Valois of France and the Hapsburgs of Austria and Spain, to the rich possibilities of Italian art and led to the importation of Italian art and artists to their courts. The spread of humanism and double entry accounting to the major urban and political centers of Europe – facilitated by Italian publishing, commerce, and banking – further fostered a taste for Italian art. Non-Italian church officials, especially cardinals, who traveled to or resided in Rome, merchants who had commercial offices and contacts within Italy, and students of the universities in Padua, Pavia, and Bologna often developed a taste for Renaissance art and patronized both Italian artists and Italianate styles in their countries of origin. Widely circulated Italian theoretical treatises on architecture, especially those of Alberti and Serlio, stimulated a demand for classicizing architecture. As classicism gained acceptance over local varieties of medieval styles, non-Italian artists increasingly traveled to Italy to train directly under Italian masters or to study their works and the remains of classical antiquity. The Reformation with its attendant iconoclasm and Wars of Religion (1562–98) sharply curtailed the spread of Italian Renaissance art in Protestant areas, but in those regions that remained Catholic and connected to Italy by commercial and political ties the prestige and impact of Italian art remained strong.

Since much of sixteenth-century Italian classicistic art was directed toward supporting ducal or papal claims to temporal and spiritual sovereignty and toward demonstrating the truth of Catholic doctrines and traditions, in areas with similar religious and political ideology, notably Spain, Italian classicizing art was often appropriated with little change in form or content. Thus, Charles V's Palace in

Granada and Philip II's Escorial, for example, have been successfully studied mostly in terms of Italian Renaissance paradigms by Earl Rosenthal, Manfredo Tafuri, George Kubler, Catherine Wilkinson-Zerner, Rosemarie Mulcahy, and many others. The tendency of both Italian and European sixteenth-century rulers to support claims to legitimacy and authority by boasting genealogical roots back to antiquity and association with the Roman Empire also led to similar references to classical forms and imperial themes in the art they commissioned.

But for the most part Italian classicism outside of Italy was radically transformed by a continuing taste for local Gothic styles, long-standing craft and guild practices, and differing functional needs. (See the essay by Peter Burke above.) Almost no Renaissance artist outside of Italy, with the exception of a few architects like Philibert de l'Orme who worked for the French court in the third quarter of the sixteenth century, and Inigo Jones employed by the English Stuart court in the early seventeenth century, ever fully absorbed the vocabulary, grammar, and syntax of Italian classicizing art. Thus, the study of non-Italian Renaissance art, including the many surveys of this material, has been plagued by the tendency to use the aims and ideals of Italian Renaissance art as the yardstick to measure success or failure, leading inevitably to viewing non-Italian variations negatively as inferior hybrids. The reverse of the same coin is to plot classicism as an international style (with Baroque, Rococo, or Neoclassical variations) triumphally marching across Europe over three centuries, gradually defeating or absorbing all other alternative styles. What has been lacking until recently are studies that move beyond comparative formal (and sometimes iconographical) analyses and interpret non-Italian Renaissance art in terms of its own peculiar local needs and circumstances, examining especially the resistance to and suspicion of Italian culture.

Again it was Michael Baxandall who paved the way for a contextual approach to non-Italian art in his magisterial 1980 *Limewood Sculptors of Renaissance Germany*. After introducing the history, the settlement patterns, and the political, social, and economic structure of the urban centers of upper Germany, as well as their sculptural traditions, he studied limewood sculpture in terms of material, functions, the market, the period eye, and four of the leading practitioners. Only in one chapter does he discuss Italian art, mostly to dismiss its importance. One might expect the development of distinct individual styles in limewood sculpture to result from the importation of Italian art theory, which attempted to raise the status of artists by championing originality. But Baxandall shows that, in music, German Mastersingers had developed a concept of personal patterning within their craftsman's aesthetic much more closely related to the novel styles of limewood sculptors than to Italian Greco-Roman art theory, which sprang from an elite literary aesthetic. When he does discuss the first clear-cut case of Italianate sculpture, in the Fugger Chapel in Augsburg (1512–18), it is to show that there was resistance to the alien *Welsch* (Italianate style); for this was seen by nationalistic German humanists as part of a general subversion of the simplicity and piety of German culture and society by Italian luxury, commercialism, immorality, and neo-Roman law.

In the 1993 *Moment of Self-Portraiture in German Renaissance Art*, a book of great methodological sophistication and interpretative subtlety, Joseph Koerner also addresses the discovery of the unique artistic self and style in Dürer's self-portraits, examples of the quintessential Renaissance art form. While Dürer traveled to Italy, studied Italian art, and knew that Italian humanists often championed artists' individuality and genius, Koerner shows in great detail that Dürer's self-portraits, which are generally considered to begin the German Renaissance, had almost nothing to do with Italian classicizing art. Rather, they grew from northern visual and iconographical traditions within specific German circumstances of piety, labor, patronage, and self-understanding. The second half of this extensive and brilliant book – which offers the most convincing demonstrations of reception theory yet to appear in Renaissance studies – treats Dürer's most talented pupil, Hans Baldung, and how he deconstructed in his art Dürer's confident, rational, and optimistic sense of an ideal artistic self by opposing degeneration, decay, and death – a dialectic, Koerner argues, that was embedded in the inherent instabilities and polarities of Reformation theology.

Two other notable contextual contributions to northern art that make almost no reference to Italian art are Christopher Wood's 1993 *Albrecht Altdorfer and the Origins of Landscape*, and, for Netherlandish Renaissance art, Elizabeth Honig's 1998 *Painting and the Market in Early Modern Antwerp*. The latter is particularly notable in that Honig shows more convincingly than any study of the Italian art market how painting, especially the work of Aertsen, not only reflects and absorbs financial, social, and ethical attitudes toward the market and commodities, but serves as the very visual locus where these issues are mediated.

The impact of Italian classicism in France was profound, but compared to the supposed "authentic" seventeenth-century classicism, sixteenth-century French art has usually been viewed as the inferior product of largely uncomprehending artists and patrons. But Henri Zerner in his excellent 1996 *L'Art de la Renaissance en France* shows that the paradigms of Italian classicism were self-consciously modified by local craft skills, visual traditions, and symbolic associations to meet very different aesthetic and ideological needs. Furthermore, the social, political, religious, and linguistic instabilities and insecurities of Renaissance France fostered greater experimentation than in Italy, resulting in many more modes of classicism. French patrons also valued much more than their Italian counterparts the so-called minor arts, such as stained glass and tapestries, where the direct connection between an artist's mental design and manual execution was usually not readily apparent, a situation devaluing the importance of *disegno* upon which Vasari believed artistic originality and genius depended. In addition, the function of the decorative arts was to embellish space for various court rituals rather than engage the minds of individual viewers though an Italian-like *istoria* seen though a perspectival frame. In other words, Zerner interprets French Renaissance art within the contingencies and contexts of France, not Italy.

Conclusion

In spite of a large quantity and wide diversity of research in Italian and European Renaissance art, scholarship has not yet achieved, with very few exceptions, the interpretative sophistication of which the field is capable. The reason, I believe, is that either the material and aesthetic qualities of the art have been emphasized over its conceptual and circumstantial aspects, or vice versa, and that individual works have not been approached from a sufficient number of relevant perspectives.

In the face of the almost bewildering number of approaches to art currently available and the difficultly of mastering their jargon and philosophical underpinnings, some art historians have recommended that we retreat to what we are best trained to do – use our eyes to analyze the aesthetic, formal, or stylistic qualities of art – and leave the social, political, economic, religious, intellectual, and literary contexts to the historians and scholars of literature whose archival, philological, statistical, and linguistic skills are usually more highly developed. Historians and literary scholars for their part are increasingly turning to visual materials as primary documentary evidence for their interpretive studies, but most are woefully unprepared to handle the material and aesthetic aspects of art, often reducing it to mere illustration. But if the study of Renaissance visual culture is to realize its full potential, then future scholars, in my view, must be able to perform equally competently as historians, literary historians, and art historians. This suggests the necessity to develop programs in Renaissance area studies with interdisciplinary team teaching, where students can be trained to bridge traditional departmental specialties. One way or another, in any case, they must acquire the highest degree of methodological and philosophical sophistication, gather new empirical data from the widest possible primary and secondary sources, and proceed on all fronts simultaneously, from the work of art out to the cultural context and from the cultural context back to the work of art. All the while they must be responsible for the work's unique materiality and most subtle aesthetic properties, and sensitive as well to the ambiguities and conflicts of its circumstances. Finally, students must demonstrate – and this is most difficult – how the culture registers *formally* in the work of art and how the work of art *interactively* informs and shapes the culture. The interpretations that result from this process – a process that I believe will inevitably have to concentrate much more on single works or separate genres of art than in the past – must be multileveled, nuanced, open-ended, and articulate. Scholarship of this nature is enormously challenging. Easy formulas or shortcuts will not serve. Only wide and multidimensional research, close and prolonged scrutiny, repeated questioning, and extensive practice will succeed in elevating research in Renaissance art to its full potential.

NOTE

I wish to thank Professor Guido Ruggiero, whose comments and suggestions have much improved this essay, and Leslie Martin whose keen editorial eye clarified my writing.

FURTHER READING

Ames-Lewis, Francis, *Drawing in Early Renaissance Italy* (New Haven: Yale University Press, 1981).
—— , *The Intellectual Life of the Early Renaissance Artist* (New Haven: Yale University Press, 2000).
Barkan, Leonard, *Unearthing the Past: Archaeology and Aesthetics in the Making of Renaissance Culture* (New Haven: Yale University Press, 1999).

Barolsky, Paul, *Michelangelo's Nose: A Myth and its Maker* (University Park: Pennsylvania State University Press, 1990).

——, *Why Mona Lisa Smiles and Other Tales by Vasari* (University Park: Pennsylvania State University Press, 1991).

——, *Giotto's Father and the Family of Vasari's "Lives"* (University Park: Pennsylvania State University Press, 1992).

——, *The Faun in the Garden: Michelangelo and the Poetic Origins of Italian Renaissance Art* (University Park: Pennsylvania State University Press, 1994).

Baskins, Cristelle, *"Cassone" Painting, Humanism, and Gender in Early Modern Italy* (Cambridge: Cambridge University Press, 1998).

Baxandall, Michael, *Giotto and the Orators* (Oxford: Oxford University Press, 1971).

——, *Patterns of Intention* (New Haven: Yale University Press, 1985).

Blunt, Anthony, *Philibert de l'Orme* (London: Zwemmer, 1958).

Brown, Patricia Fortini, *Venice and Antiquity* (New Haven: Yale University Press, 1996).

Brunner, H. H., *The Statue Court in the Vatican Belvedere* (Stockholm: Almqvist and Wiksell, 1970).

Burroughs, Charles, *From Sign to Design* (Cambridge, MA: MIT Press, 1990).

Bush, Virginia, "Bandinelli's *Hercules and Cacus* and Florentine Traditions," *Studies in Italian Art and Architecture 15th through 18th Centuries*, ed. Henry Millon, vol. 35 of *Memoirs of the American Academy in Rome* (Rome: Edizioni dell'Elefante, 1980), pp. 163–206.

Cropper, Elizabeth, "On Beautiful Women, Parmigianino, *Petrarchismo*, and the Vernacular Style," *Art Bulletin* 58 (1976), pp. 374–94.

Edgerton, Samuel, Jr., *The Renaissance Rediscovery of Linear Perspective* (New York: Basic Books, 1975).

Findlen, Paula, *Possessing Nature: Museums, Collecting, and Scientific Culture in Early Modern Italy* (Berkeley: University of California Press, 1994).

Garrard, Mary, "Leonardo da Vinci: Female Portraits, Female Nature," *The Expanding Discourse: Feminism and Art History*, ed. Norma Broude and Mary Garrard (New York: HarperCollins, 1992), pp. 58–85.

Goldthwaite, Richard, "The Building of the Strozzi Palace: The Construction Industry in Renaissance Florence," *Studies in Medieval and Renaissance History* 10 (1973), pp. 98–185.

Gombrich, E. H., *Art and Illusion* (Princeton: Princeton University Press, 1960).

Hall, Marcia, *After Raphael: Painting in Central Italy in the Sixteenth Century* (Cambridge: Cambridge University Press, 1999).

Hood, William, "The State of Research in Italian Renaissance Art," *Art Bulletin* 69 (1987), pp. 174–86.

Kaufmann, Thomas DaCosta, *Variations on the Imperial Theme in the Age of Maximilian II and Rudolf II* (New York: Garland, 1978).

——, *The School of Prague: Painting at the Court of Rudolf II* (Chicago: University of Chicago Press, 1988).

——, *Court, Cloister and City: The Art and the Culture of Central Europe, 1450–1800* (Chicago: University of Chicago Press, 1995).

Kemp, Martin, *The Science of Art: Optical Themes in Western Art from Brunelleschi to Seurat* (New Haven: Yale University Press, 1990).

Kent, F. W. and Simons, Patricia, eds., *Patronage, Art, and Society in Renaissance Italy* (Oxford: Clarendon Press, 1987).

Kubler, George, *Building the Escorial* (Princeton: Princeton University Press, 1982).

Landau, David and Parshall, Peter, *The Renaissance Print 1470–1550* (New Haven: Yale University Press, 1994).

Miles, Margaret, "The Virgin's One Bare Breast," *The Expanding Discourse: Feminism and Art History*, ed. Norma Broude and Mary Garrard (New York: HarperCollins, 1992), pp. 26–37.

Millon, Henry A., "Art and Architectural History in the Twentieth Century," *Useful Knowledge*, ed. Alexander Bearn (Philadelphia: American Philosophical Society, 1999), pp. 199–225.

Mulcahy, Rosemarie, *The Decoration of the Royal Basilica of El Escorial* (Cambridge: Cambridge University Press, 1994).

Panofsky, Erwin, *Studies in Iconology* (Oxford: Oxford University Press, 1939).

——, *Early Netherlandish Painting: Its Origins and Character* (Cambridge, MA: Harvard University Press, 1953).

——, *The Life and Art of Albrecht Dürer* (Princeton: Princeton University Press, 1955).

——, *Renaissance and Renascences in Western Art* (Stockholm: Almqvist & Wiksell, 1960).

——, *Perspective as Symbolic Form*, trans. Christopher S. Wood (New York: Zone Books, 1991).

Podro, Michael, *The Critical Historians of Art* (New Haven: Yale University Press, 1982).

Reilly, Patricia, "Grand Designs: Alessandro Allori's *Discussions on the Rules of Drawing*, Giorgio Vasari's *Lives of the Artists*, and the Florentine Visual Vernacular" (Ph.D. dissertation, University of California at Berkeley, 1999).

Rosand, David, *Painting in Sixteenth-Century Venice: Titian, Veronese, Tintoretto*, rev. edn. (Cambridge: Cambridge University Press, 1997).

Rosenthal, Earl E., *The Palace of Charles V in Granada* (Princeton: Princeton University Press, 1985).

Rubin, Patricia, *Giorgio Vasari: Art and History* (New Haven: Yale University Press, 1995).

Shearman, John, *Mannerism* (Harmondsworth: Penguin, 1967).

——, *Raphael's Cartoons in the Collection of Her Majesty the Queen and the Tapestries of the Sistine Chapel* (London: Phaidon, 1972).

——, *Only Connect . . . Art and the Spectator in the Italian Renaissance* (Princeton: Princeton University Press, 1992).

Silver, Larry, "The State of Research in Northern European Art of the Renaissance Era," *Art Bulletin* 68 (1986), pp. 518–35.

Simons, Patricia, "Women in Frames: The Gaze, the Eye, the Profile in Renaissance Portraiture," in *The Expanding Discourse: Feminism and Art History*, ed. Norma Broude and Mary Garrard (New York: HarperCollins, 1992), pp. 39–57.

——, "Portraiture, Portrayal, and Idealization: Ambiguous Individualism in Representations of Renaissance Women," in *Language and Image of Renaissance Italy*, ed. A. Brown (Oxford: Clarendon Press, 1995), pp. 263–311.

Summerson, John N., *Inigo Jones* (Harmondsworth: Penguin Books, 1966).

Trachtenberg, Marvin, "Some Observations on Recent Architectural History," *Art Bulletin* 70 (1988), pp. 208–41.

Trexler, Richard, "Florentine Religious Experience: The Sacred Image," *Studies in the Renaissance* 19 (1972), pp. 7–14.

——, *Public Life in Renaissance Florence* (New York: Academic Press, 1980).

Weil-Garris, Kathleen, "On Pedestals: Michelangelo's *David*, Bandinelli's *Hercules and Cacus* and the Sculpture on the Piazza della Signoria," *Römisches Jahrbuch für Kunstgeschichte* 20 (1983), pp. 377–415.

White, John, *The Birth and Rebirth of Pictorial Space* (Boston: Boston Book and Art Shop, 1967).

Wigley, Mark, "Untitled: The Housing of Gender," in *Sexuality and Space: Princeton Papers on Architecture* (New York: Princeton Architectural Press, 1992), pp. 327–89.

Wilkinson-Zerner, Catherine, *Juan de Herrera: Architect to Philip II of Spain* (New Haven: Yale University Press, 1993).

Williams, Robert, *Art, Theory, and Culture in Sixteenth-Century Italy: From Techne to Meta-techne* (Cambridge: Cambridge University Press, 1997).

Wittkower, Rudolf, *Architectural Principles in the Age of Humanism* (New York: W. W. Norton, 1971).

Woods-Marsden, Joanna, *Renaissance Self-Portraiture* (New Haven: Yale University Press, 1998).

CHAPTER TWENTY-ONE

Literature

JAMES GRANTHAM TURNER

Though the term "Renaissance" raises troublesome issues of definition and interpretation, it still conjures up a handful of great names in literature. Certain imaginative authors, steeped in a long tradition of tale-telling, carnival humor, and chivalric romance, nevertheless seem to tower above their medieval sources: Giovanni Boccaccio, Lodovico Ariosto, François Rabelais, Miguel de Cervantes. Others devote their lives to recreating the epic forms of classical literature (Torquato Tasso, John Milton). Petrarch himself (Francesco Petrarca, 1304–74) provides the model for all impassioned poets of the love sonnet and lyric, including the versatile Pierre de Ronsard. France also produced the heteroclite Michel de Montaigne, inventor of the modern essay; Germany on the other hand produced the prolific Meistersinger Hans Sachs, the mystic scientist Paracelsus, and the world-changing theologian Martin Luther, but nothing now recognizable as "Renaissance literature." In other vernacular cultures, heroic figures such as Edmund Spenser and Sir Philip Sidney attempt the whole range of genres from pastoral to epic without achieving a reputation beyond their own language-group; this category includes dramatists from the outer edges of Italocentric Europe, such as Lope de Vega and William Shakespeare. The international medium of Latin favored mercurial intellectuals like Desiderius Erasmus and Sir Thomas More, whose *Utopia* gave a new word to the world.

Alongside these well-known names, specialists recognize literally thousands of authors performing in dozens of genres. Following the lead of Boccaccio's *Decameron* we find many confabulations or gatherings of stories loosely held together by a meta-narrative device: Queen Marguérite of Navarre's *Heptameron*, Cervantes's *Novelas ejemplares*, the novel-collections of Matteo Bandello and Giambattista Giraldi Cinthio, raided by Shakespeare for *Othello* and *Measure for Measure*. (Cinthio also wrote gruesome tragedies and two critical treatises – a range typical of many Renaissance authors.) Ariosto's *Orlando furioso*, equally loose in structure and derivative from earlier chivalric poems in the same stanza, bred imitations from Lorenzo Veniero's obscene *La puttana errante* to Spencer's allegorical *Faerie Queene*, in which all the virtues would have been embodied by Arthurian knights and Amazons. (Like many ambitious narrative projects of the period it remained unfinished.) Many writers emulated More's *Utopia* by inventing fantastic alternative societies,[1] or (like the uneducated but "divine" Pietro Aretino) worked with popular genres such as pornography and scurrilous satire. Meanwhile, more "correct" authors tried to construct epics around a single massive action, anticipating Tasso's *Jerusalem Liberated* and Milton's *Paradise Lost*; examples include Ronsard's abandoned *Franciade* and a blank-verse epic by Giangiorgio Trissino that narrates, and supposedly exemplifies, *Italy Liberated from the Goths* (1547–8). (Trissino's best-remembered monument is his famous pupil Andrea Palladio, whose name is taken from the guardian angel in his teacher's epic.) The amorous sonnet takes on other subjects, "heroic" (Tasso, Cervantes, Milton), religious (Donne), and contemplative-descriptive (Joachim Du Bellay's *Antiquitez de Rome*, later translated by Spenser). Other serious genres develop, like the blank-verse tragedy in classical form inspired by the recently recovered *Poetics* of Aristotle, the Pindaric ode (Ronsard again), and the biblical epic – including poetic versions of the Genesis creation-myth.

But "Renaissance" or "rebirth" must mean a self-conscious movement of cultural renewal, rather than a mere cluster of famous names or catalogue of titles. Paradoxically, this period venerated "classical" antiquity even though most of its distinctive achievements used brand-new forms and techniques: oil paintings, maps, perspective, epics, and cycles of love poetry in set rhymed stanzas, artillery and geometrical fortification, ships that could navigate to Goa and Acapulco. Stable and affordable printed texts of classics like Horace or the Bible made possible "a library which knows no walls save those of the world itself," as Erasmus said in praise of the Venetian publisher Aldus.[2] (Some scholars would add the Self to this list of Renaissance inventions, believing that it emerges from the soliloquies of Hamlet or the shifting moods of Montaigne's introspective essays; typically, however, Montaigne's intense probing of his own foibles is sustained by a densely-woven web of classical quotation. (See the essay of John Martin above.)) This imagery of innovation and cosmic expansion clearly excited thinkers of the time as well as in Burckhardt's day. It resonates with Emperor Charles V's emblem "Plus Ultra," going beyond the Pillars of Hercules into a brave new world, and with another response to a German invention, the powerful magician whose "dominion . . . stretcheth as far as does the mind of man" (Marlowe, *Doctor Faustus* I. i). But it would be naive to posit a direct relation between new discoveries and cultural brilliance. Print, travel, and gunpowder propagate the miseries of disease, intolerance, and religious war as well as the triumphs of Erasmus and Ariosto.

Even though Burckhardt left the visual arts out of his influential *Cultur der Renaissance in Italien*, it is obvious that art, not literature, defines this culture for most observers. The Renaissance can be *seen*, directly and palpably, by anyone visiting a National Gallery, but identifying an equivalent, self-evident "Renaissance" mode in writing is more difficult. One of the few writers actually to use the R-word in the period was Giorgio Vasari, whose *Lives* of Italian painters, sculptors, and architects founded art history. Vasari argues forcefully for a *renascita* or "rebirth" of visual art from the abyss that falls between glorious antiquity and glorious modernity – the essential fiction behind all notions of a renaissance, a kind of dark rainbow that shifts with the eye of the beholder – and he identifies the specific features that mark off "reborn" art from the horrors of mediaeval barbarism, which he describes as clumsy, "Greek" (i.e. Byzantine), and "modern" in the bad sense (*Vite* II. 31, 36). If

"Renaissance literature" means anything, it must refer to creative texts that display the same qualities that Vasari saw gradually emerging since the "rebirth" of art: confident movement, coherent design, self-conscious emulation of classic models (inventing them where they did not survive), idealized grace combined with psychological expression, and the manifestation of "genius."

Sixteenth-century writers looked for these qualities of gracious confidence in the person as well as the text. Rhetoric treatises recreated the ideal of the ancient orator in elocution and gesture as well as in verbal technique. Rabelais dramatizes this with his usual wise exaggeration when he presents the medieval schoolboy as a slovenly lout, expert only in children's games; in contrast the newly educated youth, beautiful as a picture, delivers impromptu speeches in perfect Latin without the slightest hesitation. (Gargantua's letter to his son Pantagruel, marveling at the advance of learning, stands out for its heartfelt sincerity in the midst of Rabelais's ironic fantasy.[3]) Renaissance self-definition celebrates the happy fusion of "reborn" present with classic past, starkly defined against an intervening "middle" or "dark age" of intellectual torpor, "Gothic" superstition and ignorance, closed horizons, mechanical repetition of musty authorities, gawky cluttered style, indifference to the splendor of Augustan antiquity. The Renaissance-effect, in contrast, exemplifies "classical" matter and manner, using the Olympic pantheon and personifications sanctioned by ancient poets rather than allegory and dream-vision. It synthesizes Christianity with ancient mythology, and avows a quasi-religious respect for Vergil and "Saint Socrates" (as Erasmus calls him in a dialogue called "The Religious Symposium"), as well as for the more urbane Church Fathers.[4] Style aspires to rhetorical *copia* or varied abundance, to a kind of golden or laureate effulgence. (One marker of the new period is the ceremony of crowning the poet with laurel, revived in the fourteenth century.) The "Renaissance" poet combined an external and an internal concern with glory, the self-crowning of the *literatus* as a high-cultural achiever coinciding with the desire to deploy all the resources of the language for maximum effect. In a word, eloquence.

Renaissance aesthetics also proclaims the interrelation of the arts. Lyric and dramatic poets cooperate with music and emulate its melody. Literature compares itself to the work of painters (starting with Petrarch's sonnets on Simone Martini) and introduces elaborate *ecphrases* or verbal descriptions of pictures. Some artists even launch their own literary careers: Cellini writes a famously egotistic autobiography and the base-born Aretino became a leading art critic, composing a program for Michelangelo's *Last Judgment* (which he later denounced for its obscenity). Though he is isolated among his German contemporaries, Dürer wrote treatises on proportion, draughtsmanship, and measurement that often rise above the mechanical. Michelangelo's own sonnets include intense evocations of homoerotic love (varying the Petrarchan norm) and one of the most powerful myths of creativity – when he conceives himself chiselling away the *soverchio* or "superfluity" to release the already-perfect sculpture from inside the block of marble.

Renaissance scholars are no longer content, however, to eulogize the great geniuses and neglect the difficult questions lurking in the margins. How far did the period extend? When and how did it end? Protestant reformers celebrated *la renaissance* of religion from the abyss of ignorance and superstition,[5] but it was a rebirth in blood; was the Reformation the fruit of the Renaissance or its ghastly nemesis?

And can the term be applied at all to "belated" cultures like England, with no significant visual art and a growing Protestant-nationalist suspicion of continental influence?

"Renaissance"? "Literature"?

Both the period concept and the definition of literature have come under heavy fire, but they enjoy new vitality as objects of study rather than answers to questions. The new *Cambridge History of Early Modern English Literature*, for example, drops the word "Renaissance" from its title completely, and promises to define literature very broadly, comprising all writing and the cultural sites that produce it. At the same time, however, the editors explicitly recognize that the term still means "poems, plays, fiction and essays." It is important to recognize that Renaissance theory *did* recognize a category that corresponds to the autonomous aesthetic concept "literature," namely "poetry" or *poesia*, corresponding to the modern "creative writing" rather than strictly to compositions in verse. Assembling the perfect library at Urbino, Federico da Montefeltro "began with the Latin poets," implying priority and categorical distinction; the woodcut titlepage to Erasmus's best-selling *Adagia* places Homer, Solomon, and Hesiod at the very top, and gives them twice the space allotted to other authors. Sir Philip Sidney, distilling the neo-classical treatises of sixteenth-century Italy, sharply distinguishes "Poesie" from history and philosophy on the grounds that it creates its own reality: the poet "lifted up with the vigour of his own invention, doth grow in effect into another nature; . . . [nature's] world is brazen, the poets only deliver a golden." Fiction does not merely differ in degree or surface ornament, but constitutes a distinct epistemic field; poetry cannot be condemned for lying, since it delivers a different, non-literal kind of truth, "nothing affirms, and therefore never lieth."[6]

Literary studies of the later twentieth century attacked, not only this concept of literature, but virtually every aspect of Burckhardt's idealized Renaissance. Hostility to western values offset the Euro-triumphalism of earlier accounts. Humanism (in the sense of glorifying "man") was demolished by discourse-based theories of subject-formation, though paradoxically the critics most keen to demolish essentialist notions of Renaissance individualism discovered its "construction" in the discourse of Shakespeare, restoring the prestige of the period and the canon they wish to question. The most influential new ideas often involved discovering some atrocity. The correction or "castigation" of corrupt classical texts was interpreted as corporal punishment launched against a female body, the Petrarchan *blason* or catalogue of beautiful features as violent dismemberment. Renaissance readers, who witnessed the "ferocious spectacle" of real bodies hacked apart and displayed in the piazza, might have been unimpressed by this interpretation. The most thoughtful literary scholars tended to value conflict, anxiety, and non-meaning over the (equally fictitious) qualities of confidence, harmony, the dignity of man, the Golden Age of letters, and the apotheosis of individualism. Ariosto's *Orlando furioso*, once the epitome of a higher harmony that transcends the turmoil of its narrative, now resonated with every kind of crisis and achieved at most what Ariosto himself calls a "bitter concord, horrible harmony."[7]

The worship of "Renaissance Man," culminating in studies such as Joan Kelly Gadol's *Leon Battista Alberti, Universal Man of the Early Renaissance*, was decisively undercut by asking "Did Women Have a Renaissance?" (the title of a famous article by the same Joan Kelly). As if in reaction to Kelly's negative answer, literary scholarship turned its productive energies to the recovery and canonization of women authors, from the Latinist Cassandra Fedele to the feminist Moderata Fonte, from the courtesan-poets Tullia d'Aragona and Veronica Franco to the nuns who wrote plays in Italy and scholarly epistles in Germany. French theorists studied narrative in Marguérite de Navarre or rhetoric in Louise Labé and Pernette du Guillet, while English specialists, despite the paucity of women writers in Britain before 1600, turned to royal polyglots such as Mary Queen of Scots, Catherine Parr, and Elizabeth I. This revival continues to the present. (See the essay by Elissa Weaver above.)

The uniqueness of the Renaissance period had already been questioned by medievalists, who showed that the idea of a revival or rebirth never entirely disappeared from poetic diction. A beautifully crafted imitation of Vergil's fourth eclogue, applying Vergil's "Golden Age restored" motif to the current regime and declaring Rome "reborn" (*Aurea Roma renascitur*), seems like the quintessential Renaissance text, not only using the rebirth-word but re-enacting cultural renewal in the elegance of its style and the aptness of its allusion. But the date is AD 810 and the emperor is Charlemagne. Late antiquity also bequeathed the counter-intuition that birth means pain and that growth brings problems: "ordo renascendi est crescere posse malis"; the rule of rebirth is to grow with your misfortunes.[8] This could be the motto for the new, troubled conception of the "early modern."

Powerful statements of innovation do mark the thresholds of "Renaissance literature." Dante's *Vita nuova* associates the beginning of his love for Beatrice with a new epoch in vernacular poetry – assembling his sonnets and *canzone* into a sequence about her, as Petrarch would do for Laura and as hundreds of imitators would do for their Delias and Stellas – and it ends by hoping "to compose concerning her what has never been written in rhyme of any woman" (section XLII). Ariosto promises "something never before said in prose or rhyme" at the beginning of *Orlando furioso* (I. ii). We should not take these gestures at face value, however. The period's absolute individualism and innovation diminish once we learn to recognize the rhetorical tropes and ornaments that persist throughout late antiquity and the so-called Middle Ages; Ernst Robert Curtius's magisterial *European Literature and the Latin Middle Ages* shows, for example, that the promise to "bring things never said before" was a standard *topos* or commonplace, a time-honored way of beginning a full-scale poem.[9] Despite Burckhardt's impassioned eulogy of the *Vita nuova* as "a mighty step towards 'modern' subjectivity,"[10] no historian or textbook-writer would now begin the Renaissance/"early modern" period in the thirteenth century. The high points of literature are either too early (Dante, Boccaccio, and Petrarch) or too late (Shakespeare and Milton) to confirm the idea of a single epoch glorious in every art; Milton himself feared that he was born in "an age too late" for the epic, and translates his confident promise to create "Things unattempted yet in Prose or Rhime" verbatim from Ariosto, belying its originality (*Paradise Lost* IX. 44 and I. 16). Other great figures are too skeptical, lewd or satirical to fit the category, belonging more to a "counter-Renaissance."

The concept of "literature" proves unstable, too. In antiquity the term meant "letters" or "literacy," though it could refer to the body of writing in a given language. In early modern usage, as late as Samuel Johnson, "literature" was something you *had*, not something you wrote – the higher literacy, "polite" learning, the cultural competence deriving from mastery of a select Latin and Greek canon. It denoted something pure and noble, and could therefore always be associated with its degraded and perverse opposite; in one of the earliest Italian uses of the word, Dante complains that worldly men have turned *litteratura* into a whore ("l'hanno fatto di donna meretrice," *Convivio* I: ix: 5). The key word "humanist" likewise first appears in shady company; Ariosto's sixth satire records (and proliferates) popular jokes about the "vices of the *umanisti*" (anyone with "a vein of poetry" must be an inveterate sodomite, so don't turn your back if you have to share a bed with one).[11] "Rebirth" gives art a body, which can turn grotesque. In an era that staked its highest philosophical hopes on Eros, this betrayal inevitably took the form of comic, perverse desire.

Endless Play: Renaissance Dialogism

Definitional problems are helped by recognizing that Renaissance *poesie* – golden rather than brazen, "freely ranging only within the zodiac of wit" rather than affirming literal truth – already resembles the romantic idea of literature as an autonomous art-form, creative and imaginative rather than instrumental and didactic. This distinction has ostensibly been abolished by literary theorists, but it continues to work for the vast majority of the reading public and their booksellers. Authors and readers like Sidney did separate the ornamental-recreational genres of poetry, fiction, and theater from the expository and instructional treatise, the history, the letter.[12] In the classical paradigm exemplified by Horace's *Ars Poetica* the best writing is supposed to combine delight *and* instruction. Nevertheless, the proportion of each varies dramatically from genre to genre.

The distinction between true literature and expository discourse certainly existed in the Renaissance, then, but it was never watertight. Some genres slip between communication and belle-lettrism, such as the "essay" and the "familiar letter" written for future public consumption (the most famous being Petrarch's Latin *Familiares*, though Aretino later turned his own vernacular letters to kings and courtesans into a modern best-seller). And poetry still performed many functions that would later be classified as prosaic: the middling class of poem, corresponding to the agricultural *Georgics* that Virgil wrote in mid-career, applied high literary craft to stubbornly material subjects, as in Marco Girolamo Vida's *Bombyx* (*The Silkworm*) or Girolamo Fracastoro's *Syphilis*, a mythological account of the venereal disease that still bears the name of that poem's hero-victim. (Sidney typically denied that such philosophical verse was true poetry, since it remains "wrapped within the fold of the proposed subject" rather than following "the course of invention."[13]) Furthermore, many poetic products that we would generically label "creative" rather than "instrumental" – comedies, masques, pastoral eclogues, epics – were produced for specific court occasions at the command of powerful patrons. Heroic poems explicitly glorify current rulers by narrating the exploits of their mythic ancestors (Ariosto, the d'Este of Ferrara; Spenser, Queen Elizabeth I of England), and some treat contemporary affairs directly. Even lighter genres (elegies for pets, descriptions of gardens) served dynastic legitimation and consolidation of cultural capital, as well as celebrating the social gathering or the beauty of the spot.

On the other hand, treatises and conduct-books like Castiglione's *Cortegiano* or *Book of the Courtier* (not to be confused with Aretino's *Cortegiana* or high-class prostitute) can be seen aspiring to the condition of literature. The often-quoted recommendation that the courtier must practice a graceful carelessness or *sprezzatura* proves the point by citing the ancient maxim that "art must conceal art" – hinting that Castiglione's treatise is itself a kind of *ars poetica* for what Stephen Greenblatt calls "self-fashioning"; the imagined courtier becomes a total artwork of which the individual arts, from swordplay to sonneteering, are partial instances. Many treatises also took the form of dialogues, bringing intellectual discourse closer to a drama of ideas and (potentially) creating characters with their own perspective rather than mere mouthpieces of a single dominant truth. Examples include most of the major expositions of Platonic philosophy, Alberti's *Book of the Family*, Machiavelli's *Art of War*, Erasmus's *Colloquia* and *Julius Exclusus* (a hilarious exchange in which St. Peter refuses to let the militant pope into Heaven), Leone Ebreo's *Dialoghi d'amore* (an important treatise on Eros originally written in Hebrew or Spanish but surviving in an Italian version), Tullia d'Aragona's *On the Infinity of Love*, Giordano Bruno's *Expulsion of the Triumphant Beast*, most of the feminist texts studied by Constance Jordan, and pornographic works such as Aretino's *Ragionamenti* and Antonio Vignali's *Cazzaria*. In some cases the speakers are clearly fictional (like Nanna and Pippa, Aretino's irrepressible whores), while in others real persons are transformed into semi-fictions: in d'Aragona's *Infinità* "Tullia" herself becomes a vibrant, interactive character, and in Lodovico Dolce's *Aretino* the great scoundrel-connoisseur appears posthumously to discuss aesthetics.

We can find this dialogic and fictive element in the most instrumental genres, for example in the formal Latin orations that every elite schoolboy had to compose as *progymnasmata* or warm-up exercises for public life, marshalling the most eloquent arguments on both sides of a set question. These questions can be deliberately frivolous (whether day or night is more excellent) or alarmingly serious: the boy-king Edward VI of England is made to debate whether the ruler should inspire love or fear,[14] precisely what Machiavelli was investigating in chapter 17 of *The Prince*. The formal pairing of arguments detaches discourse from conviction, effectively subordinating its truth-value to the ingenious play of contrast, and this in some ways anticipates Kant's description of the pure artwork as purposive without purpose. Generations of American students learn about the Renaissance from Pico della Mirandola's oration on the dignity of man, assigned no fixed position in the chain of being, but instead gifted with the protean and creative ability to fashion himself an angel or a beast. But we should not simply deduce beliefs from these performances. Ciceronian platitudes on the dignity of man were often paired with equally eloquent demonstrations of the misery of the human condition. These two contrasting extremes ricochet back and forth in the dazzling self-contradictions of Montaigne and in Hamlet's manic-depressive speech "What piece of work is a man," declaring him an angel, a divinity, and at the same time the wretched "quintessence of dust" (II. ii).

Decorative chains of demonstration pro and con were spun out on a grand scale, as when the German philosopher Cornelius Agrippa created two massive but self-cancelling treatises, one devoted to the efficacy of the magic arts, one to the vanity of all arts. Other ostensibly single-voiced treatises imply their own opposites too, encouraging counter-eloquence by deliberately espousing lost causes or praising contemptible objects. Another influential treatise by Cornelius Agrippa argues for "The Supremacy of the Female Sex," an exercise in pushing arguments over the edge which, ironically, became a foundation for Renaissance feminism.[15] The typical Renaissance text is "jocoserious," cunningly poised between jest and earnest, and many more of them might be rescued from literal exposition and replaced in the category of playful paradox: the notorious eighteenth chapter of Machiavelli's *Prince*, recommending lies and hypocrisy in the new ruler, begs to be read as a world-upside-down satire or as Swiftian irony, a modest proposal on behalf of republicanism masquerading as an ultra-realistic manual for the dictator.

Even resolutely practical texts gesture towards poetry. *The Prince* ends with a stirring quotation from Petrarch's *canzone* "Italia mia." (This might be an added ornament, but the previous chapter too ends with a highly "literary" effect, the notorious allegory of Fortune as a woman who must be raped and subjugated by the aggressive young male ruler.) The "objective" genre of historiography aspires to the condition of poetry when it describes battles and imagines speeches that could not possibly have been recorded verbatim, or when it appeals to the emotions of the reader through the same rhetorical devices used to turn poetry into eloquence. Machiavelli pours scorn on the imaginative, utopian streak in other writers – particularly in chapter 15 of *The Prince*, where like Sidney he enforces the distinction between "what is done" in the real world and "what ought to be done" in the never-never land of imagination. But when he comments on the imaginary speech that Livy gives to Camillus, proposing to treat the defeated enemy with the utmost generosity after decisively punishing their leaders, Machiavelli has no hesitation in proposing this (fictive) speech as a (prescriptive) model for how new rulers "ought" to behave. (Compare a moment of historical seriousness embedded in the most playful text of the Renaissance; in the strangely moving conclusion to a clownish war between two villages, Rabelais's Gargantua does exactly what Camillus recommends (I. 1).) Machiavelli's *History of Florence* adopts the same goals as Horace's *Ars poetica*, delighting and instructing, moving the passions as well as marshaling the facts. Even though he blames the disastrous decadence of the Florentine state on "literature," his famous character of Cesare Borgia is itself a masterpiece of dramatization as well as a masterly analysis of a leader who turned politics into drama. Cesare employed a draconian official to subjugate the province of Romagna and then destroyed him, to "purge" the people's mind of the idea that he himself might be guilty of cruelty: one morning he has his officer "placed on the piazza in two pieces with a block of wood and a bloody sword beside him. The ferocity of such a spectacle left those people satisfied and amazed at the same time" (*satisfatti e stupidi*). This coup seems modeled on Aristotle's theory of tragedy, its ruthless logic leading to an astonishing climax that maximizes "pity and fear" but through *catharsis* or purgation turns them into an aesthetically satisfying conclusion. Machiavelli's studiedly casual description does the same to us, the readers; his words *perform* what they describe, achieving not only *mimesis* (imitation) but *poesis*, a kind of making or creation.

Machiavelli himself felt quite hurt when Ariosto left him out of the roll-call of contemporary poets in *Orlando furioso*.[16]

Even though it is not formally set out as a dialogue, Thomas More's Latin prose fiction *Utopia* represents the high point of Renaissance dialogism. More's protean text has often been simplified by paraphrasing the second part – the sober description of the island republic of Utopia (from a Greek word meaning No-place) – without regard to its ironic setting. This ordered kibbutz-like state, however stifling to late-twentieth-century notions of individuality, must have seemed exhilaratingly free from class-inequality, corruption, starvation amidst opulence, religious persecution, and capital punishment (reserved for party politicians and serial adulterers); everyone wears simple earth-tones, everyone enjoys moderate labor and moderate sensory pleasure, apart from a few scholars and ascetics who volunteer for dirty work. (Slaves and foreigners are treated quite differently, however.) This calm, rational narrative is punctuated by bursts of carnival humor that drive home a bitter critique of capitalism: in Utopia gold is the basest metal, used only for chamber-pots and shackles; a foreign ambassador dripping in silks and jewels is identified as the court fool; in England, racked by mass unemployment caused by enclosures, the sheep devour the men. And the entire book constitutes a play of contrasting voices that suspend and unsettle the reader's judgment. The description of Utopia in Part II is delivered by an unreliable narrator: a member of Amerigo Vespucci's expedition named Raphael Hythlodaeus ("Bringer of Nonsense"), who seems to have been crazed by his experience of European courts. In Part I the frame-narrative dramatizes a meeting between "Morus" and a group of sophisticated friends, who invite the Ancient Mariner Hythlodaeus to debate the burning issue of More's own life: whether the intellectual should enter public service or keep a critical distance from the abuses he sees all around him. This convivial setting returns in the beautifully-poised ending, when Morus (who represents the conventional side of More himself) gently steers the fanatical utopianist to the supper-table, promising to discuss everything later. Rabelais's chronicle of Gargantua and Pantagruel, themselves inhabitants of Utopia, likewise ends with an amused shrug and a Dionysian invitation; after long debate on the pros and cons of marriage, with innumerable side-episodes that parade yet more great issues in absurd form, the travelers finally reach the oracular Holy Bottle, which simply orders them to "*Trink!*"

Mondo Latino

More's *Utopia* and Erasmus's *Praise of Folly* have survived the eclipse of Latin as the international language of intellectuals and literati, so it takes some effort to reconstruct the huge reputation and scope of neo-Latin literature. This *lingua franca* allowed gifted students to travel anywhere in Europe, joining both the private academies and the universities (though admittedly foreigners did form their own "nations" there), and it sustained an equally wide culture of fame: the Welsh John Owen was known throughout Europe for his epigrams; the astonishing Scots polymath George Buchanan – playwright, historian, critic, erotic and salacious poet, nemesis of Mary Queen of Scots, theologian, and republican theorist – was universally respected and his tragedies repeatedly translated. Latin sustained a broad range of genres too, including prose fiction such as the *Hypnerotomachia* (published with beautiful woodcuts in 1499), and it encouraged versatility in modes and personae. The French divine Théodore Beza wrote Catullus-like poems about the "little slit" of a lady and the problems of satisfying his boyfriend and his mistress at the same time (as his enemies loved pointing out when he became head of the Calvinist Church). Konrad Celtis – the low-born German who rose to be imperial Poet Laureate, professor of poetry, and a proud member of the "commonwealth of letters" – composed *Amores*, odes, epigrams, a pastoral music-drama performed at the Viennese court, an unfinished epic on Theodoric, and wild vituperations against Italian buggery.[17] (German writers found Latin particularly useful for parody and gross humor.) Like many other authors who influenced Sidney, Fracastoro published literary theory as well as original poetry like *Syphilis*. Jacopo Sannazaro's *De partu virginis* (*The Birth of the Virgin*, 1526) adapts the Vergilian epic to Christian subject-matter, and Vida likewise wrote a classicizing *Christiad* (1535) as well as his poems on silkworms and chess and a new *Ars poetica*. Another imperial Poet Laureate, the splendidly-named Aeneas Silvius Piccolomini, composed wordly erotic verse, a Terentian comedy, and a racy short novel about two lovers who overcome social and architectural obstacles; when he came to choose the name Pius II after being elected Pope, he punned on the famous line in Vergil, "I am *pius Aeneas*." Though he later urges himself to reject the "Aeneas" and assume the "Pius" (in *Commentaries*), the entire choice of name still derives from the literary allusion.

The same ideal of versatility stimulated experiments in the vernacular. Prose fictions such as More's *Utopia* and Pope Pius's *Two Lovers* were avidly translated into modern languages, but the flow went in both directions: Johannes Reuchlin translated the popular French farce *Maitre Pathelin* into perfect Latin in imitation of Terence, and Buchanan converted a Scots satire by his countryman William Dunbar into an epigram in the style of Martial.[18] Most authors wrote in Latin as well as the mother tongue, and works such as Boccaccio's *Genealogy of the Gods* and Petrarch's *Africa* (an imitation of Vergil, proposing Scipio Africanus as a heroic model for modern Italy) were valued as highly as their Italian tales and sonnets. Keeping the torch alive, Milton's Latin poems on his father and his closest male friend are significantly more personal than anything he wrote in English.

The bilingual literary career encouraged the playful command of multiple voices. Archbishop Giovanni della Casa produced urbane Latin poems, the manners-treatise *Galateo*, and a range of Italian verse including the notorious *Capitolo del forno*, which praises a "baker's oven" that turns out to mean his favourite boy's bottom. Sannazaro fashioned a literary oeuvre that resembles Vergil's – adapting the pastoral to fishermen and the epic to the Virgin Mary – but he also invented the prose-and-verse novel: *Arcadia*, which celebrates the Naples area and the school of poets that flourished there. Giordano Bruno wrote not only the Latin and Italian philosophical dialogues that caused him to be burnt as a heretic, but the sonnet-sequence *Eroici furori* (with prose interpretation) and one of the most successful comedies of the later sixteenth century *The Candle-Maker* (*Il Candelaio*). Even in the fifteenth century – not especially distinguished for vernacular literature, except for outsiders like Jacques Villon or Robert Henryson who revitalized medieval modes rather than attempting the new classicism – Latinists made fresh inventions in the mother-tongue. Angelo Poliziano (also known as "Politian") created a beautiful fragment on the jousts organized by the Medici in 1475 (the source of Botticelli's *Primavera* and *Birth of Venus*) and the secular drama *Orfeo*, all in Italian except for Orpheus's Latin canticle in praise of the patron. This direct ancestor of Monteverdi's opera ends not with lament, apotheosis, or neo-classical poetic justice but with the Bacchae triumphantly flaunting Orpheus's severed head in a drunken dance, a truly Dionysiac origin for Renaissance drama.

Latin also gave the freedom to vituperate and to explore the most pornographic aspects of sexuality. The epigrams of Martial and Catullus brought bawdy no-holes-barred sexual insult to a high polish, and literary "decorum" allowed the Renaissance poet equally hair-raising obscenity provided he paid stylistic homage to those originals. The Sicilian humanist Antonio Beccadelli conceived his epigrams as active "hermaphrodites" endowed with the organs of both sexes, and they certainly present sexual problems and deformities as frankly as Martial. The epic poet Bishop Janus Pannonius produced a whole range of sex-lyrics and epigrams including one about the obvious maleness of Pope Paul II, and the saintly Thomas More wrote a distasteful poem about a rape victim who begs her assailant to stay on the job. The most successful erotic poet of the Renaissance was the Dutch Johannes Secundus, who composed Ovidian elegies (episodes from a young man's sexual prowling), the sensuous lyrics *Basia* (kisses), and cheeky epigrams, one of which is endlessly quoted in libertine literature: separating sex from gender at a stroke, Secundus poses the question, why is *cunnus* (vulva) grammatically masculine and *mentula* (penis) feminine?[19] Secundus's frank "epithalamium" or wedding song reminds us that married love generated its own literature, including Giovanni Pontano's *De amore conjugali* and Spenser's *Amoretti*.

It is misleading, therefore, to refer to Renaissance love-poetry as purely "Petrarchan." Petrarch's poetry of infinite yearning, freezing, burning non-fulfilment, and quasi-religious worship of Laura exerted an immense influence, over treatises on ideal beauty as well as over poetry; a small copy of Petrarch became the obligatory accessory for high-class courtesans and sensitive young men. Petrarchism confirmed Dante's founding observation, in *La vita nuova*, xxv, that vernacular rhymed poetry evolved *solely* to express this kind of adoration (any other subject requiring Latin). France and England, too, created poetry of respectful adoration whose object is as much Petrarch as the idealized beloved; Maurice Scève of Lyons, for example, celebrates his Délie (anagram of *l'idée*) in ten-line stanzas, as if the master's fourteen-line sonnet were too much for him. Meanwhile, Latin depicts every other form of desire, illicit, corporeal, consummated, and sated: *La vida loca* rather than *La vita nuova*.

The vernacular soon began to catch up. Aretino's infamous *sonetti lussuriosi* (1524?) describe the "Modes" of genital performance in detail, aptly using seventeen-line "sonnets with a tail." Women poets such as Tullia d'Aragona, Gaspara Stampa, Veronica Franco, and Louise Labé brought physical gratification and longing back into sonnet and *terza rima*, without resorting to verbal obscenity. French poets expanded the lyric range to include every aspect of the love-affair: Clément Marot expanded the *blason* into an encyclopaedia of erotic zones; Pierre de Ronsard dramatized the rivalry of phallus and dildo, the bliss of love-making and the wistfulness of the older man inviting a young mistress to "gather the roses" before she too grows old. The literary stars that called themselves the Pléiade under Ronsard's leadership elaborated these themes *ad infinitum*, as did John Donne in England. And Montaigne recreated Latinate erotic culture in his worldly, capricious essay on sexuality (III. v), interweaving his own fluid prose with an array of verse quotations from Vergil and Martial to Secundus and Beza. English poets such as Sidney also tried to reintroduce the body into the sonnet-sequence (*Astrophil and Stella* 71 ends when the voice of Desire cries "Give me some food"). But this anti-Petrarchanism still exhibits the master's stamp, as when Shakespeare declares "My mistress's eyes are nothing like the sun" (sonnet 130), when Donne writes "Against Constancy," or when Sidney refuses to replicate "Petrarch's long-deceased woes" (*Astrophil and Stella* 15). Even Sidney's dramatic opening, when the Muse tells him to abandon set phrases and "Look in thy heart and write," revives a *topos* going back to Petrarch.

The physicality of sexually explicit discourse allies it to the carnival and to playful, world-upside-down genres like the mock encomium, which clothes trivial or shameful subjects in literary grandeur. Examples include eulogies of the bread-oven, the paint-brush, or the onion (all concealing a sexual meaning), of nothing, of fleas and gout (by Johann Fischart, who also translated Rabelais into German). Sir John Harington's *Metamorphosis of Ajax* concerns not the Greek hero but "a jakes" or lavatory. Bawds and whores become the heroines of Buchanan's Latin "Pro Lena apologia," Du Bellay's French "La Vieille Courtisanne," the Spanish *Celestina* written or expanded by Fernando de Rojas, and Aretino's Italian *Ragionamenti*. Mock-praise flourished as far afield as Scots Gaelic, where Sir Duncan Campbell's ironic tribute to a dead beggar shows affinities with Erasmus and Rabelais, the supreme authors in this genre.

Erasmus in Latin and Rabelais in French, like their Greek model Lucian, suffuse mere mockery with the surreal humor of intellectuals taking a holiday that may suddenly turn serious. Erasmus's *Encomium moriae* (*The Praise of Folly*, 1509, dedicated to the "man for all seasons" Thomas More) begins with a relatively lucid irony, in which the truth is reached by simply turning the Goddess Folly's self-praise upside down, but it evolves into a genuine eulogy that exalts the folly of Christ's sacrifice above the prudence of the secular world. Taking the jester's licence, Erasmus critiques not only the passions of the secular world (sex, money, celebrity) but those abuses of the Church that would soon fuel the Protestant Reformation. The *Praise of Folly*'s influence can still be felt in the wise fooleries of Shakespeare: Hamlet seems to be reading it when he teases Polonius about the ever-shifting shapes visible in the clouds (III. ii), and Jacques cites it in *As You Like It* when he declares "All the world's a stage" (II. vii).

Rabelais likewise mixes ecclesiastical satire, mock-encomium, and evangelism into his retelling of popular folk-tales about the giants Gargantua and Pantagruel, who cover the French landscape with traces of their exploits and emissions. Gigantic in style as well as content, the sprawling, drunken narrative turns every incident into an occasion for elaborate verbiage and extravagant praise, sometimes straight (as in the glowing tributes to humanist learning or the utopian Abbey of Theleme) and sometimes poised between jest and earnest. Panurge's praise of debt is so fiendishly eloquent and ingenious that after a while the reader starts to believe it, to glimpse a larger, cosmic economy of Debt behind the scrounger's casuistry; his litany of the testicle, containing over two hundred fantastic and absurd epithets, becomes itself a verbal icon of fertility. Erasmus spells out his strategy by evoking "The Sileni of

Alcibiades," applying to his own comic text Plato's interpretation of Socrates, grotesque and satyr-faced on the outside, but concealing precious wisdom within.
Rabelais adopts exactly this image when he prepares the reader to find deep truths
beneath the tall tales and torrential obscenity of *Gargantua*, though here the irony is
harder to fix: is he *recommending* an esoteric reading of his carnivalesque discourse (as
high-minded "Christian humanist" scholars assume), or is he *mocking* the whole
attempt to peer beneath the surface or crack the bone to suck out the marrow of
wisdom?[20]

Latin and vernacular culture seem to feed each other, then. But we must also
be aware of their rivalry. "Humanism" is generally regarded as the driving force of
Renaissance literature, and certainly an expert like Ariosto equated the *humanisti*
with poetry (and pederasty). Much humanist activity went into creating the *support
system* for literature: improved editions of the classics (with standardized line- and
page-numbers made possible by print), manuals of style and grammar, line-by-line
commentaries, endowed chairs in Poetry and Dante Studies. But metacritical awareness of rhetoric and poetics could harden into the neo-classicism of Rules and Unities;
Tasso, for example, is often blamed for revising the life out of his own *Gerusalemme
liberata* and crushing invention with prescriptive theory. And renewed respect for the
classics could disparage the "modern" tongue.

A great effort did go into theorizing the vernacular, creating a national literary
language that could stand beside classical Latin and Greek, eliminating (or promoting) regional dialects and archaisms. This happened first in treatises on Tuscan
(simultaneously defended against Latin and against other forms of Italian), then in
the linguistic and metrical reforms of the Pléiade in France (Du Bellay, *Défense et
illustration de la langue française*, 1549), and finally in Spenser's attempt to create a
literary English that combined Chaucerian archaism and Ariostan modernity. (The
result is a stately, encrusted style and a unique stanza that grafts a six-beat Alexandrine
onto the *ottava rima*, moving like an elephant hung with cloth of gold.) Manuals
introduced the rhetorical figures into English and Welsh, and numerous mid-sixteenth-century anthologies showed off the new lyric resources of the British vernaculars. Once Buchanan had transposed the Psalms into respectable Latin meter stanzaic
translations followed, not only in French and German but in English, in Welsh, and in
Yiddish.

Some humanists deplored this modern diaspora, however. In an eloquent lament
quoted by Burckhardt, Paolo Giovio denounces a collapse of literary standards so
complete that "the plays of Plautus and Terence, once a school of Latin style for
the educated Romans, are banished to make room for Italian comedies." His worst
fears would have been confirmed when, in 1524, Plautus' masterpiece *Menaechmi*
was performed back to back with Machiavelli's wicked new *Mandragola* (*The Man-
drake Root*), and the vernacular comedy stole the show.[21] *Mandragola*'s mad spiral of
inventive trickery uses the standard Plautine cast – parasite, desperate young man,
clever go-between – but absorbs classical allusion effortlessly into colloquial impro-
visation: the trembling lover describes his symptoms in words taken from Sappho via
Catullus, the crafty friar evokes the neo-Aristotelian unities between the acts, but
only to remind the audience that nobody is getting any sleep. Machiavelli gives his
comedy an ending almost as Dionysian as Politian's *Orfeo*, without loss of blood; the
trickery works, the idiot husband remains happily deceived, and the virtuous wife

(ironically named Lucrezia) enjoys her clandestine lover and agrees to continue the deception.

Mandragola contributes to a wave of vernacular drama that absorbs classical practice but goes beyond it, including court comedies like Ariosto's *I suppositi*, Cardinal Bibbiena's *Calandra*, and Aretino's *Cortegiana*, the popular theatre of Angelo Beolco ("Il Ruzzante"), gory tragedies in the manner of Seneca, and pastoral shepherd-plays like Tasso's much-imitated *Aminta*. This Italian coterie drama prepared the way for the public theater of Spain and England, even though Lope de Vega, Marlowe, and Shakespeare mingled it with popular modes and departed much further from ancient models. Elizabethan playwrights, flying by the seat of their breeches, left little commentary on their own art (considered hopelessly incorrect by Italian observers). But Lope explicitly states that he "banishes" Plautus and Terence when he sits down to write a working play, definitively breaking from the Latin world.[22]

Beyond Italy

The cultural hegemony of Italy, which grew as its political condition worsened, left its mark on aspiring poets in many barbarian lands. Italian served as a kind of modern classical language alongside Latin and Greek. Luís de Camões (or Camoens) wrote his fiercely national and modernist epic *Os Lusíadas* in Portuguese, heroizing the Indian voyage of Vasco da Gama that had given Portugal a stake in world empire barely sixty years earlier. Heavily dependent on Italian stanza form and on classical mythology (Venus and Bacchus fight over the action, answering prayers that the sailors *think* they are addressing to the Christian God), Camoens nevertheless asserts that he has transcended and defeated all previous literature. But in the highly erotic closing episode, when Venus rewards the Portuguese crew with an island full of available nymphs, the one sailor unsuccessful in his wooing articulates his despair with a line from Petrarch in the original Italian (IX. lxxviii). Louise Labé, a leading poet of Lyons, starts her sonnet sequence by writing one in Italian, as if to show her credentials at the threshold of a poetic career that goes on to adapt the Petrarchan sonnet of frustration to the sensuous immediacy expected of her as a French woman poet. Even as late as the 1620s, on the outer fringes of the empire of letters, an idealistic and backward-looking English poet felt the need to compose sonnets and *canzone* in Italian because "this is the language that Love takes pride in" ("Questa è lingua di cui si vanta Amore": Milton, *Canzone*).

Between the center and the periphery flowed a constant but uneven interchange of ideas, technologies, and texts. (See the essay by Peter Burke above.) Just as Greek scholarship and German printing poured into Italy, so literary influence from Italy (and later France) irradiated native talent in Dutch, English, Romansch, Hungarian, Polish, Croatian, and modern Greek.[23] Poets little known in Anglo-American anthologies still embody the Renaissance in their own national literatures, like the versatile lyricist and dramatist Jan Kochanowski (still a household name for Poles) and the dashing aristocrat Bálint Balassi (1554–94). Poised between East and West, Balassi wrote Hungarian poetry for tunes with titles in Polish, Romanian, and Turkish (from which he also translated); he composed familiar letters, a classical comedy, military songs, the obligatory cycle of love-poems (to "Julia"), and self-castigating devotional lyrics, manifesting a powerful voice through heavy rhymes and grammatically identical word-endings. (This presumably gave Sidney the impression that Hungarian poetry, which he heard *in situ*, expressed only fierce martial sentiments.[24]) Latin was still the passport for Europeans from non-translated language groups (like another Hungarian, Stephen Parmenius, who wrote a Latin poem boosting the English colonial expedition to North America and died in a shipwreck during one such voyage). But the will to create a vernacular "Renaissance literature" could be felt even on the margins of Europe, as we see in the case of Alexander Barclay (1475?–1552). Conversant in the late-medieval German tradition and in the international Latin culture that flourished in Tudor Britain, Barclay is the first English-language writer to adopt the Vergilian "Eclogue," the pastoral that deals with serious matters of Church and state, and his source materials are impeccably "Renaissance": he versifies Pius II's Latin prose letter about the miseries of serving at the imperial court, and translates the highly-regarded Latin poet Baptista Mantuanus (later imitated by Spenser in his *Shepherd's Calendar*). The result is Renaissance in content but provincial in form, written in a kind of rhymed prose with no sense of poetic meter. The serious verse of John Skelton (Oxford Poet Laureate), and the lyrics of the court poet Sir Thomas Wyatt, still suffer from this inability to grasp the basic English pentameter.[25] Even after these technical problems were solved by Surrey and Sackville, English poetry sounds graceless and labored until the advent of Sidney.

The "belated" cultures of Spain and England, opposite in many ways, turn marginality into a triumph that signals the apex and the death of Renaissance literature. Both draw on indigenous traditions of popular drama and fiction, rather than perfecting classical forms. Don Quixote does own several Spanish colonial epics, but he and his contemporaries give more credence and affection to prose romances like the Catalan *Tirant lo Blanc* (1455) and Montemayor's Castilian pastoral *Diana* (1559) – which Sidney imitates in both versions of his novel *Arcadia*, one as tightly-plotted as an Aristotelian drama, the other so inventive that it breaks the pastoral frame and could never be finished. Quixote is starstruck by Montemayor and Ariosto as well as by old-fashioned ballads and tales (I. v, x, xxv); he consciously emulates the canonical madness of Orlando, and expresses himself in eloquent, courtly prose. A surprising number of the other characters share the Renaissance side of his delusion, dressing as shepherds, pining with Petrarchan desire, or discoursing like Tullia d'Aragona on the Infinity of Love (I. xiii).

England's brief "Renaissance" vanished almost as soon as it occurred: *The Faerie Queene* ran into the sand, Sidney was killed fighting for Dutch independence at the Byronic age of 32, Marlowe died in a fight leaving *Doctor Faustus* a thing of shreds and patches, unworthy of its promised challenge to "the mind of man." Like Don Quixote, the next generation (Donne, Shakespeare, Jonson) haunts the ruins of Renaissance magnificence. Shakespeare's characters constitute a kind of meta- or post-Renaissance, ironizing, elegizing, or outdoing its now-problematic certainties. Richard III, a popular "Vice" villain straight out of the old morality plays, confronts Renaissance individualism when he promises to change shapes more often than Proteus and "set the murderous Machiavel to school" (*3 Henry VI*, III. ii). Romeo and Juliet perform a perfectly rhymed sonnet on their first encounter, but never again achieve that harmony (I. v). Hamlet embodies, then deconstructs, the perfect courtier and the heroic lunatic. Macbeth turns Machiavellian success into a tale told by an idiot, signifying nothing. Meanwhile, Donne laments that "new philosophy puts all in doubt," crumbles all collective enterprise into "atomies," and makes every man a "phoenix" alone with his individualism.[26] Scientists from Bacon onwards use the rebirth trope for their own achievement, but for them the dark age *was* the Renaissance; everything they hated can be summed up in two words: *eloquence* and *literature*.

NOTES

1   Firpo, "Political Philosophy"; Hale, *Civilization*, pp. 416–19.
2   Erasmus, *Collected Works*, XXX. 10.
3   Rabelais, I. xv, xxi–ii, II. viii; the most influential critic of Rabelais, Mikhail Bakhtin, tends to associate him with medieval festive culture rather than Renaissance intellectual play.
4   Erasmus, *Collected Works*, XXXIX. 194–5; cf. *On Copia*, where Erasmus generates page after page of Monty Pythonesque variants on one simple sentence, "I enjoyed getting your letter."
5   Théodore Beza, cited in Kerrigan and Braden, *Idea*, p. 9.
6   Jardine, *Worldly Goods*, pp. 188, 157; Sidney, *Apology*, pp. 100, 123.
7   I am alluding to (among others) Jed, *Chaste Thinking*, Vickers, "Body Re-Membered," Ascoli, *Ariosto's Bitter Harmony* (citing *Orlando furioso* XIV. cxxxiv); for public dismemberment, see p. 373.
8   Cited in Kerrigan and Braden, *Idea*, pp. 6, 221 n. 9.
9   Curtius, *European Literature*, p. 86.
10 Burckhardt, *Civilization*, p. 186.
11 Ariosto, Satire VI.
12 Sidney, *Apology*, p. 100.
13 Ibid., p. 102 (and cf. p. 100).
14 Jardine, *Worldly Goods*, p. 262.
15 Jordan, *Renaissance Feminism*, pp. 122–7; Sidney, *Apology*, p. 121 classifies Agrippa's *De Incertitudine* as a "merry" work alongside Erasmus's *Praise of Folly* and Rabelais's praise of debt.
16 Machiavelli, *Portable Machiavelli*, p. 328 (*Discorsi*), pp. 552–3, 558–9 (*History of Florence*), pp. 99–100 (*Il Principe*, ch. 7); letter of 17 December 1517; cf. Ascoli and Kahn, *Machiavelli and the Discourse of Literature*, Introduction.
17 Beza, *Juvenilia*, epigrams LXXIV, XC; Hale, *Civilization*, p. 282; Abbé, *Drama*, p. 4; Rowland, "Revenge," pp. 321–2.
18 Abbé, *Drama*, p. 1; Macqueen, "Renaissance in Scotland," pp. 44–5.
19 Kirkconnell, *Hungarian Helicon*, p. 198 (and cf. pp. 2–7); More, "De puella quae raptum finxit," in Nichols, *Neo-Latin Poetry*, pp. 465–6 (a reference I owe to Amy Greenstadt); Secundus, *Opera*, p. 141.
20 Rabelais, III. ii-4, xxvi (and cf. xxviii), I Prologue; Erasmus, *Praise of Folly*, p. 28.
21 Burckhardt, *Civilization*, p. 144.
22 Hale, *Civilization*, pp. 205, 345; cf. Cohen, *Drama of a Nation*, pp. 96–185, 88–9.
23 Thorlby, *European Literature*, under "Noot, Junker Jan van der," "Romansch Literature," "Dalmatian and Dubrovnik Literature," "Hortatzis, Georgios," "*Erotokritos*"; for Edmwnd Prys's failed attempt to create a new Renaissance poetry in Welsh, see Gruffydd, "Renaissance and Welsh Literature," pp. 26–31.

24   Peterkiewicz and Singer, *Polish Poetry*, Kochanowski selections; Cohen, *Drama of a Nation*, pp. 87–8; Balassi, *Összes Versei* (with thanks to Martha Pollak for translations); Kirkconnell, *Hungarian Helicon*, pp. 208–13 (and pp. 8–9, 200–8 for contemporary poets); Sidney, *Apology*, p. 118. Like his contemporary Spenser, Balassi invented a stanza that still bears his name.

25   Hanson, "From Dante to Pinsky," pp. 72–3.

26   Donne, *An Anatomie of the World* ("The First Anniversary"), ll. 205–18. Bacon opposed true science to the "incumbr[ance of] literature and book-learning," as Greenblatt points out in "Literature?," p. 471, and the Royal Society banished "eloquence" altogether; it seems unwise to cram mid-seventeenth-century science into a discussion of the "Renaissance," as Kerrigan and Braden do in *Idea*, ch. 8.

REFERENCES

Abbé, Derek van, *Drama in Renaissance Germany and Switzerland* (Melbourne: University of Melbourne Press, 1961).

Ariosto, Ludovico, *The Satires of Ludovico Ariosto: A Renaissance Autobiography*, trans. Peter DeSa Wiggins (Athens, OH: Ohio University Press, 1976).

Ascoli, Albert Russell, *Ariosto's Bitter Harmony: Crisis and Evasion in the Italian Renaissance* (Princeton: Princeton University Press, 1987).

—— and Kahn, Victoria, eds., *Machiavelli and the Discourse of Literature* (Ithaca, NY: Cornell University Press, 1993).

Balassi, Bálint, *Összes Versei, szép magyar comoediája és levelezése*, ed. Béla Stoll and Sándor Eckhardt ([Budapest]: Magyar Helikon, 1974).

Beza (Bèze), Théodore de, *Juvenilia* [1578], ed. and trans. Alexandre Machard (Paris: Liseux, 1879).

Burckhardt, Jacob, *The Civilization of the Renaissance in Italy*, trans. S. G. C. Middlemore (Oxford: Phaidon, 1945).

Cohen, Walter, *Drama of a Nation: Public Theater in Renaissance England and Spain* (Ithaca, NY: Cornell University Press, 1985).

Curtius, Ernst Robert, *European Literature and the Latin Middle Ages*, trans. Willard R. Trask (Princeton: Princeton University Press, 1990).

Donne, John, *Complete Poetry*, ed. John T. Shawcross (New York: New York University Press, 1968).

Erasmus, Desiderius, *Collected Works* (Toronto: University of Toronto Press, 1974–).

——, *The Praise of Folly and Other Writings*, trans. and ed. Robert M. Adams (New York: W. W. Norton, 1989).

Firpo, Luigi, "Political Philosophy: Renaissance Utopianism," in *The Late Italian Renaissance, 1525–1630*, ed. Eric Cochrane (London: Macmillan, 1970).

Greenblatt, Stephen, "What Is the History of Literature?," *Critical Inquiry* 23 (1997).

Gruffydd, R. Geraint, "The Renaissance and Welsh Literature," in *The Celts and the Renaissance*, ed. Glanmore Williams and Robert Owen Jones (Cardiff: University of Wales Press, 1990).

Hale, John, *The Civilization of Europe in the Renaissance* (New York: Atheneum, 1994).

Hanson, Kristen, "From Dante to Pinsky: A Theoretical Perspective on the History of the Modern English Iambic Pentameter," *Rivista di Linguistica* 9/1 (1997).

Jardine, Lisa, *Worldly Goods: A New History of the Renaissance* (New York: Doubleday, 1996).

Jed, Stephanie H., *Chaste Thinking: The Rape of Lucretia and the Birth of Humanism* (Bloomington: Indiana University Press, 1989).

Jordan, Constance, *Renaissance Feminism: Literary Texts and Political Models* (Ithaca, NY: Cornell University Press, 1990).

Kerrigan, William and Braden, Gordon, *The Idea of the Renaissance* (Baltimore: Johns Hopkins University Press, 1989).

Kirkconnell, Watson, ed. and trans., *The Hungarian Helicon: Epic and Other Poetry* (Calgary: Széchenyi Society, 1985).

Machiavelli, Nicolò, *The Portable Machiavelli*, ed. and trans. Peter Bondanella and Mark Musa (New York: Viking Penguin, 1979).

Macqueen, John, "The Renaissance in Scotland," in *The Celts and the Renaissance*, ed. Glanmore Williams and Robert Owen Jones (Cardiff: University of Wales Press, 1990).

Nichols, Fred J., ed. and trans., *An Anthology of Neo-Latin Poetry* (New Haven: Yale University Press, 1979).

Peterkiewicz, Jerzy and Singer, Burns, *Five Centuries of Polish Poetry* (London: Oxford University Press, 1970).

Rabelais, François, *Œuvres complètes*, ed. Guy Demerson (Paris: L'Intégrale/Seuil, 1973). The five books that make up the chronicles of Gargantua have separate titles, but are cited by volume and chapter.

Rowland, Ingrid D., "Revenge of the Regensburg Humanists, 1493," *Sixteenth-Century Journal* 25 (1994).

Secundus, Johannes (Jan Nicholaus Everaerts), *Opera*, ed. Petrus Scriverus (Leiden, 1619).

Sidney, Sir Philip, *An Apology for Poetry* (*The Defence of Poesie*), ed. Geoffrey Shepherd (London: Nelson, 1965).

Thorlby, Anthony, ed., *The Penguin Companion to European Literature* (New York: McGraw-Hill, 1969).

Vickers, Nancy J., "The Body Re-Membered: Petrarchan Lyric and the Strategies of Description," in *Mimesis: From Mirror to Methos, Augustine to Descartes*, ed. John D. Lyons and Stephen G. Nichols (Hanover, NH: University of New England Press, 1982).

FURTHER READING

Ferguson, Margaret, Quilligan, Maureen, and Vickers, Nancy, eds., *Rewriting the Renaissance: The Discourses of Sexual Difference in Early Modern Europe* (Chicago: University of Chicago Press, 1986).

Greenblatt, Stephen, *Renaissance Self-Fashioning, from More to Shakespeare* (Chicago: University of Chicago Press, 1980).

Hollier, Denis, ed., *A New History of French Literature* (Cambridge, MA: Harvard University Press, 1989).

Jones, Ann Rosalind, *The Currency of Eros: Women's Love Lyric in Europe, 1540–1620* (Bloomington: Indiana University Press, 1990).

Kritzman, Lawrence D., *The Rhetoric of Sexuality and the Literature of the French Renaissance* (Cambridge: Cambridge University Press, 1991).

Rosenthal, Margaret F., *The Honest Courtesan: Veronica Franco, Citizen and Writer in Sixteenth-Century Venice* (Chicago: University of Chicago Press, 1992).

Waddington, Raymond, "Rewriting the World, Rewriting the Body," in *The Cambridge Companion to English Literature 1500–1600*, ed. Arthur F. Kinney (Cambridge: Cambridge University Press, 2000).

Wind, Edgar, *Pagan Mysteries in the Renaissance* (Oxford: Oxford University Press, 1980).

Chapter Twenty-Two

Political Ideas

John M. Najemy

Renaissance politics and political thought have an old reputation for the pursuit of power and the means to its unfettered exercise. Much of this reputation centers on a narrow and even distorted reading of Machiavelli, and indeed of only one of his books (*The Prince*), but it also reflects a generalized view of the politics of the period – mostly in Italy, but to a certain extent in the so-called Renaissance monarchies of England, Spain, and France – as dominated by princes who embodied a ruthless and single-minded lust for power. In his *Civilization of the Renaissance in Italy* (1860) Jacob Burckhardt created unforgettable images of amoral and all-powerful princes who rose from the ranks of petty tyrants and condottieri by means of guile and cruelty. And a powerful – albeit inaccurate – historiographical tradition of the Renaissance as a period whose politics and culture were liberated from ethical restraints has perpetuated these notions. To see Renaissance politics and political ideas on their own terms, we need first to notice that the attention to princes and their modes of (mis)conduct recedes to one, by no means negligible, but hardly dominant feature of the period. Side by side with the interest in establishing the claims and criteria of princely power was a broader, more searching, and far more innovative project that sought, for the first time since antiquity, to link the social and the political – to explore the ways in which the organization of society conditioned political authority and power. Such exploration for the most part took the form of inquiries into the nature and rules of self-governing polities, or republics. But even republicanism was a subset of a larger effort to ground ideas about all political authority – republics and monarchies alike – in a deeper understanding of the nature, characteristics, and specific requirements of different types of societies, and even of individual communities. Linking ideas about political organization and leadership to an analytical awareness of social structures and differences was the most significant achievement of Renaissance political thinkers.

The Emergence of Republicanism in Italy

Around 1300 there were three principal languages, or discourses, of politics in Europe. The oldest was the tradition of Roman imperial sovereignty, in which rule was command and the *princeps* the source of law: ideas embraced by medieval emperors and defended by Dante in the *Monarchia* (ca. 1314), but which perhaps only Frederick II (d. 1250) came close to realizing. Feudal lordship and kingship constituted a second and very different political language, in which personal and contractual obligations created dependent, hierarchical relationships between lords and vassals and gave the former jurisdiction – the authority to define rights and resolve conflicts – over the latter. The feudal monarchies of France and England attempted to build a large-scale system of political organization on these grounds by making the king the chief lord in a complex pyramid of such ties. Feudal kings thus had no unconditional powers: their authority derived from mutually respected contractual obligations.

The third discourse of politics emerged from the experiments of self-governing associations in thousands of towns and cities all over Europe, but especially in Italy. Such associations could be formed by citizens in a town, by the members of a trade or profession in their guild, or indeed by any group of persons who wished to enter into an organization, create rules for the regulation of their common activity and an authority to enforce their own observance of those rules. They did so by means of sworn voluntary mutual oaths that brought into being a legal entity, generically called an *universitas*, to which the members pledged their obedience. Jurists devised the theory of the *universitas* as a fictive person in the eyes of the law, distinct from the actual persons who created it, that could, like a living person, assume rights and obligations and appoint representatives, or procurators, to act on its behalf. A *universitas* could do these things only with the consent of its members, and the authority of those who acted in its name was limited by the terms of a delegation of power approved by the members and codified in statutes. While small associations were sometimes able to bring together all, or a majority, of their members to approve laws and elect officials, larger corporations, including guilds with hundreds of members and especially the city-wide associations of citizens called communes, accomplished these tasks not by direct participatory democracy, but by systems of representation whereby one or more councils represented the *universitas* and acted on behalf of all, as if the council(s) were the whole corporation: a notion encapsulated by the jurist Bartolus of Sassoferrato (1314–57) in the principle that "the council represents the mind of the people." Although the executive committees (of priors, consuls, or elders) exercised authority in day-to-day administration and had the power to propose legislation, it was the councils that converted proposals into laws and created the commune's constitutional framework. A *universitas* was in effect a miniature proto-republic in which political authority reflected the will of the members, and the specific forms of representation that resulted in councils and executive committees of varying composition and size depended on the differences in the social and professional organization of the members, which varied from guild to guild and from commune to commune. Thus, to determine and conceptualize the nature of political authority in such communities necessarily required some understanding of their social organization.

The proto-republicanism of the twelfth- and thirteenth-century Italian cities was a novel element in European political discourse. It had no articulated theoretical foundation, no canonical enunciation of underlying principles. Before it became the object of formal political theory, the republicanism of the communes was an ongoing collective effort by their citizens to articulate and codify the procedures of self-government in a working dialogue with everyday political practice. A good example comes from Florence, where, in November 1292, the representatives of the twelve major guilds gathered for an open debate on the procedures to be adopted for the election of the commune's chief executive magistracy, the priorate. The victory of those who favored elections involving a larger group of guilds resulted in a priorate representing a broader range of social groups. This priorate then authorized a committee of jurists to draft the *Ordinances of Justice,* which established the legal basis of the guild federation by invoking the definition of justice in Roman law: "the constant and unfailing disposition to secure to each his own right," and asserting that the *Ordinances* are "deservedly called of justice" because their aim is the "utility of the republic." The federation, created by the sworn oaths of a representative of each guild, is declared "most perfect" because it "consists of all its parts and is approved by the judgment of them all": an echo of the Roman law maxim, "that which touches all must be approved by all," commonly used by this time to affirm the principle of consent. This example shows how the production of theory around the political experiments of the communes began with the participation of citizens in electoral and legislative functions. Their decisions were then given more precise legal grounding by notaries and jurists who applied to them the appropriate notions from Roman law. And the concepts and vocabularies worked out in such texts became the building blocks of the earliest chapter of formal political theory.

The final step toward theory involved the dialogue with the texts of antiquity. In Aristotle's *Politics,* translated into Latin for the first time around 1260, theorists found a teleology of the natural origins and purposes of political communities and an anthropology of political participation and citizenship, both crucial to the development of Renaissance republicanism and constitutionalism. In Cicero and Roman moral philosophy they found historical precedent for a political ethics grounded in the virtuous ends to be achieved for and by self-governing societies and their citizens. Renaissance political thought was born in the late thirteenth- and early fourteenth-century exploration of these texts as sources of historical and theoretical legitimation of the political practices of self-governing cities. The *Politics* offered the potential for an analytical approach to the different kinds of government and modes of rule. Particularly influential was Aristotle's distinction between the "regal" or unlimited rule of one man over a free people (and its "despotic" variant of rule over an unfree people) and the "political" rule exercised among a free people by citizens who assume and relinquish office by turns. Through commentators on Aristotle the term *politicus* gradually entered Italian and European thought as a way of talking about governments limited by law and statutes, dedicated to the common good, and characterized by alternation of office among citizens. Among the earliest to apply this language to the Italian communes was Bartolomeo (or Tolomeo, hence Ptolemy in English) of Lucca (1236–1327), who around 1300 completed Thomas Aquinas's *On the Government of Rulers* and redirected its argument to a fully elaborated republicanism that rejected regal rule as in essence always despotic. Governance "according to the statutes" was the essence of "political" rule for Ptolemy: rulers must be bound by the laws, even in matters of justice. Ptolemy's analysis of political rule as the expression of the collective virtue of a people, combined with his praise of the ancient Roman Republic as the model for such rule and his condemnation of Caesar for having transformed Rome from a "polity" into tyranny, marks the real beginning of Renaissance republican thought. "Polity," for Ptolemy, was not just the best form of rule; it was the best because it embodied the collective virtues, nature, and will of the citizens over whom – and by whom – it was exercised.

Marsilius of Padua (d. 1342) elaborated a theory of popular sovereignty around the representation of socially and institutionally distinct "parts of the state." *The Defender of Peace*, written in the 1320s, reveals the imprint of the guild-based governments that came to power in Florence, Bologna, Perugia, and other cities, including his native Padua. Marsilius defines the *civitas* (which he implicitly assumes to be a self-governing entity and thus, in our terms, a state) as an assemblage or combination of parts, in turn defined by the professional and economic activities of its inhabitants, which, following Aristotle, he identifies as the agricultural, artisan, military, financial, priestly, and judicial or deliberative (1.5). Marsilius's political theory thus begins with a consideration of the nature of the society, or community, to be governed. Whereas households and small villages could be governed by the patriarchal authority of elders, in cities the "differentiation and ordering of the parts" makes it necessary to "regulate matters of justice and benefit by some reasonable ordinance" (1.3). He conceives of the growth of communities as a process entailing the development of "more perfect arts [*artes*] and rules and ways of living" and the ever greater differentiation of the parts: "the things which are necessary for living and living well were brought to full development by men's reason and experience, and there was established the perfect community, called the state [*civitas*], with the differentiation of its parts" (1.3). *Artes* – which also means guilds – and *partes*, with their distinct identities within the framework of a larger whole, were central to the political language of guild-based governments, which asserted the right of each guild to send representatives to (or to participate in the election of) the councils or governing committees of the commune (as in Florence in 1292).

Because the whole and the authority that governs it emerge from the community of parts, for Marsilius, legitimate government depends on consent: "Every government is over either voluntary or involuntary subjects. The first is the genus of well-tempered governments, the second of diseased governments... It is the consent of the subjects which is the distinguishing criterion... The elected kind of government is superior to the non-elected" (1.9). Election and consent should be the foundation of all governments, no matter what their form. But the government (or ruler, the *pars principans*), whether a monarch or a republican magistracy, cannot be the author of the laws by which both the community and the government are bound (1.11). That function belongs to the *legislator*, which Marsilius defines as the "populus seu civium universitas" – the people or corporation of citizens (1.12). Marsilius thus borrowed the central term and concept through which the communes created legitimate authority from the consent of citizens. In defining the sovereignty of the people in terms of law-making powers, he echoed the practices of the communes in which councils made the laws that the executive committees of government enforced. To his definition of the *legislator* Marsilius added the words "or the weightier part thereof," whose exact meaning has been much debated. But when he explains that the weightier part "represents the whole *universitas*," it becomes clear that he is referring to the practices by which a numerical minority, elected to the councils and representing the corporation of citizens, acted as if they were the whole people. Even as the drafting of laws required trained experts, final approval depended on the consent of the "multitude," whose collective judgment is best because "no one knowingly harms himself" – a crucial assumption underlying Marsilius's optimistic view of participatory politics as sustained by the civic education of citizens who know and can defend their interests. The culture of the multitude – the combination of literacy, speech, education, the varieties of professional training and work, and the capacity to represent individual, corporate, and collective interests – thus determines the specific configuration of political authority and the content of the laws in each community. Laws must be made, changed, and interpreted "insofar as the exigencies of time or place or other circumstances make any such action opportune for the common benefit."[1]

Constitutionalism in the Northern Monarchies and the Church

A comparable brand of constitutionalism, similarly inspired by the application of Aristotelian categories to the nature of particular communities, also took hold in the political thought of northern Europe. James Blythe has recently shown that even among theorists who believed that monarchy was ideally the best form of government, local conditions and social customs had to be taken into account in determining what was best for a particular community. The Austrian Engelbert of Admont (d. 1331) was impressed by what he knew of the Italian cities and suggested that some form of mixed government, in which the people had their part, would produce the result that corresponded, in each case, to what the citizens held to be the common good. In France Jean Buridan (d. 1370) and Nicole Oresme (d. 1382) also underscored the diversity of customs and conditions and thus the need for different laws and forms of government, and indeed for changes in law and government as circumstances required. According to Oresme, the multitude should choose the form of government, and what is suitable in each case will be determined by the size of regions, historical circumstances, and traditions. The king, he insisted, must not be a source of law; the law itself is sovereign, and the multitude has "dominion" in the approval of laws and the chastisement of kings, "because it is said that that which touches all ought to be approved by all."[2]

Even before the Schism in the Church (1378–1417) produced the scandal of rival popes, critics of papal monarchy had applied constitutionalist ideas to the Church. Marsilius argued that, just as the *universitas civium* had sovereign authority in the state, so the *universitas fidelium* – the corporation of the faithful, both clerics and laypersons – represented by a general council should govern the Church and limit papal power. Similarly, Oresme proposed that the Church ought to be thought of as a city, and thus as a "polity" in Aristotelian terms. The Schism lent greater urgency to the rethinking of the Church's constitutional structure. In his *Treatise on the Authority of the Church*, Pierre D'Ailly (1350–1420), chancellor of the University of Paris in the early 1390s, advocated a mixed constitution for the Church, with councils meeting on their own authority two or three times each century and a smaller council of cardinals selected by, and representing, their local churches, governing with the Pope and limiting his "plenitude of power." D'Ailly's pupil and successor as university chancellor, Jean Gerson (1363–1429), who played a leading role at the Council of Constance (1414–18) that declared the supremacy of the general council over the Pope, also argued that the Church ought to be a mixed government, with sovereign power vested in the general council. Gerson's conciliarism rests on an understanding of the Church as a free community whose power to correct or depose its rulers was inalienable. The canonist Francesco Zabarella (1339–1417) applied the legal concept of *universitas* to the Church to argue that papal power was, as in any corporation, delegated by the community and ultimately dependent on its consent. In the early 1430s Nicholas of Cusa (1401–64) defended conciliarism in his *On Catholic Concordance* with the argument that all men are naturally free and the legitimacy of any government must rest on concord and consent. Even into the 1450s, after extremists at the Council of Basel had discredited the movement, conciliarism still found a major defender in Juan de Segovia (1386–1458).

Among English theorists too, constitutionalist notions of monarchy took hold. William of Ockham (d. 1349), who wrote his political works at the court of the emperor Ludwig in Munich, and Walter Burley (d. 1345) described the best kingdom as one in which the king cooperated with the multitude in ruling. Burley thought that the true ruler was the multitude, which included the king, and that a well-run polity with a virtuous ruler entailed a sharing of governance between king and people. In the fifteenth century, these ideas were further refined and integrated with the Aristotelian language of politics by John Fortescue (1394–1476), who described the English kingdom as a *dominium politicum et regale*: *regale* because it was a monarchy, but *politicum* because the king had his power from the people and could rule only with the laws to which they had given their assent, as he wrote in *The Governance of England*. In *dominium regale*, which Fortescue identified with the French kingdom, kings seeking their own glory rule by laws they themselves make, whereas under *dominium regale et politicum* the people are organized into a *corpus politicum* and elect their kings. Fortescue also underscored the historically specific characteristics of English law. In *In Praise of the Laws of England*, a dialogue between a Prince of Wales and a Lord Chancellor, the latter urges the former to study the laws as much as the military arts. Because England's laws are a combination of customs and statutes, to understand them requires seeing their intimate relationship to the particular character and circumstances of England. Usage and time determine whether laws are good, and judgments about laws must be relative to their specific historical and social setting. When laws must be made or revised, this is best done by the prudence of the many and thus with the approval of the whole realm.

Humanist Political Thought in Italy

Although jurists – chiefly Bartolus and Baldo degli Ubaldi (d. 1400) – continued to refine the legal concepts surrounding the sovereignty of the communes, communal liberties were in crisis in the fourteenth century. In the cities of the Po Valley (including Milan, Verona, Mantua, Ferrara, and Padua), defensive reactions against guild governments and factional struggles within the elite led to the emergence in each city of one faction or family, usually led by a strongman who became *signore* or lord, first on a de facto basis or for a limited period of time, and then on more permanent, *de jure*, and ultimately hereditary foundations. The victory of "despotism" was almost everywhere achieved with the support of elites. Even the cities that retained a republican constitution – particularly Venice and Florence – saw a concentration of power in the hands of elites seeking to protect themselves from challenges from below. Under the impact of these developments, the character of Italian political thought underwent a transformation that coincided with the affirmation of humanism.

Humanists were drawn to politics both because their favorite Roman texts were imbued with the celebration of ancient Rome's power and liberty, but also because the Ciceronian texts were immersed in questions pertaining to the duties and proper conduct of citizens. Ancient traditions of rhetoric emphasized the citizen's duty in terms of public speech and participation, providing yet another natural connection between humanism and politics. As early as the thirteenth century, the notary and chancellor of the first Florentine popular government, Brunetto Latini (d. 1295), combined speaking well and governing men as in effect a single art. The history of early humanism can in fact be traced against the background of the prominence in culture and politics of notaries whose knowledge of Roman law and mastery of the correct formulas of public discourse (for, among other things, the drafting of communal legislation) drew them ineluctably to Cicero and the Roman historians. The attraction of the notary/humanist to politics is evident in a line that stretches from Latini to Coluccio Salutati. In 1314 Albertino Mussato wrote his *Ecerinis*, a dramatization of the defense of Padua's liberty against tyrants, at the request of the Paduan guild of notaries of which he was a member. The Roman notary and epigrapher Cola di Rienzo led a rebellion in Rome in the 1340s against the power of barons and popes alike and briefly restored republican government. Francesco Petrarca (known as Petrarch, 1304–74), the son of a notary who owned the works of Cicero and Vergil, enthusiastically hailed Cola's restoration of liberty, and in 1375 Petrarch's most important follower, the notary Coluccio Salutati (1331–1406), took the central concerns of humanism – Roman history, moral philosophy, rhetoric, and poetry – with him into the office of chancellor of the Florentine republic, where he defended Florentine "liberty," with frequent appeals to ancient history, for more than thirty years.

Humanists approached politics more as a field of moral action than of legal or constitutional principles. But this was still – no less than for Marsilius or the jurists – grounded in an interpretation of the relationship between the social and the political. Humanists were typically less concerned with the parts of the state or the interests of different classes. In part because humanism achieved real prominence when the communes were in decline and both oligarchy and "despotism" on the rise, and in part because Roman political ideas stressed the personal attributes of good leaders and citizens and the affective ties of friendship and patronage that bound citizens to their leaders, humanist political thought tended toward building consensus – the absence of class conflict – and inculcating attitudes of loyalty, duty, and deference toward authority. This was so whether they were praising republics or princes. Petrarch, who had lauded Cola di Rienzo's revolution for its ethic of civic duty commanding the loyalty of every citizen, similarly praised the rule of the lord of

Padua, Francesco Carrara, for the affective bonds that, according to Petrarch, he cultivated *vis-à-vis* his subjects. In a metaphor destined for a long life in humanist political ideas, Petrarch likened the relationship between ruler and devoted subjects to that of a father and his children, thus making of the state a family writ large. The successful ruler treats his subjects as he would his own children and thus earns their love as the father of all his people. Such notions had no room for dissent or conflicts of opinion or policy. For Petrarch, citizens were those who sought to protect the state, not those who thirsted for change, whom he denounced as rebels and enemies.

The Florentine civic humanists – Salutati to a degree, more fully Leonardo Bruni (1370–1444), himself chancellor from 1427 until his death, and Matteo Palmieri (1406–75) – and their Venetian counterparts Giovanni Caldiera (ca. 1400–74) and Lauro Quirini (1420–75) celebrated their republics as ideal communities in which good citizens gave loyalty and fulfilled their civic duty without questioning the authority of their leaders. They all employed the analogy of family and republic to reinforce the expectation of deference to authority, to discourage and delegitimate dissent, to underscore the importance of consensus and unity, and to define good leadership as a species of benevolent paternalism. And they all decried political divisions of any kind. Virtuous citizenship consisted in a willingness to serve when called upon, accompanied by a dutiful passivity that made officeholders reluctant to express dissenting views or to represent the interests of, or even identify with, any social class or constituency. Bruni could find no higher praise for the Florentine constitution than to say that "under these magistracies this city has been governed with such diligence and competence that one could not find better discipline even in a household ruled by a solicitous father."[3] Giovanni Caldiera similarly stressed the parallel between family and state, emphasizing principles of natural hierarchy in both, and lauded the Venetian republic as worthy of the almost religious devotion of its loyal citizens.

While most of the attention in studies of civic humanism has been to the "civic" component, its accompanying "humanism" must also be taken seriously. Civic humanists insisted that culture and education must serve the republic, both in preparing the individual to assume his civic responsibilities and in reinforcing the consensus: the unified vision of origins, institutions, and historical destiny that was the oligarchical republic's ideological foundation. Humanist education privileged those texts of antiquity that taught moral lessons of exemplary sociability and citizenship. Matteo Palmieri's *Vita civile* of the 1430s, a veritable compendium of civic humanist wisdom and advice, much of it organized around an explication of the cardinal virtues of prudence, justice, fortitude, and temperance, is in long stretches almost a paraphrase of Cicero's *On Duties*. Palmieri explains that such a book was needed in order to make accessible to those of his fellow citizens who knew no Latin the wisdom of the ancients concerning citizenship and the precepts and rules required for living in an "excellent republic." Humanism thus turned politics toward moral philosophy and a concern with the needed qualities of temperament and behavior of the good citizen (and, in non-republican contexts, of the just prince). In his *Life of Dante*, also written in the 1430s, Bruni provided a somewhat fictionalized and idealized portrait of Dante as a dutiful citizen and family man, who was however unable to maintain his quiet civic loyalty in an admittedly unmerited exile and became, through his intemperate denunciations of the republic's leaders, the cause of his own permanent banishment. In Bruni's hands political disputes always turned on what he saw as the moral imperatives facing the citizen, and never on legitimate grievances over the organization, distribution, and exercise of power. For as long as civic virtue was defined in terms of loyalty to constituted power, humanist political discourse ultimately tended toward the protection of that power.

Some writers saw through the idealizations and pieties of civic humanism. Because some of the speakers in Leon Battista Alberti's *Books on the Family* (1430s) echo the civic humanists, Alberti (1404–72) is often assumed to have accepted the civic humanist paradigm of politics and society. But other speakers express serious doubts about whether the family should be thought of as so reassuringly analogous to the larger civic community. Families, they point out, can be loci of alienation, and benevolent paternalism can easily slip into punitive patriarchy. The chief character of the third book, Giannozzo, often taken to be the exemplar of the diligent paterfamilias, is in fact alienated from his Alberti elders, deeply distrustful of the civic world, and suspicious of the humanists' optimistic conviction that the wisdom of antiquity could make better citizens or republics. The elements of civic humanism break apart in the character of Giannozzo, and through him Alberti underscores the instability of the humanist construction of the good society. Alamanno Rinuccini (1426–99) was more openly hostile in his dialogue *On Liberty*, written around 1480 after his humiliation and (temporary) banishment from the favor of Florence's leading citizen, Lorenzo de' Medici. One speaker naively defends the validity of civic humanism as if Lorenzo's unofficial but unmistakable power had changed nothing; a second defends civic humanist ideals while acknowledging that Medici rule had undermined them; and a third, called a lover of liberty, dismisses the entire ideology as a mystification of the true nature of an always and inevitably corrupt political world from which the virtuous man can only take refuge in complete withdrawal and philosophical cultivation of the inner life. Even for an angry critic of the way civic humanist ideals had betrayed good men, there was no solution except self-exile from politics. Humanism did not generate a discourse of engaged dissent and programmatic reform.

Political Thought in the Crisis of Italy

A tougher republicanism that put something stronger than citizen duty and humanist education at the center of its defense of the republic emerged in Florence under the pressure of events that began with the French invasion of 1494, the collapse of the Medicean regime, and the creation of a more broadly based republican constitution under the influence of the millenarian preaching of the charismatic Dominican Girolamo Savonarola (1452–98). Although Savonarola believed that monarchy was generally the best form of government, in the case of the Florentines he adduced particular circumstances – their intellectual characteristics and long history, indeed their habit, or second nature, of republican government – as reasons why only a "civil form of government" would ever work in that city. He assured them that the creation and preservation of a government with a large and powerful Great Council at its center was the first step that the Almighty wanted them to take toward the purification of their city and subsequently of the Church and Christendom, and that their reward would be the realization of some decidedly secular Florentine dreams – prosperity and political power. Essential to their success, he argued, was the rejection of both oligarchic factionalism and tyranny, especially a tyranny that resembled the rule of the Medici. Savonarola skillfully combined an appeal to Florentine popular political traditions with a captivating millenarianism to fashion a new republicanism; its influence must be measured not only in the republic that lasted until the return of the Medici in 1512, but even more in the radical last republic of 1527–30, which resisted a papal-imperial assault for ten arduous months under the banner of the friar's memory.

After 1494, the facade of consensus in Florentine political life dissolved and yielded three distinct trajectories, each mistrustful of the other two and all three expressions of social conflicts exposed by the expulsion of the Medici. The first was the popular republicanism, liberated from the myth of consensus, whose chief theorists were Savonarola, later Niccolò Machiavelli (1469–1527), and in the next generation Donato Giannotti (1492–1573). The second was an aristocratic republicanism that distilled from the previous hundred years of oligarchic hegemony in both Florence and Venice a theory, most evident in the writings of Francesco Guicciardini (1483–1540), that sought new criteria and legitimacy for power in the hands of social elites. And the third was the emerging attempt, in the circles around the Medici, to theorize the introduction and benefits of a principate and courtly society. All three discourses, like so much of the political thought of the preceding two centuries, were rooted in interpretations of the social order; the underlying disagreements were more about the nature of society and the relations among its component parts than about the perceived advantages of this or that form of government in the abstract.

The popular republicans were critical of the elite and its tendencies to create factions that undermined public authority and to ally strategically with tyranny in order to defend elite interests. One of the consistent threads of Machiavelli's political theorizing was the need to contain the *ottimati* – not to destroy them as a class, but to balance their advantages of wealth and patronage networks by giving the people a major share of power in government and in the army, as the Romans had done. Machiavelli assumed as axiomatic that all states have serious internal divisions that cannot be reduced, as the civic humanists thought, to the misbehavior of malcontents who had somehow failed to absorb the virtuous consensus. Machiavelli saw these divisions as emerging from the "grave and natural enmities between the people [*gli uomini popolari*] and the elite [*i nobili*], brought about by the elite's wish to rule and the people's wish not to obey them," as he says in the *Florentine Histories* (3.1). A healthy republic must rein in the arrogance and lust to rule of its social elites. Against the prevailing admiration among the Florentine *ottimati* of the Venetian constitution in which the people had no such role, Machiavelli championed the ancient Roman Republic, in which the people, or plebs, filled the ranks of the army and had a political voice through their tribunes.

In the *Discourses on Livy* (1517) Machiavelli argues (I.55) that republics cannot exist where "gentlemen" who live off the land exercise jurisdiction in the manner of feudal lords, as in Milan and Naples. True republics are only possible where legal equality prevails. But even in republics the wealthy and powerful will – by the very nature of their class – seek to dominate the rest of society, and Machiavelli insisted that, as in ancient Rome, it was necessary to allow the classes to compete with each other, but not to permit either the elite or the people to achieve hegemonic power. He believed that, at least until the social wars that began with the Gracchi, the Romans successfully maintained this balance, and that Roman liberty was actually made possible by those constant quarrels between the nobility and the people that so many others mistakenly decried (I.4–6). Even in *The Prince* (1513), a book mostly concerned with defining the qualities and strategies of a successful ruler of a new principality, Machiavelli advises princes – and thus the Medici to whom the book was addressed – to base their rule on an alliance with the people rather than the elite, because these *grandi* will consider themselves his equal and not be so easily governed by him, and also because, since the aim of the *grandi* is to oppress others while the people have the "more honorable" aim of merely wishing not to be oppressed, the prince cannot please the *grandi* without offending the rest of his subjects (ch. 9). If not on every page of *The Prince*, certainly throughout the *Discourses* and the *Florentine Histories*, Machiavelli's political ideas were regularly shaped by his perceptions of the aims and fears of the social classes whose conflicts largely determined the configuration of politics and exercise of power. Many of these ideas, particularly the military role of the people, were further elaborated by the last of the great Florentine republican theorists, Donato Giannotti, who held one of Machiavelli's former positions in government – secretary to the Ten of War – under the last republic.

The aristocratic republicans wanted real power in the hands of an elite of the "best" and most "experienced and diligent" men, as Guicciardini put it in the *Discorso di Logrogno* (1512), one of the foundational texts of the school of thought that included other *ottimati* and most of the Venetian theorists. Although Guicciardini's notorious realism and sometimes cynical unmasking of all pretence to high-minded principle might seem to be the antithesis of civic humanism's lofty ideals of participatory republicanism with its appeals to the exemplarity of a mythical past, in one crucial respect he was civic humanism's true heir: namely, in the argument that republics needed to be controlled by elites defined by their collective virtue. "It has always been the case," he wrote in the *Discorso*, "that the virtue of a few citizens is the mainstay of a well-ordered republic, and that glorious deeds and great works are invariably brought about and accomplished by a few" who "must be moved not only by devotion to their city but also by the spur of ambition: a desire for greatness and the prospect of supreme rank." Bruni and Palmieri would have set aside the emphasis here on the inevitably small number of such men (even while quietly agreeing with it), but otherwise Guicciardini's statement is perfectly compatible with their view that republics should be governed by virtuous men who prove their worth through deeds, and that more such men could be found in the class that had the requisite education and experience. Civic humanists and aristocratic republicans shared both a visceral fear of the lower classes and the optimism that the middle orders of society would be content to enjoy occasional participation in some office or council while acquiescing in the leadership of a meritocracy of their social betters.[4]

The line from the civic humanists to the Florentine aristocratic republicans led straight on to the flowering of Venetian political thought. Venetian theorists from Henry of Rimini (ca. 1300) to Caldiera, Quirini, and Domenico Morosini (1417–1509) had long praised the city's successful combination of republican institutions, aristocratic control, and civic peace. In the sixteenth century these same virtues were elaborated into the full-blown state ideology of Venice's mixed constitution in which, as so often in Renaissance political thought, the legitimacy and character of government rested on a connection between politics and culture and an interpretation of the social order. Andrea Navagero, appointed as Venice's official state historian in 1515, published an edition of Cicero's orations in which he echoed Bruni's contention that only in republics was there a sufficient degree of liberty for the flowering of culture; as in ancient Rome, so in Venice, liberty, eloquence, the arts, and letters all flourished together. In the mid-1520s, Gasparo Contarini (1483–1542) drafted the central text of what came to be known as the myth of Venice, his *On the Magistrates and the Republic of the Venetians*, published in 1543 and soon thereafter made available throughout Europe in many translations, including one into English in 1599. Contarini rejected the model of Rome because of the ancient republic's militarism and constant class warfare. Venice, he argued, was by contrast organized for the peace and well-being of its citizens through its mixed constitution, which harmoniously combined monarchy in its doge, the rule of the few in its senate, and the rule of the many in the Great Council. Contarini's "many" were still a restricted elite of families distinguished by the nobility of their blood, exceptional virtue, and service to the state. Those with no place in the Council – the true many – Contarini divided into two groups: "citizens," to whom the republic entrusted certain administrative offices, which satisfied the popular desire for some role in public affairs, but who, lacking any real share in rule, did "not disturb the state of the nobles," and wage laborers and guildsmen, who "ought to be considered public servants." Contarini's view of Venetian society was, to be sure, an idealization, and a deeply conservative and fundamentally ahistorical one. Later in the century Paolo Paruta (1540–98) also rejected the Roman model – and thus Machiavelli's arguments for a political and military role for the people – and again praised Venice for its social concord. Harmony among hierarchically arranged social orders was the underlying assumption of Venice's mixed constitution, as it had been in the more muted fashion of the Florentine civic humanists and aristocratic republicans.

The third contender in the great debate over the fate of republicanism – a view absent in Venice but with many voices in the rest of Italy – was the emerging theory of a principate buttressed by a domesticated, courtly aristocracy. Whereas Machiavelli still thought of his prince within the terms of the social conflict between the *grandi* and the *popolo*, others began to theorize a radically different kind of principate. In 1516 Lodovico Alamanni addressed a policy memorandum to Lorenzo de' Medici the younger, whose proto-princely style of governance had already offended traditional Florentine republican sensibilities. Recognizing that the Florentines were "more alien to the ways of the court than any other people," reluctant to show "reverence" or to remove their hoods, and uncomfortable in conversing with princes, he advised Lorenzo to forget about the older men, who would never let go of this "fantasia," and to concentrate on "weaning" the young men from their civic ways (*civiltà*) and accustoming them to courtly manners (*costumi cortesani*). Once they were in his service, his first aim would be to remove their *habito civile*: "for, to those who for His Excellency's sake will take the cape and leave aside the hood, it will be as if they had become members of a religious order, because they will renounce the republic and make a profession [of faith] to him and to his order of things, and never again will they be able to lay claim to the status of citizens or to the good graces of the people." Eventually, with time and the ever greater presence in government of men "who will have been brought up in his [the prince's] school, our city will soon not know how to live without a prince who sustains them all."[5] Alamanni aimed at nothing less than the cultural and social conversion of a republican into a courtly society, and here too it is culture, education in the broadest sense, and relations among classes that determine the nature of the political regime.

Far from being simply the manual of good courtiership it is sometimes thought to be, the *Courtier* of Baldassare Castiglione (1478–1529) is actually a critical and worried meditation on the politics and political ideas produced by the established courtly societies of northern Italy. The worries surface briefly and unexpectedly in book I, when Count Lodovico da Canossa, to whom the task of defining the perfect courtier had been entrusted, warns against effeminacy in courtiers and later expresses a convergent worry about whether dedication to "letters" – humanist education – has diminished Italian military valor. These anxieties resurface in book IV, when Ottaviano Fregoso argues that all the courtier's skills and graces, if not directed to a worthy end, would be "vain and frivolous" and would "belong to the world of women and romance ... and serve simply to make men effeminate, to corrupt the young and to lead them into dissolute ways. And the consequences are that the name of Italy is brought into disgrace." To save him from "this kind of sterile courtier-ship," Ottaviano assigns the courtier a higher purpose: "so to win for himself the mind and favour of the prince he serves that he can and always will tell him the truth about all he needs to know"; he will correct and teach the prince, prevent him from being deceived, and help him to distinguish good from evil. This is particularly necessary today, Ottaviano continues, because princes are for the most part ignorant, conceited fools, easily swayed by lies and flattery, whose "ignorance of how to govern peoples gives rise to so many evils, so much death, destruction, burning, and ruin-ation, that it may be said to be the deadliest plague of all." This is a very different view of princes and their courts – lies, flatteries, deceptions, the hollowness of a *false* school of manners – and even Ottaviano knows that the courtier's truth-telling function will require some "beguilements" and the practice of "healthy deception." Even this newly refashioned civic courtier is still practicing the arts of simulation and conceal-ment – the essence of *sprezzatura*, as presented in book I – with the heavy implica-tion, in the wake of the warnings about effeminacy, that these are in essence womanly ways of seduction. Still, Ottaviano insists that his courtier can give to the prince a gift of "what is doubtless the greatest and rarest of all human virtues: the manner and method of good government." But when the Duchess Elisabetta Gonzaga, who presides over the discussions, asks Ottaviano exactly what such a courtier should say to his prince, Ottaviano answers, smiling: "If I had the favour of some of the rulers I know, and were to speak my mind freely, I imagine I would soon lose [the prince's favor] again." Only in a joke can Ottaviano face the improbability and even unreality of his truth-telling courtier. As another speaker then puts it, urging Ottaviano not to pursue his ideal courtier any further, "I am afraid that he is like Plato's republic, and that we shall never see the like of him, except perhaps in heaven." If the courtier is a deluded figure chasing phantasms, perhaps he is after all nothing more than a graceful flatterer and skillful dissimulator. This is the fear that pervades the *Courtier*. Casti-glione was writing out the anxiety, even the agony, of courtly elites who knew that they had failed to advise their princes wisely or to protect Italy.[6]

The Political Thought of Northern Humanism

Although attention to the social conditions of government was already well established in northern European thought, it received added stimulus from developments
in Italy after 1500. When the adviser and diplomat of Louis XII, Claude de Seyssel
(1450–1520), praised the French monarchy as free of all tyranny because of its mixed
constitution in which the king's power was properly limited by good laws and
officials, he was echoing constitutionalist arguments that went back to Oresme and
Fortescue. But in *The Monarchy of France*, Seyssel focused on harmony among the
social classes, in terms more reminiscent of humanist discourse, as the key to a healthy
monarchy or republic. Such harmony, he says, depends on an acceptance by the three
estates of the role appropriate to each. Seyssel in fact admired the Venetian constitution and, like Contarini and Guicciardini, assumed that the superior virtues of those
born to privilege justified their preponderant role in government. But privileges of
noble birth had in turn to be maintained by service to the state and the common
good: hence the importance of education in training this elite to assume its proper
role.

The two most celebrated northern humanists, Desiderius Erasmus (1466–1536)
and Thomas More (1478–1535), adopted more critical stances toward contemporary
social problems. Erasmus's book of advice to the future Emperor Charles V, the
Education of a Christian Prince (1516), followed one aspect of humanist tradition in
preaching to the prince all the virtues necessary to rule for the common good, which
becomes an occasion for rehearsing the injustices of European society and urging his
virtuous prince to exercise humanity and wisdom to remedy inequities of taxation,
excessively harsh penal systems, and above all the plague of war regularly inflicted on
society by princes and ruling classes in their own selfish interests. Erasmus's solution –
a prince educated in the humanist and Christian virtues – is perhaps disappointingly
conventional, but his diagnosis of social ills brings him close to More's more famous
and imaginative assessment of the same issues.

Utopia (1516) was a fierce polemic against Europe's social ills and the shortsight-
edness – even hypocrisy – of its political leaders. Although Morus – the participant in
the dialogue – argues against Raphael Hythloday's refusal to enter political service,
More the author gives ample space to Hythloday's reasons for shunning involvement
in politics. Like Ottaviano in his moment of truth in the *Courtier*, Hythloday despairs
of the very possibility of speaking truth to princes and decries the corruption sustained by such fears and the consequent sycophancy of courtiers. His indictment of
misguided policies that ensure the prevalence of poverty, crime, and war accompanies
a denunciation of indolent nobles and ineffectual rulers who impose burdensome
taxes, drive peasants off the land with enclosures, thus increasing unemployment and
poverty and generating crime from desperation, and then punish that crime in the
most inhumane manner. The kings and ruling classes who styled themselves "noble"
were in fact responsible for a social catastrophe. This radical critique of England's and
Europe's flawed social and political system is underscored in book II by Hythloday's
description of the "ideal state of a commonwealth" (the *optimus reipublicae status*)
achieved by the Utopians, who permit no hereditary nobility and recognize as noble
only those who work for the common good. Indeed, private property is prohibited

and all goods held in common. Utopia is a federated republic of fifty-four identical cities, with a minimum of central governance, and all with the same constitution: two assemblies of representatives elected by small groups of households, and a governor chosen by the assemblies. The representatives consult regularly with their households and send recommendations to the assemblies.

Although Utopia seems to embody an ideal of government as the expression of the will of the people, the improbable uniformity of the Utopians makes one wonder whether More thought he was outlining a workable system of government. With all the Utopian cities identical in language, traditions, customs, and laws, the representatives presumably hear the same things and make the same recommendations over and over. Despite the radicalism of More's critique of European social ills, the vision of a different political order is stunted by the assumption – at least among the Utopians – that the "best state of a commonwealth" must be built on the most absolute homogeneity, on a consensus so powerful as to preclude the slightest degree of individuality or difference. Of course, even the character Morus expresses doubts about the viability of Utopian communism, which Hythloday presents as evidence of their devotion to the common good. The mystery of *Utopia* persists, but its attempt to link political arrangements to social conditions ensures its place in the Renaissance tradition of political thought.

Religious Conflicts and the End of the Renaissance

With the confessional struggles of the sixteenth century, political thought underwent a major reorientation. While it would be reductive to divide Renaissance from Reformation political ideas with any simple secular/religious dichotomy, it is nonetheless the case that theology played a larger role in the political thought of Reformation Europe than it had previously, especially on the Protestant side of the confessional split. Martin Luther (1483–1546) approached politics from a neo-Augustinian perspective that emphasized humankind's fallen nature and thus the impossibility of constructing just political rule from anything like the Aristotelian natural impulse to associate. For Luther, political authority emanates from God's will, and the political duty of the good Christian is to submit to the powers ordained by God. But he also argued that the only legitimate princes are those who manifest godliness and righteousness and that no obedience is due to an ungodly ruler. Despite the tension between these positions, the constant in Luther's thinking about politics is that God's will defines both the political order and the subject's duty. With politics in effect a branch of theology, the social or historical characteristics of particular communities slipped into insignificance compared to the task of divining God's purposes.

Here and there Renaissance political ideas managed to survive the theological tidal wave. The assumption that legitimate political power had either directly or indirectly to belong to the people continued to find occasional expression, for example, among French Calvinists who theorized resistance to a "tyrannical" monarchy. In the *Francogallia* of 1573, François Hotman (1524–90) reviewed French constitutional history and decided that the monarchy, which he believed to be in origin an elective office, was subordinate to the Public Council, or Estates General, which protected the basic laws, made and deposed kings, and ruled with them. Hotman praised the mixed constitution with the authority of Aristotle and Polybius, and with yet another paraphrase of the maxim that that which touches all must be approved by all.

Another area in which echoes of Renaissance political ideas survived was the "constitutionalism" of the so-called "School of Salamanca," mostly Spanish Dominicans and Jesuits concerned with refuting Luther's thesis that legitimate political authority depends on the ruler's godliness. They argued that natural law and right reason are impressed on all human minds even in the pre-political state of nature. Thus the transition from pre-political to political societies is a rational decision to limit the absolute freedom of the state of nature in favor of the greater collective benefits to be secured by the institution of government and positive law. Hence political authority receives its legitimacy from consent, not from the divine will. From this school also came the major arguments in defense of the American Indians in the great debate over the claims of the Spanish crown and conquerors to an alleged right to dispossess and rule the Indians. Against the thesis advanced in 1550 by Juan Ginés de Sepúlveda that the practice of human sacrifice and cannibalism deprived them of the status of civil beings endowed with rights, the Indians were defended by Juan de la Pena who countered that, whatever their "errors," they remained rational men with rights to their property, and by the Dominican Bartolomé de las Casas (1474–1566), whose treatise *In Defence of the Indians* forcefully argued that their ignorance of Christianity had not prevented them from constituting a political society "with sufficient natural knowledge and ability to rule and govern itself."

Perhaps the greatest late Renaissance theorist of politics as a reflection of the social was the German-Dutch legal scholar Johannes Althusius (1557–1638), who, building on the experience of the city-states of western and southern Germany and influenced by the Calvinist revolt in the Dutch provinces, postulated the origin of the state and the sovereignty of the people in small associations – the various forms of *consociatio* (including guilds) – in which groups of people "undertake mutual obligation to one another to communicate to each other those things that are useful and necessary for the maintenance and sharing of social life." Very much in the spirit of Marsilius of Padua, Althusius argued in his *Systematic Analysis of Politics*, first published in 1603, that the commonwealth is an emanation of this *consociatio*. Sovereignty belongs to "the whole body of the association...all of [which] together acknowledge its unity in the consent and accord of the associated bodies." Government, for Althusius, results from a contract between the sovereign people and a supreme magistrate, and "from this contract...it is clear that the people...is complete lord of all authority and power. Therefore the prince does not have equal power with the people...in this, but a far less and inferior power."[7]

By the last quarter of the sixteenth century, however, the dominant discourses of politics were moving in very different directions. In many quarters, the pull of religious absolutisms gradually drew political thought toward the unquestioned and unconditioned power of rulers as a reflection or instrument of God's will. A different approach, but equally corrosive of the Renaissance link between the social and the political, was the notion of "reason of state," popularized by the Piedmontese Giovanni Botero (1544–1617) in his *Ragione di stato* (1589), the first of a series of treatises all over Europe that defined the state as dominion over peoples and "reason of state" as the science or art of maintaining power, of applying proper rules of prudence, and of knowing when and how *not* to remain within the limits of law and constitutional norms. Finally, perhaps the most influential of the new directions of thought was the assertion of the necessity of the state's absolute power over its subjects as a way of muting the claims and counterclaims of competing confessional communities. Chief among the theorists of unbridled state power was Jean Bodin (1530–96), whose *Six Books of the Commonwealth* (1576) argued that in any state worthy of the name there must be a single, unambiguous sovereignty – "the most high, absolute and perpetual power over the citizens and subjects in a common-wealth" – a power that gives the laws as a function of its sovereignty (and not by virtue of any presumed consent on the part of those who receive them) and is not itself bound by those laws; a sovereignty against which no resistance is permitted, and which cannot be shared by social groups or estates in any mixed constitution. Bodin's absolute ruler was in no way limited by the wishes or customs of his subjects: "We thus see that the main point of sovereign majesty and absolute power consists of giving the law to subjects in general without their consent" (1.8). Such views became popular among French political thinkers, and subsequently in other areas of Europe that also experienced turmoil spawned by religious conflicts. The ascendancy of the idea – common to *ragion di stato* and to Bodin and his followers – that the chief task of political thought is to define and defend sovereign political power without refer-ence to the consent or custom of the society it rules was the beginning of a long dormancy for Renaissance political thought, a dormancy briefly, if brilliantly, inter-rupted by English republicans in the mid-seventeenth century and finally brought to an end by the Enlightenment's revived interest in the Renaissance legacy.

NOTES

1 Marsilius of Padua, *Defender of Peace*, pp. 10–12, 31–2, 45–7.
2 Blythe, *Ideal Government*, pp. 118–38, 177–9, 203–40.
3 Bruni, *Panegyric to the City of Florence*, in Kohl and Witt, *Earthly Republic*, p. 173.
4 Text in Moulakis, *Republican Realism*, pp. 134, 136.
5 Albertini, *Firenze*, pp. 383–4 (my translation).
6 Castiglione, *The Courtier*, pp. 61, 90, 284–9, 296, 302, 315.
7 Black, *Guilds*, pp. 133–4, 139–40.

REFERENCES

Albertini, Rudolf von, *Firenze dalla repubblica al principato*, trans. Cesare Cristofolini (Turin: Einaudi, 1970).
Black, Antony, *Guilds and Civil Society in European Political Thought from the Twelfth Century to the Present* (Ithaca, NY: Cornell University Press, 1984).
Blythe, James M., *Ideal Government and the Mixed Constitution in the Middle Ages* (Princeton: Princeton University Press, 1992).
Castiglione, Baldassare, *The Book of the Courtier*, trans. George Bull (London: Penguin, 1976).

Kohl, Benjamin and Witt, Ronald, *The Earthly Republic: Italian Humanists on Government and Society* (Philadelphia: University of Pennsylvania Press, 1978).

Marsilius of Padua, *The Defender of Peace*, ed. and trans. Alan Gewirth (New York: Columbia University Press, 1956).

Moulakis, Athanasios, *Republican Realism in Renaissance Florence: Francesco Guicciardini's* Discorso di Logrogno (Lanham, MD: Rowman and Littlefield, 1998).

FURTHER READING

Baron, Hans, *The Crisis of the Early Italian Renaissance: Civic Humanism and Republican Liberty in an Age of Classicism and Tyranny* (Princeton: Princeton University Press, 1966).

——, *In Search of Florentine Civic Humanism*, 2 vols. (Princeton: Princeton University Press, 1988).

Bouwsma, William J., *Venice and the Defense of Republican Liberty: Renaissance Values in the Age of the Counter Reformation* (Berkeley: University of California Press, 1968).

Cambridge History of Medieval Political Thought, c.350–c.1450, ed. J. H. Burns (Cambridge: Cambridge University Press, 1988).

Cambridge History of Political Thought, 1450–1470, ed. J. H. Burns and M. Goldie (Cambridge: Cambridge University Press, 1991).

Canning, Joseph, *The Political Thought of Baldus de Ubaldis* (Cambridge: Cambridge University Press, 1987).

Davis, Charles T., *Dante's Italy and Other Essays* (Philadelphia: University of Pennsylvania Press, 1984).

Gilbert, Felix, *Machiavelli and Guicciardini: Politics and History in Sixteenth-Century Florence* (Princeton: Princeton University Press, 1965).

——, "The Venetian Constitution in Florentine Political Thought," in *Florentine Studies: Politics and Society in Renaissance Florence*, ed. Nicolai Rubinstein (Evanston: Northwestern University Press, 1968), pp. 463–500.

Hankins, James, ed., *Renaissance Civic Humanism: Reappraisals and Reflections* (Cambridge: Cambridge University Press, 2000).

Hexter, J. H., *More's Utopia: The Biography of an Idea* (New York: Harper Torchbooks, 1952).

King, Margaret, *Venetian Humanism in an Age of Patrician Dominance* (Princeton: Princeton University Press, 1986).

Libby, Lester J., Jr., "Venetian History and Political Thought after 1509," *Studies in the Renaissance* 20 (1973), pp. 7–45.

Muir, Edward, *Civic Ritual in Renaissance Venice* (Princeton: Princeton University Press, 1981).

Najemy, John M., *Corporatism and Consensus in Florentine Electoral Politics, 1280–1400* (Chapel Hill: University of North Carolina Press, 1982).

Pagden, Anthony, ed., *Languages of Political Theory in Early Modern Europe* (Cambridge: Cambridge University Press, 1987).

Pocock, J. G. A., *The Machiavellian Moment: Florentine Political Thought and the Atlantic Republican Tradition* (Princeton: Princeton University Press, 1975).

Skinner, Quentin, *The Foundations of Modern Political Thought*, 2 vols. (Cambridge: Cambridge University Press, 1978).

Tierney, Brian, *Religion, Law, and the Growth of Constitutional Thought, 1150–1650* (Cambridge: Cambridge University Press, 1982).

Ullmann, Walter, "De Bartoli sententia: Concilium repraesentat mentem populi," in *Bartolo da Sassoferrato: Studi e documenti per il VI centenario*, vol. 2 (Milan, 1962), pp. 707–33.

Weinstein, Donald, *Savonarola and Florence: Prophecy and Patriotism in the Renaissance* (Princeton: Princeton University Press, 1970).

Witt, Ronald, "The *De Tyranno* and Coluccio Salutati's View of Politics and Roman History," *Nuova Rivista Storica* 53 (1969), pp. 434–74.

CHAPTER TWENTY-THREE

The Scientific Renaissance

WILLIAM EAMON

Toward the end of the sixteenth century, the French humanist Louis Le Roy surveyed the discoveries and inventions of his age and concluded that

> All the mysteries of God and secrets of nature are not discovered at one time ... How many have been first known and found out in this age? I say, new lands, new seas, new forms of men, manners, laws, and customs, new diseases and new remedies, new ways of the heaven and of the ocean, never before found out, and new stars seen? Yea, and how many remain to be known by our posterity? That which is now hidden, with time will come to light, and our successors will wonder that we were ignorant of them. (*De la vicissitude ou varieté des choses*, 1575, English translation 1594)

Le Roy's exultation in the ability of moderns to surpass the knowledge of antiquity may initially strike us as contrary to everything we have learned about Renaissance humanism. According to conventional wisdom, the humanists regarded classical culture as the pinnacle of the human achievement, a view that left little room for intellectual progress. In fact, however, Le Roy's insistence that there were new things to discover underscores one of the most distinctive features of the Renaissance sensibility: its sense of delight in and fascination with novelty. Nowhere, perhaps, was this attitude more apparent than in the Renaissance perspective on the natural world. Whether in the form of exotic plants and animals from the New World or the discovery of the "secrets of nature," delight in novelty was a hallmark of Renaissance science.

Despite the widespread enthusiasm with novelty that is evident during the period, Renaissance natural philosophy, as the study of nature was then called, was by no means a matter of "out with the old, in with the new." Classical antiquity still mattered deeply to natural philosophers both as a source of information about nature and as a methodological guide. Most scientists were also humanists, and were inspired by the humanist ideal of reviving classical culture as a model for contemporary life and letters. Consequently, natural philosophy retained its traditional bookish flavor well into the Renaissance, even if eventually reading the "book of nature" gained more importance than reading ancient books. The new was relatively comfortably folded into the old, novelty assimilated into the familiar until, eventually, the classical envelope burst. The accumulation of novelties in the heavens and new worlds that Europe's cosmographers and explorers discovered made it seem unlikely that any single cosmology could comprehend the universe. At the end of the Renaissance, skeptics such as Montaigne could write that "philosophy is but sophisticated poetry," while in 1611 the English poet John Donne reflected that "new Philosophy calls all in doubt . . . 'Tis all in pieces, all coherence gone." What began as a humanist recovery of classical science ended not only with the overthrow of the ancient cosmos but also with widespread doubt about the classical way of knowing nature.

Humanism and Science

Traditional accounts of the relationship between humanism and science stressed fundamental incompatibilities between the two movements. Earlier generations of historians of science portrayed the relationship between science and humanism as a collision of two different worlds, one literary, rarified, and tradition-bound, the other empirical, practical, and innovative. Lynn Thorndike, in his monumental *History of Magic and Experimental Science*, characterized humanism by "its emphasis on style rather than science, and show rather than substance."[1] Instead of valuing innovation and progress, he asserted, the humanists complacently looked backward to a Golden Age unsurpassed by subsequent generations.

More recently, this negative assessment of Renaissance humanism has been revised in favor of a more balanced interpretation. Modern scholars have shown that earlier historians of science failed to do justice to the complexity of the humanist movement and seriously distorted the character of Renaissance science. In the first place, humanists did not confine themselves to strictly literary studies. They applied their critical methods to scientific texts with as much enthusiasm as they did to a treatise by Livy or a poem of Horace. Moreover, because they advocated an active civic life in opposition to the medieval contemplative ideal, the humanists turned their attention to writings on the practical arts as well as to the literary and scientific works of antiquity. They wrote on specialized subjects ranging from metallurgy to distillation and edited ancient treatises on engineering and technology. Ancient learning was thus deployed to serve modern needs. Humanists argued forcefully for the dignity of the mechanical arts. The German humanist Georgius Agricola (1494–1555), in his landmark book on mining, *De re metallica* (On Metals, 1556), challenged the prevailing view that the occupation of mining "is one of sordid toil and altogether a kind of business requiring not so much skill as labour." In such works, the humanists forged a new definition of the relationship between the mechanical arts and philosophy.

The search for ancient texts generated tremendous excitement in the fifteenth century, and each new discovery was hailed as a major achievement. (See the essay by Ingrid Rowland above.) The humanists salvaged intellectual traditions whose very survival was precarious. In 1417, Poggio Bracciolini (1380–1459) brought back from Constantinople what was found to be the only manuscript of Lucretius's *De rerum naturae* to have survived from antiquity. Little read in the Middle Ages, Lucretius's poem expounding an atomistic view of the universe would have a major influence on matter theory down through the seventeenth century. By the middle of the sixteenth century, western Europe had recovered most of the major mathematical works of antiquity, including the writings of Euclid, Apollonius, and Archimedes, along with major treatises in astronomy, medicine, and natural history.

As knowledge of the Greek language expanded in Europe, the medieval translations of the ancient scientific works were deemed unsatisfactory, and efforts turned to translating the ancient writings directly from the Greek originals. In the 1450s, Pope Nicholas V commissioned George Trebizond (1396–1472) to make a new version of Ptolemy's *Almagest* from the Greek. Then, in the 1460s, Johannes Regiomontanus (1436–76) completed an abridgement of the *Almagest* that had been begun by his teacher Georg Peurbach (1423–61). Contemporaries saw Peurbach and Regiomontanus as "restorers" of ancient astronomy. Writing in 1545, Philip Melanchthon remarked that astronomy "had lain for centuries without honour, but has recently flowered again in Germany restored by those two great men Peurbach and Regiomontanus." Nearly every Renaissance astronomer, including Copernicus, learned his Ptolemy from Regiomontanus's *Epitome of the Almagest*.

In 1471, Regiomontanus moved to Nuremberg with his great collection of Greek scientific manuscripts. There he set up a printing press and began an ambitious program to print, for the first time, the mathematical and astronomical works of antiquity. Regiomontanus in fact established the first scientific publishing house. In 1474 he issued a prospectus of what he intended to print, a list that included virtually the entire mathematical corpus of classical antiquity, plus a number of modern works. Unfortunately, Regiomontanus died before completing the project, but his manuscripts continued to be consulted, translated, and published.

As Regiomontanus's ambitious publishing program suggests, Renaissance humanists enthusiastically embraced the new medium of printing. Humanists frequently associated themselves with the new presses as editors and proofreaders, and as translators and popularizers made ancient and modern science accessible to an entirely new audience. The question of the impact of printing on the emergence of the "new science" of the early modern period has been much debated in recent historiography. Elizabeth Eisenstein, in her influential *The Printing Press as an Agent of Change*, argued that the humanist recovery of classical antiquity was merely a prelude to an era of revolutionary change. Typography, by fixing classical scientific texts in print, made that recovery permanent, and created a foundation upon which natural philosophers could begin to develop doubts about ancient authority.[2] Eisenstein's thesis has been challenged from a number of different directions, and subsequent historians of printing have produced a more balanced analysis of "print culture" and of the shift from script to print.[3] (See the article by Randolf Starn above.) But few historians would argue with the claim that printing radically altered the conditions under which scientific knowledge was produced and disseminated.

The Renaissance Worldview

The worldview that the Renaissance intellectuals inherited was based essentially on the philosophy of Aristotle, whose works on natural philosophy comprised the core of the scientific curriculum of the universities. Aristotle's natural philosophy was based upon a fairly simple, "commonsense" view of the world. Its empiricism was both Aristotelianism's major strength and, in the long run, its chief weakness. According to Aristotle and the scholastic commentators, the universe formed a great sphere at whose center the earth sat immobile, while the sun, planets, and stars revolved around it in a uniform circuit that defined the days and nights and the seasons of the year. Accompanied by Ptolemy's mathematical astronomy, Aristotelian natural philosophy developed into a sophisticated cosmology that both accounted for terrestrial phenomena and enabled astronomers to make accurate stellar predictions.

The placement of the heavenly and earthly spheres also established the hierarchy of the elements, earth, air, fire, and water, of which all material things were made and which defined the physical properties of things. The spheres of the elements, extending from earth at the center of the universe to fire at its outer regions, not only defined the basic order of the terrestrial universe, but also endowed material things with their qualities and attributes. Thus motion was defined as the tendency of things toward their natural place; hence heavy, earthy things move naturally downward toward the center of the universe, while fiery things go upwards toward the heavens. Similarly, plants, animals, and minerals are composed of mixtures of the four elements, which determined their properties and medical virtues.

The Renaissance concept of human physiology, inherited from Galen, was closely related to the theory of the elements. Physical life begins with food, which is made of the four elements. Once ingested, food passes through the stomach to the liver, where it is converted into four fluids, or humors, each of which has its own counterpart among the elements. Melancholy corresponds to earth because it is cold and dry, phlegm to water (cold and moist), blood to air (hot and moist), and choler to fire (hot and dry). It was generally understood that every person had a characteristic complexion or temperament determined by the mixture of the four elements and their corresponding qualities in the human body, a commonplace that underlay Antony's tribute to the dead Brutus in the closing scene of Shakespeare's *Julius Caesar*:

> His life was gentle, and the elements
> So mix'd in him, that Nature might stand up
> And say to all the world, "This was a man!"

For their conception of the earth and the creatures that inhabited it, Renaissance intellectuals again looked back to the ancients, especially to the great encyclopedic *Natural History* of the elder Pliny and to Ptolemy's *Geography*. Drawing on a rich heritage of scientific, historical, and ethnographic writing stretching all the way back to Herodotus, Pliny had compiled vast amounts of information and misinformation about the flora, fauna, and races of people that inhabited the world.[4] For all its faults, Ptolemy's *Geography* was considered by humanists to be the most advanced treatise on the subject available and was a standard text in the geographical curriculum of the universities. Although the earth that Ptolemy described was tiny by comparison to what it was soon to become, Renaissance cartographers recognized that his geography, however coherent and sophisticated, was imperfect. Thus, as if to invite exploration and discovery, they designated the lands beyond the Indian Ocean as "Terra incognita secundum Ptolemaeum" – "unknown land, according to Ptolemy."

Such, in general, was the worldview that dominated European intellectual life until the seventeenth century. The Aristotelian-Ptolemaic-Galenic worldview became the shared intellectual property of educated Europeans not because they felt compelled to submit to the authority of the ancients but because this cosmology offered a compelling and satisfying account of the world as they perceived it. (See the essay by Peter Burke above.)

Plato and the Renaissance Hermes

One of the first signs of the weakening of Aristotelianism was the revival of interest in Plato. The moving spirit of the Platonic revival was the Florentine humanist Marsilio Ficino (1433–94), who in 1484 produced a monumental Latin edition of Plato's *Opera omnia*. In 1462, as Ficino was deep into the Plato manuscripts, his patron, Cosimo de' Medici, interrupted his work with something he found even more momentous. Cosimo had obtained the Greek text of an eclectic group of writings that he, Ficino, and their contemporaries believed were the work of Hermes Trismegistus, venerated by the Egyptians as the god Thoth, who was thought to have lived just after the time of Moses. In fact, the hermetic writings were composed during the early centuries of the Christian era, and were an amalgam of Platonic, gnostic, Christian, and Egyptian philosophy. Despite its fraudulent origin (which was not proven until 1614), the *Corpus Hermeticum* exerted a profound, if intermittent, influence on Renaissance natural philosophy. Long after its false pedigree was revealed, natural philosophers continued to be intrigued and inspired by the magical ideas that sprang from the hermetic corpus. No less a figure than Isaac Newton was absorbed by the religious and philosophical implications of hermeticism.

What accounts for the widespread appeal of this strange and incoherent doctrine? One reason, certainly, was hermeticism's alleged ancient pedigree, which Renaissance intellectuals were convinced led all the way back to that *prisca theologia*, or original theology, that they believed was the source of all true philosophy. A second reason was one compellingly advanced by the late Dame Frances Yates in her pioneering book, *Giordano Bruno and the Hermetic Tradition*.[5] Yates argued that the magical ideas that saturated the hermetic writings produced a new conception of humans as operators on nature. This re-evaluation of the human self-image, according to Yates, was a powerful stimulus to a kind of natural philosophy that emphasized the search for hidden forces in nature. The image of the human as a magus capable of transforming nature and making nature work "wonders" was an essential part of a newly emerging view of the relation of humanity to the cosmos.

Ever since the publication of her book in 1964, the Yates thesis has stimulated spirited debate over the origins and nature of early modern science. Although historians acknowledge that astrology and magic were central concerns for Renaissance natural philosophers, it is now generally agreed that Yates overemphasized the extent to which hermeticism, specifically, was the source of these ideas. Many of the concepts associated with Renaissance natural magic, for example, can be traced to authors such as Pliny or other ancient sources and bear little relation to specifically hermetic ideas. When early modern natural philosophers used the adjective "hermetic," they were often referring to a style of thinking rather than a distinct philosophical tradition. In his debate with the English philosopher Robert Fludd (1574–1637), Johannes Kepler (1571–1630) used the expression "hermetic manner" (*mos Hermeticus*) to characterize Fludd's mystical and esotericist style. Others used the term to mean alchemical, as when Andreas Libavius (1540–1616) employed it against the Paracelsians. Such imprecision in the use of the term "hermetic" also seems to characterize much of modern historical commentary on the supposed influence of hermeticism on early modern science. For this reason, some historians have urged that the term "hermetic" should be used to refer specifically to the *Hermetica* or to ideas demonstrably owing their origins to those writings.[6] Otherwise, the term has little explanatory significance.

Magic and the Occult

Whatever the status of hermeticism in the Renaissance, there can be little doubt that magic and astrology appealed widely to Renaissance intellectuals. What did Renaissance natural philosophers mean by "magic" (*magia*)? In general, they recognized two forms, one demonic and the other involving the use of natural forces. Henricus Cornelius Agrippa's (1486–1535) definition of "natural magic" (*magia naturalis*) was consistent with what other Renaissance intellectuals understood by that term. "That magic is natural," he explained,

> which, having observed the forces of all things natural and celestial and having examined by painstaking investigation the sympathy among those things, brings into the open powers hidden and stored away in nature; thus, magic links lower things (as if they were magical enticements) to the gifts of higher things . . . so that astonishing miracles thereby occur, not so much by art as by nature to which – as nature works these wonders – this art of magic offers herself as a handmaiden. (*De occulta philosophia*, 1533)

Although the proponents of natural magic fervently denied consorting with demons and vigorously defended their orthodoxy, the connection between magic and demonology was more than merely theoretical. Theologians agreed that demons could not do things by supernatural means, but were essentially very adept natural magicians. Surely, they argued, demons were clever enough to fool the magi into doing their work for them. It was not helpful to serious students of the occult sciences that persons of dubious character went about proclaiming themselves to be great magi. Georg Helmstetter, a Heidelberg student who adopted the Latin name Georgius Faustus, is reported to have offered his services as a necromancer, astrologer, magus, and expert in the arts of chiromancy (palm reading), pyromancy (divination from fire), and hydromancy (divination from water). The original "Doctor Faustus," Helmstetter was so notorious that he entered popular culture in chapbooks about him and became the infamous anti-hero of Christopher Marlowe's *Tragicall Historie of Doctor Faustus*.

The natural magicians all agreed that their art demanded proficiency in many sciences. High on their list was alchemy, the science of metallic transmutations, which they believed would help them to uncover the "secrets of nature." Always controversial and perennially beguiling, alchemy had as its main goal the search for the Philosopher's Stone or the Elixir, the agent of transmutation. Because alchemy offered a short-cut to wealth in the form of transmuting base metals into silver and gold, alchemists found a welcome reception at many Renaissance courts. Yet the appeal of alchemy, especially in the German courts, went beyond its promise of wealth gained at little cost. As Bruce Moran has shown, alchemy was part of an occult system that was based on the belief that every part of the universe reflected the cosmos as a whole. Such a view of the interrelation of microcosm and macrocosm "offered precisely the right sort of analogy for German princes seeking to justify personal claims to individual authority within the political universe of the Holy Roman Empire."[7] The chemical philosophy of nature appealed to many Renaissance natural philosophers as an alternative to Aristotelian physics, while the alchemical laboratory became a symbol of a new, experimental approach to natural philosophy.[8]

In describing magic as a linking of inferior entities to superiors, Agrippa underscored its connection with astrology. "Anyone who professes magic without astrology," he wrote, "accomplishes nothing." Despite Giovanni Pico della Mirandola's (1463–94) sustained critique of astrology, written in 1494, astrology continued to occupy the minds of some of the most accomplished Renaissance natural philosophers. Humanists, merchants, princes, and popes consulted astrologers for nativities and to learn propitious days for weddings and feasts, thus making astrology one of the most lucrative scientific professions of the day. Johannes Kepler practiced astrology in the court of the Holy Roman Emperor Rudolf II and cast the horoscope of Count Albrecht von Wallenstein, while Queen Elizabeth I consulted with John Dee (1527–1608) about the most propitious time for her coronation.

At the level of popular culture, astrological forecasts were widely published in cheap almanacs and prognostications. As early as 1499, German astrologers were predicting that a planetary conjunction in the sign of Pisces foretold that catastrophic floods would take place in the year 1524. News of the prediction quickly spread through sermons and printed broadsides, and in January 1524 the Venetian chronicler Marin Sanudo reported that the mainland "is in great fear" over the impending flood. However, other evidence suggests that the urban population did not take the science of astrology very seriously. Niccolò Machiavelli reported in 1521 that "flood stories" were part of ordinary tavern talk, suggesting that the subject had become banal. Meanwhile, ballad singers satirized the astrologers in carnival songs such as one by "Doctor Master Pegasus Neptune" that predicted "conjunctions of cheese and lasagna" and "a flood of Dalmation wine," followed by "horrendous winds shot off like bombards sending off stupendous stenches."[9]

The New Cosmology

Astrology was part of the mathematics curriculum of every Renaissance university; *mathematicus* was a synonym for an astrologer. It is thus one of the ironies of the history of Renaissance science that the reform of astronomy, which began as an attempt to make astrological forecasting more reliable, destroyed the foundations upon which astrology rested.

Humanist astronomers were keenly aware of the discrepancies between mathematical models and cosmology. They hoped to reform the Ptolemaic system by

eliminating the eccentrics, epicycles, and other geometrical devices that stood in the
way of a unified picture of the cosmos. Yet the obstacles to reforming astronomy were
formidable. On one hand, Ptolemaic astronomy made possible relatively accurate
predictions of celestial events, so any reform of astronomy would have to preserve its
mathematical precision. On the other hand, there were fundamental inconsistencies
between Ptolemaic astronomy and Aristotelian natural philosophy. Aristotle had put
forth the doctrine that the heavens were made of an entirely unworldly substance,
aether, a perfect and invisible substance whose natural motion was uniformly circular.
But the epicycles, eccentrics, and equants that gave Ptolemaic astronomy its predictive accuracy were incompatible with the homocentric crystalline spheres proposed by
Aristotle. Johannes Peurbach, in his *Theoricae novae planetarum* (New Theory of
Planets, 1472), had managed to reconcile eccentrics and epicycles with Aristotelian
cosmology, but Ptolemy's equants continued to be particularly troublesome, since
motion around the equant was necessarily non-circular.

Against this background, the work of the Polish astronomer Nicolaus Copernicus
(1473–1543) can be seen as a continuation of the tradition of astronomical humanism begun by Peurbach and Regiomontanus. A canon of the bishopric of Frauenberg,
Copernicus was a church administrator concerned with overseeing various practical
and financial affairs of the diocese. In his spare time he concerned himself with
calendar reform, an astronomical problem that involved such matters as predicting
holy days such as Easter.

Copernicus was no revolutionary. His stated aim in his great work, *De revolutionibus orbium coelestium* (On the Revolutions of the Heavenly Spheres, 1543) was to
reform astronomy within the constraints of the classical tradition. Although he is best
known today for his introduction of heliocentricism, contemporaries were deeply
ambivalent about the theory, and saw his chief contribution as having eliminated the
equant. Nor did Copernicus abolish the distinction between the heavens and the
earth simply by making the earth a planet, as is commonly thought. Insofar as he
had anything to say about the matter, his physics was staunchly Aristotelian, and he
still imagined the planets as embedded in solid crystalline spheres. As a conservative
reformer, he appealed to antiquity as the source of authority for his innovation and
argued against Ptolemaic astronomy principally on the grounds of seeking simpler
and more unified explanations for celestial motions.

If Copernicus's theory did not immediately overthrow the existing order of the
heavens, it did pose a challenge to the traditional ordering of the disciplines. For in
propounding the earth's status as a planet by appealing to arguments from *mathematics*, he "shifted the weight of evidence for the earth's planetary status to the
lower discipline of geometry, thereby violating the traditional hierarchy of the disciplines."[10] When, at the very end of his life, he was finally persuaded to publish his
book, he entrusted the manuscript to one of his disciples, Georg Joachim Rheticus
(1514–74), a Protestant mathematician from the University of Wittenberg. While
overseeing the publication of the book, Rheticus accepted a professorship at Leipzig
and turned the job over to a fellow Lutheran, Andreas Osiander (1498–1552). Upon
reading the work, Osiander became convinced that Copernicus would be attacked by
scholars on the grounds that "the liberal arts . . . should not be thrown into confusion." To avert such criticism, he appended to the work an unsigned preface stating
that Copernicus's new theory, like all astronomical hypotheses, was intended solely

for computation and was not to be considered as physically true. This was not Copernicus's position at all. But he was probably unaware of what Osiander had done, since he suffered a stroke in December 1542 that left him comatose and was given a copy of his book on his deathbed.

Copernicus's heliocentric model of the universe was widely disseminated through Erasmus Reinhold's (1511–53) *Prutenic Tables* (1551), which demonstrated that the theory could be used to make accurate stellar predictions. As it was not required that one endorse Copernicus's earth-centered hypothesis to use his model for computational purposes, Reinhold and many others happily used Copernicus's mathematics without abandoning allegiance to Aristotle's physics. Because this approach first developed at the University of Wittenberg, where Reinhold taught mathematics, it is today known as the "Wittenberg Interpretation" of the Copernican theory.[11] The Wittenberg Interpretation of the Copernican theory dominated discussion until about the 1580s. Although *De revolutionibus* was widely read during the second half of the sixteenth century, relatively few astronomers openly adopted its radical proposal for a heliocentric cosmos. According to one authority, we can identify only ten full-fledged Copernicans between 1543 and 1600 (seven Protestants and three Catholics).[12] Some sought compromises between the two world systems. The Danish astronomer Tycho Brahe (1546–1601) proposed a cosmology that left the earth at the center of the universe with the moon and the Sun revolving around it and with the Sun as the center of the five planetary orbits. Brahe's cosmology was quite popular among astronomers until the early seventeenth century because it had the advantage of simplifying astronomy without abandoning Aristotelian physics. Of greater significance in the long run, however, was the extraordinary body of astronomical data that Brahe gathered at his observatory at Uraniborg, using new instruments of his own design. Brahe's data showed, for example, that the novae of 1572 and 1577 were supralunar, contradicting Aristotle's doctrine that the celestial region was the place of perfectly circular motion.

In 1599, Brahe moved to the Hapsburg court in Prague to assume the position of imperial astronomer. Rudolf II, the Holy Roman Emperor, was one of Europe's most generous benefactors, and his patronage of scientific enterprises made his court a vibrant center of astronomical research. It was also a magnet for all sorts of occultists, astrologers, alchemists, and natural magicians. One of Brahe's assistants at Prague, Johannes Kepler, found the Rudolfine court especially receptive to his mystical approach to astronomy. Preoccupied with the idea of universal celestial harmony, Kepler had already published a précis of his ideas in a bold and original work, *Mysterium cosmographicum* (Cosmographic Mystery, 1596), which tried to establish a connection between the six primary planets and the five regular solids. In Kepler's radical new approach, astronomy was developed in the context of cosmology rather than as a strictly computational science. In shifting the focus of astronomy to cosmology, Kepler laid the groundwork for the undermining of astrology.

De revolutionibus was published at a time when two powerful socioreligious movements converged. The first was the Protestant Reformation, which challenged the scholastic monopoly over theological discourse. The second was the Catholic reform program known as the Counter-Reformation, which reaffirmed the doctrine that matters of biblical hermeneutics were to be referred to the patristic and scholastic traditions. The Catholic Church did not make an official pronouncement on the Copernican system until 1616, when the Congregation of the Index ruled that the work be "suspended until corrected." But this official response masks a long and complex history of conflict and accommodation. On one side were liberals such as Galileo Galilei (1564–1642), who argued in his *Letter to the Grand Duchess Christina* (1615) that the Bible accommodated itself to the language of common people. Because Holy Scripture concerned itself with the salvation of souls and not with physics and astronomy, the two realms of discourse cannot be mixed. On the other side of the argument were conservatives such as the Jesuit controversialist Cardinal Robert Bellarmine (1542–1641), who replied that astronomers should speak "hypothetically and not absolutely." The decree of 1616, essentially a nod to Bellarmine's authority, set the stage for Galileo's trial.

In traditional accounts of the history of early modern science, physics and astronomy tended to dominate, and the "Copernican revolution" took center stage. Since the history of Renaissance science was usually written as a prelude to the "Scientific Revolution" of the seventeenth century, the emphasis was on the rise of the mathematical disciplines, the "mechanization of the world picture," and the centrality of figures like Copernicus, Kepler, and Galileo. Yet until the trial of Galileo made Copernicanism the focus of a public spectacle, debates over the new cosmology were confined mainly to small circles of mathematicians and astronomers. Nor did the new cosmology seem to offer any significant advantages to those who brought the science of astronomy down to earth in the form of astrological forecasts and nativities, although at least one Venetian astrologer thought he could appeal to more readers by calculating his prognostication for 1581 "according to the new and more true Copernican motions." As long as people could buy their almanacs, what did they care whether it was Ptolemy's or Copernicus's mathematics that astrologers employed in making them?

Medical Learning and Practice

During the Renaissance, the most widely discussed and hotly debated issues in natural philosophy were not in the domain of cosmology but in the fields of medicine and natural history. Two developments were of critical importance for the development of medicine in the Renaissance. One was the humanist revival of classical antiquity, with its insistence on the superiority of the Greek medical writers. The other was the changing medical marketplace, which accelerated the demand for quick cures rather than prolonged dietary and behavioral regimens. These two forces working in tandem changed the character of medicine and paved the way for a new, empirical approach to natural philosophy.

By the late fifteenth century, medical learning became permeated with the humanist insistence upon direct study of the ancient Greek medical writings. In 1525 the Aldine Press of Venice published the complete works of Galen in Greek, marking a major step in the attempt to retrieve the pure medicine of the ancients. In the following year the first Greek edition of Hippocrates appeared. No wonder that in 1531 the Paris doctor Johann Guinther von Andernach (1487–1574) could exclaim that in his day medicine had been "raised from the dead" and that Hippocrates and

Galen were "only now at last rescued from perpetual darkness and silent night."[13] Between 1500 and 1600 around 590 editions of Galen's works were printed.

The development of anatomy in the sixteenth century was a direct result of the humanist recovery and subsequent critique of Galen's anatomical works. To be sure, academic physicians were not the only people to perform human dissections. Contrary to the persistent misconception that there was a deep-seated medieval "taboo" against opening the body, dissections and autopsies were in fact regular and integral aspects of legal procedures long before they were practiced in the medical schools.[14] The practice of performing anatomies as part of university instruction began in the fourteenth century. By the early sixteenth century, human dissections (mainly on bodies of executed criminals) were regularly done in most medical schools as part of the medical curriculum, and were attended by citizens as well as medical students.

The humanist revival of Galenic anatomy culminated in the work of the Flemish physician Andrea Vesalius (1514–64). Like Copernicus, Vesalius was a reformer rather than a revolutionary. Born in Brussels and trained in humanist medicine, he became a skilled dissectionist while a student of Guinther von Andernach at Paris. In 1537 he was invited to teach anatomy and surgery at the university of Padua, marking the first time a humanist physician rather than a lowly surgeon was hired to teach anatomy at one of Europe's premier medical schools. His experience led him to the crucial realization that Galen's anatomical knowledge was founded solely on the dissection of animals, which, he insisted, was no substitute for human dissection.

Although Vesalius saw himself as correcting many of Galen's errors in anatomy, it would be a mistake to characterize his famous work, *De fabrica* (1543), as symbolizing anatomy's "liberation from Galen's authority."[15] In fact, Vesalius worked very much within the Galenic tradition and conceived of his own anatomical project as completing that begun in antiquity. Although he challenged Galen on points of detail, he remained squarely within the Galenic physiological paradigm. He defended Galen's physiology as vigorously as anyone and forcefully argued for humoral pathology against the Arabs. Indeed, Vesalius's own critics charged him with adhering too closely to Galen.

De fabrica marks a turning point in the creation of the *medical* view of the human body. With its meticulously-drawn images (executed by an artist from Titian's workshop), the book supported the idea that to treat disease the physician must understand how the body functions at the most intimate level. Vesalius also made an important contribution to raising the status of anatomy. By proclaiming the dignity of anatomy against detractors who, as the German anatomist Volcher Coiter observed in 1572, "assert that it is disgraceful to touch the parts of a dead body polluted with blood and dirt," Vesalius and his followers emphasized that their discipline proclaimed the dignity and excellence of the human body. After Vesalius, anatomy increasingly became part of learned medicine.

Galenic medicine encountered its stiffest opposition not from the anatomists but from the followers of the iconoclastic Swiss physician and reformer Theophrastus Philippus Aureolus Bombastus von Hohenheim (ca. 1493–1541), who called himself Paracelsus, meaning "surpassing Celsus," the ancient Roman medical writer. The son of a physician, he prided himself on his rough and rustic manner and his defiant stance against traditional medicine. Openly contemptuous of the Greek and Arabic medical writers, he claimed to have learned more from peasants and miners than from books.

Nor did the new anatomy then being promoted in the universities impress him – "dead anatomy," he called it, because it did not disclose how the living body functioned.

Rejecting Aristotelian materialism and Galenic humoral medicine, Paracelsus argued that the real causes of organic phenomena, including diseases, were spiritual. Comparing the human body to an alchemical laboratory, he saw metabolic processes such as digestion and respiration as alchemical operations produced by spiritual agents that he likened to what alchemists called *archei*. Paracelsus believed that every disease has a specific cause or disease agent, a radical departure from the Galenic view of diseases as humoral imbalances. Because diseases were specific entities with specific causes, Paracelsus maintained that they had to be attacked with specific cures. For serious illnesses he recommended potent, sometimes poisonous drugs to destroy or expel morborific impurities.

Paracelsus's ideas, combining radical spirituality with a deep animus toward the medical establishment, found broad support in early modern Europe. Some physicians were sympathetic to his stress on chemical drugs, while others constructed from his ideas a full-fledged "chemical philosophy" of nature. Paracelsus's complex and often confusing cosmology had considerable appeal at princely courts in Germany. Princes could disregard the entrenched authority of medical faculties, and Paracelsian natural philosophy appealed to the political identity of Renaissance rulers.[16] The ideological appeal of Paracelsianism crossed religious lines: while Paracelsus himself remained steadfastly Catholic, his spiritualist natural philosophy gained many adherents among Protestants and Catholics alike.

Outside the courts, the popularity of Paracelsianism in early modern Europe may have owed less to the "chemical philosophy" than to changes in the medical marketplace. No less than the economy at large, the medical economy underwent a dramatic transformation with the growth of money, which facilitated exchanges and accelerated the demand for certain types of medical services. In particular, it furthered the demand for active remedies for specific ailments as opposed to passive regimens for living. "Empirical" healers delivered with an imposing arsenal of drugs that produced dramatic results, and Paracelsianism supplied many of them with a ready-made theory of disease to match: that of illness as a morborific agent that had to be forcefully expelled from the body. The appeal of Paracelsianism and the growth of alternative medical practices was not simply a matter of people making choices about competing natural philosophies and medical systems. It was also about people taking advantage of the possibilities for self-fashioning opened up by a rapidly changing medical marketplace.

Like society in general, the medical profession was organized in a hierarchy ranging from empirics and cunning people (often women) at the bottom to university-educated physicians at the top. Internal ailments were generally the domain of the physicians, but for wounds, fractures, and skin conditions, people consulted surgeons. Empirics offered remedies for particular diseases or specialized in a single category of ailment, such as fistulas, hernias, cataracts, or kidney and bladder stones. Apothecaries sold drugs and provided medical advice, while barbers bled patients, pulled teeth, and provided other kinds of minor medical care. Midwives attended birthing and provided obstetrical care. Most cities provided at state expense licensed physicians to administer to the needs of the poor, while hospitals were normally charitable institutions run by the Church or by confraternities. In theory, the medical hierarchy was regulated by town guilds, colleges of physicians, or community health boards, but in reality, often that regulation was quite loose.

Multiple routes led to the practice of medicine in the Renaissance. The education of physicians took place in the universities, where aspiring doctors were trained in a curriculum that continued to be dominated by the medical texts of antiquity. As we have seen, anatomy became an important part of the medical curriculum during the sixteenth century, as did the study of botany with the establishment of botanical gardens. A somewhat more subtle but equally important change in the medical curriculum was the expansion of interest in the branch of medical knowledge known as *practica*, which concerned the diagnosis and treatment of specific diseases.[17] *Theoria*, by contrast, dealt with more general and abstract questions regarding physiology and the nature of illness and health. Whereas during the Middle Ages medical education allied itself with natural philosophy, the growing demand for professional medical services forced changes in the focus of medical training toward developing effective therapeutic measures as opposed to teaching theory.

Surgeons, by contrast, were normally trained as artisans under an apprenticeship system and practiced their trade within the context of guilds. Although by the middle of the sixteenth century surgery was beginning to be integrated into the medical school curriculum, the Renaissance surgeon was schooled by experience, and he contrasted himself to physician by his courage and knowledge of the real world. Warfare was the surgeon's best school, said the Italian surgeon Leonardo Fioravanti (1517–ca. 1588), and the battlefields of Renaissance Europe fostered the development of innovative surgical techniques. Experience taught the French surgeon Ambrose Paré (1510–90) that the accepted and extremely painful method of treating gunshot wounds, cauterization with hot oil, did more harm than good, and his advocacy of simpler treatments with unguents and salves eventually won over the surgical community.

Although the orthodox medical community was essentially a male domain, women had a virtual monopoly over the delivery of infants. Like surgeons, midwives were trained in an apprentice-like system, where older, more experienced midwives passed on their knowledge to younger women, often daughters, nieces, or other relatives. Only a few obstetrical manuals were in print by the sixteenth century, the most famous being those of the French midwife Louise Bourgeois (1564–1640) and the German popularizer Walther Hermann Ryff. Although it is difficult to gauge the impact of these works upon the practice of midwifery, it was in part through such printed works that the technical aspects of midwifery passed from female culture into the professional culture of physicians. Meanwhile, orthodox medical writers grew increasingly critical of midwives. The French physician Laurent Joubert (1529–82), in his work, *Popular Errors*, reserved special contempt for midwives, who "go about [childbirth] blindly like empirics, without knowing what they are doing." In the struggle between orthodox medicine and empirical practice, women healers became symbolic of the ignorant intruder into the domain of official medicine. The hierarchy of medicine demanded that midwives, surgeons, and barbers be instructed and overseen by physicians. By the end of the eighteenth century, the "reform" of midwifery culminated in the emergence of the male midwife as the dominant birth attendant.

The expanding market for medical services resulted in an explosion of opportunities for self-trained, half-trained, and barely trained popular healers, empirics, and charlatans. Although they were rebuked by the medical establishment, empirics filled an important niche in the medical economy. Often the main providers of medical services to the poor, they were consulted by members of all classes for their "secrets" to cure skin diseases, eye ailments, and general aches and pains. For most of these healers, medicine was probably a sideline to some other activity, but itinerant healers also wandered from town to town selling their wares (often including household articles as well as remedies) in the marketplaces and piazzas. Although their cures appear to have been based on a kind of "popular Galenism," enough borrowing of popular remedies and techniques by elite physicians suggests that the communication between orthodox doctors and irregular practitioners was a two-way street.

In the urban marketplace, empirical medicine shaded into charlatanism. Practitioners of a kind of anti-medicine, charlatans were everything that official doctors were not.[18] While the physician prized stability and ordered hierarchy, the charlatan was itinerant, rootless, and often foreign. Where the physician was grounded in book-learning, the charlatan was steeped in oral tradition. Where the physician prided himself on his erudition and reasoned method, the charlatan mocked the doctor's learning in ridiculous burlesques. And if the physician, at least in his own eyes, practiced his art according to the rules of charity and the moral economy, the charlatan unabashedly vended his nostrums for lucre. Charlatans brought to light society's uncertainties about a still relatively new and morally ambiguous commercial economy, and gave a novel, medical meaning to the timeworn maxim "Caveat emptor." (See the essays below by Mary Lindemann and Guido Ruggiero.)

Wonder and the Secrets of Nature

Many Renaissance intellectuals believed that the common people were more likely than others to be taken in by the deceptions of mountebanks and charlatans because, as Scipione Mercurio said, the people lack judgment and hence are readily "enchanted" by the charlatans. Yet wonder was by no means an exclusive preserve of popular culture. Roundly condemned by the medieval scholastics as a sign of ignorance and credulity, wonder was reclaimed in the Renaissance as a legitimate philosophical emotion. Fascinated by marvelous phenomena, Renaissance natural philosophers "rehabilitated wonders as useful objects of philosophical reflection."[19] In the process, they dramatically expanded the purview of natural philosophy to include marvelous phenomena of all kinds.

One event more than any other catapulted wonder into the Renaissance consciousness. From the moment when, in 1492, Christopher Columbus reported back to Europe that he had arrived at what he thought was the outer reaches of Asia, talk of the wonders of the "Indies" was on everyone's lips. In 1565 the Sevillan physician Juan de Monardes published his famous survey of the medicinal plants of the New World, and at the end of the century José de Acosta's great *Natural and Moral History of the Indies* opened Europeans' eyes to a vast panoply of exotic natural wonders. To some, the "discovery" of the lands that became known as America merely confirmed what Pliny, Solinus, and other ancient authors said about the prodigiousness of nature. But to others, the new discoveries demonstrated the inadequacies of ancient knowledge. Far from being authoritative, they argued, the ancients were wholly ignorant of what moderns know. In the words of Girolamo Cardano, "Among the extraordinary, though quite natural circumstances of my life, the first and most unusual is that I was born in this century in which the whole world became known; whereas the ancients were familiar with but little more than a third of it" (*Book of My Life*).

The voyages of discovery not only yielded a cornucopia of exotic naturalia for study, but also prompted a reconsideration of how nature might best be explored. The barrage of objects that poured into Europe from all over the world induced naturalists to comprehensively describe and categorize natural phenomena. The focus on particulars was nowhere more evident than in the collections of natural and artificial objects that were assembled by humanists, naturalists, physicians, and apothecaries throughout Europe. Described by contemporaries as *Wunderkammern* ("wonder rooms"), "cabinets of curiosities," and "theaters of nature," these early museums displayed fossils, exotic animals, antiquities, carved gems, and "rarities" of all sorts. The Mannerist juxtaposition of naturalia and artificialia that was characteristic of the curiosity cabinets not only blurred the traditional boundary between art and nature but also drew attention to particular kinds of "facts," namely, what the English philosopher Francis Bacon (1561–1626) called "singular instances," or anomalies that challenged existing theories. Visual tributes to the variety and plenitude of nature, the museums and curiosity cabinets confirmed Hamlet's reproach that "There are more things in heaven and earth, Horatio, | Than are dreamt of in your philosophy."

Another sign of the emerging "factual sensibility" was the vogue for books of secrets retailing craft and household recipes, virtues of plants and stones, "experiments," tricks of the trades, and natural magic. The prototype of these works, the immensely popular *Secrets* (1555) of "Alessio Piemontese," opened up to readers an entire New World of exotic secrets and practical recipes. Alessio's "secrets" included remedies unknown to the doctors, exotic perfumes and oils, dyeing techniques, tricks of the metalworking trades, and alchemical secrets tried out by Alessio himself. An instant best-seller, the work unleashed a torrent of books of secrets. So sensational were these works in their day that Tommaso Garzoni (1549–89), writing in 1585, identified their authors as making up a new profession, dubbing them the "professors of secrets."

The valorization of secrets and natural particulars gave rise to a novel view of scientific discovery, an approach that might be called the epistemology of the hunt. In the new methodology, the aim of science was not to give demonstrations of the known facts of nature, as the scholastics had done, but to seek out the hidden secrets of nature. To the professors of secrets, nature was like a dense wood hiding its secrets from whomever might seek them. The experimenter was a hunter who tracks his quarry following the signs it leaves behind. Particulars pointed the way to new particulars, just as the hunter extrapolates the presence of his quarry from its footprints and other clues left in its trail.

The discovery of the New World coincided with a programmatic effort by humanists to reform the field of *materia medica*, the science of the ingredients used in making medicinal drugs. Although classical works on natural history provided the model for reform, naturalists soon concluded that the ancient texts had to be supplemented by observations made in the field. In 1530, the German humanist Otto Brunfels (1489–1534) published his monumental *Herbarum vivae eicones* (Living Images of Plants, 1530), a work that supplemented the ancient authors with illustrations of some 500 plants drawn from nature. A flurry of botanical activity followed the appearance of Brunfels's herbal. With the publication of Pier Antonio Mattioli's translation of Dioscorides's *De materia medica* (The Materials of Medicine) in 1544, natural history became an increasingly important part of the university medical curriculum and began to emerge as a full-fledged scientific discipline.

Nevertheless, in many respects plants and animals remained part of what William B. Ashworth has called the "emblematic worldview," an intricate language of metaphor and symbol.[20] Renaissance naturalists believed that all natural objects had hidden meanings, and that knowledge of nature consisted of comprehending these myriad symbols. Thus to know a peacock was to know not only what it looked like but what its name meant, what proverbial associations it had, what it symbolized in mythology and history, and with what other natural objects it had sympathies or antipathies. The emblematic worldview prevailed through the first half of the seventeenth century, and was eventually eroded under the combined influence of the voyages of discovery, skepticism, and the Baconian philosophy. The plants and animals of the New World were so novel that they had no proverbial meanings attached to them, while Bacon and the skeptics denuded nature of its similitudes and symbolic intentions.

The Engineering Renaissance

An important result of humanism's continual refashioning of itself was the increasing attention paid to technology. Although the humanists were not responsible for the technological innovations of the fifteenth and sixteenth centuries – they were the products of the economic and social transformation of the commercial cities of Europe – humanists made important contributions to technology. In linking technology with the classics, they gave technology an ancient pedigree, thereby elevating the mechanical arts to a place of dignity alongside philosophy. Humanists also gave technology a theoretical foundation by laying down the mathematical principles of arts that were hitherto considered purely manual. Finally, the humanist movement contributed to the construction of the figure of the heroic artist-engineer, a topos developed to its most refined degree in Giorgio Vasari's life of the Florentine architect-engineer Filippo Brunelleschi (1377–1446). Vasari records that Brunelleschi, a supreme example of the "Tuscan genius," took mathematics lessons from the learned humanist Paolo Toscanelli, reformed the art of perspective, studied natural philosophy and mechanics, and undertook, despite protestations that his scheme was the work of a "madman," to construct the massive dome of the Florence cathedral without internal framework (*Lives of the Artists*).

In cities and princely courts throughout Europe, engineers found employment not only as architects, but also as designers of siege engines, fortifications, and monumental civic projects such as the great network of underground water canals in Siena (the so-called *bottini*), built between 1200 and 1400. With the introduction of gunpowder in the fifteenth century, techniques of warfare changed rapidly. Cannon largely negated the value of traditional castle fortifications, thus tipping the balance toward besiegers. In response, Italian architects and engineers developed a new fortification system known as the *trace italienne*. The key element of the new design, a polygonal bastion with a gun platform, developed between about 1450 and 1530 and spread from Italy to every corner of the globe where Europeans established their presence.

In addition to new technologies, the Renaissance saw the birth of a new kind of technological treatise. Lavishly illustrated, suffused with classical references, and often containing imaginative or fantastic designs of dubious utility, the Renaissance technological writings seem contrived almost as much to promote the self-image of the engineer as to impart technical information. The close parallel between the magus and engineer suggested in these writings was based on the notion that technical skill (*ingegno*), like magic, alters and bends nature to serve human needs. If he did not portray himself as a magus, the Renaissance engineer often projected himself as a mathematical wonder-worker. Mariano di Jacopo, known as Taccola (1382–ca. 1453), styled himself "the Archimedes of Siena." By becoming authors and adopting the sobriquet "engineer" (*ingeniarius*), the Renaissance inventors fashioned themselves as men of learning, ingenuity, and action.

Although the classics fueled the Renaissance machine books, early modern engineers were not content merely to ape their predecessors; they used ancient sources as guides to new experiments and inventions. Guidobaldo dal Monte's *Liber mechanicorum* (Book on Mechanics, 1577) was a creative and largely successful attempt to fuse the science of machines with Archimedean statics. Giovanni Battista Aleotti's Italian translation of Hero of Alexandria's *Pneumatica*, which appeared in 1589, stimulated scores of experiments, from the fantastic to the practical, with wind- and water-powered machines. Throughout the sixteenth century, lavish printed "theaters of machines" such as Agostino Ramelli's (1531–90) *Le diverse et artificiose machine* (The Various and Ingenious Machines, 1588) exhibited the marvelous inventions and technological wonders that would become stock productions of the Baroque.

We know a good deal about the technological work of Renaissance inventors from the detailed notebooks kept by one of the age's most accomplished engineers, Leonardo da Vinci (1452–1519). Although Leonardo is best known as an artist, his main source of livelihood was as an engineer in the service of various patrons, including the city of Florence, the Duke of Milan, Cesare Borgia, and King François I of France. Among Leonardo's multitude of projects were converting the Arno river to a navigable canal from Pisa to Florence, designs for court spectacles and theatrical performances, battleships and submarines, and a treadmill-powered multiple crossbow. However, Leonardo went beyond the design of machines to investigate the theoretical principles of mechanics. In a planned treatise on the "elements of machines" (*elementi macchinali*), he proposed to investigate the principles of mechanics, including its mathematical foundations, methods for calculating centers of gravity, and the four "powers" of nature, motion, weight, force, and impact. This boldly original approach bears witness to Leonardo's attempt to reconcile the practical work of craftsmen with classical statics. No one since Archimedes had attempted to subject mechanical operations to such rigorous theoretical analysis.

In a seminal work, Paolo Rossi argued that a radically new appraisal of labor and technical knowledge appeared in the writings of the sixteenth-century humanists and engineers. Rejecting the classical valuation of the mechanical arts as impure and base, humanists praised the arts for their dignity and usefulness, and insisted that they were necessary subjects in the philosopher's curriculum. The increased attention to the mechanical arts resulted in a new emphasis on empiricism in natural philosophy. In blurring the traditional distinction between nature and art, the humanists prepared the way for the experimental natural philosophies of the seventeenth century.[21]

The New Philosophy of Nature

By the middle of the sixteenth century, a group of thinkers, mainly but not exclusively Italian, were beginning to elaborate a new natural philosophy. Renouncing Aristotle, they tried to imagine a philosophy of nature, in the words of Bernardino Telesio (1509–80), one of the founders of the movement, "according to its own principles." Rejecting the forms and essences of Peripatetic philosophy, Telesio insisted that observation alone, not reason or authority, was the path to true knowledge. When we let things speak for themselves, he thought, nature presented itself as a single, unitary physical substratum activated by the forces of heat and cold. For him, nature was not only concrete and physical, but alive and sentient.

Telesio's iconoclastic spirit reverberated in the thought of the naturalists. It was as if, in liberating themselves from Aristotle, the nature philosophers opened their eyes to a universe that teemed with strange and unheard-of phenomena, and to a sentient cosmos pulsating with activity. Cataloging and making sense of such a universe proved to be a hopeless task, but among those who tried the physician and polymath Girolamo Cardano stands out as one of the most ambitious. The titles of his encyclopedic works on natural philosophy, *De subtilitate* (Of Subtlety, 1550) and *De rerum varietate* (On the Variety of Things, 1557) acknowledge his interest in understanding the boundaries of the natural, the preternatural, and the miraculous. "Our age has seen nothing that is not marvelous," he reflected at one point, "nor does nature play less wonderfully in small things than in large." Cardano's admiration for the inexhaustible variety and beauty of nature was characteristic of the Renaissance naturephilosophers.

For the Calabrian philosopher and Dominican friar Tommaso Campanella, the same living and thriving nature that produced Cardano's "subtlety" became at once the metaphysical substratum of a universal philosophy of nature and a manifesto for political action. From his first published book, *Philosophy Explicated According to the Senses* (1591), until the end of his career, Campanella remained fanatically devoted to one cause: opposition to Aristotelianism, which he saw as an intellectual addiction that corrupted philosophy, the Church, and the state. His magical worldview framed the ideology behind the abortive conspiracy to overthrow the Spanish government in Calabria that Campanella led in the spring of 1599. With this absurd plot, Campanella had hoped to establish a quasi-communist state along the lines later outlined in his utopian tract *The City of the Sun*. The revolt was a complete failure. Betrayed by co-conspirators, Campanella was arrested and charged with heresy and insurrection. He spent the next twenty-seven years in the jails of Naples, where, despite long periods of barbaric detention and torture, he composed the bulk of his voluminous *oeuvres* of scientific, religious, and political writings. Among these works was an impassioned defense of Galileo. Despite their shared anti-Aristotelianism, however, Campanella and Galileo in reality stood worlds apart. Campanella remained wedded to Telesio and continued to set astrological priorities above mathematical ones. His *Apology for Galileo* (1616) was not so much a defense of Copernicanism as it was an affirmation of freedom of thought, and was one of the first sustained arguments defending the liberty of the philosopher, which he held to be absolute.

While Campanella languished in the Neapolitan dungeon, another southern Italian nature-philosopher, Giordano Bruno, was rounded up by the Venetian Inquisition and extradited to Rome, where, in 1600, he was tried for a long list of heresies and burned alive in the Campo de' Fiori. Unlike Campanella, Bruno was an avowed Copernican. Yet it was not Copernicanism that led him to the stake: he was no scientific martyr, as legend holds. It was, rather, his religious and political activities, above all his scheme to employ astrology and magic in a bizarre plot to establish a new universal religion, that caused his downfall. Inspired by the idea that Moses and Christ were magi, Bruno apparently felt that as a magician he would play a special role in preparing the way for a new millennium.

If Bruno was hopeful of a more liberal religious environment in Italy, he was sadly mistaken. Yet he was certainly not the last to make that miscalculation. Galileo, too, thought he had grounds to anticipate a more tolerant atmosphere when, in 1623, Urban VIII became Pope. Indeed, throughout the process of licensing and publishing the *Dialogue on the Two Chief World Systems* (1633), Galileo's great work on cosmology, Urban had seemed to encourage Galileo. Then, something happened to enrage him, and he ordered proceedings against the astronomer. After a trial lasting several months, Galileo was forced to recant his Copernican beliefs and placed under house arrest, where he devoted the remainder of his life to technical problems and eschewed cosmology. Symbolically, at least, the era of Renaissance Italian science had come to an end.

The End of the Renaissance

In his *New Organon* (1620), Francis Bacon wrote that three inventions unknown to the ancients, printing, gunpowder, and the compass, "have changed the whole face and state of things throughout the world." Bacon believed that science should progress like the mechanical arts and, like the arts in general, should be productive of useful things. He saw the geographical revolution as a symbol for intellectual progress: just as mariners had sailed beyond the Pillars of Hercules, the fabled limits of navigable waters, so should philosophers advance beyond adherence to ancient dogmas. While moderns had outdistanced the ancients, he implied, they still had not reformed the method of natural philosophy, and hence continued to chase chimeras such as occult qualities. Thus he praised the experimental work on the magnet by his countryman William Gilbert (1544–1603) but criticized Gilbert's magnetic natural philosophy, which he said was like trying to build a ship from a row-lock, i.e., attempting to construct a comprehensive worldview on the basis of a few isolated experiments.[22]

Bacon distanced himself from both Renaissance magic and the naturalist tradition of Cardano, Campanella, and Bruno. He attacked magic for its megalomania and its tendency to exalt individual genius over the cooperative efforts of many individuals. In reality, Bacon was undermining not only a style of thinking but an institutional context that promoted it. Whether as astrologers, engineers, physicians, or magi, by necessity Renaissance natural philosophers had to accommodate their styles of scientific thinking to court culture, where scientific discourse was framed by considerations of "honor." In place of the swaggering, contentious magus, Bacon proposed a new kind of natural philosopher with a new institutional context, that of the experimenter within a community of experimenters. During the scientific revolution of the seventeenth century, patrons progressively disappeared from the stage, and the establishment of more circumscribed and less contentious experimental "matters of fact" (as opposed to sweeping cosmological theories) became the goal of natural philosophy.

NOTES

1   Thorndike, *History of Magic*, vol. 5, p. 5.
2   Eisenstein, *Printing Press*, p. 573.
3   Johns, *Nature of the Book*; Eamon, *Secrets*, pp. 3–12.
4   Nauert, "Humanists, Scientists."
5   Yates, *Giordano Bruno*.
6   Copenhaver, "Natural Magic," p. 289.
7   Moran, *Alchemical World*, p. 25.
8   Debus, *Chemical Philosophy*.
9   Quoted in Niccoli, *Prophecy*, p. 158.
10   Westman, "Copernicus," p. 78.
11   Westman, "Melanchthon Circle."
12   Westman, "Copernicus," 85.
13   Quoted in Wear, "Medicine," p. 253.
14   Park, "Saintly Body."
15   O'Malley, *Andreas Vesalius*, p. 61.
16   Trevor-Roper, "Court Physician."
17   Siraisi, *Medicine*, p. 152.
18   Brockliss and Jones, *Medical World*, pp. 230–4.
19   Daston and Park, *Wonders*, p. 137.
20   Ashworth, "Natural History."
21   Rossi, *Philosophy, Technology*, pp. 137–45.
22   Rossi, *Francis Bacon*.

REFERENCES

Ashworth, William B., "Natural History and the Emblematic World View," in *Reappraisals of the Scientific Revolution*, ed. David C. Lindberg and Robert S. Westman (Cambridge: Cambridge University Press, 1990), pp. 303–32.
Brockliss, Laurence and Jones, Colin, *The Medical World of Early Modern France* (Oxford: Oxford University Press, 1997).

Copenhaver, Brian P., "Natural Magic, Hermetism, and Occultism in Early Modern Science," in *Reappraisals of the Scientific Revolution*, ed. David C. Lindberg and Robert S. Westman (Cambridge: Cambridge University Press, 1990), pp. 261–301.

Daston, Lorraine and Park, Katharine, *Wonders and the Order of Nature, 1150–1750* (Cambridge, MA: Zone Books, 1998).

Debus, Allen G., *The Chemical Philosophy: Paracelsian Science and Medicine in the Sixteenth and Seventeenth Centuries*, 2 vols. (New York: Science History Publications, 1977).

Eamon, William, *Science and the Secrets of Nature: Books of Secrets in Medieval and Early Modern Culture* (Princeton: Princeton University Press, 1994).

Eisenstein, Elizabeth, *The Printing Press as an Agent of Change* (Cambridge: Cambridge University Press, 1979).

Johns, Adrian, *The Nature of the Book: Print and Knowledge in the Making* (Chicago: University of Chicago Press, 1998).

Moran, Bruce, *The Alchemical World of the German Court: Occult Philosophy and Chemical Medicine in the Circle of Moritz of Hessen, 1572–1632* (Stuttgart: Franx Steiner, 1991).

Nauert, Charles, "Humanists, Scientists, and Pliny: Changing Approaches to a Classical Author," *American Historical Review* 84 (1979), pp. 72–85.

Niccoli, Ottavia, *Prophecy and the People in Renaissance Italy*, trans. L. G. Cochrane (Princeton: Princeton University Press, 1990).

O'Malley, C. D., *Andreas Vesalius of Brussels, 1514–1564* (Berkeley: University of California Press, 1964).

——, "The Criminal and the Saintly Body: Autopsy and Dissection in Renaissance Italy," *Renaissance Quarterly* 47 (1994), pp. 1–33.

Rossi, Paolo, *Philosophy, Technology, and the Arts in the Early Modern Era*, trans. S. Attansio (New York: Harper & Row, 1970).

——, *Francis Bacon: From Magic to Science*, trans. S. Rabiniovitch (Chicago: University of Chicago Press, 1972).

Siraisi, Nancy, *Medieval and Early Renaissance Medicine: An Introduction to Knowledge and Practice* (Chicago: University of Chicago Press, 1990).

Thorndike, Lynne, *A History of Magic and Experimental Science*, 8 vols. (New York: Columbia University Press, 1923–58).

Trevor-Roper, Hugh, "The Court Physician and Paracelsianism," in *Medicine at the Courts of Europe, 1500–1837*, ed. Vivian Nutton (London: Routledge, 1990), pp. 79–94

Wear, Andrew, "Medicine in Early Modern Europe, 1500–1700," in *The Western Medical Tradition 800 BC to AD 1800* (Cambridge: Cambridge University Press, 1995).

Westman, Robert S., "The Melanchthon Circle, Rheticus, and the Wittenberg Interpretation of the Copernican Theory," *Isis* 66 (1975), pp. 165–93.

—— "Copernicus and the Churches," in *God and Nature: Historical Essays on the Encounter between Christianity and Science* (Berkeley and Los Angeles: University of California Press, 1986), pp. 76–113.

Yates, Frances A., *Giordano Bruno and the Hermetic Tradition* (Chicago: University of Chicago Press, 1964).

FURTHER READING

Biagioli, Mario, *Galileo Courtier: The Practice of Science in the Culture of Absolutism* (Chicago: University of Chicago Press, 1993).

Carlino, Andrea, *Books of the Body: Anatomical Ritual and Renaissance Learning*, trans. J. and A. T. Tedeschi (Chicago: University of Chicago Press, 1999).

Ferrari, Giovanna, "Public Anatomy Lessons and the Carnival: The Anatomy Theatre of Bologna," *Past and Present* 117 (1987), pp. 51–106.

Findlen, Paula, *Possessing Nature: Museums, Collection, and Scientific Culture in Early Modern Italy* (Berkeley and Los Angeles: University of California Press, 1994).

Galluzzi, Paolo, *Renaissance Engineers from Brunelleschi to Leonardo da Vinci* (Florence: Istituto e Museo di Storia della Scienza, 1996).

Gatti, Hilary, *Giordano Bruno and Renaissance Science* (Ithaca, NY: Cornell University Press, 1999).

Grafton, Anthony, *New Worlds, Ancient Texts: The Power of Tradition and the Shock of the New* (Cambridge, MA: Harvard University Press, 1992).

——, *Cardano's Cosmos: The Worlds and Works of a Renaissance Astrologer* (Cambridge, MA: Harvard University Press, 1999).

Grant, Edward, *Planets, Stars, and Orbs: The Medieval Cosmos, 1200–1687* (Cambridge: Cambridge University Press, 1996).

Hall, Bert S., *Weapons and Warfare in Renaissance Europe: Gunpowder, Technology, and Tactics* (Baltimore: Johns Hopkins University Press, 1997).

Headley, John M., *Tommaso Campanella and the Transformation of the World* (Princeton: Princeton University Press, 1997).

Langford, Jerome J., *Galileo, Science, and the Church* (Ann Arbor: University of Michigan Press, 1966).

Pagel, Walter, *Paracelsus: An Introduction to Philosophical Medicine in the Era of the Renaissance* (Basel: S. Karger, 1958).

Park, Katharine, *Doctors and Medicine in Early Renaissance Florence* (Princeton: Princeton University Press, 1985).

Redondi, Pietro, *Galileo Heretic*, trans. R. Rosenthal (Princeton: Princeton University Press, 1987).

Rose, Paul L., *The Italian Renaissance of Mathematics: Studies on Humanists and Mathematicians from Petrarch to Galileo* (Geneva: Librarie Droz, 1975).

Thoren, Victor, *The Lord of Uraniborg: A Biography of Tycho Brahe* (Cambridge: Cambridge University Press, 1990).

PART V

Anti-Worlds

CHAPTER TWENTY-FOUR

Plague, Disease, and Hunger

Mary Lindemann

Plague, disease, and hunger are as central to the Renaissance as the *Divine Comedy* and the opening of the Atlantic. The grisly trio did not merely symbolize a life that was nasty, brutish, and short; plague, disease, and hunger were realities that evoked creative responses and interacted with other momentous events. Plague and syphilis arose from the multiple encounters with new regions of the globe that profoundly altered Europe and the world in these centuries. Both diseases were first observed in Italy and then spread outward. All three Renaissance "pestilences" – plague, disease, and famine – shook social, economic, demographic, and cultural structures to their foundations; the Europe that emerged was forever changed.

During the Renaissance, attitudes toward pestilence began to assume the meanings that would persist throughout early modern times. Plague and syphilis, for instance, called into question received medical thinking about disease causation and appropriate treatments. In a period of ever greater exposure to the rest of the world – to the Muslim East and South, to China, and, later, to the Americas – Europeans became tremulously sensitive to the dangers an expanding world posed. Contact with new worlds raised questions about some of Europe's most deeply held beliefs, bared Europe to new menaces, and produced new fears along with new knowledge and great new wealth; what fructified could also frighten.

In several other ways as well, these three horrors shaped European life. Plague, for instance, may have fostered a sense of personhood separate from others and threatened by them. Plague evoked bureaucratic measures (quarantine and boards of health are only the most obvious) and these worked to enhance – eventually – the power of the state and to enlarge the role of government in daily life. Syphilis nurtured a more skeptical perspective on sexuality and stiffened an already existing bond between immorality and disease. Famine was beginning to yield to increased production, vigorous government intervention, and better transportation, although progress was barely discernible in the 1500s and the subsistence crises of an old demographic regime persisted until the 1740s.

Plague

> That Omnipotence which has called the world with all its living creatures into one
> animated being, especially reveals himself in the desolation of great pestilences. The
> powers of creation come into violent collision; the sultry dryness of the atmosphere; the
> subterraneous thunders; the mist of overflowing waters, are the harbingers of destruc-
> tion. Nature is not satisfied with the alternations of life and death, and the destroying
> angel waves over man and beast his flaming sword.[1]

Thus did J. F. C. Hecker in 1832 relate the coming of the sickness commonly known
as the Black Death. As the "Schwarzer Tod," Hecker popularized a name that was,
however, never current before the nineteenth century. Contemporaries knew the
disease that ravaged Europe from 1347 to 1352 as a pestilence. In the middle of
the fourteenth century, this *pestis* was a new disease with shocking symptoms and
grievous mortality. Agnolo di Tura, a citizen of Siena, lamented that "it is impossible
for the human tongue to recount the awful truth. . . . the victims died almost immediately. They would swell beneath the armpits and in their groins, and fall over while
talking. Father abandoned child, wife husband, one brother another; for this illness
seemed to strike through breath and sight. And so they died. And none could be
found to bury the dead for money or friendship."[2] Mortality in di Tura's home town
may have been as high as 60 percent, but enormous death tolls were widespread and
so, too, was the consternation they roused. The last large-scale pestilence had vanished from the Mediterranean world almost five hundred years earlier. After 1347–8,
however, pestilence would recur often in the fifteenth and sixteenth centuries
throughout Europe (there were, for example, more incidents in the fifteenth than
in the fourteenth century in Italy). It diminished in frequency and brutality over the
next two centuries and disappeared from western Europe, somewhat mysteriously, by
1721.

If the disease was new and chillingly mortal, its provenance seemed plain. This
pandemic (an epidemic dispersed over a vast geographical area) had come from the
distant East and moved inexorably through the caravansarais to the West. Two years
before it invaded Italy, it was in the Crimea at the siege of Kaffa, where the Muslim
threat was military and biological. "Oh God!" commented Gabriele de Mussis in
1348,

> See how the heathen Tartar races, pouring together from all sides . . . besieged the
> trapped Christians there for almost three years. . . . but behold, the whole army was
> affected by a disease which overran the Tartars and killed thousands among thousands
> every day.[3]

Those fleeing Kaffa carried the plague with them, seeding it everywhere along the
Mediterranean littoral. It first struck Messina and Sicily in 1347, then nosed into
southern Spain and Italy, spread relentlessly north into France, the Germanies, the
Low Countries, Sweden, and finally entered Russia in 1351. Not all areas were
equally affected; some escaped entirely. Italy suffered grave demographic losses and
recovered slowly as the pestilence settled in for a long stay. Before the plague, Prato
(in 1339), for example, had about 10,600 inhabitants; after, about 6,000. Demo-

graphic rebound was slow and in 1427, the *catasto* (tax records) found only 3,533. Some large urban centers paid uncommonly high bills of mortality, declining to less than 60 percent of their pre-plague population. Florence, for example, lost about 40 percent of its inhabitants. Subsequent incursions of plague wasted more lives and hamstrung demographic recovery. In the early fourteenth century, Florence probably held more than 100,000 people: in 1427, 37,000; 1480, 41,000; and in 1552, two centuries after the first shock, just 59,000.[4] The great plague of 1347–52 probably wiped out one-third of the European population as a whole, although mortality varied significantly from place to place.

Plague also slew differentially. Those confined together – the aged in pensionary homes, monks and nuns, lepers – succumbed quickly. Curiously, the most robust seemed more susceptible than their weaker brethren. Plague, moreover, struck and killed children more frequently than adults. Even if mortality among children from plague was misreported – in that the children who died *during* plague epidemics did not always die *of* plague – plague must have enhanced the feeling that children were frail creatures and may well have contributed to the early modern tendency to view children as, quite literally, not long for this world. This does not, however, imply that children were neither valued nor loved or that adults neglected and ignored them. Biographical and autobiographical writings on plague testify to the burning anguish of parents who buried their children, carrying them to the pits or digging graves themselves when necessary. Thus it may well be that during the Renaissance a sense of childhood ephemerality increased at the very same moment that literary depictions of parental love became more frequent. On the other hand, David Herlihy has suggested that as children became scarcer, they also become more cherished commodities. If the precise effect of plague on families and on the valuation of children remains enigmatic, most historians concur that it was not negligible.

Historians and demographers have frequently – perhaps facilely – assumed this great "dying" to have been an outbreak of bubonic plague mixed, in some cities, with pneumonic plague. Scholars by no means agree, however, that the "pestilence" of the mid fourteenth century was in truth bubonic (or pneumonic) plague. Medical historians are chary of diagnosing diseases in the past (a practice known as retro-diagnosis) and are also acutely aware of the ability of bacilli and viruses to mutate over time. In addition, misdiagnoses of plague, or rather the diagnosis of all deaths (or almost all deaths) occurring during an epidemic as caused by the pestilence, often artificially elevated mortality rates; indeed, "a plague was many plagues."[5] If many scholars feel fairly confident identifying the disease that ravaged Italy between 1347 and 1352 as bubonic/pneumonic plague, dissenters have been vocal and, at times, persuasive. The epidemiologist Graham Twigg hypothesized that the fourteenth-century *pestis* might have been anthrax, although "historically, [anthrax] has certainly never struck human populations in epidemic proportions."[6] Perhaps more important to remember, however, is that Renaissance people did not conceive of plague in the same way that twentieth-century medical science does: as a unique disease arising from a specific pathogen, *Yersina pestis*.

Evidence on the bacteriological causes of plague and its vectors of dissemination only yielded to scientific inquiry in the late nineteenth century, during the 1894 outbreak in China when researchers discovered the bacillus responsible: *Yersina pestis* (often still identified by its older name, *Pasturella pestis*). The epidemiology that eventually developed and became ruling orthodoxy presented a rather elegant story of how what was essentially an epizootic (a plague of animals) among the European black rat (*Rattus rattus*) became a human epidemic when infected rat fleas (*Xenopsylla cheopis*) left their dying animal hosts and bit humans. The disease becomes epidemic when conditions that facilitate this transferal exist: an active epizootic; a close proximity of rats, fleas, and humans; and a sufficient population of each to sustain the chain of events.

Once the bacillus enters the human bloodstream, the progress of the disease is swift. The case mortality of untreated patients varies between 60 and 80 percent. The initial, mild symptoms quickly worsen. A high temperature of 103–4 °F (almost 40°C) ensues and accompanies intense pains in the limbs, splitting headaches, and nausea. The lymph nodes in the armpits and groin often swell, producing extremely painful *buboes*; these buboes are what give bubonic plague its name. Such form the classic symptoms of bubonic plague, although early modern people spoke, of course, of signs or tokens rather than symptoms. Still, the clinical presentation is not always complete and unambiguous. An acute form of bubonic plague, where the bacilli multiply rapidly in the bloodstream before the telltale buboes can appear, is called *septicemic plague*. A highly lethal form of plague, *pneumonic plague*, is more distinct and occurs when plague is complicated by pneumonia. With each cough, the victim expels bacilli which then enter the airways of others, evoking a progressive and almost always fatal disease. Considering overall mortality rates and the speed with which death ensued, as well as the frequent notation in the sources that "people fell over while talking," it seems probable that pneumonic plague played a major role in the mid-fourteenth century but was less significant in the outbreaks of the sixteenth and seventeenth centuries, including during the Great Plague of London (1666). Moreover, the existence of two separate forms of plague helps account for disproportionately high death rates in certain places as well as for seasonal variations. Bubonic plague tends to dominate the epidemiological profile in the warm months; pneumonic in the late fall, winter, and early spring.

Although modern epidemiological research has caused several parts of this simple story of rats, fleas, and humans to be questioned (and offered other variables involving, for example, the intermediary of the human flea, *Pulex irritans*), it seems clear that an epidemic of rodents – mostly rats – forms the necessary precondition for plague to occur. In the 1970s, William H. McNeill crafted a provocative macrohistorical interpretation of why plague "broke out" in the fourteenth century. He coupled plague's appearance in the West to the new "permeability" of the Eurasian heartland prompted by the empire-building of the Mongols and the establishment of a vast communication and trade network that stretched from China to Europe.[7] Plague was, therefore, probably never endemic nor even enzootic in Europe, but was always reintroduced through the Middle East or over the Europe–Asia land-routes. Plague remained an alien invader, dependent on the very expansion of European horizons and the broadening perspectives that hallmarked Renaissance art and endeavor.

Renaissance people faced with plague sought to unravel its meaning. Whereas we today want to track down the "germ" responsible and to identify its "means of transmission," our early modern ancestors concerned themselves with ultimate origins and avoidance as well as with prophylactic measures and treatments. Academic, lay, and governmental groups differed in their responses, but their explanations demonstrated a certain convergence of beliefs. Each was interested in remote and proximate causes: God; perturbations in the celestial and terrestrial spheres; and human agency, including sin. At the same time, contemporaries divided on whether pestilences spread directly from person to person (contagion) or arose from and were transmitted through the air. The schism between the two positions was never, however, absolute and steps taken to combat the plague mixed both approaches.

The experience of plague reinforced the conviction that God was the *causa finalis* of all disease. Almost everyone accepted that the ultimate origin of plague bedded in God's inscrutable will and was his chosen weapon for punishing sin. Plague was, according to Boccaccio, "the just anger of God . . . sent upon us mortals." Gabriele de Mussis, a Piacenza lawyer, saw plague as an obvious manifestation of divine wrath.

> God said, "The exercise of justice belongs to me. I am the life of the living. I bear the keys of death. I bring retribution, giving each individual his due . . . The sight of the vanities and lecheries to which you have abandoned yourself [however] has provoked me to fury. May evil spirits arise with the power to devour you. May you have no escape from this time forward.[8]

When William Zouche, Archbishop of York, called for an intercessionary procession in July, 1348, he hoped that "orisons and prayers" to God might "turn away his anger and remove the pestilence and drive away the infection from the people whom he redeemed with his precious blood."[9] Thus appeals to God's mercy and attempts to rectify the sinfulness of self and society were shock-troops in the Renaissance war against disease.

Another remote but puissant force lay in the skies; the disordered movements of the heavenly bodies could raise pestilences. A Shakespeare character mused on how the unfavorable conjunction of the celestial orbs bred disease:

> when the Planets
> In evil mixture to disorder wander,
> What Plagues, and what portents, what mutiny. . .
> Divert, and crack, rend and deracinate
> The unity, and married calm of States
> Quite from their fixture!
> (*Troilus and Cressida*, I. iii. 94–101)

The earth, too, bore her share of guilt: earthquakes and tremors; ash- and gas-belching volcanoes; floods and droughts; unnatural heat or cold; and even ill winds could all "on Prosper fall, and make him by inch-meal a disease" (*The Tempest*, II. ii. 2–3). Terrestrial accidents like celestial anomalies could "poison" the very atmosphere and spew forth plagues in humans and animals as well as other afflictions: flies and toads, toadstools and "unsavory" meats.

Although plague was a new disease and a harrowing one, the reaction of laypeople and physicians alike was never merely sheer terror and paralysis. (See the essay above by William Eamon.) The learned doctors who composed the Paris *Consilium* in October 1348, while never questioning the divine origins of disease and while doubting that human reason could ever fully grasp its true cause, also grappled with understanding what was happening and why. Not too surprisingly, their explanations drew on academic theories and assumptions inherited from medieval scholarship. During the first onslaught of plague, ideas of how the pestilence propagated and its proximate cause were linked to older Galenic and Hippocratic concepts of disease and, especially, of epidemics; both resulted from a corruption of the air. The Hippocratic/Galenic tradition that had dominated medieval academic medicine tied disease chiefly to the environment but also worked in concepts of pollution and impurity to clarify disease occurrences. Ficinus noticed that "when the ayer of that place varyeth from his naturall temperature, declyning to heate and moysture . . . When the Wyndes are grosse and hoat . . . strange Agewes arise, raging continuall, burning, phrantike, when the small Pockes, and Mesels are rife, and wormes abound in children and old folkes," and plague, too, strikes.[10] The equally archaic notion of complexion or temperament explained why some people got the plague and others did not, even while breathing the same corrupted air. Health lay in the proper balancing of the four humors: black bile, yellow (or red) bile, blood, and phlegm. Disease resulted from humors that had tipped "out of balance," grown corrupt, or had come to putrefy; the state of the environment could precipitate constitutional disequilibriums or promote putrefaction. Thus preventives and cures were concerned with trying to purify corrupted air by fumigating houses, clothing, and goods, setting bonfires, or discharging cannon. In addition to lightening or sweetening the atmosphere, physicians modified diets to readjust humoral imbalances. Galenic medicine also taught that each disease was unique to an individual and diseases or disease entities as we normally speak of them today – as AIDS, influenza, or measles that someone "catches" – did not exist. In short, physicians and medical commentators deployed older categories of disease causation and treatment to deal with this new menace (although some steadfastly denied its novelty).

The experience of several plagues, however, slowly bolstered the idea of contagion; that is, that plague passed directly from person to person. Such concepts stimulated the development of measures – such as quarantine and the establishment of plague hospitals – to prevent contact between the infected and the healthy. Strictly speaking, bubonic plague is not contagious; it does not spread by human contact (although the less frequent pneumonic plague does). Moreover, these three manners of explaining the spread of plague – contagion, miasma, and predisposing causes – often converged for "both miasma and contagion were thought to arise from ill-defined processes of corruption and putrefaction, either in the heavens, in the air or in terrestrial or human bodies, and thus they had the same root." Moreover, sinfulness – spiritual unwholesomeness – was intimately related to physical unhealthfulness for "the corruption which lay at the root of plague was not only a physical process but also a moral one."[11]

The repeated encounters with plague powerfully affected medical theory, without causing Europeans to jettison the older Hippocratic/Galenic framework entirely. Girolamo Fracastoro (1478–1553) developed his famous "seeds of contagion" in response to plague. Likewise, plague conditioned physicians to think in terms of specific diseases rather than humoral imbalances. Still, therapeutics continued to rely on the old standbys of bleeding and purging, and everyone knew that the best way to avoid plague was to "flee far, stay long, and come back slowly."

As learned opinion gradually and by no means *en masse* migrated in the direction of contagion, the everyday experience of plague worked to reweave the social fabric of Renaissance societies. Plague (and later, syphilis) reinforced the already-existing inclination to regard disease as an intruder (both into a society and into a body) and to underscore the fact that a more open world was also a more parlous one. Renaissance pestilences significantly altered attitudes toward the poor, itinerants, and Jews and larded them with harsher implications. Contagion could shade over into fear of "others" and even nourish conspiracy theories. (See the essay below by Linda Woodbridge.) Herman Gigas, a Franciscan friar from Franconia, reported how many Jews had confessed under torture to having "bred spiders and toads in pots and pans" after "obtain[ing] the poison from overseas" and then contaminated wells and springs with it. Persecutions in many parts of Europe sprung up almost spontaneously; in 1348–9, for example, the Jewish community in the Rhineland suffered grievously. Similar attacks and pogroms occurred elsewhere. Yet some secular and religious authorities did their best to quell the hysteria and protect the Jews. Pope Clement VI, while typically abhorring the "deceit of the Jews," also extended the Church's protection to them and condemned those who "out of their own hot-headedness ... have impiously slain many Jews."[12]

Plague came to be associated with other groups of people: with the poor, with vagabonds, and especially with the many malnourished or starving drifters who took to the roads in times of famine. So was forged a link between poverty and plague, or rather between poverty and the bearers of the "seeds" of disease, which became a permanent part of early modern social welfare and sanitary policies, as "plague controls became social controls."[13] (Yet at the same time many people sought to placate God's anger by directing more acts of charity toward the poor.) Very often those ill with plague and those connected with its victims were stigmatized and cast into the role of outsiders. This had, of course, happened before with lepers, but plague – and then syphilis – firmed up the connection between disease (and especially a "loathsome" disease) and social undesirability. Syphilis and other "unclean" afflictions became terms of abuse. In 1612, for example, a citizen of Cologne, Antonius Schwartz, suffered personally and occupationally from the rumor that he had "the foul pox or the French disease."[14]

For a long time, historians have credited plague with forcing the first discernible steps toward the creation of municipal public health legislation and enforcement. Carlo Cipolla argued that "it all started with the great pandemic of 1347–51." While there is no doubt that cities, such as Florence, set up temporary measures to deal with the threat, no public health bureaucracy developed during the initial wave of infection. Florence, for example, did not empanel a permanent board of health until 1527. The Renaissance public health machinery arose piecemeal, coaxed into being by repeated biological disasters. Cities throughout Europe over the course of the fifteenth and sixteenth centuries began to put more robust bureaucratic apparatuses in place to administer a series of steps that – from the perspective of some five hundred years later – we label "public health." In fact, like the maturation of the Renaissance state more generally, such steps were far less integrated and purposeful than the passage of time makes them appear. Still, quarantines, pesthouses, and cordons sanitaires did in fact grow out of the plague experience of two centuries and continued to form an important part of the European armamentarium against disease well into the nineteenth century.

Scholars dispute the long- and short-term economic consequences of plague. (See the essay above by Karl Appuhn.) Obviously population declined dramatically during the initial onslaught of 1347–52 and recovered only haltingly. Whether plague contributed to a rise in real wages or whether it spelled the end of medieval serfdom – as some historians have asserted – still remain open questions complicated by the fact that the 1300s suffered endemic warfare, famine, and population decline even before the mid-century biological disaster. Herlihy has argued that the considerable decline in population spurred the development of new, labor-saving devices and fostered a technological mini-revolution, but other historians have not eagerly followed his lead. The most convincing economic studies have addressed specific localities and particular occupations rather than macro-historical shifts.

The social and cultural repercussions of plague were intense and long-lasting, although they, too, probably evolved slowly and as a result of repeated incursions of plague. Isolated catastrophes had less impact than common sense might suggest. The influence of plague on the artistic imagination was profound. Boccaccio set his *Decameron* in Florence during the plague. His characters, a *brigata* of young men and women, had fled the city for a pastoral haven. Others have documented how plague stamped western iconography with the dance of death motif and nurtured a fascination with images of the apocalypse and memento mori figures. Johan Huizinga's famous argument that plague throttled the vibrant culture of the High Middle Ages, and ushered in a period where art became morbid and people less creative, has not stood the test of time and additional archival research very well. Samuel Cohn, for instance, has argued persuasively that plague actually stimulated an artistic revival and that plague's survivors became ardent patrons of the arts. Such an interpretation surely fits better with the undoubted artistic florescence of the Renaissance. On the other hand, one might agree with other scholars that the rise of more pronounced senses of fear and guilt accompanied plague and came to constitute a major part of the European psyche thereafter.

The plagues of Renaissance Europe – whether they were in fact what science today identifies as bubonic plague or whether they were something else entirely – left lasting scars. Whenever death rates soared dramatically, whenever news of a mysterious "dying" leaked out, the first suspicion that popped, almost unbidden, into everyone's mind was that plague had returned. Although plague's virulence and frequency waned with time, it haunted the eastern and southern edges of Europe, always ready, it seemed, to venture forth and kill again. Even in the nineteenth century plague had by no means lost all its menace.

Disease

Plague indelibly imprinted Renaissance life and sensibilities, but we should not forget that "many epidemic crises . . . could not possibly have been due to plague alone."[15] Especially during epidemics subsequent to the great "dying" of 1347–52, other diseases contributed to what was generally viewed as plague mortality. Dysentery, smallpox, influenza, and perhaps also typhus inflated the supramortality of "plague years." Diseases that we do not regard today as epidemic – such as syphilis – were so viewed in the Renaissance. Moreover, we must remember that the meaning of disease did not depend solely on the epidemic experience.

Syphilis harrowed the imagination of Renaissance people as much as plague did, although its demographic weight was always slight. If few people died of syphilis (at least in the short run), the disease nevertheless reinforced ideas about medicine and social organization born with plague. Even more than plague, syphilis was a new disease that came "from the outside"; it helped solidify the perception of a disease as a specific thing; it exacerbated fear of "others"; it yoked disease and sin tightly together; and it affected European perceptions on sexuality deeply.

Syphilis apparently first broke out during the French king's Italian campaign of 1494–5. The disease was frightful in all its aspects. Ser Tommaso di Silvestro recounted his own episode of pox:

> all my head became covered with blemishes or scabs, and the pains appeared in my right and left arms... [and] the bones ached so that I could never find rest. And then my right knee ached, and I became covered with boils, all over my front and back...[16]

In 1498, Joseph Grünpeck moaned that "the disease launched its first arrow into my Priapic glans which ... became so swollen that both hands could scarcely circle it."[17] Girolamo Fracastoro named the disease *Syphilis sive morbus Gallicus* (1546) in an epic poem of that title, but most people called it the great pox, the French itch, the French boils, or the French or the Neapolitan disease. Fracastoro's poem was only one literary manifestation of the pox in Renaissance literature. In northern Europe, for example, the humanists Rudolf Agricola, Ulrich von Hutten, Johann Reuchlin, and Sebastian Brant graphically portrayed its ravages.

The great pox (to distinguish it from the "small" pox) seemed previously unknown in Europe. The names that described and labeled the disease reflect its novelty and the perception of its character as an invader, its origins in "foreign lands," and its spread by outsiders: *mala franzosa* or *morbus gallicus* were the commonest. That it first emerged during the French invasion of Italy led quickly to its Gallification. Its character as an intruder and a stranger was also evident in writings that made the Arabs, the Jews, or the Ethiopians its progenitors.

Today syphilis is a chronic disease. As many as two-thirds of all those infected suffer few problems and little or no impairment, although the symptoms demonstrated by others can be severe: blindness, paresis, cardiovascular distress, and motor dysfunctions. Renaissance chroniclers viewed syphilis in a very different light, one more consistent with the incursion of a new disease in a biologically unseasoned population. The disease killed in its early stages, which modern chronic syphilis does not. Moreover, it seemed that casual contact alone spread the misery like wildfire. Even in the Renaissance sex was not regarded as the only (or even the principal) means of transmission. The Bolognese Friano degli Ubaldini believed that syphilis could be contracted "through eating, drinking and through sexual relations."[18] Others believed that it was produced by an infection of the air. It was also, as the Dominican reformer Girolamo Savonarola preached, a punishment for sin but not only for sins of a fleshy or sexual nature. That unnatural sex could breed disease was an old idea registered in the belief that oral sex spawned leprous children. The same circular ties between natural and supernatural causes that plague evoked worked for syphilis as well.

The suddenness with which the disease appeared in the late fifteenth and early sixteenth centuries quickly led some to speculate that Columbus's sailors had brought it back with them from the Indies. Roderigo de Isla widely publicized his conjectures in the *Treatise on the Serpentine Malady*, which appeared in 1539. If this theory is true (and there is much dissent), then syphilis was one of the first diseases in Europe (along with plague) begot by contact with other parts of the globe. At the same time syphilis nicely illustrates the consequences of communication between two parts of the world once separated. The opening of the Atlantic and the development of a regular traffic between the Old World and the New inaugurated a new biological regime that sent Old World diseases, like smallpox, measles, and influenza to the New World where they wreaked frightful havoc among the as-yet epidemiologically un-touched populations of central America. (See the essay above by Matthew Restall.)

If Renaissance peoples believed that syphilis came from the realm of Eldorado (and contemporary opinion diverged on this point), medical historians and demographers since then have been more incredulous. Barrels of ink have been splashed about trying to verify either the Columbian or the non-Columbian (unitarian) origin of syphilis. Irrefutable proof is not to be found. Paleopathologists who have examined bones from excavations of pre-Columbian cultures have discovered lesions character-istic of syphilis there but not among equally ancient European remains. Such evidence is hardly conclusive, however, as several diseases produce similar pathological traces. Other scholars have argued for the unitarian viewpoint that syphilis was always present in the Old World in the form of the milder spirochete diseases of bejel, yaws, and pinta, which predominate in hot dry climates such as the Middle East. In wetter climates, the spirochetes retreat deeper into the body and nest in the human genitals and other mucous membranes. The unusual violence and almost endemic warfare of the late fifteenth and early sixteenth centuries certainly propagated the disease rapidly. Neither theory – the Columbian or the unitarian – is totally satisfac-tory in epidemiological terms. But this does not in many ways matter. Many, perhaps even most, Europeans were convinced that syphilis was a new disease and that it came from the Indies.

Treatment of syphilis combined the old and the new in ways that typified Renais-sance medicine. The earliest therapeutic interventions sought to remove or purify corrupted humors from the sufferer's body; he was bled or administered a sudorific, purge, or emetic. Other, newer remedies soon became popular. Some healers came to favor a decoction made from the wood of the guaiac tree from Hispaniola, arguing that the cure for a disease should be sought in the region that was home to the disease. The therapy that soon triumphed, partly under the influence of Paracelsian teaching, was mercury. Mercury salves and ointments, first introduced in the six-teenth century, would become the preferred remedy, giving rise to the catch-phrase "a night with Venus, a lifetime with mercury."

Syphilis, of course, also transformed the sexuality of Europeans as it "settled" into a venereal condition. Sexuality became fraught in previously unimagined ways (des-pite the long-term presence of other venereal maladies such as gonorrhea) and linked not only to "others" – such as "the French," prostitutes, and wanderers – but also to sinfulness. Syphilis was important in cementing the links between sin and disease that had always been around but which now drew tighter. A culture of guilt became a culture of shame.

Of course, we must remember that we have not "told" the disease story of the Renaissance by reviewing the impact of plague and syphilis. If plague and syphilis illustrate best how "new" diseases transformed European ways of thinking about a whole range of issues, other diseases – such as tuberculosis – demonstrated a strong continuity reaching from the Middle Ages through to modern times. Tuberculosis is apparently one of humankind's oldest afflictions: the Egyptians knew it. Still, the demographic impact of tuberculosis and consciousness of it seem modern phenomena, more reminiscent of nineteenth-century Romanticism than Renaissance humanism. Pulmonary tuberculosis was undoubtedly prevalent in Renaissance cities but earned little mention and no concerted response. More than most diseases, consumption appeared to be due to an infirmity of constitution or misaligned humors. Only in its glandular form, as scrofula (which produces swellings of the lymph nodes of the neck), did tuberculosis mark Renaissance society culturally and politically. This impact, however, remained virtually unchanged from the twelfth to the seventeenth century. For some five hundred years, monarchs "touched" for scrofula. Those who possessed the "royal touch" thereby demonstrated their thaumaturgic and sacred powers. The ability of a monarch to "cure" scrofula testified to his legitimacy and, as Marc Bloch pointed out, this legacy of sacred royalty was ancient and persisted well into the early modern period.

Influenza is another very old disease that apparently became epidemic in Europe only toward the end of the fourteenth century; all Europe seemed to have been affected in 1387, for example. Epidemics in the fifteenth and especially in the sixteenth centuries often proved quite lethal. As a medical event, however, influenza has received far less attention than the splashier episodes of plague and syphilis, possibly because observers could easily confuse its symptoms with those of other illnesses. In addition, and despite the virulence of some early modern outbreaks (England in 1557–9), influenza has always been more important as a contributor to European morbidity rather than mortality. Influenza causes many people to fall ill but relatively few to die. Moreover, deaths from influenza generally cluster among the elderly, the malnourished, the very young, or the already ill and it has thus not received as much attention as diseases – such as plague – that abruptly deprived society of its young, strong, and productive members.

Scholars once frequently identified influenza as the mysterious "sweating sickness" or "English sweat" that first appeared in Renaissance England in 1485–6. It then returned to England, and appeared elsewhere (including Hungary), at the beginning of the sixteenth century. Epidemiologists and medical historians today are convinced that this was not in fact a particularly vicious manifestation of influenza but perhaps a totally new virus that killed so effectively that it rapidly sucked dry the pool of susceptibles. These types of diseases were wild cards, but the names they bore – the English or Hungarian sweat – testify to the deepening conviction that killing diseases were imported ones.

Epidemics are flashy. They evoke horror and dread. Still, as the Renaissance ordeal with plague has demonstrated, the impact of epidemics relies on repeated encounters with the disease and not merely on one event, no matter how horrifying. A series of far more "common" diseases and afflictions always blighted people's existences and shaped their view of the world they inhabited and their perceptions of when and how they would sicken and die. Infant mortality was always high and parents anticipated that many of their offspring would never reach adulthood. Yet the mass of documentation we possess on epidemics has skewed our perceptions of the impact of disease even more than this slaughter of innocents. The list of diseases that Renaissance people suffered ran long; many could be completely incapacitating, while some were merely irritating. Running sores (ulcerated varicose veins), skin infections (like the "itch"), tumors and cancers, gout and other nutritionally related ailments (such as rachitis, scurvy, and ergotism), fractured and poorly-healed limbs, cataracts and other eye afflictions, troubled the lives of millions but we know little about them. It is also instructive to recall that a meaningful difference exists between "being sick" and "falling sick." In the Renaissance, as throughout early modern times, the odds on falling sick were high. Sicknesses were often acute, so that death followed swiftly if the person did not recover. Thus the time spent "being sick" was probably not as long as we generally assume.[19]

Finally, we must also consider how people felt about illness and what they believed could be done to cure them, blunt their pain, and soothe their discomfort. Frequently, historians have argued that Renaissance people endured intermittent or constant pain stoically or fatalistically. Certainly, the evidence of wills and bequests, like the numbers of fraternal organizations dedicated to burials and perpetual masses, suggest that Renaissance people always kept at least one ear cocked for the flutter of death's wings. Yet they did not sit still.

Few people accepted Providence's verdict without trying to plea-bargain by seeking assistance, whether medical, pastoral, or magical. Most medical care began at home and women played an important role, not only in home-nursing, but also in the concoction and administration of medicines. If home remedies failed, people quickly reached outward, first trying friends and neighbors, before striking out into the medical marketplace. The time and money they spent seeking cures from a wide variety of practitioners and sources, and the flood of writing about preventives and treatments that circulated at least one level below that of a highly educated academic elite, however, indicate that health was not a matter of indifference to most. In short, when faced with illness and affliction, early modern people were assiduous in seeking to alleviate it and while what one did when one fell ill always depended to a degree on individual inclinations, much was tried to restore the health of self, friends, and family.

Hunger

One of the most persistent images of early modern times is a Malthusian one that spins people about in a maelstrom between the Scylla of overpopulation and the Charybdis of famine. In Thomas Malthus's grim vision of a world where population growth inevitably outstripped food supplies, famine and pestilence were positive checks that re-established demographic equilibrium. Until something interrupted the Malthusian grind, Europeans were doomed to endure an endless cycle of demographic booms and busts. This rather crude Malthusian model – and more subtle variations – has persisted long after historians have demolished most of its premises probably because the correlation between hunger and disease seems so commonsensical; "first famine then fever." Renaissance eyewitnesses reflexively coupled famine and disease, as the Florentine physician Antonio Benevieni made clear in his comments on the 1496 eruption of syphilis:

almost all Italy was stricken with such widespread and enormous hunger that everywhere many people died in the streets and public squares, and many others fell prey to various diseases as a result of having consumed bad and unhealthy food.[20]

In fact, the links between nutrition and disease are by no means simple or direct.

Famine was a severe problem in both northern and southern Europe in 1346–7 directly before the plague. The Frenchman Simon de Couvin was quick to note that "the one who was poorly nourished...fell victim to the merest breath of the disease." Others believed that famine emptied a body which then drew in the "stinking commixed vapors of the air."[21] The major famine of 1314–17, known as "the great hunger," however, did not precede a pestilence. For Italy, the Malthusian pressures on food supply were already extremely high in the pre-plague period. The general consensus that has now emerged among scholars, therefore, is that famine does not "cause" or necessarily precede plague and that the connections between disease and malnutrition are far more intricate than the easy formulation of "first famine then fever" allows. Indeed, malnutrition may protect against plague as the bacillus requires an iron-sufficient environment in which to grow. In conclusion, then, we must accept pestilences and plagues as exogenous elements, and disease "as an autonomous influence on population growth."[22] No clear synergistic relationship existed between famine and pestilence.

More recently, however, demographers have framed another interpretation that portrays connections between famine and epidemic disease in a more complex and subtle manner. John D. Post argued, for example, that "epidemics were promoted chiefly by the altered social matrix engendered by famine conditions."[23] Climactic disasters (flood or drought, for example) caused harvest failures that quickly and dramatically elevated the price of grain, drove people off the land, and forced them to roam, to steal, and to beg; in short, they created social disorder. This situation bred other negative social conditions – overcrowding in poorly ventilated and constructed housing, for example – that facilitated the spread of disease. Thus, the "critical link was not a biological...but rather a social structural one which determined how the impact of food shortage would be distributed."[24] Short-term and localized famines could result from wartime pilfering and destruction. These incidents, too, were particularly frequent in the military jostling common in Renaissance Europe, if obviously more disruptive and pronounced in some places than others. (See the essay by Thomas Arnold below.)

Famine, of course, was not a chimera, although it never affected population size or demographic growth with the catastrophic force that plague did. Hunger and the fear of hunger were persistent features of all premodern societies. Subsistence crises were regular demographic, social, and psychological events in western Europe at least through 1740s. Famine in the countryside drove starvelings into the cities, and when famine and plague coincided – as they often did in northern Italy, for example, between 1385 and 1393 – responses included bureaucratic measures to deal with the poor, such as organizing distributions of grain and alms and endowing charitable fraternities. Yet such repeated incidents also indurated attitudes toward the needy and the homeless. Dirty, withered, disgusting, smelly, and now perceived as diseased as well, migrants reinforced the tendency to see cleanliness and continence (societal and personal) as ways to avoid sickness and as emblems of health. Poor relief became an

integral and unquestioned part of plague prophylaxis. In 1596 the Hamburg physician, Johannes Böckel, warned against beggars who "carried the plague seed with
them" and passed it to those who "with good will" took them into their homes. He
also cautioned against "begging Jews." By the early eighteenth century, city fathers in
Hamburg – and not only there, of course – were convinced that they had "learned
from experience . . . that such contagions spring from the poor and are spread by
wandering rabble."

Famine was all too common, especially in the countryside. In the fourteenth
century, for instance, in 1314–17 a massive famine ravaged all Europe; in 1347,
after a series of fat years, there was famine in Italy, in the Lyonnais, and in Aquitaine;
in 1372–4, the areas that suffered in 1347 were hit again, but so, too, were the Levant
and north Africa; in 1383, southern Europe, and especially Italy, France, and Spain,
starved once more. The fifteenth century supplied little relief. All of eastern Europe
suffered in 1424; then from 1438 to 1441, a general famine spared almost no part of
western Europe. The end of the century was marked by repetitions of dearth that
struck especially hard in the Mediterranean lands.[25] In these years one in every six
harvests was failed. One need not multiply numbers and incidents endlessly to
demonstrate that food shortages, famine, and even starvation were common experiences for all Renaissance people whether they themselves hungered or not. Those
who did not encounter want personally, nevertheless knew its effects: hordes of the
poor and famished crowded highways and filed into cities clamoring vociferously for
what succor could be found.

The direct impact of famine in cities was becoming seldom and muted. A siege
might induce famine, but in times of peace, cities were far better provisioned than
rural areas. Already perceptible was the urban/rural split that separated the cultured
city from the rude hinterlands. Such divisions involved ideas of plenty and want, as
well as differences in how people dressed, worked, and lived. Food – surfeit and
shortage – fed the Renaissance imagination. The Rabelaisian grotesque vision was
intimately tied to food and "gargantuan" meant not only "giant" but also "big
meal." Images of skinny Lent and fat Carnival were so obviously food-related that it
seems superfluous to mention them. Happiness was fullness and dreams were made of
bread. Even Paradise was gustatory. Giacomino da Verona's dream of a "heavenly
Jerusalem" was a delight to the nose, the eyes, the ears, and the palate.[26] The earthier
Land of Cockaigne in less elevated literature also abounded in food. Here, hunger
was not merely banished; it was indulged. One ate until the buttons popped. Harvest-
time was rich with fat and meat; early spring, lean with bitter herbs, shriveled roots,
and little else. The seasons themselves became metaphors for plenty and dearth,
comfort and hardship.

If the harsher, more straitened times of the thirteenth and fourteenth centuries
produced natural and man-made famines, they also stimulated the spread of voluntary
hunger: fasting. According to Caroline Bynum, "[t]o repress eating and hunger was
to control the body in a discipline far more basic than any achieved by shedding the
less frequent and essential gratifications of sex and money." Fasting became a central
component of religious piety and one that showed a strong gender identity; fasting
was more important to women saints – such as Catherine of Siena (d. 1380) and
Catherine of Genoa (d. 1510) – than to men because for them "flesh was suffering
and fertility." If food was the token of bliss for the many, the withholding of food

facilitated religious transcendence for the few.[27] Denying the body food – albeit on a more moderate scale – could also be wholesome. Luigi Cornaro and Sanctorius Sanctorius (early investigators of metabolic processes) believed that strictly restricting what one ate was the golden road to a long life.

If famine and subsistence crises were by no means banished during the Renaissance, at least mechanisms came into place to alleviate local needs. Better forms of transportation and bureaucratic procedures to ensure steady bread prices and ship emergency provisions assuaged the sharpness of a crisis, even if they rarely stopped one. Hunger did not perish during the Renaissance, of course, although the opening of the Atlantic began the long process that contributed to ending the cycle of European subsistence crises. The trade between the Old World and the New was already funneling massive wealth into the continent. New World plants would later substantially enlarge food stores for both animals and humans. Renaissance exploration prompted the agricultural revolution that would, eventually, profoundly affect European food supplies and European tastes as well as European life spans.

The traditional view of the Renaissance as representing a "rebirth of learning" or a "rupture" with the medieval world has been challenged, revised, and to some extent refuted. In terms of human biology – plague, disease, and hunger – the Renaissance, however, was a time of profoundly new experiences. Episodes of pestilence conditioned how Europeans "handled" disease, and especially epidemic disease, in the future: administratively, medically, and ideologically. Of course, many of the older causes of mortality common since antiquity – infantile diarrheas, tuberculosis, smallpox, and vaguely defined yet often deadly "fevers" – persisted throughout the Middle Ages, the Renaissance, and far into the more modern world. These were always notable killers, even during epidemic times. Hunger was a chronic problem. Little happened in these centuries to improve European nutrition and food supplies. While contact with the New World, for example, would eventually transform both dramatically, those improvements lay in the future and for the next two hundred years cycles of feast and famine would continue.

NOTES

1   Hecker, *Black Death*, p. 1.
2   Quoted in Bowsky, *Black Death*, pp. 13–14.
3   Quoted in Horrox, *Black Death*, p. 17.
4   Hohenberg and Lees, *Urban Europe*, p. 74.
5   Carmichael, *Plague*, pp. 14–18.
6   Herlihy, *Black Death*, p. 30.
7   McNeill, *Plagues*, ch. 4.
8   Quoted in Horrox, *Black Death*, p. 15.
9   Ibid., p. 111.
10 Quoted in Wilson, *Plague*, p. 5.
11 Slack, *Impact*, pp. 28–9.
12 Quoted in Horrox, *Black Death*, pp. 207, 221.
13 Carmichael, *Plague*, pp. 108–26.
14 Jütte, *Ärzte*, p. 169.

15 Carmichael, *Plague*, p. 8.
16 Quoted in Arrizabalaga et al., *Great Pox*, pp. 26–7.
17 Quoted in Quétel, *Syphilis*, p. 17.
18 Arrizabalaga et al., *Great Pox*, p. 35.
19 Riley, *Sickness*.
20 Arrizabalaga et al., *Great Pox*, p. 35.
21 Quoted in Herlihy, *Black Death*, p. 32; Slack, *Impact*, p. 28.
22 Appleby, "Nutrition," p. 19.
23 Post, "Nutritional Status," pp. 241–2.
24 Walter and Scofield, "Crisis Mortality," pp. 53–4.
25 Biraben, *Les Hommes*, vol. 1, pp. 147–8.
26 Camporesi, *Incorruptible Flesh*, pp. 242–3.
27 Bynum, *Holy Feast*, pp. 2, 5.

REFERENCES

Appleby, Andrew B, "Nutrition and Disease: The Case of London, 1550–1750," *Journal of Interdisciplinary History* 6 (1975), pp. 1–22.

Arrizabalaga, Jon, Henderson, John, and French, Roger, *The Great Pox: The French Disease in Renaissance Europe* (New Haven: Yale University Press, 1997).

Biraben, Jean Noël, *Les Hommes et la peste en France et dans les pays européens et méditerranéens*, 2 vols. (Paris: Mouton, 1975–6).

Bowsky, William, ed., *The Black Death: A Turning Point in History?* (New York: Holt, Rinehart and Winston, 1971).

Bynum, Caroline Walker, *Holy Feast and Holy Fast: The Religious Significance of Food to Medieval Women* (Berkeley: University of California Press, 1987).

Camporesi, Piero, *The Incorruptible Flesh: Bodily Mutation and Mortification in Religion and Folklore*, trans. Tania Croft-Murray (Cambridge: Cambridge University Press, 1983).

Carmichael, Ann, *Plague and the Poor in Renaissance Florence* (Cambridge: Cambridge University Press, 1986).

Hecker, J. F. C., *The Black Death*, trans. B. G. Babbington (Lawrenceville, KS: Coronado Press, 1972).

Herlihy, David, *The Black Death and the Transformation of the West*, ed. Samuel K. Cohn Jr. (Cambridge, MA: Harvard University Press, 1997).

Hohenberg, Paul M. and Lees, Lynn Hollen, *The Making of Urban Europe, 1000–1950* (Cambridge, MA: Harvard University Press, 1985).

Horrox, Rosemary, ed. and trans., *The Black Death* (Manchester: Manchester University Press, 1994).

Jütte, Robert, *Ärzte, Heiler und Patienten: Medizinischer Alltag in der frühen Neuzeit* (Munich: Artemis and Winkler, 1991).

McNeill, William H., *Plagues and Peoples* (New York: Anchor Books, Doubleday, 1976).

Post, John D., "Nutritional Status and Mortality in Eighteenth-century Europe," in *Hunger in History: Food Shortage, Poverty, and Deprivation*, ed. Lucile F. Newman (Oxford and Cambridge, MA: Blackwell Publishers, 1990), pp. 241–280.

Quétel, Claude, *History of Syphilis*, trans. Judith Braddock and Brian Pike (Baltimore: Johns Hopkins University Press, 1990).

Riley, James C., *Sickness, Recovery and Death: A History and Forecast of Ill Health* (Iowa City: University of Iowa Press, 1989).

Slack, Paul, *The Impact of Plague in Tudor and Stuart England* (Oxford: Clarendon Press, 1985).

Walter, John and Schofield, Roger, "Famine, Disease and Crisis Mortality in Early Modern Society," in *Famine, Disease and the Social Order in Early Modern Society*, ed. John Walter and Roger Schofield (Cambridge: Cambridge University Press, 1989), pp. 1–73.

Wilson, Frank Percy, *The Plague in Shakespeare's London* (Oxford: Clarendon Press, 1927).

FURTHER READING

Calvi, Giulia, *Histories of a Plague Year: The Social and the Imaginary in Baroque Florence* (Berkeley: University of California Press, 1984).

Camporesi, Piero, *Bread of Dreams: Food and Fantasy in Early Modern Europe* (Chicago: University of Chicago Press, 1989).

Dols, Michael, *The Black Death in the Middle East* (Princeton: Princeton University Press, 1977).

Jordan, William C., *The Great Famine: Northern Europe in the Early Fourteenth Century* (Princeton: Princeton University Press, 1996).

Journal of Interdisciplinary History 14 (1983). Special issue, "Hunger and History."

Newman, Lucile F., gen. ed., *Hunger in History: Food Shortage, Poverty, and Deprivation* (Cambridge, MA: Blackwell Publishers, 1990).

Siraisi, Nancy G., *Medieval and Early Renaissance Medicine: An Introduction to Knowledge and Practice* (Chicago: University of Chicago Press, 1990).

CHAPTER TWENTY-FIVE

Renaissance Bogeymen: The Necessary Monsters of the Age

LINDA WOODBRIDGE

Renaissance Europe needed enemies. Maybe every culture defines itself against what it is not. Anyway, Renaissance Europe was preoccupied with an assortment of pariahs or demonized enemies: Jews, Muslims, black Africans, Gypsies, aboriginals, Catholics, vagrants, beggars, accused witches, sodomites, cross-dressing women, the physically deformed. I will call them bogeymen – feared and monstrous beings concocted from an ounce of reality and a gallon of imagination.

Bogeymen uncannily resembled each other. The word "monster" was applied to the handicapped and to cross-dressed women. The charge of "sodomy" was leveled at same-sex lovers, heretics, and witches. Thinking that "thieves' cant" – underground lingo ascribed to vagrants – sounded Jewish, Luther extended his anti-Semitism to vagrants. Witches, like beggars, were often depicted as lame, and similar fears attended both: John Taylor's nurse, he reports in "The Praise, Antiquity, and Commodity of Beggary, Beggars, and Begging," frightened him into behaving by threatening him with abduction by "the beggar." Could the "bogeyman" of nursery imaginings, whose etymology is unknown, be a variant of "beggarman"? Thomas Harman identified vagrants with "outsiders" residing in England: Gypsies, the Irish, the Welsh. Gypsies, vagrants, and Jews were suspected of baby-stealing. Reformation rhetoric stigmatized Catholic clerics as "sturdy beggars" and "vagabonds." When Elizabethans encountered nomadic people in the New World, they identified them with English vagrants. Diverse groups blended together in moments of fear and paranoia because the same anxieties projected onto various groups effaced their differences.

Bogeymen as Outsiders

Many feared groups seemed "foreign." Even paranoids can have real enemies, and some opponents actually *were* outsiders. The French really did invade Venetian territory in 1494. Spain's Armada really did try to invade England in 1588. Islam really was, as Edward Said has argued, a defining other for all of Europe; the Ottoman

Empire invaded Hungary in 1526 and three years later threatened Vienna. Further, texts such as Hakluyt's *Principal Navigations* and Leo Africanus's *A Geographical History of Africa* heightened a sense of Moors' "outsider" status by emphasizing exotic differences and effacing areas of similarity in which Moors were competitors of Christian Europeans.[1]

Some categories of outsidership preceded the Renaissance and transcended boundaries; heretics and witches were enemies of all Christendom. But the emergence of nation-states, the stirrings of a new sense of nationhood throughout Europe, imparted a peculiar flavor to Renaissance "othering." Within Europe, national differences were heightened in what John Hale calls a "cartography of insult," a lexicon of nasty stereotypes: Germans saw Bohemians as heretics, Poles as thieves, the Swiss as boors, Spaniards as pimps, natives of Saxony as drunkards, Florentines as sodomites; the French found the Spanish haughty, the English proud, the Greeks subtle; in *Antipathy between the Spanish and French Peoples*, 1617, the Spaniard Carlos García maintained that these peoples differed not only culturally but physiologically. Eastern Europeans were decidedly outsiders: western Europeans regarded Hungarians as "ferocious people who wore stove-pipe hats and flapped their arms while drinking" and Russians as "slavish, cantankerous drunks".[2]

Though nations defined themselves against foreign nations, many bogeymen were foreigners – or seeming foreigners – residing *within* a nation. In Spain, the fetishizing of "pure blood" led to exclusion of non-Spaniards from public office.[3] French nationalism was fueled by anti-Italian xenophobia, directed at "the many Italian merchants, financiers, and civil servants who held influential and well-remunerated positions in France."[4] Proclamations and orders issued in 1596 and 1601 expelled "Negroes and blackamoors" from England.[5] Early Tudor poor legislation (like much European poverty legislation) provided for expelling beggars from towns and parishes, but from 1597, beggars (now *national* enemies) were deported from England.

One could demonize foreign nationals living within one's borders, or manufacture outsiders artificially: some internal bogeymen were local residents, made to seem foreign. Marranos, Christians of Jewish ancestry, were persecuted as alien crypto-Jews in Spain and Portugal, and in the trial of Queen Elizabeth's physician Roderigo Lopez, his Jewish/Portuguese origins were held against him. Although many Moors had lived in Spain for centuries, after the fall of Granada in 1492 they were forced to convert to Christianity or be expelled; during Philip II's reign Spanish Moors were expelled from what by then amounted to their ancestral home. Amsterdam punished sex between a Christian and a Jew with whipping or even death.[6] Few members of monastic orders were foreign nationals, but the Reformation stigmatized them as minions of a foreign power, the papacy in Rome. Accused witches, often victims of localized village rivalries and suspicions, were denounced as minions of another foreign power, the dominions of Hell. Beggars supposedly spoke virtually a foreign language, thieves' cant. Luther counseled German municipalities to deny poor relief to those not on parish rolls, as if poverty were foisted on parishes by strangers and foreigners. Few European vagrants were real foreigners; most were local or from neighboring towns, thrown out of work by enclosures or depressions in local industries. Many outsiders were insiders branded as foreign. As Richard Helgerson shows, nationhood deals in "a rhetoric of uniformity and wholeness; the unified self of the Englishman or Frenchman, the Italian or German, is founded on the political and cultural unity of the nation to which each belongs."[7] Domestic embarrassments were made to seem foreign.

A sense of beleaguerment by outsiders resulted also from unsettled social hierarchies: social climbers disturbed borders between classes just as "foreigners" troubled borders between nations. In a *crise de classe*, the French nobility, seriously in debt, intermarried with wealthy *roturiers* (non-nobles), creating ambiguity about the class status of offspring; the nobility, many complained, thus "became 'bastardized'." And Claude de Seyssel, a sixteenth-century French official, reported that "every day we see men of the popular estate ascend by degrees, some to nobility and innumerable to the middling estate."[8] Tracking new social mobilities in England, David Palliser notes, "the tiresomely frequent disputes over church pews...occurred because men and women rising in wealth and respect demanded better seats". England's Edward VI expressed dismay at newfangled social mobility ("the grazier, the farmer, the merchant become landed men, and call themselves gentlemen, though they be churls."[9] Norbert Elias sees social climbing, the threat of upstarts bounding up from below, as the engine driving increased refinement of manners, as the elite sought distinction from lower orders. In an upward spiral, aristocrats made refined manners their badge, and middle classes upped the ante by imitating them. Though English sumptuary laws aimed to force people to identify their social class by clothing, many successfully infiltrated a higher class through dressing richly, changing their manners and their accents. As Frank Whigham shows, handbooks of civility were two-edged: aimed at buttressing the position of the elite by "describing" their polite behavior, civility manuals became how-to books for the socially ambitious. Across Europe, restrictions sought to re-erect eroding class barriers. Charles V forbade the granting of nobility to any newcomers; Henri IV of France closed off military service as a route to ennoblement.[10]

Amid worry about class infiltration, the idea of "passing" was born. In Shakespeare's *Titus Andronicus*, a black husband and white wife have a baby so light it can "pass," and the play provokes fear of secret Moors. The heroine of Walter Smith's *Twelve Merry Jests of the Widow Edith* is a vagrant who passes as a wealthy widow. The Spanish *Guzman de Alfarache* suggests that society abounds in criminals, passing for pillars of society, "great rich thieves, such as ride on their foot-cloths of velvet, that hang their houses with hangings of tissue and costly arras, and cover the floors of their chambers with gold and silk."[11] Anticipating 1950s nightmare visions of Communist infiltrators, Edward Hext, an English justice, described the infiltration of decent society by well-dressed beggars: "They have intelligence of all things intended against them," are "present at every assize, sessions, and assembly of justices, and will so clothe themselves for that time as any should deem him to be an honest husbandman; so nothing is spoken, done, or intended to be done but they know it."[12] Even the ubiquitous concern with cuckoldry bespeaks fear of "passing": men suspected that even their children were strangers, *passing* as their own.

Fear of one's territory being invaded by Moors, vagrants, or witches was fantastic. More likely was invasion by people one rung lower on the social ladder than oneself. "Rogue literature" – the *Liber Vagatorum* in Germany, *Guzman de Alfarache* in Spain, Teseo Pini's *Il Libro dei Vagabondi* in Italy – dealt in some seedy specimens of the "bogeyman" class. But Gilbert Walker's *Manifest Detection of Diceplay*, an early English rogue text, features only "respectable" rogues, who have once been genteel:

they were recruited into the dicing underworld after dicing away their fortunes. Here we glimpse economic changes which shifted wealth away from the landed, who were being displaced into a supposed underworld of criminal bogeymen. In another rogue piece, John Awdeley describes "courtesy men" who pass as respectable citizens, "cleanly appareled" and able to "behave [themselves] mannerly" because before losing their fortunes they were "wealthily brought up." Trusted in hostelries because they behave like "right good gentlemen," they slip away early, stealing the sheets. Another group, "cheaters or fingerers," almost undetectable as "idle vagabonds," go about "gorgeously, sometime with waiting men."[13] Renaissance literature abounds in impostors. Masetto da Lamporecchio in Boccaccio's *Decameron* feigns dumbness to take a job in a convent, where the nuns are quite willing to befriend a gardener able to kiss but not to tell (third day, novel one). The well-dressed cutpurse Edgeworth in Ben Jonson's *Bartholomew Fair* passes as a gentleman. Smith's vagrant Widow Edith infiltrates the household of Sir Thomas More, receiving marriage proposals from his wellborn followers.

The well-dressed "rogue" who spoke in refined accents and infiltrated polite society was a fantastic imaginary figure, considering the degraded condition of actual poor folk. Such figures sprang from an othering process, projecting "bad" social climbing onto members of a criminal underworld, to protect the position of "good" social climbers, who as it happens were the authors of such literature. Aleman, author of *Guzman de Alfarache*, rose from humble origins to obtain a university degree and success as an administrator. Johann Grimmelshausen, author of the German picaresque novel *Simplicius Simplicissimus* and of a life of the vagabond woman Courage, rose from penniless musketeer to estate administrator. Walter Smith, author of *Widow Edith*, attained an important office, Sword-Bearer to the Lord Mayor.[14] Rogue literature was not written by rogues. Out of the anxieties of the elite (defending class boundaries) and of the socially ambitious (queasy about their own social bounding) was born the fantastic figure of the "rogue" who infiltrated polite society. (See James Amelang's essay above.)

In *Passing and the Fictions of Identity*, Elaine Ginsberg shows why the prospect of passing – a black person passing for a white, a female for a male, a rogue for a genteel man – so unsettles those with any stake in society: "Passing challenges a number of … assumptions about identities, the first of which is that some identity categories are inherent and unalterable essences."[15] Fear of "passers" makes sense only in a society that lives in fear that traditional boundaries, classifications, and hierarchies will be eroded or penetrated.

Bogeymen as Hybrids

The humanist explanation of poverty – that the poor were to blame for having ruined their fortunes by profligacy – unintentionally effaced social boundaries. It implied that the poor were not a permanent, fixed group but simply those who had slipped out of gentility through moral weakness. This effacement caused logical problems for conceptions of social order like Jean Bodin's in France or Sir Thomas Elyot's in England, which posited God-given social estates, some fit to rule, others to be ruled. The logical contradiction here resembles the period's insistence on God-given heterosexual roles, and its simultaneous definition of sodomy as a potentiality, not an identity; or its essentialist insistence on fixed gender roles, and its simultaneous belief that a woman could physically turn into a man through over-exertion, or a man turn psychologically into a woman by transvestism. In New World contexts, belief in the innate superiority of white Europeans coexisted with fear that white Europeans might "go native" in a land of savages. In each of these cases, insistence on the fixity and divine sanction of boundaries, coexisting with fear of slippage across them, is not as illogical as it looks: fear that a married man turn into a sodomite, a man into a woman, a humanist into a beggar, a European into an Indian, actually *provokes* essentialist pronouncements about the immutability of such boundaries.

Such border-patrolling anxieties generated not only invaders and infiltrators, but also bogeymen who were hybrids. Surveying societies afflicted with insecure borders, anthropologist Mary Douglas argues that border defense produces both pollution beliefs and fear of boundary-defying hybrids. To Douglas, Hebrew dietary proscriptions are attempts to keep categories clear: animals too unclean to eat are those unassignable to a clear category: "any class of creatures...not equipped for the right kind of locomotion in its element...anything in the water which has not fins and scales." Humans can also elude clear categories: "persons in a marginal state," hybrids who live in cracks between categories. Witches, for example, "are the social equivalents of beetles and spiders who live in the cracks of the walls." Joan of Arc, "a peasant at court, a woman in armour, an outsider in the councils of war," was accused as a witch.[16] Jeffrey Cohen argues that physiological monsters "generally...are disturbing hybrids whose externally incoherent bodies resist attempts to include them in any systematic structuration....The monster notoriously appears at times of crisis,"[17] and rapid changes certainly qualify the Renaissance as a time of crisis.

Many Renaissance bogeymen are hybrids. Anti-Semites pictured Jewish men as hermaphrodites who menstruated,[18] and charged Jews with cannibalism, erasing the line between human and beast. Witches too were human/animal hybrids, suckling animal/demon familiars from their own breasts. Vagrants seemed animal-like, sleeping in barns and indulging animal-like sexuality; Harman says "they couch comely together...[like] dog and bitch"; they resemble his cow, "that goeth to bull every moon, with what bull she careth not."[19] Sodomites blurred the boundary between male and female, and were sometimes thought physically hermaphroditic. Londoners were outraged by women's fashion of male attire. Phillip Stubbes foregrounded its hybridity: "Our apparel was given us as a sign distinctive to discern between sex and sex, and therefore one to wear the apparel of another sex, is to participate with the same, and to adulterate the verity of his own kind. Wherefore these women may...be called Hermaphrodita, that is, monsters of both kinds, half women, half men.[20] Stubbes's diction is typical: cross-dressers were routinely labeled "monsters" by furious pamphleteers.

Hybridity became a figure for evil in general. In Spenser's *Faerie Queene*, Una the heroine of holiness possesses a unitary nature, as her name suggests, but the forces of sin, as Duessa's name hints, are double and hybrid. Archimago can become bird, fish, or fox; Error is half woman, half snake; Duessa is part fox, part eagle, part bear. Here members of a specific group stand in for large, amorphous forces of wickedness: Archimago allegorically represents both Catholic priestcraft and evil magic in general; Duessa represents that Whore of Babylon, the Catholic Church, and also duplicity in general; Error represents Catholic pamphleteering in particular and religious error in general. In all three cases, evils afflicting humanity in general are particularized in bogeymen from a specific group – Catholics; and in all three, bogeymen are hybrids.

Bogeymen as Disturbingly Mobile

Many Renaissance bogeymen were conspicuous for their mobility. Legislation lumped vagrants together with time-honored figures of the oral tradition (wandering minstrels, ballad singers, and actors) as suspicious "vagabonds." Any itinerant worker could be caught by Elizabethan vagrancy laws, which cast suspicion on such tradesmen as tinkers and pedlars. France enacted repressive legislation against the *porteballe* (packman) and the *marcelot* (wandering trader), considered tricksters and cheats. Contemporaries suspected (with some justification) not only itinerant pedlars but all traveling merchants of working "on the fringes of the law"; Laurence Fontaine documents constant friction between traveling and sedentary merchants in Germany, France, Italy, and other parts of Europe, the latter accusing the former of smuggling, tax evasion, and general bad citizenship.[21] Gypsies, the quintessential wanderers, were identified with economic migrants. The wandering Jew was a figure of folklore, and Jews, so often expelled from various locales, could hardly help wandering. Witches were feared for flying, and out-of-body travel. Preachers and satirists condemned London women for "gadding" about the streets when good women should stay modestly home. To Barnabe Rich, the good woman was no "gadder about the streets" (*Excellency of Good Women*, 1613); in Thomas Heywood's play *How a Man May Choose a Good Wife from a Bad*, a bad wife "never keep[s] home, but [will] always be a-gadding" (Act I). Italian conduct books exhorted wives to stay strictly at home, while Spanish moralists were exercised about gentlewomen's attendance at theaters, which tended to be rowdy.

Suspicion of mobility generated many bogeymen. Jesuits, traversing Europe to make converts to Catholicism, helped put mobility in bad odor with Protestants. One of the English Reformation's most terrifying bogeymen was the black-garbed Jesuit smuggled into the country and hidden in priest holes. One reason for suspicion of friars – the most demonized of religious orders – was their mobility as itinerant preachers. In the colloquy "Well-to-do Beggars" by the Dutch scholar Erasmus, an innkeeper asks two Franciscan friars, "What kind of men are you, anyway, to wander like this without packhorse, without purse, without servants, without arms, without provisions?", and calls this "a life of vagabonds" (*Colloquies*). Early on, the French antifraternal writer Rutebeuf had identified friars with vagabonds.[22] Even cloistered monks' mobility was denounced: an opening move in the English Reformation was to forbid monks to travel out of monasteries; another was the assault on pilgrimages, which had been central to medieval religion. In England in 1536 and 1538, injunctions were issued against "wandering to pilgrimages." One Reformation ballad linked pilgrims to those other bogeymen, beggars, applying to both the term "gadding,"[23] which was also applied to footloose London women.

Mobility's fearsomeness reflected its novelty. Medieval folk had often been closely bound to land and village; few traveled more than 30 or 40 miles from home in a lifetime. As changing economic and social conditions produced more traveling merchants and more vagrants, long-distance travel became more common. Many, though, still led a settled life. As Peter Laslett has shown, early modern workers seldom commuted: they worked where they lived, a baker living above the bakery with his family and apprentices. In so settled a society, itinerant strangers provoked more unease than in our commuting age. The Venetian chronicler Marino Sanudo wrote of the unease of local people in Venice, accosted by "foreign" beggars, "the poor from Burano, with their scarves wrapped around their heads and their children in their arms, begging for alms. Many also come from as far as Vincenze and Brescia."[24]

More metaphorically, I suggest that anxiety about economic migrants or itinerant preachers and tradesmen – all geographically mobile – projected fear of other forms of change and mobility: religious and intellectual change, social mobility. "Place" meant both social rank and geographic location, and those with no fixed place to live, or who frequently wandered, came to represent cultural dislocations occasioned by the Reformation, economic recessions, educational and technological change, or govern- mental innovations.

The mobile, like hybrids, were sometimes figures of power: literature sometimes idealized beggars. Texts glamorizing vagrants' freedom, like Brome's *A Jovial Crew* and Fletcher and Massinger's *Beggar's Bush*, reveal a fissure in Renaissance attitudes. Should mobility be feared or envied? Travel sparked great excitement in this age of global exploration. Hakluyt's accounts of voyages thrilled English readers. Marlowe's imagination was fired by "huge argosies," and the wealth Spain garnered in America reminded him of Jason's golden fleece (*Dr. Faustus*, Bowers edition, I. i. 131–2). Many writers transmuted real travel into fantastic travelers' tales: Astolfo in Ariosto's *Orlando furioso* travels the world and visits the moon upon a hippogriff; Shakespeare endowed supernatural agents with powers of globetrotting travel: in *A Midsummer Night's Dream* Puck cries, "I'll put a girdle round the earth/ In forty minutes" (II. i. 175–6) and Titania jets between Athens and India; in *The Tempest*, Ariel runs errands to Bermuda (I. ii. 230).[25] But despite all this, the era was edgy about mobility, and anti-travel literature flourished. Travel corrupted the young; it could turn a manly English Protestant into a downright Italian. Roger Ascham had known many who, "parting out of England fervent in the love of Christ's doctrine, and well furnished with the fear of God, returned out of Italy worse transformed, than ever was any in Circe's court" (*The Schoolmaster*). In Nashe's *Unfortunate Traveller*, a banished earl lectures a compatriot on the evils of travel: "What is the occasion of thy straying so far out of England? . . . The first traveler was Cain, and he was called a vagabond runa- gate . . . .God had no greater curse to lay upon the Israelites, than by leading them out of their own country." Sara Warneke traces a common English image of the traveler, "the dissolute Englishman corrupted by the pleasures and temptations freely available on the Continent."[26] In Spain, moralistic writings such as Fray Luis de Leon's *Vida Retirada* condemned the rush to the New World for its materialism and greed. In anxiety about travel, distrust of mobility combined with distrust of foreigners.

Laboring to stabilize slippery ideas about mobility, contemporaries pitted good mobility against bad. Tension between domestic home-keeping ideology and new practices of international trade was eased by distinguishing between good merchants and bad. The former included wealthy international traders and settled city and town shopkeepers, and the latter itinerant salesmen (pedlars, chapmen) and itinerant tradesmen (tinkers, cobblers), who were consigned to the category of vagabond: a particularly clear example of the privileged projecting onto bogeymen qualities they felt uneasy about in themselves. Each group valued mobility for itself but proscribed mobility in the group just below. Well-to-do international traders valued their own freedom of travel, but sought to immobilize "illegitimate" merchants like pedlars or chapmen by supporting legislation defining them as vagrants. The male sex cherished its own right to move freely about London, but enjoined women to stay at home, and criticized them for "gadding."

Bogeymen as Keepers of Secrets

The characteristic bogeymen seized on or manufactured by the Renaissance imagination, then, reflect some of its typical anxieties. Bogeymen who were outsiders or hybrids, I have argued, reflect anxieties of a border-patrolling age, preoccupied with defining and defending national and class borders. Bogeymen who were highly mobile reflect anxieties about travel, social mobility, and other kinds of cultural change. Another commonly imagined attribute of "bogeymen" was their inveterate secretiveness and proclivity for dark and sinister practices. They had something to hide, and were fiendishly clever about hiding it. Jews, having pretended to convert to Christianity, allegedly practiced Jewish rites behind closed doors, from simple religious rituals to the sacrifice of kidnapped Christian children. Gypsies and vagrants skulked about stealing babies. Beggarly "rogues" practiced sexual orgies in secluded barns, hid their healthy bodies under bandages to beg alms more effectively, and conveyed secret messages in thieves' cant. Witches stuck pins into wax images in the secrecy of their dwellings, convened for secret witches' sabbaths in out-of-the-way spots, and performed unspeakable acts with animal familiars and with Satan himself, under cover of darkness. Catholics were suspected of harboring Jesuits in priest holes and moving them from house to house by night. New World aboriginals and black Africans were said to practice barbaric rites – cannibalism, witchcraft, orgies – in the dark forests of mysterious continents. Understanding the cultural preoccupation with exposing secrets takes us into the period's theories of knowledge and its notions of individual subjectivity.

Rogue literature promotes itself as exposé. In *A Caveat for Common Cursetors*, billed as an exposé of rogues' secret practices, Harman italicizes his conviction that *something lurk and lay hid that did not plainly appear* (1567 edn.), alluding to the Latin tag *Aliquod latet quod non patet*. The same tag is cited by Jack Wilton as he unveils his occulted history at the beginning of Nashe's *Unfortunate Traveller*. Another version, *Multa latent quae non patent*, "Many things lie hidden which are not exposed," accompanies a decoding of thieves' cant in Robert Greene's rogue piece, *A Notable Discovery of Cozenage*. The lantern shedding light on dark practices was a controlling image of rogue literature (as in Thomas Dekker's title *Lantern and Candlelight*), but writers in many genres claimed to be smoking out what was hidden. Exploring the period's fascination with bringing secret things to light, Patricia Parker sees a link between "the anatomist's opening and exposing to the eye the secrets or 'privities' of women and the 'discovery' or bringing to light of what were from a Eurocentric perspective previously hidden worlds," in the age of exploration. Their "shared language of opening, uncovering or bringing to light" also characterizes monster literature, to which exploration narratives were related; a 1600 geographical history of Africa contained "a map of Africa folded and closed upon itself, which, when opened up, brings before the reader's gaze the land of monsters, of Amazons, of prodigious sexuality and of peoples who expose those parts which should be hid." Parker relates this cluster of ideas to the age's passion for eye-witness accounts and to the growth of domestic informing and spying: "This shared language of 'discovery' as informing or spying on something hid . . . [gives] many of these exotic histories their affinities with the ocular preoccupations of the growing domestic network of . . . informers and spies, charged with reporting on the secret or hid." Jonathan Sawday notes the many "teasing titles" of works which "hinted at revelation, or access to secret knowledge."[27] John Davies of Hereford wrote of those who "desire to *know*," to "break through the *bound* that *human knowledge* bars,| To pry into His *breast* which doth infold| *Secrets* unknown" (*Microcosmos*, 1603). (See William Eamon's essay above.)

A rhetorical habit was developing, of appeal to direct observation; for example, the Holinshed chroniclers' devotion to eye-witness testimony. But in rogue literature, witchcraft exposés, and travelers' reports of monsters, "empirical" language is little but rhetorical window dressing. The sixteenth century did not distinguish firmly between discovery and invention; indeed, several discourses used the two words interchangeably. Renaissance rogue literature may represent itself as tough-minded investigative reporting, but in fact most of it is plagiarized from earlier rogue literature, suggesting that most of its discoveries were in fact inventions, as was the case with witchcraft and travelers' marvels.

The repeated stripping of Widow Edith, to expose her deceitful social climbing, belongs (like that of Spenser's Duessa) to the same realm as the folktale (re-familiarized in A. S. Byatt's *Possession*) of Melusine, a bride whose clothes conceal a snaky tail of spectacular length. In some versions the husband finally sees Melusine in the bath, her tail touching the ceiling. (One is not supposed to ask what was wrong with his sense of touch in the bedroom; this is a folktale after all.) Edith's nature is only metaphorically snaky, but the old tales often expressed, by naive snaky appendages, something metaphoric and inward. Renaissance interest in the physiologically monstrous can project fear of the monstrous outsider who has become an insider. The Melusine tale, like related tales of the monster bridegroom tale type, expresses newly-wed anxiety: the fear of finding something monstrous in the beloved, an outsider in one's bedroom. Practical reasons were given for stripping beggars and accused witches, but I suspect the practice stemmed ultimately from folk fear of hidden monstrosity. The period's fascination with physical monstrosity gave corporeal form to anxieties that also generated bogeymen figures of less material monstrosity.

The Renaissance penetrated dark recesses of interiors, from human entrails to darkest Africa, from scientific discovery to geographical exploration. The search for knowledge was figured as penetrative, violative, an extraction of secrets by force. The adversarial stance of investigators and knowledge-seekers mirrors the representation of society's enemies as devious secret-keepers. But enemies are in part created as heightened projections of what we fear or loathe in ourselves, and these secret-keeping enemies look like caricatures of everyday individual subjectivity, which must somehow have seemed fearsome.

Whether personalities were growing more individualized has long been debated. The fascination with *prodigies*, one-of-a-kind monsters, might manifest uneasiness over increasingly individualized personalities that could seem antisocial. Certainly some Shakespearean figures awakened suspicion by their individuality. It is the antisocial fratricide Richard III who declares "I have no brother, I am like no brother;| . . . I am myself alone" (*3 Henry VI*, v. vi. 81–4). In the case of Richard (as of other Shakespearean loners, like the villainous Edmund in *King Lear*), suspicion proves justified, and other "bogeyman" stigmata appear: Richard is physically handicapped, and epithets brand him animal-like: boar, toad, spider. To be individual was to be monstrous. But though people are still debating whether or not personalities were growing more individualized and alienated, most agree that personalities were growing more private. (See John Martin's essay above.)

Recent scholars link the period's fascination with dissection, with probing of entrails, to new interiority of personality. Jonathan Sawday documents the rise of cultural institutions of dissection; Michael Neill explores the language of the dissecting theater as it was applied in the *dramatic* theater; tragedy, in the words of Sidney's *Defense of Poesy*, "openeth the greatest wounds, and sheweth forth the ulcers that are covered with tissue." David Hillman argues that owing to "materialist habits of early modern thought," bodily interiority "seems to have been practically inseparable from spiritual inwardness"; he notes that "several of Shakespeare's characters seem to imagine that penetrating the other's body [will] somehow solve the riddle of knowing the other." Katharine Eisaman Maus maintains that in "sixteenth- and early seventeenth-century speech and writing, the whole interior of the body – heart, liver, womb, bowels, kidneys, gall, blood, lymph – quite often involves itself in the production of the mental interior, of the individual's private experience."[28] As geographic wandering can be a material embodiment of social mobility, so material entrails can stand in for an interiorized sense of self. The Renaissance, when witch persecution climaxed, when empiricism was born and the New World explored, when rogue exposés had a literary vogue, and writers rejoiced in a rhetoric of bringing dark things to light, was also an age of a new interiority. Puritans saw God by their own inner light; diary-keeping flourished; houses began evolving private rooms; private, silent reading began to replace more gregarious reading aloud. People had secret inner selves to protect, as never before. And if they cherished this inwardness in themselves, they feared it in others. It was all very well to love thy neighbor, but what secrets was thy neighbor harboring? Was this neighbor a witch? Did that neighbor practice sodomy in the dark, or lock himself in the bowels of the house to utter Jewish prayers? Was this neighbor a social upstart, masking lowly origins behind a fancy farthingale? Did that wife meet secret lovers in a garden house?

Eavesdropping was a major literary motif. The Spanish drama has a rich tradition of the *mirón*, a peeping tom cum eavesdropper. Authors imagined spying on "gadding" bogeywomen: the Scottish William Dunbar positions himself as an eavesdropper on women's conversation in *The Two Married Women and the Widow*. In England, Samuel Rowlands's *'Tis Merry When Gossips Meet* is prefaced by a conversation wherein a bookseller's apprentice makes a sale of *'Tis Merry* by advertising it as a chance for male readers to eavesdrop on women's conversation. A host of male authors created scenes in which sequestered groups of women (who often have been out gadding and have met at a tavern) chat privately about their latest lovers or their husbands' sexual inadequacies. In Shakespeare, Beatrice and Benedick in *Much Ado About Nothing* are brought together when their friends deliberately stage eavesdroppings; Malvolio in *Twelfth Night* is humiliated by a similar manipulation. Iago encourages Othello to smoke out sexual infidelity by spying on his wife.

Perhaps the phenomenon of *passing* – a Moor passing for white, a vagrant for a respectable woman – interested the Renaissance because to some degree, nearly *everybody* was passing, preparing a face to meet the faces that they met; protecting a newly privatized heart. A suspicion was abroad in the land that nobody really knew his neighbor, that any seeming insider might prove to be an outsider.

The ubiquity of investigation, spying, surveillance in Renaissance culture raises a chicken and egg question about subjectivity and interiority. Though Foucault argues that surveillance causes publicly-sponsored values to become internalized, transforming public shame to private guilt, it is equally possible that the heart's increasingly private, guarded condition created or fostered the urge to investigate, to spy, and so created a culture of surveillance. The sixteenth century was preoccupied with imposture and with infiltration. Impostors were potentially everywhere; you couldn't be sure who anyone was. Was your neighbor a witch, a rogue/confidence man, a light-skinned Moor, or at the very least a social climber who had covered her tracks well? Rogues and confidence men had infiltrated polite society, cony-catching pamphleteers claimed to have infiltrated the rogue underworld to expose its practices. The proto-scientific urge to probe nature's secrets, to expose principles of magnetism or blood circulation, was akin to the urge to probe other people's secrets, to expose truths and practices underlying genteel clothes and refined accents. Was it the nosiness of the age, its mistrust of surfaces, that gave rise to a particular closeted heart? Or did the closeting provoke the nosiness? Or were nosiness and closeting mutually constitutive?

With regard to secret sexual practices, the demonizing of bogeymen could help clarify the messy borders left by changing notions of what should be public and what private. The impulse to pry into and spy upon sexual practices of rogues and vagabonds or of newly-discovered nomads is colored by a newly private sexuality. Where once servants had shared bedchambers with masters, house design now encouraged more private sexuality. Noting that the influential architect Alberti recommended separate bedrooms for husband and wife with a connecting door "to enable them to seek each other's company unnoticed," Mark Wigley sees domestic architecture as "the agent of a new kind of modesty" which "played an active part in the constitution of the private subject."[29] It is against a newly private sexuality that we should view charges that vagrants' sexuality was animal-like in its publicness. And insofar as prurience thrives on inhibition, the impulse to expose the sexual practices of others, whether vagrants or New World natives, was in part an artifact of the new, inhibiting imperatives to keep one's own sexual activity hidden. Again, closeting and nosiness were mutually constitutive: closeting of one's own sexual practices, nosiness about the practices of others.

Natives of exotic lands, and vagrants at home, were said to observe no sexual privacy. Depicting "the land of Negroes," Leo Africanus describes (or fantasizes) a "brutish and savage life"; come nightfall, black Africans "resorted ten or twelve both men and women into one cottage together, using hairy skins instead of beds, and each man choosing his leman which he had most fancy unto." In a similar fantasy of rogue life, Harman pictures vagrants bedding down in a barn; a typical vagrant woman, in a parody of domestic bustling, "shuffles up a quantity of straw or hay into some pretty corner of the barn . . . and well shaketh the same, making the head somewhat high, and drives the same upon the sides and feet like a bed: then she layeth her wallet, or some other little pack of rags or scrip under her head in the straw, to bear up the same, and layeth her petticoat or cloak upon and over the straw, so made like a bed, and that serveth for the blanket. Then she layeth her slate (which is her sheet) upon that. And she have no sheet, . . . she spreadeth some large clouts or rags over the same, and . . . layeth her drowsily down." But once settled, she becomes the sexual prey of a bullying alpha rogue and then (like the leftovers of a sordid meal) is enjoyed by rank-and-file rogues: "The rogue hath his leavings."[30] Vagrant women are envisioned as a public sexual utility for men on the road, and Harman renders their sex life the more public by printing his account. But insistence that decent sexuality was to be strictly private was in fact rather new in Harman's time, and demonizing those who didn't observe the privacy rules was part of the process Norbert Elias describes, by which higher classes differentiated themselves from lower by increasing refinement of manners.

Because the private/public boundary was being renegotiated, bogeymen got blamed for behavior that was too secret and private, and for behavior not secret or private enough. Eve Kosofsky Sedgwick writes of a similar situation involving a *modern* figure with a hidden life: the closeted homosexual. One court upheld the firing of a teacher for discussing his homosexuality on television, "on the grounds that he had failed to note on his original employment application that he had been, in college, an officer of a student homophile organization – a notation that would, as school officials admitted in court, have prevented his ever being hired." Paradoxically, "the rationale for keeping [the teacher] out of his classroom was . . . no longer that he had disclosed too much about his homosexuality, but . . . that he had not disclosed enough." While the closeted homosexual did not exist in his modern form in the Renaissance, what Sedgwick calls "an excruciating system of double binds"[31] is highly visible in Renaissance anxieties about sexuality in general, anxieties projected onto "outsiders" such as aboriginal peoples and vagrants, whose lives were paradoxically condemned as both disgracefully public and suspiciously secretive. The ambiguity of public sex within a cottage or barn reflects this contradictory thinking: vagrant and aboriginal sexuality seemed shockingly public because in European polite society, sex was becoming more private; but the concealing of this group sex enacts the stereotype of devious, secretive vagrants and aboriginals. Stigmatizing these devious deviants, Renaissance writers worked through changes in their own culture, projecting "bad" publicness or privateness onto bogeymen.

Bogeymen were also condemned for both deceptive clothing and nakedness. Accused witches were strip-searched for demonic tokens such as extra teats; vagrants were stripped to increase the pain of whipping and to expose feigned disability. Widow Edith often uses a good dress, obtained through trickery, to impersonate higher social class. When her cheats are exposed, she is stripped to her petticoat and sent packing. Since Edith never feigns disability, her frequent stripping as a method of "outing" her as a vagrant seems a symbolic disclosure of deceit. But contemporaries who worried about deceptive clothing were also scandalized by nakedness: in an age concerned about modesty, beggars wore rags through which their nakedness peaked. Like their "public" sexuality, sartorial immodesty marked them as alien, just as the nakedness of many aboriginal people coded them savage.

Both being clothed and being naked could be offensive, too private or too public – an "excruciating double bind" indeed.

The era was fascinated by that French cause célèbre, the trial of an impostor who for years impersonated Martin Guerre. Combining mobility with imposture, a wanderer infiltrated a village, stole a man's identity, and succeeded in "passing," even with Guerre's wife. The language surrounding the case was redolent of wondrous New World monstrosities, "brought to light" by investigative travel literature. The 1561 account by the trial judge, Jean de Coras, was billed as *une histoire prodigieuse*, "a prodigious history." As Natalie Zemon Davis notes, "very much in the air these days were collections of 'prodigies' – of wondrous plants and animals, of double suns and monstrous births,"[32] and an impostor husband was in the category of the monstrous. Figures like sea monsters, two-headed calves, and sexually-rampant rogues and nomads were really outsize caricatures projecting some everyday fears: fear of mobility and social change; fear that people you think you know are hiding something terrible. The possibility of hidden monstrosity below a normal skin haunted the age, from Spenser's Duessa hiding bestial body parts under fine clothes to Shakespeare's Othello's suspicion of monstrous sexuality under his wife's devotion and finding monstrous lies under his friend's "honesty." No wonder Othello cries "O monstrous! monstrous!" (III. iii. 442). The dark side of cherishing the new privacies of one's own bosom was the fear of finding a monster impostor in somebody else's.

Bogeymen are the stuff of nightmare, and in Renaissance fear of monstrous births, of witches flying, of cannibal Jews, of skulking vagrants, of evil Catholics creeping out of priest holes after dark, speak the evil dreams of an age. The bogeymen who haunted the Renaissance unconscious illuminate the doubts and anxieties of Renaissance consciousness. O monstrous! Monstrous!

NOTES

I am grateful to my colleagues Mary Barnard-Quinones, Laura Giannetti, and Gerhard Strasser for helping to remedy this English professor's deficiencies in knowledge of Spanish, Italian, and German cultural developments. I am also grateful for permission to reprint portions of this essay which have appeared in my book *Vagrancy and Homelessness in English Renaissance Literature* and in my essay "Nomads Meet Vagrants: Elizabethan Anxieties about Mobility and Hidden Realities, at Home and Abroad."

1   See Bartels, "Making More."
2   Hale, *Civilization of Europe*, p. 61.
3   Sicroff, *Les Controverses*, p. 21; see also García, *Ideas*.
4   Marcus, *Nationalism*, p. 60.
5   Hughes and Larkin, *Tudor Proclamations* III, pp. 221–2.
6   Spierenburg, *Spectacle*, p. 170.
7   Helgerson, *Forms of Nationhood*, p. 22.
8   Bitton, *French Nobility*, pp. 1–2, 92–3; Seyssel, *Monarchy of France*, pp. 62–3.
9   Palliser, *Age of Elizabeth*, pp. 83–4.
10 Dewald, *European Nobility*, pp. 21–2. See also Whigham, *Ambition and Privilege*.
11 Aleman, *Guzman*, vol. 3, pp. 338–42.

12 Tawney and Power, *Tudor Documents*, vol. 2, p. 345. Of beggars' alleged ability to feign poverty and disability on the one hand and gentility on the other, William Carroll notes, "There seems little, in these accounts, that such beggars cannot do: they can forge official documents, feign disease and mutilation . . . even 'play' the role of middle-class citizen. . . . Rarely has any culture fashioned so wily and powerful an enemy out of such degraded and pathetic materials" (*Fat King*, p. 47).

13 Awdeley, "Vacabondes," pp. 1–16.

14 Ward, *Early Tudor Drama*, p. 154.

15 Ginsberg, *Fictions of Identity*, p. 4.

16 Douglas, *Purity and Danger*, pp. 55, 95, 102, 103. The ambivalence of responses to Joan of Arc – national hero or witch? – is a common feature of responses to hybridity. As Douglas writes (drawing on Van Gennep) of initiates in transition to adulthood, "danger lies in transitional states. . . . To go out of the formal structure and to enter the margins is to be exposed to power that is enough to kill them or to make their manhood" (*Purity and Danger*, p. 96). Just as category transitions like initiation involve both danger and power, in some Renaissance contexts hybridity can be a positive good. Peter Stallybrass and Allon White write of festive "hybridization" as well as inversion within topsy-turvy festive traditions such as the Lord of Misrule and festive seasons such as the twelve days of Christmas. Other positively inflected hybrids of the period include symbolic hermaphrodites; Robin Hood (outlawed aristocrat identifying with the poor); the *puer senex* trope, the trope of the *renouveau*, an old man turned young. Hybridity characterized some of the period's heroes, as well as some of its bogeymen, and indeed culture heroes as a rule have much in common with bogeymen – but that is matter for another essay.

17 Cohen, "Monster Culture," p. 6.

18 Shapiro, *Shakespeare*, pp. 37–8.

19 Harman, *Caveat*, pp. 70, 99.

20 Stubbes, *Anatomy*, Sig. [F5] – F5]ᵛ.

21 Fontaine, *Pedlars*, pp. 1, 32.

22 Szittya, *Antifraternal Tradition*, p. 185.

23 Duffy, *Stripping of the Altars*, pp. 398–409 and 408–9.

24 Geremek, *Poverty*, p. 132.

25 All Shakespeare references are to Bevington's *Complete Works*, 4th edn.

26 Warneke, *Educational Traveller*, p. 191.

27 Parker, *Shakespeare from the Margins*, pp. 240–1; Sawday, *Body Emblazoned*, p. 143.

28 Hillman, "Visceral Knowledge," p. 82; Maus, *Inwardness*, p. 195.

29 Wigley, "Untitled," p. 345.

30 Harman, *Caveat*, p. 108.

31 Sedgwick, *Epistemology*, pp. 69, 70.

32 Davis, *Martin Guerre*, pp. 105–6. The changing meanings of the word "prodigy" itself track the shift in sensibility; meaning "omen, portent" from medieval times onward, the word came by the late sixteenth century to denote a person regarded as a monster (Richard III is called a "crook-backed prodigy" in *3 Henry VI*, ca. 1594 (I. iv. 75)); not until the mid-seventeenth century, in English, did "prodigy" acquire its laudatory, modern sense of precocious genius (OED).

REFERENCES

Aleman, Matheo, *The Rogue: or the Life of Guzman de Alfarache* [1623], trans. James Mabbe (London: Constable, 1924).

Awdeley, John, "Fraternity of Vacabondes, Harman's Caveat, Haben's Serman," etc., ed. Edward Viles and F. J. Furnivall (London: Early English Text Society, 1869).

Bartels, Emily C., "Making More of the Moor: Aaron, Othello, and Renaissance Refashionings of Race," *Shakespeare Quarterly* 41 (1990), pp. 433–54.

Bitton, Davis, *The French Nobility in Crisis 1560–1640* (Stanford: Stanford University Press, 1969).

Carroll, William C., *Fat King, Lean Beggar: Representations of Poverty in the Age of Shakespeare* (Ithaca, NY: Cornell University Press, 1996).

Cohen, Jeffrey Jerome, "Monster Culture (Seven Theses)," in *Monster Theory: Reading Culture*, ed. Jeffrey Jerome Cohen (Minneapolis: University of Minnesota Press, 1996).

Davis, Natalie Zemon, *The Return of Martin Guerre* (Cambridge, MA: Harvard University Press, 1983).

Dewald, Jonathan, *The European Nobility, 1400–1800* (Cambridge: Cambridge University Press, 1996).

Douglas, Mary, *Purity and Danger: An Analysis of the Concepts of Pollution and Taboo* (London: Routledge, 1966).

Duffy, Eamon, *The Stripping of the Altars: Traditional Religion in England 1400–1580* (New Haven: Yale University Press, 1992).

Elias, Norbert, *The Civilizing Process*, trans. Edmund Jephcott (New York: Urizen, 1978).

Fontaine, Laurence, *A History of Pedlars in Europe*, trans. Vicki Whittaker (Durham, NC: Duke University Press, 1996).

García, Miguel Herrero, *Ideas de los Españoles del Siglo XVIII* (Madrid: Editorial Gredos, 1966).

Geremek, Bronislaw, *Poverty: A History*, trans. Agnieszka Kolakowska (Oxford: Blackwell Publishers, 1994).

Ginsberg, Elaine K., ed., *Passing and the Fictions of Identity* (Durham, NC: Duke University Press, 1996).

Hale, John, *The Civilization of Europe in the Renaissance* (New York: Simon and Schuster, 1995).

Harman, Thomas, *A Caveat for Common Cursetors, Vulgarly called Vagabonds* [1567], in *The Elizabethan Underworld*, ed. A. V. Judges (New York: Octagon, 1964), pp. 61–118.

Helgerson, Richard, *Forms of Nationhood: The Elizabethan Writing of England* (Chicago: University of Chicago Press, 1992).

Hillman, David, "Visceral Knowledge: Shakespeare, Skepticism, and the Interior of the Early Modern Body," in *The Body in Parts: Fantasies of Corporeality in Early Modern Europe*, ed. David Hillman and Carla Mazzio (New York: Routledge, 1997), pp. 81–105.

Hughes, Paul L. and Larkin, James F., eds., *Tudor Royal Proclamations*, 3 vols. (New Haven: Yale University Press, 1964–9).

Laslett, Peter, *The World We Have Lost* (New York: Scribner, 1965).

Macfarlane, Alan, "A Tudor Anthropologist: George Gifford's *Discourse and Dialogue*," in *The Damned Art: Essays in the Literature of Witchcraft*, ed. Sydney Anglo (London: Routledge and Kegan Paul, 1977), pp. 140–55.

Marcus, E. D., *Sixteenth Century Nationalism* (New York: Abaris, 1976).

Maus, Katharine Eisaman, *Inwardness and Theater in the English Renaissance* (Chicago: University of Chicago Press, 1995).

Neill, Michael, *Issues of Death: Mortality and Identity in English Renaissance Tragedy* (Oxford: Clarendon Press, 1997).

Palliser, David M., *The Age of Elizabeth: England under the Later Tudors, 1547–1603* (London: Longman, 1983).

Parker, Patricia, *Shakespeare from the Margins: Language, Culture, Context* (Chicago: University of Chicago Press, 1996).

Sawday, Jonathan, *The Body Emblazoned: Dissection and the Human Body in Renaissance Culture* (London: Routledge, 1995).

Sedgwick, Eve Kosofsky, *Epistemology of the Closet* (Berkeley: University of California Press, 1990).

Seyssel, Claude de, *The Monarchy of France*, trans. J. H. Hexter, ed. Donald R. Kelley (New Haven: Yale University Press, 1981).

Shapiro, James S., *Shakespeare and the Jews* (New York: Columbia University Press, 1996).

Sicroff, A. S., *Les Controverses des Statuts de "Pureté de Sang" en Espagne du XVe au XVIIe siècle* (Paris: Études de Littérature Étrangère et Comparée, 1960).

Spierenburg, Pieter, *The Spectacle of Suffering: Executions and the Evolution of Repression: From a Preindustrial Metropolis to the European Experience* (Cambridge: Cambridge University Press, 1984).

Stallybrass, Peter, and White, Allon, *The Politics and Poetics of Transgression* (Ithaca, NY: Cornell University Press, 1986).

Stubbes, Philip, *The Anatomy of Abuses* (London, 1583).

Szittya, Penn R., *The Antifraternal Tradition in Medieval Literature* (Princeton: Princeton University Press, 1986).

Tawney, R. H. and Power, Eileen, eds., *Tudor Economic Documents*, 3 vols. (London: Longman Green, 1963).

Ward, A. W., *Early Tudor Drama: Medwall, the Rastells, Heywood, and the More Circle* (London: Methuen, 1926).

Warneke, Sara, *Images of the Educational Traveller in Early Modern England* (Leiden: E. J. Brill, 1995).

Whigham, Frank, *Ambition and Privilege: The Social Tropes of Elizabethan Courtesy Theory* (Berkeley: University of California Press, 1984).

Wigley, Mark, "Untitled: The Housing of Gender," in *Sexuality and Space*, ed. Beatriz Colomina (Princeton: Princeton University School of Architecture, 1992), pp. 327–89.

Woodbridge, Linda, *Vagrancy and Homelessness in English Renaissance Literature* (Urbana: University of Illinois Press, 2001).

——, "Nomads Meet Vagrants: Elizabethan Anxieties about Mobility and Hidden Realities, at Home and Abroad," in *Making Contact*, ed. Lesley Cormack and Glenn Burger (Edmonton: University of Alberta Press, forthcoming).

CHAPTER TWENTY-SIX

Violence and Warfare in the Renaissance World

THOMAS F. ARNOLD

The author of this essay has little personal experience of violence, and none of war. It can be safely assumed that the western, middle-class, university-educated editors and readers of this piece share that lack of experience. We are sheltered, and we feel lucky to be so sheltered: we have been taught to despise personal violence, and we only reluctantly – if at all – respect the possibility of state-sanctioned political violence – that is, war – in very particular circumstances and with great regret. Our society, our civilization, is deeply irenic and even pacifistic. As a result, those of us who write and read history, with a very few exceptions, only really know about violence and war from afar: these are things that happen to other people in other places, in Brixton and the Bronx, Chechnya and the Congo. There are consequences of this distance and distaste: we assume, above all, that violence and warfare are social pathologies, and we associate both with the ill-educated and with the socially and politically disadvantaged. War and violence are problems for poor people, and poor places.

Such assumptions, based on our own world, can make it very difficult to understand the place of violence and warfare in the world of the Renaissance. First of all, our humane prejudices have led to scholarly neglect. Violence in its purest social sense has received some attention, beginning with a 1972 volume of essays edited by Lauro Martines and based on a May, 1969 academic conference that exactly coincided with current headlines and editorial hand-wringing over civil riot and escalating crime rates.[1] Suddenly, violence seemed an obvious historical theme. Since then, Guido Ruggiero, Edward Muir, and Robert Davis, among others, have ably continued this research and publication possibility.[2] But the closely related subject of warfare in the Renaissance has achieved almost no attention, especially if British university faculty are omitted, the most outstanding of whom are Michael Mallett and the late John Hale.[3] This curious, willful neglect of a powerful theme in actual Renaissance lives has greatly distorted our understanding of the Renaissance past. For example, there is not one recent treatment of the Italian Wars of 1494–1559 as a whole, and very few select studies, while my university electronic library catalogue lists 489 works on the subject of "Michelangelo" and 673 on "Leonardo da Vinci." To compare the sixteenth century with the twentieth, this is as if there were hundreds of books on Picasso, but not a single book on the First or Second World War, to say nothing of the Spanish Civil War. How then could we possibly understand the *Guernica*, if it were impossible to really learn about the Condor Legion, carpet bombing, Adolf Hitler, or Mussolini?

Secondly, our present-day assumptions regarding violence and warfare can cause us to fundamentally misunderstand how the actual human beings of the Renaissance understood those forces in their own, real lives. Between four and seven hundred years ago (to give the Renaissance its broadest possible temporal limits), no one made the mistake of thinking violence was a social pathology, though many did understand anger and murder to be sins, which is not at all the same thing. And no one associated violence and warfare exclusively with misfortune, the poor, or with the criminal classes. Rather, the opposite was more common: there was an entire European social order, the nobility, whose special rights were founded on their special privileges to wear arms, to use arms, and to think in terms of blows. If anything, to resort to force was a sign of social ascendancy; to be bellicose, quarrelsome, prickly, touchy, and otherwise always ready to take offense and fight was to ape the behavior of the great and the good, not the low and the obscure. So even if it is doubtless true that the grinding harshness of daily and seasonal life – floods, hard frosts, blights in the field, visitations of plague, etc. – drove individuals to want, and thus to crime, and as criminals to violence, the behavior of social unfortunates or marginals is not the place to look to find the cause, or the essence, of a truly violent Renaissance world.

An Angry Age?

Renaissance tempers were hot. If we first look at artists, we find that Mantegna hired thugs to beat up a rival; that Michelangelo had his nose broken in a fist-fight; and that Caravaggio killed a man over a tennis match. In his autobiography, Benvenuto Cellini bragged that during the siege of the Castel' San Angelo during the 1527 sack of Rome he served as a gunner, and that with a trick shot he managed to cut in half an enemy officer at an extreme range. Whether true or not, the relish with which Cellini recounts the story tells us a lot. Cellini's enthusiastic military service was not exceptional. Brunelleschi, Leonardo, and Michelangelo, to name only three of the most prominent and influential Florentine artists of the entire period, all served as military architects and engineers. Indeed, it was Leonardo's most conspicuous line of work, and he served in turn the Sforza Duke of Milan, the Venetian Republic, the Florentine Republic, and Cesare Borgia. Leonardo also wrote a letter offering his engineering services to the sultan in Constantinople, an extraordinary testament to his real interests and ambitions. He was, of course, barely capable of finishing a painting in the same years, even avoiding the possibility of becoming the court painter at Mantua, a nice enough sinecure if he had been willing to take it. Leonardo may have been a vegetarian and an animal-lover, but that did not prevent him from filling his notebooks with page after page of designs for ingenious killing machines.

The extent to which violent instincts saturated Renaissance life is clear from a look at the behavior of the clergy: an ecclesiastical career was not necessarily an impediment to a militant life. One fifteenth-century Italian visitation discovered an abbot wearing armor and prosecuting a private, local feud. Pope Julius II directed his own armies personally, and notoriously wore armor at the siege of Bologna in 1510. His predecessor, Alexander VI, and his successors, Clement VII and Paul III, were equally devoted to military affairs, even if not as personally active as the Della Rovere Pope. A century later, even after Trent, Borromeo, and a renewed Catholic emphasis on parochial and episcopal good-shepherdship, Cardinal Richelieu wore armor as he stood on the dike at La Rochelle, personally directing the reduction of the greatest French Protestant stronghold. The Reformation of course brought Christian militancy to the fore, as arms quickly and inevitably supplemented words. Huldrych Zwingli, a soldier in his youth, died (as a chaplain) on the battlefield of Kappel in 1531. Reform came to Geneva by war, and Calvin in his preaching recognized that Christendom was aflame:

> "Since a good part of the world is not only contrary [to the Gospel] but fights against it, we cannot serve Christ without conflict and without attracting the hate of many. So Christ warns his disciples to prepare themselves for battle: since it is necessary to fight to give witness to the truth."[4]

The Huguenot nobility of France heeded Calvin's words exactly, and eagerly went to war for their faith, singing psalms in the saddle as they prepared for the charge. Catholics took up the struggle with equal intensity, and a military spirit often colored the reformed Catholic Church. The ex-soldier Ignatius Loyola found a personal mission for God while recovering from a frightful leg wound received at the siege of Pamplona, and he composed a spiritual drill manual for his adherents, the *Spiritual Exercises*, to gird them for their fight against sin – and Protestantism. The new church discipline had more than a whiff of the drill-square to it.

Of course, many prominent clergy – including Loyola – brought the instincts of the nobility, particularly the lesser nobility, to their clerical careers. And it is with the mores of the nobility that we find the deep-seated heart of Renaissance rage and violence. Evidence for the instinctive, casual violence and militancy of the nobility is simply overwhelming.

An easy example is the house of Gonzaga, first captains, then marquesses, and finally dukes of Mantua and Montferrat. Their control of Mantua began in 1328 when the Gonzaga and their supporters rode into town and dragged the members of the previous ruling dynasty, the Bonacolsi, from their palace and massacred them in the main square. Far from forgetting or burying this initial, violent act of expropriation, at the end of the century the *capitano* Francesco commissioned the artist Domenico Morone to paint a busy and explicit painting – all hacking arms and milling limbs – to celebrate this bloodshed. The Gonzaga never lost their violent ways, even beyond their ceaseless military service as mercenary commanders. Good taste – the sophisticated patronage of numerous excellent poets, painters, and musicians – never erased a fundamentally angry streak. In 1391, Captain Francesco had his wife Agnese Visconti executed on an accusation of adultery. A century later, Rodolfo Gonzaga, brother of the Marquess Federico, had his wife Antonia Malatesta summarily beheaded on the same charge. Several Gonzaga had a knack for brawling. In 1582 the young Vincenzo Gonzaga, son of the ruling duke and later duke himself, murdered the Scottish intellectual prodigy "the admirable" James Creighton in a midnight encounter in the streets of Mantua. Vincenzo's own son Ferdinando as a teenager stalked the streets of Rome at night with a band of companions, beating up and even stabbing stray Spaniards. At the time, it is worth emphasizing, Ferdinando was in Rome to prepare for his future church career, and he was the Gonzaga cardinal from 1608 to 1615.

Other noble families were as violent, and as quickly so. Duke Ercole I d'Este once spotted an accused murderer, seized him, and threw him out of a castle window – a remarkably swift and simultaneous apprehension, judgment, and execution. In the last days of the long siege of Florence in 1530, the republic's frustrated mercenary commander, Malatesta Baglioni, lost his temper and stabbed to death a representative of the regime who had called to formally relieve him of his command. Baglioni then turned the city over to its besiegers.

Noble women could be as violent as men. In Faenza in 1488 the 20-year-old Francesca Bentivoglio, angered at her husband Galeotto Manfredi's dalliances, engaged four servants to kill him. When they hesitated, she cried "You swore you would kill him!," grabbed a knife herself, and plunged it into her husband's heart, murdering him on the spot.[5] Francesca's near contemporary Caterina Sforza, who was also married to a Romagnol princeling, had no less than two husbands assassinated, and when she was implicated in one of these murders she coolly noted that "neither [she] nor any other Sforza had ever found it necessary to hire assassins when they wanted someone dead."[6]

It is the explosive, murderous quickness of the Renaissance temper that is perhaps most shocking and foreign to us today. The best explication of this hair-trigger sensitivity, this easy and complete loss of self-control, is in Edward Muir's examination of the angry nobleman Antonio Savorgnan during the so-called "Cruel Carnival" that convulsed the city of Udine in Friuli in February of 1511.[7] There were many roots to this extraordinary outbreak of violence, but the main provocation was a simple incident: a boy from the Della Torre family, enemies of the Savorgnan, attempted to paint his own house's heraldic device on the well-head in front of the Savorgnan townhouse. The boy was caught. Incensed, the supporters of the Savorgnan attacked the Della Torre. Rather than working with the Venetian authorities to suppress this riot, Antonio Savorgnan, leader of his clan, complained that he was powerless to control his own or his followers' angry emotions: "I am so angry that I am beside myself, and I don't know myself what I'm doing."[8] His supporters went on to tear the Della Torre palace apart, slaughtering all those within with particular violence, hacking the bodies to bits and even feeding the cut-up pieces to animals. Antonio didn't even profit much from this indulgence; he paid for his temper. In a little over a year he was assassinated by men seeking revenge for family members killed during the Cruel Carnival. Mindful of how vendetta worked, the Venetian authorities granted Savorgnan's killers the perpetual right to wear arms, as they now would need to defend themselves from further rounds of revenge.

What made such brutality possible? Most important was the nobility's insistence on their right to a temper, and their right to confront and solve problems with violence. Europe's social and political elite were personally violent, and respected violence as both honorable – even superior to other forms of confrontation and solution – and also right in itself. Here it is impossible to separate social violence from political violence – that is, war. Warfare in the Renaissance must be understood as a spectrum that stretched from the petty and the provincial – such as the Della Torre versus Savorgnan in Friuli – to the feuds and arguments of the truly powerful: Francis I of

France versus the Emperor Charles V, for example. The latter struggle was fought out by armies and fleets, great operations with costs in the millions, but it was also an intensely personal struggle. Habsburg and Valois hated each other the way Della Torre hated Savorgnan, and vice versa, and this hatred was inherited and passed from father to son, uncle to nephew. Francis I and Charles V were both raised from boyhood to be skilled warriors, not just future strategic commanders. Both knew how to fight, and were willing to do so, even to the extent of agreeing to a single combat. This idea seems preposterous today, but it was a serious possibility, though councillors were obviously frightened of the risks, and consistently preached composure. Sometimes their princes could not, would not listen. Flush with his victory over Tunis in 1535, and exasperated and supremely angry with his rival Francis, in Easter of 1536 Charles V stood in St. Peter's in Rome and formally challenged the King of France to a duel with sword and dagger and without armor: terms that meant a fight to the death. At its deepest level, Renaissance competition between European princes was almost always physical, emotional, and personally agonistic: hence the celebrated wrestling match between King Francis and Henry VIII at the "field of the cloth of gold."

Renaissance noble culture was founded on skill at arms. The rising civilization of humanism, the spread of literacy and literary appreciation among the ruling elite, did not erase, but only supplemented, an older medieval and knightly nobiliar culture. A new fascination with Caesar, Hannibal, and Alexander replaced the hero-worship of an earlier age (Arthur and Amadis de Gaul), but did not remove the underlying fascination with military deeds and topics. *Orlando furioso* is as bloody as the *Song of Roland*. Humanistic debates over whether the art of love or the art of war was the superior should not lead us to conclude that Europe's aristocracy were foregoing their ancestors' rough ways for a softer, gentler sense of nobility. (The important athletic dimension of Renaissance martial and noble culture has only recently been carefully explored by Sydney Anglo.[9]) Though high culture changed remarkably, a particular kind of military identity remained the essence of being a noble. Lorenzo de' Medici, "the Magnificent," announced the new political direction of his family not only by being the first to marry into the Italian feudal nobility (Clarice Orsini, from an extremely bellicose Roman clan), but by being the first of his family to appear in the streets of Florence at a difficult political moment riding a horse and wearing a suit of armor.

If there is one peculiarity of Renaissance noble culture that proves the typical noble's easy anger and violence, it is the duel; participation in this exploded exactly as earlier tournament customs were waning, and therefore other options for displaying bravery and skill at arms in peacetime were disappearing. A survival and outgrowth of the deep-seated, medieval principle of a trial by combat, the duel is almost impossible for a present-day, western person to understand, even though it survived in modern culture until almost recent times. In its original and legally recognized form, Renaissance dueling depended on the court of honor, presided over by the local feudal authority – for example, in Ferrara by the duke, who would recognize an insult and authorize a combat. This was public and open. Spectators attended. The combatants would have to be equally armed and armored, and an inspection of each duelist's person was mandatory to ensure there were no hidden coats of mail or magical charms.

This earlier, more formal dueling was eclipsed by a more spontaneous dueling culture from the early sixteenth century, particularly after dueling was denounced by the council of Trent. The new dueling culture may have developed first in Naples, where the fashion became to fight *alla macchia*, that is, in the scrublands outside the city, and it became a further point of honor to fight as quickly as possible after an insult was given and satisfaction demanded. Taking time to think was tantamount to a declaration of cowardice. From Naples and Italy the new dueling ethics and fashion spread to Spain and France, England and the rest of Europe. Spontaneous dueling demanded a new kind of sword, and a new kind of sword fighting. Carrying a heavy military broad sword was both clumsy and awkward, if one had to be prepared for sudden encounters. Instead, a long, slender, and elegant new sword type, the rapier, was not encumbering, could be drawn with speed, and in skilled hands its piercing point could be as fatal as a great slashing blow, and much quicker. Combats were rough. Fencing masters taught how to fight with a rapier, with a sword and a parrying dagger, with two daggers, with a rapier and a rolled-up cloak, and with kicks and throws as well as thrusts. Late Renaissance gentlemen did not wear swords for decoration, but for savage and sudden use.

Spontaneous dueling also encouraged the existing tendency for noblemen, especially the rowdy young men, to travel in packs, as it could mean death to be caught on the streets undermanned. Dueling and brawling mixed; two on two and crowd on crowd encounters were common; the duelists "seconds" participated, they did not just watch. In times of civil discord and trouble, large retinues walked the streets at night with torches and weapons. They were a law unto themselves. Here is the perspective of an outraged citizen of Brescia in 1611:

> No one living in the city can be sure of his life or his home if he does not join one of the many factions. People elect to join one so that they do not have to fear them all. Women live in constant peril of rape. Crimes go unpunished because the men of importance march through the city flanked by twenty to forty armed supporters. If the Venetian officers of justice order them to stay in their homes, they send out their hired reinforcements to carry out their misdeeds, and the Venetian Republic lacks both the men and the resources to control the situation. In fact, the [nobles] so intimidate public officials that the latter prefer to stay in their palaces.[10]

Of course, the young man, the *bravo* who found employment in a noble's entourage, could best distinguish himself by proving himself eager to fight. How else was a poor boy from the country, the landless younger son, to make a name for himself? Join the church? Bah!

Noble familiarity with bloodshed and the sensations of inflicting physical hurt on another living thing were first won, and most often reinforced, by the experience of the hunt – another violent activity central to the Renaissance world that is increasingly anathema, even unfathomable, to the present-day mind. Hunting was no casual activity enjoyed by a few, but an essential part of what it meant to live like a noble, and the central experience of the hunt was understood to be the act of killing other living things, and taking pleasure in that act. In the Renaissance, hunters frankly and openly enjoyed killing animals; Queen Elizabeth at least once used a crossbow to shoot deer driven into an enclosure for her ease of slaughter. The blood of the hunt was not held at a distance, and no one pretended that hunting was really about riding horses, or liking dogs, or being out of doors. There were important hunting rituals particular to the enjoyment of a kill. Turberville's 1576 *Book of Hunting* explains that once a hart or hind is dead, the huntsman presents a sharp knife to the leading personage present (the huntsman must kneel if it is a royal), who takes the blade and then personally slits the deer's chest and belly. Head, feet, and horns are cut off and set aside for distribution, and a particularly gruesome package of membranes, tongue, ears, genitals, and parts of the gut are put "in a fair handkerchief altogether, for the Prince." What exactly "the Prince" would do with this little bundle of blood and guts is not specified – throw it to the barking, leaping dogs with a laugh? By the time a young noble saw his first battle or siege, or was old enough to fight a duel in the streets, he was already long familiar with what killing violence to large animals actually looked like. There would have been little shock or horror at the sight of a man pierced with a rapier through the eye-socket or under the soft part of the jaw (two killing thrusts taught in the fencing schools), or smashed to pieces by a cannon ball on the field of battle. In fact, he had already been taught to think and act as something of a hunting, killing animal himself. In Italy, the toughs who made up a nobleman's entourage might be known as his loyal "dogs."

Violence against animals was merely a prologue to violence against man. If it was a common street game to bury a cat up to its neck in the dirt and then throw rocks at its skull, then it is easy to see how people could watch with amusement, and even take part in, the brutal carnival game of blind man's bluff: take an earthenware pot, put it upside down on the ground with the prize within, and then blindfold a group of men and give them long cudgels. The first man to break the pot wins the game. The fullest treatment to date of Renaissance sporting violence – if that is the right term – is Robert Davis's discussion of the organized factional brawls between Venetian neighborhoods.[11] These were fought by small armies of tradesmen, fishermen, apprentices, and other hardy types, originally armed with sticks, but weapons were outlawed in 1574 and the participants were only allowed to use their fists. The combats were still brutal enough. Venetian and foreign nobles were enthusiastic spectators. Exceptional combatants could find a job in a nobleman's retinue, further proof that violent behavior could be the path to fame and even upward social mobility.

The circumstances of criminal justice and execution allow us to go even further, and suggest there was a scent of sanctioned sadism to the culture of the Renaissance. Testimony of course was often given under torture. When poor Machiavelli was hauled before the restored Medici regime on accusation of having plotted against them as a former republican official, he had to endure three jerks of the strappado, a common if vicious judicial procedure in Florence and elsewhere: a person's hands were secured behind the back; a rope was tossed over a high beam and then tied to the bound wrists; then the accused was lifted up and suddenly dropped, violently wrenching the shoulders. Public executions were common, there being few institutions and little patience for long-term incarceration. In Ferrara between 1460 and 1500 there were a total of 293 executions.[12] These were public, of course, and were sometimes especially elaborate, drawn out, and humiliating. In Ferrara, one man executed for murdering two German students at the university was first dragged alive through the streets of the city, then decapitated, then quartered, and finally the parts were put on public display. There is no doubt that people flocked in crowds to enjoy the entertainment value of public executions: to see Jan Hus burned in 1415, or Savonarola in 1498, Michael Servetus in 1553, Giordano Bruno in 1600 (just to list some of the more interesting religious examples). The crowd could even participate, and make it a frolic. Boys dragged through the streets and played with the bodies of those killed in Florence in 1478 for the Pazzi conspiracy assassination of Giuliano de' Medici, and the attempted assassination of Lorenzo. Assassination, of course, is a long and full sub-chapter of the history of Renaissance violence, from the murder of Galeazzo Maria Sforza in 1476 through the knifing of Henri IV of France in 1610 (it was the twentieth attempt on that king's life). As in our own times, assassins were almost always caught, and they paid for their crime with exquisitely drawn-out public executions: first torture (hot pincers, chopping off of hands), then death, then dismemberment. Finally, all executed criminal's dead bodies (or body parts) would be put on public display, for all to see as the sun, wind, rain, crows, dogs, and marketplace pigs took care of the remains. In northern Europe any visitor to a town would have frequent, casual exposure to rotting bodies hanging from the gibbet, and the wheels on poles where the bodies of those sentenced to be broken at the wheel would disintegrate.

So violent death was a Renaissance commonplace. Regimes, even as they employed torturers and hangmen, naturally sought to control the violence that swirled within and around every Renaissance state. Unable – or unwilling – to control people, governments attempted to control weapons, the tools of violence. In the Netherlands, there would sometimes be a representative iron dagger hanging on a chain at the town hall; any knife longer than this measure would be illegal. In Genoa it was illicit to own a dagger with a point. When long rapiers became the preferred gentleman's side arm, there were rules to limit the length of swords. In northern Italy, travelers arriving at a town might have to surrender their weapons. They would receive a chit as a receipt, like a coat check, and when passing out of town the travelers would turn this chit in and a boy would be sent running to retrieve the party's weaponry. When firearms became common, the short-barreled pistol immediately became a law and order issue. In fact, one of the very first mentions of a pistol comes from a German brothel incident in which a young man accidentally shot and killed a prostitute while playing with – or showing off – his novelty. Soon highwaymen and assassins were using pistols, and the barrel lengths of firearms came to be subject to the same type of limiting legislation as blade weapons. Of course, none of it did any good. If pistols were sniffed at as a low-born weapon by a gentleman of the 1540s, they would soon come to be seen as an honorable alternative to a sword for a duel. When the Elizabethan sea dog Martin Frobisher posed for his portrait carrying an elaborate and elegant little pistol, a type known as a dag, he was emphasizing what a dog he really was – a man of violence, in a violent time.

Tempering War

Renaissance patterns of social violence infected military operations. Again, there was no clear line of separation demarcating the limits of private violence on the one hand, and legitimate public violence, that is military action, on the other: the two could overlap and intertwine in various ways, several of them against the interest of the states and rulers in whose names full-scale wars were supposedly fought. Noble participation in war was often for personal, rather than patriotic or even professional reasons. Castiglione, who captained a squadron of men-at-arms before writing his influential *Courtier*, hinted that it was necessary for military deeds to be seen to be worth doing. A gentleman needed an audience; this is why late medieval and earlier Renaissance battle accounts bristle with the details of how individual noble participants behaved and fared in the encounter. Tactics had not yet really been invented, or rather, reinvented, after the ancient example (one great project of the Renaissance military reformers).

Medieval and humanistic genres for the intellectual understanding of warfare mingled, or stayed on parallel tracks within the same larger privileged cultural milieu; Paolo Giovio wrote both real humanist history, and a long discussion of the *imprese*, the involved and purposely difficult-to-decipher heraldic devices of notable warriors. For many, what mattered about the battlefield was that here was another, sanctioned place to prove one's personal valor and thus increase one's personal honor. (See the essay above by James Farr.) Though to our eyes foolish, Renaissance warfare could be as much a social practice as a political necessity. Thus Henri IV of France, after winning one battle, elected not to follow up the victory by a vigorous pursuit of the enemy, but rather gathered the captured standards and literally draped them at the feet of his teenaged mistress. If we ignore or minimize such incidents we risk confusing our sense of war for theirs.

The culture of the tournament, and the duel, affected the military behavior of the most prominent members, and even the leaders of armies. Such men often found the hurly-burly of open warfare less than satisfactory, or too haphazard for their personal need to seek death or glory – and often both. Full-scale warfare would therefore be punctuated by arranged combats: for the real hot-heads, war itself wasn't deadly enough. At Barletta in 1503 two evenly matched bodies of French and Spanish knights decorated a truce by engaging in a spectacular and ferocious staged combat that was fought to the death. The fame of this *disfida* overshadowed memories of the lackluster larger campaign. A century later, at the close of the period, and after many military reforms aimed at increasing the state's political and hierarchical control over warfare and noble warriors, it was still possible for gentlemen to see combat in overwhelmingly personal terms. At the siege of Breda in the Netherlands in 1625, an arranged duel took place between Dutch and Spanish gentlemen. For many noble participants, warfare was not something to be fought and won to allow a return to civilian life; rather, warfare was life itself, formal campaigning providing just another murderous arena for the display of pride, courage, and skill at arms.

Such attitudes colored the very tip-top levels of command, and could completely overshadow any sense of nation, state, or strict feudal obligation. Francis I's highest military commander, the constable Bourbon, fell out with his sovereign and changed sides to join the army of the Emperor Charles V. Over a century later, the Great Condé, who first won renown by destroying a Spanish army at the battle of Rocroi (1643), fell out with the government of the boy-king Louis XIV, joined the Fronde, and then fought for Spain against France before finally being reconciled and finishing his glorious professional career with his natural lord. As far as the prickly, fickle loyalty of the noble military commander goes, the stories of the Italian *condottiere* provide almost limitless examples. At heart it was their personal view of war, and certainly not their timidity, that encouraged Bruni and Machiavelli and others to explore the possibilities of reviving the lost ancient traditions of militarily disciplined and politic-ally loyal citizen infantry armies.

Given this almost inexhaustible elite enthusiasm for combat, it is not surprising that warfare was common. The major wars are well known: the Reconquista in Spain up to 1492, the last campaigns of the Hundred Years War in France until 1453, the later fifteenth-century northern wars between Burgundy and the king of France or the Swiss, and then the Italian Wars themselves from 1494 to 1559, which were followed by the Eighty Years War in the Netherlands (1567–1648), the French Religious Wars (inter-mittently from 1562 to 1629) and the Thirty Years War in Germany (1618–48). If none of these were hot enough at the moment, one could always join the Knights of St. John on Malta, and so join the endless Mediterranean war of casual *razzia* and episodic, more serious crusade campaigning. The instinct to go to war so saturated the nobility of Renaissance Europe that it was exported to every point of the compass, thanks to the new oceanic discoveries. Noble warriors who went to North Africa or New Spain seeking glory and wealth chaffed at royal restrictions against raiding or designs of further conquest. Risk was nothing to such men, just as it meant nothing to fight a duel in the streets of Seville. The against-all-odds exploits of Cortez in Mexico and Pizarro in Peru are well known, even notorious, but we must also remember the equally audacious but failed expeditions that brought bands and even armies of would-be conquistadors to their deaths in Morocco, Angola, Ethiopia, India, Siam, and elsewhere.

If war in Europe was nearly omnipresent, it was also a heavy presence. An army that seems tiny to us – 10,000 men was a good-sized force – was the equivalent of a major town in most of the Renaissance world. The demands of such a force could be heavy, draining a district of the necessary food and supplies. The demand for forage was particularly ravenous; armies were crowds of animals as well as of men. A company of properly mounted, heavily armed and armored men-at-arms required two or three horses, one or two of them large and valuable warhorses, for every combatant. The enormous artillery pieces of the fourteenth and especially fifteenth century required a dozen pair or more of oxen to pull them, and dozens more to cart their enormous stone cannonballs; the lighter pieces of the sixteenth and seventeenth century re-quired rather less, but there were now more guns all told. A siege train could easily include over a thousand draft animals. Outriders searching for these animals' feed cut a wide swath; armies were locusts.

Wise peasants knew enough to flee to marshes and high ground when armies approached. Townsmen trusted in their walls. When those defenses failed, the conse-quences could be catastrophic: the details of the sack of Prato in 1512, or Rome in 1527, or Lyons in 1562 still shock today. Custom demanded a three day ravaging to sate the soldiers, who were often so far in arrears of pay that their generals and captains were hardly in control, anyway. The French lost Milan in 1522 because their Swiss mercenary infantry, unpaid, insisted on attacking a well-emplaced Imperial army: either let us have plunder in lieu of pay, or we march home, they said. Shrugging, the French commander gave them their wish, and many paid with their lives in the hopeless battle that followed. Perhaps these poor Swiss soldiers' choice tells us something about the real poverty in the proud mountain forests and valleys of their homeland. Even when paid, there were few armies that were ever really on good behavior. Stray rapes, murders, and other sundry outrages were a constant. One poetic scrap captures the soldiery's casual savagery:

> We'll move against your enemy,
> 'till the very women and little children cry murder,
> That is what we long for and [take] joy in.[13]

Captains might hang the rascals responsible (hangmen were among an army's attending professionals), but this only delayed the next incident.

Armies spread more than destruction: they spread disease, too. Syphilis came to Italy, and from Italy was spread to the rest of Europe, by the marching soldiers of the Italian Wars. The Swiss artist Urs Graf has left us a brutal sketch of a soldier's girl, a prostitute certainly, ravaged by the disease with only stumps for arms, and one leg a wooden stick. Commanders hated these women and the trouble they brought. The Venetian reformer Alviano had the noses of prostitutes slit and drummed them from camp, and one French commander, according to Brantôme, had more than 800 camp-following women pushed over the edge of a bridge along the route of march so that they drowned: "and it might have happened that many soldiers, friends of their trollops, would have mutinied, if order had not been restored."[14] We should not doubt the severity by which that "order" was restored. To be a soldier – or to follow with soldiers – was to suffer as much as to cause suffering.

Not everyone reveled in the seething warfare. Particularly those exposed to the history and the military theory of the ancient world conceived of different martial values, and wished for different kinds of military institutions. We are only starting to understand and appreciate the work and worldview of these "military humanists" (the phrase is that of Frederic Verrier, one of the few scholars to have labored on this potentially great historical project).[15] For those Renaissance intellectuals who were dissatisfied with existing military practice, and existing military culture, the surviving ancient technical manuals, such as those by Vegetius and Aelian the Tactician, and the surviving Greek and Roman historians, particularly Livy's and Polybius' descriptions of ancient Roman republican armies, hinted at a very different world in which governments and generals were in control, not the armies themselves. By the turn of the sixteenth century it was common, at least in Italy, for a noble military professional to be literate and exposed to the ancient military classics. Connecting theory with practice was the next step. For many, there was an obvious and desirable military parallel between the ancient prowess of pike-armed infantry (associated with the victories of Alexander the Great and Pyrrhus of Epirus, besides lesser-known Hellenistic commanders) and the recent success of pike-armed Swiss and German infantry, particularly after the Swiss victories over the Burgundians in the 1470s. To recover ancient military skill, therefore, the project became the duplication of Swiss and German infantry warfare – as analyzed by those steeped in the ancient military classics.

There were problems with this mimesis. Small numbers of Swiss and Germans could be recruited as a training cadre; however, to copy the field discipline and ferocity of the Swiss and landsknecht mercenaries also meant to risk copying other, less desirable aspects of their peculiar military culture: their strange costumes with enormous plumes, slashed jackets, and pantaloons, and gigantic, suggestive codpieces – plus their habit of refusing irksome tasks (anything to do with digging, for example). A better solution was to blend ancient and modern practice intellectually and put the results down in drill books which would spread the ideal of a disciplined, ancient-style infantry warfare, a warfare that was firmly under the control of the treatise writers and readers – and, it was hoped, under the control of generals and rulers, too. There were practical experiments in this direction. The most famous is Machiavelli's reform of the Florentine militia before 1512, but equally based on ancient precedent were the Venetian reforms of Bartolomeo d'Alviano in 1513, and the most far-reaching and ambitious scheme of all was Francis I's 1534 plan to raise six "legions" of loyal, native infantry based on six different regions of France. An important detail of this French legionary scheme was that officers were to be of the local, native gentry; their bellicosity would now be steeled by the discipline of a hierarchical, codified infantry drill and regulation. In the end, none of these deliberate schemes *all'antica* single-handedly satisfied the desire for disciplined armies (or ever really worked), but these practical fantasies sketched the evolutionary direction of modern European or western militaries down to the present day: the humanistic reformers insisted that soldiers must be technically, behaviorally, and politically subservient to governments and high commanders. These goals or values seem obvious to us today, but only because of the Renaissance reformers' remarkable eventual success.

The technical demands of reform forced cultural changes. First of all, the tripartite social division of all modern, western armies emerged: simple soldiers, who were formation place-holders and fighters, and then two classes of controlling supervisors, first the noble officers who supplied the moral discipline, and then the technical specialists, the sergeants, who supplied the technical discipline. The medieval sergeant had been an assistant or partner to the man-at-arms; the Renaissance, modern sergeant was a hands-on, low-level leader whose job was to monitor a unit's formation, man by man. The new sergeantry became a military middle class (as they still are today), and it is important to note that their technical demands were such that they needed to be literate, at least ideally, and numerate to the extent of calculating square roots – not a light skill, at the time. For their part, the noble officers supplied a different kind of direction complementary to the sergeant's pokes and threats. Here the existing noble culture of individual, extreme physical bravery was made useful in a new system of war dedicated to overall cohesion and command control. Already indifferent to the chance of his own death, scornful of the enemy's swords and pikes, musket and cannon fire, the officer gained a new battlefield role. It became his duty to stand at the front of his company, battalion, or regiment, wearing his best suit of clothes and a conspicuous sash and plume, and nonchalantly lead his men into battle. An officer might have technical skills, might himself lend a hand at the drilling and the marshaling of his men, but he most of all supplied the raw physical courage that served as the galvanizing moral example for an entire formation. This is where and how, in his own mind, the European noble would prove his social and moral superiority – and therefore his right to rule – down to the First World War: by standing at the head of his command, and accepting the horrendous casualty rates that went with that exposure and with that honor. (There is an awful lineage in the front-line carnage of junior officers from the sixteenth century, at such blood-baths as Ravenna, the Somme or Verdun in the twentieth century.)

For the nobility, then, the new infantry service delivered a new sense of military identity. By the second half of the sixteenth century there is already a subtle, though certainly still incomplete shift in the heroics of warfare: forbearance and self-discipline are becoming more valuable than an aggressive thirst for blood. The Renaissance invention of the infantry officer and his superior, the general as a battle director, was one of the crucial first steps toward the creation of modern, restrained notions of warfare, and of war as subservient to the interests of policy. How did this this new officer ethic based on infantry service clash with older martial traditions? And did principles of restraint and forbearance on the battlefield affect European nobles' more general attitudes toward violence in society as a whole?

This possibility, and other possible consequences of Renaissance-era military reform, are due a wider and more detailed examination. A host of similar, currently unanswered questions await research and publication. There is in fact an historiographical framework in place for a fuller discussion of the military history of the period, though it has not yet been well connected with the broader issues of cultural and social history. For almost fifty years now historians have been discussing an "early modern military revolution," which, it is posited, created modern warfare. To date, almost the entirety of the debate has been argued with an emphasis on the rubric "early modern."[16] The leading theorist is Geoffrey Parker, who firmly places his proposed military revolution in the context of Europe's growing position on the world stage, and extends the revolutionary process from the sixteenth through the eighteenth century.[17] The stoutest criticism of the Parker thesis has come from the community of medievalist military historians. Scholars of the Renaissance have largely ignored the discussion. The greatest military historian of the Renaissance to date, John Hale, himself avoided, and even challenged, the term revolution, and instead promoted the idea of a "military reformation," a comparison with the simultaneous religious Reformation being implicit.[18] The idea has not caught fire.

The evidence of the larger period – Renaissance, Late Medieval, Reformation, or Early Modern, however it is named – does suggest that there are very strong connections between what are traditionally considered the defining topics and movements of a European Renaissance – particularly humanism – and the military technical changes of the era. But there is equal evidence that the revolution, if it can be so called, was incomplete, and that medieval, for lack of a better word, conceptions of military identity and service continued well past the period of decisive change, and are still with us today. How exactly did Europe's nobility both direct a military transformation, and allow that transformation to challenge and change their own identities as Europe's military, political, and social elite? To this question, as to so many others, we have as yet no answers. The cultural and social history of Renaissance warfare, something we do not yet possess, is only beginning to be written. What is needed, as always, is more research and more publications that do not privilege the assumptions of the author's world, but seek to honestly explicate the worlds of the past.

NOTES

1   Martines, *Violence and Civil Disorder*.
2   Ruggiero, *Violence*; Muir, *Mad Blood*; Davis, *War of the Fists*.
3   Mallett, *Mercenaries*; Hale, *War and Society*; Mallett and Hale, *Military Organization*.
4   Quoted in Higman, " 'I Came'," p. 123.

5   Larner, "Order and Disorder," p. 60.
6   Pitkin, *Fortune*, p. 250.
7   Muir, *Mad Blood*.
8   Ibid., pp. 7–8.
9   Anglo, *Martial Arts*.
10 Quoted in Ferraro, *Family and Public Life*, pp. 133–4.
11 Davis, *War of the Fists*.
12 Gundesheimer, "Crime and Punishment."
13 Hale, *Artists and Warfare*, p. 34.
14 Quoted in Wood, *King's Army*, p. 305.
15 Verrier, *Les Armes*.
16 Rogers, *Military Revolution Debate*.
17 Parker, *Military Revolution*.
18 Hale, *War and Society*, p. 46.

REFERENCES

Anglo, Sydney, *The Martial Arts of Renaissance Europe* (New Haven: Yale University Press, 2000).

Davis, Robert C., *The War of the Fists: Popular Culture and Public Violence in Late Renaissance Venice* (New York: Oxford University Press, 1994).

Ferraro, Joanne M., *Family and Public Life in Brescia, 1580–1650* (Cambridge: Cambridge University Press, 1993).

Gundesheimer, Werner L., "Crime and Punishment in Ferrara, 1440–1500," in *Violence and Civil Disorder in Italian Cities, 1200–1500*, ed. Lauro Martines (Berkeley: University of California Press, 1972).

Hale, John R., *War and Society in Renaissance Europe, 1450–1620* (Baltimore: Johns Hopkins University Press, 1985).

——, *Artists and Warfare in the Renaissance* (New Haven: Yale University Press, 1990).

Higman, Francis, "'I Came Not to Send Peace, but a Sword'," in *Calvinus Sincerioris Religionis Vindex*, ed. Wilhelm H. Neuser and Brian G. Armstrong (Kirksville, MO: Sixteenth Century Journal, 1997).

Larner, John, "Order and Disorder in Romagna, 1450–1500," in *Violence and Civil Disorder in Italian Cities, 1200–1500*, ed. Lauro Martines (Berkeley: University of California Press, 1972).

Mallet, Michael, *Mercenaries and their Masters: Warfare in Renaissance Italy* (Totowa, NJ: Rowman and Littlefield, 1974).

Mallet, Michael and Hale, John R., *The Military Organization of a Renaissance State: Venice c. 1400 to 1617* (Cambridge: Cambridge University Press, 1984).

Martines, Lauro, ed., *Violence and Civil Disorder in Italian Cities, 1200–1500* (Berkeley: University of California Press, 1972).

Muir, Edward, *Mad Blood Stirring: Vendetta and Factions in Friuli during the Renaissance* (Baltimore: Johns Hopkins University Press, 1993).

Parker, Geoffrey, *The Military Revolution: Military Innovation and the Rise of the West, 1500–1800* (Cambridge: Cambridge University Press, 1988).

Pitkin, Hanna Fenichel, *Fortune is a Woman* (Berkeley: University of California Press, 1984).

Rogers, Clifford J., ed., *The Military Revolution Debate* (Boulder, CO: Westview Press, 1995).

Ruggiero, Guido, *Violence in Early Renaissance Venice* (New Brunswick, NJ: Rutgers University Press, 1980).

Verrier, Frederic, *Les Armes de Minerve: l'humanisme militaire dans l'Italie du XVIe siècle* (Paris: Université de Paris-Sorbonne, 1997).

Wood, James B., *The King's Army: Warfare, Soldiers, and Society during the Wars of Religion in France, 1562–1576* (Cambridge: Cambridge University Press, 1996).

CHAPTER TWENTY-SEVEN

Witchcraft and Magic

GUIDO RUGGIERO

In the famous fifteenth-century treatise the *Malleus maleficarum* or *Hammer of Witches* (1486) by the Dominicans Heinrich Kramer and Jacob Sprenger, there is a memorable story about a man who found one day that "he had lost his member." Suspecting foul play he asked a local witch for help and she without hesitation sent him to a nearby tree where he found a collection of phalluses hidden in a bird's nest and selected the largest to replace his loss.[1] A century later a parish priest in Chioggia, near Venice, was accused of witchcraft and magic for a similar deed. He informed local officials that he had found many men magically bound and unable to use their phalluses to consummate their marriages. He restored functioning phalluses to them with a little holy magic that involved dust from a church bell mixed with broth while saying a psalm, and he reported that his cure had worked miracles.[2]

The ups and downs of Renaissance phalluses – because both stories are represented as true – suggest that some serious rethinking is in order about magic and witchcraft in the Renaissance. Traditionally historians have looked at Renaissance witches and witchcraft from two perspectives. First, they have studied prescriptive literature – especially from the fifteenth century, when the Renaissance stereotype of the witch was formalized, and the long seventeenth century (ca. 1570–1700) when that litera-ture spread across Europe and beyond. Second, they have examined the prosecutions of witches, which gained momentum in northern Italy, Switzerland, and bordering areas in southern France and Germany from the late thirteenth century; these seemed to die out at the end of the fifteenth century and then exploded again in a series of witch-hunts that spread out from the heartland of Europe from about 1570. Pros-ecutions started becoming common in German territories, Switzerland, and bordering areas especially in France, then included most of Europe, although Eng-land, Scotland, and the Scandinavian countries practiced relatively milder repression; finally, as the seventeenth century progressed, they moved into eastern Europe, with special violence in Poland, and reached as far as Russia. Estimates vary widely, but it appears that these waves of repression resulted in perhaps as many as 60,000 execu-tions and well over double that number of prosecutions.[3]

Curiously, however, in many modern studies the witch and the practices of witch-craft seem largely invisible, and the repressive activities of governments, churches, and the opinions of intellectuals about witches and witchcraft hold center stage. There are some good reasons for this. Most notably, the most extensive records that we have on witchcraft come from sources – prescriptive literature and trial records – that do not have much to say about actual practices. Even the trial, often based on torture, induced testimonies where witches were pressed to confirm the vision of witchcraft purloined from prescriptive literature; as a result one finds in both sources less what witches did, and more what intellectual and ruling elites feared they did. But signifi-cantly in certain areas of Europe such as Italy, Spain, and England, torture was used less frequently,[4] so by focusing on prosecutions in those areas – especially on the rich testimony of everyday people talking about what they saw as witchcraft and magic – it is possible to construct a series of profiles of practices and practitioners that moves beyond fears and stereotypes. In turn insights gained from such cases can be used to re-read even cases where torture was used to look for hints of practices hidden in the seams of torture-induced testimony. Of course, this is not to imply that testimony collected without torture is unproblematic and can be read as straightforward fact; most testimony in such cases had an agenda and must be read closely and critically. Crucially, looking first at the practice and practitioners of the magic associated with witchcraft changes dramatically our understanding of these phenomena and the way that they fit into Renaissance culture and society.

One thing is clear at the start when one looks at witchcraft from this perspective: few of the people accused of witchcraft thought of themselves as the classic witch of prescriptive literature – the person who had renounced God to form an alliance with the devil, who went to the Sabbat, who destroyed babies and crops and rode on a broom. Rather, the common element in both self-portrayal and neighborly fears was that those labeled witches were practicing magic. And the central issue was often whether that magic was good (natural or white magic) or evil (black magic used to harm others: *maleficium*, *maleficia*, a term closely related to that used in the title of Kramer and Spengler's *Malleus maleficarum*). The key to understanding the practices of those accused of witchcraft may well be the developing of a better understanding of *maleficium* and how this term was used in the Renaissance. Often scholars have dismissed *maleficia* as simple, unsophisticated spells and half-understood magical formulas that deluded only the poor and ignorant. At times that may have been the case, but I would argue that there was a rich and deep significance to much of this magic that integrated it deeply into Renaissance life and gave it meaningful resonances with both high culture and everyday culture in ways that have been largely overlooked.[5]

The Spiritual World of *Maleficium*

One key to understanding how deeply and intimately *maleficia* were intertwined with Renaissance life is to see the way in which the spiritual and material worlds were understood at the time. Simply, the deep and absolute Cartesian split between the material and spiritual was still in the future. In such a world phalluses could be freed by a psalm and the dust of a church bell or spirited away by a witch. In fact, to understand the Renaissance one has to recognize that the boundaries between the spiritual and material were fragile and contested – contested because the spiritual world was widely accepted as possessing superior power. This was so whether one was thinking in terms of theology (with an omnipotent God creating and actively inter-fering in the material world with miracles, portents, and punishments), philosophy (with a great chain of being where power descended and the spiritual world consti-tuted a superior reality), politics (where governments strove to co-opt the spiritual) or everyday practice (with prayers, relics, shrines, icons, portents, miracles, magic, and witchcraft constantly showing the power of the spiritual in the material world). In sum, across a host of Renaissance discourses, the power of the spiritual over the material was recognized, and magic and *maleficia* provided merely another set of opportunities for utilizing such power.

Not all magic was spiritual in the Renaissance, but a great deal of even herbal and alchemical magic was heavily reliant on spiritual forces. And while some practitioners of everyday magic may have made no spiritual claims, most people expected that their magic would have a significant spiritual dimension, and it usually did. Ultimately the spiritual realm was too close and too powerful to be ignored by any discourse of power in the Renaissance and magic was no exception; in fact, in many ways it was a discourse whose claims to power were based upon translating the superior powers of the spiritual world to the material and that was true whether one is talking about the high magic of intellectuals and philosophers like the Neoplatonist Marsilio Ficino or everyday healers and magicians. Perhaps the most significant area of contact and power was to be found in religion; in Christianity the relationship between religion and spiritual magic was clearly close and rich. This was especially true in the fifteenth century before Christianity split into camps, each to some degree having a different view about the relationship between the spiritual world and religious practices.

But in Catholic Europe before and after that divide, the Church stressed the closeness of the spiritual and the way it regularly penetrated the material world. Most notably the sacrament of the Eucharist at the heart of the Mass and Catholic ritual miraculously and regularly transformed the substance of bread and wine into the substance of Christ's blood and body, a ritual that for believers represented the most profound eruption of the spiritual into the material world since the act it recalled and in a way replayed: God becoming man, the Spirit becoming flesh. Significantly, in the High Middle Ages, as the Eucharistic ritual was expanded and dramatized, we find almost immediately evidence of the Eucharist itself being used for magic. Already in the twelfth century priests were being warned to keep the host under lock and key to protect it from illicit use by local magicians, and miracle stories begin to appear about consecrated hosts carried off for magical purposes bleeding miraculously or otherwise showing their disapproval.[6] The spiritual powers associated with holy water, holy oil, relics, and a host of things associated with churches, shrines, and holy people also reinforced the proximity of the spiritual to the material world, and offered opportunities for magicians to utilize such spiritual things for their magic.

And in a way the Catholic Church encouraged such thinking, with its own rather syncretistic approach to many forms of spiritual power: blessing animals, crops, and homes; recognizing and celebrating the power of local saints, holy people, shrines, and holy places; developing and following local rituals and calendars; accepting practices and rituals that turned on the miraculous powers of local icons and symbols of spiritual power; and many other practices that integrated Christianity into the daily life of communities. Such local practices and beliefs suggest that rather than labeling the Renaissance Christian we might label it a time of many "christianities": local variations on Christianity dominated by local spiritual beliefs and traditions. Simply put, the Catholic Church had great trouble imposing its vision of Christianity on society, even in larger urban centers, never mind the countryside. And in Protestant areas after the initial enthusiasm for reform and Bible reading cooled, it was equally difficult to disseminate from the top down the official reformed view of Christianity. But this did not mean, as some have argued, that rural populations and the lower classes in cities and towns were ignorant and mired in a material culture of survival; rather, I would argue, such people had constructed their own rich local cultures in which the spiritual world played a vital role. Religious life was actually based upon a series of working relationships between locals recognized for their holiness, often women, more active local clergy (if they existed), leaders of the community, and local traditions and practices. (See the essays of R. Po-chia Hsia and David Gentilcore above.) And this was most significant for everyday magic, both good and evil, because just as local christianities were built on locally constructed discourses on spiritual life and the power of holy things and people, so too was much magic and *maleficia* constructed from the same raw materials.

Honor, Violence, Love, and Health

Much of this magic, whether it was seen as good or a form of *maleficium* was concerned with four crucial domains of Renaissance life: honor, violence, love, and health. (See the essays above, on honor by James Farr; on violence by Gregory Hanlon and Thomas Arnold; on love by Joanne Ferraro and Elissa Weaver; and on health by Mary Lindemann and William Eamon.) In a public and hierarchical society like that of the Renaissance, one of the most important dynamics of daily life was that of honor/shame. Recent studies have emphasized that honor was not a prerogative solely of the upper classes or men; in fact, across the social spectrum and across genders virtually everyone saw their honor as something "more dear than life itself."[7] Clearly the honor of a noble or a gentleman was different from that of an artisan or a thief, a wife's different from that of an unmarried girl or a servant, but maintaining honor was crucial for one's public place in communities that were often small-scale, personal, and that closely monitored honor. In such a world insults were never mere words or deeds, they were the stuff of dishonor and to be avoided at all costs. A noble or a gentleman ideally would not be dishonored in part because of a behavioral code that forbade it and in part because of support networks that would punish such deeds. From vendetta and duels with peers to violence against inferiors – even occasionally using litigation – notable people cultivated a range of powers and used them regularly to protect their honor.

But what happened lower down the social scale? Where did lesser mortals get the power to defend their honor? Violence, of course, was central; fists, various weapons, even bread knives served; and, of course, family and friends offered crucial resources, while women (and men) could attempt to mould the gossip networks that evaluated honor with defamation, insults, cruel jokes, and more moderate explanations. But not everyone at the bottom of society had the physical strength, the family supports, or other sources of power to defend their honor. In this context local witches or cunning people were very useful. They could be employed, often at modest expense, to threaten and, if necessary, punish dishonoring enemies with *maleficia*. In turn honor was often also deeply intertwined with violence. In fact, violence in the form of vendetta was a primary tool in restoring honor. Dishonoring deeds were punished and zeroed out by violent acts of vendetta which re-established the balance of honor in a community. And once again here the witch's use of *maleficia* was a crucial resource for waging vendetta. A rich man could rely on family and retainers to carry out his vendettas, a poor widow on her own, or a humble peasant, might have more luck with the negative spiritual powers of a local witch. And the mere fear of such powers could be a positive force, for the threat of vendetta, even magical vendetta, was a powerful force restricting the level of violence in society. When everyone had access to some form of punishing power, everyone had to treat their neighbors with a certain restraint. Such balanced threats of violence – rather like balanced nuclear deterrents of the Cold War – did not create a society without violence or eliminate tensions, but they did limit levels of violence. From that perspective witches and magicians who could deploy punishing magic were a positive and virtually essential part of Renaissance society. In sum, the desire to preserve honor and limit violence required that every community have its witch.[8]

An interesting confirmation of this hypothesis is the fact that when one looks more closely at when witches were accused by their neighbors, it often occurred when a witch appears to have run amok. Frequently, in such cases people talked about how a witch had begun to overreact: by punishing affronts too severely, targeting victims indiscriminately, or with high-handed threats and deeds that reflected a dangerous lack of moderation. In short, when the symbiotic relationship between the witch's power to punish and the community's need for that power broke down, the community turned against them, denouncing them to authorities. Another sign of this dynamic at work is that often the community actually tried to get such people on track before turning them in, encouraging them or warning them about inappropriate magic, even at times calling in other local magicians to solve the problem before going to the authorities.

Love

Love might seem less significant in power strategies, but, of course, love was one of the most powerful forces in the Renaissance. And tellingly, its spiritual dimensions made it a natural target for those who manipulated the spiritual. Most visible perhaps was the role love played or did not play in marriage (see the essay by Joanne Ferraro above). Although marriages were formally arranged by parents or relatives, a moderate, affection-like love was nonetheless the ideal; those making matches sought to select partners who were well suited to each other in terms of family, status, wealth, and even temperament and interests. More passionate forms of love were dangerous for marriage, because on the one hand they could disrupt it and on the other they could lead couples to upset family strategies by running off together or initiating sexual relations clandestinely. Love magic clearly had many roles to play in this complex dynamic. People on the make used love magic to marry their daughters or sons up the social scale; others used it to reinforce unions that were threatened; and many used it to break apart families and marriages. Witches and magicians (not to mention priests and clerics plus a whole range of marriage brokers, charlatans, and mountebanks) sought to manipulate marriage using the spiritual power of love.

One popular form of such control was based on a form of punishing magic called "hammering," which was designed to make someone suffer until they either fell in love or gave up on love. This type of magic helped form many Renaissance marriages and break up many others, playing a central role even in the matchmaking strategies of the rich and powerful.[9] But the power of love could be used in many other ways, both positive and negative, and again magic and witchcraft were regularly involved. Prostitutes and concubines, whose livelihood depended directly on the attraction their clients felt for them, regularly used a wide range of love magic to hold their clients and lovers. Very popular were little spells with a strong religious or spiritual component written out on paper or parchment that were used to touch a lover and bind their love to the person who did the touching. Such spiritually induced attraction was not limited to illicit love, however; often such magic was used by men to cement friendships, especially in the area of client–patron relationships, courtly networks, or business relationships. In a very personal world where friendship was essential for the functioning of a host of informal relationships, magic that could create bonds of friendship was crucially important. Again it was a service that witches and magicians could provide, which served everyone from those at the bottom of society to those at the top seeking the good wishes of patrons, princes, and popes. And that means in turn that witchcraft and magic added another dimension to the way such relationships were seen and understood; it linked them in a deep way to the spiritual world which underlay everyday practice.

Healing

Medicine and spiritual magic were also closely aligned in the Renaissance, largely because illnesses were seen as much broader and more spiritually influenced afflictions than they are today. Illnesses could have physical causes, but equally if not more important were spiritual causes. For when facing illness Renaissance people felt that they were dealing with phenomena that easily crossed the boundaries between the material and the spiritual worlds. As a result even formally trained doctors regularly used spiritual cures and prayers in their healing. Most people, however, did not have access to doctors or even formally trained practitioners, especially in rural areas; and therefore they sought cures elsewhere. Perhaps the most important healers in the Renaissance were women, usually wives or mothers responsible for the health of their households. This day-to-day healing role of women was so informal that it hardly appears in the records, but it is a kind of background noise in many descriptions of Renaissance healing: women providing the first cures in cases referred to doctors; women discussing remedies for family members in church or in the streets; women passing on healing remedies from generation to generation and through women's networks. A number of women, however, took these skills beyond the home and became healers in their communities. In fact, working as a healer was an especially good option for older women on their own or with limited resources; it was a form of labor that usually did not require great strength or formal training. As a result, across Renaissance Europe there was a major medical world parallel to the formal one of doctors, surgeons, and university medical schools – a much more popular, accessible, and affordable world of wives, mothers, and women healers.

Most of these women saw no reason to limit their cures to the use of simple herbs and potions. Just as doctors were willing to use the spiritual to help empower their cures, women turned to the spiritual world. Simple prayer was available to everyone and, of course, widely respected as an aid in curing, but it was not a long step from such unquestioned uses of the spiritual realm to more questionable ones. Things with recognized spiritual power such as holy oil, holy water, the Eucharist, rosaries, relics, and even bits of the holy like the dust from a church bell, could all be diverted by healers to their task. In turn, many believed prayers could be made more powerful by pressuring saints, angels, and perhaps demons and devils to come to the aid of the sick. Healers in the Renaissance who were willing to use the spiritual world to aid in their healing found no lack of opportunities, manipulating everything from simple prayer to the deeper spiritual powers of Christianity, and on to some of the strongest spiritual powers in the cosmos including the Virgin Mary and Christ himself. These were heavy weapons, indeed, against illness.

Yet at the same time these were exactly the kind of incursions into the spiritual realm to summon power that created fears of witchcraft and *maleficia*. Often it was assumed that the power to heal was reversible: those who had the spiritual power to heal, had the spiritual power to make people fall sick. To the extent that this was believed this whole parallel world of women healers had the potential to dissolve into one where women, as practitioners of *maleficia*, made others fall ill. Once again this vision is confirmed by the myriad denunciations of women healers as witches by their communities, when people began to suspect that they had turned to harming others. One might well ask why a woman earning her living as a healer would want to harm people; for many in the Renaissance the answer lay in the question itself. If money was made healing the sick, what better way to increase income than to make more people sick, especially when having caused the illness, one could easily cure it. It was a perfect scam, Renaissance style! And, of course, the healer with her reversible knowledge was the perfect source of vendetta magic as well. As a result, when fear of evil witches spread through a community, there usually was no lack of local women available to accuse. And although such accusations did not lack misogynistic elements, in a way they also reflected a reasonable fear of the widely recognized forms of power and authority that women to a great extent at that time had.

In sum, witchcraft and magic were involved in a wide range of Renaissance ways of thinking about and dealing with the everyday world. And crucially they played a central role in emphasizing the way in which that everyday world – often assumed to be materialistic, static and limited – was closely and deeply integrated with a complex, dynamic, and powerful spiritual world. Ordinary people understood and were prepared to use the spiritual to protect their honor, to gain and wield power, and be healed. To gain these Renaissance necessities they went to others, often women, who specialized in crossing the close and permeable boundary that separated the material from the spiritual even if (or even because) they were labeled witches or magicians.

The Repression of Witchcraft and Magic

Of course, the story of witchcraft and magic in the Renaissance is not only the story of practice and thinking about the spiritual world from the perspective of the everyday culture of the period, it is also the much better-known story of repression, and of the way high culture understood the impact of the spiritual world (particularly the evil spiritual world) on daily life. At one time that story was dominated by the way in which prescriptive texts of the late Middle Ages and Renaissance came together in the fifteenth century, at the heart of the Renaissance, to transform *maleficia* into witchcraft, creating the stereotype of the witch aligned with the forces of evil against an embattled Christian community. The primary villain of the tale was the *Malleus maleficarum*, published in 1482 and reprinted at least thirteen times by 1520, which was seen as providing the stereotype of the witch and the program for repressing witchcraft. Recent scholarship, however, has tended to downplay the significance of the *Malleus*. The book did not stress the crucial connection between witchcraft and worshipping the Devil, that is, witchcraft's connection with the supreme spiritual force of evil that made *maleficia* much worse than a simple manipulation of spiritual (and material) forces to harm others, transforming it from just another form of assault, into the most serious crime of all: the renunciation of God to worship the Devil. This association between witchcraft and extreme evil had in fact been made much earlier, at least as far back as the High Middle Ages; it was then that theologians began to fear that the most serious forms of *maleficia* were based not simply on manipulating the spiritual, but on a formal alliance with the Devil. Up through the fourteenth century, however, most theologians saw such relationships as limited primarily to practitioners of higher forms of magic. But in the late fourteenth and early fifteenth centuries the logic of an empowering alliance with the Devil began to find its way back into the discussion of everyday magic practiced by humble people. The reasons for this are not clear, but one may have been the association of lesser forms of *maleficia* with contemporary heresies like those of the Albigensians and Waldensians, heretical movements that were perceived as misusing the spiritual and often accused of being aligned with the Devil against Christianity.

It was not hard to place witches in the same context as they too seemed to be using spiritual forces for evil, and that logically implied some form of alliance with the Devil himself, even if witches were unwilling to admit it or even realize it. Significantly, the repression of heresy from the late thirteenth into the fifteenth century spawned a number of handbooks on the nature of heresies and techniques for destroying them, often written by members of the mendicant orders, especially Dominicans. In this literature we see the progressive stressing of *maleficia* as another form of heresy, one based upon an alliance with the Devil, and the gradual formation of the stereotype of a devil-worshipping witch who attended the Sabbat, and renounced God to gain the use of evil spiritual power. In this context the *Malleus*, written by two Dominicans who had hunted heretics and witches, was actually a late and slightly flawed contribution, lacking as it did an emphasis on the witch's formal alliance with the Devil. Its unmistakably misogynistic tone, however, creates a strong association between witchcraft and women, and its pervasive hostility to sex may also have added a sexual dimension to fear of witchcraft.

But repression requires more than prescriptive texts, it requires the ability to act; and from this standpoint the repression of witchcraft and magic in Europe from the fourteenth to the mid-seventeenth centuries takes on a decidedly Renaissance tone. For it is the changing bureaucratic nature of Renaissance society that may have made the famous witch-hunts possible. It is a familiar story, but across Europe, where the economic flourishing of the High Middle Ages had the greatest impact, and especially in northern Italy, towns and cities grew up with a much more complex and conflicted social and economic life. Such growth stimulated the development of increasingly articulated bureaucracies to discipline urban life (see the essays by Muir, Hanlon, and Appuhn above). Discipline was the key here – and the term was, in fact, often evoked at the time – discipline provided by stricter policing, more aggressive laws controlling dress and behavior, and a whole panoply of new courts and magistracies controlling urban life, where residents could litigate their disputes rather than fight them out in the streets.

For the repression of witchcraft two crucial aspects of this bureaucratic Renaissance – and often bureaucratic changes were modeled on ancient models – were the revival of Roman Law and the development of torture as an evidentiary tool in criminal procedure. From the late thirteenth century the revival of Roman Law profoundly changed the nature of governance, first in Renaissance cities and then across society. And one of the most influential changes was a gradual replacement of an accusatorial system of justice with an inquisitorial system. The older accusatorial system of justice was much more community based; many crimes were settled outside the courts via customary and personal ways of settling disputes. In disputes that went to court, the accused were denounced by victims, their families or supporters, and guilt or innocence was usually settled by ordeal, combat, or other form of confrontation that ultimately turned on a theory of divine intervention deciding guilt. In the inquisitorial system the process could be initiated by government itself (although accusations still often figured prominently), officials collected proofs of guilt and judges decided on guilt and penalties. In reality, this apparent sharp contrast between systems was seldom so neat; by the early Renaissance most systems of justice were more complex than the simple accusatorial model and local customs, especially in cities, had developed many elements that could be labeled as inquisitorial. But with the reintroduction of Roman Law – a law that presupposed an inquisitorial system – inquisitorial forms began a process of conquering first the cities of Europe and then the countryside. The one exception was England, where a jury system followed a rather different course and significantly, the prosecution of witchcraft seems to have been different there as well, as noted earlier.

One problem, however, with the inquisitorial system as it developed in a Roman Law context was that with the de-emphasis on divine judgment in the form of ordeals or combats, guilt had to be proven in other ways. Roman Law stressed confession and, given the difficulty of obtaining confessions, most inquisitorial tribunals turned to torture as a tool for securing them. Many understood that torture was unreliable and its use was carefully restricted, at least in theory; thus courts had to provide strong evidence of guilt before torture could be used; torture had to be limited (the ability of the accused to withstand torture and the evidence suggesting guilt were crucial limiting factors); if torture did not produce a confession the accused was to be released; and confessions gained under torture had to be confirmed afterwards. When such restrictions were followed judicial torture seemed to limit the problem of proving guilt and provided a tool for obtaining convictions with inquisitorial procedure. In sum, it helped make inquisitorial procedure effective and efficient enough to serve the desire for more ordered and controlled urban environments in the Renaissance.

But the problem was that when society seemed to be seriously threatened it was easy to forget restrictions on the use of torture and, together with the inquisitorial system, it could lead to fearsome repression. Already in the fifteenth century, in the cities of northern Italy, this was occasionally the case for sodomy. In Venice, for example, there were a number of large trials where individuals accused of sodomy were tortured to extract confessions, following inquisitorial forms, and torture was continued to extract the names of other accomplices. When the accomplices were then rounded up and in turn tortured a chain reaction of accusations and convictions was created that led to the conviction and burning alive of "schools of sodomites," mini-witch-hunts in form at least.[10] Moreover, as city-states and then developing nation states tried to bring the countryside under inquisitorial forms of justice, central authorities were often unable to ensure the required procedural safeguards. And, in fact, it is significant that witch-hunts often occurred in remote areas, minimally controled by central authorities, even while they used the newer Renaissance forms of inquisitorial justice and torture. But in the fourteenth century and early fifteenth century as these reforms were being introduced in the context of broader bureaucratic reforms associated with the early Renaissance, prosecutions for *maleficia* remained relatively rare and focused on such crimes in the context of assault or vendetta using illicit spiritual or material powers.

Clearly something more was necessary to set in motion the Renaissance machinery of repression and the new learned vision of the evil witch, successfully theoretized and ready to be applied. It may well be that what was lacking still was consent; even in the most strictly controlled societies, repression needs a certain level of broader acceptance to function. Although many factors may have played a role in building consent for repression, three stand out: the regular return of the plague, aggressive preaching campaigns by reform-minded clerics, and a growing anxiety about the power of the spiritual and the Devil in daily life. Scholars are beginning to re-evaluate the impact of the first wave of the plague that swept through Europe in 1347–8. While the massive die-off of a third to a half or more of Europe's population cannot be denied, the idea of a similarly massive wave of anxiety and fear sweeping Europe in its aftermath seems more difficult to sustain. It may be that the first wave of the plague actually fitted well with widespread expectations in the thirteenth and fourteenth century that Europe with all its rapidly changing, untraditional, and "sinful" ways would be punished by God. In essence, the apocalyptical assumptions that seem to closely shadow periods of change were seen as merely fulfilled by the plague. Significantly, however, when the plague returned in the 1370s and continued to return thereafter (see the essay above by Mary Lindemann) other explanatory scenarios had to be imagined. God's wrath with a sinful world began to seem not a once-only cleansing, but a continuing eruption of the spiritual in this world, in an ongoing epic battle between the forces of good and evil: a battle where that wrath might well be triggered by local heretics, sodomites, or witches who worshipped the Devil.

Such spiritual uncertainties were expressed and given new meanings and form by militant reforming movements and fire-breathing preachers, who became very popular in the last decades of the fourteenth and the first decades of the fifteenth century, and continued popular even in the most sophisticated urban centers of Renaissance Italy. Perhaps the best known of these preachers was Bernardino of Siena (1380–1444) who, like many others, moved from city to city delivering sermons that instructed in fear and called for reform and a return to a more God-fearing way of life, and invoked a close God hovering ever near the boundary between the spiritual and material world, ready to make his wrath felt. And tellingly, one of the preacher's favorite targets was witchcraft and heretical alliances with the Devil. Preaching widely in Italy in the early fifteenth century he proclaimed, "There is neither town nor castle nor state that is not filled with seers, sorcerers, diviners and witches." Witchcraft, he argued, was one of the top sins of man "for which God frequently condemns and punishes states and kingdoms,"[11] and in the context of the time plague seemed the punishment that God preferred. The repressive intention of this logic was well exemplified by a sermon that Bernardino preached in his home city of Siena in 1427, where he referred with great enthusiasm to his success in having a number of witches burnt in Rome a few years before. Similar fires, he argued needed to be lighted in Siena to save the city from God's wrath and he concluded "To the fire! . . . If I could only make the same thing happen here . . . Oh, let's send up to the Lord God some of the same incense right here in Siena!"[12]

Bernardino's preaching was highly visible and influential, but it was merely a part of a larger preaching movement and a broader fear of God's wrath that helped raise the witch as a priority for repression, both in the prescriptive literature of the fifteenth century and in the bureaucratic drives of urban governments in Italy and elsewhere. It is significant that many city governments strengthened their laws against witchcraft and black magic in direct response to demands from impassioned preachers and popular expressions of mass piety. Also significant is the fact that while in most of the rest of Europe the mass hysteria associated with witch-hunting came later (ca. 1570–ca. 1650), in the urban areas of Italy, the first larger trials, which occurred in the fifteenth century, were often associated with preachers like Bernardino.[13] In fact, it is arguable that Rome and the papacy's later reluctance to support witch-hunts may have been in part due to their earlier and not entirely satisfactory experience with what they perceived as the dangers of powerful (and difficult to discipline) popular preachers and the popular piety that fired such hunts in fifteenth-century Italy.

Evaluating the anxiety level of a society or a period is a highly risky business, but nonetheless I want to suggest, sinning boldly as Luther recommended, that this level of fear, disseminated in the wake of the plague by preachers and reformers, grew in the sixteenth century and became a kind of sea-change in Europe. And that sea-change was deeply associated again with events that were central to the Renaissance: the invasions of Italy that began in 1494 and involved most of Europe; the reform and division of Christianity (see the essay by Hsia above) that enveloped the sixteenth and first half of the seventeenth centuries in confessional strife and further war and violence; the encounter with "new" worlds, which problematized yet further man's place in the world and relationship with God; and a growing inner sense of self and self-evaluation associated with reformed Christianity on both sides of the confessional divide. In sum, the very stuff of this volume. In this short essay I cannot sustain the bold assertion that the sixteenth century ushered in an age of deeper anxiety by considering all these changes or illustrating with the necessary detail the way this anxiety was manifested throughout society. Others have attempted the task with mixed results, perhaps because proving such sweeping assertions satisfactorily is virtually impossible.[14]

In this climate of fear and repression in the second half of the sixteenth century, the anti-heretical literature that focused on the witch and pacts with the Devil expanded exponentially. Witches became the anti-world *par excellence*, literally the dialectical opposite of all that was good in God's creation. First, they rejected God to worship the Devil; turning one's back on God to follow the Devil was the basis of all sin, echoing the Original Sin in the Garden of Eden. But the witch's anti-world was all-encompassing. While mankind's goal after the Fall was to multiply and make the earth fruitful, the goal of witches was to destroy both babies and the fruits of the earth. As the godly went to Mass and ritually united with God via the mystery of the Eucharist, witches went to the Sabbat and ritually united with the Devil via orgiastic rites of submission. In fact this dialectic vision was rife with reversals at every level, from the most cosmic to the most comic (to modern eyes at least): if at the Mass Christians united with God in purity, at the Sabbat witches united with the Devil via sodomy; if at the Mass Christians exchanged the kiss of peace, at the Sabbat witches kissed the ass of the devil; if at the Mass the faithful sang the praises of God with decorum and discipline, at the Sabbat the Devil's horde dissolved in orgy and disorder to discordant music. And beyond the Sabbat, while the faithful humbly walked the paths of everyday life as servants of God, witches flew above those paths, overthrowing the rules of daily existence with pride and wrath as servants of Satan. While Christians remained what they were, human and God-fearing, witches transformed themselves into animals, often of the most frightening or distasteful sorts. The anti-world of this prescriptive view of witchcraft is so rich with apparent reversals that it has been argued it provides a crucial window on the dialectical nature of the Renaissance mind.[15]

But timing was important here. For there was a significant gap between the creation of the bureaucratic tools for repression and the development of the diabolical vision of the witch and this second wave of repressive literature and repression. In the first half of the sixteenth century the Italian Wars and the Reformation itself focused fears and bureaucracies on more immediate problems, and as a result witches to a great extent had to await their repression. But that time of turmoil if anything strengthened the forces of fear and repression. In 1542 the Catholic Church, notably, reformed the medieval Inquisition, giving it new powers, new funding, and strong support to wipe out heresy. And in much the same time-frame at the Council of Trent (1545–7, 1551–2, 1562–3) it reorganized and strengthened its own theological underpinnings and bureaucratic structure, with an eye to making it an efficient and compact Church Militant that would be capable of standing up to heresy and would discipline Catholics as never before. Meanwhile, in Protestant Europe similar drives to discipline a new Christian society took different forms but were often in alliance with developing urban and national bureaucracies – frequently using inquisitorial procedure and torture – to produce structures of power with great repressive potential.

In sum, by the second half of the sixteenth century Europe had articulated a vision of witchcraft that required its repression; developed a strong reservoir of fear of heresy and heretics aligned with the Devil; and had had experience with the violent extirpation of heresy; these things in conjunction with newly articulated bureaucracies prepared the way for the witch-hunts that followed. Curiously, in Italy, which in many ways created the tools for repression, prosecutions were more moderate and less lethal. The renewed Inquisition, after an aggressive period of policing confessional "heresy," began in the mid-1570s to discipline the more "minor" misuses of the spiritual in the everyday world of people in the town and country. Although witchcraft was a major concern it seems that the Inquisition acted with a considerable bureaucratic rigor and restraint, most notably using torture sparingly. As a result witches tried by the Inquisition in Italy seldom referred to pacts with the Devil and most were convicted for *maleficia* and at worst "suspicion of heresy," crimes requiring correction rather than severe punishment. Executions were rare and usually the work of local secular courts acting on their own and using torture.

Turning to the North, the bureaucratic context of witch-hunts seems again central. Especially in Protestant towns and cities, reformed communities attempting to create the City of God on earth (focused on Christian community and a more godly way of life) were susceptible to being sidetracked into panics about hidden diabolical sects and witches bent on undermining their success. Although it is a facile generalization it still needs to be said that communities of saints have difficulty dealing with the fact that the visible signs of a community's saintliness never seem enough; there seems to be too much evil in everyday life to sustain such a faith. A strong Devil and diabolical traitors working against the community are easy to imagine and can focus fears in a wide range of circumstances. It might be fear of the "new" poor in England; fear of old, no longer fertile women; fear of seemingly vengeful lower-class people; fear of marginal people; or fear of outsiders and vagabonds. Both rising and lowering expectations – really, any perceived disruption of community – could trigger such fears and an ensuing discovery of Satan's followers. This may well be the reason that scholars have posited so many different reasons for witch-hunts; simply, there were many different local reasons and broader generalizations will always have limited value for explaining local situations. Having said that, however, the common factors in the witch-hunts of northern Europe were fear – focusing on a witchly pact with the Devil – and newer more aggressive bureaucracies – relying on torture to discover and convict witches.

Not surprisingly this Renaissance fear and bureaucracy both jumped the Atlantic without great difficulty and continued to have an impact in the New World. In Protestant-dominated areas of North America fears fastened on threats to the community of saints, and purges could consist of swift fires burning through communities in the classic mode of northern European witch-hunts, even without extensive use of torture. In the areas conquered by Catholic countries the relationship was more complex, because large numbers of the indigenous populations were thought to practice diabolical magic. From virtually the first contact some Europeans feared that natives worshipped the Devil, which explained their seemingly strange and incomprehensible religious beliefs. Still, on the whole, the ideal that prevailed was one of conversion. As time wore on, however, fears began to grow, especially as it became clear that many converts – perhaps encouraged by Catholic tendencies to accept syncretism – continued "strange" practices and ways of understanding the spiritual world that could be interpreted as witchcraft and diabolical magic. Crucially, the conquerors had brought with them the institutional forms of the Spanish Inquisition and in the New World it pursued this "witchcraft" with zeal. With time, however, it seems that it became more interested in investigating native spiritual beliefs in order to repress and control more effectively native populations and create the disciplined Christian society that they envisioned. (See the essay by Matthew Restall above.)

But it must be kept to the fore that all these witch-hunts, especially those of northern Europe and the New World, were less about witchcraft and more about who would control the power the spiritual world had to offer. It seems clear that few witches lived down to the models created by the prescriptive literature of the fifteenth and sixteenth centuries. In fact, it may be argued, as some have done, that if we measure witchcraft by the definitions of that literature witches hardly existed at all. Be that as it may, I think it is safe to assume that the classic witch of prescriptive literature hiding men's phalluses was largely the stuff of fantasy – a fantasy both interesting and dangerous. But that does not mean we should forget the many women and men who actually attempted to manipulate the spiritual world for power and profit. In a way, in the Renaissance, every town and village needed its witches and magicians, for they provided a crucial source of the absolute necessities of Renaissance society: honor, love, health, and power. And neatly, they found it right at the heart of everyday life, just across that very close and permeable border that all humans straddled between the material world and the spiritual world. When everyday life slowly withdrew from that border and the spiritual became a distant territory mediated by priests and clerics or simply an alien territory dominated by the word of a distant God (or when it was to a great extent marginalized by the new materialistic powers of science and technology), witchcraft and magic quietly died, along with witch-hunts and the Renaissance.

NOTES

1   *Malleus maleficarum* as quoted in Kors and Peters, *Witchcraft*, p. 151. Note that this was a perfect Renaissance place to hide stolen male members, given the metaphorical association of phalluses, birds, nests, and codpieces at the time.
2   Archivio di Stato, Venezia, Sant'Ufficio, busta 62, Case of Fra Gabriele Garofolo, 1588, unfoliated.
3   These figures are based on Brian Levack's calculations in Levack, *Witch-hunt*, pp. 23–5.
4   For England see: Macfarlane, *Witchcraft* and Thomas, *Decline of Magic*; for Spain Henningsen, *Basque Witchcraft* and Monter, *Frontiers*; and for Italy, Ruggiero, *Binding Passions*, Ginzburg, *Night Battles*, and O'Neil, "Magical Healing."
5   See Ruggiero, *Binding Passions*, especially chs. 3 and 4.
6   Bynum, *Holy Feast*, p. 64 and more generally pp. 54–65.
7   See Ruggiero, "More Dear to Me Than Life Itself," in *Binding Passions*, pp. 57–87.
8   Ibid., pp. 74–5.
9   Ibid. pp. 88–129, 213–17 for examples; such problems were not limited to Italy, as the insistent rumors about the use of love magic to force royal marriages suggests, most notably perhaps in the woes of the wives of Henry VIII of England. At a more humble level even the famous Martin Guerre suffered from love magic; see Davis, *Return*, pp. 19–21, 28.
10 Ruggiero, *Boundaries*, pp. 137–45.
11 Mormando, *Preacher's Demons*, p. 52 and in general pp. 52–108.
12 Ibid., p. 52.
13 Kieckhefer, *European Witch Trials*, pp. 10–26.
14 Perhaps most notably Delumeau, in *Sin and Fear*.
15 See Clark, *Thinking with Demons*.

REFERENCES

Bynum, Caroline Walker, *Holy Feast and Holy Fast: The Religious Significance of Food to Medieval Women* (Berkeley: University of California Press, 1987).

Clark, Stuart, *Thinking with Demons: The Idea of Witchcraft in Early Modern Europe* (Oxford: Clarendon Press, 1997).

Davis, Natalie Z., *The Return of Martin Guerre* (Cambridge, MA: Harvard University Press, 1983).

Delumeau, Jean, *Sin and Fear: The Emergence of a Western Guilt Culture, 13th–18th Centuries*, trans. Eric Nicholson (New York: St. Martin's Press, 1990).

Ginzburg, Carlo, *The Night Battles: Witchcraft and Agrarian Cults in the Sixteenth and Seventeenth Centuries*, trans. John and Anne Tedeschi (Baltimore: Johns Hopkins University Press, 1983).

Henningsen, Gustav, *The Witches' Advocate: Basque Witchcraft and the Spanish Inquisition, 1609–1614* (Reno: University of Nevada Press, 1980).

Kieckhefer, Richard, *European Witch Trials: Their Foundation in Popular and Learned Culture, 1300–1500* (Berkeley: University of California Press, 1976).

Kors, Alan C. and Peters, Edward, eds., *Witchcraft in Europe, 1100–1700* (Philadelphia: University of Pennsylvania Press, 1972).

Kramer, Heinrich and Sprenger, James, *The Malleus maleficarum*, trans. and ed. M. Summers (New York: Dover, 1971).

Levack, Brian P., *The Witch-hunt in Early Modern Europe* (London: Longman, 1994).

Macfarlane, Alan, *Witchcraft in Tudor and Stuart England* (London: Routledge, 1970).

Monter, E. William, *Frontiers of Heresy: The Spanish Inquisition from the Basque Lands to Sicily* (New York: Cambridge University Press, 1990).

Mormando, Franco, *The Preacher's Demons: Bernardino of Siena and the Social Underworld of Early Renaissance Italy* (Chicago: University of Chicago Press, 1999).

O'Neil, Mary, "Magical Healing, Love Magic and the Inquisition in Late Sixteenth-Century Modena," in *Inquisition and Society in Early Modern Europe*, ed. Stephen Haliczer (Totowa, NJ: Barnes and Noble, 1987).

Ruggiero, Guido, *The Boundaries of Eros: Sex Crime and Sexuality in Renaissance Venice* (New York: Oxford University Press, 1985).

——, *Binding Passions: Tales of Magic, Marriage and Power at the End of the Renaissance* (New York: Oxford University Press, 1993).

Thomas, Keith, *Religion and the Decline of Magic* (New York: Macmillan, 1971).

FURTHER READING

Ankarloo, Bengt and Henningsen, Gustav, eds., *Early Modern Witchcraft: Centres and Peripheries* (Oxford: Clarendon Press, 1990).

Boyer, Paul and Nissenbaum, Stephen, *Salem Possessed: The Social Origins of Witchcraft* (Cambridge, MA: Harvard University Press, 1974).

Briggs, Robin, *Witches and Neighbors: The Social and Cultural Context of European Witchcraft* (New York: Viking, 1996).

Demos, John P., *Entertaining Satan: Witchcraft and the Culture of Early New England* (New York: Oxford University Press, 1982).

Gentilcore, David, *From Bishop to Witch: The System of the Sacred in Early Modern Terra d'Otranto* (Manchester: Manchester University Press, 1992).

Hsia, R. Po-chia, *The Myth of Ritual Murder: Jews and Magic in Reformation Germany* (New Haven: Yale University Press, 1988).

Larner, Christina, *Witchcraft and Religion: The Politics of Popular Belief* (Oxford: Blackwell Publishers, 1984).

Midelfort, H. C. Eric, *Witch Hunting in Southwestern Germany, 1562–1684: The Social and Intellectual Foundations* (Stanford: Stanford University Press, 1971).

Monter, E. William, *Witchcraft in France and Switzerland: The Borderlands during the Reformation* (Ithaca, NY: Cornell University Press, 1976).

Moore, R. I., *The Formation of a Persecuting Society: Power and Deviance in Western Europe, 950–1250* (Oxford: Blackwell Publishers, 1987).

Roper, Lyndal, *Oedipus and the Devil: Witchcraft, Sexuality and Religion in Early Modern Europe* (London: Routledge, 1994).

Silverblatt, Irene, *Moon, Sun and Witches: Gender Ideologies and Class in Inca and Colonial Peru* (Princeton: Princeton University Press, 1987).

CHAPTER TWENTY-EIGHT

The Illicit Worlds of the Renaissance

IAN FREDERICK MOULTON

Among the Locrensians the adulterers have both their eyes thrust out. The Romans, in times past, punished whoredom sometimes by fire, sometimes by the sword. If any man among the Egyptians had been taken in adultery, the law was that he should openly in the presence of the people be scourged naked with whips, unto the number of a thousand stripes. The woman that was taken with him had her nose cut off, whereby she was known ever after to be a whore ... Among the Turks, even at this day, they that be taken in adultery, both man and woman, are stoned straightaway to death without mercy.

Thus we see what godly acts were devised in times past of the high powers for the putting away of whoredom and for the maintaining of holy Matrimony.

("The Sermon against Adultery," in *The Book of Homilies* of the
Church of England, 1547, 1623)

Although adulterers were sometimes whipped and even mutilated in Renaissance Europe, they were seldom blinded, burned alive, or stoned. In fact, if the adulterer was male, he was often not punished at all. This passage thus does not accurately reflect early modern practice, but in its harsh rhetoric it does reflect early modern ways of thinking. Despite its gleeful advocacy of violent punishment, this text is not a rant or a marginal extremist view. It is taken from *The Book of Homilies* of the Church of England (a moderate denomination, after all) and as such reflects that Church's considered and measured opinion on the issue of adultery. As part of the *Homilies*, it was frequently read to congregations all across England. Its judgments are canonical and familiar. It thus provides a useful reminder of the seriousness with which illicit activities were treated in the Renaissance. Our own culture has a tendency to celebrate the illicit, in the same way that it tends to idealize rebellion. In the Renaissance, although illicit activities could be seen humorously or ironically, they did not tend to be idealized (neither, incidentally, was rebellion).

We must put the harsh rhetoric in context. Illicit activities were harshly condemned in part because in a society with relatively little law enforcement, the authorities, both sacred and secular, relied on harsh warnings and highly visible punishments to maintain public order. English adulterers may not have been stoned or blinded, but they were told they deserved to be, and they were publicly shamed, forced to sit in church dressed in a white sheet while the preacher denounced their sins.[1] In Italy, women taken in adultery were frequently publicly whipped, and often had their heads shaved or their clothes torn as a sign of shame. Men were also shamed in similar ways, but unlike women they sometimes had the option of paying a fine instead. Thus although adultery was universally condemned, punishment was, by modern stand-ards, uneven and erratic. Much depended on circumstance, on the gender of the offender, on their social status, on their class.

As the example of adultery demonstrates, what constituted the "illicit" in early modern Europe is a complex question. Nonetheless, it is possible for the purposes of analysis to divide illicit activity into a number of distinct categories: (1) illicit sexual activity: prostitution, adultery, same-sex relations, anything, in fact, outside the bonds of lawful marriage; (2) unfair or corrupt ways of making money: usury, gambling, cheating, stealing, smuggling; (3) inappropriate habits of consumption: excessive drinking or eating, the new vice of tobacco smoking.

An illicit activity is one that is forbidden or unlawful. But forbidden by whom? And how effectively? In modern society, generally speaking, illicit activity is illegal activity: actions that go against the laws of a given state. Thus for adults in western culture, drinking beer is not illicit, but smoking marijuana is – at least for now. The situation in the early modern period is somewhat more complex. State laws governing illicit activities were, by modern standards, weakly and erratically enforced. In comparison with contemporary society, state police played a much smaller role in social control; a far larger role was played by the Church, and also by communal organizations such as urban craft guilds. Thus an activity could be illicit if it was illegal, if it was sinful, or if it transgressed community norms.

Activities denounced as sinful by the Church were not necessarily illegal, and might even be generally accepted within a given community; drunkenness and smoking were widely decried, for example, but there were few laws against either. Other activities, although sinful and illegal, were nonetheless granted a degree of toleration in practice. Both usury and sodomy, for example, were universally condemned but widely practiced. Sex between men was forbidden by the Church and punishable by law, and yet in England few accusations of sodomy were brought before the courts, and even fewer led to convictions. In Renaissance Florence, possibly the state in which sodomy was most extensively prosecuted, it seems that as many as two of every three adult men were implicated in the practice. Similarly, despite English laws prohibiting premarital sex, engaged couples had sexual relations so frequently that, to judge by parish records, as many as 30 percent of brides – like Shakespeare's bride Anne Hathaway – were pregnant on their wedding day.[2]

To understand the social dynamics of illicit activity in the Renaissance, one must understand the various mechanisms of control and punishment that condemned certain actions. First of all, and perhaps most importantly, there was the Church. Whether Catholic or Protestant, the various Churches of Renaissance Europe rou-tinely condemned a vast array of human activity as sinful and damnable. There was of course local, doctrinal, and communal variation on where exactly the boundaries of the illicit began, but generally speaking the Churches condemned a wider range of activity than did the state or other secular authorities such as guilds. Having said that, it is also true that the Renaissance saw a general secularization of the justice system as monarchies exerted increasing control over their subjects' lives. (See the essays above by James Farr and Gregory Hanlon.) In England, for example, sodomy went from being a sin punished by church courts to being a crime punished by civil courts. Sorcery and heresy became felonies under civil law at the same time.

In a traditional society, informed at all levels by religion and religious belief, there was a great difference in valence between sin and crime, though the same activity could fit into both categories. To a devout believer, sin was much more serious than crime, for it was not only a transgression of human law, but went against the nature of the universe and the will of God. Human laws could be unjust or corrupt, but God's law was unimpeachable. Sin could not be avoided, but it had to be recognized and sincerely repented – though the precise mechanism for this was a matter of intense and violent conflict in the period following Luther's break with the Church. Of course, the doctrine of sin and salvation was taken with different degrees of seriousness by different people, but as a cultural model it was powerful and pervasive. While many people were not especially devout, there were few self-identified atheists in early modern Europe, and public order was maintained by sermons as well as by policing.

Beyond the ministers of Church and state, order was also enforced communally, both by social organizations such as guilds and by the community at large. Scolding women were ducked in ponds; quarrelsome spouses were shamed by "rough music" and charivaris; similar punishments were sometimes meted out to widows who remarried, or to husbands who beat their wives. In France, husbands who had failed to produce children could be subjected to public "trials of impotence" to prove their virility.[3]

Whatever form of authority they transgress, all illicit activities share certain common characteristics. First, they are pleasure-driven. Illicit acts are all designed to satisfy bodily lusts and desires. As such, they stand in opposition to the rational control of the passions which was believed crucial to orderly human society. Based as they are on a rejection of rational self-government, illicit acts threaten the basis of social order and human community; and thus even the most seemingly trivial of them can have great symbolic power. Their rebellious quality is paradoxical, however, for to a certain extent they constitute a rebellion of the privileged: illicit activities were primarily, though not exclusively, aimed at gratifying the desires of men, in many cases upper-class men attempting to gain freedom and reject responsibilities. Though there were women swindlers, women who had sexual relations with other women, and women who drank and smoked, the larger social structures that facilitated illicit activities were primarily designed for and by men: there were no brothels for women to be serviced by men; women were strongly discouraged from smoking tobacco; and women were far more harshly and frequently punished for adulterous relations. As well, the commercial structures that supported illicit activity were predominantly, though not always, male controlled: courtesans depended on powerful male protectors, prostitutes worked for male pimps, female thieves worked for male masters.

Second, illicit activity, while in fact widely distributed throughout the countryside, was most often and most powerfully imagined as urban. London, Paris, Venice, Rome – these were the sites of iniquity. In a period of fairly rapid urban growth and a relative shift of political power from the country to the city, the urban world was an exciting and terrifying site of social dislocation. The relative anonymity of city life, the mixing of high and low classes, the daily proximity of rich and poor, the presence of foreigners – all these combined to make the early modern city a place of social uncertainty and potential danger. The urban environment also offered many options for masculine pleasure. Thomas Nashe, the English satirist, describes an idle gentleman in London dividing his leisure time "either into gaming, following of harlots, drinking, or seeing a play."[4] Even the theater, the most "innocent" of these diversions, was known as "Venus' palace"[5] and was frequently equated with brothels in contemporary polemic. Cities concentrated a wide variety of vice in a small space. And thus, while the most notorious sexual crime in early modern England – the Earl of Castlehaven's sodomitical abuse of his wife and servants[6] – took place on a country estate, in the popular imagination it was the liberties of London, not secluded castles, which were the quintessential site of sexual depravity.

Third, there was a strong tendency to imagine that illicit activity was highly organized – that it did, in fact, constitute an illicit world which mirrored and parodied the structures of respectable life. There were persistent rumors of the existence of a thieves' guild, and thieves' cant, or slang, was seen as constituting a language all its own. Moralists spoke metaphorically of "schools" of abuse, in which young people would learn to become corrupt and lascivious.[7] Prostitutes, pimps, innkeepers, and swindlers were widely imagined to be working in league, in a smoothly coordinated operation designed to separate fools from their money with almost clinical precision. English stage plays presented their spectators with secret societies of young men devoted to drinking and smoking as if to some arcane cult.[8] Dutch sermons compared brothels to the stock exchange. Although it is difficult to find hard evidence to substantiate rumors of secret criminal societies, their importance in the popular imagination cannot be overstressed.

If people living at the time did not have a clear and accurate idea about the extent and organization of illicit activities in their own culture, how is an historian to excavate them four hundred years later? Broadly speaking, there are three sources of information on illicit activities in the period: court records, moralistic attacks, and fictional accounts. All three are, in different ways, problematic. But despite methodological difficulties, each of these sources contains a wealth of information, and if read with an awareness of their limitations and an appropriate degree of skepticism, they can tell us much about the illicit worlds they represent.

There are some obvious problems with court records: they are often biased or incomplete, statements are often coerced or of questionable accuracy, and – after all – they offer a record only of those who got caught. Moralistic attacks, either satires or sermons or pamphlets, can tell us a lot about common attitudes towards illicit activity. But besides being prone to exaggeration, they are also frequently formulaic, organized by a set of generic and rhetorical principles rather than being based on accurate or specific description. We also lack strong evidence on how such tracts were received. Did their readers and auditors always take them seriously, accept their claims, and agree with their judgments? The third source of evidence is fictional representation, in poems, prose narratives, and drama, or visual representations such as prints or paintings. Erotic texts, in particular, offer valuable insights into illicit activity in the period. Although it was frequently criticized, sexually explicit writing was not generally subject to strict control in the early modern period; broadly speaking, governments were much more concerned to limit the circulation of heretical or politically inflammatory texts than they were about erotic writing. In any case, much erotic writing was circulated in manuscript rather than print, and thus was free from most forms of censorship. But while such materials can tell us much about how illicit activity was imagined and understood, like all fictional accounts their accuracy is always in question, as is the nature of their reception by their original audiences.

The most notorious illicit world in the Renaissance imagination was that associated with prostitution. In the popular imagination, the brothel constituted a parodic mirror image of the respectable world. In aristocratic court societies such as papal Rome, the brothel was an anti-court, where women ruled and men were hopeful suitors. In more bourgeois societies, such as the Netherlands, the brothel became an "anti-home," a domestic space in which domestic values such as thrift, sobriety, and fidelity were mocked and negated. Prostitution in various forms was ubiquitous in early modern society; in villages too small to have a permanent brothel prostitutes would often work out of the local inn or tavern. Although in larger cities such as London, there were districts, such as Shoreditch and the Bankside, which were known for their high concentration of brothels, bawdy houses were to be found in all neighborhoods. One was so close to the Guildhall that the Lord Mayor himself was disturbed by the noise.[9]

In the late Middle Ages in France, Italy, and England, prostitution had often been licensed by civic authorities – and even by the Church – on the theory that it was a lesser evil than the seduction of the wives or marriageable daughters of respectable citizens. The licensing of brothels did not, however, mean that prostitution was an honored or accepted profession. And all over Europe the religious turmoil of the sixteenth century was marked by an increasing judicial and social crack-down on prostitution. Although it is debatable whether or not the levels of prostitution decreased, there is no question that prostitution at all levels became less acceptable and increasingly illicit. In many cities practicing prostitutes had to be registered with the civic authorities, and there were efforts to make them wear distinctive clothing. Although the male clients of prostitutes were not similarly shamed, frequenting brothels gradually became less openly acceptable, at least for married men in respectable society.

Throughout Italy, "charitable" institutions were established by the Catholic Church in an attempt to control the social and economic conditions that gave rise to prostitution. To give them their Venetian names: the *Convertite* was for those who had given up their profession; the *Incurabile*, for those afflicted by syphilis; the *Zitelle* for unmarried girls who might be tempted to turn to prostitution; and the *Malmaritate*, for women whose marriages had foundered. In Protestant England a similar function was performed by Bridewell, a "hospital" founded in 1553 for the correction of scolds, whores, and vagrants. Theoretically a place of refuge, Bridewell was actually a brutal prison, in which inmates were regularly whipped and poorly fed. And it was the Bridewell authorities who led a crack-down on the London brothels in the years after 1570.

Like most other aspects of early modern society, prostitution was a hierarchical profession, with enormous differences in wealth and status between the high and low ends of the market. At the highest end were kept women, who often lived in great comfort, rode in coaches, and wore fine clothes. These women tended to have some level of control over their own finances, and restricted themselves to a small number of clients at any one time. Next came brothel whores, who lived and worked out of a bawdy house owned and operated by male pimps and female bawds. These women were often exploited by their employers, and their wages were dependent on volume: the more clients they serviced, the more money they made. Other whores were not affiliated with permanent brothels, but worked out of inns and rented rooms. These women too were employed and often exploited by pimps, and were reliant on the good will of their landlords to stay in business. At the bottom of the heap were street whores, who serviced clients in alleyways and dark corners, and were often homeless themselves.

The courtesans of Rome and Venice were another matter altogether. Both these cities had high populations of well-educated, wealthy, unattached men: either clerics who were unable to marry or visiting merchants, living far from both their country and their family. While the precise origins of courtesan culture remain obscure, it seems clear that courtesans responded to a demand for sophisticated female companionship: artistic and intellectual, as well as sexual. Courtesans were not only sexually skilled; they were well educated, and could knowledgeably discuss poetry and philosophy. They often wrote poetry – the Venetian courtesans Gaspara Stampa and Veronica Franco were both published authors – and many courtesans were trained to sing and play instruments, sometimes at a very high level of proficiency. They lived in gorgeous houses, wore sumptuous clothes of the finest fabrics, dyed their hair, wore exquisite makeup, and kept exotic pets like monkeys, tropical birds, and rare breeds of dog.

In their heyday, the courtesans of Venice and Rome were renowned from one end of Europe to the other. They served as models for the greatest Renaissance painters: Leonardo, Carpaccio, Raphael, Titian, Tintoretto. They inspired an outpouring of literature: Pietro Aretino's *Ragionamenti* (1534, 1536), which recounted the scandalous and hilarious career of a fictional courtesan named Nanna; the Dutch *Spiegel der Vermaarde Courtesanen* (The Mirror of the Most Celebrated Courtesans, 1630), a collection of courtesan's biographies; Gervase Markham's English poem *The Famous Whore, or Noble Curtizan* (1609), which recounts the career of "Paulina, the famous Roman Curtizan, sometimes mistress unto the great Cardinal Ippolito d'Este"; and Lorenzo Veniero's Italian poems "La trentuna di Zaffetta" (The Gang Rape of Zaffetta, ca. 1533) and "La puttana errante" (The Wandering Whore, ca. 1533). Travelers from Michel de Montaigne to Thomas Coryat recounted their experiences of meeting the great courtesans of Venice. Catalogues such as the *Dialogo di Zoppino* (The Lame Man's Dialogue) and the *Tariffa delle puttane di Venetia* (The Prices of Venetian Whores) – both ca. 1535 – which listed the most famous attributes of Roman and Venetian courtesans, were widely circulated and were later imitated in other cities such as Amsterdam (*t'Amsterdamsch Hoerdom* (The Hague, 1694)).

The social position of the courtesan was profoundly ambiguous. Elegant, entertaining, sophisticated, and seductive, she circulated in the most exclusive levels of society, present at great feasts, highly visible at court, and even entertained royalty. Although courtesans and whores may have had, at the height of their careers, greater freedom of action and movement than some respectable women, their profession was a dangerous one and a courtesan's status was never secure. If she angered her powerful lovers, they were free to take savage revenge on her. The Roman courtesan Antea, who served as the model for Parmigianino's portrait *La Bella*, was later disfigured by an angry client. The Venetian Angela Zaffetta was abducted and gang-raped by a group of up to eighty men. In times of social crisis, a courtesan's very prominence and attractiveness could be turned against her as moralists looked for sinners to blame for the bad times that had befallen the state. As a courtesan aged and her physical attractiveness waned, she was likely to fall out of favor, her place taken by younger women. In many cases, prostitutes ended badly. Even a woman lucky enough to avoid imprisonment, syphilis, rape, or beating, would eventually see her status decline as she aged. By the time she reached her mid-thirties, a prostitute's career was effectively over and, if she had no network of kin to care for her, she faced almost certain poverty and misery. Though some courtesans managed to provide for their retirements, many women who began as courtesans ended their lives as vagrants and streetwalkers.

Despite their great fame, courtesans – like common prostitutes – were subject to increasing restrictions in the course of the sixteenth century. Whereas in 1502 fifty "decent prostitutes" had danced naked in the presence of Pope Alexander VI on the occasion of his daughter's wedding,[10] the vigorous reforms of the Counter-Reformation ensured that by the 1560s courtesans were no longer welcome at the papal court. In 1566 Pope Pius V actually attempted to banish all courtesans from Rome, though he was ultimately dissuaded by the citizenry, who argued that such an exodus of labor and capital would be ruinous for the local economy. Still, the social and religious upheavals of the Reformation and Counter-Reformation destroyed the relatively lax society that had allowed courtesans to flourish. Prostitution persisted as ever, but its shamefulness was firmly established.

One of the reasons prostitution flourished in the early modern period was the generally lengthy period between the age of sexual maturity and the common age of marriage. While aristocratic marriages were often arranged early, at other social levels young men could not marry until they had completed their apprenticeship or were otherwise capable of supporting their wife and future family. Though both men and women tended to become sexually active in their early teens, the average age of marriage for men was 25, for women 22.[11] The late age of marriage meant there were many young, sexually active men with no licit outlet for their sexual drives. Inevitably, this meant that young men engaged in various forms of illicit sex: with prostitutes, with unmarried women, with other men's wives, and with other men.

Same sex relations – especially between men – seem to have been quite common in early modern Europe, though they were not structured or understood in the same ways that they are today. In the Renaissance, there was no such thing as a "gay" identity, uniting those who shared an exclusive preference for sex with members of their own gender. In early modern culture, sex roles were more important than object choice; that is, whether a person took the active or passive role in sexual activity was more important than whom they had sex with. Men were thought to be naturally active; that is, their natural sexual role was to penetrate the bodies of others. If a man took the active role in sex with other men, he was seldom harshly punished, despite the savage laws against sodomy that were enacted all over Europe in the sixteenth century. On the other hand, men who let their bodies be penetrated by taking the passive role in anal intercourse were seen as effeminate. In prosecutions of male homosexual activity, adult men who "took the woman's part" were often much more harshly punished than their partners.[12] Sodomy, which was a catch-all category for sexual offenses, was punishable by death, and although in England almost no one was convicted as a sodomite, in Italy executions were not uncommon.

Homoerotic relations between men tended to be hierarchically structured: one partner, usually several years older than the other and possibly of higher social status, would consistently take the active role. While there may well have been exceptional cases in which two men of the same age were sexually involved, most relationships seem to have been between adult men and adolescent boys. Though some men were no doubt sexually attracted exclusively to other men, many men engaged in homo-erotic activity during their youth or before their marriage, and then less and less in later life. That is, young men had homosexual relations at the same time in their lives that they frequented prostitutes. Both activities were seen as part of the natural, if reprehensible, wildness of masculine youth. Just as married men were more likely to be criticized for having sex with prostitutes, so too male homoeroticism was seen as especially socially disruptive if it prevented a man from fulfilling his marital obliga-tions and begetting legitimate children. But in many cases if an upper-class man had a wife and children he was not strongly persecuted for also having male lovers.

Upper-class male friendship was idealized in the period, and often described in highly eroticized language, though it is impossible at this remove to tell how often this language of love and spiritual unity reflected an erotic relationship. Montaigne's famous essay on friendship shies away from the homoerotic potential of the passionate relationship it recounts (*Essays*, 1.28); Shakespeare's sonnets to the fair young man tend to flirt with the possibility without ever confirming it. Texts actually describing sexual desire or relations between men, such as Antonio Vignali's *La cazzaria* (1525) or the sonnets of Richard Barnfield, tend to be more straightforward in tone and less idealistic.

Much less is known, and much less written, about sexual relations between women. Though penalties for lesbian sex also became harsher during the sixteenth century, women were often not subject to general laws against homosexual relations. It is a telling fact that those women who were punished were generally prosecuted for using a dildo rather than for their sexual activity as such. That is, they were punished for usurping the penetrative male role, rather than for taking pleasure with members of their own sex. In a culture that put so much emphasis on both phallic penetration and the proper use of masculine seed to generate children, it may be that activity that involved neither penetration nor male ejaculation was not thought of as "sexual" at all. Besides lesbian sex, oral sex and masturbation are subjects on which documents from the period are relatively silent.

Modern readers of Dante are often puzzled by the fact that in the *Inferno* (cantos 15–17) sodomy and usury are seen as analogous sins. Are there any two human activities which seem more disparate to the modern mind than homosexuality and banking? But in the late Middle Ages, usury, like sodomy, was seen as a sin against nature: if sodomy turned the fertility of semen to sterility by diverting it from the vagina, so usury turned the sterility of gold into fertility by unnaturally breeding money. Given the economic dynamism of the Renaissance, such scholastic notions were bound to be radically re-evaluated. In the world of the Medici and the Fuggers, of Potosì and the spice trade, mere lending at interest could not long remain a sin.

Nonetheless, it is important to remember that even the most rudimentary of modern financial practices posed a threat to traditional notions of just prices and trust among neighbors. In the common mind, interest-bearing loans were associated with Jews, the quintessential European outsiders. Beyond certain bounds, profit was easily seen as a sign of sinful greed rather than godly reward.

Perhaps as a result of the influx of New World silver, the sixteenth century was marked by sustained price inflation. (See the essay above by John Marino.) Massive rises in the cost of living, combined with the terrifying and exhilarating fluidity of capitalist profit and loss contributed to a pervasive sense of economic uncertainty. Anxieties about financial ruin and the dangers of city life combined to produce an outpouring of writings warning of highly organized swindles and cons. In London in the 1590s, pamphlet after pamphlet warned of the dangers of "coney-catching," the conning of inexperienced young men by cheats, tricksters, and bawds operating in seemingly respectable city taverns. The "coney-catching" pamphlets revealed the secret language of thieves: a complex slang dialect said to be spoken only by the initiates of the Elizabethan underworld. Thomas Harmon's *Caveat for Common Cursetors* provides a glossary of cant terms: day was "the lightmans"; night, "the darkmans"; "to myll a ken" meant "to rob a house"; "to nyggle" was "to have to doo with a woman carnally." The same pamphlet lists twenty-three different kinds of thief, each with a bizarre and colorful name, from a "prigger of Praunces" (a horse thief) to a "Kinchin mort" (a thieving girl). In these pamphlets the underworld is imagined as a parodic mirror of respectable society. In *A Notable Discovery of Cozenage* (London, 1591), Robert Greene claims that coney-catchers give their code of criminal conduct "an honest & godly title, calling it by the name of a law" (sig. C3r), and he fears that criminals will enforce their law by amputating his hand as punishment for writing coney-catching pamphlets (A4v) – precisely the penalty the Elizabethan state meted out to those who wrote seditious pamphlets. As is the case with prostitution, the world of thieves and con artists is seen as an alternative society, an illicit world of the night which mocks daytime respectability.

"Coney-catching" refers specifically to cheating a man at cards. Other forms of deceit described in pamphlets are given similarly slangy names, such as "cross-biting" and "Barnard's law." In "Cross-biting" a man was approached by a prostitute in a tavern, and eventually taken upstairs to her room. Then, just as he had removed all his clothes, the woman's husband would burst in with his friends, beating and robbing the client. "Barnard's law" is the name of a more elaborate con: a country man visiting the city is accosted by the "Taker Up," who quickly determines from the stranger's accent and other regional characteristics what part of the country he is from. The "Taker Up" poses as a long-lost neighbor, and offers to buy the victim a drink. In the tavern they are joined by the "Verser," who seems a gentleman of quality, and the "Barnard," who appears to be a foolish, drunken country bumpkin. The Barnard, spending money right and left, offers to buy the others a drink. The Verser talks the victim into agreeing to play cards with the Barnard, so that they will be able to get some easy money off him. At first, the Barnard loses, but eventually, his "luck" begins to turn. Just as he has won all the money the victim has, the fourth member of the gang, the "Rutter" arrives. The "Rutter" storms into the tavern, picking fights with all and sundry, and as the room erupts in chaos, the Barnard sneaks off with the loot, which will be shared later between all four gang members (sig. A3v). Many similarly elaborate tricks are described in contemporary pamphlets, and plays like Ben Jonson's *The Alchemist* (1610) exploit the satiric possibilities of the world of the trickster by focusing not only on the wit of the con artists, but on the credulity of the people who fall for their lies. In *The Alchemist*, the con-game becomes a powerful metaphor for new forms of social relations, based on self-interested market exchange of commodities rather than traditional obligations of service and duty.

Concerns about illicit profit were matched by anxieties about inappropriate habits of consumption. Gluttony had always been condemned in sermons and homilies; moderation in eating was related not only to Christian abstinence from the pleasures of the flesh, but also to stoic virtue and martial fortitude. In early modern Germany, the vomiting that inevitably followed a gluttonous feast was seen as emblematic of a loss of rational control; gorging and spewing reduced men to the level of beasts.[13] Not surprisingly, the aspect of gluttony that provoked the most serious concern was drunkenness. Excessive drinking was a frequent cause of social disorder: drunken men fought each other, broke the peace, railed against their superiors, and beat their wives and children.

Along with Rabelais's giants, the greatest portrait of a glutton from early modern Europe is Shakespeare's Falstaff, and more than Gargantua or Pantagruel the character of Falstaff provides a telling glimpse of the social anxieties surrounding gluttony in the period. A glutton, drunkard, swindler, and a thief, he lives at the center of one of the most vividly imagined illicit worlds of the Renaissance, the Boar's Head Tavern in Eastcheap. Despite his dissolute urban life-style, it is important to remember that Falstaff is not a commoner, but a decayed aristocrat: a corrupt and impoverished knight, living proof of the ability of illicit activity to undermine the social order. Falstaff's role is always parodic: he puts a pillow on his head and imitates the King; he mocks and refutes the notions of aristocratic honor idealized by the other members of his class. He is also a corrupter of youth, whose designs on Prince Hal threaten to undermine national stability and royal justice. Falstaff's excessive appetites are manifest in his excessive body, a leaky vessel always on the verge of spewing forth.[14]

Drunkenness was often imagined as a social, rather than purely personal vice, and it was the central feature of a tavern-based subculture – an illicit world of whoring, gorging, gambling, cheating, and stealing. Just as Falstaff parodies King Henry, so the tavern world parodied the structures of respectable life. As a public meeting place consecrated to pleasure and dissipation, the alehouse was at once the opposite of the church and a parody of the household. Students even imagined the tavern as an alternate university. In the English pamphlet *The Law of Drinking* (1617), the anonymous author imagines the tavern as a parodic "College of Hilarity" which produces graduates in the "liberal sciences of wine and beer." The volume – which purports to have been translated out of the original Latin – parodies legal diction and takes the form of a scholarly disputation on the "laws" governing drinking. Questions debated include whether or not it is dishonorable to vomit in front of your friends ("The common opinion is that it [is] not, being such a necessarie consequence as it cannot be prevented"); whether it is dishonorable to vomit in the presence of women ("Yes surely...for...many to their griefe, have had experience hereof: being by this meanes estranged from their *Sweethearts* love"); and whether "hee who by vomiting hath besprinted the face or garment of another, may be sued for an action of trespasse?" ("And this is denied: because the will and purpose distinguish offences. Now, he had no purpose to offend, being compelled by necessity to cast, or else to burst out his teeth") (sig. D4v–D5r).

This volume also includes a companion piece dealing with a vice that was becoming increasingly linked with drinking in the early modern period: the smoking of tobacco. In northwest Europe, especially England and the Netherlands, tobacco use became widespread after 1570. The introduction of tobacco into alehouse culture is drama-tized in an anonymous English dialogue, entitled *Wine, Beere, Ale, and Tobacco Contending for Superiority*, published in 1630. Characters representing Wine, Beer, and Ale brawl in a tavern until they are reconciled by Water (the parson), who mediates their quarrel by assigning a special role to each. Each alcoholic beverage is associated with a specific class and social space: wine is for the gentry and nobility; beer, by contrast, is a bourgeois beverage, "in most grace with the Citizens," and ale (a more traditional beverage than beer) is a country drink (sig. C2r). This vision of hierarchical harmony – celebrated by the singing of a communal song – is rudely interrupted by the entrance of Tobacco, who insists that he is ruler of them all: "the soveraigne drinke Tobacco" (sig. C4v). Though the assembled company protest strongly, they eventually admit Tobacco to their fellowship, noting that he is in favor with "the greatest" and that even "the ladies begin to affect him" (sig. D2r). The dialogue (perhaps performed as a masque?) ends with a dance of reconciliation.

Novel, much sought after, and highly addictive, tobacco fundamentally changed the social habits of early modern Europe. Although it may seem a relatively mild drug in comparison with those that came after – opium, heroin, and cocaine – tobacco's arrival in Europe marks a crucial phase in the history of drug use in western culture. It was the first of many exotic substances unknown to the ancient and medieval worlds whose use promised new forms of pleasure and consciousness. In the Americas tobacco was only one of many different narcotic substances used by native cultures in ritual and religious ceremonies. Migrating to Europe, tobacco was commodified, moving from the realm of religion to that of the marketplace. In England and the Netherlands it quickly became an integral part of the national economy. Reflecting a larger conflict between capitalist profit and traditional values, economic incentives and government protection encouraged the sale and use of tobacco, while at the same time smoking was widely condemned, not least by James I of England, who published his famous *Counterblaste to Tobacco* in 1604. There was a great debate over whether or not tobacco was harmful, and what its proper use might be in a "civilized" Christian society. Poems both praising and condemning tobacco are common in English manuscript collections of poetry and, again reflecting the cultural ambiva-lence about this new drug, poems for and against it are sometimes found on the same page (see for example, Bodleian Library MS Rawl. poet 153 (c. 1640), fol. 21v).

Religious authorities condemned tobacco as a satanic, barbarous innovation. Joshua Sylvester's 1614 poem *Tobacco Battered and the Pipes Shattered* locates to-bacco smoking in brothels, gambling dens, and public theaters, and claims smokers are "Blasphemers, Ruffians, Atheists, [and] Damn'd *Libertines*." Tobacco is seen as an alien substance; Sylvester calls it "a *Drugge* for *Jewes*" and claims that its American origin means it is unnatural for Europeans. Anti-tobacco texts are often racist, linking tobacco with blackness and barbarism. A poem entitled "Plutoes Proclamation" (1614) by the populist poet John Taylor associates tobacco use with "blacke Nations" such as native Americans, and argues that smoking is Satan's way of making white people black. As Sylvester's odd association of tobacco with Jews suggests, tobacco is seen not just as foreign but profoundly unchristian.[15]

Given cultural stereotypes linking Jews and usury, Sylvester's notion that tobacco is "for Jewes" may also suggest the harmfulness of tobacco as a commodity. Like other commentators, he certainly sees tobacco use as economically dangerous: the money wasted on it ruins young noblemen and leads to decline in hospitality, thus disrupting the traditional social fabric.[16] Similarly, John Deacon's 1616 tract *Tobacco Tortured* argues that tobacco is unhealthy, a waste of money, and "pestiferous to the publike State."

In a passage that admirably demonstrates the early modern tendency to see all forms of vice as fundamentally linked, Deacon argues that the use of tobacco will lead to other abuses, especially drunkenness and lechery:

> This burning and scorching flame being once inwardly taken into the bowels; there must necessarily follow, an insatiable quaffing up of wine, ale, or beere at the least, to allay and quench the excessive heate of the stomacke. And by the insatiable quaffing in these strong drinks, Dame Venus her selfe beginneth eftsoones so fiercely to be enflamed and set on fire. (sig. L4r–L4v)

Smoking tobacco was often equated with drinking alcohol; in fact, in the early seventeenth century, before the term "smoking" came into use, one was said to "drink" tobacco. And while there was some suspicion that tobacco caused impotence, smoking was often associated with lechery. An anonymous English manuscript riddle calls the penis "the kindest true tobacco pipe"[17] and phallic pipes frequently appear held at suggestive angles in Dutch paintings.

Ironically, medical authorities tended to praise tobacco, seeing it as a useful and powerful medicine. They usually insisted that it should be taken in moderation, as a medicinal rather than recreational drug. The key text in this tradition is a survey of New World herbs written by the Spanish physician Nicholas Monardes in 1571 and widely disseminated, translated, and imitated thereafter. An English translation, entitled *Joyfull Newes out of the New Found Worlde*, appeared in 1577. Monardes related tobacco to the humoral paradigm which dominated Renaissance medicine, arguing that since tobacco was hot and dry, it was therefore effective in the treatment of diseases that involved an excess of cold, wet humors (sig. I2r–M1r). This logical, yet perverse analysis paradoxically led commentators to recommend smoking tobacco as a cure for coughs and chest congestion.

Ultimately, tobacco was seen as a volatile substance whose effects often depended on the nature of the person using it.

> In some great Tobacconists, you shall see them staringly wilde, their face troubled, their voyce frightfull, and distempered. They foame at the mouth, they startle and quake, rage and ruffle, and wordes escape them, that they afterwards repent. But in others againe it causeth a pleasant humour, and cleane contrary usages, humours, and passions.[16]

And though many authorities felt tobacco was harmful, it was too economically profitable to ban, and its use throughout Europe only increased during the seventeenth century. As a proclamation by England's Charles I dated February 17th, 1626 admitted, "because the immoderate desire of taking of Tobacco hath so farre prevailed in these Our Kingdomes...it cannot on a sodaine bee utterly suppressed."

If there is a common fear or anxiety expressed in early modern accounts of illicit behavior, it is that personal failings and self-indulgence will lead to a general social breakdown. In the rhetoric of the period, the fact that young men have sex with prostitutes, for example, is not merely a matter of personal morality. Of course, by engaging in illicit sex, these young men are going against God's commandments restricting sexual activity to the generation of children in lawful wedlock. But they are also dissipating their masculine vigor in effeminate pleasure, and this waste of masculine energy ultimately weakens the commonwealth. In a patriarchal culture in which social mastery is based on the putative superiority of masculine rationality, the individual failure of masculine will – the surrender of the rational faculty to sensual pleasure – constitutes a larger social failure. Men made effeminate by pleasure will be too soft and weak to defend the state against its enemies. Men who waste their seed in illicit sex will not have enough to spend in the getting of lawful children. From the point of view of the commonwealth, prostitution not only wastes sperm, it also wastes money: parents' fortunes are dissipated by their ungrateful sons and powerful families are brought low by "the expense of spirit in a waste of shame."[19] The same arguments were used against drinking and smoking: young heirs pissed their honor and their fortune away in wine and transformed their landed property into airy smoke.

Ironically, few of these social fears had much basis in reality. Far from being drains on the economy, both prostitution and the new trade in tobacco were sources of enormous wealth. Military success depended on many factors, but the level of sexual activity in contending armies was not one of them. And despite drunkenness, increased consumption of tobacco, and a thriving trade in sex, the patriarchal system held up well enough in the sixteenth and seventeenth centuries. Illicit activity harmed individuals: countless women were physically and psychologically destroyed by the hard life of the brothels; they and their male clients died of syphilis; then as now tobacco ruined smokers' lungs; and men and women lived lives ravaged by alcohol abuse. But social breakdown in the sixteenth and seventeenth centuries was far more likely to result from conflicts over religion than from the vices of individuals. The sack of Rome, the French wars of religion, the English Civil War, and the Thirty Years War in Germany caused immeasurably greater suffering and social dislocation than all the brothels, alehouses, and tobacconists of Europe combined.

NOTES

1 Cooke, *White Sheet.*
2 Cressy, *Birth, Marriage, and Death*, p. 277.
3 Darmon, *Trial by Impotence.*
4 Nashe, *Piers Penniless*, p. 112.
5 Stubbes, *Anatomy of Abuses*, sig. L7v–L8v.
6 See *Arraignment and Conviction.*
7 Gosson, *Schoole of Abuse.*
8 Middleton and Rowley, *A Fair Quarrel*, IV. i.
9 Archer, *Pursuit*, pp. 211–13.
10 Lawner, *Courtesans*, p. 36.
11 Laslett, *World We Have Lost*, pp. 84–91.

12 But see Ruggiero, *Boundaries*, p. 121.
13 Roper, *Oedipus and the Devil*, p. 153.
14 Traub, *Desire and Anxiety*, pp. 56–61.
15 Sylvester, *Tobacco*, pp. 97, 98, 82, 83.
16 Ibid., pp. 109–10.
17 Rosenbach MS 1083/15, fol. 37v, Rosenbach Library, Philadelphia.
18 Gardiner, *Trial of Tabacco*, sig. P1v.
19 Shakespeare, Sonnet 129.

REFERENCES

Archer, Ian, *The Pursuit of Stability: Social Relations in Elizabethan London* (New York: Cambridge University Press, 1991).

The Arraignment and Conviction of Mervin Lord Audley, Earl of Castlehaven (London, 1642).

Cooke, Richard, *A White Sheet, or a Warning for Whoremongers* (London, 1629).

Cressy, David, *Birth, Marriage, and Death: Ritual, Religion, and the Life-cycle in Tudor and Stuart England* (New York: Oxford University Press, 1997).

Darmon, Pierre, *Trial By Impotence: Virility and Marriage in Pre-Revolutionary France*, trans. Paul Keegan (London: Chatto & Windus, 1985).

Gardiner, Edmund, *The Trial of Tabacco* (London, 1610).

Gosson, Stephen, *The Schoole of Abuse* (London, 1579).

Laslett, Peter, *The World We Have Lost* (London: Methuen, 1971).

Lawner, Lynne, *Lives of the Courtesans: Portraits of the Renaissance* (New York: Rizzoli, 1987).

Middleton, Thomas and Rowley, William, *A Fair Quarrel* [1617], ed. R. V. Holdsworth (London: Ernest Benn, 1974).

Nashe, Thomas, *Piers Penniless*, in *The Unfortunate Traveler and Other Works*, ed. J. B. Steane (New York: Penguin, 1972).

Roper, Lyndal, *Oedipus and the Devil: Witchcraft, Sexuality, and Religion in Early Modern Europe* (New York: Routledge, 1994).

Ruggiero, Guido, *The Boundaries of Eros: Sex, Crime, and Sexuality in Renaissance Venice* (New York: Oxford University Press, 1985).

Stubbes, Philip, *The Anatomy of Abuses* (London, 1583).

Traub, Valerie, *Desire and Anxiety: Circulations of Sexuality in Shakespearean Drama* (New York: Routledge, 1992).

FURTHER READING

Ben-Amos, Ilana Krausman, *Adolescence and Youth in Early Modern England* (New Haven: Yale University Press, 1994).

Brown, Judith C., *Immodest Acts: The Life of a Lesbian Nun in Renaissance Italy* (New York: Oxford University Press, 1986).

Burford, E. J., *Bawds and Lodgings: A History of the London Bankside Brothels c.100–1675* (London: Peter Owen, 1976).

Clegg, Cyndia, *Press Censorship in Elizabethan England* (New York: Cambridge University Press, 1997).

Davis, Natalie Zemon, *Society and Culture in Early Modern France* (Stanford: Stanford University Press, 1975).

Geremek, Bronislaw, *The Margins of Society in Late Medieval Paris*, trans. Jean Birrell (New York: Cambridge University Press, 1987).

Goodman, Jordan, *Tobacco in History: The Cultures of Dependence* (New York: Routledge, 1993).

Karras, Ruth Mazo, *Common Women: Prostitution and Sexuality in Medieval England* (New York: Oxford University Press, 1996).

McMullan, John L., *The Canting Crew: London's Criminal Underworld 1500–1700* (New Brunswick: Rutgers University Press, 1984).

Masson, Georgina, *Courtesans of the Italian Renaissance* (New York: St. Martin's, 1975).

Masten, Jeff, *Textual Intercourse: Collaboration, Authorship, and Sexualities in Renaissance Drama* (New York: Cambridge University Press, 1997).

Moulton, Ian Frederick, *Before Pornography: Erotic Writing in Early Modern England* (New York: Oxford University Press, 2000).

Muir, Edward and Ruggiero, Guido, eds., *History from Crime: Selections from Quaderni Storici* (Baltimore: Johns Hopkins University Press, 1994).

Rappaport, Steve, *Worlds within Worlds: Structures of Life in Sixteenth Century London* (New York: Cambridge University Press, 1989).

Rocke, Michael, *Forbidden Friendships: Homosexuality and Male Culture in Renaissance Florence* (New York: Oxford University Press, 1996).

——, "Gender and Sexual Culture in Renaissance Italy," in *Gender and Society in Renaissance Italy*, ed. Judith C. Brown and Robert C. Davis (New York: Longman, 1998).

Rosenthal, Margaret, *The Honest Courtesan: Veronica Franco, Citizen and Writer in Sixteenth-century Venice* (Chicago: University of Chicago Press, 1992).

Rossiaud, Jacques, *Medieval Prostitution*, trans. Lydia G. Cochrane (New York: Blackwell, 1988).

Ruggiero, Guido, *Binding Passions: Tales of Magic, Marriage and Power at the End of the Renaissance* (New York: Oxford University Press, 1993).

——, "Marriage, Love, Sex, and Renaissance Civic Morality," in *Sexuality and Gender in Early Modern Europe*, ed. James Grantham Turner (New York: Cambridge University Press, 1993), pp. 10–30.

Schama, Simon, *The Embarrassment of Riches: An Interpretation of Dutch Culture in the Golden Age* (New York: Vintage, 1987).

Smith, Bruce, *Homosexual Desire in Shakespeare's England* (Chicago: University of Chicago Press, 1991).

Sylvester, Joshua, *Tobacco Battered and the Pipes Shattered* (London, 1614).

Talvacchia, Bette, *Taking Positions: On the Erotic in Renaissance Culture* (Princeton: Princeton University Press, 1999).

Traub, Valerie, "The (In)significance of Lesbian Desire in Early Modern England," in *Erotic Politics: Desire on the Renaissance Stage*, ed. Susan Zimmerman (New York: Routledge, 1992).

Consolidated Bibliography

Abbé, Derek van, *Drama in Renaissance Germany and Switzerland* (Melbourne: University of Melbourne Press, 1961).

Abu-Lughod, Janet L., *Before European Hegemony: The World System AD 1250–1360* (New York: Oxford University Press, 1989).

Ackerman, James S. and Rosenfeld, M. N., "Social Stratification in Renaissance Urban Planning," in *Urban Life in the Renaissance*, ed. S. Zimmerman and R. F. E. Weissman (Newark, DE: University of Delaware Press, 1989).

Agnew, John A., "The Devaluation of Place in Social Science," in John A. Agnew and James S. Duncan, *The Power of Place: Bringing Together Geography and Sociological Imaginations* (Boston: Unwin Hyman, 1989).

Alberti, Leon Battista, *I libri della famiglia*, ed. Cecil Grayson, in *Opere volgari*, vol. 1 (Bari: Laterza, 1960).

Albertini, Rudolf von, *Firenze dalla repubblica al principato*, trans. Cesare Cristofolini (Turin: Einaudi, 1970).

Aleman, Matheo, *The Rogue: or the Life of Guzman de Alfarache* [1623], trans. James Mabbe (London: Constable, 1924).

Allegra, Luciano, "Oltre le fonti criminale: Chieri nel '500'," *Quaderni Storici* 17 (1982).

——, *La città verticale: usurai, mercanti e tessitori nella Chieri del Cinquecento* (Milan: Franco Angeli, 1987).

Ambrosoli, Mauro, *The Wild and the Sown: Botany and Agriculture in Western Europe, 1350–1850*, trans. Mary McCann Salvatorelli (Cambridge: Cambridge University Press, 1997).

Amelang, James, *Honored Citizens of Barcelona: Patrician Culture and Class Relations, 1490–1714* (Princeton: Princeton University Press, 1986).

——, *The Flight of Icarus: Artisan Autobiography in Early Modern Europe* (Stanford: Stanford University Press, 1998).

Ames-Lewis, Francis, *Drawing in Early Renaissance Italy* (New Haven: Yale University Press, 1981).

——, *The Intellectual Life of the Early Renaissance Artist* (New Haven: Yale University Press, 2000).

Amussen, Susan, "The Gendering of Popular Culture in Early Modern England," in *Popular Culture in England, c.1500–1850*, ed. Tim Harris (London: Macmillan, 1995).

Anderson, Benedict, *Imagined Communities: Reflections on the Origin and Spread of Nationalism* (London: Verso, 1983).

Anderson, M. S., *The Origins of the Modern European State System, 1494–1618* (London: Longman, 1998).

Anderson, Perry, *Lineages of the Absolutist State* (London: Verso, 1974).

Andrews, Walter G., "Literary Art of the Golden Age: The Age of Süleymân," in *Süleymân the Second and His Time*, ed. Halil Inalcık and Cemal Kafadar (Istanbul: Isis Press, 1993).

Anglo, Sydney, *The Martial Arts of Renaissance Europe* (New Haven: Yale University Press, 2000).

Ankarloo, Bengt and Henningson, Gustav, eds., *Early Modern Witchcraft: Centres and Peripheries* (Oxford: Clarendon Press, 1990).

Appleby, Andrew B., "Nutrition and Disease: The Case of London, 1550–1750," *Journal of Interdisciplinary History* 6 (1975).

Appuhn, Karl, "Inventing Nature: Forestry and State Power in Renaissance Venice," *Journal of Modern History* 72 (2000).

Archer, Ian, *The Pursuit of Stability: Social Relations in Elizabethan London* (New York: Cambridge University Press, 1991).

Arditi, Jorge, *A Genealogy of Manners: Transformations of Social Relations in France and England from the Fourteenth to the Eighteenth Century* (Chicago: University of Chicago Press, 1998).

Ariès, Philippe and Duby, Georges, eds., *A History of Private Life*, vols. II and III, trans. Arthur Goldhammer (Cambridge, MA: Harvard University Press, 1988–9).

Ariosto, Ludovico, *The Satires of Ludovico Ariosto: A Renaissance Autobiography*, trans. Peter DeSa Wiggins (Athens, OH: Ohio University Press, 1976).

The Arraignment and Conviction of Mervin Lord Audley, Earl of Castlehaven (London, 1642).

Arriaza, Armand, "Adam's Noble Children: An Early Modern Theorist's Concept of Human Nobility," *Journal of the History of Ideas* 55/3 (1994).

Arrizabalaga, Jon, Henderson, John, and French, Roger, *The Great Pox: The French Disease in Renaissance Europe* (New Haven: Yale University Press, 1997).

Asch, Ronald G. and Birke, Adolf M., eds., *Princes, Patronage and the Nobility: The Court at the Beginning of the Modern Age* (Oxford: Oxford University Press, 1991).

Ascoli, Albert Russell, *Ariosto's Bitter Harmony: Crisis and Evasion in the Italian Renaissance* (Princeton: Princeton University Press, 1987).

Ascoli, Albert Russell and Kahn, Victoria, eds., *Machiavelli and the Discourse of Literature* (Ithaca, NY: Cornell University Press, 1993).

Ashley, Robert, *Of Honour* (San Marino, CA: Huntington Library, 1947).

Ashworth, William B., "Natural History and the Emblematic World View," in *Reappraisals of the Scientific Revolution*, ed. David C. Lindberg and Robert S. Westman (Cambridge: Cambridge University Press, 1990).

Astarita, Tommaso, *The Continuity of Feudal Power: The Caracciolo di Brienza in Spanish Naples* (Cambridge: Cambridge University Press, 1992).

——, *Village Justice: Community, Family and Popular Culture in Early Modern Italy* (Baltimore: Johns Hopkins University Press, 1999).

Atıl, Esin, "Ottoman Miniature Painting under Sultan Mehmed II," *Ars Orientalis* 9 (1973).

——, *Süleymanname: The Illustrated History of Süleyman the Magnificent* (Washington, DC: National Gallery of Art; New York: Harry N. Abrams, 1986).

Awdeley, John, "Fraternity of Vacabondes, Harman's Caveat, Haben's Sermon," etc., ed. Edward Viles and F. J. Furnivall (London: Early English Text Society, 1869).

Babinger, Franz, *Mehmed the Conqueror and His Time*, trans. Ralph Manheim, ed. William C. Hickman (Princeton: Princeton University Press, 1978).

Balassi, Bálint, *Összes Versei, szép magyar comoediája és levelezése*, ed. Béla Stoll and Sándor Eckhardt ([Budapest]: Magyar Helikon, 1974).

Balestracci, Duccio, *The Renaissance in the Fields: Family Memoirs of a Fifteenth-Century Tuscan Peasant*, trans. Paolo Squatriti and Betsy Merideth (University Park, PA: Pennsylvania State University Press, 1999).

Barbagli, Mario, *Sotto lo stesso tetto. Mutamenti della famiglia in Italia dal XV al XX secolo* (Bologna: Il Mulino, 1984).

Barkan, Leonard, *Unearthing the Past: Archaeology and Aesthetics in the Making of Renaissance Culture* (New Haven: Yale University Press, 1999).

Barolsky, Paul, *Michelangelo's Nose: A Myth and its Maker* (University Park: Pennsylvania State University Press, 1990).

——, *Why Mona Lisa Smiles and Other Tales by Vasari* (University Park: Pennsylvania State University Press, 1991).

——, *Giotto's Father and the Family of Vasari's "Lives"* (University Park: Pennsylvania State University Press, 1992).

——, *The Faun in the Garden: Michelangelo and the Poetic Origins of Italian Renaissance Art* (University Park: Pennsylvania State University Press, 1994).

Baron, Hans, *The Crisis of the Early Italian Renaissance: Civic Humanism and Republican Liberty in the Age of Classicism and Tyranny*, rev. edn. (Princeton: Princeton University Press, 1966).

——, *In Search of Florentine Civic Humanism*, 2 vols. (Princeton: Princeton University Press, 1988).

Barry, Jonathan and Brooks, C., eds., *The Middling Sort of People: Culture, Society and Politics in England, 1550–1800* (New York: St. Martin's Press, 1994).

Bartels, Emily C., "Making More of the Moor: Aaron, Othello, and Renaissance Refashionings of Race," *Shakespeare Quarterly* 41 (1990).

Baschet, Jérôme, *Les Justices de l'au-delà. Les représentations de l'enfer en France et en Italie (XIIe-XVe siècle)* (Rome: École Française de Rome, 1993).

Baskins, Cristelle, *"Cassone" Painting, Humanism, and Gender in Early Modern Italy* (Cambridge: Cambridge University Press, 1998).

Baxandall, Michael, *Giotto and the Orators* (Oxford: Oxford University Press, 1971).

——, *Painting and Experience in Fifteenth Century Italy* (Oxford: Clarendon Press, 1972).

——, *Patterns of Intention* (New Haven: Yale University Press, 1985).

Becker, Marvin, "Individualism in the Early Italian Renaissance: Burden and Blessing," *Studies in the Renaissance* 19(1972).

Beik, William, *Urban Protest in Seventeenth-Century France: The Culture of Retribution* (Cambridge: Cambridge University Press, 1997).

Bell, Rudolph M., *How To Do It: Guide to Good Living for Renaissance Italians* (Chicago: University of Chicago Press, 1999).

Bellomo, Manlio, *The Common Legal Past of Europe, 1000–1800* (Washington, DC: Catholic University of America Press, 1991).

Ben-Amos, Ilana Krausman, *Adolescence and Youth in Early Modern England* (New Haven: Yale University Press, 1994).

Benigno, Francesco, *Specchi della rivoluzione: Conflitto e identità politica nell'Europa moderna* (Rome: Donzelli, 1999).

Berengo, Marino, *Nobili e mercanti nella Lucca del Cinquecento* (Turin: Einaudi, 1965).

——, *L'Europa delle città: Il volto della società urbana europea tra medioevo ed età moderna* (Turin: Einaudi, 1999).

Berger, Harry, *Second World and Green World: Studies in Renaissance Fiction-Making* (Berkeley: University of California Press, 1988).

Beza (Bèze), Théodore de, *Juvenilia* [1578], ed. and trans. Alexandre Machard (Paris: Liseux, 1879).

Biagioli, Mario, *Galileo Courtier: The Practice of Science in the Culture of Absolutism* (Chicago: University of Chicago Press, 1993).

Bialostocki, Jan, *Art of the Renaissance in Eastern Europe* (Ithaca: Cornell University Press, 1976).

——, "The Baltic Area as an Artistic Region in the Sixteenth Century," *Hafnia* (1976).

——, "Some Values of Artistic Periphery," in *World Art: Themes of Unity and Diversity*, vol. 1, ed. Irving Lavin (University Park: Pennsylvania State University Press, 1986).

Biraben, Jean Noël, *Les Hommes et la peste en France et dans les pays européens et méditerranéens*, 2 vols. (Paris: Mouton, 1975–6).

Bitton, Davis, *The French Nobility in Crisis 1560–1640* (Stanford: Stanford University Press, 1969).

Bizzocchi, Roberto, *Genealogie incredibili: Scritti di storia nell'Europa moderna* (Bologna: Il Mulino, 1995).

Black, Antony, *Guilds and Civil Society in European Political Thought from the Twelfth Century to the Present* (Ithaca, NY: Cornell University Press, 1984).

Black, Jeremy, *Maps and History: Constructing Images of the Past* (New Haven: Yale University Press, 1997).

Blickle, Peter, "The Popular Reformation," in *Handbook of European History, 1400–1600: Late Middle Ages, Renaissance, and Reformation*, ed. Thomas A. Brady Jr., Heiko A. Oberman, and James D. Tracy (New York: E. J. Brill, 1994), vol. 2.

——, *Obedient Germans? A Rebuttal: A New View of German History*, trans. Thomas A. Brady Jr. (Charlottesville, VA: University of Virginia Press, 1997).

Bloch, Marc, *French Rural History: An Essay on its Basic Characteristics*, trans. Janet Sondheimer (Berkeley: University of California Press, 1966).

Blockmans, Wim, "Patronage, Brokerage and Corruption as Symptoms of Incipient State Formation in the Burgundian-Habsburg Netherlands," in *Klientelsysteme im Europa der Frühen Neuzeit*, ed. Antoni Maczak (Schriften des Historischen Kollegs, Herausgegeben von der Stiftung Historisches Kolleg, Kolloquien) (Munich: R. Oldenbourg Verlag, 1988).

Blunt, Anthony, *Philibert de l'Orme* (London: Zwemmer, 1958).

Blythe, James M., *Ideal Government and the Mixed Constitution in the Middle Ages* (Princeton: Princeton University Press, 1992).

Bobbioni, Maria Teresa, "Conflittualità e amministrazione della giustizia in un feudo padano tra la fine del '500 e il primo trentennio del '600," in *Persistenza feudale e autonomie comunitative in stati padani fra Cinque e Settecento*, ed. Giovanni Tocci (Bologna: CLUEB, 1988).

Bohanan, Donna, *Old and New Nobility in Aix-en-Provence 1600–1695: Portrait of an Urban Elite* (Baton Rouge: Louisiana State University Press, 1992).

Bonfil, Robert, "Aliens Within: The Jews and Anti-Judaism," in *Handbook of European History, 1400–1600*, 2 vols., Thomas A. Brady Jr., Heiko A. Oberman, James D. Tracy (Leiden and New York: E. J. Brill, 1994–5), vol. 1.

Bornstein, Daniel and Rusconi, Roberto, eds., *Women and Religion in Medieval and Renaissance Italy* (Chicago: University of Chicago Press, 1996).

Bouwsma, William J., *Venice and the Defense of Republican Liberty: Renaissance Values in the Age of the Counter Reformation* (Berkeley: University of California Press, 1968).

——, "The Renaissance and the Drama of Western History," *American Historical Review* 84 (1979).

——, *A Usable Past* (Berkeley: University of California Press, 1990).

——, *The Waning of the Renaissance* (New Haven: Yale University Press, 2001).

Bowsky, William, ed., *The Black Death: A Turning Point in History?* (New York: Holt, Rinehart and Winston, 1971).

Boyer, Paul and Nissenbaum, Stephen, *Salem Possessed: The Social Origins of Witchcraft* (Cambridge, MA: Harvard University Press, 1974).

Brackett, John, *Criminal Justice and Crime in Late Renaissance Florence, 1537–1609* (Cambridge: Cambridge University Press, 1992).

Brady, Thomas, *Turning Swiss: Cities and Empire, 1450–1550* (Cambridge: Cambridge University Press, 1985).

Brady, Thomas A., Jr., Oberman, Heiko A., and Tracy, James D., *Handbook of European History 1400–1600: Late Middle Ages, Renaissance and Reformation*, 2 vols. (New York: E. J. Brill, 1994–5).

Braudel, Ferdinand, *The Mediterranean and the Mediterranean World in the Age of Philip II*, 2 vols., trans. Sian Reynolds (New York: Harper and Row, 1972 and Berkeley: University of California Press, 1995).

Brenner, Robert, "The Agrarian Roots of European Capitalism," in *The Brenner Debate: Agrarian Class Structure and Economic Development in Pre-Industrial Europe*, ed. T. H. Ason and C. H. E. Philpin (Cambridge: Cambridge University Press, 1985).

Briggs, Robin, *Communities of Belief: Cultural and Social Tension in Early Modern France* (Oxford: Clarendon Press, 1989).

——, *Witches and Neighbors: The Social and Cultural Context of European Witchcraft* (New York: Viking, 1996).

Brockliss, Laurence and Jones, Colin, *The Medical World of Early Modern France* (Oxford: Oxford University Press, 1997).

Brown, Alison, *The Renaissance*, 2nd edn. (London: Longman, 1999).

Brown, Judith C., *Immodest Acts: The Life of a Lesbian Nun in Renaissance Italy* (New York: Oxford University Press, 1986).

Brown, Judith C. and Davis, Robert C., eds., *Gender and Society in Renaissance Italy* (London: Longman, 1998).

Brown, Patricia Fortini, *Venice and Antiquity* (New Haven: Yale University Press, 1996).

Browne, Walden, *Sahagún and the Transition to Modernity* (Norman: University of Oklahoma Press, 2000).

Brucker, Gene, *The Society of Renaissance Florence* (New York: Harper and Row, 1971).

——, "The Florentine *Popolo minuto* and its Political Role, 1340–1450," in *Violence and Civil Disorder in Italian Cities, 1200–1500*, ed. Lauro Martines (Berkeley: University of California Press, 1972).

——, *Renaissance Florence*, 2nd edn. (Berkeley: University of California Press, 1983).

——, *Florence: The Golden Age (1138–1737)* (Berkeley: University of California Press, 1998).

Brummett, Palmira, *Ottoman Seapower and Levantine Diplomacy in the Age of Discovery* (Albany: State University of New York Press, 1994).

Brunner, H. H., *The Statue Court in the Vatican Belvedere* (Stockholm: Almqvist and Wiksell, 1970).

Brunner, Otto, *Land and Lordship: Structures of Governance in Medieval Austria*, trans. Howard Kaminsky and James Van Horn Melton (Philadelphia: University of Pennsylvania Press, 1992).

Buisseret, David, *Monarchs, Ministers and Maps: The Emergence of Cartography as a Tool of Government in Early Modern Europe* (Chicago: University of Chicago Press, 1992).

Burckhardt, Jacob, *The Civilization of the Renaissance in Italy*, trans. S. G. C. Middlemore (Oxford: Phaidon, 1945 and New York: Harper, 1958, 1971).

Burford, E. J., *Bawds and Lodgings: A History of the London Bankside Brothels c.100–1675* (London: Peter Owen, 1976).

Burke, Peter, *Culture and Society in Renaissance Italy* (New York: Scribners, 1972).

——, *Tradition and Innovation in Renaissance Italy: A Sociological Approach* (London: Fontana, 1974).

——, *Popular Culture in Early Modern Europe* (New York: New York University Press, 1978).

——, *The Italian Renaissance* (Princeton: Princeton University Press, 1986).

——, *The Historical Anthropology of Early Modern Italy: Essays on Perception and Communication* (Cambridge: Cambridge University Press, 1987).

——, "L'homme de cour," in *L'Homme de la Renaissance*, ed. Eugenio Garin (Paris: Seuil, 1990).

——, *Popular Culture in Early Modern Europe* (Aldershot: Scolar Press, 1994).

——, "Hosts and Guests: A General View of Minorities in the Cultural Life of Europe," in *Minorities in Western European Cities*, ed. Hugo Soly and Alfons K. L. Thijs (Brussels: Institut Historique Belge de Rome, 1995).

——, *The Fortunes of the Courtier: The European Reception of Castiglione's "Cortegiano"* (University Park, PA: Pennsylvania State University Press, 1995 and Cambridge: Cambridge University Press, 1995).

——, "The Renaissance, Individualism, and the Portrait," *History of European Ideas* 21 (1995).

——, "The Myth of 1453: Notes and Reflections," *Querdenken: Festschrift Hans Guggisberg*, ed. Michael Erbe et al. (Mannheim: Palatium Verlag, 1996).

——, "Learned Culture and Popular Culture in Renaissance Italy," in *Varieties of Cultural History* (Oxford: Polity Press, 1997).

——, "Representations of the Self from Petrarch to Descartes," in *Rewriting the Self: Histories from the Renaissance to the Present*, ed. Roy Porter (London: Routledge, 1997).

——, *The European Renaissance: Centres and Peripheries* (Oxford: Blackwell Publishers, 1998).

——, "Les langages de la politesse," *Terrain* 33 (1999).

Burroughs, Charles, *From Sign to Design* (Cambridge, MA: MIT Press, 1990).

Bush, Virginia, "Bandinelli's *Hercules and Cacus* and Florentine Traditions," *Studies in Italian Art and Architecture 15th through 18th Centuries*, ed. Henry Millon, vol. 35 of *Memoirs of the American Academy in Rome* (Rome: Edizioni dell'Elefante, 1980).

Bynum, Caroline Walker, *Holy Feast and Holy Fast: The Religious Significance of Food to Medieval Women* (Berkeley: University of California Press, 1987).

Cahill, James F., *The Compelling Image: Nature and Style in Seventeenth-Century Chinese Painting* (Cambridge, MA: Harvard University Press).

Calasso, Francesco, *I glossatori e la teoria della sovranità. Studio di diritto comune pubblico* (Milan: Giuffrè, 1951).

Calvi, Giulia, *Histories of a Plague Year: The Social and the Imaginary in Baroque Florence* (Berkeley: University of California Press, 1984).

Cambridge History of Medieval Political Thought, c.350–c.1450, ed. J. H. Burns (Cambridge: Cambridge University Press, 1988).

Cambridge History of Political Thought, 1450–1470, ed. J. H. Burns and M. Goldie (Cambridge: Cambridge University Press, 1991).

Camporesi, Piero, *The Incorruptible Flesh: Bodily Mutation and Mortification in Religion and Folklore*, trans. Tania Croft-Murray (Cambridge: Cambridge University Press, 1983).

——, *Bread of Dreams: Food and Fantasy in Early Modern Europe* (Chicago: University of Chicago Press, 1989).

Canning, Joseph, *The Political Thought of Baldus de Ubaldis* (Cambridge: Cambridge University Press, 1987).

Capp, Bernard, "Separate Domains? Women and Authority in Early Modern England," in *The Experience of Authority in Early Modern England*, ed. P. Griffith, A. Fox, and S. Hindle (New York: St. Martin's Press, 1996).

Cardan, Jerome (Cardano, Girolamo), *The Book of My Life*, trans. Jean Stoner (New York: E. P. Dutton, 1930).

Carlino, Andrea, *Books of the Body: Anatomical Ritual and Renaissance Learning*, trans. J. and A. T. Tedeschi (Chicago: University of Chicago Press, 1999).

Carmichael, Ann G., *Plague and the Poor in Renaissance Florence* (Cambridge: Cambridge University Press, 1986).

Carroll, Stuart, *Noble Power during the French Wars of Religion: The Guise Affinity and the Catholic Cause in Normandy* (Cambridge: Cambridge University Press, 1998).

Carroll, William C., *Fat King, Lean Beggar: Representations of Poverty in the Age of Shakespeare* (Ithaca, NY: Cornell University Press, 1996).

Casagrande, Carla, "La donna custodita," in *Storia delle donne in Occidente*, vol. 2: *Il Medioevo*, ed. Christiane Klapisch-Zuber (Bari: Laterza, 1990).

Castelnuovo, Enrico and Ginzburg, Carlo, "Centre and Periphery," in *History of Italian Art*, ed. P. Burke (Cambridge: Polity Press, 1996).

Castiglione, Baldasar, *Il libro del cortegiano* (Turin: Unione tipografico, editrice torinese, 1964).

——, *The Book of the Courtier*, trans. George Bull (London: Penguin, 1976).

Cavallo, Sandra, *Charity and Power in Early Modern Italy: Benefactors and Their Motives in Turin, 1541–1789* (Cambridge: Cambridge University Press, 1995).

Cellini, Benvenuto, *The Autobiography*, trans. George Bull (Harmondsworth and New York: Penguin, 1985).

Chambers, David, *The Imperial Age of Venice 1380–1580* (London: Thames and Hudson, 1970).

Chaudhuri, K. N., *Trade and Civilisation in the Indian Ocean: An Economic History from the Rise of Islam to 1750* (Cambridge: Cambridge University Press, 1985).

——, *Asia Before Europe: Economy and Civilisation of the Indian Ocean from the Rise of Islam to 1750* (Cambridge: Cambridge University Press, 1990).

Chelkowski, Peter J., *Mirror of the Invisible World: Tales from the Khamsah of Nizami* (New York: Metropolitan Museum of Art, 1975).

Chiappelli, Fredi, ed., *First Images of America*, 2 vols. (Berkeley: University of California Press, 1976).

Chojnacki, Stanley, "Patrician Women in Early Renaissance Venice," *Studies in the Renaissance* 21 (1974).

——, "Dowries and Kinsmen in Early Renaissance Venice," *Journal of Interdisciplinary History* 4 (1975).

——, "Kinship Ties and Young Patricians in Fifteenth-Century Venice," *Renaissance Quarterly* 38 (1985).

——, " 'The Most Serious Duty': Motherhood, Gender, and Patrician Culture in Renaissance Venice," in *Refiguring Woman: Perspectives on Gender and the Italian Renaissance*, ed. M. Migiel and J. Schiesari (Ithaca, NY: Cornell University Press, 1991).

——, *Women and Men in Renaissance Venice: Twelve Essays on Patrician Society* (Baltimore: Johns Hopkins University Press, 2000).

Christian, William, *Local Religion in Sixteenth-Century Spain* (Princeton: Princeton University Press, 1981).

Cicchetti, Angelo and Mordenti, Raul, *I libri di famiglia in Italia* (Rome: Edizioni di storia e letteratura, 1985).

Cipolla, Carlo M., "The Diffusion of Innovations in Early Modern Europe," *Comparative Studies in Society and History* 14 (1972).

——, *Guns and Sails in the Early Phase of European Expansion, 1400–1700* (London: Collins, 1965).

——, *Before the Industrial Revolution: European Society and Economy 1000–1700* (New York: W. W. Norton, 1994).

Clark, H. Wilberforce, *The Iskandar nama, e bara, or Book of Alexander the Great* (London: W. H. Allen, 1881).

Clark, Stuart, *Thinking with Demons: The Idea of Witchcraft in Early Modern Europe* (Oxford: Clarendon Press, 1997).

Clarke, Michael, "On the Concept of 'Sub-Culture'," *British Journal of Sociology* 25 (1974).

Clegg, Cyndia, *Press Censorship in Elizabethan England* (New York: Cambridge University Press, 1997).

Cochrane, Eric, *Italy 1530–1630* (London: Longman, 1988).

Cochrane, Eric and Kirshner, Julius, eds., *The Renaissance* (University of Chicago Readings in Western Civilization) (Chicago: University of Chicago Press, 1986).

Coe, Michael D., *Breaking the Maya Code*, rev. edn. (New York: Thames and Hudson, 1999).

Cogolludo, Fray Diego López de, *Historia de Yucatán* [1654] (Mexico City: Editorial Academia Literaria, 1957).

Cohen, Jeffrey Jerome, "Monster Culture (Seven Theses)," in *Monster Theory: Reading Culture*, ed. Jeffrey Jerome Cohen (Minneapolis: University of Minnesota Press, 1996).

Cohen, Thomas, "The Case of the Mysterious Coil of Rope: Street Life and Jewish Persona in Rome in the Middle of the Sixteenth Century", *Sixteenth Century Journal* 19 (1988).

——, "A Long Day in Monte Rotondo: The Politics of Jeopardy in a Village Uprising (1558)", *Comparative Studies in Society and History* 33 (1991).

——, "Social Memory as Festive Therapy in Village Politics," *Histoire sociale: Social History* 24 (1992).

——, "Three Forms of Jeopardy: Honor, Pain, and Truth-Telling in a Sixteenth-Century Italian Courtroom," *Sixteenth Century Journal* 29/4 (1998).

Cohen, Thomas V. and Cohen, Elizabeth S., *Words and Deeds in Renaissance Rome: Trials before the Papal Magistrates* (Toronto: University of Toronto Press, 1993).

Cohen, Walter, *Drama of a Nation: Public Theater in Renaissance England and Spain* (Ithaca, NY: Cornell University Press, 1985).

Cohn, Norman, *The Pursuit of the Millennium* (New York: Harper, 1961).

Cohn, Samuel K., Jr., *The Laboring Classes of Renaissance Florence* (New York: Academic Press, 1980).

——, *The Cult of Remembrance and the Black Death: Six Renaissance Cities in Central Italy* (Baltimore: Johns Hopkins University Press, 1992).

——, "Burckhardt Revisited from Social History," in *Language and Images of Renaissance Italy*, ed. Alison Brown (Oxford: Clarendon Press, 1995).

——, "Women and Work in Renaissance Italy," in *Gender and Society in Renaissance Italy*, ed. Judith C. Brown and Robert C. Davis (London: Longman, 1998).

——, *Creating the Florentine State: Peasants and Rebellion, 1348–1434* (Cambridge: Cambridge University Press, 1999).

Connell, William J. and Zorzi, Andrea, eds., *Florentine Tuscany: Structures and Practices of Power* (Cambridge: Cambridge University Press, 2000).

Cooke, Richard, *A White Sheet, or a Warning for Whoremongers* (London, 1629).

Copenhaver, Brian P., "Natural Magic, Hermetism, and Occultism in Early Modern Science," in *Reappraisals of the Scientific Revolution*, ed. David C. Lindberg and Robert S. Westman (Cambridge: Cambridge University Press, 1990).

Cortés, Hernán, *Letters from Mexico*, trans. and ed. Anthony Pagden (New Haven: Yale University Press, 1986).

Cox, Virginia, "The Single Self: Feminist Thought and the Marriage Market in Early Modern Venice," *Renaissance Quarterly* 48 (1995).

Cressy, David, *Birth, Marriage, and Death: Ritual, Religion, and the Life-cycle in Tudor and Stuart England* (New York: Oxford University Press, 1997).

Cropper, Elizabeth, "On Beautiful Women, Parmigianino, Petrarchismo, and the Vernacular Style," *Art Bulletin* 58 (1976).

Crosby, Alfred W., *The Columbian Exchange, Biological and Cultural Consequences of 1492* (Westport, CT: Greenwood Press, 1972).

——, *The Measure of Reality: Quantification and Western Society, 1250–1600* (Cambridge: Cambridge University Press, 1997).

Crouzet, Denis, *Les Guerriers de Dieu. La violence au temps des troubles de religion, vers 1525 – vers 1610*, 2 vols. (Seyssel: Camp Vallon, 1990).

Cruz, Anne J. and Perry, M. E., eds., *Culture and Control in Counter-Reformation Spain* (Minneapolis: University of Minnesota Press, 1992).

Cummins, Tom, "Representation in the Sixteenth Century and the Colonial Image of the Inca," in *Writing Without Words: Alternative Literacies in Mesoamerica and the Andes*, ed. Elizabeth Hill Boone and Walter D. Mignolo (Durham, NC: Duke University Press, 1994).

Curtius, Ernst Robert, *European Literature and the Latin Middle Ages*, trans. Willard R. Trask (Princeton: Princeton University Press, 1990).

Cust, Richard, "Honour and Politics in Early Stuart England: The Case of Beaumont v. Hastings," *Past and Present* 149 (1995).

Cutrera, Antonio, *Cronologia dei giustiziati di Palermo, 1541–1891* (Palermo, 1917).

D'Amico, John F., *Renaissance Humanism in Papal Rome. Humanists and Churchmen on the Eve of the Reformation* (Baltimore: Johns Hopkins University Press, 1983).

Darab Khan, Gholam Hossain, *The Treasury of Mysteries* (London: A. Probsthain, 1945).

Darling, Linda T., "Rethinking Europe and the Islamic World in the Age of Exploration," *Journal of Early Modern History* 2 (1998).

Darmon, Pierre, *Trial By Impotence: Virility and Marriage in Pre-Revolutionary France*, trans. Paul Keegan (London: Chatto & Windus, 1985).

Daston, Lorraine and Park, Katharine, *Wonders and the Order of Nature, 1150–1750* (Cambridge, MA: Zone Books, 1998).

Davidson, Nicolaus S., "An Armed Band and the Local Community on the Venetian Terra Ferma in the Sixteenth Century," in *Bande armate, banditi, banditismo e repressione di giustizia negli stati europei di antico regime*, ed. Gherardo Ortalli (Rome: Jouvence, 1986).

Davies, Norman, *God's Playground: A History of Poland*, rev. edn., 2 vols. (Oxford: Clarendon Press, 1982).

Davis, Charles T., *Dante's Italy and Other Essays* (Philadelphia: University of Pennsylvania Press, 1984).

Davis, John C., *The Decline of the Venetian Nobility as a Ruling Class* (Baltimore: Johns Hopkins University Press, 1962).

——, *A Venetian Family and its Fortune, 1500–1900* (Philadelphia: American Philosophical Society, 1975).

Davis, Natalie Zemon, "City Women and Religious Change," in *Society and Culture in Early Modern France* (Stanford: Stanford University Press, 1965).

——, *Society and Culture in Early Modern France* (Stanford: Stanford University Press, 1975).

——, *The Return of Martin Guerre* (Cambridge, MA: Harvard University Press, 1983).

——, "Boundaries and the Sense of Self in Sixteenth-Century France," in *Reconstructing Individualism: Autonomy, Individuality, and the Self in Western Thought*, ed. Thomas C. Heller, Morton Sosna, and David E. Wellbery (Stanford: Stanford University Press, 1986).

——, *Fiction in the Archives: Pardon Tales and their Tellers in Sixteenth-Century France* (Stanford: Stanford University Press, 1987).

Davis, Ralph, *The Rise of the Atlantic Economies* (Ithaca, NY: Cornell University Press, 1973).

Davis, Robert C., *Shipbuilders of the Venetian Arsenal: Workers and Workplace in the Preindustrial City* (Baltimore: Johns Hopkins University Press, 1992).

——, *The War of the Fists: Popular Culture and Public Violence in Late Renaissance Venice* (New York: Oxford University Press, 1994).

Dean, Trevor, "The Courts," in "The Origins of the State in Italy, 1300–1600," *Journal of Modern History*, supplement 67 (December 1995).

Debus, Allen G., *The Chemical Philosophy: Paracelsian Science and Medicine in the Sixteenth and Seventeenth Centuries*, 2 vols. (New York: Science History Publications, 1977).

De Gaetano, Armand, *Giambattista Gelli and the Florentine Academy: The Rebellion Against Latin* (Florence: Olschki, 1976).

Dekker, Rudolf, "Egodocuments (Autobiographies, Diaries, Travel Journals) in the Netherlands, 1500–1814," *Dutch Crossing* 39 (1989).

Delumeau, Jean, *Sin and Fear: The Emergence of a Western Guilt Culture, 13th–18th Centuries*, trans. Eric Nicholson (New York: St. Martin's Press, 1990).

Demos, John P., *Entertaining Satan: Witchcraft and the Culture of Early New England* (New York: Oxford University Press, 1982).

De Roover, Raymond, *The Rise and Decline of the Medici Bank, 1397–1494* (Cambridge, MA: Harvard University Press, 1963 and New York: W. W. Norton, 1966).

Descimon, Robert, "The Birth of the Nobility of the Robe: Dignity versus Privilege in the Parlement of Paris, 1500–1700," in *Changing Identities in Early Modern France*, ed. Michael Wolfe (Durham, NC: Duke University Press, 1997).

de Tocqueville, Alexis, *The Old Regime and the French Revolution*, trans. Stuart Gilbert (Garden City, NY: Doubleday, 1955).

de Vries, Jan, "The Population of Europe," in *Handbook of European History, 1400–1600*, 2 vols., ed. Thomas A. Brady Jr., Heiko A. Oberman, James D. Tracy (Leiden: E. J. Brill, 1994–5 and Grand Rapids, MI: Eerdmans, 1996), vol. 1.

Dewald, Jonathan, *The Formation of a Provincial Nobility: The Magistrates of the Parlement of Rouen, 1499–1610* (Princeton: Princeton University Press, 1980).

——, *The European Nobility, 1400–1800* (Cambridge: Cambridge University Press, 1996).

Diaz, Bernal, *The Conquest of New Spain* (London: Penguin, 1963).

Diefendorf, Barbara and Hesse, Carla, eds., *Culture and Identity in Early Modern Europe: Essays in Honor of Natalie Zemon Davis* (Ann Arbor: University of Michigan Press, 1993).

Dionisotti, Carlo, "La letteratura italiana all'epoca del Concilio di Trento," in *Geografia e storia* (Turin: Einaudi, 1967).

Di Simplicio, Oscar, "La giustizia ecclesiastica e il processo di civilizzazione," *Bollettino Senese di Storia Patria* 97 (1990).

——, *Peccato, penitenza, perdono: Siena 1575–1800. La formazione della coscienza dell'Italia moderna* (Milan: Franco Angeli Storia, 1994).

Dolan, Claire, "The Artisans of Aix-en-Provence in the Sixteenth Century: A Micro-Analysis of Social Relationships," in *Cities and Social Change in Early Modern France*, ed. Philip Benedict (London: Unwin Hyman, 1989).

Dols, Michael, *The Black Death in the Middle East* (Princeton: Princeton University Press, 1977).

Donne, John, *An Anatomy of the World* (Cambridge: Printed for the Roxburghe Club, 1951).

——, *Complete Poetry*, ed. John T. Shawcross (New York: New York University Press, 1968).

Douglas, Mary, *Purity and Danger: An Analysis of the Concepts of Pollution and Taboo* (London: Routledge, 1966).

——, *Natural Symbols: Explorations in Cosmology* (London: Barrie and Rockcliff, 1970).

Doria, Giorgio, *Uomini e terra di un borgo collinare, dal XVI al XVIII secolo* (Milan: A. Giuffrè, 1968).

Duffy, Eamon, *The Stripping of the Altars: Traditional Religion in England 1400–1580* (New Haven: Yale University Press, 1992).

Duplessis, Robert S., *Transitions to Capitalism in Early Modern Europe* (Cambridge: Cambridge University Press, 1997).

Du Rousseau de la Combe, Guy, *Traité des matières criminelles* (Paris: 1757).

Dykema, Peter A. and Oberman, Heiko A., eds., *Anticlericalism in Late Medieval and Early Modern Europe* (Leiden: E. J. Brill, 1993).

Eamon, William, "'With the Rules of Life and an Enema': Leonardo Fioravanti's Medical Primitivism," in *Renaissance and Revolution: Humanists, Scholars, Craftsmen and Natural Philosophers in Early Modern Europe*, ed. J. V. Field and F. A. J. L. James (Cambridge: Cambridge University Press, 1993).

——, *Science and the Secrets of Nature: Books of Secrets in Medieval and Early Modern Culture* (Princeton: Princeton University Press, 1994).

Early Modernities, Daedalus: Journal of the American Academy of Arts and Science 127/3 (Summer 1998).

Edgerton, Samuel, Jr., *The Renaissance Rediscovery of Linear Perspective* (New York: Basic Books, 1975).

Egmond, Florika and Mason, P., *The Mammoth and the Mouse: Microhistory and Morphology* (Baltimore: Johns Hopkins University Press, 1997).

Eisenbichler, Konrad and Publiese, Olga Zorzi, eds., *Ficino and Renaissance Neoplatonism* (Ottawa: Dovehouse Editions, 1986).

Eisenstein, Elizabeth, *The Printing Press as an Agent of Change* (Cambridge: Cambridge University Press, 1979).

Elias, Norbert, *The Civilizing Process*, I: *The History of Manners*, II: *State Formation and Civilization* [1939], trans. Edmund Jephcott (New York: Urizen Books, 1978 and Oxford: Blackwell Publishers, 1994).

——, *The Norbert Elias Reader: A Biographical Selection*, ed. Johan Goudsblom and Stephen Mennell (Oxford: Blackwell Publishers, 1998).

Elliott, John H., *Imperial Spain, 1469–1716* (New York: Penguin, 1970).

——, *The Old World and the New, 1492–1650* (Cambridge: Cambridge University Press, 1970).

——, *Richelieu and Olivares* (Cambridge: Cambridge University Press, 1984).

——, "A World United," in *Circa 1492: Art in the Age of Exploration*, ed. Jay A. Levenson (Washington and New Haven: National Gallery and Yale University Press, 1991).

Epstein, Steven A., *Wage Labor and Guilds in Medieval Europe* (Chapel Hill: University of North Carolina Press, 1991).

——, *Genoa and the Genoese 958–1528* (Chapel Hill: University of North Carolina Press, 1996).

Erasmus, Desiderius, *Collected Works* (Toronto: University of Toronto Press, 1974–).

——, *The Praise of Folly and Other Writings*, trans. and ed. Robert M. Adams (New York: W. W. Norton, 1989).

Erauso, Catalina de, *Lieutenant Nun: Memoir of a Basque Transvestite in the New World*, trans. and ed. Michele and Gabriel Stepto (Boston: Beacon, 1996).

Ertman, Thomas, *The Birth of the Leviathan: Building States and Regimes in Medieval and Early Modern Europe* (Cambridge: Cambridge University Press, 1997).

Eurich, S. Amanda, *The Economies of Power: The Private Finances of the House of Foix-Navarre-Albret during the Religious Wars* (Kirksville, MO: Sixteenth Century Texts and Studies, 1994).

Evans, Richard J., *Rituals of Retribution: Capital Punishment in Germany from the Thirty Years War to 1945* (Oxford: Oxford University Press, 1995).

Faralli, Carla, "Le missioni dei Gesuiti in Italia (sec. XVI–XVII): Problemi di una ricerca in corso," *Bolletino della società studi valdesi* 138 (1975).

Farr, James R., *Hands of Honor: Artisans and Their World in Dijon, 1550–1650* (Ithaca, NY: Cornell University Press, 1988).

——, *Authority and Sexuality in Early Modern Burgundy (1500–1730)* (New York: Oxford University Press, 1995).

——, "Parlementaires and the Paradox of Power: Sovereignty and Jurisprudence in Rapt Cases in Early Modern Burgundy," *European History Quarterly* 25/3 (1995).

Febvre, Lucien and Martin, Henri-Jean, *The Coming of the Book*, trans. David Gerard (London: NLB, 1976).

Fentress, James and Wickham, Chris, *Social Memory* (Oxford: Blackwell Publishers, 1992).

Ferguson, Margaret, Quilligan, Maureen, and Vickers, Nancy, eds., *Rewriting the Renaissance: The Discourses of Sexual Difference in Early Modern Europe* (Chicago: University of Chicago Press, 1986).

Ferguson, Wallace K., *The Renaissance in Historical Thought: Five Centuries of Interpretation* (Cambridge, MA: Riverside Press, 1948).

Fernández-Armesto, Felipe, *Before Columbus: Exploration and Colonization from the Mediterranean to the Atlantic, 1229–1492* (Philadelphia: University of Pennsylvania Press, 1987).

Fernández de Orviedo y Valdés, Gonzalo, *Natural History of the West Indies*, trans. and ed. Sterling Stoudemire (Chapel Hill: University of North Carolina Press, 1959).

Ferrari, Giovanna, "Public Anatomy Lessons and the Carnival: The Anatomy Theatre of Bologna," *Past and Present* 117 (1987).

Ferraro, Joanne M., *Family and Public Life in Brescia, 1580–1650: The Foundations of Power in the Venetian State* (Cambridge: Cambridge University Press, 1993).

——, *Marriage Wars in Late Renaissance Venice* (New York: Oxford University Press, 2001).

Filhol, René, "The Codification of Customary Law in France in the Fifteenth and Sixteenth Centuries," in *Government in Reformation Europe, 1520–1560*, ed. Henry Cohn (London: Macmillan, 1971).

Findlen, Paula, *Possessing Nature: Museums, Collecting, and Scientific Culture in Early Modern Italy* (Berkeley: University of California Press, 1994).

Findlen, Paula and Gouwens, Kenneth, eds., "AHR Forum: The Persistence of the Renaissance," *American Historical Review* 103/1 (February 1998).

Findlen, Paula, et al., eds., *Beyond Florence* (Palo Alto: Stanford University Press, forthcoming).

Finucci, Valeria, *The Lady Vanishes: Subjectivity and Representation in Castiglione and Ariosto* (Stanford: Stanford University Press, 1992).

Firdausi, *The Epic of the Kings*, trans. Reuben Levy (London: Routledge and Kegan Paul, 1967).

Firpo, Luigi, "Political Philosophy: Renaissance Utopianism," in *The Late Italian Renaissance, 1525–1630*, ed. Eric Cochrane (London: Macmillan, 1970).

——, ed., *Relazioni di ambasciatori veneti al senato*, vol. II: *Savoia (1496–1797)* (Turin: Bottega d'Erasmo, 1983).

Fleischer, Cornell H., "The Lawgiver as Messiah: The Making of the Imperial Image in the Reign of Süleymân," in *Soliman le Magnifique et son temps*, ed. Gilles Veinstein (Paris: École des Hautes Études en Sciences Sociales, 1992).

Fletcher, Anthony, "Honour, Reputation, and Local Office Holding in Elizabethan and Stuart England," in *Order and Disorder in Early Modern England*, ed. Anthony Fletcher and John Stevenson (Cambridge: Cambridge University Press, 1985).

——, *Gender, Sex and Subordination in England 1500–1800* (New Haven: Yale University Press, 1995).

Fletcher, Richard, *Moorish Spain* (Berkeley: University of California Press, 1992).

Fontaine, Laurence, *A History of Pedlars in Europe*, trans. Vicki Whittaker (Durham: Duke University Press, 1996).

Frangsmayr, Tore, Heilbron, J. L., and Rider, Robin E., *The Quantifying Spirit of the Eighteenth Century* (Berkeley: University of California Press, 1990).

Frank, Andre Gunder, *ReOrient: Global Economy in the Asian Age* (Berkeley: University of California Press, 1998).

Fraser, Valeri, "Architecture and Imperialism in Sixteenth-Century Spanish America," *Art History* 9 (1986).

——, *The Architecture of Conquest: Building in the Viceroyalty of Peru* (Cambridge: Cambridge University Press, 1990).

Freedman, Paul, *Images of the Medieval Peasant* (Stanford: Stanford University Press, 1999).

Fuentes, Carlos, *The Buried Mirror: Reflections on Spain and the New World* (Boston: Houghton Mifflin, 1992).

Furbini, Riccardo, *Quattrocento fiorentino* (Pisa: Pacini, 1996).

Galluzzi, Paolo, *Renaissance Engineers from Brunelleschi to Leonardo da Vinci* (Florence, Istituto e Museo di Storia della Scienza, 1996).

García, Miguel Herrero, *Ideas de los Españoles del Siglo XVIII* (Madrid: Editorial Gredos, 1966).

Gardiner, Edmund, *The Trial of Tabacco* (London, 1610).

Gardner, Victoria C., "*Homines non nascuntur, sed finguntur*: Benvenuto Cellini's *Vita* and Self-Presentation of the Renaissance Artist," *Sixteenth Century Journal* 28 (1997).

Garrard, Mary, "Leonardo da Vinci: Female Portraits, Female Nature," *The Expanding Discourse: Feminism and Art History*, ed. Norma Broude and Mary Garrard (New York: HarperCollins, 1992).

Gatti, Hilary, *Giordano Bruno and Renaissance Science* (Ithaca, NY: Cornell University Press, 1999).

Geertz, Clifford, *Negara: The Theatre State in Nineteenth-Century Bali* (Princeton: Princeton University Press, 1980).

——, " 'From the Native's Point of View': On the Nature of Anthropological Understanding," in *Culture Theory: Essays on Mind, Self, and Emotion*, ed. Richard Shweder and Robert Levine (Cambridge: Cambridge University Press, 1984).

Geldner, Ferdinand, *Die deutsche Inkunabeldrucker*, 2 vols. (Stuttgart: A. Hiersemann, 1968–70).

Gentilcore, David, *From Bishop to Witch: The System of the Sacred in Early Modern Terra d'Otranto* (Manchester: Manchester University Press, 1992).

——, " 'Adapt Yourselves to the People's Capabilities': Missionary Strategies, Methods and Impact in the Kingdom of Naples, 1600–1800", *Journal of Ecclesiastical History* 45 (1994).

——, *Healers and Healing in Early Modern Italy* (Manchester: Manchester University Press, 1998).

Geremek, Bronislaw, *The Margins of Society in Late Medieval Paris*, trans. Jean Birrell (New York: Cambridge University Press, 1987).

——, *Poverty: A History*, trans. Agnieszka Kolokowska (Oxford: Blackwell Publishers, 1994).

Gilbert, Felix, *Machiavelli and Guicciardini: Politics and History in Sixteenth-Century Florence* (Princeton: Princeton University Press, 1965).

——, "The Venetian Constitution in Florentine Political Thought," in *Florentine Studies: Politics and Society in Renaissance Florence*, ed. Nicolai Rubinstein (Evanston: Northwestern University Press, 1968).

Gilmore, Myron, *Argument from Roman Law in Political Thought 1200–1600* (New York: Russell and Russell, 1967).

Ginsberg, Elaine K., ed., *Passing and the Fictions of Identity* (Durham, NC: Duke University Press, 1996).

Ginzburg, Carlo, *The Cheese and the Worms: The Cosmos of a Sixteenth-Century Miller*, trans. J. and A. Tedeschi (Baltimore: Johns Hopkins University Press, 1980; Harmondsworth: Penguin, 1982).

——, *The Night Battles: Witchcraft and Agrarian Cults in the Sixteenth and Seventeenth Centuries*, trans. J. and A. Tedeschi (Baltimore: Johns Hopkins University Press, 1983).

Ginzburg, Carlo and Ferrari, M., "The Dovecote has Opened its Eyes," in *Microhistory and the Lost People of Europe*, ed. E. Muir and G. Ruggiero, trans. E. Branch (Baltimore: Johns Hopkins University Press, 1991).

Goffman, Daniel, *Britons in the Ottoman Empire, 1642–1660* (Seattle: University of Washington Press, 1998).

Goffman, Erving, *Interaction Ritual* (Garden City, NJ: Anchor Books, 1967).

Goldthwaite, Richard, *Private Wealth in Renaissance Florence: A Study of Four Families* (Princeton: Princeton University Press, 1968).

——, "The Building of the Strozzi Palace: The Construction Industry in Renaissance Florence," *Studies in Medieval and Renaissance History* 10 (1973).

——, *Wealth and the Demand for Art in Italy, 1300–1600* (Baltimore: Johns Hopkins University Press, 1993).

Gombrich, Ernst H., *Art and Illusion* (Princeton: Princeton University Press, 1960).

——, "The Leaven of Criticism in Renaissance Art," in *The Heritage of Apelles* (Oxford: Phaidon, 1976).

Goodman, Anthony and McKay, Angus, eds., *The Impact of Humanism on Western Europe* (London: Longman, 1990).

Goodman, Jordan, *Tobacco in History: The Cultures of Dependence* (New York: Routledge, 1993).

Goodwin, Godfrey, "Art and Creative Thinking in the Reign of Süleymân the Lawgiver," in *Süleymân the Second and His Time*, ed. Halil Inalcık and Cemal Kafadar (Istanbul: Isis Press, 1993).

Goody, Jack, *The European Family: An Historico-Anthropological Essay* (Oxford: Blackwell Publishers, 2000).

Gosson, Stephen, *The Schoole of Abuse* (London, 1579).

Goubert, Pierre, *The French Peasantry in the Seventeenth Century*, trans. I. Patterson (Cambridge: Cambridge University Press, 1986).

Grabar, Oleg, "Persian Miniatures: Illustrations or Paintings," in *The Persian Presence in the Islamic World*, ed. Richard G. Hovannisian and Georges Sabagh (Cambridge: Cambridge University Press, 1998).

Grabar, Oleg and Blair, Sheila, *Epic Images and Contemporary History: The Illustrations of the Great Mongol Shahnama* (Chicago: University of Chicago Press, 1980).

Grafton, Anthony, *Defenders of the Text: Traditions of Scholarship in an Age of Science* (Cambridge, MA: Harvard University Press, 1991).

——, *New Worlds, Ancient Texts: The Power of Tradition and the Shock of the New* (Cambridge, MA: Harvard University Press, 1992).

——, ed., *Rome Reborn: The Vatican Library and Renaissance Culture* (Washington, DC: Library of Congress, 1993).

——, *Cardano's Cosmos: The Worlds and Works of a Renaissance Astrologer* (Cambridge, MA: Harvard University Press, 1999).

Grafton, Anthony and Blair, Ann, eds., *The Transmission of Culture in Early Modern Europe* (Philadelphia: University of Pennsylvania Press, 1990).

Grafton, Anthony and Jardine, Lisa, *From Humanism to Humanities: Education and the Liberal Arts in Fifteenth- and Sixteenth-Century Europe* (Cambridge, MA: Harvard University Press, 1986).

Graham-Dixon, Andrew, *Renaissance* (Berkeley: Univerity of California Press, 1999).

Grant, Edward, *Planets, Stars, and Orbs: The Medieval Cosmos, 1200–1687* (Cambridge: Cambridge University Press, 1996).

Greenblatt, Stephen, *Renaissance Self-Fashioning: From More to Shakespeare* (Chicago: Chicago University Press, 1980).

——, "What Is the History of Literature?," *Critical Inquiry* 23 (1997)

Greif, Avner, "Reputations and Coalitions in Medieval Trade: Evidence on the Maghribi Traders," *Journal of Economic History* 49 (1989).

Grendi, Edoardo, "Profilo storico degli Alberghi genovesi," *MEFRM* 87 (1975).

——, "Il sistema politico di una comunità ligure: Cervo fra Cinquecento e Seicento," *Quaderni storici* 46 (1981).

——, "Sulla 'storia criminale': risposta a Mario Sbriccoli," *Quaderni Storici* 73 (1990).

Grendler, Paul F., *Schooling in Renaissance Italy: Literacy and Learning, 1300–1600* (Baltimore: Johns Hopkins University Press, 1989).

Griffiths, Paul, "Secrecy and Authority in Late Sixteenth- and Seventeenth-Century London," *The Historical Journal* 40 (1997).

Grubb, James S., "Memory and Identity: Why Venetians Did Not Keep *Recordanze*," *Renaissance Studies* 8 (1994).

——, *Provincial Families of the Renaissance: Private and Public Life in the Veneto* (Baltimore: Johns Hopkins University Press, 1996).

Grube, Ernst J., "Notes on Ottoman Painting in the 15th Century," in *Essays in Islamic Art and Architecture in Honor of Katharina Otto-Dorn*, ed. Abbas Daneshvari (Malibu, CA: Undena Publications, 1981).

Gruffydd, R. Geraint, "The Renaissance and Welsh Literature," in *The Celts and the Renaissance*, ed. Glanmore Williams and Robert Owen Jones (Cardiff: University of Wales Press, 1990).

Gruzinski, Serge, *Painting the Conquest: The Mexican Indians and the European Renaissance* (Paris: Flammarion, 1992).

——, *The Conquest of Mexico: The Incorporation of Indian Societies into the Western World, 16th–18th Centuries* (Cambridge: Polity Press, 1993).

——, *La Pensée métisse* (Paris: Fayard, 1999).

Guarini, Fasano, "Produzione di leggi e disciplinamento nella Toscana granducale tra Cinque e Seicento. Spunti di ricerca," in *Disciplina dell'anima, disciplina del corpo e disciplina società tra medioevo ed età moderna*, ed. Paolo Prodi (Bologna: Il Mulino, 1994)

Guicciardini, Francesco, *Storia d'Italia*, 5 vols. (Bari: La Terza, 1929).

Guidi, José, "Baldassar Castiglione et le pouvoir politique: du gentilhomme de cour au nonce pontifical," in *Les Écrivains et le pouvoir en Italie à l'époque de la Renaissance* (Paris: Université de la Sorbonne, 1973).

——, "Castiglione, mythe et réalité de la vie de cour," unpublished thesis, the Sorbonne, 1983.

Gundesheimer, Werner L., "Crime and Punishment in Ferrara, 1440–1500," in *Violence and Civil Disorder in Italian Cities, 1200–1500*, ed. Lauro Martines (Berkeley: University of California Presss, 1972).

Gurr, Andrew, *Playgoing in Shakespeare's London* (Cambridge: Cambridge University Press, 1987).

Gusdorf, George, "Conditions and Limits of Autobiography," in *Autobiography: Essays Theoretical and Critical*, ed. James Olney (Princeton: Princeton University Press, 1980).

Hägerstrand, Torsten, *Innovation Diffusion as a Social Process*, trans. Allan Pred (Chicago: University of Chicago Press, 1967).

——, "Survival and Arena," in *Human Activity and Time Geography*, ed. Tommy Carlstein, Don Parker, and Nigel Thrift (New York: Wiley, 1978).

——, "Some Unexplored Problems in the Modeling of Culture Transfer and Transformation," in *The Transfer and Transformation of Ideas and Material Culture*, ed. Peter J. Hugill and D. Bruce Dickson (College Station, TX: Texas A and M Press, 1988).

Hajnal, J., "Two Kinds of Pre-industrial Household Formation Systems," in *Family Forms in Historic Europe*, ed. R. Wall, J. Robin, and P. Laslett (Cambridge and New York: Cambridge University Press, 1983).

Hale, John, ed., *A Concise Encyclopedia of the Italian Renaissance* (New York: Oxford University Press, 1981).

——, *War and Society in Renaissance Europe, 1450–1620* (Baltimore: Johns Hopkins University Press, 1985 and Leicester: Leicester University Press, 1985).

——, *Artists and Warfare in the Renaissance* (New Haven: Yale University Press, 1990).

——, *The Civilization of Europe in the Renaissance* (London: HarperCollins, 1993 and New York: Atheneum, 1994, Simon and Schuster, 1995).

Hall, Bert S., *Weapons and Warfare in Renaissance Europe: Gunpowder, Technology, and Tactics* (Baltimore: Johns Hopkins University Press, 1997).

Hall, Marcia, *After Raphael: Painting in Central Italy in the Sixteenth Century* (Cambridge: Cambridge University Press, 1999).

Hall, Peter Geoffrey, *Cities in Civilization* (London: Weidenfeld and Nicolson, 1988).

Hall, Peter Geoffrey and Preston, P., *The Carrier Wave: New IT and the Geography of Innovation, 1846–2003* (London: Unwin Hyman, 1988).

Hampton, Timothy, *Writing from History: The Rhetoric of Exemplarity in Renaissance Literature* (Ithaca, NY: Cornell University Press, 1990).

Hanke, Lewis, *The Spanish Struggle for Justice in the Conquest of America* (Boston: Little, Brown, 1965).

Hankins, James, ed., *Renaissance Civic Humanism: Reappraisals and Reflections* (Cambridge: Cambridge University Press, 2000).

Hanley, Sarah, "Social Sites of Political Practice in France: Lawsuits, Civil Rights, and the Separation of Powers in Domestic and State Government, 1500–1800," *American Historical Review* 102 (1997).

Hanson, Kristen, "From Dante to Pinsky: A Theoretical Perspective on the History of the Modern English Iambic Pentameter," *Rivista di Linguistica* 9/1 (1997).

Harman, Thomas, *A Caveat for Common Cursetors, Vulgarly called Vagabonds* [1567], in *The Elizabethan Underworld*, ed. A. V. Judges (New York: Octagon, 1964).

Harris, Tim, ed., *Popular Culture in England, c.1500–1850* (London: Macmillan, 1995).

Harrington, J. F., "Escape from the Great Confinement: The Genealogy of a German Workhouse," *Journal of Modern History* 71 (1999).

Hattox, Ralph S., "Mehmed the Conqueror, the Patriarch of Jerusalem, and Mamluk Authority," *Studia Islamica* 90 (2000).

Haussherr, Renier, "Kunstgeographie: Aufgaben, Grenzen, Möglichkeiten," *Rheinische Vierteljahrblätter* 34 (1970).

Hay, Denys, *The Italian Renaissance in its Historical Background* (Cambridge: Cambridge University Press, 1961).

——, *The Church in Italy in the Fifteenth Century* (Cambridge: Cambridge University Press, 1977).

Hay, Denys and Law, John, *Italy in the Age of the Renaissance 1380–1530* (London: Longman, 1989).

Head, R. C., *Early Modern Democracy in the Grisons: Social Order and Political Language in a Swiss Mountain Canton, 1470–1620* (Cambridge: Cambridge University Press, 1995).

Headley, John M., *Tommaso Campanella and the Transformation of the World* (Princeton: Princeton University Press, 1997).

Hecker, J. F. C., *The Black Death*, trans. B. G. Babbington (Lawrenceville, KS: Coronado Press, 1972).

Helgerson, Richard, *Forms of Nationhood: The Elizabethan Writing of England* (Chicago: University of Chicago Press, 1992).

Henningsen, Gustav, *The Witches' Advocate: Basque Witchcraft and the Spanish Inquisition, 1609–1614* (Reno: University of Nevada Press, 1980).

Herlihy, David, *The Black Death and the Transformation of the West*, ed. Samuel K. Cohn Jr. (Cambridge, MA: Harvard University Press, 1997).

Herlihy, David and Klapisch-Zuber, Christiane, *Tuscans and their Families: A Study of the Florentine Castato of 1427* (New Haven: Yale University Press, 1985).

Hexter, J. H., *More's Utopia: The Biography of an Idea* (New York: Harper Torchbooks, 1952).

Higman, Francis, "'I Came Not to Send Peace, but a Sword',," in *Calvinus Sincerioris Religionis Vindex*, ed. Wilhelm H. Neuser and Brian G. Armstrong (Kirksville, MO: Sixteenth Century Journal, 1997).

Hill, Christopher, *The English Bible and the Seventeenth-Century Revolution* (London: Allen Lane, 1994).

Hill Boone, Elizabeth, *Stories in Red and Black: Pictorial Histories of the Aztecs and Mixtecs* (Austin: University of Texas Press, 2000).

Hillenbrand, Robert, "The Uses of Space in Timurid Painting," in *Timurid Art and Culture: Iran and Central Asia in the Fifteenth Century*, ed. Lisa Golombek and Maria Subtelny (Leiden: E. J. Brill, 1992).

Hillman, David, "Visceral Knowledge: Shakespeare, Skepticism, and the Interior of the Early Modern Body," in *The Body in Parts: Fantasies of Corporeality in Early Modern Europe*, ed. David Hillman and Carla Mazzio (New York: Routledge, 1997).

Hodgson, Marshall G. S., *The Venture of Islam: Conscience and History in a World Civilization*, 3 vols. (Chicago: University of Chicago Press, 1974).

Hoffman, Philip T., *Growth in a Traditional Society: The French Countryside 1450–1815* (Princeton: Princeton University Press, 1996).

Hohenberg, Paul M. and Lees, Lynn Hollen, *The Making of Urban Europe, 1000–1950* (Cambridge, MA: Harvard University Press, 1985).

Hollier, Denis, ed., *A New History of French Literature* (Cambridge, MA: Harvard University Press, 1989).

Hood, William, "The State of Research in Italian Renaissance Art," *Art Bulletin* 69 (1987).

Horrox, Rosemary, ed. and trans., *The Black Death* (Manchester: Manchester University Press, 1994).

Houston, Robert A., *Literacy in Early Modern Europe: Culture and Education, 1500–1800* (London: Longman, 1988).

Howard, Deborah, *The Architectural History of Venice* (New Haven: Yale University Press, 1980).

——, *Venice and the East: The Impact of the Islamic World on Venetian Architecture, 1100–1500* (New Haven: Yale University Press, 2000).

Howard, Jean, "Crossdressing, the Theatre, and Gender Struggle in Early Modern England," *Shakespeare Quarterly* 39/4 (1988)

Hsia, R. Po-chia, *The Myth of Ritual Murder: Jews and Magic in Reformation Germany* (New Haven: Yale University Press, 1988).

——, *Trent 1475: Stories of a Ritual Murder Trial* (New Haven: Yale University Press, 1988).

——, "Die Sakralisierung der Gesellschaft. Blutfrömmigkeit und Verehrung der Heiligen Familie in der Reformation," in *Kommunalisierung und Christianisierung Voraussetzungen und Folgen der Reformation 1400–1600* (Zeitschrift für Historische Forschung, Beiheft 9, 1989).

——, *Social Discipline in the Reformation: Central Europe, 1550–1750* (London: Routledge, 1989).

Hufton, Olwen, *The Prospect Before Her: A History of Women in Western Europe*, I: *1500–1800* (London: HarperCollins, 1995).

Hughes, Paul L. and Larkin, James F., eds., *Tudor Royal Proclamations*, 3 vols. (New Haven: Yale University Press, 1964–9).

Hugill, Peter J. and Dickson, D. Bruce, eds., *The Transfer and Transformation of Ideas and Material Culture* (College Station, TX: Texas A and M Press, 1988).

Huizinga, Johan, *The Autumn of the Middle Ages*, trans. Rodney J. Payton and Ulrich Mammitzsch (Chicago: University of Chicago Press, 1996).

Hull, Suzanne, *Chaste, Silent and Obedient: English Books for Women 1475–1640* (San Marino, CA: Huntington Library, 1982).

Humfrey, Peter, *Lorenzo Lotto* (New Haven: Yale University Press, 1997).

Imbert, Jean, *La Pratique judiciaire* (Paris, 1609).

Inalcık, Halil, "The Policy of Mehmed II toward the Greek Population of Istanbul and the Byzantine Buildings of the City," *Dumbarton Oaks Papers* 23/24 (1969/70).

——, *The Ottoman Empire: The Classical Age, 1300–1600*, trans. Norman Itzkowitz and Colin Imber (London: Weidenfeld and Nicolson, 1973; repr. London: Orion Books/Phoenix, 1994).

Isom-Verhaaren, Christine, "Ottoman–French Interaction 1480–1580: A Sixteenth Century Encounter," Ph.D. dissertation, University of Chicago, 1997.

Israel, Jonathan, *The Dutch Republic: Its Rise, Greatness, and Fall, 1477–1806* (Oxford: Clarendon Press, 1995).

Jackson, Peter and Lockhart, Laurence, eds., *Cambridge History of Iran*, 7 vols. (Cambridge: Cambridge University Press, 1968–91).

James, Mervyn E., *English Politics and the Concept of Honour, 1485–1642* (Oxford: Past and Present Society, 1978).

Jane, Cecil, ed., *Selected Documents Illustrating the Four Voyages of Columbus*, 2nd ser., nos. 65 and 70 (London: Hakluyt Society, 1930–2).

Jardine, Lisa, *Worldly Goods: A New History of the Renaissance* (New York: Doubleday, 1996).

Jardine, Lisa and Brotton, Jerry, *Global Interests: Renaissance Art between East and West* (London: Reaktion Books, 2000).

Jayyusi, Salma Khadra, ed., *The Legacy of Muslim Spain*, 2 vols. (Leiden: E. J. Brill, 1992).

Jed, Stephanie H., *Chaste Thinking: The Rape of Lucretia and the Birth of Humanism* (Bloomington: Indiana University Press, 1989).

Johns, Adrian, *The Nature of the Book: Print and Knowledge in the Making* (Chicago: University of Chicago Press, 1998).

Jolly, Anna, "Netherlandish Sculptors in Sixteenth-Century Northern Germany and their Patrons," *Simiolus* 27 (1999).

Jones, Ann Rosalind, *The Currency of Eros: Women's Love Lyric in Europe, 1540–1620* (Bloomington, IN: Indiana University Press, 1990).

Jones, E. L., *The European Miracle: Environments, Economies and Geopolitics in the History of Europe and Asia*, 2nd edn. (Cambridge: Cambridge University Press, 1987).

Jones, Philip, "Florentine Families and Florentine Diaries in the Fourteenth Century," in *Studies in Italian Medieval History Presented to Miss E. M. Jamison*, ed. Philip Grierson (Rome: British School at Rome, 1956).

——, *The Italian City-State* (Oxford: Clarendon Press, 1997).

Jordan, Constance, *Renaissance Feminism: Literary Texts and Political Models* (Ithaca, NY: Cornell University Press, 1990).

Jordan, William C., *The Great Famine: Northern Europe in the Early Fourteenth Century* (Princeton: Princeton University Press, 1996).

Jouanna, Arlette, *Le Devoir de révolte. La noblesse française et la gestation de l'état moderne (1559–1661)* (Paris: Fayard, 1989).

Journal of Interdisciplinary History 14 (1983). Special issue, "Hunger and History."

Jütte, Robert, *Ärzte, Heiler und Patienten: Medizinischer Alltag in der frühen Neuzeit* (Munich: Artemis and Winkler, 1991).

——, *Poverty and Deviance in Early Modern Europe* (Cambridge: Cambridge University Press, 1994).

Kafé, Esther, "Le mythe turc et son déclin dans les relations de voyage des européens de la Renaissance," *Oriens* 21/2 (1968–9).

Kagan, Richard L., *Lawsuits and Litigants in Castile, 1500–1700* (Chapel Hill: University of North Carolina Press, 1977).

Kantorowicz, Ernst H., "Kingship under the Impact of Jurisprudence," in *Selected Studies*, ed. Ernst H. Kantorowicz (Locust Valley, NY: J. J. Augustin, 1965).

——, *The King's Two Bodies: A Study in Medieval Political Theology* (Princeton: Princeton University Press, 1957).

Kaplan, Stephen, ed., *Understanding Popular Culture: Europe from the Middle Ages to the Present* (Berlin: Mouton, 1984).

Karli, Pierre, *Animal and Human Aggression*, trans. S. M. Carmona and H. Whyte (Oxford: Oxford University Press, 1991).

Karras, Ruth Mazo, *Common Women: Prostitution and Sexuality in Medieval England* (New York: Oxford University Press, 1996).

Kaufmann, Thomas DaCosta, *Variations on the Imperial Theme in the Age of Maximilian II and Rudolf II* (New York: Garland, 1978).

——, *The School of Prague: Painting at the Court of Rudolf II* (Chicago: University of Chicago Press, 1988).

——, *Court, Cloister and City: The Art and Culture of Central Europe, 1450–1800* (Chicago: University of Chicago Press, 1995).

——, "Italian Sculptors and Sculpture Outside of Italy," in *Reframing the Renaissance*, ed. Claire Farago (New Haven: Yale University Press, 1995).

Kaye, Joel, *Economy and Nature in the Fourteenth Century: Money, Market Exchange and the Emergence of Scientific Thought* (Cambridge: Cambridge University Press, 1998).

Kedar, Benjamin, *Merchants in Crisis: Genoese and Venetian Men of Affairs and the Fourteenth-Century Depression* (New Haven: Yale University Press, 1976).

Kelley, Donald R., *Foundations of Modern Historical Thought* (New York: Columbia University Press, 1970).

——, " 'Second nature': The Idea of Custom in European Law, Society, and Culture," in *The Transmission of Culture in Early Modern Europe*, ed. Anthony Grafton and Ann Blair (Philadelphia: University of Pennsylvania Press, 1990).

Kellog, Susan, "Depicting *Mestizaje*: Gendered Images of Ethnorace in Colonial Mexican Texts," *Journal of Women's History* 12/3 (Autumn 2000).

Kelly, Joan, "Did Women Have a Renaissance?" in *Women, History and Theory: The Essays* (Chicago: University of Chicago Press, 1984).

——, "Early Feminist Theory and the *querelle des femmes*, 1400–1789," in *Women, History and Theory: The Essays* (Chicago: University of Chicago Press, 1984).

Kelly, Kathleen Coyne, ed., *Menacing Virgins: Representing Virginity in the Middle Ages and Renaissance* (Newark, DE: University of Delaware Press, 2000).

Kelso, Ruth, *Doctrine of the English Gentleman in the Sixteenth Century* (Urbana: University of Illinois Press, 1929).

——, *Doctrine for the Lady of the Renaissance* (Urbana: University of Illinois Press, 1956; repr. 1978).

Kemp, Martin, *The Science of Art: Optical Themes in Western Art from Brunelleschi to Seurat* (New Haven: Yale University Press, 1990).

——, "The Mean and Measure of All Things," in *Circa 1492: Art in the Age of Exploration*, ed. Jay A. Levenson (Washington and New Haven: National Gallery and Yale University Press, 1991).

Kent, Francis William, *Household and Lineage in Renaissance Florence: The Family Life of the Capponi, Ginori, and Rucellai* (Princeton: Princeton University Press, 1977).

Kent, Francis William and Simons, Patricia, eds., *Patronage, Art and Society in Renaissance Italy* (New York and Oxford: Oxford University Press, 1987).

Kent, Francis William, et al., *A Florentine Patrician and his Palace* (London: Warburg Institute, 1981).

Kerrigan, William and Braden, Gordon, *The Idea of the Renaissance* (Baltimore: Johns Hopkins University Press, 1989).

Kertzer, David I., *Ritual, Politics, and Power* (New Haven: Yale University Press, 1988).

Kieckhefer, Richard, *European Witch Trials: Their Foundation in Popular and Learned Culture, 1300–1500* (Berkeley: University of California Press, 1976).

King, Margaret, *Venetian Humanism in an Age of Patrician Dominance* (Princeton: Princeton University Press, 1986).

——, *Women of the Renaissance* (Chicago: University of Chicago Press, 1991).

Kirkconnell, Watson, ed. and trans., *The Hungarian Helicon: Epic and Other Poetry* (Calgary: Széchenyi Society, 1985).

Kirshner, Julius, "Introduction: The State is 'Back In'," *Journal of Modern History* 67, supplement (1995).

——, ed., *The Origins of the State in Italy, 1300–1600* (Chicago: University of Chicago Press, 1995).

Kirshner, Julius and Molho, Anthony, "The Dowry Fund and the Marriage Market in Early *Quattrocento* Florence," *Journal of Modern History* 50 (1978).

Kjaergaard, Thorkild, *The Danish Revolution, 1500–1800*, trans. David Hohen (Cambridge: Cambridge University Press, 1994).

Klapisch-Zuber, Christiane, *Women, Family and Ritual in Renaissance Italy*, trans. L. Cochrane (Chicago: University of Chicago Press, 1985).

Klein, Robert and Zerner, Henri, *Italian Art 1500–1600* (Englewood Cliffs, NJ: Prentice Hall, 1966).

Koenigsberger, Helmut G. and Mosse, George L., *Europe in the Sixteenth Century* (London: Longman: 1968).

Koerner, Joseph Leo, *The Moment of Self-Portraiture in German Renaissance Art* (Chicago: University of Chicago Press, 1993).

Koestler, Arthur, *The Act of Creation* (London: Hutchinson, 1964).

Kohl, Benjamin and Witt, Ronald, *The Earthly Republic: Italian Humanists on Government and Society* (Philadelphia: University of Pennsylvania Press, 1978).

Kollmann, Nancy Shields, *By Honor Bound: State and Society in Early Modern Russia* (Ithaca, NY: Cornell University Press, 1999).

Kors, Alan C. and Peters, Edward, eds., *Witchcraft in Europe, 1100–1700* (Philadelphia: University of Pennsylvania Press, 1972).

Kostof, Spiro, *The City Shaped: Urban Patterns and Meanings Through History* (Boston: Bulfinch, 1991).

——, *The City Assembled: The Elements of Urban Form Through History* (Boston: Bulfinch, 1992).

Kraemer, Joel L., *Humanism in the Renaissance of Islam: The Cultural Revival during the Buyid Age* (Leiden: E. J. Brill, 1986; 2nd edn. 1992).

Kramer, Heinrich and Sprenger, James, *The Malleus Maleficarum*, trans. and ed. M. Summers (New York: Dover, 1971).

Kraye, Jill, ed., *The Cambridge Companion to Renaissance Humanism* (Cambridge: Cambridge University Press, 1996).

Kritovoulos, *History of Mehmed the Conqueror*, trans. Charles T. Riggs (Princeton: Princeton University Press, 1954).

Kritzman, Lawrence D., *The Rhetoric of Sexuality and the Literature of the French Renaissance* (Cambridge: Cambridge University Press, 1991).

Kruger, Lorenz, et al., *The Probabilistic Revolution* (Cambridge MA: MIT Press, 1987).

Kubler, George, *Building the Escorial* (Princeton: Princeton University Press, 1982).

Kuehn, Thomas, *Law, Family, and Women: Towards a Legal Anthropology of Renaissance Italy* (Chicago: University of Chicago Press, 1991).

Kunt, Metin and Woodhead, Christine, eds., *Süleyman the Magnificent and His Age: The Ottoman Empire in the Early Modern World* (London: Longman, 1995).

Labalme, Patricia, "Venetian Women on Women: Three Early Modern Feminists," *Archivio veneto* 5th ser. 117 (1981).

Labib, Subhi, "The Era of Süleyman the Magnificent: A Crisis of Orientation," *Saeculum* 29 (1978).

Labrot, Gérard, *Quand l'histoire murmure: Villages et campagnes du royaume de Naples, XVe–XVIIIe siècles* (Rome: École Française de Rome, 1995).

Lach, Donald, *Asia in the Making of Europe*, 3 vols. (Chicago: University of Chicago Press, 1965).

Landa, Fr. Diego de, *Yucatan Before and After the Conquest*, ed. William Gates (New York: Dover, 1978).

Landau, David and Parshall, Peter, *The Renaissance Print 1470–1550* (New Haven: Yale University Press, 1994).

Landes, Joan and Knoppers, Laura, eds., *Monstrous Bodies/Political Monstrosities in Early Modern Europe* (forthcoming).

Lane, Frederic C. and Mueller, Reinhold, *Money and Banking in Medieval and Renaissance Venice: Coins and Moneys of Account* (Baltimore: Johns Hopkins University Press, 1985).

Langford, Jerome J., *Galileo, Science, and the Church* (Ann Arbor: University of Michigan Press, 1966).

Langford, Paul, *A Polite and Commercial People* (Oxford: Oxford University Press, 1989).

Laqueur, Thomas, *Making Sex: Body and Gender from the Greeks to Freud* (Cambridge, MA: Harvard University Press, 1990).

Larme, Père, "Relation de la mort du Président Giroux," Bibliothèque Municipale de Dijon, Manuscript 328.

Larner, Christina, *Witchcraft and Religion: The Politics of Popular Belief* (Oxford: Blackwell Publishers, 1984).

Larner, John, "Order and Disorder in Romagna, 1450–1500," in *Violence and Civil Disorder in Italian Cities, 1200–1500*, ed. Lauro Martines (Berkeley: University of California Press, 1972).

——, "Europe of the Courts," *Journal of Modern History* 55 (1983).

——, *Marco Polo and the Discovery of the World* (New Haven: Yale University Press, 1999).

Laslett, Peter, *The World We Have Lost* (New York: Scribner, 1965; London: Methuen, 1971).

——, "Family and Household as Work Group and Kin Group: Areas of Traditional Europe Compared," in *Family Forms in Historic Europe*, ed. R. Wall, J. Robin, and P. Laslett (Cambridge: Cambridge University Press, 1983).

Latour, Bruno, *We Have Never Been Modern*, trans. Catherine Porter (Cambridge, MA: Harvard University Press, 1993).

Lavrin, Asunción, ed., *Sexuality and Marriage in Colonial Latin America* (Lincoln, NE: University of Nebraska Press, 1989).

Lawner, Lynne, *Lives of the Courtesans: Portraits of the Renaissance* (New York: Rizzoli, 1987).

Lebigre, Arlette and Leguai, André, *Histoire du droit pénal* (Paris: Cujus, 1979).

Leedham-Green, Elisabeth, *Books in Cambridge Inventories*, 2 vols. (Cambridge: Cambridge University Press), 1987).

Leinwand, Theodore, "Shakespeare and the Middling Sort," *Shakespeare Quarterly* 44 (1993).

Lentz, Thomas W. and Lowry, Glenn D., *Timur and the Princely Vision: Persian Art and Culture in the Fifteenth Century* (Los Angeles: Los Angeles County Museum of Art, 1989).

Le Roy Ladurie, Emmanuel, *Montaillou: village occitan de 1294 à 1324* (Paris: Gallimard, 1975).

——, *The Beggar and the Professor: A Sixteenth-Century Family Saga*, trans. Arthur Goldhammer (Chicago: University of Chicago Press, 1997).

Lestringant, Frank, *Mapping the Renaissance World: The Geographical Imagination in the Age of Discovery*, trans. D. Fausett (Berkeley: University of California Press, 1994).

Levack, Brian P., *The Witch-hunt in Early Modern Europe* (London: Longman, 1994).

Libby, Lester J., Jr., "Venetian History and Political Thought after 1509," *Studies in the Renaissance* 20 (1973).

Lindley, Keith, *Popular Politics and Religion in Civil War London* (Aldershot: Scolar Press, 1997).

Lindsay, Mark C., "Spanish Merida: Overlaying the Maya City," Ph.D. dissertation, University of Florida, 1999.

Lockhart, James, "Double Mistaken Identity: Some Nahua Concepts in Postconquest Guise," in *Of Things of the Indies: Essays Old and New in Early Latin American History* (Stanford: Stanford University Press, 2000).

Lopez, Robert S., "European Merchants in the Medieval Indies: Evidence of Commercial Documents," *Journal of Economic History* 3 (1943).

——, *The Commercial Revolution of the Middle Ages, 950–1350* (Cambridge: Cambridge University Press, 1976).

——, "The Dawn of Medieval Banking," in *The Dawn of Modern Banking*, Center for Medieval and Renaissance Studies, University of California (New Haven: Yale University Press, 1979).

Low, Setha M., *On the Plaza: The Politics of Public Space and Culture* (Austin: University of Texas Press, 2000).

Lubkin, Gregory, *A Renaissance Court: Milan under Galeazzo Maria Sforza* (Berkeley: University of California Press, 1994).

Macfarlane, Alan, *Witchcraft in Tudor and Stuart England* (London: Routledge, 1970).

——, "A Tudor Anthropologist: George Gifford's Discourse and Dialogue," in *The Damned Art: Essays in the Literature of Witchcraft*, ed. Sydney Anglo (London: Routledge and Kegan Paul, 1977).

——, *The Origins of English Individualism: The Family, Property and Social Transition* (Cambridge: Cambridge University Press, 1978).

Machiavelli, Niccolò, *The Prince*, trans. Mark Musa (New York: St. Martin's Press, 1964).

——, *The Portable Machiavelli*, ed. and trans. Peter Bondanella and Mark Musa (New York: Viking Penguin, 1979).

——, *Lettere*, ed. Franco Gaeta (Milan: Feltrinelli, 1981).

——, *The Prince*, ed. Quentin Skinner, trans. Richard Price (Cambridge: Cambridge University Press, 1998).

Mackenney, Richard, *Tradesmen and Traders: The World of the Guilds in Venice and Europe, c.1250 – c.1650* (London: Croom Helm, 1987).

Maclean, Ian, *The Renaissance Notion of Woman: A Study in the Fortunes of Scholasticism and Medical Science in European Intellectual Life* (Cambridge: Cambridge University Press, 1980).

McManners, John, *Church and Society in Eighteenth Century France*, 2 vols. (Oxford: Clarendon Press, 1999).

McMullan, John L., *The Canting Crew: London's Criminal Underworld 1500–1700* (New Brunswick: Rutgers University Press, 1984).

McNeill, William H., *Plagues and Peoples* (New York: Anchor Books, Doubleday, 1976).

——, "Diffusion in History," in *The Transfer and Transformation of Ideas and Material Culture*, ed. Peter J. Hugill and D. Bruce Dickson (College Station, TX: Texas A and M Press, 1988).

Macqueen, John, "The Renaissance in Scotland," in *The Celts and the Renaissance*, ed. Glanmore Williams and Robert Owen Jones (Cardiff: University of Wales Press, 1990).

Maczak, Antoni, "La cour et l'espace du pouvoir entre l'Italie du Pô et l'Europe du Centre-Est," in *La corte et lo spazio: Ferrara estense*, ed. Giuseppe Papago and Amedeo Quondam (Rome: Bulzoni, 1982).

——, "From Aristocratic Household to Princely Court: Restructuring Patronage in the Sixteenth and Seventeenth Centuries," in *Klientelsysteme im Europa der Frühen Neuzeit*, ed. Antoni Maczak (Schriften des Historischen Kollegs, Herausgegeben von der Stiftung Historisches Kolleg, Kolloquien) (Munich: R. Oldenbourg Verlag, 1988).

Major, J. Russell, *From Renaissance Monarchy to Absolute Monarchy: French Kings, Nobles, and Estates* (Baltimore: Johns Hopkins University Press, 1994).

Makdisi, George, *The Rise of Humanism in Classical Islam and the Christian West: With Special Reference to Scholasticism* (Edinburgh: Edinburgh University Press, 1990).

Malik, Iftikhar Haider, "Muslims' Contribution in the European Renaissance," *Pakistan Journal of History and Culture* 3 (1982).

Mallet, Michael, *Mercenaries and their Masters: Warfare in Renaissance Italy* (Totowa, NJ: Rowman and Littlefield, 1974).

Mallet, Michael and Hale, John R., *The Military Organization of a Renaissance State: Venice c.1400 to 1617* (Cambridge: Cambridge University Press, 1984).

Marcus, E. D., *Sixteenth Century Nationalism* (New York: Abaris, 1976).

Marcus, Joyce, *Mesoamerican Writing Systems: Propaganda, Myth, and History in Four Ancient Civilizations* (Princeton: Princeton University Press, 1992).

Marinella, Lucrezia, *The Nobility and Excellence of Women and the Defects and Vices of Men*, trans. and ed. Anne Dunhill (Chicago: University of Chicago Press, 1999).

Marino, John, *Pastoral Economics in the Kingdom of Naples* (Baltimore: Johns Hopkins University Press, 1988).

——, "Administrative Mapping in the Italian States," in *Monarchs, Ministers and Maps: The Emergence of Cartography as a Tool of Government in Early Modern Europe*, ed. David Buisseret (Chicago: University of Chicago Press, 1992).

Marrone, Giovanni, *Città, campagna e criminalità nella Sicilia moderna* (Palermo: Palumbo, 1955).

Marsilius of Padua, *The Defender of Peace*, ed. and trans. Alan Gewirth (New York: Columbia University Press, 1956).

Martin, John Jeffries, *Venice's Hidden Enemies: Italian Heretics in a Renaissance City* (Berkeley: University of California Press, 1993).

——, "Inventing Sincerity, Refashioning Prudence: The Discovery of the Individual in Renaissance Europe," *American Historical Review* 102 (1997).

Martines, Lauro, ed., *Violence and Civil Disorder in Italian Cities, 1200–1500* (Berkeley: University of California Press, 1972).

——, *Power and Imagination: City States in Renaissance Italy* (New York: Knopf, 1975).

Martz, Linda, *Poverty and Welfare in Habsburg Spain: The Example of Toledo* (Cambridge: Cambridge University Press, 1983).

Mascuch, Michael, *The Origins of the Individualist Self: Autobiography and Self-Identity in England* (Stanford: Stanford University Press, 1996).

Massey, Doreen, "Places and their Pasts," *History Workshop Journal* 39 (1995).

Masson, Georgina, *Courtesans of the Italian Renaissance* (New York: St. Martin's, 1975).

Masten, Jeff, *Textual Intercourse: Collaboration, Authorship, and Sexualities in Renaissance Drama* (New York: Cambridge University Press, 1997).

Maus, Katharine Eisaman, *Inwardness and Theater in the English Renaissance* (Chicago: University of Chicago Press, 1995).

Mauss, Marcel, "The Category of the Person," in *The Category of the Person*, ed. Michael Carrithers (Cambridge: Cambridge University Press, 1985).

Mayer, Thomas and Woolf, D. R., eds., *The Rhetorics of Life-Writing in Early Modern Europe* (Ann Arbor: University of Michigan Press, 1995).

Mazzacane, Aldo, "Law and Jurists in the Formation of the Modern State in Italy," in *The Origins of the State in Italy, 1300–1600*, ed. Julius Kirshner (Chicago: University of Chicago Press, 1995).

Medick, Hans, "Village Spinning Bees: Sexual Culture and Free Time among Rural Youth in Early Modern Germany," in *Interest and Emotion: Essays on the Study of Family and Kinship*, ed. H. Medick and D. Sabean (Cambridge: Cambridge University Press, 1984).

Meiggs, Russell, *Trees and Timber in the Ancient Mediterranean World* (Oxford: Clarendon Press, 1982).

Meisami, Julie Scott, *The Haft Paykar: A Medieval Persian Romance* (Oxford: Oxford University Press, 1995).

Mez, Adam, *The Renaissance of Islam*, trans. Salahuddin Khuda Bukhsh and D. S. Margoliouth (London: Luzac, 1937).

Mezzadri, Luigi, "Le missioni popolari dei lazzaristi nell'Umbria (1675–1797)," *Vincent de Paul: Actes du Colloque International d'Études Vincentiennes* (Rome: Edizioni Vincenziane, 1981).

Middleton, Thomas and Rowley, William, *A Fair Quarrel* [1617], ed. R. V. Holdsworth (London: Ernest Benn, 1974).

Midelfort, H. C. Eric, *Witch Hunting in Southwestern Germany, 1562–1684: The Social and Intellectual Foundations* (Stanford: Stanford University Press, 1971).

——, *Mad Princes of Renaissance Germany* (Charlottesville: University of Virginia Press, 1996).

Mignolo, Walter D., *The Darker Side of the Renaissance: Literacy, Territoriality, and Colonialization* (Ann Arbor: University of Michigan Press, 1995).

Milàn, Luis, *Il libro intitulado el Cortesano* (Valencia, 1561).

Miles, Margaret, "The Virgin's One Bare Breast," *The Expanding Discourse: Feminism and Art History*, ed. Norma Broude and Mary Garrard (New York: HarperCollins, 1992).

Miller, Mary Ellen, *Maya Art and Architecture* (New York: Thames and Hudson, 1999).

Miller, Naomi, *Renaissance Bologna: A Study in Architectural Form and Content* (New York: P. Lang, 1989).

Millon, Henry A., "Art and Architectural History in the Twentieth Century," *Useful Knowledge*, ed. Alexander Bearn (Philadelphia: American Philosophical Society, 1999).

Mintz, Sidney W., *Sweetness and Power: The Place of Sugar in Modern History* (New York: Elizabeth Sifton Books-Viking Penguin, 1985).

Misch, Georg, *Geschichte der Autobiographie*, 4 vols. (Bern: Francke, 1949–70).

Miskimin, Harry A., *The Economy of Early Renaissance Europe, 1300–1460* (Cambridge: Cambridge University Press, 1975).

Miskimin, Harry A., *The Economy of Later Renaissance Europe, 1460–1600* (Cambridge: Cambridge University Press, 1977).

Modena, Leone, *Life of Judah: The Autobiography of a Seventeenth-Century Venetian Rabbi*, ed. and trans. Mark R. Cohen (Princeton: Princeton University Press, 1988).

Molà, Luca, *The Silk Industry in Renaissance Venice* (Baltimore: Johns Hopkins University Press, 1999).

Molho, Anthony, "Patronage and the State in Early Modern Italy," in *Klientelsysteme in Europa der Frühen Neuzeit*, ed. Antoni Maczak (Schriften des Historischen Kollegs, Herausgegeben von der Stiftung Historisches Kolleg, Kolloquien) (Munich: R. Oldenbourg Verlag, 1988).

Monfasani, John and Musto, Ronald G., eds., *Renaissance Society and Culture: Essays in Honor of Eugene F. Rice* (New York: Italica Press, 1991).

Monson, Craig, *Disembodied Voices: Music and Culture in an Early Modern Italian Convent* (Berkeley: University of California Press, 1995).

Montaigne, Michel de, *The Complete Essays* [1585] (Stanford: Stanford University Press, 1958).

Monter, E. William, *Witchcraft in France and Switzerland: The Borderlands during the Reformation* (Ithaca, NY: Cornell University Press, 1976).

——, *Frontiers of Heresy: The Spanish Inquisition from the Basque Lands to Sicily* (New York: Cambridge University Press, 1990).

Moore, R. I., *The Formation of a Persecuting Society: Power and Deviance in Western Europe, 950–1250* (Oxford: Blackwell Publishers, 1987).

Moore, Sally Falk, *Law as Process* (London: Routledge, 1978).

Moran, Bruce, *The Alchemical World of the German Court: Occult Philosophy and Chemical Medicine in the Circle of Moritz of Hessen, 1572–1632* (Stuttgart: Franz Steiner, 1991).

More, Thomas, *Utopia* [1516] (New York: Penguin, 1961).

Moretti, Franco, *Atlas of the European Novel 1800–1900* (London: Verso, 1998).

Mormando, Franco, *The Preacher's Demons: Bernardino of Siena and the Social Underworld of Early Renaissance Italy* (Chicago: University of Chicago Press, 1999).

Moulakis, Athanasios, *Republican Realism in Renaissance Florence: Francesco Guicciardini's Discorso di Logrogno* (Lanham, MD: Rowman and Littlefield, 1998).

Moulton, Ian Frederick, *Before Pornography: Erotic Writing in Early Modern England* (New York: Oxford University Press, 2000).

Mozzarelli, Cesare, "Aristocrazia e borghesia nell'Europa moderna," in *Storia d'Europa*, vol. 4, ed. Maurice Aymard (Turin: Einaudi, 1995).

Muchembled, Robert, *Popular Culture and Elite Culture in France, 1400–1750*, trans. L. Cochrane (Baton Rouge, LA: Louisiana State University Press, 1985).

——, *L'Invention de l'homme moderne: Culture et sensibilités en France du XVe au XVIIIe siècle* (Paris: Hachette, 1994).

——, *La Société policiée: Politique et politesse en France du XVIe au XXe siècle* (Paris: Seuil, 1998).

——, "Paroles d'inceste: Les jeunes et l'honneur maternel en Artois aux XVe et XVIIe siècles," *Equinoxe, Revue des Sciences Humaines* 20 (1998).

——, *Une histoire du diable XIIe-XXe siècle* (Paris: Seuil, 2000).

Mueller, Reinhold, *The Venetian Money Market: Banks, Panics and the Public Debt, 1200–1500* (Baltimore: Johns Hopkins University Press, 1997).

Muir, Edward, *Civic Ritual in Renaissance Venice* (Princeton: Princeton University Press, 1981).

——, *Mad Blood Stirring: Vendetta and Factions in Friuli during the Renaissance* (Baltimore: Johns Hopkins University Press, 1993).

——, "The Double Binds of Manly Revenge in Renaissance Italy," in *Gender Rhetorics: Postures of Dominance and Submission in History*, ed. Richard C. Trexler (Binghamton, NY: Medieval & Renaissance Texts & Studies, 1994).

——, "The Sources of Civil Society in Italy," *Journal of Interdisciplinary History* 29 (1999).

Muir, Edward and Ruggiero, Guido, eds., *Sex and Gender in Historical Perspective* (Baltimore: Johns Hopkins University Press, 1990).

—— and——, eds., *History from Crime: Selections from Quaderni Storici* (Baltimore: Johns Hopkins University Press, 1994).

Mulcahy, Rosemarie, *The Decoration of the Royal Basilica of El Escorial* (Cambridge: Cambridge University Press, 1994).

Muyart de Vouglans, François, *Instruction criminelle* (Paris, 1762).

Nader, Helen, *Liberty in Absolutist Spain: The Habsburg Sale of Towns, 1516–1700* (Baltimore: Johns Hopkins University Press, 1990).

Najemy, John M., *Corporatism and Consensus in Florentine Electoral Politics, 1280–1400* (Chapel Hill: University of North Carolina Press, 1982).

Naphy, William and Roberts, Penelope, eds., *Fear in Early Modern Society* (Manchester: Manchester University Press, 1997).

Nashe, Thomas, *Piers Penniless*, in *The Unfortunate Traveler and Other Works*, ed. J. B. Steane (New York: Penguin, 1972).

Nasr, Seyyid Hossain, *An Introduction to Islamic Cosmological Doctrines* (Albany: State University of New York Press, 1993).

Nauert, Charles, "Humanists, Scientists, and Pliny: Changing Approaches to a Classical Author," *American Historical Review* 84 (1979).

Necipoğlu, Gülrü, "The Süleymaniye Complex in Istanbul: An Interpretation," *Muqarnas* 3 (1985).

——, "Süleyman the Magnificent and the Representation of Power in the Context of Ottoman-Hapsburg-Papal Rivalry," *Art Bulletin* 71 (1989).

——, "From International Timurid to Ottoman: A Change of Taste in Sixteenth-Century Ceramic Tiles," *Muqarnas* 7 (1990).

——, *Architecture, Ceremonial, and Power: The Topkapi Palace in the Fifteenth and Sixteenth Centuries* (Cambridge, MA: MIT Press, 1991).

Neill, Michael, *Issues of Death: Mortality and Identity in English Renaissance Tragedy* (Oxford: Clarendon Press, 1997).

Neuschel, Kristen B., *Word of Honor: Interpreting Noble Culture in Sixteenth-Century France* (Ithaca, NY: Cornell University Press, 1989).

Newman, Lucile F., ed., *Hunger in History: Food Shortage, Poverty, and Deprivation* (Cambridge, MA: Blackwell Publishers, 1990).

Niccoli, Ottavia, *Prophecy and the People in Renaissance Italy*, trans. L. G. Cochrane (Princeton: Princeton University Press, 1990).

——, *Il seme della violenza: Putti, fanciulli e mammoli nell'Italia tra '500 e '600* (Bari: Laterza, 1995).

Nichols, Fred J., ed. and trans., *An Anthology of Neo-Latin Poetry* (New Haven: Yale University Press, 1979).

Nicolas, Jean, Baruque, Julio Valdón, and Vilfan, Sergij, "The Monarchic State and Resistance in Spain, France, and the Old Provinces of the Habsburgs, 1400–1800," in *Resistance, Representation, and Community*, ed. Peter Blickle (Oxford: Clarendon Press, 1997).

Nizam al-Mulk, *The Book of Governance: or, Rules for Kings*, trans. Hubert Darke (London: Routledge and Kegan Paul, 1978).

Nizami Ganjavi, *Le Roman de Chosroes et Chirin* (Paris: G. P. Maisonneuve et Larose, 1970).

Nussdorfer, Lauri, *Civic Politics in the Rome of Urban VIII* (Princeton: Princeton University Press, 1992).

Oestreich, Gerhard, "The Structure of the Absolute State" [1964], in *Neostoicism and the Early Modern State*, ed. B. Oestreich and H. G. Koenigsberger (Cambridge: Cambridge University Press, 1982).

O'Malley, C. D., *Andreas Vesalius of Brussels, 1514–1564* (Berkeley: University of California Press, 1964).

——, "The Criminal and the Saintly Body: Autopsy and Dissection in Renaissance Italy," *Renaissance Quarterly,* 47 (1994).

O'Malley, John, ed., *Humanity and Divinity in Renaissance and Reformation* (Leiden: E. J. Brill, 1993).

O'Neil, Mary, "Magical Healing, Love Magic and the Inquisition in Late Sixteenth-Century Modena," in *Inquisition and Society in Early Modern Europe*, ed. Stephen Haliczer (Totowa, NJ: Barnes and Noble, 1987).

Orgel, Stephen, *Impersonations: The Performance of Gender in Shakespeare's England* (Cambridge: Cambridge University Press, 1997).

Osorio Romero, Ignazio, *La enseñanza del Latín a los Indios* (Mexico City: Centro de Estudios Clásicos, 1990).

Owen-Hughes, Diane, "Representing the Family: Portraits and Purposes in Early Modern Italy," *Journal of Interdisciplinary History* 17 (1986).

Ozment, Steven, *When Fathers Ruled: Family Life in Reformation Europe* (Cambridge, MA: Harvard University Press, 1983).

——, *Magdalena and Balthasar: An Intimate Portait of Life in Sixteenth-Century Europe* (New York: Simon and Schuster, 1986).

Pagden, Anthony, *The Fall of Natural Man: The American Indian and the Origins of Comparative Ethnology* (Cambridge: Cambridge University Press, 1982).

——, ed., *Languages of Political Theory in Early Modern Europe* (Cambridge: Cambridge University Press, 1987).

——, *Lords of All the World: Ideologies of Empire in Spain, Britain and France c.1500–c.1800* (New Haven: Yale University Press, 1995).

Pagel, Walter, *Paracelsus: An Introduction to Philosophical Medicine in the Era of the Renaissance* (Basel: S. Karger, 1958).

Palmer, William, "That 'Insolent Liberty': Honor, Rites of Power, and Persuasion in Sixteenth-Century Ireland," *Renaissance Quarterly* 46/2 (1993).

Palliser, David M., *The Age of Elizabeth: England under the Later Tudors, 1547–1603* (London: Longman, 1983).

Pancaroğlu, Oya, " 'A World Unto Himself': The Rise of a New Human Image in the Late Seljuk period (1150–1250)," Ph.D. dissertation, Harvard University, 2000.

Pandimiglio, Leonida, "Ricordanze e libro di famiglia: il manifestarsi di una nuova fonte," *Lettere italiane* 39 (1987).

Panofsky, Erwin, *Studies in Iconology* (Oxford: Oxford University Press, 1939).

——, "Renaissance and Renascenses," *Kenyan Review* 6 (1944).

——, *Early Netherlandish Painting: Its Origins and Character* (Cambridge, MA: Harvard University Press, 1953).

——, *The Life and Art of Albrecht Dürer* (Princeton: Princeton University Press, 1955).

——, *Renaissance and Renascences in Western Art* (Stockholm: Almqvist and Wiksells, 1960 and New York: Harper and Row, 1969).

——, *Perspective as Symbolic Form*, trans. Christopher S. Wood (New York: Zone Books, 1991).

Paravicini, Werner, "Structure et fonctionnement de la cour bourguignonne au XVe siècle," in *A la cour de Bourgogne: Le duc, son entourage, son train*, ed. Jean-Marie Cauchies (Turnhout: Brepols, 1998).

Park, Katharine, *Doctors and Medicine in Early Renaissance Florence* (Princeton: Princeton University Press, 1985).

——, "The Criminal and the Saintly Body: Autopsy and Dissection in Renaissance Italy," *Renaissance Quarterly* 47 (1994).

Parker, Geoffrey, *The Dutch Revolt*, rev. edn. (Harmondsworth: Penguin, 1988).

——, *The Military Revolution: Military Innovation and the Rise of the West, 1500–1800* (Cambridge: Cambridge University Press, 1988).

——, *The Grand Strategy of Philip II* (New Haven: Yale University Press, 1998).

Parker, Patricia, *Shakespeare from the Margins: Language, Culture, Context* (Chicago: University of Chicago Press, 1996).

Parker, Patrica and Quint, David, eds., *Literary Theory/Renaissance Texts* (Baltimore: Johns Hopkins University Press, 1986).

Parrott, David, "A 'Prince Souverain' and the French Crown: Charles de Nevers, 1580–1637," in *Royal and Republican Sovereignty in Early Modern Europe: Essays in Memory of Ragnhild Hatton*, ed. Robert Oresko, G. C. Gibbs, and H. M. Scott (Cambridge: Cambridge University Press, 1997).

Partner, Peter, *The Pope's Men: The Papal Civil Service in the Renaissance* (Oxford: Clarendon Press, 1990).

Patterson, Annabel, *Reading Holinshed's Chronicles* (Chicago: University of Chicago Press, 1994).

Pennington, Kenneth, *The Prince and the Law, 1200–1600* (Berkeley: University of California Press, 1993).

Perosa, Alessandro, ed., *Giovanni Rucellai ed il suo Zibaldone* (London: Warburg Institute, 1960).

Perry, Mary E., *Gender and Disorder in Early Modern Seville* (Princeton: Princeton University Press, 1990).

Peterkiewicz, Jerzy and Singer, Burns, *Five Centuries of Polish Poetry* (London: Oxford University Press, 1970).

Pevsner, Nikolaus, *The Englishness of English Art* (London: Architectural Press, 1956).

Pitkin, Hanna Fenichel, *Fortune is a Woman* (Berkeley: University of California Press, 1984).

Pizan, Christine de, *La Cité des dames*, ed. Earl Jeffrey Richards, published with the Italian translation: Christine de Pizan, *La città delle dame*, ed. Patrizia Caraffi (Milan: Luni Editrice, 1997).

Pocock, John G. A., *The Ancient Constitution and the Feudal Law* (Cambridge: Cambridge University Press, 1957).

——, *The Machiavellian Moment: Florentine Political Thought and the Atlantic Republican Tradition* (Princeton: Princeton University Press, 1975).

Podro, Michael, *The Critical Historians of Art* (New Haven: Yale University Press, 1982).

Politi, Giorgio, *Aristocrazia e potere politico nella Cremona di Filippo II* (Milan: SugarCo, 1976).

Polverini Fosi, Irene, *La società violenta: Il banditismo nello stato pontificio nella seconda metà del Cinquecento* (Rome: Edizioni dell'Ateneo, 1985).

Pomeranz, Kenneth, *The Great Divergence: Europe, China, and the Making of the Modern World Economy* (Princeton: Princeton University Press, 2000).

Porter, Roy and Teich, Mikulás, eds., *The Renaissance in National Context* (Cambridge: Cambridge University Press, 1992).

Post, John D., "Nutritional Status and Mortality in Eighteenth-century Europe," in *Hunger in History: Food Shortage, Poverty, and Deprivation*, ed. Lucile F. Newman (Oxford and Cambridge, MA: Blackwell Publishers, 1990).

Post, R. R., *The Modern Devotion* (Leiden: E. J. Brill, 1968).

Pred, Allan Richard, *Place, Practice and Structure* (Cambridge: Polity Press, 1987).

Prestwich, Michael, "Italian Merchants in Late Thirteenth- and Early Fourteenth-Century England," in *The Dawn of Modern Banking*, Center for Medieval and Renaissance Studies, University of California (New Haven: Yale University Press, 1979).

Prodi, Paolo, *The Papal Prince: One Body and Two Souls: The Papal Monarchy in Early Modern Europe*, trans. Susan Haskins (Cambridge: Cambridge University Press, 1987).

Prosperi, Adriano, ed., *La corte e il "Cortegiano," II: Un modello europeo* (Rome: Bulzoni, 1980).

Pullan, Brian, *Rich and Poor in Renaissance Venice: The Social Institutions of a Catholic State, to 1620* (Cambridge, MA: Harvard University Press, 1971).

——, *A History of Early Renaissance Italy* (London: Allen Lane, 1973).

——, " 'A Ship with Two Rudders': 'Righetto Marrano' and the Inquisition in Venice," *The Historical Journal* 20 (1977).

——, "Plague and Perceptions of the Poor in Early Modern Italy," in *Epidemics and Ideas: Essays on the Historical Perception of Pestilence*, ed. T. Ranger and P. Slack (Cambridge: Cambridge University Press, 1992).

Pumfrey, Stephen, Rossi, Paolo, and Slawinski, Maurice, eds., *Science, Culture and Popular Belief in Renaissance Europe* (Manchester: Manchester University Press, 1991).

Quale, Gladys Robina, *A History of Marriage Systems* (New York: Greenwood Press, 1988).

——, *Families in Context: A World History of Population* (New York: Greenwood Press, 1992).

Quétel, Claude, *History of Syphilis*, trans. Judith Braddock and Brian Pike (Baltimore: Johns Hopkins University Press, 1990).

Rabelais, François, *Œuvres complètes*, ed. Guy Demerson (Paris: L'Intégrale/Seuil, 1973).

Rabasa, José, *Inventing America: Spanish Historiography and the Foundation of Eurocentrism* (Norman: University of Oklahoma Press, 1993).

Rabil, Albert, Jr., ed., *Renaissance Humanism: Foundations, Forms, and Legacy* (Philadelphia: University of Pennsylvania Press, 1988).

Raggio, Osvaldo, *Faide e parentele: Lo stato genovese visto dalla Fontanabona* (Turin: Einaudi, 1990).

Rapp, Richard T., *Industry and Economic Decline in Seventeenth-Century Venice* (Cambridge, MA: Harvard University Press, 1976).

Rappaport, Steve, *Worlds within Worlds: Structures of Life in Sixteenth-Century London* (Cambridge: Cambridge University Press, 1989).

Redondi, Pietro, *Galileo Heretic*, trans. R. Rosenthal (Princeton: Princeton University Press, 1987).

Reeves, Majorie, ed., *Prophetic Rome in the High Renaissance Period* (Oxford: Clarendon Press, 1992).

Reilly, Patricia, "Grand Designs: Alessandro Allori's *Discussions on the Rules of Drawing*, Giorgio Vasari's *Lives of the Artists*, and the Florentine Visual Vernacular," Ph.D. dissertation, University of California at Berkeley, 1999.

Restall, Matthew, "Heirs to the Hieroglyphics: Indigenous Writing in Colonial Mesoamerica," *The Americas* 54/2 (October 1997).

——, *The Maya World: Yucatec Culture and Society, 1550–1850* (Stanford: Stanford University Press, 1997).

——, *Maya Conquistador* (Boston: Beacon, 1998).

——, "A History of the New Philology and the New Philology in History," *Desacatos* 2 (2001).

Revel, Jacques, "The Uses of Civility," in *A History of Private Life*, vol. III: *The Passions of the Renaissance*, ed. Roger Chartier, trans. Arthur Goldhammer (Cambridge, MA: Belknap Press, 1989).

Richter, Jean Paul, ed., *The Literary Works of Leonardo da Vinci* (London: Phaidon, 1970).

Riley, James C., *Sickness, Recovery and Death: A History and Forecast of Ill Health* (Iowa City: University of Iowa Press, 1989).

Riley-Smith, Jonathan, *Atlas of the Crusades* (London: Times Books, 1991).

Rivière, Claude, *Les Rites profanes* (Paris: PUF, 1995).

Robinson, B. W., *Fifteenth-Century Persian Paintings: Problems and Issues* (New York: New York University Press, 1991).

Robinson, Michael, "The Arts under Süleymân the Magnificent," in *Süleymân the Second and His Time*, ed. Halil Inalcik and Cemal Kafadar (Istanbul: Isis Press, 1993).

Rocke, Michael, *Forbidden Friendships: Homosexuality and Male Culture in Renaissance Florence* (New York: Oxford University Press, 1996).

——, "Gender and Sexual Culture in Renaissance Italy," in *Gender and Society in Renaissance Italy*, ed. Judith C. Brown and Robert C. Davis (New York: Longman, 1998).

Rogers, Clifford J., ed., *The Military Revolution Debate* (Boulder, CO: Westview Press, 995).

Rogers, Michael, "The Arts under Süleymân the Magnificent," in *Süleymân the Second and His Time*, ed. Halil Inalcık and Cemal Kafadar (Istanbul: Isis Press, 1993).

Romagnoli, Daniela, ed., *La Ville et la cour: Des bonnes et des mauvaises manières* (Paris: Fayard, 1995).

Romani, Marzio, "Criminalità e giustizia nel ducato di Mantova alla fine del Cinquecento," *Rivista Storica Italiana* (1980).

Romano, Dennis, *Patricians and Poplani: The Social Foundations of the Venetian Renaissance State* (Baltimore: Johns Hopkins University Press, 1987).

——, *Housecraft and Statecraft: Domestic Service in Renaissance Venice, 1400–1600* (Baltimore: Johns Hopkins University Press, 1996).

Roper, Lyndal, *Oedipus and the Devil: Witchcraft, Sexuality and Religion in Early Modern Europe* (London and New York: Routledge, 1994).

Rosand, David, *Painting in Sixteenth-Century Venice: Titian, Veronese, Tintoretto*, rev. edn. (Cambridge: Cambridge University Press, rev. ed. 1997).

Rose, Mark, *Authors and Owners: The Invention of Copyright* (Cambridge, MA: Harvard University Press, 1993).

Rose, Mary Beth, "Women in Men's Clothing: Apparel and Social Stability in *The Roaring Girl*," *English Literary Renaissance* 14 (1984).

Rose, Paul L., *The Italian Renaissance of Mathematics: Studies on Humanists and Mathematicians from Petrarch to Galileo* (Geneva: Librarie Droz, 1975).

Rosenthal, Earl E., *The Palace of Charles V in Granada* (Princeton: Princeton University Press, 1985).

Rosenthal, Margaret F., *The Honest Courtesan: Veronica Franco, Citizen and Writer in Sixteenth-Century Venice* (Chicago: University of Chicago Press, 1992).

Rossi, Paolo, *Philosophy, Technology and the Arts in the Early Modern Era*, trans. S. Attanasio, ed. B. Nelson (New York: Harper and Row, 1970).

——, *Francis Bacon: From Magic to Science*, trans. S. Rabiniovitch (Chicago: University of Chicago Press, 1972).

Rossiaud, Jacques, *Medieval Prostitution*, trans. Lydia G. Cochrane (New York: Blackwell, 1988).

Rowland, Ingrid D., "Revenge of the Regensburg Humanists, 1493," *Sixteenth-Century Journal* 25 (1994).

Rowlands, A., "The Conditions of Life for the Masses," in *Early Modern Europe: An Oxford History*, ed. E. Cameron (Oxford: Oxford University Press, 1999).

Rubin, Patricia, *Giorgio Vasari: Art and History* (New Haven: Yale University Press, 1995).

Rubio Mañé, Ignacio, *La Casa de Montejo* (Mexico City: Imprenta Universitaria, 1941).

Ruggiero, Guido, *Violence in Early Renaissance Venice* (New Brunswick, NJ: Rutgers University Press, 1980).

——, *The Boundaries of Eros: Sex, Crime, and Sexuality in Renaissance Venice* (New York: Oxford University Press, 1985).

——, *Binding Passions: Tales of Magic, Marriage, and Power at the End of the Renaissance* (New York: Oxford University Press, 1993).

——, "Marriage, Love, Sex, and Renaissance Civic Morality," in *Sexuality and Gender in Early Modern Europe*, ed. James Grantham Turner (New York: Cambridge University Press, 1993).

Runciman, Steven, *The Fall of Constantinople, 1453* (Cambridge: Cambridge University Press, 1965).

Sabatini, Gaetano, "Fiscalità e banditismo in Abruzzo alla fine del Seicento," *Nuova Rivista Storica* 79 (1995).

Sabean, David, *Power in the Blood: Popular Culture and Village Discourse in Early Modern Germany* (Cambridge: Cambridge University Press, 1984).

Sadiq, Isa, "Le rôle de l'Iran dans la Renaissance," *Acta Iranica*, ser. 1, vol. 3 (1974).

Safley, Thomas and Rosenband, Leonard, eds., *The Workplace before the Factory: Artisans and Proletarians, 1500–1800* (Ithaca, NY: Cornell University Press, 1993).

Sahlins, Peter, *Boundaries: The Making of France and Spain in the Pyrenees* (Berkeley: University of California Press, 1989).

Saliba, George, "Seeking Science from the Lands of Islam," in *Visions of Islam in Renaissance Europe*, http://www.columbia.edu/~gas1/project/visions/visions.html, November 20, 2000.

Salomon, Frank, "Testimonies: The Making and Reading of Native South American Historical Sources," in *Cambridge History of the Native Peoples of the Americas*, vol. III: *South America*, ed. Frank Salomon and Stuart Schwartz (New York: Cambridge University Press, 1999).

Sanders, Eve, *Gender and Literacy on Stage in Early Modern England* (Cambridge: Cambridge University Press, 1998).

Sawday, Jonathan, *The Body Emblazoned: Dissection and the Human Body in Renaissance Culture* (London: Routledge, 1995).

Sbriccoli, Mario, "Fonti giudiziarie e fonti giuridiche. Riflessione sulla fase attuale degli studi," *Studi Storici* 29 (1988).

Schalk, Ellery, *From Valor to Pedigree: Ideas of Nobility in France in the Sixteenth and Seventeenth Centuries* (Princeton: Princeton University Press, 1986).

Schama, Simon, *The Embarrassment of Riches: An Interpretation of Dutch Culture in the Golden Age* (New York: Vintage, 1987).

——, *Rembrandt's Eyes* (New York: Knopf, 1999).

Schilling, Heinz, "Confessional Europe", in *Handbook of European History, 1400–1600*, 2 vols., ed. Thomas A. Brady Jr., Heiko A. Oberman, and James D. Tracy (Leiden: E. J. Brill, 1994–5), vol. 2.

Schmitt, Jean-Claude, *Mort d'une hérésie. L'Église et les clercs face aux béguines et aux béghards du Rhin supérior du XIVe au XVe siècle* (Paris: Mouton, 1978).

Schurman, Anna Maria van, *Whether a Christian Woman Should Be Educated* [1632], ed. and trans. Joyce L. Irwin (Chicago: University of Chicago Press, 1998).

Schutte, Anne Jacobson, *The Autobiography of an Aspiring Saint: Cecilia Ferrazzi* (Chicago: University of Chicago Press, 1996).

Schwartz, Stuart B., ed., *Implicit Understandings: Observing, Reporting, and Reflecting on the Encounters between Europeans and other peoples in the Early Modern Era* (Cambridge: Cambridge University Press, 1994).

Scott, Joan W., *Gender and the Politics of History* (New York: Columbia University Press, 1988).

Scott, Tom, ed., *The Peasantries of Europe from the Fourteenth to the Eighteenth Centuries* (London: Longman, 1998).

Scribner, Robert W., *Popular Culture and Popular Movements in Reformation Germany* (London: Ronceverte, 1987).

——, "Is a History of Popular Culture Possible?," *History of European Ideas* 10 (1989).

——, "The Impact of the Reformation on Daily Life," in *Mensch und Objekt in Mittelalter und in der frühen Neuzeit: Leben-Alltag-Kultur* (Vienna: Verlag der Österreichischen Akademie der Wissenschaften, 1990).

Secundus, Johannes (Jan Nicholaus Everaerts), *Opera*, ed. Petrus Scriverus (Leiden, 1619).

Sedgwick, Eve Kosofsky, *Epistemology of the Closet* (Berkeley: University of California Press, 1990).

Seed, Patricia, *Ceremonies of Possession in Europe's Conquest of the New World, 1492–1640* (Cambridge: Cambridge University Press, 1995).

Seyssel, Claude de, *The Monarchy of France*, trans. J. H. Hexter, ed. Donald R. Kelley (New Haven: Yale University Press, 1981).

Shapin, Steven, *The Scientific Revolution* (Chicago: University of Chicago Press, 1996).

Shapiro, James S., *Shakespeare and the Jews* (New York: Columbia University Press, 1996).

Shatton, Arthur, *Sinan* (New York: Scribner, 1972).

Shearman, John, *Mannerism* (Harmondsworth: Penguin, 1967).

——, *Raphael's Cartoons in the Collection of Her Majesty the Queen and the Tapestries of the Sistine Chapel* (London: Phaidon, 1972).

——, *Only Connect... Art and the Spectator in the Italian Renaissance* (Princeton, Princeton University Press, 1992).

Sicroff, A. S., *Les Controverses des Statuts de "Pureté de Sang" en Espagne du XVe au XVIIe siècle* (Paris: Études de Littérature Étrangère et Comparée, 1960).

Sidney, Sir Philip, *An Apology for Poetry (The Defence of Poesie)*, ed. Geoffrey Shepherd (London: Nelson, 1965).

Silver, Larry, "The State of Research in Northern European Art of the Renaissance Era," *Art Bulletin* 68 (1986).

Silverblatt, Irene, *Moon, Sun and Witches: Gender Ideologies and Class in Inca and Colonial Peru* (Princeton: Princeton University Press, 1987).

Simons, Patricia, "Women in Frames: The Gaze, the Eye, the Profile in Renaissance Portraiture," in *The Expanding Discourse: Feminism and Art History*, ed. Norma Broude and Mary Garrard (New York: HarperCollins, 1992).

——, "Alert and Erect: Masculinity in Some Italian Renaissance Portraits of Fathers and Sons," in *Gender Rhetorics: Postures of Dominance and Submission in History*, ed. Richard C. Trexler (Binghamton, NY: Medieval & Renaissance Texts & Studies, 1994).

——, "Portraiture, Portrayal, and Idealization: Ambiguous Individualism in Representations of Renaissance Women," in *Language and Image of Renaissance Italy*, ed. A. Brown (Oxford: Clarendon Press, 1995).

Siraisi, Nancy, *Medieval and Early Renaissance Medicine: An Introduction to Knowledge and Practice* (Chicago: University of Chicago Press, 1990).

Skinner, Quentin, *The Foundations of Modern Political Thought*, 2 vols. (Cambridge: Cambridge University Press, 1978).

——, *Liberty before Liberalism* (Cambridge: Cambridge University Press, 1998).

Slack, Paul, *The Impact of Plague in Tudor and Stuart England* (Oxford: Clarendon Press, 1985).

Smith, Bruce, *Homosexual Desire in Shakespeare's England* (Chicago: University of Chicago Press, 1991).

Smith, Pauline, M., *The Anti-Courtier Trend in Sixteenth Century French Literature* (Geneva: Droz, 1966).

Soly, Hugo and Thijs, Alfons, eds., *Minorities in Western European Cities (Sixteenth–Twentieth Centuries)* (Rome: Institut historique belge de Rome, 1995).

Soman, Alfred, "Deviance and Criminal Justice in Western Europe, 1300–1800: An Essay in Structure," *Criminal Justice History* 1 (1980).

Soucek, Priscilla, "The New York Public Library *Makhzan al-Asrah* and its Importance," *Ars Orientalis* 18 (1988).

Sperling, Jutta, *Convents and the Body Politic in Late Renaissance Venice* (Chicago: University of Chicago Press, 1999).

Spierenburg, Pieter, *The Spectacle of Suffering: Executions and the Evolution of Repression: From a Preindustrial Metropolis to the European Experience* (Cambridge: Cambridge University Press, 1984).

Springborg, Patricia, *Western Republicanism and the Oriental Prince* (Austin: University of Texas Press, 1992).

Stallybrass, Peter, and White, Allon, *The Politics and Poetics of Transgression* (Ithaca, NY: Cornell University Press, 1986).

Starn, Randolph, "Who's Afraid of the Renaissance?," in *The Present and Future of Medieval Studies*, ed. John Van Engen (South Bend, IN: University of Notre Dame Press, 1996).

Starr, June and Collier, Jane F., "Introduction: Dialogues in Legal Anthropology," in *History and Power in the Study of Law: New Directions in Legal Anthropology*, ed. J. Starr and J. F. Collier (Ithaca, NY: Cornell University Press, 1989).

Steiner, George, *The New Yorker*, January 13, 1997, pp. 76–7.

Stella, Alessandro, *La Révolte des Ciompi. Les hommes, les lieux, le travail* (Paris: Éditions de l'École des hautes études en sciences sociales, 1993).

Stern, Steve J., "Paradigms of Conquest: History, Historiography and Politics," *Journal of Latin American Studies* 24, Supplement (1992).

Stewart, Frank Henderson, *Honor* (Chicago: University of Chicago Press, 1994).

Stinger, Charles L., *The Renaissance in Rome* (Bloomington, IN: Indiana University Press, 1985).

Stone, Lawrence, *Family, Sex and Marriage in England* (New York: Harper and Row, 1979).

Strauss, Gerald, "Ideas of *Reformatio* and *Renovatio* from the Middles Ages to the Reformation," in *Handbook of European History, 1400–1600*, vol. 2, ed. Thomas A. Brady Jr., Heiko A. Oberman, and James D. Tracy (Leiden and New York: E. J. Brill, 1994–5 and Grand Rapids, MI: Eerdmans, 1996).

Strauss, Gerald, *Law, Resistance, and the State: The Opposition to Roman Law in Reformation Germany* (Princeton: Princeton University Press, 1986).

Strozzi, Alessandra Macinghi, *Lettere di una gentildonna fiorentina del secolo XV ai figliuoli esuli*, ed. Cesare Guasti (Florence: G. C. Sansoni, 1877).

Stubbes, Philip, *The Anatomy of Abuses* (London, 1583).

Subrahmanyam, Sanjay, *The Political Economy of Commerce: Southern India, 1500–1650*, (Cambridge: Cambridge University Press, 1990).

Summerson, John N., *Inigo Jones* (Harmondsworth: Penguin, 1966).

Sydow, Carl Wilhelm von, "Geography and Folk-Tale Oicotypes," in *Selected Papers on Folklore* (Copenhagen: Rosenkilde and Bagger, 1948).

Sylvester, Joshua, *Tobacco Battered and the Pipes Shattered* (London, 1614).

Szittya, Penn R., *The Antifraternal Tradition in Medieval Literature* (Princeton: Princeton University Press, 1986).

Talvacchia, Bette, *Taking Positions: On the Erotic in Renaissance Culture* (Princeton: Princeton University Press, 1999).

Tarabotti, Arcangela (pseud. Galerana Baratotti), *La semplicità ingannata* (Leiden, 1654).

Tavakoli-Targhi, Mohamad, "Orientalism's Genesis Amnesia," *Comparative Studies of South Asia, Africa and the Middle East* 16/1 (1996).

Tawney, R. H. and Power, Eileen, eds., *Tudor Economic Documents*, 3 vols. (London: Longman Green, 1963).

Taylor, Larissa, *Soldiers of Christ: Preaching in Late Medieval and Reformation France* (New York: Oxford University Press, 1992).

Te Brake, Wayne, *Shaping History: Ordinary People in European Politics, 1500–1700* (Berkeley: University of California Press, 1998).

Terraciano, Kevin, "Ñudzahui History: Mixtec Writing and Culture in Colonial Oaxaca," Ph.D. dissertation, University of California, Los Angeles, 1994.

Thomas, Keith, *Religion and the Decline of Magic* (New York: Scribner and Macmillan, 1971).

Thompson, E. P., *Customs in Common: Studies in Traditional Popular Culture* (New York: New Press, 1991).

Thoren, Victor, *The Lord of Uraniborg: A Biography of Tycho Brahe* (Cambridge: Cambridge University Press, 1990).

Thorlby, Anthony, ed., *The Penguin Companion to European Literature* (New York: McGraw-Hill, 1969).

Thorndike, Lynn, *A History of Magic and Experimental Science*, 8 vols. (New York: Columbia University Press, 1923–58).

Tierney, Brian, *Religion, Law, and the Growth of Constitutional Thought, 1150–1650* (Cambridge: Cambridge University Press, 1982).

Törnqvist, Gunnar, "Creativity and the Renewal of Regional Life," in *Creativity and Context*, ed. Anne Buttimer (Lund: University of Lund, 1983).

Torre, Angelo, "Il consumo di devozione: Rituali e potere nelle campagne piemontese nella prima metà del Settecento," *Quaderni Storici* 20 (1985).

——, "Politics Cloaked in Worship: State, Church and Local Power in Piedmont, 1570–1770," *Past and Present* 134 (1992).

Trachtenberg, Marvin, "Some Observations on Recent Architectural History," *Art Bulletin*, 70 (1988).

Tracy, James D., *A Financial Revolution in the Habsburg Netherlands: "Renten" and "Renteniers" in the County of Holland, 1515–1566* (Berkeley: University of California Press, 1985).

——, ed., *The Rise of Merchant Empires: Long-Distance Trade in the Early Modern World, 1350–1750* (Cambridge: Cambridge University Press, 1990).

——, *The Political Economy of Merchant Empires* (Cambridge: Cambridge University Press, 1991).

Traeger, Jörg, *Renaissance und Religion. Die Kunst des Glaubens im Zeitalter Raphaels* (Munich: C. Beck, 1997).

Traub, Valerie, *Desire and Anxiety: Circulations of Sexuality in Shakespearean Drama* (New York: Routledge, 1992).

——, "The (In)significance of Lesbian Desire in Early Modern England," in *Erotic Politics: Desire on the Renaissance Stage*, ed. Susan Zimmerman (New York: Routledge, 1992).

Trevor-Roper, Hugh, "The Court Physician and Paracelsianism," in *Medicine at the Courts of Europe, 1500–1837*, ed. Vivian Nutton (London: Routledge, 1990).

Trexler, Richard, "Florentine Religious Experience: The Sacred Image," *Studies in the Renaissance* 19 (1972).

——, *Public Life in Renaissance Florence* (New York: Academic Press, 1980).

——, "Neighbours and Comrades: The Revolutionaries of Florence, 1378," *Social Analysis* 14 (1983).

Trinkaus, Charles, *In Our Image and Likeness: Humanity and Divinity in Italian Renaissance Thought*, 2 vols. (Chicago: University of Chicago Press, 1970).

——, *The Scope of Renaissance Humanism* (Ann Arbor: University of Michigan Press, 1983).

Truant, Cynthia, *Rites of Labor: Brotherhoods of Campagnonnage in Old and New Regime France* (Ithaca, NY: Cornell University Press, 1994).

Tunçer, O. Cezmi, "Rönesans ve Klasik Osmanlı Dönemi Dînî Yapılarda Kubbenin Amaç ve Uygulanış Açısından Karşılaştırılmasi," *Vakıflar Dergisi* 18 (1984).

Turner, Colin, *Laila and Majnun* (London: Blake, 1997).

Turner, James Grantham, ed., *Sexuality and Gender in Early Modern Europe: Institutions, Texts, Images* (Cambridge: Cambridge University Press, 1993).

Ullmann, Walter, "De Bartoli sententia: Concilium repraesentat mentem populi," in *Bartolo da Sassoferrato: Studi e documenti per il VI centenario*, vol. 2 (Milan, 1962).

Urton, Gary, "From Knots to Narratives: Reconstructing the Art of Historical Record Keeping in the Andes," *Ethnohistory* 45/3 (summer 1998).

Valone, Carolyn, "Roman Matrons as Patrons: Various Views of the Cloister Wall," in *The Crannied Wall: Women, Religion, and the Arts in Early Modern Europe*, ed. Craig Monson (Ann Arbor, MI: University of Michigan Press, 1992).

Van Deursen, Arie T., *Plain Lives in a Golden Age: Popular Culture, Religion and Society in Seventeenth-Century Holland* (Cambridge: Cambridge University Press, 1991).

Vauchez, André, *La Sainteté en Occident aux derniers siècles du moyen âge* (Rome: École française de Rome, 1981). English translation: *Sainthood in the Later Middle Ages* (Cambridge: Cambridge University Press, 1997).

——, *Les Laïcs au moyen âge. Pratiques et expériences religieuses* (Paris: Cerf, 1987). English translation: *Laity in the Middle Ages: Religious Beliefs and Devotional Practices* (South Bend, IN: University of Notre Dame Press, 1993).

Vegas, Federico, et al., eds., *El Continente de Papel: Venezuela en el Archivo de Indias* (Caracas: Neumann, 1984).

Verdon, Timothy and Henderson, John, eds., *Christianity and the Renaissance: Image and Religious Imagination in the Quattrocento* (Syracuse, NY: Syracuse University Press, 1990).

Verrier, Frederic, *Les Armes de Minerve: l'humanisme militaire dans l'Italie du XVIe siècle* (Paris: Université de Paris-Sorbonne, 1997).

Vickers, Nancy J., "The Body Re-Membered: Petrarchan Lyric and the Strategies of Description," in *Mimesis: From Mirror to Methos, Augustine to Descartes*, ed. John D. Lyons and Stephen G. Nichols (Hanover, NH: University of New England Press, 1982).

Villari, Rosario, *La rivolta antispagnola a Napoli: Le origini (1585–1647)* (Bari: Laterza, 1964).

——, *The Revolt of Naples*, trans. J. Newell and J. A. Marino (Cambridge: Polity Press, 1993).

Vives, Juan Luis, *Women and Gender in Early Modern Europe* (Cambridge: Cambridge University Press, 1993)

——, *The Education of a Christian Woman, a Sixteenth-century Manual* [1523], ed. and trans. Charles Fantazzi (Chicago: University of Chicago Press, 2000).

Von Pastor, Ludwig, *History of the Popes*, 16 vols. (London and St. Louis: Herder, 1898–1953).

Waddington, Raymond, "Rewriting the World, Rewriting the Body," in *The Cambridge Companion to English Literature 1500–1600*, ed. Arthur F. Kinney (Cambridge: Cambridge University Press, 2000)

Walker, D. P., *Spiritual and Demonic Magic from Ficino to Campanella* (London: Warburg Institute, 1958).

Wallerstein, Immanuel, *The Modern World-System*, vols. 1–2 (New York: Academic Press, 1974–80).

Walter, John and Schofield, Roger, "Famine, Disease and Crisis Mortality in Early Modern Society," in *Famine, Disease and the Social Order in Early Modern Society*, ed. John Walter and Roger Schofield (Cambridge: Cambridge University Press, 1989).

Walzer, Michael, "On the Role of Symbolism in Political Thought," *Political Science Quarterly* 82 (1967).

Warburg, Aby, "Flemish Art and the Florentine Early Renaissance" [1902], translated in *The Renewal of Classical Antiquity* (Los Angeles: Getty Research Institute, 1999).

Ward, A. W., *Early Tudor Drama: Medwall, the Rastells, Heywood, and the More Circle* (London: Methuen, 1926).

Warneke, Sara, *Images of the Educational Traveller in Early Modern England* (Leiden: E. J. Brill, 1995).

Wear, Andrew, "Medicine in Early Modern Europe, 1500–1700," in *The Western Medical Tradition 800 BC to AD 1800* (Cambridge: Cambridge University Press, 1995).

Weber, Max, *Economy and Society*, 3 vols., ed. Guenther Roth and Claus Wittich (New York: Bedminster Press, 1968).

Weil-Garris, Kathleen, "On Pedestals: Michelangelo's *David*, Bandinelli's *Hercules and Cacus* and the Sculpture on the Piazza della Signoria," *Römisches Jahrbuch für Kunstgeschichte* 20 (1983).

Weinstein, Donald, *Savonarola and Florence: Prophecy and Patriotism in the Renaissance* (Princeton: Princeton University Press, 1970).

Weinstein, Donald and Bell, Rudolph M., *Saints and Society: The Two Worlds of Western Christendom, 1000–1700* (Chicago: University of Chicago Press, 1982).

Weintraub, Karl Joachim, *The Value of the Individual: Self and Circumstance in Autobiography* (Chicago: University of Chicago Press, 1978).

Weissman, Ronald F. E., "The Importance of Being Ambiguous: Social Relations, Individualism, and Identity in Renaissance Florence," in *Urban Life in the Renaissance*, ed. Susan Zimmerman and Ronald F. E. Weissman (Newark: University of Delaware Press, 1989).

Westman, Robert S., "The Melanchthon Circle, Rheticus, and the Wittenberg Interpretation of the Copernican Theory," *Isis* 66 (1975).

——, "Copernicus and the Churches," in *God and Nature: Historical Essays on the Encounter between Christianity and Science* (Berkeley and Los Angeles: University of California Press, 1986).

Whigham, Frank, *Ambition and Privilege: The Social Tropes of Elizabethan Courtesy Theory* (Berkeley: University of California Press, 1984).

White, John, *The Birth and Rebirth of Pictorial Space* (Boston: Boston Book and Art Shop, 1967).

Whitlock, Keith, ed., *The Renaissance in Europe: A Reader* (New Haven: Yale University Press, 2000).

Wiesner, Merry, "Corpi separati. Le associazioni dei lavoranti nella Germania moderna," *Memoria* 27 (1989).

——, *Women and Gender in Early Modern Europe* (Cambridge: Cambridge University Press, 1993).

Wigley, Mark, "Untitled: The Housing of Gender," in *Sexuality and Space*, ed. Beatriz Colomina (Princeton Papers on Architecture) (Princeton: Princeton University School of Architecture, 1992).

Wilkins, Ernest Hatch, *Life of Petrarch* (Chicago: University of Chicago Press, 1961).

Wilkinson-Zerner, Catherine, *Juan de Herrera: Architect to Philip II of Spain* (New Haven: Yale University Press, 1993).

Williams, Robert, *Art, Theory, and Culture in Sixteenth-Century Italy: From Techne to Meta-techne* (Cambridge: Cambridge University Press, 1997).

Williamson, Dean V., "The Design of Agency Relations: Four Essays on Contract Theory, Applications, and Experimentation," Ph.D. dissertation, California Institute of Technology, 1999.

Wilson, Adrian, "The Ceremony of Childbirth and its Interpretation," in *Women as Mothers in Pre-industrial England: Essays in Memory of Dorothy McLaren*, ed. V. Fildes (London: Routledge, 1990).

Wilson, Frank Percy, *The Plague in Shakespeare's London* (Oxford: Clarendon Press, 1927).

Wind, Edgar, *Pagan Mysteries in the Renaissance* (Oxford: Oxford University Press, 1980).

Witt, Ronald, "The *De Tyranno* and Coluccio Salutati's View of Politics and Roman History," *Nuova Rivista Storica* 53 (1969).

Wittkower, Rudolf, *Architectural Principles in the Age of Humanism* (New York: W. W. Norton, 1971).

——, *Gothic vs. Classic: Architectural Projects in Seventeenth-Century Italy* (New York: G. Braziller, 1974).

Wood, James B., *The King's Army: Warfare, Soldiers, and Society during the Wars of Religion in France, 1562–1576* (Cambridge: Cambridge University Press, 1996).

Woodbridge, Linda, *Women and the English Renaissance: Literature and the Nature of Womankind, 1540–1620* (Urbana: University of Illinois Press, 1986).

——, *Vagrancy and Homelessness in English Renaissance Literature* (Urbana: University of Illinois Press, 2001) .

——, "Nomads Meet Vagrants: Elizabethan Anxieties about Mobility and Hidden Realities, at Home and Abroad," in *Making Contact*, ed. Lesley Cormack and Glenn Burger (Edmonton: University of Alberta Press, forthcoming).

Woods-Marsden, Joanna, *Renaissance Self-Portaiture: The Visual Construction of Identity and the Social Status of the Artist* (New Haven: Yale University Press, 1998).

Woolf, Stuart J., *Studi sulla nobiltà piemontese nell'epoca dell'assolutismo* (Turin: Einardi, 1983).

Wunder, Heide, "Considerazioni sulla costruzione della virilità e dell'identità maschile nelle testimonianze della prima età moderna," in *Tempi e spazi di vita femminile tra medioevo ed età moderna*, ed. Silvana Seidel Menchi, Anne Jacobson Schutte, and Thomas Kuehn (Bologna: Il Mulino, 1999).

Xenophon, *The Education of Cyrus*, trans. Henry Graham Dakyns (London, 1914).

Yarshatar, Ehsan, "The Persian Presence in the Islamic World," in *The Persian Presence in the Islamic World*, ed. Richard G. Hovannisian and Georges Sabagh (Cambridge: Cambridge University Press, 1998).

Yates, Frances A., *Giordano Bruno and the Hermetic Tradition* (Chicago: University of Chicago Press, 1964).

——, *Astraea: The Imperial Theme in the Sixteenth Century* (London: Routledge and Kegan Paul, 1975).

Zarri, Gabriella, *Le sante vive. Profezie di corte e devozione femminile tra '400 e '500* (Turin: Rosenberg and Sellier, 1990).

——, "Living Saints: A Typology of Female Sanctity in the Early Sixteenth Century," in *Women and Religion in Medieval and Renaissance Italy*, ed. Daniel Bornstein and Roberto Rusconi (Chicago: University of Chicago Press, 1996).

——, "Gender, Religious Institutions and Social Discipline: The Reform of the Regulars," in *Gender and Society in Renaissance Italy*, ed. Judith C. Brown and Robert C. Davis (London: Longman, 1998).

——, *Recinti. Donne, clausura e matrimonio nella prima età moderna* (Bologna: Il Mulino, 2000).

Zerner, Henri, ed., *Le stampe e la diffusione delle immagini e degli stili* (Bologna: CLUEB, 1983).

Ziman, John, "Ideas move around inside People," in *Puzzles, Problems and Enigmas* (Cambridge: Cambridge University Press, 1981).

Zmora, Hillay, *State and Nobility in Early Modern Germany: The Knightly Feud in Franconia, 1440–1567* (Cambridge: Cambridge University Press, 1997).

Zorzi, Andrea, "La politique criminelle en Italie (XIIIe–XVIIe siècles)," *Crime, Histoire et Sociétés* 2 (1998).

Index